CONIECTANEA BIBLICA ● NEW TESTAMENT SERIES 6

BIRGER OLSSON

Structure and Meaning in the Fourth Gospel

A TEXT-LINGUISTIC ANALYSIS
OF JOHN 2:1–11 AND 4:1–42

CWK GLEERUP LUND SWEDEN

Translated by Jean Gray, B.A., B.D.

© Birger Olsson 1974
Printed in Sweden 1974
TEXTgruppen i Uppsala AB
ISBN 91—40—03344—9

Contents

1   Introduction 1

1.1   General Approach 1
1.2   A Text-Linguistic Analysis 8

2   A "Narrative" Text, Jn 2:1—11 18

2.1   Introduction 18
2.2   The Statement Units of the Text (U 1—U 31) 21
2.3   The Structure of the Text 77
2.3.1 Terminal Features 78
2.3.2 Spatial Features 79
2.3.3 Logical Features 80
2.3.4 Temporal Features 82
2.3.5 The Roles of the Participants 84
2.3.6 The Information Flow 88
2.3.7 The Point of View 92
2.4   The Message of the Text 94
2.4.1 Preliminary Remarks 94
2.4.2 An Interpretation of the Text as a Whole 97
2.4.3 The Sinai Screen in Jn 1:19—2:11(22) 102
2.4.4 Some Other Textual Features 109
2.4.5 The Question of Text Type 114

3   A "Dialogue" Text, Jn 41:1—42 115

3.1   Introduction 115
3.2   The Event Structure 124
3.2.1 A Survey of the Event Units (E 1—E 32) 124
3.2.2 Terminal Features 133
3.2.3 Spatial Features 138
3.2.4 Temporal Features 147
3.2.5 Some Other Features 152
3.2.6 Preliminary Summary 159
3.2.7 Excursus I. The Well in Jewish tradition 162
3.3   The Dialogue Structure of vv. 7—26 173
3.3.1 The Quotation Formulae 173
3.3.2 The Speeches (S 1—S 13) 175

3.3 3 The Junction of the Speeches 193
3.3 4 The Dialogue and Its Context 208
3.3 5 Preliminary Summary . . . . ˙. . . 210
3.3 6 Excursus II. "Living Water" in Jn 212
3.4   The Dialogue Structure of vv. 31—38 218
3.4 1 Dialogue or Monologue 219
3.4 1 The Speeches (S 1—S 4) 220
3.4.3 The Junction of the Speeches 233
3.4.4 The Dialogue and Its Context 238
3.4.5 Preliminary Summary 239
3.4.6 Excursus III. Mission in Jn 241
3.5   The Message of the Text 249
3.5.1 An Interpretation of the Text as a Whole 249
3.5.2 The Question of Text Type . . . . ˙. 256

4   The Interpretative Character of the Text and the Paraclete 259

4.1   Interpretative Elements in Jn 259
4.2   The Remarks of the Narrator 262
4.3   The Paraclete as the Interpreter 266
4.4   Excursus IV. The Beloved Disciple in Jn 272

5   Epilogue 275

       Bibliography 291
       Index of Authors 313
       Index of Passages 319

1

Introduction

1.1 General Approach

The individual Bible texts have through the centuries acquired *a multitude of interpretations,* primarily as regards details within them, but also concerning each text taken as a whole.[1] Even a consideration of works of our own time and of scientific, exegetical commentaries indicates that the suggested interpretations are still numerous, and that the commentators frequently omit to select one of the proposals they present. The reader finds it difficult to arrive at an understanding of a text as a whole. This applies not least to Johannine texts where, *inter alia,* the question of the degree and the nature of the symbolism makes a decision particularly difficult.[2]

Are then the Biblical texts invariably ambiguous? Why this multitude of interpretations? It would seem to result from both the nature of the research material[3] and the research methods.[4] Unfortunately there is, so far as I know, no detailed analysis available of the elementary arguments and the most important criteria in the exegetical literature of today.[5] Discussions of method exist, however, even reported in monographs,[6] and these have become more frequent in recent years, in connection with various attempts to apply structuralist methods to exegesis or take advantage of results in generative grammar, in literary science or in communication theory.[7] We have here a confrontation between exegetical

[1] I have in 2.1 and 3.1 to some extent illustrated this and in the comments on the units of my first text in 2.2.

[2] On symbolism and allegory in Jn, see especially Bacon 1910, pp. 332ff, Howard 1931, pp. 181ff, Dodd 1953, pp. 133ff, Feuillet 1965, pp. 527ff, Stemberger 1970, pp. 12ff, the references to Jn 2:1—11 and 4:1—42 mentioned below (2.1, 3.1) and the bibliographical notes in Malatesta 1967, p. 36.

[3] Our extant material is highly fragmentary, so that the possibilities of combination are many, the texts consist sometimes of several layers, the Bible is today linked with specific functions, etc.

[4] Differing *points de départ* with regard to linguistic theory, philosophy of history, hermeneutics, etc.

[5] Note, however, Palmer 1968: "The Logic of Gospel Criticism: An account of the methods and arguments used by textual, documentary, source, and form critics of the New Testament". Cf. Rohde 1966, Koch [2]1967 and Perrin 1972.

[6] See Kieffer 1972 and the bibliographical references in his book.

[7] See especially Güttgemanns [2]1971 and the papers and discussions in *Linguistica Biblica* 1—

research and modern linguistics, which run parallel with the general debate on the place and function of linguistics in text interpretation overall.[8] The background is not least the expansion of the research field and the theoretical debate which has been in progress in linguistics during the last decade.[9]

The purpose of this investigation is not an attempt to arrive at new interpretations of a text but, as far as possible, to find *internal (textual) criteria* allowing of a choice between the many suggestions. However, this does not prevent the result from consisting, to some extent, in new combinations of earlier interpretations. I am interested to discover which criteria are to be found in the actual text and must find a way of working with the text which will allow me to assess and to sort out the many alternative interpretations. To arrive at such a "method", as I shall show below under section 1.2, I turned first of all to the field of linguistics dealing with semantic structures, analysis of discourse and textual problems.

The multitude of interpretations of Johannine texts appears to be chiefly dependent on uncertainty concerning *the environment and situation(s) of the text* and *the nature of the text,* (often described in the following pages as *the text type*). There are a number of unknown factors which influence the determination of the Gospel's origin, environment, author, potential readers etc., which have led to many hypotheses concerning the probable external situation(s) of the text.[10] I am unwilling—so far as reluctance is feasible—to use any of these as a basis for my investigation; I would rather begin with an analysis of the extant text and only discuss as they arise those problems of the environment and situation of the text which essentially affect the linguistic analysis. As a result of this procedure, many questions of detail which, seen from a definite theory of the origin and situation of the text, are considered solved, are mentioned and discussed together with other problems, in an attempt to arrive at an analysis of the text as a whole. Thus my investigation is concerned with the message and the nature of the text,

(1972—), Greenwood 1970, Richter 1971, Bovon (ed.) 1971, Léon-Dufour (ed.)1971, Schenk 1973. Cf. also an interesting attempt to combine old and new methods in Theissen 1974 (with a methodological discussion on pp. 11ff) and a communicative approach to OT quotations and allusions in Mt in Hartman 1972. See also the literature mentioned in the following notes. Jn is analysed as a short story in Henriksen 1971.

[8] The recent literature on linguistics and text interpretation is immense. See, for example, Ihwe 1971, 1972, Lagerroth 1974, and the many new periodicals on this subject: *Language and Style* (1968ff), *Semiotica* (1969ff), *Zeitschrift für Literaturwissenschaft und Linguistik* (LiLi) (1971ff), *Poetics* (1971ff), and also the Danish *Kritik* (1967ff) and *Poetik* (1968ff). On exegetics and linguistics see, besides the literature mentioned above, Alonso-Schökel 1963, Richter 1970, Nielsen 1971, Ringgren 1971, Nida 1972a, Sawyer 1972, Tångberg 1973 (and the works of James Barr mentioned by him) and Doty 1973.

[9] See Lyons (ed.) 1970.

[10] See Feine-Behm-Kümmel, pp. 135ff, Wikenhauser-Schmid, pp. 327ff, Schnackenburg, Comm., pp. 46ff, and Brown, Comm., pp. xliff.

and not with its situation, insofar as these two elements can be kept separate. *From an analysis of the constitutive elements in the text I shall try to determine its message and then describe its linguistic and literary form (text type).*[11] Thus I join the ranks of the few scholars who hold that the Johannine problem must first of all be solved from an analysis of the "Darstellungscharakter" of the Gospel.[12] My investigation is primarily *linguistic* in character, although the message of the extant text which I am trying to establish is that inherent in the historical situation of the text and not in a setting contemporary to us.

The linguistic problems occupy little space in *modern Johannine research.* This is dominated by Source Criticism[13] and *Religionsgeschichte.*[14] The perspective is almost invariably comparative and historico-genetic. To arrive at analyses of Johannine language and style one must, if one ignores the commentaries, go back to works published at the turn of the century and the decades immediately thereafter,[15] or, for investigations of "style statistics", to Schweizer 1939 and Ruckstuhl 1951 and some papers in between.[16] Among later monographs I can here only mention Leroy (1968) on misunderstandings in Jn, and Wead (1970) on literary devices in Jn.[17] Commentaries[18] make little mention of such subsidiary problems as the Semitic character of Johannine language,[19] certain lexicographical and syntactic peculiarities, poetic qualities such as parallelism and rhythm, variation of expression,[20] repetitions, use of inclusions, chiasms and structural patterns,[21] ambiguity,[22] misunderstanding, "irony", dramatic qualities,[23]

[11] I try to determine "le 'sens'" of the text, according to Kieffers terminology (1972, pp. 46ff), which is "le premier but d'une recherche exégétique", p. 49. Generally on "das geschichtliche Verstehen", Coreth 1969, pp. 68ff, and on the importance of the total aspect (text type), Lagerroth 1974, pp. 79ff.

[12] Thus already von Aberle 1868 and also Stange 1914, Bruns 1969 and Lindars 1971. For a concrete problem in Jn, see Riesenfeld 1965.

[13] See, for example, Fortna 1970, 1970a, 1973, Robinson 1970, 1971 (referring to Haenchen's commentary, not yet published), and Kysar 1973. Cf. 3.1, note 15.

[14] See, for example, Schulz 1960, Käsemann 1966, Meeks 1967, MacRay 1970, Martyn 1970 and Schottroff 1970.

[15] Schlatter 1902, Abbott 1905, 1906, Stange 1914, Burney 1922, Windisch 1923, Colwell 1931. Note also the works of Kundsin (1939, 1954) and the references in Malatesta 1967, pp. 31ff.

[16] See the references in Ruckstuhl 1951.

[17] See also Bruns 1969 and Lindars 1971, pp. 43ff.

[18] See especially Wellhausen 1908, pp. 133ff, Lagrange, Comm., pp. lxxxiff, Barrett, Comm., pp. 5ff, Schnackenburg, Comm., pp. 88ff, Brown, Comm., pp. cxxvixff.

[19] A survey in S. Brown 1964. I assume that there is a Semitic influence on the Johannine language. For arguments, see Schnackenburg, Comm., pp. 88ff, and Brown, Comm., pp. cxxvixff.

[20] See also Morris 1969, pp. 293ff.

[21] For special references, see below note 39.

[22] See also Cullmann ²1950, 1966, pp. 176ff.

[23] Further references in Muilenburg 1932 and Connick 1948. The dramatic qualities are especially stressed by Thompson 1918 and Windisch 1923.

personal roles,[24] dialogue structure, narrative style, line of thought in the monologues, figurative language, minor literary forms, cross-references, remarks in the text,[25] composition[26] etc. Nevertheless there is no investigation incorporating these subsidiary problems, or a part of them, into a collated linguistic survey, based on what we now know of how language and texts function.[27]

The earlier *research into the Johannine language* was almost always dependent on comparisons with the Synoptic writers, and mainly concerned with minor linguistic units and more formal features of the text.[28] With regard to its language and its special style—there seem to be no close parallels in extant Greek literature—Jn is best served by an *internal analysis*. In contrast to the trend in earlier research toward "atomism", I have chosen in the following linguistic analysis to start from a larger linguistic unit (the discourse) and analyse it *in toto*, in order to arrive at *a view of the text as a whole,* its linguistic and its literary character: indeed my analysis includes the subsidiary problems listed above insofar as they are encountered in the texts I have selected. There they are seen in a wider perspective, which is essential in most cases, even if the subsidiary problems are analysed separately in Jn as a whole. The problem of text type also brings out the *semantic aspects* of the text, which were often neglected formerly, since it is mainly the semantic structure which determines the character of the text as a whole.[29]

As linguistic units for my analysis, I have chosen sections with definite beginnings and endings, which the reader naturally understands as a unit, at the same time as they are part of Jn as a whole, being equivalent to what we often call "pericopes".[30] I selected a short text about one of Jesus' "signs", which has clear narrative features and is therefore designated as a "narrative" text, 2:1—11, and a longer text containing passages of dialogue, called a "dialogue" text, 4:1—42. Thus two important textual groups in Jn are represented, narrative texts with isolated speeches but no detailed dialogue and narrative texts in which the dialogue dominates.[31]

---

[24] See also Krafft 1956 and Oehler 1956.

[25] Tenney 1960.

[26] The structure of the Gospel has been described in very different ways; see Willemse 1965, pp. 13ff.

[27] The linguistic orientation in Wead 1970 is very old. — For further references to articles on Johannine language and style, see Malatesta 1967, pp. 32ff.

[28] See, for example, Abbott 1905, 1906, Wellhausen 1908, pp. 133ff, and for the "style statistics", Ruckstuhl 1951.

[29] See below, 1.2.

[30] A similar choice of "pericopes" in Louw 1973.

[31] My analysis does not cover the third group, namely the so-called Johannine discourses (expositions). If we follow Schnackenburg's division into "Rede- und Erzählungsgut" (Comm., pp. 97ff), my analysis would concern only "Erzählungsstoff" and not "Reden".

My analysis does not stop at isolated words, phrases, clauses, sentences, paragraphs, but deals with *the discourse* as a whole, often merely designated *text* in the following pages, and is thus a form of discourse analysis.[32] By allowing the investigation to aim at a description of the text as a whole, I have at the same time chosen the linguistic problem which is perhaps related more closely than all others to the interpretation of the texts, and the problems thereby involved which are listed above.

The interest in the larger units of the text, in their structure and their literary form, has a great deal in common with *Formgeschichte, Redaktionsgeschichte,* structural analyses inspired by the New Criticism and with Fnglish and American investigations of the texts' literary qualities.

According to Schulz' methodological survey, *Formgeschichte* is a dead branch of the history of Johannine research.[33] He alleges that Dibelius only encountered one literary form in Jn, corresponding to what Windisch calls "die dramatisch ausgesponnene Novelle", and that Bultmann found 'no use for the form-critical method in his work on Jn. According to Schulz the "style statistics" is the Johannine analogy to the Synoptic *Formgeschichte.*

Bultmann's main reason for his omission to work with form criticism in Jn is his source criticism, but perhaps also his derivation of his literary forms to a great extent from outside and not from an analysis of the texts themselves: there are in Greek literature—the Semitic was of less interest to him—no given equivalents of the Johannine forms. Indeed Leroy, in his analysis of the Johannine misunderstandings, entitled "Ein Beitrag zur Formgeschichte des Johannesevangeliums", starts from a form outside the texts, from the riddle, ("die Form des Rätsels"),[34] This particular part of his analysis is not convincing, while his analysis of the Johannine texts on the other hand, which resulted in a Johannine "Sondersprache", is a vital contribution to the attempts to define Johannine text. A Johannine *Formgeschichte* is, to a great extent, referred to the Johannine texts themselves and, secondly, if the Gospel is rooted in a strong Jewish/Christian environment, to Jewish writings and the literary forms to be found there.

In *Redaktionsgeschichte* the interest is instead concentrated on the larger literary units and the composition of the text as a whole, and on the theological trends underlying the final editing.[35] In my investigation I share this interest, but I do not see the text primarily from the point of view of history and origin, of its

[32] I use "text" in more than one meaning: of the formal concept of text as the basic linguistic unit, of discourse as a manifestation of text in this first meaning—see van Dijk 1972, p. 3—and of a specific text, e.g. Jn 2:1—11.

[33] Schulz 1957, pp. 75f. "Aufs Ganze gesehen stellt die Formgeschichte im Joh-Ev einen toten Zweig dar", p. 76.

[34] Leroy 1968, pp. 13ff. Cf. R.E. Brown's recension in *Biblica* 51 (1970), pp. 152ff.

[35] See the extended presentation in Rohde 1966 and Stein 1969. For "redaction criticism" in Jn, see Martyn 1970 and Fortna 1970a, 1973. Critique in Greenwood 1970.

creation through tradition and redaction,[36] but as an independent language unit, calling for a detailed analysis of all its parts and not merely of transitions between traditions and editorial additions to see how the traditions were reinterpreted. The traditions, more or less fixed in form, which were somehow or other taken over, are seen, not as passages alien to the text, but as essential, functional parts of it.[37] Thus I start from the belief that the final product, i.e. the text as we now have it, functioned as a text from the very beginning—and not only in later use of Jn—and that it is in some sense homogenous and coherent. Only when an analysis from this *point de départ* proves impossible should, for example, the prehistory of the text be taken into account for its interpretation.[38] Naturally this does not mean that I regard a diachronic investigation—"eine traditionsgeschichtliche Untersuchung"—as unimportant, merely that a synchronic analysis of the extant text *in toto* is a justifiable exegetical project, not least as regards Jn. Such an analysis should usually be included in an investigation based on the history of tradition too, as I see it, since we generally possess the largest quantity of empirical (linguistic) data concerning just the final text, and every diachronic investigation presumes synchronic analyses.

The *structural analysis* inspired by the New Criticism is practiced primarily by a number of scholars at the Pontifical Bible Institute in Rome.[39] By an analysis of "structural devices"[40] they try to arrive at a description of the structure of the text, which then provides a basis for their interpretation. One of the most valuable features of this method is the weight attributed to the text as a whole, to the internal features, to its starting point in an analysis of the literary composition of the text without too many preconceived ideas on how the text was written, and also to its concentration on many formal features inherent in the textual structure.[41] Nevertheless there is a tendency to emphasize formal and explicit features at the expense of the semantic and implicit traits; a strict parallelism between syntactic and semantic structures is far too lightly assumed.[42]

[36] There are tradition and redaction in Jn too. See the introductions of the recent commentaries, especially Schnackenburg, Brown and Lindars, and Lindars 1971.

[37] This assertion is perhaps easier to make in the case of Jn, as being linguistically homogenous, than in that of, for example, Mk.

[38] We have the same problems in some parts of the NT epistles. See Olsson 1972—73, pp. 255ff.

[39] See, for example, Vanhoye 1963, Alonso-Schökel 1963, Lohfink 1963, de la Potterie 1969, also Laruentin 1957, Janssens de Varebeke 1962, Lambrecht 1967, Simonis 1967, Malatesta 1971 and Sibinga 1970, 1972.

[40] Announcement of theme, hookwords, moods, thematic vocabulary, inclusions, chiastic patterns, distribution of words, formal parallelisms, etc. See Janssens de Varebeke 1962, pp. 513ff, and Vanhoye 1963, pp. 37f.

[41] An excellent example of the usefulness of this method in Lofink 1963 (with discussion of the method on pp. 10ff). For an example of how this structural approach solves textual problems, see Lohfink's analysis of Jon 4:5 (1961).

[42] See Topel 1971, pp. 213, 219f.

The structure of a text—this applies to most text types—is determined mostly by its semantic structure. In any case, I am of the opinion that a structural analysis should embrace *both* the expression (form) *and* the content of the text and not merely the former.[43]

Questions concerning *the literary form of the NT texts* in a more general sense[44] have long been discussed in the English-speaking world, nowadays not least in the USA.[45] My questions on the nature of the text are the same type of problem. The American investigations are often influenced by general literary research and rhetorics. I have tried to start from the "textual linguistics", *sensu lato*.

In my view, the general approach described here involves some difficulties, which should perhaps be mentioned here. The analysis concentrates on the NT texts themselves, and refrains from comprehensive comparative studies,[46] being focused on two very well known and often quoted texts, the narrative of the wedding at Cana and the account of the meeting with the woman of Samaria. The interpretation tradition is here especially massive, and intensive research is still in progress to explain these texts and determine their message. Moreover, I shall allow the analysis to incline toward a description of the literary character of the texts, and thus touch on the heart of the interpretation of these passages. A delimitation, or even a change in the concept of the text type, generally involves a revision of the interpretation of the text as a whole. Thus the analyses must be said to concern the texts in one of their most comprehensive aspects. To determine the text type I use a method based on linguistic results concerning texts in general, yet in a situation in which the "textual science" is still in the making.[47] Finally, the investigation will fall within a no-man's-land between exegesis and linguistics, with the border feuds now raging there. All this leads to certain problems, not least as regards the disposition and presentation of my material. I will comment on these problems separately in the following analyses and also in the description of my method, which now follows.

[43] For further discussion, see below 1.2.

[44] On composition, genre, style, literary forms, etc.

[45] See Muilenburg 1932 (with references), Wilder 1964, Baird 1969 and Greenwood 1970 (with references).

[46] I mean the very common exegetical studies including one part concerning non-Biblical material and one part concerning some problems or passages in the Bible. My comparative analyses in, for example, 2.4.3 are jusitifed by a thorough textual analysis, which comes first.

[47] On "textual science", see Scherner 1972, pp. 58f (with references) and the presentation of textual linguistics and discourse analysis below, 1.2. A determination of text type is crucial to an interpretation of a text, Lagerroth 1974, pp. 79 (referring to Hirsch 1967, pp. 113f), 92ff.

1.2 A Text-Linguistic Analysis

When, with some reservations, I describe my book as a text-linguistic analysis, I do not envisage a theoretical and highly formalised investigation, but an exegetical analysis in which *the text* itself is placed in the centre, and some general *linguistic* conclusions on how texts are constituted and understood are applied. This must be made clear, as the German term "textlinguistisch" is, to a great extent, associated with theoretical and often formalised analyses of textual problems.[48] As shown by 1.1 above, my work is practically oriented to an analysis of the texts, in order to determine their message and their literary character.

Textual linguistics, *sensu lato,* are today studied in several places and in different ways, and I shall mention three such trends before I define my own method: French structuralism, German "Textlinguistik" and American discourse analysis.

The *French structuralist method,* advocated by such scholars as C. Lévy-Strauss, R. Barthes, A.J. Greimas, T. Todorov and J. Kristeva,[49] has perhaps been the most used in textual interpretation and has also gained ground in exegetical research.[50] Here we are chiefly interested in the structural analysis of narrative texts.[51]

First of all, the French method is completely internal in the sense that historical, biographical, psychological, sociological and anthropological aspects of the texts are wholly neglected. The analysis must not refer to any factor beyond the text but remains within it, so to speak, in describing the "coherence" of the text and its internal organization of "meanings".[52] Therefore it has in different contexts been criticized for "geschichtsfeindlichen Agnostizismus".[53] Secondly, the structural analysis is intended to describe cer-

[48] See van Dijk-Ihwe-Petöfi-Rieser 1972 (with references).

[49] See the surveys in Bovon (ed.) 1971, pp. 9ff, Dressler 1972, p. 106, van Dijk 1972, pp. 273ff, and Galland 1973, p. 35. This method is derived from de Saussure's linguistic theory, the Russian Formalism and the Prague School. For material on this tradition, see Madsen (ed.) 1970 and Aspelin-Lundberg (eds.) 1971.

[50] Chabrol-Marin (eds.) 1971, Léon-Dufour (ed.) 1971, Bovon (ed.) 1971, Marin 1971, Schnider-Stenger 1972 and the illuminating article on the situation in France by F. Refoulé (1973, pp. 11ff, with references to recent literature).

[51] The main contribution of the French school concerns narrative texts. For work on poetic texts, see Greimas (ed.) 1972.

[52] Galland 1972, pp. 36f, and also Bovon (ed.) 1971, pp. 11f, 24f, Schnider-Stenger 1972, pp. 94ff. The text is defined as a system of functions, Schnider-Stenger 1972, pp. 94f, referring to R. Barthes: "So verlangt etwa R. Barthes eine 'immanente Analyse'. Die Analyse soll 'in einem Bereich... arbeiten, der ganz und gar innerhalb des Werkes liegt'. ... Als 'phänomenologische Kritik' will sie 'das Werk explicit machen, statt es zu erklären', als 'strukturale Kritik' hält sie 'das Werk für ein System von Funktionen'."

[53] Schnider-Stenger 1972, p. 95, Refoulé 1973, p. 112, Lagerroth 1974, pp. 65ff.

tain "translinguistic" structures, which may also be manifested in, for instance, films, dances and dreams.[54] Thus the results are strongly general, abstract patterns, possessing validity for all kinds of narrative. Greimas says that narrative structures are "located at a deeper level than deep linguistic structures" and "enjoy a certain autonomy with regard to linguistic structures".[55] The temporalization and the spatialization coincide with the transition from narrative to linguistic structures, as do the linguistic expansion and condensation and the stylistic distancing.[56] The analysis seeks to penetrate beyond these linguistic processes. The background is to a great extent V. Propp's analysis of Russian folk tales.[57] He asserted that there is a limited number of recurrent characteristics (31 in all) in the tales and that these are always found in a specific sequence. Regarding narratives, Greimas similarly tries to establish a far more limited number of characteristics, which often consist of binary oppositions.[58] A narrative is defined as "a sequence of narrative énoncés". Enoncés, which are thus the invariants of the narrative, must possess a determined and predictable canonic form and the relations between them must be capable of being explicit and described. An énoncé is defined as actants (subjects, objects, senders, receivers) tied together by a function, such as *Peter hits Paul,* where *Peter* and *Paul* are actants and the verb *hit* is regarded as a function. Once the minimal units of a narrative have been so defined, we are left with a classification of different kinds of énoncés and a determination of the syntagmatic organization thereof. Thus, by means of a determination of different functions, actants and sequences of énoncés, we arrive at the main categories needed for each analysis of a narrative text.

My investigation is but little influenced by the French structuralist method, although my division of the text into minimal units bears certain resemblances to it, and even the general orientation to the text as such is the same. This depends above all on the inclination of the structural analysis toward the highly abstract translinguistic structures in the text and its non-historical and strictly internal character. These two characteristics render the method less useful as a means of determining the message of the text in the historical situation to which it belongs. The results tend to be very general, to some extent already known basic structures, which may then be padded with different meanings. With this latter quality in mind, it is not surprising that the analysis method has provoked some interest

[54] Greimas 1971, p. 793.

[55] Greimas 1971, p. 794.

[56] Greimas 1971, p. 797.

[57] An excellent presentation of Greimas' method in Galland 1973, a more theoretical description in van Dijk 1972, pp. 283ff.

[58] Greimas' main works are from 1966 and 1970. I follow here a shorter presentation of his from 1971.

in the ecumenical work.[59] My interest in the historical interpretation of the text means that I stay within the lingusitic levels and try to determine the semantic structures of the text, and also that I am obliged to take into consideration some external conditions and relations.[60]

The German term *Textlinguistik* nowadays covers a series of linguistic investigations, mostly papers, which have recently been published in Germany during the years I have spent working on my texts.[61] Other designations also occur: "Textsyntax", "Suprasyntax", "Supersyntax", "Hypersyntax", "Makrosyntax".[62] Following Peter Hartmann's programmatic use of the expression "Textlinguistik", in two papers from 1968, however, this term is the one most commonly used.[63] All these investigations are concerned with the linguistic phenomena beyond the sentences, i.e. questions which were previously discussed within the ancient rhetorics and in different forms of stylistics.[64] As in the case of French structuralism, the background of this increasingly fashionable discipline of Lnguistics is to be found, to some extent, in Russian Formalism and the Prague School, together with the glossematics and other structural currents in linguistics.[65] Research on text grammars is now in progress[66] and comprehensive theoretical systems have been presented by H. Rieser, J.S. Petöfi and T.A. van Dijk.[67] In the following presentation, my greatest dependence is on the brief general introduction to "textual linguistics" (1972) by Wolfgang Dressler, now working in Vienna, and on Teun A. van Dijk's great work on text grammars (1972). Both of them choose the Generative Semantics as the general linguistic theory for a text grammar.

[59] See, for example, *The Ecumenical Review* 23 (1971), no. 4, and Léon-Dufour (ed.) 1971, p. 7.

[60] A broadening of the structural analysis to include also some pragmatic components is foreshadowed in Galland 1973, p. 48.

[61] See, besides the literature mentioned in the following notes, the bibliographies in Brinker 1971, pp. 235ff, Dressler 1972, pp. 116ff, and van Dijk 1972, pp. 343ff.

[62] Fries 1971, p. 219, with references.

[63] Hartmann 1971, p. 9. The first paper had the title: "Textlinguistik als linguistische Aufgabe", published in *Konkrete Kunst, konkrete Dichtung* (ed. S.J. Schmidt, Karlsruhe 1968, pp. 62—77), the second "Textlinguistik als neue linguistische Teildisziplin", published in *Replik* 2 (1968), pp. 2—7. See also Stempel (ed.) 1971.

[64] A short survey of some traditional approaches in van Dijk 1972, pp. 23ff, and Dressler 1972, pp. 5f.

[65] Dressler 1972, pp. 6ff, van Dijk 1972, pp. 25ff, and for a survey of structural linguistics, see Lepschy 1972.

[66] Mainly at the Universities of Münster (Peter Hartmann, Roland Harweg, Walter Koch), Constanza (Wolf-Dieter Stempel, Jens Ihwe, Hannes Rieser) and Bielefeld (Elisabeth Gülich, Wolfgang Raible, Siegfried J. Schmidt), according to Dressler 1972, p. 8.

[67] See van Dijk-Ihwe-Petöfi-Rieser 1972 (with references). van Dijk 1972, pp. 25ff, distinguishes between a structuralist and a generative-transformational approach to textual analysis.

German textual linguistics are perhaps best presented by the questions listed by Dressler in the introduction to his book.[68] In his view textual linguistics are primarily concerned with such problems as

1. Was ist ein Text? Wodurch wird ein Text konstituiert?
2. Wann ist ein Text abgeschlossen?
3. Was ist der Sinn eines Textes? Wie wird er vom Empfänger des Textes (Hörer/Leser) verstanden?
4. Wozu äussert man einem mündlichen oder schriftlichen Text?
5. In welchem aussersprachlichen, gedanklichen und gesellschaftlichen Kontext ist ein bestimmter Text erst sinnvoll?
6. Inwiefern ist jeder Satz eines Textes unvollständig und sein notwendiger Bezug auf den Gesamttext erkennbar?
7. Wie wird ein Text von seinem Sender (Sprecher/Schreiber) programmiert und realisiert?
8. Welche Funktion haben die verschiedenen Sprachelemente im Text?
9. Welche Relationen bestehen zwischen Text und Satz und welche hierarchische Zwischenstufen gibt es?
10. Welche Texttypen (Textsorten) gibt es und wie kann man sie voneinander abgrenzen?
11. Welche sprachlichen Gesetze lenken den Ablauf einer Konversation?
12. Welche Rolle spielt die Ebene des Textes beim kindlichen Spracherwerb, beim Fremdsprachenlernen, ... beim Übersetzen?
13. Welche textlinguistischen Gesetzmässigkeiten und Regeln ändern sich nicht in der historischen Entwicklung der Sprachen?

Even this cursory list of questions suggests that textual linguistics, in their German manifestation, is a very comprehensive discipline, and Dressler also mentions that it is relevant to many other fields of knowledge: communication theory, sociology, comparative literary history, stylistics, folkloristics, rhetorics, logic, psychology, documentation analysis, the art of translation and language teaching.[69] Many of the problems are not new,[70] but here they are combined with other problems under a general premise: *the text is the primary, basic unit of the language.*[71] The interest has clearly shifted from sentences, via utterances, to discourses.[72] Dressler allows "Textgrammatik" to embrace "Textsemantik"

[68] Dressler 1972, pp. 1ff.
[69] Dressler 1972, pp. 102ff ("Zur interdiziplinären Rolle der Textlinguistik").
[70] See Brinker 1971, pp. 217ff.
[71] The text is "das primäre sprachliche Zeichen, die grundlegende Einheit der Sprache", Dressler 1972, p. 3; cf. pp. 12ff. See also Brinkmann [2]1971, p. 723, and the survey of different definitions of text in Brinker 1971, pp. 217ff. T.A.van Dijk 1972 gives his arguments for a text grammar on pp. 1ff. He will "introduce the concept of *text* as the basic linguistic unit manifesting itself, as *discourse*, in verbal utterances" (p. 3).
[72] See Dressler 1972, pp. 10ff. van Dijk opposes sentence grammars and text grammars (1972, pp. 12ff).

11

(concerned with the question "Was ist die Bedeutung eines Textes und wie konstituiert sie sich?"), and "Textsyntax" (on the question "Wie wird die Bedeutung eines Textes syntaktisch ausgedrückt und wie kann sie ausgedrückt werden?"), distinguishing them from "Textpragmatik", which deals with "die Beziehung eines sprachlichen Elements zu seinen Erzeugern, Verwendern und Emphängern in der Kommunikationssituation".[73] He shows how the development within textual linguistics has progressed from "Textsyntax" by "Textsemantik" to "Textpragmatik".[74] This gradual expansion and inclusion of the pragmatic properties of speech acts is also marked in the many attempts to define a text. An internal definition, such as "a text is a coherent sequence of clauses" has proved insufficient.[75] This extension is essential, not least considering the practical use of textual linguistics in the interpretation of texts.[76]

German textual linguistics seems to be much more useful in NT exegetics than French structuralism[77] The main reason for this is the communicative aspect, which is to be found in this discipline, the combination of internal and external categories used in the discussion of texts, surely beginning with an internal analysis but also including pragmatic properties. According to K. Brinker, the primary task of textual linguistics is *die Beschreibung der Korrelation von Text-konstitution und Textrezeption. Dabei ist von der Analyse von Einzeltexten auszugehen. Bei der Analyse der Textstruktur ist — methodisch gesehen — unter steter Reflexion und Beobachtung des Ablaufs der Textverstehensprozesse bei sich und anderen Sprachteilhabern von der Analyse der 'Informationsstruktur' zur Beschreibung der die 'Information' (= das was der Leser oder Hörer einem Text als Mitteilung entnimmt) jeweils signalisierenden festen sprachlichen Mittel vorzugehen*.[78] This practical, textual and communicative approach in German

---

[73] "Textpragmatik" is concerned with the question: "Was ist die Funktion eines Textes im (aussersprachlichen) Kontext?", Dressler 1972, p. 4, and pp. 92ff.

[74] Dressler 1972, pp. 12ff; cf. Brinker 1971 and Scherner 1972. van Dijk's Text Grammar also includes a pragmatic component (1972, pp. 313ff). An immanent definition of text (excluding the pragmatic properties) has been given especially by Peter Hartmann and Roland Harweg, van Dijk 1972, pp. 29f.

[75] See especially Brinker 1971, pp. 220ff, Scherner 1972, pp. 52ff, and Faiss 1972, pp. 117ff. Dressler gives the following definition of text: "Text ist eine nach der Intention des oder der Sender und Empfänger sprachlich abgeschlossene Spracheinheit, die nach den Regeln der Grammatik der jeweils verwendeten Sprache gebildet ist" (1972, p. 1).

[76] See, besides the references in Dressler 1972, pp. 105ff, some papers of Maximilian Scherner (1970, 1971, 1972), referring especially to H. Brinkmann and S.J. Schmidt. For my use of Scherner 1972, see below 2.4.1.

[77] Dressler 1972, p. 108, also notes the relevance of textual linguistics for the theology, referring to Chabrol-Marin (eds.) 1971 and E. Güttgemanns' project "Generative Poetik des Neuen Testaments" and his periodical "Linguistica Biblica", but they are not depending on German textual linguistics. —A number of the questions mentioned above are already part of the exegetical work.

[78] Brinker 1971, p. 233 (my italics).

textual linguistics, together with the interest in the problem of different text types,[79] are also to be found in my investigation, although I am primarily inspired by some results within the American discourse analysis.

The discipline which I here call *the American discourse analysis* embraces different methods, all of which are based on the discourse as a primary unit of language. The methods vary according to the grammatical model on which the analysis is based, e.g. whether one chooses a structuralist (like Z.S. Harris), a tagmemic (K.L. Pike, R. Longacre),[80] a stratificational (S. Lamb, H.A. Gleason),[81] or a generative-transformational grammar (E.A. Nida).[82] As in German textual linguistics, there is here a clear shift from a non-semantic, non-mentalistic formalism, represented mainly by Zelling S. Harris' famous paper "Discourse Analysis" from 1952,[83] to a discourse analysis in which the semantics are treated as an autonomous domain, advocated by, for example, Eugene A. Nida.[84] The general approach of my work, and also the disposition, was at first dependent on the short discussion of the discourse and discourse analysis in Nida-Taber 1969.[85]

A well-constructed discourse in any language will, according to Nida and Taber, abide by a variety of constraints, designed to give it structure. They call these constraints "universals of discourse", assuming at least eight, two relative to the discourse as a whole, three to the events therein, two to objects within it and one to the author. They are:

---

[79] Both Dressler and van Dijk refer to a colloquium in Rheda 1972: "Differenzierungskriterien für Textsorten aus der Sicht der Linguistik und einzelner Textwissenschaften". The papers from this conference have, as far I know, not yet been published. On types of text, see also Reiss 1971 ("Die Bedeutung von Texttyp und Textfunktion für den Übersetzungsprozess").

[80] A tagmemic method is applied in Longacre 1968 and Pike-Pike 1972 (with references to other tagmemic works).

[81] See Nida 1972b, pp. 303f (with references).

[82] See the general surveys in Dressler 1972, pp. 6f, and van Dijk 1972, pp. 26ff. On E.A. Nida, see below, note 84.

[83] Published in *Language* 28 (1952), pp. 1–30. He presents an analysis of a text on pp. 474ff in the same periodical and both papers are reprinted in *Discourse Analysis Reprints* (The Hague 1963). For a critique of Harris' "formalistic" approach, see Pak 1972 and van Dijk 1972, pp. 26ff.

[84] There is also such a shift from syntactic to semantic structures in the works of E.A. Nida (1964, 1969, pp. 487ff, 1972a, pp. 74, 80ff, 1972b, pp. 304ff, and Nida-Taber 1969), as in the American linguistics the last years, Chafe 1970, pp. 1ff, 59ff (from structuralism, via syntacticism, to semanticism). Unfortunately I cannot quote Nida's latest detailed discussion of semantic structures and discourse analysis, which will be published in *Exploring Semantic Structures* (in press). I owe a great debt of gratitude to Dr Nida for his course on semantic structures at a Translators' Seminar, held in Halle in the summer of 1971, for private conversations and for the opportunity to read two earlier versions of the book mentioned above.

[85] See pp. 131–133, 152–154. Cf. Nida 1964, pp. 210–213. See also Wonderly 1968, pp. 182ff.

1. The marking of the beginning and end of the discourse, which I shall call *terminal* features.
2. The marking of major internal *transitions* (by phrases, clauses etc.).
3. The marking of *temporal* relations between events (by temporal conjunctions, temporal phrases, relative tenses, sequence of tenses and order of events, on the assumption that, unless otherwise stated, the linguistic order is also the historical order).
4. The marking of *spatial* relations between events and objects (by special particles, e.g. prepositions, expressions of distance, words of motion, etc.).
5. The marking of *logical* relations between events (by so-called adverbial sentences, conjunctions, forms of verbs and by many other devices).
6. *The identification of participants* (by pronominal references, deictic references, synonyms, etc. Events may also be referred to by successive references).
7. *The foregrounding and backgrounding* of successive series of participants and events (high-lighting, focusing, emphasis, point of view etc.).[86]
8. *The involvement of the author* (autobiographical notes in the first person, personal judgements etc.).

The formal features reported here mark semantic relations between different elements in the text. Since 1969 E.A. Nida has laid increasing emphasis on the independent status of semantics in the analysis of a discourse, and tried to devise a method of dividing a text into nuclear structures, or primary and secondary semantic configurations, and to determine the various semantic relations between these structures.[87] This method is to some extent applied to NT text in Louw 1973. The combination of theory and practice in Nida, and his emphasis on the semantic aspects of the language, render his work on method particularly valuable for all textual interpretation, including that of Bible texts. Nida himself applied his method to a passage from The Times. Yet if it is to be used for ancient texts belonging to a distant culture, such as the Bible, it should be supplemented with some form of hermeneutic interpretation model, offering scope for the philological analysis necessary in the treatment of discourse, and allowing a possibility of filling in the cultural gap between the NT and our own time, by incorporating an analysis of the situational and linguistic context of the discourse.[88] The analyses of Johannine text which here follows seems to me to suggest that the pragmatic dimension is indispensable in every theory of how a text is to be described and understood.[89]

With reference to this rough sketch of text-oriented linguistics and to the description of the general approach of my work (1.1), I wish, finally, to point out some characteristic features of my method of analysing the texts, already partly presented above. It is a form of exegetic analysis which could be described as "textual exegetics".

[86] Cf. Gleason 1965, pp. 329ff, 419ff, Wonderly 1968, pp. 182ff.
[87] See above, note 84.
[88] For further discussion, see below 2.4.1.
[89] This is also stressed by E.A. Nida, for example, in Nida 1964, pp. 242ff, and Nida 1972c.

Firstly, the analysis is *heavily oriented toward the text*. This means that I start from *the text as we now have it*, i.e. from that which is usually described as the final stage in the history of the text, attributed sometimes to the evangelist, sometimes to a redactor.[90] This layer, which I regard as a functioning text from the start, with the demand for consistency which this poses, must be considered as important, not merely because it is the layer which has been in use through the centuries,[91] but also because, as I have already said (1.1), we tend to possess the largest amount of empirical data on just this layer. The orientation to the text means that I start from an *internal (textual) analysis*, in contrast to various kinds of comparative analysis common in exegesis. This does not mean an internal approach in the sense used by French structuralism, but an attempt to derive criteria and confirmation primarily from the texts analysed and their linguistic contexts. The latter means that a philological material from Jn, or the Johannine writings, or a Semitically influenced Greek-speaking environment,[92] takes priority in the interpretation of the linguistic elements in the text. The concentration on the text also involves an *holistic trend:* I shall try to do justice to *all* the parts of the text and to the different relationships between them.[93] The text acts as a model: I first take the model (the text) to pieces, analyse each component separately (for content and form) and then put them together again, after I have examined all the joints and the construction as a whole. The final interpretation of the text, therefore, claims to interpret the text as a whole.

Secondly, the method of analysis now figuratively presented is not only a way of arranging my book; it is justified by an essential tenet of *modern linguistics:* the *semantic structure* is the crucial component of language.[94] Language is a way of converting meaning into sound, a truth which is often considered in ancient handbooks on rhetorics.[95] Anyone who wishes to speak is faced with the problem of

---

[90] See the discussion below in 3.1 and 5.

[91] There may be some alternations in the text, depending on the history of the text (including glosses).

[92] See above, note 19.

[93] A holistic method is best applied to Jn as a whole, but it is possible to use it also for pericopes if their linguistic contexts are noted.

[94] See especially Chafe 1970, pp. 55ff, 346ff, and on semantic recurrences in a text, Cummings-Herum-Lybbert 1971.

[95] In the interest in determining the linguistic processes possibly underlying the production of specifically 'well-formed' texts and in assigning the text to its place in the total communication process. See Lausberg 1960 and the assessment in van Dijk 1972, pp. 24f, referring also to the current re-evaluation of rhetorics. Cf. Dressler 1972, p. 5: "Zwei wichtige Aufgaben des Redners fallen (zumindest teilweise) in den Bereich der Textlingustik: die Anordung der Gedanken oder Disposition und die sprachliche Formulierung oder Elokution. ... In *dispositio, elocutio* und in der Lehre von den Gedanken- oder Redefiguren und vom kunstvollen Periodenbau hat die Rhetorik auch Gebiete der späteren Stilistik umfasst. Bei der mittelalterlichen Einteilung der Freien Künste in Rhetorik, Grammatik und Dialektik (Logik) usw. fiel das heutige Gebiet der Textlinguistik also

how to express his thought. He must select words from his store of concepts, decide on a certain sequence and compose his material. Indeed his language generally offers him a wide range of possible sequences.[96] His arrangement of the material is essential, because it tends to be crucial for the communicative effect.[97] The semantic structure of a text is therefore very closely related to the intention of the author and to the message of the text.[98] Indeed when interpreting a text, we are referred first to the linguistic manifestation of the semantic process just mentioned, to what is sometimes called the surface structure, but an understanding of the author's intention in fact involves a reconstruction of his path from the semantic to the phonetic structure. "This procedure is more informative and is precisely what discourse analysis is trying to do, for it reveals the selections, orderings and arrangements made by the author in moving from deep to surface structure. These also have semantic function. Therefore, *the structure* has a very important function in the semantics of the discourse".[99] In his short paper from 1973 on discourse analysis and the Greek New Testament Johannes P. Louw sums up: "The structure of a discourse is a vital point in determining its intentions. It is the hinge on which the communication turns; it is part and parcel of the semantics of a discourse. For in order to understand its meaning, one has to analyse the basis for selecting a particular structure. Unless we know the nature of a semantic structure, we cannot describe in any adequate way the postsemantic processes which operate upon it, for we are ignorant of the input to those processes".[1]

There appear to be several methods of applying this semantics-to-phonetics directionality in a textual analysis.[2] In my analyses of Jn 2:1—11 (ch. 2) and Jn 4:1—42 (ch. 3), I wish first *to establish "die Textkonstitution"* by means of a review of the minor elements of the text, which are determined in slightly different ways in the two texts, and then of the structure of the text.[3] In the first text I start from those elements which give a limited information, so-called information units or statement units. In the second I follow the same procedure for the event struc-

im wesentlichen der Rhetorik zu." The classical rhetorics was applied not only to literary texts; see Birgit Stolt's analysis of Luther's "Ein Predigt, dass man Kinder zur Schulen halten solle", Stolt 1970.

[95] This applies especially to texts.

[97] "The structure, in which a notion is communicated, is the heart of its effectiveness", Louw 1973, p. 101. Cf. Chafe 1970, p. 59: "It is in semantic structure that the well-formedness of sentences is determined".

[98] Dressler 1972, pp. 17ff. Semantic structure is here regarded not as something very abstract but as a first level abstraction which bears a direct relation to the world of observable thoughts and ideas, Chafe 1970, p. 351.

[99] Louw 1973, p. 102.

Louw 1973, p. 104. On postsemantic processes, see Chafe 1970.

Cf. Louw 1973, who analyses two texts, Lk 9:57—62 and Rom 5:12—21.

See below, 2.2 and 3.2.

ture, but in the dialogue sections I begin from the different speeches, which are naturally understood as delimited units.[4] In both cases, bearing in mind the well known problem of symbolism or allegory in Jn, I often report symbolical interpretations of various elements in the texts and in the first passage I also mention a number of suggestions which later on in the interpretation of the text as a whole prove to be erroneous. I base my analysis of the structure of the text on what Nida and Taber call "the universals of discourse", sometimes complemented with what is said of these markings of semantic relations in text-linguistic studies. While the terminology differs, there are many similarities between American discourse analysis and German textual linguistics.[5]

After these subsidiary analyses, I endeavour *to establish the connection between "die Textkonstitution" and "die Textrezeption"*,[6] with an "ideal receiver" in mind, i.e. chiefly between the structure and the message of the text, defined as the "message" which the author intended to convey.[7] This give rise to some short comparative studies. This method of analysis involves a certain circular progress (or rather spiral progress) in the manner of presentation as regards the whole and the parts of the text, as regards "Vorverständnis" and "Sachverständnis" and as regards the linguistically manifested communication and "die Sache", which seems, however, to belong to "die Grundstrukturen des Verstehens".[8]

Finally, on the basis of such an analysis of the text and determination of its message, I have tried to describe its linguistic and literary character (*text type*), which prompted me to discuss certain elements in Jn as a whole, which "express an opinion" concerning the text (interpretative elements, the Paraclete, ch. 4). The results in chs. 2—4 give some preliminary results concerning Johannine language and text and they are shortly summarized in ch. 5, where I also touch on some questions of the origin of Jn and its religious and historical environment.

[4] Other segmentation of, for example, Jn 2:6, would lead to the same result.
[5] See, for example, Dressler 1972, pp. 20ff, 42ff, 47ff, 57ff, and the references on these pages.
[6] A strict division between these two is impossible; see Brinker 1971, p. 233.
[7] See below, 2.4.1.
[8] See Coreth 1969, pp. 115ff, and also Lagerroth 1974, pp. 80ff.

2

A "Narrative" Text, Jn 2:1—11

2.1 Introduction

The story of the miracle of the wine at Cana is one of the most mysterious texts in the NT. I have chosen it for analysis here because it is short and well delimited, especially by v. 11. Moreover it constitutes an example of a "narrative" text, related to an important group of Johannine texts on Jesus' signs (σημεῖα).[1] It is marked and focused as a *semeion* text in a special way in Jn, partly by its position at the beginning of Jesus' public ministry, partly by its numbering, ἀρχὴ τῶν σημείων, qualities which link it with the end of the Gospel.[2]

The evangelist therefore assigns great significance to the narrative, a fact which should reasonably be balanced by the weight of meaning of the text itself. In contrast to most *semeion* texts this cardinal text is not interpreted by any monologue or detailed dialogue.[3] Thus there appears to be special reason to analyse the individual statement units and the structure of the text, in order to arrive at a more accurate assessment of its meaning in the Johannine context. The result of such analysis as regards the character of the text cannot be transferred without more ado to other *semeion* texts, but it may provide an essential contribution to a more detailed examination of them.

Jn 2:1—11 has often been discussed in the exegetical literature.[4] The multitude of interpretations is overwhelming. This is true both of the interpretation as a

[1] Especially Jn 2:1—11; 4:46—54; 5:1—9; 6:1—15; 9:1—7; 11:1—44. See also 2.2, U 29.

[2] At the same time as the Cana narrative ends the "second prologue" in Jn (1:19—2:11), it is the introduction to chs. 2—4 (chs. 2—12 and chs. 2—20). Here the reader meets the disciples for the first time as a group. We find the mother of Jesus only here in the end of the first week and then in the last week (19:25—27). The formulation of 2:11 points forward to 20:30f. On the position of the narrative in the Johannine composition as a whole, see also below, 2.2, U 1, 3, 4, 6, 9c, 11, 17 and 27—31.

[3] Cf. 5:1ff; 6:1ff; 9:1ff, and 11:1ff. The second Cana narrative (4:46—54) has no interpreting dialogue or monologue either. See 2.2, U 27.

[4] For surveys of how the text has been interpreted, especially in the first centuries and in our own century, see Schnackenburg 1951, pp. 10ff, and Smitmans' dissertation from 1966, which has an excellent bibliography. See also Malatesta's bibliography of books and periodical literature on the Fourth Gospel 1920—1965 from 1967 and the literature mentioned in the following notes. A survey and summary of the studies of the last decade on Mary in Jn 2, see Collins 1972, pp. 117ff.

whole and of individual details in the text. There are still scholars who place the main emphasis on the actual physical miracle: some 600—700 litres of water turned into choice wine. The great miracle of transformation reveals Jesus' power and supernatural ability and gives rise to the beginning of faith in the great wonder-worker.[5]

The majority of scholars nowadays however would see some sort of deeper meaning in this miracle. Some emphasize the comment in v. 11, with the key words $\sigma\eta\mu\varepsilon\tilde{\iota}o\nu$, $\delta\acute{o}\xi\alpha$ and $\pi\iota\sigma\tau\varepsilon\acute{\upsilon}\varepsilon\iota\nu$, link the text with the promise in Jn 1:51 and cite the words on the "hour" of Jesus ($\dot{\eta}$ $\overset{\backprime}{\omega}\rho\alpha$ $\mu o\upsilon$) and the question "whence" ($\pi\acute{o}\vartheta\varepsilon\nu$) in v. 4 and v. 9 respectively. The miracle is then able to reveal a profound secret concerning the person of Jesus, something of his union with the Father. The revelation of the *doxa* of Jesus does not create faith directly but it is linked with faith in that the secret is only revealed to those who believe. The disciples' faith is in this text not only an initial faith but a total faith in Jesus Christ, the Son of God.[6]

This strongly Christological approach may be combined to some extent with a Messianic interpretation of the Cana narrative. The large quantity of wine in the brimming jars ($\overset{\backprime}{\varepsilon}\omega\varsigma$ $\overset{\backprime}{\alpha}\nu\omega$), its choice quality ($\dot{o}$ $\kappa\alpha\lambda\grave{o}\varsigma$ $o\overset{\backprime}{\iota}\nu o\varsigma$; cf. Mk 2:18ff) and the wedding context are regarded as evidence that the miracle at Cana is to be understood as a Messianic miracle. It created among the disciples a firm belief in Jesus as the Messiah.[7]

Other details in the text—the item $\kappa\alpha\tau\grave{\alpha}$ $\tau\grave{o}\nu$ $\kappa\alpha\vartheta\alpha\rho\iota\sigma\mu\grave{o}\nu$ $\tau\tilde{\omega}\nu$ $'Io\upsilon\delta\alpha\acute{\iota}\omega\nu$ and the turning of the water into wine—however have been cited as indications that the main message must lie in the replacement motif of the text: Judaism is replaced by a new religion which Jesus brought. There are already portents of this motif in Jn 1:17 ($\dot{o}$ $\nu\acute{o}\mu o\varsigma$ $\delta\iota\grave{\alpha}$ $M\omega\ddot{\upsilon}\sigma\acute{\varepsilon}\omega\varsigma$ $\dot{\varepsilon}\delta\acute{o}\vartheta\eta$, $\dot{\eta}$ $\chi\acute{\alpha}\rho\iota\varsigma$ $\kappa\alpha\grave{\iota}$ $\dot{\eta}$ $\dot{\alpha}\lambda\acute{\eta}\vartheta\varepsilon\iota\alpha$ $\delta\iota\grave{\alpha}$ $'I\eta\sigma o\tilde{\upsilon}$ $X\rho\iota\sigma\tau o\tilde{\upsilon}$ $\dot{\varepsilon}\gamma\acute{\varepsilon}\nu\varepsilon\tau o$) and it may be regarded as the leitmotif running through the entire introduction of the Gospel, chs. 2—4.[8] According to this interpretation the wine may, for example, represent the Spirit or the teaching of Jesus in a wider sense. For other scholars, those who interpret the text as having primarily a sacramental meaning, the wine is equivalent to the Eucharist, and the

---

[5] According to Smitmans 1966, pp. 37ff, for example, J. Michl, C.P. Ceroke, F. Büchsel and W. Grundmann. Cf. Lu 1972 on synthetic production of wine from water.

[6] See especially Schnackenburg 1951 and his commentary from 1965, also Bultmann and Barrett in their commentaries and Rengstorf in ThWNT, vol. 7, pp. 241ff. The Christological interpretation is regarded as the most important by, for example, Braun [2]1954, Boismard 1956 and Feuillet 1962, who suggest more than one interpretation of the narrative. This view is summarized in Smitmans 1966, pp. 46ff.

[7] According to Smitmans 1966, pp. 43ff, for example, J. Jeremias, H. van den Bussche, H. Noetzel and H. Sahlin.

[8] See especially Dodd 1953, Guilding 1960 and Hanhart 1970. More examples in Smitmans 1966, pp. 46ff.

miracle of the wine is a parallel to that of the bread in Jn 6 with its manifest Eucharistic overtones.[9] In such an exposition the Johannine texts may be described as having meanings on two levels, one of which deals with the "historical" Jesus while the other reveals essential features in the life of the Church of Christ.

This multitude of interpretations is increased by the obvious mariological interest inherent in the text: Mary is a partner in God's work of salvation, as mediator, intercessor, or a kind of prototype Christian, or as the mother of Jesus she represents Judaism, the Jewish Christian Church or simply, the Church.[10]

The reason why the text may be expounded in so many and various ways would seem to be found in different assumptions about relevant parallel material, about the function and significance of the context, about the history of the text and about its character (text type). The extent to which the idea of the text type governs the interpretation is shown by various attitudes to the degree of symbolism. In his expansive work on the miracles of Jesus, van der Loos repudiates every kind of symbolic interpretation. He alleges that the miracle of the wine at Cana shows how even the simple everyday things were close to Jesus' heart: Jesus has the "power to 'change' in whatsoever situation, at whatsoever place and at whatsoever time He wishes". "The miracle at Cana is rooted in Jesus' positive attitude towards the natural human values of life".[11] To counterbalance this theory we may cite K. Hanhart's thesis that Jn 1:35—4:54 is a *"midrashic comment"* on episodes from Mt, Mk, Lk and Acts with inserted *haggadahs* created by the evangelist himself. Jn 2:1—11 is described as an allegorical *haggadah* which links the theological message in Lk 1—2 and Acts 1—2, Jn 1:11f being the main theme. Each separate detail in the text has a transferred meaning.[12]

The main purpose of the following analysis is to try to describe the character of the text (text type).[13] I shall begin by analysing the individual statement units, then the various structures of the text, and after that I shall attempt to discuss the character of the text as a whole and its message in the Johannine context. This may put a strain on the reader, to try to find the real balance of the arguments and the total assessments after a long series of individual analyses of small units and of structural features, but such a procedure would seem to do the text justice, bearing in mind the purpose of my analysis.

[9] Thus Cullmann [2]1950 and Strathmann, Comm., ad loc. Some scholars have interpreted the text as referring to baptism, which purifies man from sin, or to the sanctification of marriage, Smitmans 1966, pp. 53f.

[10] See the survey in Smitmans 1966, pp. 54ff, and H. Räisänen's dissertation on the mother of Jesus in NT from 1969, and also the mariological survey of Collins 1972.

[11] van der Loos 1965, pp. 618, 615.

[12] Hanhart 1970, p. 23, note 3, pp. 38—43.

[13] See above, ch. 1.

2.2 The Statement Units of the Text (U 1–U 31)

Before analysing the structural elements of a text we must have a preliminary idea of what the text is saying, or at least of various ways of understanding its minor elements.[1] There are several ways of dividing it up. For theoretical and practical reasons I have chosen to present it in *statement* (or information) *units,* that is units which contain one statement (or a limited piece of information). In the majority of cases they are "nuclear structures", but certain simple genitive constructions, such as Jesus' mother, Jesus' disciples, the hour of Jesus, the purification of the Jews, and Jesus' *doxa,* have not been further segmented.[2] All the statements in direct speech have been linked with the quotation formulas since they do not belong to the same level as the other statement units but are subordinate to them. In order to arrive at a preliminary idea of the content of the text we intend in the following pages to discuss problems of textual criticism, of vocabulary, and, to some extent, of syntax, related to the individual statement units, and to pay special attention to the relation between the linguistic elements and the external situation presented by the text on the one hand (the reality), and the Johannine text in general on the other (parallels of form and content in Jn). The conclusions I draw in this section should be very preliminary, and in some cases I merely offer various possible interpretations. It is impossible to arrive at a comprehensive assessment, or a total interpretation, of the text, before the analysis of the statement units and the structure of the text is complete. —There is a survey of the statement units (in English translation) on the following page.

U 1 $\tau\tilde{\eta}$ $\dot{\eta}\mu\acute{\epsilon}\rho\alpha$ $\tau\tilde{\eta}$ $\tau\rho\acute{\iota}\tau\eta$
It was on the third day.
The temporal phrase U 1 links our text with the preceding passage and forms a transition. This is confirmed by, among other features, the use of the particle ($\kappa\alpha\acute{\iota}$) and the direct introduction of the new situation.[3] The point at issue is how we are to define the meaning of this Greek expression, which normally signifies "the day after the morrow".[4]

[1] See 1.2.

[2] The segmentation is justified by the belief that the verb (the verbal expression) functions as a centre, as a "nucleus" with different adjuncts—in traditional grammar subject, objects, adverbial modifiers—as "satellites". Every unit may be regarded as "a miniature drama, whose plot is given by the main predicate and whose actors (in their various roles) are the nominal expressions that occur with them", Langendoen 1970, p. 62. See also Fillmore 1968 and Chafe 1970. E.A. Nida—see 1.2, note 84—has sometimes called these structures "nuclear structures". My units in 2.2 correspond as a rule to what Nida and Taber call "kernel sentences", Nida-Taber 1969, pp. 39ff. M.A.K. Halliday focuses the information flow in the text and calls the smallest units "information units", Halliday 1967, p. 200.

[3] Schlatter, Comm., ad loc.

[4] See the material in Barrett, Comm., ad loc.

A survey
of
the statement units
in
Jn 2:1—11

	1	It was on the third day
	2	There was a wedding at Cana
	3	Cana is in Galilee
	4	The mother of Jesus was there
	5	Jesus also was invited to the wedding
	6	His disciples were invited
	7	There was no wine
	8	Jesus' mother says to him
	a	They have no wine
	9	Jesus says to her
	a	What have you to do with me
	b	O woman
	c	My hour has not yet come
	10	His mother says to the servants
	a	Do whatever he tells you
	11	There were some vessels there
	12	They were of stone
	13	There were six of them
	14	They were for the purification of the Jews
	15	They held 2 à 3 bathsfull each
	16	Jesus says to them
	a	Fill the vessels with water
	17	They filled them to the brim
	18	He says to them
	a	Now draw some out and take it to the steward of the feast
	19	They took it
	20	The Steward tasted the water
	21	The water had become wine
	22	He did not know where it came from
	23	The servants knew it
	24	They had drawn the water
	25	The steward calls the bridegroom
	26	He says to him
	a	Every man serves the good wine first and when men have drunk freely, then the poor wine
	b	You have kept the good wine until now
	27	This Jesus did at Cana
	28	Cana is in Galilee
	29	This is the beginning of the signs
	30	He revealed his glory
	31	His disciples believed in him

Hebrew and Aramaic often use phrases such as "after three days" and "on the third day" as general expressions of time, these being literally reproduced in the LXX.[5] This usage would suggest that U 1 is "ein Perikopen-Initium . . . wie ein farbloseres 'hiernach', 'in jener Zeit'".[6] This is contradicted however by the explicit counting of days in 1:19ff and perhaps also by the placing of the adjective. The usual word order in Greek, $\tau \tilde{\eta} \ \tau \rho i \tau \eta \ \dot{\eta} \mu \acute{\epsilon} \rho q$, is always used to refer to "the third day" in the NT,[7] apart from Lk 18:33 and the early formulation in 1 Cor 15:4. LXX has the same word order as the Hebrew, i.e. with adjectives following their nouns.[8] The adjective in U 1 would therefore seem either to express emphasis[9] or to be a phrase influenced by the Hebrew. Only if the former is true can the word order in U 1 be regarded as indicating that we here have a counting of days.[10]

The main reason for the translations "on the third day", "when the third day was at hand"—instead of the general "thereupon"—is to be found, however, in the composition of 1:19ff. The events are there arranged in a clearly chronological framework:

The first day: 1:19—28 (v. 28 is in the nature of a conclusion).
The second day: 1:29—34 (marked by $\tau \tilde{\eta} \ \dot{\epsilon} \pi \alpha \dot{\nu} \rho \iota \nu$).
The third day: 1:35—42 (marked by $\tau \tilde{\eta} \ \dot{\epsilon} \pi \alpha \dot{\nu} \rho \iota \nu$; cf. v. 39).
The fourth day: 1:43—51 (marked by $\tau \tilde{\eta} \ \dot{\epsilon} \pi \alpha \dot{\nu} \rho \iota \nu$).

The phrase $\tau \tilde{\eta} \ \dot{\epsilon} \pi \alpha \dot{\nu} \rho \iota \nu$ in the NT implies a clear counting of days.[11] This also applies in Jn 6:22 where 6:1—59(71) links up with a unit of two days, and in Jn 12:12 where we also have a two day framework (12:1ff). After such a marking of days it seems unnatural to interpret the opening phrase in 2:1 as a general statement of time.[12]

How then are the days to be counted? The method that comes immediately to mind is to add a sixth to the four days explicitly mentioned, that referred to in 2:1—11 as "the third day". Then as at the end of Jn (12:1—19:42), and perhaps also in Jn 11, we have a period of six days.[13] Several scholars have tried to elicit a seven day scheme from the text,

[5] The linguistic material is given in Bode 1970, pp. 105ff, and Jeremias 1971, pp. 221ff.
[6] Thus Schmidt 1921, p. 33.
[7] Mt 16:21; 17:23; 20:19; 27:64; Lk 9:22; 24:7, 46; Acts 10:40.
[8] According to Hatch-Redpath's Concordance, with some exceptions, e.g. Gen 31:12. The Hebrew text almost always has שלישי יום.
[9] Abbott 1906, pp. 63f.
[10] The word order has been noted, since there are some variant readings. See the textual apparatus in Nestle-Aland.
[11] Mt 27:62; Mk 11:12 and especially in the marking of days in Acts 10:9,23f; 14:20 (?); 20:7; 21:8; 22:30; 23:32; 25:6, 23.
[12] Cf. ($\dot{\epsilon} \xi \epsilon \lambda \vartheta \epsilon \tilde{\iota} \nu$) in 2:12, which may be a parallel expression to the vague transitional phrase $\mu \epsilon \tau \dot{\alpha} \ \tau o \tilde{\nu} \tau o$, 3:22; 5:1; 6:1; 7:1; 13:7; 19:38; 21:1. The use of $\mu \epsilon \tau \dot{\alpha} \ \tau o \tilde{\nu} \tau o$ in 2:12; 11:7,11; 19:28, however, indicates a more specific temporal marking in this expression. On different opinions, see Brown, Comm., ad 2:12. 2:12 as a transitional passage belongs more to what precedes than to what follows (persons, places).
[13] On the Passover week, see the temporal markers in 12:1,12; 13:1,30; 18:28; 19:14, 31, 42 and 20:1, 19, (26). The text, as we now have it, gives the following data: *1.* The anointing at Bethany, 12:1ff, marks the beginning of Jesus' last week—in contrast to the Synoptics. What happens on the first day is linked by v. 7 to the last day, the day of Jesus' burial, i.e. the eve of the Passover, 19:14, 31, 42. — *2.* All that "was coming upon" Jesus (18:4) happened *before* the

to allow of its interpretation as a parallel to the seven days of creation but such a solution raises various problems with the text as we now possess it.[14] Boismard's introduction of a new day in 1:47 does not accord with the structure of the text in general, and a division at 1:39/41 can hardly be supported by the variants of the text of v. 41.[15] The content of the text and the temporal marking in v. 39 would tend to indicate that the events in 1:35—42 took place within a period of two days. Since πρῶτος or πρῶτον in v. 41 invites change for linguistic reasons, it is easier to explain why πρῶτος or πρῶτον became πρωΐ than vice versa. The old variation *mane* would rather indicate that, by reason of the timing expressed in 1:35 and 1:43, 1:35—42 are to be regarded as referring to one day, since the chronological scheme does not seem to have been derived from the events themselves but to be a pattern imposed on the narrative in 1:19ff.

Thus "on the third day" means "on the sixth day". The content of 1:19ff may perhaps justify beginning the count again at 1:35: there are two parts, 1:19—34 and 1:35—41, with 1:35f as an obvious transition.[16] We should then have 2+3 days. Yet would it not be more natural to say "and (as early as) the following day" or the like in 2:1, instead of the emphatic "on the third day"? It is possible to count exclusively to seven days but the inclusive way of counting is more usual in the Biblical texts.[17]

We find an interesting parallel to this chronological pattern in Targum Pseudo-Jonathan.[18] There the events in Ex 19—24 of how Israel became the people of God is set in an eight day framework with the explicit order, first, second, third, fourth, sixth (called "the third day"), seventh and eight days. According to Jewish tradition this week was one of preparation for the Lord's revelation on Sinai and the giving of the Law.[19] Acts 2, for

Jewish Passover, which was a Sabbath (Friday - Saturday) this year, 19:31,42. His death and burial had happened before ca. 6.00 p.m. on Friday when the 15th Nisan began. — *3.* The first day of this temporally well marked period in Jesus' life was, according to 12:1, six days before the Passover, probably a Sabbath. The expression ἐπαύριον in v. 12 indicates that the meal took place in the evening, after the Sabbath, Brown, Comm., ad loc. The central event in Jn, Jesus' death on Golgotha, must have happened on the 6th day. — *4.* The day of Resurrection was the first day of the week, i.e. according to what has been mentioned here, the 8th day, 20:1,19; cf. the expression in 20:26. — Bultmann's scepticism about the possibilities of arriving at a temporal scheme for the last days of Jesus' life in Jn (Comm., ad 12:1) does not seem justified. For a six day scheme, see Westcott, Barrett and Brown, Comm., ad loc. — For the Lazarus narrative, see the temporal markers in 11:6, 17.

[14] See, for example, Bernard, Mollat and Strathmann, Comm., ad loc., Boismard 1956 and Barrosse 1959. Weise 1966, pp. 48ff, counts seven days, by interpreting μένειν as "stay during the Sabbath", which is not linguistically proved. For further arguments against a seven day scheme, see Brown, Comm., pp. 105f.

[15] Boismard 1956, p. 95. See Brown, Comm., pp. 85, 106.

[16] The first part covers two days, with John the Baptist as the main character, the second part three days (with 2:1—11) and concerns Jesus and his disciples. See 2.2, U 6.

[17] Cf. the expression "on the third day" of the resurrection of Jesus. The phrase seems to be a parallel to "after two days", Jn 4:43; (11:6). See 3.2.4.

[18] Potin 1971, pp. 314ff, and Serra 1971, pp. 1ff, refer to the Targ. Pseudo-Jonathan for the interpretation of Jn 2:1, also Grassi 1972, p. 133. For an extended analysis of the different Targum texts to Ex 19; 20; 24, see Potin 1971.

[19] See below 2.4.3.

example, seems to indicate clearly that the Early Church interpreted its origin in the light of the Sinai tradition.[20] If indeed the chronology of Jn 1:19ff is dependent on the Jewish tradition on Ex 19—24, certain features of the Johannine text may be explained by this material. A.M. Serra finds the following parallels in addition to the chronology:[21]

1. Moses and Jesus *are called* and *go down* ($\dot{\epsilon}\kappa\dot{\alpha}\lambda\epsilon\sigma\epsilon\nu$ / $\dot{\epsilon}\kappa\lambda\dot{\eta}\vartheta\eta$ and $\kappa\alpha\tau\dot{\epsilon}\beta\eta$ / $\kappa\alpha\tau\dot{\epsilon}\beta\eta$ in the LXX Ex 19:16, 20, 24, 25 and Jn 2:1f, 12).

2. People *obey* the orders given them ($\pi\dot{\alpha}\nu\tau\alpha$, $\ddot{\sigma}\sigma\alpha$ $\epsilon\tilde{\iota}\pi\epsilon\nu$ $\dot{o}$ $\vartheta\epsilon\dot{o}\varsigma$, $\pi\sigma\iota\dot{\eta}\sigma\sigma\mu\epsilon\nu$ $\kappa\alpha\dot{\iota}$ $\dot{\alpha}\kappa\sigma\upsilon\sigma\dot{o}\mu\epsilon\vartheta\alpha$ / $\ddot{o}$ $\tau\iota$ $\dot{\alpha}\nu$ $\lambda\dot{\epsilon}\gamma\eta$ $\dot{\upsilon}\mu\tilde{\iota}\nu$ $\pi\sigma\iota\dot{\eta}\sigma\alpha\tau\epsilon$ in the LXX Ex 19:8, cf. 24:3,7, and Jn 2:5).

3. The *glory* of the Lord is revealed, that men will *believe in* Moses/Jesus. (The Lord *revealed* his *glory*, that the people should *believe in* Moses, according to the Targum to 19:9,11. Cf. LXX Ex 19:9,11 and Jn 2:11).

I shall have reason to return to Serra's comparisons in order to show that a number of features in the text are best explained from a Sinai "screen".[22] Yet at this stage I may say that even apart from this Jewish material the introductory phrase, U 1 in our text, links 2:1—11 with 1:19ff in a *six* day pattern. Whether or not the phrase also refers to the Day of Resurrection[23] can only be determined on the basis of the interpretation of the text as a whole. The Gospel itself does not accentuate the third day (the expression does not occur in or before the Passion narrative) but it does have a timetable of 6 + 2 days in which the emphasis is on the sixth day and then on the eighth day, which is at the same time the first day of the week.[24]

U 2 $\kappa\alpha\dot{\iota}$ . . . $\gamma\dot{\alpha}\mu\sigma\varsigma$ $\dot{\epsilon}\gamma\dot{\epsilon}\nu\epsilon\tau\sigma$ $\dot{\epsilon}\nu$ $K\alpha\nu\dot{\alpha}$
There was a wedding at Cana.

The verb form shows rather that a wedding took place, not that it was in progress.[25] The event is seen as a whole, described only as a fact by the aorist $\dot{\epsilon}\gamma\dot{\epsilon}\nu\epsilon\tau\sigma$, which is often used in the introduction to a new section.[26]

A Jewish wedding normally consisted of a procession, in which the bridegroom's friends conducted the bride to his home, and a wedding feast.[27] According to certain sources this would begin on a Wednesday and continue for seven days. The guests, who usually brought gifts, came and went during the festivities. A considerable quantity of

---

[20] This interpretation seems to belong to traditions which Luke took over, Noack 1968, pp. 93ff, especially pp. 104f and 108f.

[21] Serra 1971, pp. 17ff.

[22] See below, 2.4.3.

[23] Dodd 1953, p. 300, and Boismard 1956, p. 136, let it refer to the Day of Resurrection. See also Smitmans 1966, p. 10.

[24] See above, note 13.

[25] Cf. Jn 1:6, 14, 17, and especially 3:25; 6:16; 7:43; 10:19,22 (the significance "became, came, appeared", not "was going on").

[26] This applies especially to the phrase $\kappa\alpha\dot{\iota}$ $\dot{\epsilon}\gamma\dot{\epsilon}\nu\epsilon\tau\sigma$; see Beyer, pp. 29ff, and in Jn also $\dot{\epsilon}\gamma\dot{\epsilon}\nu\epsilon\tau\sigma$ in 1:6, 14; 3:25; 7:43; 10:19, 22.

[27] See the texts and the literature mentioned in Schnackenburg, Comm., ad loc., and Smitmans 1966, p. 11. The wedding ceremonies had a legal, covenantal character rather than a sacral, religious meaning, Goodenough, vol. 12, p. 125.

wine was consumed. Our text makes no explicit mention of these wedding customs. Either they were assumed to be well known to the reader or the interest does not lie in the description of the situation.

In the Jewish and Christian environments of the time the word *wedding* certainly had theological associations. The covenant between the Lord and the maiden Israel was depicted as a marriage.[28] Moreover allusions to wedding feasts are to be found in the accounts of the expected eschatological age.[29] The metaphor also appears in the NT in parables of the Kingdom of God, Mt 8:11; 22:2; 25:1,5,6; Rev 19:7; Lk 12:36, in the description of Jesus, Mk 2:19f, in the account of the Church of Christ, 2 Cor 11:2; Rev 21:2,9, but in Jn only here in ch. 2 and in 3:29.[30] Jn in particular notes that Jesus acts during feasts, especially the great feasts of the Jewish calendar.[31]

The event takes place at Cana.[32] This town was obviously important to Jn. It is impressed on the reader by the repetition in 2:11 ($\dot{\epsilon}\pi o\acute{\iota}\eta\sigma\epsilon\nu$ $\dot{\epsilon}\nu$ $Kav\acute{a}$) and in 4:46 ($\pi\acute{a}\lambda\iota\nu$ $\epsilon\iota\varsigma$ $\tau\grave{\eta}\nu$ $Kav\acute{a}$ ... $\ddot{o}\pi o\nu$ $\dot{\epsilon}\pi o\acute{\iota}\eta\sigma\epsilon\nu$ $\tau\grave{o}$ $\ddot{\upsilon}\delta\omega\rho$ $o\dot{\iota}\nu o\nu$).[33] In 21:2 we are told that Nathanael, who is linked with our text by 1:45ff, came from Cana. It is difficult to arrive at a certain identification of the town. The Greek transcription suggests Khirbet Kana, some 13 km north of Nazareth.[34]

The evangelist's method of emphasizing the site, and his exegesis of, for instance, Siloam in 9:7[35] poses the question of whether the name Cana was used in any way allusively. It is generally derived from קנה "acquire" and may be translated *property, possession*.[36] The idea of Jesus and "his own sheep", his own people ($o\dot{\iota}$ $\ddot{\iota}\delta\iota o\iota$), which the Son received from the Father, is predominant in Jn, cf. 1:10f; 4:44; 10:1ff; 13:1;17, partly because of the severe tension in the Gospel between the Synagogue and the Church.[37] Who were in fact the real people of God? How could a "new" people of God be created from the "old"? Why did "his own" not receive Jesus? Reflection on questions such as these seems to underlie much of John's writing,[38] which may support the belief that the very name Cana was significant for the *narrator*. Hanhart also associated the second miracle at Cana, Jn 4:46ff, with Is 11:11 *en passant*: "In that day the Lord will extend

---

[28] E Stauffer in ThWNT, vol. 1, pp. 651f, Knight 1959, pp. 177ff, 219ff, 323f, and below, 2.4.4, and the passages cited there.

[29] Is 54:4ff; 62:4f, Batey 1971, pp. 2ff.

[30] See J. Jeremias in ThWNT, vol. 4, pp. 1092ff. The text is rich in associations, but this is not sufficient reason for describing the text as an allegory; against Holtzmann, Comm., ad loc.

[31] Schlatter, Comm., ad loc.

[32] The events in Jn very frequently include a notice as to place, Kundsin 1925, pp. 10ff. His explanation is that the texts have been bound to certain places as cult legend.

[33] See 2.2, U 27 and 3.2.3.

[34] See the material and literature mentioned in Schnackenburg, Comm., ad loc. Cana may have been the seat of one of the 24 priestly divisions, Kundsin 1925, pp. 15, 22f.

[35] Cf. also 1:47; 3:22 (?); 5:1(?).

[36] Thus always in the Church Fathers (Origen, Epiphanius, Gaudentius, Jerome), Smitmans 1966, pp. 82f. Kreyenbühl, Comm., ad loc., links the name Cana to קנה "create (Gen 14:19; Dt 32:6; Ps 139:13; Pr 8:22; Ps 104:24).

[37] See 3.2.3.

[38] See ch. 5.

his hand yet *a second time to recover*(לִקְנוֹת)the remnant which is left of his people".[39] The possibility of a symbolic use of Cana is apparent, at least to the narrator, but only the determination of the function and the character of the total text can provide us with additional criteria.[40]

Hanhart takes a further step towards an ingenious symbolic interpretation in deriving Cana from *Capernaum* and *Nazareth*, referring to the mention of these towns in the text (1:45f and 2:12), and to their association with rejection (Nazareth, e.g. Lk 4:16ff; Mk 6:1ff) and acceptance (Capernaum, Lk 4:31ff). Jn 2:1–11 would then link the "theology" of the two places.[41] Such an interpretation however must clearly prove that some contemporary writers did deal with texts in such a way and that Jn is such a type of text.

The naming of the place in 2:1–11 is usually explained by mention of the fact that the name is found in the traditional material at the evangelist's disposal and is thus, so to speak, part of the "scenery", or that it belongs to his narrative style.[42] As we said above, Jn gives very precise data about the site of events,[43] and in some cases the place is extremely important for the text as a whole, in ch. 4 for example.[44] The association of the attribute τῆς Γαλιλαίας with Cana may indicate that the naming of the place is not solely ornamental.

U 3 τῆς Γαλιλαίας

Cana is in Galilee.

Jn always specifies that Cana is in Galilee.[45] It seems far-fetched to assume that the evangelist only used this attribute to exclude the Cana mentioned in Jos 19:28.[46] Either the attribute is part of the actual name, *or* Jn wished to inform the readers in, for instance, Asia Minor where this place, which would be unknown to them, was situated (a geographical indication) *or* he is emphasizing that the event described in our text occurred in Galilee.[47]

The immediate setting of the text is clearly associated with Galilee. Jesus *decided* to go to Galilee, 1:43.[48] He himself came from Nazareth, 1:45f. The Galilean origin of the dis-

[39] Hanhart 1970, p. 43, note 3.

[40] See the further discussion below, 2.4.4.

[41] Hanhart 1970, p. 43. He asserts that the text does not refer to a specific town. The name Cana has only a symbolic function.

[42] Some scholars suppose that the tradition behind Jn 2:1–11 comes from Cana, Kundsin 1925, pp. 22ff, Bultmann and Schnackenburg, Comm., ad loc.

[43] See above, note 32.

[44] See below, 3.2.3, and compare the notice as to place in 3:22ff; 5:1ff and chs. 7–9.

[45] Jn 2:1,11; 4:46; 21:2. Josephus, Vita 86, mentions κώμη τῆς Γαλιλαίας ἣ προσαγορεύεται Κανά, a night's march from Tiberias (Vita 90). For the grammatical construction, see Mt 21:11 (Ναсαρὲϑ τῆς Γαλιλαίας); 2:1; Mk 1:9; Acts 16:12; 22:3.

[46] Such an explanation is given in, for example, Bultmann and Lindars, Comm., ad loc.

[47] On supporters of different views, see Smitmans 1966, p. 28.

[48] The formulation is remarkable: Jesus *wanted to* (ἠϑέλησεν) set out (   ) for Galilee. The wanderings of Jesus in Jn seem to be narrated as conscious parts of the salvation work of the Son. See 4:44; 7:1 and on the whole the consciousness of the Son in all his acts, for example, in 2:24; 13:1, 3, 18; 14:31; 18:1ff. All that happens has a touch of divine "programming". See also below, 3.2.3.

ciples is mentioned, 1:45 (21:2). Jesus is going down to Capernaum, 2:12, before Jerusalem and "the Jews" are referred to. There is some doubt as to where Nathanael was when Jesus saw him under the fig tree, but the mention in 21:2 may be taken as an indication that in Johannine circles the event was regarded as taking place in Cana.

What part then does Galilee play in St. John's Gospel? If we analyse the geographical details and the events occurring in the various places a certain pattern emerges: Jesus wanders in a circle, from the land beyond Jordan/the Sea of Galilee, to Galilee (possibly through Samaria) and to Judea up to Jerusalem.[49]

> A. 1:19—3:21: *Bethany* (1:28f, 35), toward *Galilee* (1:43), *Cana in Galilee* (2:11), down to *Capernaum* (2:12) and up to *Jerusalem* (2:13, 23).
>
> B. 3:22—5:47: *the countryside of Judea, Aenon near Salim*, probably in Samaria (3:22f, reference to the land beyond Jordan),[50] leaves *Judea* (4:3) and goes through *Samaria* to *Galilee* (4:45f, 40, 45, 47, 54), back to *Cana in Galilee* (4:46) and thence to *Capernaum* (4:46, 47, 49, 51) and then goes up to *Jerusalem* (5:1).
>
> C. 6:1—10:39: On the other side of the Sea of Galilee/Lake Tiberias (6:1), across to *Capernaum* (6:19, 21, 24, 59), around *Galilee* (7:1,9) and up to *Jerusalem* (7:10ff).
>
> D. 10:40—20:31: *Bethany* beyond Jordan (10:40), to *Bethany* near Jerusalem (11:17f, 20, 30, 32, 38), to *Ephraim* near the wilderness (11:54), to *Bethany* near Jerusalem (12:1), to *Jerusalem* (12:12).

This circular pattern may be entirely fortuitous and lacking in any function but its special nature and its connections with the reaction to Jesus should be noted.

All four circles begin with a mention of the region on the other side (πέραν 1:28, 3:26, 6:1; 10:40; cf. 18:1) and there are three explicit references to the activity of John the Baptist, first in general terms, 1:19—35, then a minor episode before John is thrown into prison, 3:22—30, and finally a brief item in the third person, the wording of which suggests that John is dead, 10:40f. John "is decreasing" but Jesus "is increasing", 3:30. The closest parallel is in the first two cycles in which Jerusalem is far less important than in the last two. The omission of Galilee from the last cycle is striking: there Jesus circles round Jerusalem, more and more hidden from those who did not belong to him (11:54; 12:36). The separation between those who are his own and those who are not has already taken place.

Jesus' main work is done in Jerusalem in Judea, chs. 13—20. Jerusalem/Judea is designated Jesus' own country in Jn (ἡ ἰδία πατρίς) a country which does not accept its prophet, 4:44.[51] His own (οἱ ἴδιοι) received him not, 1:11f. The people of Jerusalem do not believe, or some of them believe but their faith will not hold in the face of the revelation which is to come, 2:23ff; 7:31ff; 8:30ff; 12:42. Above all it is the leaders (of the Jewish people) in Jerusalem who do not wholeheartedly believe. They have the words and

---

[49] For this geographical pattern, see some articles by Rafael Gyllenberg (1960, 1965, 1967).
[50] See 3.2.3.
[51] On Jesus "own country", see 3.2.3.

works of Jesus before their eyes (ἔμπροσθεν αὐτῶν, 12:37),[52] but they do not receive him.

There were, however, others who received Jesus: Jn says that the majority of these came from Galilee and Samaria, from the areas of the less orthodox Jews, "Galilee of the Gentiles" and heretical Samaria, the region where John the Baptist had worked, 1:35–51; 2:11f; 3:26; 4:9,30, 39–42, 45, 50; 6:2, 14, 24. Jesus himself is a Galilean, the son of Joseph of Nazareth, 1:46, 6:42, cf. 7:41ff, a fact which provokes several suspicious queries:[53] "Can anything good come out of Nazareth?" 1:46; "Is the Christ to come from Galilee?" 7:41f; "Surely no prophet will rise in Galilee?" 7:52. When Nicodemus defends Jesus he is abused as a Galilean, 7:52.[54] Nathanael, the ideal disciple,[55] believes in Jesus despite his Galilean origin, the disciples too are from Galilee. Large crowds had followed Jesus there, 6:2, 14, 22ff, 66, and the Twelve, the genuine Israel,[56] were chosen from this Galilean throng, 6:67ff.

These features of the Gospel make it difficult to deny Galilee the role of the site of "acceptance and discipleship", also confirmed by the addition in ch. 21, the revelation beside Lake Tiberias.[57] This "geographical symbolism" seems to be specially connected with *Cana in Galilee*. There the disciples see Jesus' *doxa* for the first time and believe; Nathanael, the typical disciple, was from there, and from Cana came the life-giving word which had immediate effect, 4:46ff. Cana in Galilee is in some sense an opposite of *Jerusalem in Judea*. In the light of Jn as a whole U 3 may be intended to provide not only geographical information but also a symbolic and an interpretative element which by its "ecclesial" overtones contributes to the total understanding of the text.

U 4 καὶ ἦν ἡ μήτηρ τοῦ Ἰησοῦ ἐκεῖ

The mother of Jesus was there.

The phrase ἦν ἐκεῖ [58] in Jn introduces individuals or objects which are essential to the course of events immediately following, 2:1,6; 4:6; 5:5. The narrator does not say why Jesus' mother was there.[59] She is presented only by her relationship to Jesus. Later she

[52] Jesus had spoken openly to them in the synagogues and in the Temple, 18:20f; many had borne witness to Jesus, John the Baptist, 1:19ff; 3:22ff, the man born blind, 9:1ff, those who had seen Lazarus raised from the dead, 11:45ff; 12:9ff, all who had heard him (the disciples), 18:21.
[53] Cf. the problems of the places in Mt 1–2, Stendahl 1960, pp. 94ff.
[54] It is in this context that we have the scornful words of the Jewish leaders about the people who do not know the Law, 7:49. Cf. the accusation of Jesus that he is a Samaritan in 8:48.
[55] See 2.2, U 6.
[56] See 2.2, U 6.
[57] See Meeks 1967, pp. 313ff, and Rissi 1967, pp. 82ff. This symbolism may partly be explained by the fact that Johannine Christianity has some connections with Samaria and Galilee. For further discussion, see below 3.2.3 and ch. 5. On Galilee as a place of revelation, see Lohmeyer 1936, Lightfoot 1938 and Steinseifer 1971.
[58] Rabbinic usage according to Schlatter, Comm., ad loc.
[59] This question is, however, of interest to many readers and interpreters and was so at a very early date. There are many explanations: Jesus' family was related to the family of the bride or the bridegroom or knew them very well, the groom was a friend of Jesus, or John the Evangelist, they were invited by Nathanael who came from Cana, etc. See Holtzmann, Comm., ad loc., and Smitmans 1966, pp. 11f.

appears to know the servants of the house, v. 5.

Jn always uses the designation "the mother of Jesus", 2:1, 3, 5, 12; 6:42; 19:25—27, never the name Mary. Occasionally he gives the names of individuals, Nicodemus, Lazarus, Malchus etc, but usually contents himself with a general description: the royal official at Capernaum, 4:46ff; the man who had been ill for 38 years at the pool of Bethesda, 5:1ff; the man born blind in Jerusalem, 9:1ff; "the disciple whom Jesus loved". Jn lnks Jesus' mother with the beloved disciple, 19:25—27. He allows her to appear only at the beginning and at the end of the Gospel, 2:1—12 and 19:25—27, both times in the context of the "hour" of Jesus, both times addressed as γύναι.[60] This feature, like Jn's way of allowing certain persons to appear as types, as representatives of a group of individuals,[61] compels us to discuss in all seriousness whether Jesus' mother has a special (symbolic) role in our text.[62] Jn 6:42 and 2:12 seem to make it clear that the narrator also regards her as an historical personage.[63]

U 5 ἐκλήθη δὲ καὶ ὁ Ἰησοῦς . . . εἰς τὸν γάμον

Jesus also was invited to the wedding.

Following the usage in 3:23; 18:2, 5, 18; 19:39 and 20:6, καί should be referred to the subject as a whole and not linked with the later καί to mean "both - and". The most natural translation would be: Jesus, like Mary, was invited, or possibly to understand the text as meaning that Jesus was invited together with others.[64] In both cases U 5 emphasizes that Jesus too was among the wedding guests, but this fact is not explicitly linked with what occurred.[65] The narrator's sole interest seems to be to place the necessary persons in a wedding situation before the dialogue can begin. The phrase εἰς τὸν γάμον joins the first two verses formally into one unit (inclusion).

U 6 . . . καὶ οἱ μαθηταὶ αὐτοῦ

His disciples were invited.

The disciples have no independent status in the text: where Jesus goes they go.[66] This is

---

[50] See 2.2, U 9b.

[51] For example, Nicodemus, Thomas, the beloved disciple. See Krafft 1956, Oehler 1956 and below, the excursus on the beloved disciple (4.4).

[62] Cf. the use of "my brothers" in Jn 20:17 (and 21:23). Words denoting relatives are often used in Jn in a transferred meaning, Bouttier 1964, pp. 182ff, and Feuillet 1966.

[63] For further discussion, see 2.4.4.

[64] Καλεῖν meaning "invite" only here in Jn. Cf. Mt 22:3f, 8f; Lk 7:39; 14:7ff; Rev 19:9. Serra also here sees a connection with Ex 19:24; see above, 2.2, U 1.

[65] Commentators sometimes discuss whether Jesus was invited when he was on the way there, or since he was already there, referring, for example, to the fact that the aorist in this passage implies that Jesus was invited after the feast had begun, Meyer, Comm., ad loc., Abbott 1906, p. 335. Such an interpretation of the aorist is rightly rejected by Schmidt 1921, p. 33, and Bultmann, Comm., ad loc. Cf. Stagg 1972.

[66] Holtzmann, Comm., ad loc. Variant readings of 2:12 and the formulation in Epist. Apost. ch. 5 ("Und man lud ihn ein mit seiner Mutter und seinen Brüdern", Hennecke-Schneemelcher, vol. 1, p. 128) have been adduced as a reason for reading only οἱ ἀδελφοί αὐτοῦ as the original text,

our first encounter in Jn with the expression "Jesus' disciples".[67] 1:35 mentions two of John the Baptist's disciples who left him to follow Jesus. The entire section, 1:35—51, is later dominated by disciples and their relation to Jesus. Notwithstanding that almost every statement unit in these verses explicitly mentions one or more of them, Jesus is here singled out as *Rabbi,* 1:38, 49, interpreted "teacher", 1:38. They are with Jesus on his wanderings in 2:12. This nucleus of disciples around Jesus includes at least five persons, Andrew + an anonymous individual + Simon + Philip + Nathanael. Bearing in mind the role of the anonymous disciple and the "ecclesial" associations of the number six it is tempting to interpret the very obscure verse 1:41 — by reading πρῶτος and a reflexive meaning into ἴδιος — as suggesting yet another disciple, so that John the son of Zebedee, well known from other texts, also found his brother James. We would then have six disciples at Cana.[68] The interpretation is possible but presumes that the readers for whom the narrator was writing are very well informed about the events described and can understand his meaning from the very slight indication in v. 41.

The term "disciples" in our text may thus mean those named in ch. 1. The word may also refer to the Twelve, mentioned in 6:67 and 20:24,[69] or to a less specific group of believers; cf., for example, 6:60ff; 19:38. The latter is the least probable, while the idea of a definite group is supported by the comment in 2:11. This links the text with 20:30f, which says that Jesus did his signs "in the presence of his disciples". 20:30f and 2:11 provide some justification for assuming the same reference in 2:2. Yet whether or not we refer οἱ μαθηταί to the five or six in ch. 1 or to another specific group they would still seem, for Jn, to represent the real Israel, those who received Jesus.[70]

How did this Israel, distinct from the people of Israel and therefore often called the "new" Israel, come into existence according to ch. 1? All the disciples save Philip were brought to Jesus by the testimony of another, the first two through John the Baptist, Simon through Andrew and Nathanael through Philip. They *hear* the word of revelation, 1:36, 41, 45, and accept it. Jesus then reveals who Simon and Nathanael really are.[71] Thus we have a double meeting; first with the witness to Jesus, then with Jesus himself. A promise is also given of fuller understanding ("seeing") in the future, 1:50f. Thus: the dis-

Wellhausen 1908, p. 13, Bultmann, Comm., p. 79. The disciples, however, play a very important role in the narrative as it now stands, Schnackenburg, Comm., ad loc.

[67] So far as I know, there is only one investigation dealing with the very important term οἱ μαθηταί (and related words) in Jn, namely an article of Moreno Jiménez (1971). Cf. Rigaux 1970 on the disciples in Jn 17. Brown's suggestion (Comm., ad loc.) that Jn uses μαθηταί instead of ἀπόστολοι for historical reason— ἀπόστολοι only for the time after the resurrection—is hardly plausible. The term οἱ μαθηταί rather links the first group around Jesus to the disciples of the evangelist's own time, a usage which is partly parallel to that of Mt, Luz 1971, pp. 169f. They are Jesus' own people, the new Israel.

[68] See the arguments in Turner 1965, pp. 135ff. Schwank, Comm., ad loc., gives an ecclesiological interpretation of the Cana narrative and would, therefore, see six disciples in Cana.

[69] Note the twelve baskets in 6:13, too.

[70] This is justified by the description of the disciples in Jn, especially in ch. 17, and of Nathanael in ch. 1. See B. Gerhardsson in ²SBU, vol. 2, col. 268f, with the literature mentioned there, and Pancaro 1969—70, pp. 123ff.

[71] ἴδε functions here as a revelation formula, de Goedt 1961—62, Brown, Comm., ad loc.

31

ciples *hear of* Jesus, they *meet* Jesus personally, they *are expected to be able to see* who he really is.[72]

Nathanael is described in more detail than the other disciples: he is sitting "unter dem Baum der Erkenntnis Gottes und seines Wortes" and is thus presented as one who knows the writings of Moses and the prophets.[73] He rejects the idea that the Messiah will come from Nazareth in Galilee but still accepts the challenge to come and see. Jesus then reveals Nathanel's true being: he is truly an Israelite (ἴδε ἀληϑῶς Ἰσραηλίτης).[74] He makes the most significant confession in ch. 1: "Rabbi, you are the Son of God, you are the King of Israel". After this deep insight it is somewhat unexpected to hear that the "greater things" are in the future: Nathanael and the disciples will "see" who Jesus truly is, the Son of Man; they will understand the relationship between him and God, the union of the Father and the Son.[75]

This account makes Nathanael into an ideal figure, the representative of the Israel of which Jesus is King.[76] Some scholars hold that 1:47 is a play on the name Jacob, and perhaps also on Israel, "a man who sees God".[77] The meaning of the name Nathanael, "what God has given",[78] may also be reflected in the text. This is suggested by the most remarkable description of the disciples in Jn as "whom the Father gave to the Son", ὃ δέδωκας αὐτῷ, or a similar expression, 17:2, 6, 7, 24. The disciples, in the definite form, are, according to Jn, those whom the Son received from the Father, "his own". They are a unit which can be described either in the plural or in the singular, 1:51, 10:3f, 16; 15:1ff; 17:2, 6f, 24. In ch. 1 they are summed up in the person of Nathanael.

To sum up: The disciples in U 6 are primarily those named in ch. 1, but at the same time "the disciples" as such, often mentioned in Jn. In the story about Nathanael in particular they stand out as the true Israel.[79] They have come to belong to Jesus in three stages: the testimony about him, the meeting with him, and the "seeing" of him. The account given in our text would seem, according to 1:50, to refer to the third stage but the other two will also prove to form part of our narrative.[80]

---

[72] Bovon (ed.) 1971, pp. 21ff, shows by a structural analysis of Jn 1:35–51 how the call of the disciples is described as "un passage d'un état dans un autre sous une double impulsion", "un passage de A à B grace à C + d", but he does not note the function of vv. 50f in the description of the relation between Jesus and his disciples. On how a person becomes Jesus' disciple by "hearing", see 2.2, U 10 and U 31.

[73] Jeremias 1930, p. 3; cf. Moule 1954 and Michaels 1966–67.

[74] On the revelation formula in this verse, see above, note 71.

[75] See the further discussion of the *ergon* aspect in our text, 2.4.2.

[76] See B. Gerhardsson in ²SBU, vol. 2, col. 268f, and the literature mentioned there.

[77] Besides the commentaries, see W. Gutbrod in ThWNT, vol. 3, p. 373, who cited the interpretation of Philo (ἄνϑρωπος ὁρῶν ϑεόν).

[78] Str.-B., vol. 2, p. 317, translating the name as "den Gott gab, Gottesgabe". On the verb "give" in Jn, see the comment on S 3 below, 3.3.2.

[79] Note also Jesus' description of Simon as Cephas, which may have some "ecclesial" associations, 1:42. Cf. Mt 16:18.

[80] Further discussion in 2.2, U 31 and 2.4.

U 7 ὑστερήσαντος οἴνου

There was no wine.

The Greek wording is notably short and vague. Its position (between the setting of the scene in vv. 1f and the dialogue in vv. 3ff) and its form (genitive absolute) show that U 7 is a transitional phrase. Jn sometimes allows a speech to be preceded by a statement equivalent in content, 11:2; 5:6f, cf. 4:46f; 6:5f and 9:1ff, which may also be the case here. The exact meaning of ὑστερήσαντος is, however, difficult to establish by comparison with other texts.[81] The verb is not used in the sense of "to be wanting, to fail" until Late Greek.[82] It is found with a substantive in the nominative—and a person as accusative—in Jesus' words to the rich young man ἕν σε ὑστερεῖ in Mk 10:21, a construction which Luke, evidently for linguistic reasons, changes to ἕν σοι λείπει.[83] According to Ps 23:1 (LXX οὐδέν με ὑστερήσει) the righteous man will want for nothing since God will provide him with everything.[84] This use of the verb suggests that U 7 be translated in general terms: there was no wine, the wine failed.

A number of MSS. give us an interesting variant reading here: οἴνον οὐκ εἶχον, ὅτι συνετελέσθη ὁ οἶνος τοῦ γάμου· εἶτα, in Latin, et factum est per multam turbam vocitorum vinum consummari mater autem . . .[85] Its unusual (clumsy) form favours this version, as does the fact that the shorter reading may be explained as a linguistic polishing of the long and clumsy variant.[86] Yet the reasons for the shorter reading carry far more weight:

1. It is supported by the majority of, and the best, manuscripts, including p[66] and p[75].[87]
2. The content is vague, and calls for explanation. The longer reading gives a detailed description of the situation: the wine is presented as a wedding wine and the text makes it clear that the guests had drunk all there was, which seems to be implied by v. 10. The shorter reading may have been thought insufficient, partly because of v. 10.

[81] Comparative material is given by U. Wilckens in ThWNT, vol. 8, pp. 590ff. He gives the traditional translation "als der Wein ausgegangen war", which may be justified by a specific understanding of the context. Other possibilities: "when the wine ran out", "since they had no wine".

[82] Besides U. Wilckens in ThWNT just mentioned, see Bauer and Schnackenburg, Comm., ad loc., with such examples as Mk 10:21; Is 51:14 (see below, note 84), Josephus, Ant XV.70; XV. 200; VI.194 and Dioscurides V.86.

[83] Mt 19:20 does not have the same construction (τί ἔτι ὑστερῶ;). The peculiar use of the accusative in Mk may depend on LXX, for example, Ps 23:1 (LXX ὑστερήσει), Taylor, Comm., ad Mk 10:21.

[84] Cf. Ps 84:12 (LXX 83:12) κύριος οὐχ ὑστερήσει τὰ ἀγαθὰ τοὺς πορευομένους ἐν ἀκακίᾳ (var.) and Neh 9:21 (LXX 2 Esdr 19:21) οὐχ ὑστέρησαν (how God nourished Israel in the desert that they lacked nothing). A variant to Is 51:14 reads καὶ οὐ μὴ ὑστερήσῃ ὁ ἄρτος αὐτοῦ.

[85] See the textual apparatus in Nestle-Aland and Metzger 1971, p. 201. The Latin text quoted is from Codex Palatinus and Codex Rhedigeranus.

[86] The longer reading is preferred by Lagrange, Bultmann, Mollat and Braun. See Smitmans 1966, p. 12, note 9. It is difficult to accept that the longer reading would give the better expression of the symbolic meaning in the text, as Braun [2]1954, pp. 49, 70, suggests.

[87] Metzger 1971, p. 201. The only Greek witness for the longer reading, Codex Sinaiticus, prima manus, is "a leading Greek representative of the Western textual tradition in John i.1—viii.38", Fee 1968—69, p. 44. Cf. Kieffer 1968, pp. 144ff, who finds a connection between Sinaiticus, p[66] and D in his thorough textual examination of Jn 6:52—71.

3. The Late Greek meaning of ὑστερεῖν may have caused changes in the wording but this could hardly have been a decisive reason, since the longer reading does not reveal any great linguistic sensitivity.[88]
4. The longer reading is a paraphrase fairly typical of the Western text.[89]

Thus despite the uniqueness of its wording,[90] the shorter reading is the more original, the longer being an early exegesis by a writer who was familiar with the situation and who read the text as an "historical" narrative. The shorter reading gives the "dialogue" greater weight and the text, being less bound by the situation, is more open to theological interpretation.

The *wine* was naturally an integral part of the wedding ceremony at that time, and the situation described in our text, presumably of rare occurrence, must have been most embarrassing for the hosts.[91] The wine is mentioned from time to time as one of the "Messianic" gifts in the accounts of the age to come.[92] In our text it has also been interpreted as a symbol. It may represent, for example, joy, spontaneity and ecstasy,[93] the blood of Christ in the Eucharist,[94] ἡ γνῶσις τοῦ θεοῦ [95] or the Spirit.[96] Yet there is no statement in our passage, in contrast to the texts about water (ch. 4) and bread (ch. 6), directly suggestive of a transferred meaning. The possible symbolical significance of the wine must be chiefly derived from its function in the text, perhaps from its relation to the water.[97]

U 8 καὶ ... λέγει ἡ μήτηρ τοῦ Ἰησοῦ πρὸς αὐτόν

a. οἶνον οὐκ ἔχουσιν

Jesus' mother says to him: "They have no wine".

The passage preceding U 8, i.e. U 1—7, is so constructed by vocabulary and syntax as to lead into the "dialogue" beginning in U 8. We have the necessary framework: the wedding, Jesus' mother, Jesus, the lack of wine. As a first speech of a "dialogue" U 8 is a close parallel to 11:2f: first the scene is set, then it is reported to Jesus (ἀσθενῶν, v. 1, ἠσθένει v. 2, Κύριε, ἴδε ὃν φιλεῖς ἀσθενεῖ v. 3).[98] As in 2:1—11 Jesus does not intervene immediately. The speeches are in indicative form but need not therefore be assertions.[99]

[88] See above, note 82. This linguistic argument is found in, for example, the commentaries of Barrett and Schnackenburg, ad loc.
[89] Thus Westcott, Comm., ad loc. On the Western text, see the short characterization in Metzger 1971, pp. xviiif.
[90] "The text of this verse of simple narrative is curiously corrupt", Barrett, Comm., ad loc.
[91] Schnackenburg, Comm., ad loc.
[92] Am 9:13; Hos 2:24; Jl 4:18; Is 29:17; Jer 31:5; Enoch 10:19; 2 Baruch 29:5; SibOr II.31f; III.620ff, 744f. See Schnackenburg, Comm., p. 342: Wine, bread and water are symbols for "die umfassende Heilsgabe des göttlichen Lebens". For NT, see Mk 2:22 par. and Holtzmann, Comm., ad loc.
[93] Bultmann and Barrett, Comm., ad loc.
[94] Cullmann ²1950, pp. 69f, with a reference to Jn 6.
[95] Dodd 1963, p. 223.
[96] See, for example, Hanhart 1970, p. 41.
[97] See below, 2.4.4.
[98] Cf. Jn 5:7f and 4:46f.
[99] Jespersen 1924, pp. 301ff.

11:2f is obviously a prayer that Jesus will come to help Lazarus.[1] In both cases the opening phrases do not indicate the nature of the speech but this must be understood from the situation, from the other speeches, and from the function of the text as a whole. This, as we said, is fairly easy to see in the case of 11:2f. There is far more doubt concerning our text, which explains the scholars' diverse interpretations of this speech.[2] It is explained purely literarily by Bultmann as an introductory phrase, typical of the genre of miracle narrative; van den Bussche considers it a feature of style and narrative technique; K.L. Schmidt sees the words in the light of the resurrection and understands them as the prayer of the believer to his Risen Lord, while others interpret it as the cry of Israel for salvation[3] or as the expression of man's poverty and need.[4] If we set the speech in an historical situation in Jesus' life, it is in the eyes of most scholars a *prayer for help*, either eschatological in character ("eine Wunderbitte") or purely human in nature, while some regard it as a *reproach:* Jesus and his followers either were not expected or brought no wedding gifts, so they should leave.[5]

Further analysis of the individual statement unit, U 8, can hardly be of much help in determining its function. The fact is that Jesus' mother tells her son of the problem. The vital issue is the *lack* of wine. The Johannine parallels, together with Mt 8:6 and Mk 8:1/Mt 15:32, indicate that the words should be seen as a request to Jesus to intervene in some way. The statement is a form of prayer. In the concrete situation described in the text the prayer is, presumably, *a request for wine for the wedding guests,* while in other contexts the prayer may have a transferred meaning. Which context is relevant can only be decided on the basis of an evaluation of the text as a whole.[6]

U 9 καὶ λέγει αὐτῇ ὁ Ἰησοῦς

a. τί ἐμοὶ καὶ σοί
b. γύναι
c. οὔπω ἥκει ἡ ὥρα μου

Jesus says to her: "O woman, what have you to do with me? My hour has not yet come.

Scholars' understanding of this unit reflects, more than in other units, their total interpretation.[7] Here it is particularly difficult to decide to what extent we should use *the situation* described and implied in the text as the basis of our analysis of the linguistic elements (the historical level) or *the wider Johannine context* (the textual level). The results of the analysis of the latter half of the speech differ widely, depending on which

---

[1] Cf. Jn 4:46ff, where we find a prayer (ἠρώτα ἵνα καταβῇ . . . κύριε, κατάβηθι), with the parallel narrative in Mt 8:6, which has an assertion. Cf. also Mt 15:22.

[2] See the survey in Smitmans 1966, pp. 13ff, and the arguments and literature he mentions.

[3] For example, Krafft, Dillon, Bauer and Sahlin interpret it as the cry of Israel, Smitmans 1966, p. 13.

[4] Thus, for example, van den Bussche, Giblet and Bouyer according to Smitmans' survey, p. 15.

[5] Thus especially Derrett 1970, pp. 228ff.

[6] See below, 2.4.

[7] This is also Smitmans' judgement, having examined the early interpretations of the text (1966, pp. 16ff, 272ff).

context is given priority. I cannot discuss here the connection between the speech and the other parts of the text as I must concentrate on the individual elements of U 9, using linguistic comparisons to define their significance or to suggest possible alternatives for further analysis. Johannine parallels to the speech as a whole may also be of help in interpreting this important unit of our text.

U 9a τί ἐμοὶ καὶ σοί

This idiom is to be found in Greek, Latin (*Quid mihi et tibi*), Hebrew and Aramaic (מַה לִי ולך) language areas.[8] Since its significance is highly dependent on context and intonation[9] we should expect differing meanings and shades of meaning in different contexts rather than a single meaning, especially not in all the language areas mentioned, as Gaechter seems to presume.[10]

The construction recurs in Classical Greek in the sense "What have I in common with you?"[11] and in Hellenistic texts, such as Epictetus and the Corpus Hermeticum, as an objection in discussions or a protest in specific situations: If that is the situation what have I to do with it/him/them/you?[12] The closest parallels as regards content however should be sought in an environment using both Greek and Aramaic, and in particular in sections of dialogue resembling the Jn text.

The expressions in the LXX which are linguistically parallel—Jos 22:24; Jg 11:12; 2 Sam 16:10; 19:23 (MT 19:22); 1 Kg 17:18; 2 Kg 3:13; 9:18f; 2 Chr 35:21; Hos 14:9 and Jer 2:18—vary in meaning according to context. In Jos 22:24 the Reubenites and the Gadites from across Jordan hold a discussion with the other tribes of Israel to defend the great altar they built by the Jordan. They wish to avoid the possibility that in time to come the other tribes will come to them and say "What have you to do with the Lord (τί ὑμῖν καὶ κυρίῳ), the God of Israel? For the Lord has made the Jordan a boundary between us and you ... you have no portion in the Lord (οὐκ ἔστιν ὑμῖν μερὶς κυρίου) ". The latter clause and the general context give the phrase its meaning: 'What has *x* in common with *y*? What *share* has *x* in *y*?'. This is a rhetorical question expecting a negative answer: approx.: Surely you have nothing to do with the Lord, the God of Israel.

We find roughly the same usage in Hos 14:9 (τί αὐτῷ ἔτι καὶ εἰδώλοις) and in Jer 2:18 (τί σοι καὶ τῇ ὁδῷ Αἰγύπτου / Ἀσσυρίων), both in a context of dialogue. The succinct dialogue in 2 Kg 9:18f resembles these texts: Jehu, whom the Lord appointed King

---

[8] This idiom has been very much discussed. Malatesta 1967, pp. 83ff, lists, besides commentaries and articles to the whole narrative, more than 30 articles about Jn 2:4. Two of them are dissertations which I have had no opportunity to read. I will here especially mention Gaechter 1953, pp. 171ff, Michaud 1962, pp. 247ff, and Derrett 1970, pp. 238ff.

[9] Rightly stressed by Schnackenburg, Comm., ad loc.

[10] Gaechter 1953, p. 174. Commentaries and translations give many renderings: You must not tell me what to do. Your concern is not mine. Is that your concern, or mine? What part can I take with thee? Why dost thou trouble me with that? Do not try to direct me. Why turn to me? It is better to leave the matter in my hands. This is not your business. Etc.

[11] See Kühnert-Gert, vol. 1, p. 417, with the passages quoted there, and Tabachovitz 1956, pp. 108f.

[12] Epictetus, Diss. I.1,16; 22,15; 27,13 and II.19,16, Corpus Hermeticum XI.21.

of Israel and who was anointed by Elisha, rides with his retinue against Joram, the reigning sovereign, whose messenger goes to meet him saying "Thus says the king, is it peace?" Jehu answers "What have you to do with peace ($\tau\iota'\,\sigma o\iota\,\kappa a\iota'\,\epsilon\iota\rho\dot{\eta}\nu\eta$)? Turn round and ride behind me!" A messenger from Joram the apostate had nothing to do with peace, v. 22.

There are six more places in the LXX parallels, all of which refer to relations between persons who are present at the dialogue (the form $\tau\iota'\,\dot{\epsilon}\mu o\iota'\,\kappa a\iota'\,\sigma o\iota'\,/\,\dot{\upsilon}\mu\tilde{\iota}\nu$) and—apart from 2 Chr 35:21—take part in it. Thus they closely resemble Jn as regards form and situation and are therefore of special interest. This applies to 2 Chr 35:21; Jg 11:12; 1 Kg 17:18; 2 Kg 3:13; 2 Sam 16:10 and 19:23 (MT 19:22). In one way or another all of them express protest or objection, sometimes a certain amount of reproach or rebuke, based on a different view of the situation. We may take an example.

2 Sam 16:10 and 19:23 describe the relationship between David and Abishai, one of David's bravest followers and son of his sister Zeruiah. As in Jn 2 the speech does not come first in the dialogue but as a reply to a request. The family relationships may be concerned. The shorter text in ch. 16 tells how Shimei, Saul's kinsman, curses David during Absalom's revolt. Abishai then asks leave to kill him but David replies: "What have I to do with you, you sons of Zeruiah? Let him alone and let him curse; for the Lord has bidden him . . . and who then shall say 'Why have you done so?' " And so David allows him to continue. Thus the apparently natural and fitting request of his nephews and comrades-in-arms is rejected with the words "What has this to do with you? Do not concern yourselves with it."

In ch. 19 David returns victorious from the struggle with Absalom: Shimei meets him then and begs for mercy. Abishai protests: "Shall not Shimei be put to death for this because he cursed the Lord's anointed". David replies: "What have I to do with you, you sons of Zeruiah, that you should this day be an adversary to me (MT: ‏לשטן‎ v. 22, LXX: $\epsilon\iota\varsigma\,\dot{\epsilon}\pi\iota'\beta o\upsilon\lambda o\nu$, v. 23)? Today shall no man in Israel be put to death, for today I am King over Israel". So Shimei was pardoned. The exchange of views between the parties is here more explicit than in the previous quotation. Both passages are concerned with a request which is rejected because the parties have different attitudes to the situation. Abishai regards the whole problem from the angle of the normal and usual conditions in war, and perhaps also from the aspect of his rights as David's kinsman and comrade-in-arms, while David sees the particular situation prevailing now that he is King of Israel. The context into which our phrase fits seems to include three elements: *1.* A and B have opposite ideas about a situation, A having a more usual and "natural" attitude, B a more special view. *2.* A uses a request to try to persuade B to follow his advice. *3.* B rejects A's request, saying that he finds no reason for it, i.e. he does not accept the reasons underlying A's plea: "What right have you to make such a request? What have I to do with you . . . that you should this day be as an adversary to me?" He continues by giving his own reasons and the attitude which then determines his action.

The phrase U 9a also appears in the Synoptic Gospels: Mk 1:24; 5:7; Mt 8:29; Lk 4:34; 8:28.[13] There it always refers to the demons' appeal to Jesus. The background is their complete knowledge of Jesus' identity—his name, his origin, his mission and his being—and their realization that when the Messiah comes they will lose their power and

[13] Cf. also Mt 27:19.

be cast into Gehenna, Lk 8:31; Mt 8:29; 12:43ff. They feel themselves threatened as soon as they see Jesus. In Mt 8:29 they protest: "What have you to do with us, O Son of God? Have you come here to torment us *before the time* (ὧδε πρὸ καιροῦ)?" The phrase means: What are you doing here? You have no right/no reason to torment us here on earth before the Last Judgement.[14] This "theological" reasoning does not appear in the parallel texts, Mk 5:7 and Lk 8:28. In Mk the demons' cry takes the form of an impotent and violent protest in the face of superior force, "Jesus, Son of the Most High God".[15] The very adjuration (ὁρκίζω σε τὸν θεόν) proves their impotence: how can God fight his own Son? Supplication, knowledge of his name, and adjurations have no effect. In Lk the reaction is muted to an attempt to placate Jesus and avert the threat. Thus the episode in the synagogue at Capernaum, Mk 1:24/Lk 4:34, remains, and there the text is more succinct: "What have you to do with us, Jesus of Nazareth: You have come to destroy us.[16] I know who you are, the Holy One of God". Because of their knowledge of Jesus they understand the threat and in their terror they try in human fashion to fight and hold their own. The phrase somewhat resembles that in 1 Kg 17:18, meaning: What have you to do with us? Leave us alone.

This survey of the linguistic material confirms our earlier comment that the phrase is strongly dependent on context and intonation. Bearing Jn 2:4 in mind we can only try to sketch a general framework of the significance of Jesus' speech.

The phrase τί ἐμοὶ καὶ σοί /ὑμῖν is used in the relevant parallel material as *the opening words in a speech*, often followed by a vocative with different kinds of motivation. The context of the speech is always dominated by strong *tensions*, wherein the individual using the phrase reacts against, in his view, unjust treatment or an unjust speech by the opposing party. The phrase then marks a *protest*, a *serious objection*, often coupled with a *rebuke, amazement, a demand for an explanation, contempt, repudiation* or *rejection*. In 2 Sam 19:23, which is contextually closest to Jn 2:4, the phrase expresses a *refusal*, by referring to the prevailing situation, to comply with an inopportune *request*. The comparative linguistic material shows, therefore, that the phrase can hardly mean "What do you and I have in common?"[17] or "What have you and I to do with it?"[18] In Jn 2 it implies some kind of conflict between Jesus and his mother, which is evidently concerned with "the hour of Jesus". Jesus reprimands and rebukes her. The disagreement can hardly refer to the lack of wine as such, but to different ways of seeing or acting in the situation which has arisen. The likely explanation is that Jesus regarded his mother's words as a *request* for wine for the wedding guests, which Jesus because of his point of view, rejects. There may be more than one reason for his rejection, for example: *1*. Jesus' mother feels she can make justifiable demands on her son, or desires an immediate intervention. The reply is roughly: You cannot/need not tell me what to do. *2*. The situation which has arisen does not concern him. The reply is then approximately: That is your worry, not

---

[14] Bonnard, Comm., ad Mt 8:29.

[15] Schmid, Comm., ad Mk 5:7.

[16] This clause has also been read as a question, especially in the Lucan version.

[17] For this interpretation, see especially Gaechter 1953, pp. 174ff.

[18] See Nonnus' paraphrase (τί μοι, γύναι, ἠὲ σοὶ αὐτῇ), quoted by Michl 1955, p. 494. Burkitt chose this interpretation for linguistic reasons, according to Gaechter 1953, pp. 174f, Michaud 1962, p. 252.

mine. How can you bother me with such problems? What do you want of me? *3.* She only considers the lack of wine without understanding the more profound significance of the situation. The reply then means: You do not understand this. We do not see things the same way, you and I.[19]

In any case the first words in Jesus' reply should be considered a protest and a strong objection to the action or the ideas which emerge in his mother's words.

Thus U 9a indicates a certain relationship between the first two speeches in the text, a form of protest, opposition, repudiation, objection. Are there similar exchanges in Jn? The opening scenes in 4:46ff; 11:1ff; 9:1ff and 3:1ff are the closest parallels.

In 4:47ff a man asks Jesus for help for his sick son. There is no indication that the man's appeal should be understood in any other way than as a request for medical assistance. Jesus' reply is then abrupt and seemingly reproachful and rejecting. He seems to speak of completely different matters—that people demand miracles as proof that they should believe in him. This "faith in signs" is contrasted with belief in Jesus' word, vv. 50, 53, which is later verified and which after verification is described as Christian belief (καὶ ἐπίστευσεν αὐτὸς καὶ ἡ οἰκία αὐτοῦ ὅλη).

The situation in 11:3f is similar in nature. The sisters at Bethany tell Jesus of their brother's illness and evidently expect him to come and cure him. Nevertheless Jesus' answer suggests other lines of thought: he refers to the *doxa* of God and to the *doxa* of the Son of God and remains where he is. As in 4:46ff a positive answer to prayer is delayed because Jesus' view of the situation is different from that of the supplicants.

The account of the man born blind, 9:1ff, begins with a "theological" question about disease and sin, in which the disciples put forward views typical of the age in which they lived, 9:2. Jesus rejects their "human" viewpoints and speaks of the work of God which will be manifested on the sick man.

Nicodemus in 3:2f also receives an unexpected and abrupt repulse. When he positively confesses his faith in Jesus as a teacher come from God, Jesus begins to speak of the Kingdom of God and the need for rebirth from above.

All four passages, like Jn 2:3f, begin a narrative in which the second speech is made by Jesus and in some way contradicts and repudiates what was previously said. Apart from Jn 3, there are always three parties and the concrete problem of the third party—after some delay—is solved in a positive fashion. In the four passages analysed, the Jesus speech marks *a shift in perspective* (functions as a "shift marker"). Jesus lifts the event from the natural human context to a context concerned with faith, with the Son of God, the *doxa* of God, the work of God, that is to a level involving himself and his mission from God. Since this change of level—which is often found in Jn[20]—is frequently distinguished by an opening exchange of views it is probable that we have a similar technique in Jn 2:3f too. According to such an interpretation the opening words would mean, roughly: "You and I do not see things in the same way, woman. You are thinking of the concrete shortage of wine, I am thinking of my mission in the world and the situation it

---

[19] For the interpretation of Jesus' word as a protest and a strong objection, see the extended analysis of Michaud 1962, pp. 251ff. The idiom "garde une valeur négative et marque de soi une opposition" according to a quotation from Michaud in Salgado 1971, p. 45.

[20] Leroy 1968, pp. 1ff, and also Brown, Comm., pp. cxxxvf, and Rissi 1967, p. 85.

presupposes." The narrator, however, may not be so interested in a shift of perspective in the concrete situation in the past which the text describes, but rather in such a shift on the part of the reader who contemplates this event afterwards.[21]

U 9b γύναι

The phrase τί ἐμοὶ καὶ σοί / ὑμῖν is used both with and without a subsequent vocative. When a vocative is used its function is usually more or less clear; Jos 22:24 τῷ θεῷ Ισραηλ (part of the justification), 2 Chr 35:21 βασιλεῦ Ιουδα (part of the justification), 1 Kg 17:18 ἄνθρωπε τοῦ θεοῦ (characterization and part of the argument), 2 Sam 16:10; 19:23 υἱοὶ Σαρουιας (possibly to mark the kinship and then part of the argument), Epict. Diss. II.19,16 ἄνθρωπε (probably repudiating, derogatory). In the NT parallels the vocative plays an important part, both in the confession of Jesus' identity and in attempts to avert the threat he represents.[22] Judging by the comparative linguistic material the word γύναι in Jn 2:4 probably has a certain function and does not merely round off the statement.

It is by no means abnormal to address a woman as γύναι; the term is often used by Jesus, for example Jn 4:21; 8:10; 20:13; Mt 15:28; Lk 13:12.[23] Thus this form of address need not express harshness, contempt or lack of respect.[24] Yet the use of this title for a *mother* is unexpected.[25] In such circumstances it is abnormal and therefore has a strong impact. Many scholars have assigned an important function to the word. Most of them assume that it indicates a certain distance between Jesus and his mother. Jesus' words eliminate the mother/son relationship. More specific evaluations vary however: an honourable and ceremonial title, a suggestion of the status of Jesus' mother in the history of salvation or a description of her as a bride.[26]

Both the comparative linguistic material and the word used give the term γύναι a certain emphasis in the text. The understanding of the word only as an honorary title is in conflict with the meaning of the phrase τί ἐμοὶ καὶ σοί and Michl's attempt to place γύναι on the same level as the later use of κυρία cannot be verified.[27] To judge by the phrase beginning the speech γύναι denotes a certain distance, *either* (A) between Jesus and his mother in the parts they play in the text *or* (B) between the various roles of Jesus' mother alone, or perhaps both A and B.

Possibility A, which is supported by the comments on U 9a above, would mean that Jesus' mother, as the narrator intends, is characterised by the title as one belonging to the human order. She thinks as a human being, she speaks as a human being when she says

---

[21] See 2.4.

[22] See above the comment on U 9a.

[23] More linguistic material in ThWNT, vol 1, p. 776 (A. Oepke) and in Bultmann, Comm., ad loc.

[24] Such suggestions in commentaries of Westcott, Bauer, Hoskyns, Strathmann and Barret according to Michaud 1962, p. 254. Cf. the use of γύναι in 19:26.

[25] We have no Greek or Hebrew parallel to this usage, Brown, Comm., ad loc.

[26] See the surveys in Michaud 1962, pp. 254ff, and Smitmans 1966, p. 18. On Mary as the bride of Christ, see Charlier 1959, pp. 78f. On the interpretations of the Church Fathers, see Collins 1972, pp. 104ff.

[27] Michl 1955, pp. 498f.

"They have no wine". There is a similar contrast in v. 10: πᾶς ἄνθρωπος - οὐ.[28] According to this interpretation the narrator chose γύναι not only to indicate that Jesus' mother has a specific role but mainly to mark the shift in perspective in the opening speech. The former may also apply to the parallel use of the word in Jn 19:26 but hardly the latter, as we seem to have no change of level in Jn 19.

We arrive at possibility B if we link 2:4 with 19:26 and—with the majority of Catholic scholars—explain these passages on the history of salvation with reference to Rev 12 and Gen 3:15, 20.[29] The present composition of the Gospel indicates that to some extent 2:1–11 and 19:17–37 should be read in the light of each other,[30] yet this interpretation need not mean that γύναι has the same function in both passages. Nevertheless this possibility should be carefully considered.

The discussion of *Jn 19:25–27* here is bound to be very superficial. This scene has a deeper meaning according to the evangelist.[31] This emerges from his composition as a whole with the Passion at Golgotha (19:16b–37) as the very peak of Jesus' mission, the central event, rich in consequences, which overshadows all else; and it emerges from his placing of the scene with Jesus' mother amid the five events at Golgotha.[32] The surrounding events are highly symbolical in their different ways.[33] Why should not 19:25–27 also be symbolical? According to 19:28 (μετὰ τοῦτο) Jesus' mission ended with his "relatives" at the Cross, a conclusion which, in the light of Jn, can hardly mean that Jesus was only concerned with his earthly mother. The ἴδε- scheme introduces an aspect of revelation into the text: Jesus reveals the true inner being of his mother and of his beloved disciple.[34] These individuals can, in the Johannine fashion, act as types.[35] These circumstances make it natural to look for a deeper meaning in the scene with the mother of Jesus in ch. 19.

What then is Jn trying to say in this episode? Three interpretations would define the possibilities which are worthy of consideration:

1. Interpretation on the basis of the problem of unity in Jn: Jesus left his "family" gathered together and united as a result of his death on the Cross.[36] The question of the

---

[28] See below, 2.2, U 26.

[29] See Gaechter 1953, pp. 202ff, Braun ²1954, pp. 77ff, Feuillet 1962, pp. 29ff, 272ff, Michaud 1962, pp. 258ff, and Feuillet 1965, p. 535.

[30] Both events take place on the 6th day of the opening, or the closeing, week in Jn; only in Jn do we find the mother of Jesus, addressed as γύναι with a reference to ἡ ὥρα.

[31] See especially Brown, Comm., ad loc., and his arguments for regarding all events at Golgotha as "centered around theological symbolism" (p. 911).

[32] See the survey of the five episodes in Brown, Comm., ad loc. The introducing and concluding passages have, however, a more transitional character than Brown suggests.

[33] The interest in the proclamation of the kingship of Jesus to the whole civilized world, the witness of Jesus' garments according to the Scriptures, the completion of all that the Father had given to do by drinking the cup and handing over the Spirit, no breaking of Jesus' legs and the flow of blood and water from Jesus' side. For further discussion, see the excellent comments on these texts in Brown, Comm., ad loc.

[34] de Goedt 1961–62. Cf. above, 2.2, U 6.

[35] See the literature mentioned above in note 71 to 2.2, U 6.

[36] Brown, Comm., p. 924, refuses to discuss this interpretation saying: "Obviously we cannot

union of Jesus' disciples through the work of the Father in the Son appears in a number of the "ecclesial" sections in Jn: the union of *all* the shepherd's sheep into a single flock, 10:15f (with Jesus' death mentioned in vv. 11,15 and 17f), the gathering of all the children of God, 11:52 (in connection with Jesus' death sentence, 11:47—53) and the union of all Jesus' disciples, 17:1, 21—23 (Jesus' death is mentioned in the context, in v. 1, and suggested in v. 19).[37] This union motif recurs in the Golgotha scenes, presumably in the proclamation of the King of *the Jews* to the *whole* world and in the division of Jesus' clothing, the seamless garment.[38] Those who accept this interpretation usually allow Jesus' mother to represent Jewish Christianity, and the beloved disciple world-wide Gentile Christianity, in a Pauline sense, referring to the manifest tension in Jn between Peter and the beloved disciple.[39] Yet this distinction does not do justice to the Johannine texts, in which the true people of God somehow grows organically from the "old" Israel and where the real tension lies between these two, between Synagogue and Church, and not between the two components of the "new" Israel. Here the Johannine texts seem to be more "Jewish" than the Pauline.[40] It is also worthy of note that the woman in Rev 12 denotes the people of God in both an OT and a NT sense and that both she and her children stand for the Church of Christ.[41] A similar representative relationship would seem to be more in keeping with Jn as a whole in Jn 19:25—27 also, where the mother of Jesus stands for Israel, the true Israel, which is to be found in both the old and the new covenant, and her child, namely the beloved disciple, represents the people of God in the new covenant.

2. The interpretation based on the idea of the woman who bears a child, i.e. the mother of Jesus, as the daughter of Zion (Jn 16:21; Is 49:20—22; 54:1; 66:7—11), as the new Eve (Gen 4:1; 3:15; Rev 12:5, 17), who gives birth to a new people in the "Messianic" age. She becomes the prototype for, or the incarnation of, the Church, the mother of all believers. This interpretation, which finds in Jn 2:1—11; 16:21; 19:25—27, and Rev 12, a central Johannine theme concerning ἡ γυνή explains how the scene in ch. 19 may be regarded as a completion of the work of salvation. It also links the text with the OT quotations in the scenes immediately preceding and succeeding it. This does justice to the formula of revelation and the implicit futural aspects in the text. Catholic scholars in particular have analysed Jn on the basis of this model and we refer the reader to Gaechter, Braun, Michaud and Feuillet for more detailed arguments.[42]

3. There is a possibility of combining both these interpretations. The second interpretation reflects the idea that Jesus' mother becomes the mother of the beloved disciple, the

---

seriously discuss such a wealth of figurative possibilities", which is surprising considering what he says in pp. 921f.

[37] See my excursus on mission in Jn, 3.4.6.

[38] For justification of these interpretations, see Brown, Comm., ad loc.

[39] See especially Bultmann and Schulz, Comm., ad loc.

[40] See below, 3.4.6.

[41] Räisänen 1969, pp.187ff, and the literature he mentions. Even if Jn and Rev were written by different authors, there are so many similarities between these two books that Rev should be regarded as important parallel material to Jn.

[42] See the literature mentioned above in note 29 and Feuillet 1964, 1966, Brown, Comm., ad loc., and Collins 1972, pp. 137ff.

first refers to the fact that the beloved disciple takes care of her and they become one.[43]

A reading of Jn 2:4 with Jn 19:26 in mind therefore suggests further possible interpretations of U 9b. It is impossible to choose between them in this analysis of the individual statement unit. All that I can say is that according to all these interpretations, based on (A) a shift of perspective in the text or (B) on the parallel in Jn 19:26, γύναι in Jn 2:4 would indicate to the reader that the reference is not to Jesus' mother in the usual sense of the term. The first alternative tends to place Jesus in the centre: before him, the true revelation who knows all things, Jesus' mother is pointed out as a human being without full insight. The second alternative lays greater emphasis on the mother of Jesus: she is seen here in the light of the OT and given a specific role in God's work for the salvation of the world. This interpretation, which in contrast to the former, derives many criteria from outside the text itself, is more complicated and for this reason is not to be preferred.[44] I refer to the further treatment of Jesus' mother below.[45]

U 9c οὔπω ἥκει ἡ ὥρα μου

Many scholars are of the opinion that the interpretation of this unit, and particularly of ἡ ὥρα, is the key to the understanding of the text as a whole.[46] The interpretations suggested tend to fall into *two categories*. In the one the phrase is regarded as *a statement about the opportune moment for Jesus to intervene* in the situation reported to him by his mother (with a miracle, wedding gifts or some other means), while in the other it is *a statement about the "hour" of Jesus,* a technical expression in Jn, referring to the completion of Jesus' mission on earth, i.e. his death and glorification.

Ever since the days of the Early Church there have been those who would regard this unit as a rhetorical question[47] but this seems to be a makeshift solution.[48] Judging by Mt 16:9; Mk 4:40, and 8:17, 21,[49] it is grammatically possible but οὔπω is very seldom used in this sense.[50] This word occurs fairly frequently in Jn (13 times), always as a negation in

---

[43] Note the last words of 19:25—27. This last moment of the central event at Golgotha may have a transferred meaning, like the event as a whole, and is then a reason for the first interpretation.

[44] Cf. Brown's difficulties (Comm., ad loc.), when he argues for this interpretation, among others, of the Cana narrative.

[45] See below, 2.3.5 and 2.4.4.

[46] Smitmans 1966, pp. 272ff. Cf. his survey of different interpretations, pp. 18ff.

[47] Gregory of Nyssa and others. See Michaud 1962, p. 263, note 1, and Smitmans 1966, pp. 19f, 97f. Among modern scholars, Boismard 1956, pp. 156ff, has argued strongly for this interpretation (the use of οὐ in questions, references to the Church Fathers). The main reason for reading U 9c as a question may be a desive to arrive at a psychologically coherent text in Jn 2:1—11, not perhaps a good starting point for reading Johannine texts. Cf. below 2.4.5 and 3.5.2.

[48] Michaud 1962, pp. 263f.

[49] Note the many variant readings of some of these passages, which indicates that the use of οὔπω in questions is unusual. Does οὔπω in these passages function only as a strong negation? Cf. Liddell-Scott, s.v.

[50] I have only found these four examples from Mt and Mk. The negation οὐ is very often used in questions but this cannot be adduced as a reason for the use of οὔπω (against Boismard 1956, p. 156).

statements, in some cases in connection with the hour of Jesus, 7:6, 8, 30; 8:20; cf. 20:17.[51] The argument that U 9c as a statement would disagree with the following text is greatly weakened by the fact that we have similar "contradictions" in other passages in Jn.[52] Moreover a question would link the interpretation of ἡ ὥρα with the first category, which will prove to be the less probable.[53] There are no valid reasons for understanding U 9c as a rhetorical question. The translation becomes: "My hour has not yet come".

What is the meaning of this somewhat formal phrase? The chief justification for the first interpretation model—to understand ἡ ὥρα as the moment for Jesus to intervene—lies in the context. In order to arrive at a "natural" consequence of the timing of the event it is assumed that Jesus is here referring to his dependence on the Father: he will take action, not now, but later, at the moment decided by the Father.[54] Jesus' mother has therefore no reason to interfere, let alone tell him when he is to act. This "natural" reading, however, is not at all necessary in Jn as the evangelist often places the chief emphasis on a transferred meaning in the comments.[55] In such contexts Jesus does not mention the concrete situation described in the text but always his work of mission in general. This level of meaning links ἡ ὥρα with δόξα, σημεῖον and πιστεύειν, concepts which, according to v. 11, express the real meaning of what takes place.[56] The Johannine narrative technique and interpretation of events therefore favour the second alternative.

The use of ὥρα in Jn supports this view. The word may be used more generally of a point in time, as in 1:39; 4:6; 19:14; 4:52f; 11:9; of time, as in 16:2, 4, 21, 32, and occasionally in eschatological sayings, 4:21, 23; 5:25, 28. Yet our text most closely resembles *those passages where the word has a clear definition linking it with Jesus:*
οὔπω ἐληλύθει ἡ ὥρα αὐτοῦ (7:30; 8:20).
ἦλθεν αὐτοῦ ἡ ὥρα (13:1).
ἐλήλυθεν ἡ ὥρα ἵνα δοξασθῇ (12:23).
ἐλήλυθεν ἡ ὥρα (17:1).
πάτερ, σῶσόν με ἐκ τῆς ὥρας. ἀλλὰ διὰ τοῦτο ἦλθον εἰς τὴν ὥραν ταύτην (12:27).
At times the wording comes very close to that of 2:4. The "hour" here refers to the time for Jesus' suffering, death and resurrection, which Jn sees as a unit.[57] The entire Johan-

[51] The synoptic use of οὔπω in questions implies a strong reproach, which does not seem to be the case in U 9c. See Mk 4:40; 8:17f, 21.

[52] See, for example, 7:6ff; 4:46ff and 11:1ff.

[53] See the following analysis.

[54] Thus Bultmann, Comm., ad loc., for the evangelist's source, referring to the same characteristics in texts on θεῖος ἀνήρ. According to others, Jesus was wainting for the opportune moment to hand over the wedding gifts (J.M. Derrett), he wished the need to be stronger, etc. See Smitmans 1966, pp. 18f. According to Sanders-Mastin, Comm., ad loc., Jesus would not use his power "for so apparently trivial an object".

[55] See, for exampe, 2:13—22. "Nach dem Urteil des Evangeliums selbst ist also die historische Verstehbarkeit eines Jesus-Wortes ein ungeeigneter Auslegungsmasstab. Darüber hinaus macht das ganze Evangelium hinreichend deutlich, dass das Urteil, eine exegetische Deutung habe für ein Wort oder Gespräch einen natürlichen (d.h. im Zusammenhang zu erwartenden) Sinn gefunden, nicht für, sondern gegen diese Deutung spricht ... Weder vor noch nach der Erzählung vom Weinwunder haben die Worte ihren natürlich-wörtlichen Sinn (vgl. 2,19—21 und 1,37—39.43.46.50f.)", Smitmans 1966, p. 273. See also below, ch. 4.

[55] See the comments below on U 27—31.

[57] Thüsing ²1970, passim.

nine presentation is dominated by this "hour", the decisive boundary between the two stages of Jesus' work, the one linked with his earthly ministry, the other with his risen, glorified being. It derives its significance from Jesus' "departure" in the Johannine sense, 8:14, 21; 13:33, 36 etc., his "going to the Father", 13:1, 3; 16:28; 17:11, 13, his "lifting up", 3:14, 8:28; 12:32, 34, and his "glorification", 7:39; 12:23, 28; 13:31. All these terms in Jn refer to one and the same event: the completion of Jesus' work of mission.[58] The exclusion of 2:4 from this special usage of ἡ ὥρα τοῦ Ἰησοῦ, in a text as well constructed as is St. John's Gospel in its composition, style, cross-references, phrases and concepts, must be justified by strong arguments.[59] It is but natural to interpret the expression together with the passages quoted. U 9c should be understood primarily as a statement about the "hour" of Jesus in the special Johannine sense. The evangelist may be aware of two levels of meaning in his narrative—corresponding to the two models of interpretation—but he is definitely seeking to express ideas from the second model in his text.[60]

U 10 λέγει ἡ μήτηρ αὐτοῦ διακόνοις
a. ὅ τι ἂν λέγῃ ὑμῖν ποιήσατε

His mother says to the servants: "Do whatever he tells you."
Jesus' mother is not silenced by his rejection. She seems to play an active part in the text. Here she again points Jesus out, at the same time as she herself disappears from the scene. The servants come forward without any introduction. The quotation formula, which is asyndetically joined to the preceding phrase, was at an early stage regarded as too brusque.[61] The wording of the Greek text as we now have it is as brief as possible and the reader is rapidly led over to the speech, which thus carries the main emphasis.

The description of the servants of the house as οἱ διάκονοι does not seem to come quite naturally in the Greek,[62] but may be explained as meaning that they were serving the meal.[63] The wording has prompted some scholars to interpret the servants in the light of Acts 6:1ff; Lk 22:27 and the *diakonia* motif in the NT.[64] The wording alone does not call

---

[58] On the relations between these two stages in Jn, see Thüsing ²1970, pp. 300ff. The multitude of specifically Johannine terms connected with the "hour" of Jesus show how strongly Johannine thought is dominated by this concept.

[59] Cf. Barrett, Comm., ad loc.: "It is unthinkable that in this verse ἡ ὥρα should have a different meaning" than that in 7:30; 8:20; 12:23, 27 etc.

[60] Michaud 1962, pp. 263ff, Smitmans 1966, pp. 272ff. Ceroke 1959, pp. 338ff, sees an ambiguity in 9c: a statement about the "hour" of Jesus and a rhetorical question about the opportune moment for Jesus to perform a miracle.

[61] See, for example, Codex Palatinus (*et advocatis ad se ministris mater Jesum dixit illis*), one of the most important manuscripts of the Old Latin version (4th century), Metzger ²1968, p. 73.

[62] Abbott 1905, p. 212, Barrett, Comm., ad loc. The words οἱ δοῦλοι and οἱ παῖδες are the ordinary Greek expressions for the servants.

[63] Cf. the use of διακονεῖν in Lk 17:8; Jn 12:2; Lk 12:37; Acts 6:2, and see H.W. Beyer in ThWNT, vol. 2, pp. 81, 88, and Boulton 1959, p. 416.

[64] Abbott 1905, p. 212, Barrett, Comm., ad loc., Boulton 1959, pp. 417f, and Hanhart 1970, p. 42. Cf. Mk 9:35 par. and 10:43 par.

for such comparisons, but by reason of its special possibilities of association the word διάκονοι is more open than, for example, παῖδες or δοῦλοι. It may have been chosen because of the total message of the text.[65]

Jn also uses διάκονοι and δοῦλοι in a noteworthy fashion. In *12:26* διάκονος denotes a disciple of Jesus, in a context which clearly refers to the "hour" and the *doxa* of Jesus, *12:23—36*. The possibility of "seeing" Jesus is not realized until the "hour" of Jesus, when he is glorified; cf. the promise in *1:51*. So the man who wants to "serve" Jesus, i.e. be his disciple, must be prepared to follow him even to death. By Jesus' example the disciples must, according to *13:12ff*, behave as "servants" (δοῦλοι). *15:15* states that Jesus called his disciples "servants" (δοῦλοι) but that this designation is no longer applicable since Jesus revealed all things to them. If they follow the revelation of Jesus, here called "commandment" (ἐντολή), they are Jesus' "friends" (φίλοι μου *15:14f*), a change of title which may be connected with the designation "brothers" (ἀδελφοί) in *20:17*. Jn therefore uses *servants* (διάκονοι, δοῦλοι) as a description of the disciples, the former being a more general term, the latter on the other hand only for the time until the perfect revelation, *15:14f*. This may explain the wording of U 10.

The words of Jesus' mother to the servants express a demand for *total obedience* to Jesus and his orders: "Whatsoever at any time he says to you". The use of the present tense[66] conveys a complete parallelism between λέγῃ in this speech and the two following quotation formulae in vv. 7 and 8 (λέγει αὐτοῖς ... καὶ λέγει αὐτοῖς), and ποιήσατε corresponds to καὶ ἐγέμισαν and οἱ δὲ ἤνεγκαν in vv. 7f. This parallelism brings out the obedience inherent in the servants' actions. They are exhorted to obey Jesus' words and do so. Indeed their only characteristic mentioned in the text is that they *hear* and *do* what Jesus' mother and Jesus himself *tell* them. The text does not say that Jesus' mother obeys. Her action resembles most closely that of the many witnesses in Jn, such as John the Baptist, Moses and the OT Scriptures, *5:38ff, 45ff*; she points to Jesus.[67]

In the interpretation of this speech the reader is often referred to Gen 41:55, where Pharaoh exhorts the Egyptians: πορεύεσθε πρὸς Ιωσηφ, καὶ ὃ ἐὰν εἴπῃ, ὑμῖν, ποιήσατε, [68] and in a few isolated cases to the texts concerning the people of Israel at Sinai: Ex 19:8 LXX πάντα, ὅσα εἶπεν ὁ θεός, ποιήσομεν καὶ ἀκουσόμεθα and Ex 24:7 LXX πάντα, ὅσα ἐλάλησεν κύριος, ποιήσομεν καὶ ἀκουσόμεθα. [69] Since the words of the speech are of

---

[65] See below, 2.4.4, and compare the change of words in Mt 22:1—14 (δοῦλοι in vv. 3, 4, 6, 8, 10, and διάκονοι in v. 13), which may depend on the total message of the text (δοῦλοι refers to the prophets before Jesus and διάκονοι to Jesus' disciples).

[66] Aorist is the usual tense in these constructions, Turner, pp. 107f: "The pres. indicates that the time of subordinate clause is coincident with that of the main". See also Abbott 1906, pp. 304, 376f. — Λέγειν in the meaning "to command" is rare in Greek. The use here may depend on Semitic influence. Cf. Mk 5:8 (ἔλεγεν), in Lk 8:29 changed to παρήγγειλεν, and the variant readings to Lk 17:10.

[67] See below, 2.3.5 and 2.4.4, and compare the Samaritan woman in Jn 4, discussed below, especially in 3.2.5 and 3.4.2, S 4 and 3.5.

[68] In Nestle-Aland the speech is marked as quotation. See also Smitmans 1966, p. 24, and Brown, Comm., ad loc.: "Mary's instructions echo those of Pharaoh in Gen xli 55".

[69] Serra 1971, pp. 19f. MT has in 19:8 only נַעֲשֶׂה (Targ. נַעֲבֵיד), but in 24:7 נַעֲשֶׂה וְנִשְׁמָע (Targ. נַעֲבֵיד וּנְקַבֵּיל). The sentence quoted from 19:8 and 24:7 is repeated in the Targum in 24:3. In Ex 19—24, too, there is a stress on ποιεῖν. See all these commands (ποιήσεις) in 25:7, 8, 9,

very frequent occurrence and their content is in no way unique, an agreement almost word for word with other texts should not be assigned any great weight as evidence.[70] Possible comparative material from the OT must be linked with our text by other attributes than the form. I shall later show that Ex 19 and 24 are highly relevant for the interpretation of our text, a point which favours the Exodus parallels quoted above.[71] The aspects of obedience and revelation in this material which are missing in Gen 41 also support my argument.

Like many other NT writings, Jn places heavy emphasis on *obedience* to Jesus and his words. In Jn the theme of Jesus as the agent of the true revelation gives this obedience its unique quality. Man must hear/obey, receive and possess the word of revelation (ὁ λόγος) within himself, 5:24.[72] The damning indictment of "the Jews" is that they will not *do* what they *hear* from the Father through the Son, 8:38: Jesus' message finds no place in them (οὐ χωρεῖ) , 8:37, indeed they cannot hear/obey (ἀκούειν) Jesus' words because they are not of God, 8:43, 47. Yet the man born blind hears and does, 9:1ff, Jesus' own hear, 10:3, 16, 27. The true disciple is he who remains in the word of revelation, who knows the truth, who has kept the word given by Jesus, 17:6.[73] This means that obedience is the primary sign of a true disciple.

Obedience to God/Jesus is predominant in Jn as *obedience to the word of revelation brought by Jesus*. Jesus' message may even be described as ἡ ἐντολή or αἱ ἐντολαί , 12:49f; cf. 13:34; 14:15, 21; 15:10, 12 and 1 Jn 2:3f, 7f; 3:22ff; 4:21; 5:2f.[74] The parallel with the events at Sinai, Ex 19—24, is manifest. There the people of Israel had to make up their minds in the most final manner in their history, whether they wished to hear and do God's will as mediated by Moses. According to the passage quoted above Israel promises to do all God's bidding. The stressing of the servants' obedience in Jn 2 undoubtedly poses the question whether there is a connection between the Cana narrative, the description of the true disciples in Jn (as being those who obey the words of Jesus) and Ex 19—24. There seems to be no reason to regard U 10 as a quotation from Gen 41:55.

U 11 ἦσαν δὲ ἐκεῖ. . . ὑδρίαι . . . κείμεναι
There were some vessels there.
U 11 begins a new unit, held together by its syntax, v. 6 (= U 11—15). Its relationship to the preceding verses is marked by a δέ, which does not refer to what follows "in point of

10, 12, 16, 17, 18, 22, 23, etc., and the following chs. For the variants in the Targums, see Potin 1971, vol. 1, p. 148.

[70] Note also the different form in Gen 41:55 (ὃ ἐὰν εἴπῃ),which is the more normal expression. See note 66 above.

[71] See below, 2.4.3.

[72] The phrase ὁ τὸν λόγον μου ἀκούων is parallel to ὁ πιστεύων τῷ πέμψαντί με. To believe is in Jn primarily to hear, described by Schlier 1964, p. 280, "als Antwort oder als Ent-sprechung auf das Wort oder den Spruch der Aussage Gottes in Jesus hin". On the significance of πιστεύειν in Jn, see below, 2.2, U 31.

[73] Cf. 15:14; 8:38ff; 9:31; 6:28; 3:21. The obedience of the disciples is parallel to Jesus' obedience to his Father, 4:34; 5:19, 27, 30; 6:38; 8:28f and 17:4.

[74] The usage in LXX of ἐντέλλεσθαι, ἐντολή, referring to the commands in the Law of God, has given these words a specific character ("seinen feierlichen, religiösen Charakter"), G. Schrenk in ThWNT, vol 2, p. 542. Josephus and Philo use these words relatively seldom.

time but in point of thought".[75] The function of the verse is usually explained in one of the following ways: *1.* As an item dealing with a *contemporary custom.*[76] The narrator wishes to explain to the reader the conditions prevailing when the event took place. The reader is assumed to be at a distance, culturally speaking, from the environment of the text. *2.* As a typical *narrative feature* of the text.[77] The evangelist is remembering, seeing the situation in his mind's eye as he describes it. The result is a very lucid account. *3.* As an *interpretative,* allusive *item.*[78] Opinions differ on how many elements are allusive or conceal a deeper meaning. However, the verse is often interpreted on the basis of the contrast between Moses and Jesus, between the Jewish purification system and Jesus' saving gifts, between the old and the new orders of salvation.[79] Ὑδρίαι usually refers to small, portable (clay) pots for the transport and storage of water[80] but it may mean large containers (different kinds of vessel).[81] The latter is evidently the case here, judging by the size.[82] Jn often uses periphrasis, and also the verb κεῖσθαι, 2:6; 19:29; 20:5, 6, 7, 12; cf. 5:3, 6. The reference of ἐκεῖ is not clear.[83] The beginning of U 11 is reminiscent of v. 1, which notes that Jesus' mother was present.[84] There is a parallel in Jn 19:29 where the phrase σκεῦος ἔκειτο ὄξους μεστόν introduces a detail of the situation necessary for the following action. The conclusion from the verb form in this phrase and in U 11 (κεῖσθαι as the perfect passive of τιθέναι with God as agent)[85] that these scenes were, so to speak, arranged in advance by God with Jesus' work of mission in mind is possible but hardly likely.

U 12 λίθιναι
They were of stone.

The description of objects with adjectives is alien to Jn's style.[86] The majority of the few adjectives in Jn specify a substance as does λίθιναι.[87] Nevertheless the vessels were probably not of stone but of hard clay, roughly what we call "stone ware".[88] The archaeological material which Schnackenburg adduces—storage vessels for oil, wine or

[75] Abbott 1906, p. 104; cf., for example, Jn 6:10; 18:40.

[76] For example, Bultmann, Comm., ad loc.

[77] For example, Stauffer 1960, p. 34: "... je zwei oder (sic!) drei Mass Wasser fassten. So spricht kein theologischer Dichter, der Material für symbolistische Zahlenspielereien liefern will".

[78] For example, Strathmann, Comm., ad loc.

[79] See the introduction above, 2.1, and the literature mentioned in note 8.

[80] Jn 4:28; Gen 24:14ff, 20, 43, 45, 46; Jg 7:16, 19f; 1 Kg 17:12, 14, 16; 18:34; Ec 12:6.

[81] See Liddell-Scott, s.v.

[82] See the comments below to U 15.

[83] Westcott, Comm., ad loc., suggests "in the court of the house", Holtzmann, Comm., ad loc., "im Hochzeitssaale".

[84] See 2.2, U 4.

[85] Thus Schlatter, Comm., ad loc. Cf. also Meyer and Holtzmann, Comm., ad loc.

[86] See the survey of parts of speech in Morgenthaler, p. 164.

[87] For example, κρίθινος, ἀκάνθινος, πορφυροῦς, corresponding to a status constructus in Hebrew, Schlatter, Comm., ad loc.

[88] On כלי אבנים "stone vessels", see Krauss, Archäologie, vol. 2, p. 287. About them, he says, "neigt man auch zu der Annahme, dass sie uneigentlich 'steinern' waren, etwa wie unser Steingut, im Wirklichkeit aber etwa härtere Tonwaren".

grain, 60—120 cm high, holding 20—50 litres—is hardly relevant. They were of ordinary clay and partly buried in the earth, according to Schnackenburg's source.[89] I have found no other archaeological material which can confirm or illustrate the water vessels mentioned in our text, so we are wholly dependent on the description in the text itself.

There can hardly be any doubt that the item in U 12 should be taken together with the statement that the vessels were used at the Jewish purification ceremonies.[90] According to Jewish belief "stone vessels", Hebr. כלי אבנים, did not become ritually "unclean" and thus were especially useful for purification, unlike clay and wooden vessels.[91] According to Krauss they were often used as water containers in private houses.[92] The description in U 12 thus helps to emphasize the connection between the vessels and the "purification of the Jews", irrespective of how we interpret the function of v. 6. See the discussion of U 14 below.

U 13 ἔξ

There were six of them

Various ways of counting and comparing may easily be used to elicit a large range of numerical "structures" and allusions in a text.[93] This is also true of Jn 2:1—11 with its context: the third day as the sixth day, six days of creation, 6 = 7—1, i.e. a number of imperfection, 2+1+2+1 speeches, 2 à 3 baths full etc. Nevertheless, it is extremely difficult to decide whether any of these combinations or allusions have any relevance for author or reader. We know that figures had a part to play, even in the environment in which the Gospel material took shape.[94] It is not beyond the bounds of possibility that numerical data may have a symbolic meaning in Johannine texts, judging by the use of the figure 153 in Jn 21:11.[95] Yet this evidence does not prove a symbolic meaning in our text. When the number 6 is interpreted in terms of symbols it tends to refer to the six days of creation, which were followed by "the sabbath of the world", or to imperfection, i.e. the Jewish religious system.[96] The former springs from a total interpretation on the basis of the days of creation and falls with it.[97] Among the objections to the latter is the fact that the number 6 may be regarded as a perfect number[98] and that there is no perfection in the

[89] Galling, col. 321f.

[90] See 2.2, U 14.

[91] Lev 11:32ff; M Kel II.1; XI.1, Str.-B., vol. 2, pp. 405ff, J. Jeremias in ThWNT, vol 4, p. 273, Brown, Comm., ad loc. On stone vessels in the temple, see Krauss, Archäologie, vol. 2, pp. 287f.

[92] Krauss, Archäologie, vol. 2, p. 288.

[93] For extended—and fantastic—analyses of numerical "structures" in Jn, see Quiévreux 1953. He sees the solution of the Johannine riddle in different combinations of figures. Cf. also some results of the structural analysis mentioned above 1.1, note 39, for example Janssens de Varebeke 1962, Malatesta 1971 and Sibinga 1972.

[94] For example, in the formation of Mt 1:1—17. See Johnson 1969, pp. 139ff, especially pp. 192f.

[95] On this use of figures in Jn 21, see Brown, Comm., ad loc.

[96] Schnackenburg, Comm., ad loc., Barrett, Comm., ad loc. (with some hesitation), and also Kreyenbühl, Comm., vol. 1, p. 588, Abbott 1906, pp. 224f, Wink 1968, p. 92.

[97] See 2.2, U 1.

[98] Quiévreux 1953, pp. 132ff.

form of a seventh vessel or the like. In my opinion the number 6 may possibly have some connection with the 6 day scheme in Jn which, according to my total interpretation, is present in Jn 2:1—11.[99] Yet it is very difficult to prove such an allusion in U 13. With the material now available to us for the interpretation of the vessels in v. 6, it seems most feasible to regard U 13 only as an element in the description of volume.[1]

U 14 κατὰ τὸν καθαρισμὸν τῶν Ἰουδαίων
They were for the purification of the Jews.

This prepositional phrase may also be taken with the verb and translated "according to the purification of the Jews".[2] The above translation may be justified by linguistic parallels and the placing of the phrase in v. 6.[3] The use of Ἰουδαῖοι seems to be entirely neutral, as in the expressions, "the Passover of the Jews", 2:13; 11:55, "a feast of the Jews", 5:1; 6:4; 7:2; cf. 19:42, "an ἄρχων of the Jews", 3:1, and the phrases in 4:9 and 4:22. The wording tends to imply a certain distance between the author and the Jews and/or between his readers and the Jews.

The six "stone vessels", then, were used in the Jewish ceremonies of purification. The Jews were to cleanse themselves with their water.[4] The OT regulations on cleanness and uncleanness and the various ways of purification had, through the centuries, become a complicated casuistic system, with far-reaching distinctions between different kinds of uncleanness, sensitivity to uncleanness, the water of purification etc.[5] The Pharisees, and especially the Qumran community, were extremely zealous about purification regulations, especially the washing of hands and immersions.[6] The excavations at Masada in 1963—4 brought to light two ritual immersion baths, מקואות, from the period of the Second Temple.[7] This discovery confirms that the many regulations concerning purifications in the Mishna tractate Mikwaoth were being followed even in NT times. The purifications, including the institution of sacrifice in the Temple, were of such central significance in certain circles at this period that ὁ καθαρισμός could almost symbolize the Jewish religion as a whole.

[99] See 2.2, U 1 and 2.4.3.

[1] See 2.2, U 15.

[2] Thus, for example, Bultmann, Comm., ad loc., referring to τῶν Ἰουδαίων. These words would not be there if the prepositional phrase expressed purpose.

[3] Linguistic parallels in Bauer, Comm., ad loc. Cf. Barrett, Comm., ad loc.: the alternative "for the purpose of ... gives perhaps the simpler and more satisfactory sense".

[4] If the narrator had a single "purification" in mind it would be that of the ritual washing performed before and after a formal meal, Barrett, Comm., ad loc. Cf. the Rabbinic material mentioned in note 19 below. Schlatter, Comm., ad loc., refers to ritual baths before sexual intercourse, without giving any evidence for such a custom. Jn probably intends no particular specification. Cf. 3:25 and the analysis in 3.2.2.

[5] See R. Rendtorff in ³RGG, vol. 5, col. 942ff, R. Meyer in ThWNT, vol. 3, pp. 421ff, and Lentzen-Deis 1970, pp. 59ff.

[6] Mk 7:1 ff; Mt 23:25f and the Rabbinic material to these passages in Str.-B., vol. 1, pp. 695ff, 934ff, vol. 2, pp. 13f. For Qumran, see Ringgren 1961, pp. 172ff, Lentzen-Deis 1970, pp. 64ff.

[7] See Yadin 1965, pp. 91f, 1966, pp. 164ff. The larger had two pools, 2,3 x 1,7 m and 1,5 x 1,2 m respectively. All the rules of ritual law in the Mishna were observed in its construction.

In the Johannine writings *purification* often recurs as characteristic of both the Jews and Jesus' disciples. According to 3:25 the frequency of water baptism practised by both Jesus and John the Baptist provoked a discussion with a Jew on καθαρισμός.[8] The Jews in 11:55 go up to Jerusalem at Passover to purify themselves (ἁγνίσωσιν ἑαυτούς), and according to 19:14, 31, 42 they are very zealous in observing the Day of Preparation. Their discussion with John the Baptist deals with his baptizing with water, 1:19ff. The mention of the cleanness of the disciples should be considered with this in mind, 13:1ff; 15:2f, and 17:14ff. They are made clean both *by Jesus' word,* 15:2f and 17:14ff, and *by Jesus' death,* 13:1ff; cf. 1 Jn 1:7,9. As in the Epistle to the Hebrews the purification by Jesus' word and blood seems to be enacted against a background of the Jewish purification ritual.

The purification is a vital motif in the context of the Cana narrative. John's *baptism with water* will be replaced by Jesus' *baptism with the Spirit,* 1:29ff. The heart of John the Baptist's revelation of Jesus is that he is *the Lamb of God who takes away the sin* of the world, 1:29, repeated in 1:36, a motif which at first sight seems to be a "foreign body" in the text.[9] Yet this impels two of John's disciples to follow Jesus. Nathanael, the true Israelite, is represented as a man in whom there is *no guile:* this wording, in the light of Ps 32:2 (and Rev 14:5) and the use of the word δόλος in the LXX, may well mean that Nathanael is described as *without sin, as free from impurity.*[10] The water vessels in 2:6 are to be used to *cleanse the Jews.* Moreover the Johannine version of the purification of the Temple emphasizes the Temple's function as a *place of sacrifice*—note the mention of the sacrificial animals, vv. 14f, which is peculiar to Jn. Jesus' zeal for God's commandments will lead to his death, v. 17. Once the Jews crucify him they tear down their Temple, vv. 19f. His "resurrection body" will fully replace the Temple with its function of purification.

[8] See below, 3.2.2. Some manuscripts, inclusive p[66], read μετὰ Ἰουδαίων. The question of purification is regarded—in the text as it now stands—as one of the most important in the conflict between Jews and Jesus (Jesus' disciples, John the Baptist).

[9] According to Vermes 1961, pp. 223ff, the New Covenant is based on the fulfilment of the promise in Gen 22:8. Cf. Lentzen-Deis 1970, pp. 200ff.

[10] Thus Jeremias 1930, pp. 3f, especially referring to Ps 32:2 (LXX 31:2): "Blessed is the man to whom the Lord imputes no iniquity (ἁμαρτίαν), and in whose spirit there is no deceit (MT: ואין ברוחו רמיה, LXX οὐδὲ ἔστιν ἐν τῷ στόματι αὐτοῦ δόλος)" and to the interpretation of these words in Midr. Ps 32 § 2: "R. Jose ben R. Judah said. When a man's repentance is so complete that his heart is torn within him, the Holy One, blessed be He, forgives him" (tr. by W.G. Braude). The word "deceit(ful)" has a religious accent in OT and is used as parallel to words for impurity, falsehood, unfaithfulness, sin. See, for example, Ps 12:3; 17:1; 32:2; 43:1; 52:5f.; Pr 12:6; Is 53:9; Hos 12:1; Zeph 3:13. —As a loan-word in Aramaic it can have the meaning "imperfection, defect, impurity", Dalman, s.v., 2, ("Verfälschung"), b Pes 57a; Tos Men VIII.19; Tos B.K. VII.8. Cf. in the NT 1 Pet 2:2; Rev 14:5 (ψεῦδος, but Textus Receptus has δόλος as in LXX Ps 31:2). Nathanael seems to be described as without fault, defect, sin, not as a man with "deceitful lips and a double heart", Ps 12:3. For further discussion, see 2.4.3 about the purified people at Sinai. —There may also be a reference to the cunning of Jacob (Gen 27:35: μετὰ ἐ δόλου), Barrett, Comm., ad loc., but this comparison does not help us very much in interpreting the text, if we do not take Nathanael as a representative of the true Israel, contrasted with the "old" Israel (= Jacob).

Throughout the section 1:19—2:22 we encounter a number of references to purification and purity in a religious sense. This, like the central role of purification in contemporary Judaism and the purification problem in Jn, indicates that U 14 and the whole of v. 6 have an interpretative function and should not be regarded only as an historical note to the reader.[11] It is incontrovertible that U 14 strikingly characterizes the vessels and thus also the water which by Jesus' intervention becomes wine. Jesus' miracle is bound up with Jewish purification vessels and the filling of them. To interpret according to the Johannine pattern: a Jewish *typos* is replaced by an *antitypos* which came with Christ: this interpretation is very feasible, if we do not find other features in the text which contradict it.[12]

U 15 χωροῦσαι ἀνὰ μετρητὰς δύο ἢ τρεῖς
They held 2 à 3 bathsfull each.

According to our knowledge of the weights and measures of the time, 1 Attic μετρητής = 1 Hebrew *bath* = 39.39 litres.[13] This gives a considerable amount: 470—710 litres in all, which is surprisingly in view of the archaeological finds[14] and the reasonable requirement of wine at the wedding.[15] Each vessel held about 100 litres, having an internal volume of, for example, 40 cm in diameter by 80 cm in height. The text clearly indicates that the whole volume was used, v. 7.

This statement of volume is usually interpreted as an expression of the magnitude of the miracle and the richness and abundance of Jesus' gifts.[16] Guilding and Hanhart derive the description from two texts on the copper sea in the Temple, which, according to 2 Chr 4:6, was for the purification of the priests.[17] 1 Kg 7:26 says that it held 2 000 baths while 2 Chr 4:5 mentions 3 000 baths. A combination of these two verses would give 2—3 baths. This ingenious explanation calls for the submission of much evidence which neither Guilding nor Hanhart have put forward. The fact that in Jn 2—4 we have a contrast between the Old and the New Temple will not suffice.

Since the earlier description of the six vessels so strongly emphasized the connection with the purification rites of the Jews, the question whether or not the account of the volume is related to the ritual regulations should at least be asked. The various purifications called for a certain volume of water. According to CD X.10b—13 the amount should be such as to cover a man, a volume established in the Mishna as 40 seas, i.e. about 480 litres.[18] This was the minimum for a ritual immersion bath. Those who

---

[11] See below, 2.4.

[12] Thus Brown, and especially Vawter, Comm., ad loc.

[13] Josephus, Ant VIII.57. Further references in Schnackenburg, Comm., ad loc.

[14] See the comment above on U 12.

[15] There are many speculations which try to avoid the multitude of wine. See the examples mentioned in Holtzmann, Comm., ad loc.

[16] Smitmans 1966, p. 26.

[17] Guilding 1960, p. 184, Hanhart 1970, p. 37.

[18] M Mikw I.4,7; II.1, 2, 3, 5, 10; III.1, 2; V.6; VI.3, 6, 7, 8, 9, etc. On immersion-pools, see, for example, M Mikw I.7 ("More excellent is a pool of water containing forty *seahs*; for in them men may immerse themselves and immerse other things") and V. 6 ("any pool wherein is forty *seahs* is valid for the immersion of men or vessels. They may immerse vessels in trenches or ditches or

came from the market should immerse their hands before eating in at least 480 litres of spring, river or rain-water.[19] This regulation of volume seems to apply to all kinds of immersion and washing. Our text may be said to follow it, so that it is not improbable that U 15 is also an element in the description of the vessels' function for purification.

U 16 λέγει αὐτοῖς ὁ Ἰησοῦς

a.   γεμίσατε τὰς ὑδρίας ὕδατος

Jesus says to them: "Fill the vessels with water".

The word αὐτοῖς links U 16 very closely with the preceding speech (U 10). The whole of v. 6 takes on the nature of a parenthesis, and the direct speech is emphasized. The use of τὰς brings the description in v. 6 into Jesus' own words, so to speak.[20] As in v. 5 the need for a transitional phrase here was felt at an early stage, judging by Latin translations.[21] The wording indicates that the vessels were empty: Jesus first orders them to be filled with water. The text makes no mention of whether Jesus followed the existing regulations for the filling of purification vessels.[22]

Water is often mentioned in Jn, almost invariably in clearly theological contexts. The statement ὕδατα πολλὰ ἦν ἐκεῖ, 3:23, may be applied to the entire Gospel. In *ch. 1* we meet John the Baptist by the River Jordan with a reference to his work of baptism (ὕδωρ, 1:26, 31, 33, βαπτίζειν, 1:25, 26, 28, 31, 33), in *ch. 2*—and 4:46—we read of the water in the Jewish purification vessels which was turned into wine (ὕδωρ, 2:7, 9; 4:46, ἀντλεῖν, 2:8, 9 γεύεσθαι, 2:9, μεθύσκεσθαι, 2:10). The discussion with Nicodemus in *ch. 3* is concerned, among other points, with birth by water and Spirit, and the framework of the controversy in 3:22ff is the amount of baptising at Aenon (ὕδωρ, 3:23, βαπτίζειν, 3:22, 23, 26; 4:1, 2). The first part of the conversation at Jacob's well in *ch. 4* is based on water in different senses.[23] The sick man in *ch. 5* is lying beside a pool in Jerusalem in order to be cured (ὕδωρ, 5:3f, 7, κολυμβήθρα, 5:2, 4, 7). We hear of water flowing from Jesus (or from the heart of a believer) in *ch. 7* (διψᾶν, πίνειν, 7:37, ὕδωρ, ποταμός, ῥεῖν, 7:38), of the man born blind, *ch. 9,* who bathed in the pool of Siloam (κολυμβήθρα, 9:7, νίπτειν, 9:7, 11, 15), of baptism again in *10:40.* Then follows the washing of the disciples' feet in *ch. 13* (ὕδωρ, 13:5, νίπτειν 13:5, 6, 8, 10, 12, 14, λούειν 13:10), Jesus' work symbolized

even in donkey-tracks in the valley that are mingled /with water from a valid Immersion-pool/") and b Erub 4b; b Chag 11a; b Pes 109a; b Yom 31a.

[19] See, besides the rules for immersion-pools just mentioned, the description of "die Beschaffenheit des Tauchbades" in Str.-B., vol. 1, pp. 108f and p. 695 ("Die Untertauchung der Hände, die vor dem Genuss von Heiligem (wie Opferfleisch) nötig war und die eine Wassermenge von 40 Sea erforderte, wurde mit טבילה (von טבל untertauchen) bezeichnet"), vol. 2, p. 14, which comments on Mk 7:4 (according to Str.-B. immersion of hands). There are three forms of purification: immersions (bathing), sprinkling (as in Mt 15:2) and washing of hands.

[20] Cf. 19:29f.

[21] For example in *e: et Iesus vocatis ad se ministris,* in *ff: et vocans Iesus ministris,* in *fors: et voca tis his* (i.e. hiesus?)*ministris* and in *l: et vocavit Iesus ministris* (-*tros* cor.) according to the textual apparatus in Wordsworth's edition.

[22] See M Mikw VIf and the report on the excavations at Masada in Yadin 1966, pp. 164ff.

[23] See below, ch. 3, especially 3.3.3.

by a drink in *18:11* and *19:28—30,* water from Jesus' dead body in *19:34* and finally, if we include *ch. 21,* the catch of fish from Lake Tiberias.

It is self-evident that the terms and ceremonies dealing with water almost always have some kind of transferred meaning in these texts.[24] Water is related above all to *purification* in a wide sense, 1:19ff; 3:22ff; 13:1ff; 2:6; 5:1ff; 9:1ff; 19:34(?), and also to the *Spirit.* 7:38; 1:32f; 3:5; 4:1—42. It seems natural therefore in a Johannine context to expect a deeper meaning from our text too. If this is not the case, then Jn 2:6, 7, 9 seems to be the only passage where ὕδωρ has no symbolic or allusive function.[25]

U 17 καὶ ἐγέμισαν αὐτὰς ἕως ἄνω
They filled them to the brim.

The servants did what Jesus had told them; see U 10 above. Most scholars hold that the unusual wording ἕως ἄνω [26] emphasizes the great quantity and may call to mind the eschatological abundance of wine.[27] U 17 merely says that the Jewish purification vessels were *filled to the brim* (completely filled) with water. Only an interpretation of the text as a whole will allow of a choice between such an aspect of *completeness* and the ordinary interpretation of *abundance.* The suggestion that ἕως ἄνω is to assure the reader that there was only water in the vessels and thus prove that there was no question of deception[28] is not justified by any other features of the text and must be regarded as highly improbable.

U 18 καὶ λέγει αὐτοῖς
a.   ἀντλήσατε νῦν καὶ φέρετε τῷ ἀρχιτρικλίνῳ
He says to them: "Now draw some out and take it to the steward of the feast."
The problems of this seemingly very simple unit concern the use of νῦν, ἀντλεῖν and ἀρχιτρίκλινος.

To what extent is the word νῦν purely temporal? It may be used both as a particle and as an adverb of time, and this also applies to its use in imperative clauses.[29] When used as a continuation or logical particle νυν is enclitic or usually in certain combinations such as καὶ νῦν, νῦν οὖν, νῦν δέ, νυνί δέ.   The enclitic νυν is of very rare occurrence in the NT.[30] The use of νῦν in Mt 27:42/Mk 15:32 (καταβάτω νῦν ἀπὸ τοῦ σταυροῦ) and in Mt 27:43

---

[24] See Stemberger 1970, pp. 149ff. Robinson 1966 interprets the water as referring to the old order, the Spirit to the new. On "living water" in Jn, see below, 3.3.6.

[25] Abbott 1905, p. 237. On purification and water in Ex 19—24, see 2.4.3.

[26] Ἕως + spatial adverb is very rare. Cf. ἕως κάτω in Mt 27:51. The only parallel in LXX: κατίσχυσεν ἕως ἄνω, 2 Chr 26:8. Ἄνω "above, upward(s)" in Jn 8:23; 11:41.

[27] See above, 2.2, U 7. Cf. 3:34 about the Spirit (οὐ ἐκ μέτρου), 3:23 about water (ὕδατα πολλά) 1:14ff, about the Word (πλήρης, πληρώματος), and see also 4:14; 6:12f and 7:38.

[28] Meyer, Comm., ad loc., Smitmans 1966, p. 26.

[29] See Liddell-Scott, s.v., and W. Stählin in ThWNT, vol. 4, pp. 1101ff, and the examples given there.

[30] Possibly Jas 4:13; 5:1, and Rom 11:31 and 8:1. All passages mentioned in Liddell-Scott, s.v., have the present tense and not the aorist as in our text. There are no parallels in LXX, which almost always has a form of combination such as καὶ νῦν, νῦν οὖν, νῦν δέ, but compare Jg 16:28 (B); 1 Kg 19:4; Is 47:12 and also Is 2:10; 44:1; Jer 18:11 and 33:13.

(ῥυσάσθω νῦν εἰ θέλει αὐτόν) most nearly resemble our text.[31] In these passages νῦν has a clear temporal meaning,[32] although hardly that he will *immediately* come down[33] but as a reference to the situation then prevailing: in this crucial moment Jesus (or God) should prove who is hanging on the cross. These parallels (aorist imperative + νῦν), the minimal use of the enclitic νυν in the NT and the temporal references in the other speeches[34] make it highly probable that νῦν here is markedly temporal in meaning and is not merely emphasizing the exhortation.[35] The word then marks a certain order in time of which Jesus, according to the narrator, is aware: first he fills the vessels to the brim, then the drawing can begin. The miracle presumably took place before the drawing.[36]

Jn contains many striking temporal contrasts, using νῦν and ἄρτι very frequently.[37] The "absolute" point in time round which everything else in the Gospel revolves is the "hour" of Jesus,[38] νῦν being used on several occasions as a reference thereto. 12:27, 31; 13:31; 16:5, 22; 17:5, 13. For Jn the "hour" is the great Now. This predominant temporal pattern in Jn may perhaps also contribute to the understanding of νῦν in U 18, especially as ἡ ὥρα is mentioned in an earlier speech.[39]

The usual meaning of ἀντλεῖν is "to draw water from a spring".[40] This is always the meaning in the LXX and in the NT except for our text, vv. 8f.[41] This usage prompted Westcott's conclusion that the servants in U 18—19 fetched the water from a spring.[42] This conflicts with the rest of the passage.[43] Barrett holds that Jn uses the word "loosely" or "under the influence of his thought of Christ as the well of living water".[44] Ἀντλεῖν would then express a receiving of Jesus' saving gifts. It is quite clear that this choice of

[31] Cf. also Lk 2:29 and 22:36 with νῦν before the verb.

[32] Thus also W. Stählin in ThWNT, vol. 4, p. 1115 ("in gewisses zeitliches Gewicht").

[33] Thus Bauer, s.v.: "im Imp. um zu bez., dass d. Aufforderung sofort ausgeführt werden soll, wobei ν. nachgestellt wird (Bl.-D. § 474,3)".

[34] See below, 2.3.4.

[35] For the latter function, see W. Stählin in ThWNT, vol. 4, p. 1115 ("Dringlichmachung eines Befehls oder einer Aufforderung").

[36] Νῦν implies that the water had become wine, Weiss, Comm., ad loc. "In diesem 'nun' ist das inzwischen eingetretene Wunder, das nicht besonders erzählt ist, eingeschlossen", Schmidt 1921, p. 35. According to Schnackenburg, Comm., ad loc., the temporal adverb marks "die Zeit, die zum Füllen der Gefässe nötig war", which, however, does not seem to be its primary function.

[37] See the survey in Abbott 1905, pp. 215f.

[38] See the comments below on U 27, U 29 and U 30.

[39] For further discussion, see below 2.3.4 and 2.4.2.

[40] Liddell-Scott, s.v.

[41] Gen 24:13, 20, 40 (Rebekah at the well); Ex 2:16f, 19 (the daughters of the priest of Midian at the well) and Is 12:3 (καὶ ἀντλήσετε ὕδωρ μετ' εὐφροσύνης ἐκ τῶν πηγῶν τοῦ σωτηρίου) in NT, besides our text, only Jn 4:7,15 (the Samaritan woman at the well).

[42] Westcott, Comm., ad loc. The word νῦν marks, according to him, that we have the same kind of act in U 16 and U 18 (i.e. a drawing from the well) but a new receiver.

[43] Brown, Comm., ad loc. The etymological argument in Sanders-Mastin, Comm., ad loc., (ἀντλεῖν out of "bale out a ship" and therefore the meaning "ladling wine" in our text) is not valid.

[44] Barrett, Comm., ad loc. The latter alternative is chosen by, for example, Abbott 1906, p. 224, and Hoskyns, Comm., ad loc. Bultmann in Ergänzungsheft to his commentary (1957, p. 20) rejects Hoskyns' interpretation, referring to Theocritus 10,12 (ἀντλεῖν ἐκ πίθω).

words in a Johannine context opens the way to such associations. The fact that the drawing leads to "insight whence"[45] may be regarded as further evidence, but such an allusive use of ἀντλεῖν could only be justified on the basis of a concept of the text as a whole.

The very unusual expression ἀρχιτρίκλινος creates great difficulties in U 18. It belongs to a large category of words easily formed with the prefix ἀρχι- in the sense of "chief of, president of".[46] Such words are even found incorporated in Aramaic.[47] Τρίκλινον means "dining room with 3 couches" or "feast" in general.[48] The prefix thus marks the individual's superior status and indicates that ἀρχιτρίκλινος should be regarded as a designation of a slave who was responsible for the meal and who supervised the other servants.[49] Certain features in the text emphasize his authority: the servants are referred to him for testing of the water/the wine; he summons the bridegroom, seeming to reproach him. Other features point to a different state of affairs: he appears to be well aquainted with the bridegroom, but ill informed of what the servants were doing. Some scholars cite Sir 32:1 and regard the ἀρχιτρίκλινος as merely the host at the table or *arbiter bibendi* on the basis of Gentile customs.[50] In either case he is a person chosen from among the guests. Since this type of word allows of understanding based on word formation, I prefer the sense of "chief of the servants", in the following called *steward*. The fact remains, however, that the reference of the word, like that of βασιλικός in 4:46, cannot be clearly confirmed from what we now know of the conditions of the time.[51]

The obscurity of the reference and allusive elements of the text in general prompted some scholars to explain the choice of word from its symbolic significance, partly as a play on ἀρχιερεύς [52] and partly as an expression of the Law of Moses.[53] Previously I emphasized to some extent the prefix ἀρχι- and in any case it is worthy of note that Nicodemus, who reacted to Jesus in a similar way, 3:1ff, is described as ἄρχων τῶν

[45] See the comments below on U 22 and U 23 and also 2.3.3 and 2.4.4.

[46] Liddell-Scott, s.v., note only Jn 2:8f, Bauer, s.v., also Heliodor, 7,27,7 (ἀρχιτρίκλινοι καὶ οἰνοχόοι). On words that begin with ἀρχι- see, besides ordinary lexicons and concordances, Zahn, Comm., ad loc., and Moulton-Milligan, pp. 80f. Moulton-Milligan give only a few examples in order to show "the readiness with which any writer might coin a compound of this class. . . . The prefix ἀρχ(ι)-(*q.v.*) could be attached to any word at will."

[47] Krauss, Lehnwörter, vol. 2, p. 130.

[48] Liddell-Scott, s.v. The word τρίκλινον occurs also as a loan-word in Hebrew and Aramaic, almost always in the meaning "Speisesaal, Prunksaal", Krauss, Lehnwörter, vol. 2, p. 274.

[49] See, for example, Holtzmann, Comm., ad loc., (ἀρχιτρίκλινος=τραπεζοποιός, triclinarches), Schnackenburg, Comm., ad loc. ("der Aufseher über die Diener", "der verantwortliche Festordner"), Brown, Comm., ad loc. ("headwaiter, butler"), and also Bauer, s.v.

[50] Barrett, Comm., ad loc., Smitmans 1966, p. 27.

[51] Schnackenburg and Brown, Comm., ad loc.

[52] Hanhart 1970, pp. 42f; cf. p. 30. As reason for this he refers to the opposition to the Temple in Jn the similarity to the command "go and show yourself to the priest" (for example, Mk 1:44; Mt 8:4; Lk 17:14) and the ignorance of the steward which resembles that of the high priest in 11:51. The steward's words, recalling the accusation in Acts 3:13, are "a protest against God's gift of the Spirit at Pentecost and its consequences" (p. 43).

[53] Kreyenbühl, Comm., vol. 2, pp. 481f, referring to 3:1,10 and 4:46. "Überall ist das theokratische Gesetz gemeint, das . . . den Christen ein Urheber religiöser Knechtschaft ist." Kreyenbühl's main reason for this interpretation may be his characterization of the text as strict allegory.

'Ιουδαίων – cf. the designation in v. 10—and that the leaders of "the Jews" in Jn are mainly the high priest(s) (ὁ ἀρχιερεύς), 11:47ff; 12:10.[54] If indeed the steward in some way represents the Judaism which did not accept Jesus his speech must be interpreted as an example of "Johannine irony": "the Jews" unwittingly utter profound truths, which in fact pass judgement on Judaism, such as 11:49f; 7:35; 8:22.[55] Yet only the initiate is aware of the irony.

U 19 οἱ δὲ ἤνεγκαν

They took it.

The phrase is equivalent to our *and they did so*. Greek does not use to the same extent as English (e.g. "do") auxiliary forms with a pro-verbial function, but repeats the main verb instead. Such repetitions are also found in Jn, in 6:12f; 21:3,6f. On obedience, see U 10.

U 20 ὡς δὲ ἐγεύσατο ὁ ἀρχιτρίκλινος τὸ ὕδωρ

The steward tasted the water.

This unit is introduced by the conjunction ὡς, common in Jn,[56] which often appears in transitional sentences, such as 6:12; 2:23; 6:16.[57] The ὡς –clauses in Jn at times contain something already mentioned, 2:23; 7:10; 11:6; 18:6, at other times new information, as in our text, 6:12; 4:1; 6:16; 20:11. This hypotaxis makes the action in U 20 only a transition to the new statement, with its direct speech, in v. 10. Here too we see that the narrator is leading up to the speech.

The use of the accusative after γεύεσθαι may point to influence from the LXX and the Hebrew construction in טעם.[58] Greek usually has the genitive.[59] Both cases are used in Heb 6:4f (. . . γευσαμένους τε τῆς δωρεᾶς τῆς ἐπουρανίου . . . καλὸν γευσαμένους θεοῦ ῥῆμα δυνάμεις τε μέλλοντος αἰῶνος),   seemingly without any great shades of meaning.[60] In LXX the verb often has a sense of "taste and experience, sample, test", and may be parallel with δοκιμάζειν and διακρίνειν.[61] Such a shade of meaning also fits in here: the steward tests the wine, samples what Jesus is offering through the servants.[62]

---

[54] The conflict in chs. 18—19 is mainly between the King of the Jews (= Jesus) and the high priests of the Jews, 18:3, 10, 15, 16, 19, 22, 24, 26, 35; 19:6, 15, 21.

[55] Brown, Comm., p. cxxxvi, Wead 1970, pp. 47ff.

[56] With δέ 2:9, 23; 6:12, 16; 7:10; 8:7; with οὖν 4:1, 40, 45; 11:6; 18:6; 20:11; 21:9.

[57] According to Schlatter, Comm., ad loc.. is ὡς "als Einführung der Handlung, die die folgenden Ereignisse bedingt", characteristic of Jn.

[58] Thus J. Behm in ThWNT, vol 1, pp. 674ff, and Turner, p. 233: the use of the accusative is "a Hebraism, perhaps influenced by the constructions with טעם , (sifre Num. on 11,4 טעמו אותו), and it is fairly common in LXX". For γεύσασθαι in LXX, see below, note 61.

[59] Bl.-Debr. § 169,3, Turner, p. 233. A few examples with the accusative in Mayser II, 2,206.

[60] Thus Michel and Spicq, Comm., ad Heb 6:4f, by contrast with Abbott 1906, pp. 76ff, and Moule, p. 36.

[61] Job 12:11; 34:3; Sir 36:19 and with ὅτι Ps 34:9 (γεύσασθε καὶ ἴδετε ὅτι χρηστὸς ὁ κύριος); 1 Pet 2:3; Pr 31:18. Cf. γεύεσθαι θάνατον in Jn 8:51f as a parallel to ἰδεῖν θάνατον.

[62] Compare the Johannine way of expressing how people receive what Jesus gives: 4:7ff; 7:37; 6:53ff (πίνειν); 6:54ff (τρώγειν) and chs. 6 and 21 (ἐσθίειν). Abbott 1906, p. 77: "the grammatical evidence favours the view that John would not have used the accusative if he had not meant something different from 'tasted *of* the water' ".

In several of the miracle narratives in Jn there is a verification of the result, often associated with witness to Jesus. The most detailed example is to be found in Jn 9, where the Pharisees—according to the narrator—are forced to admit the outward event, the miracle, but (unlike the simple man who is given his sight) do not draw the right conclusions about who Jesus really is. In Jn 6:12—15 the disciples gather up the remains, thereby establishing that all have received. At the same time we have a testimony from the crowd, v. 14, a judgement about Jesus which does not however, according to v. 15, define his true identity. The reality of the miracle is confirmed in 4:51—53, as is the fact that Jesus is the agent. Here the evidence is positive: people come to believe. The tasting in U 20 and the speech following—with the comment in v. 9—may well have a similar function to these features in the Johannine miracle narratives, although it need not be the only one.[63]

U 21 οἶνον γεγενημένον
The water had become wine.

The natural sequel to U 20—in terms both of syntax and semantics—does not follow until the end of v. 9, φωνεῖ τὸν νυμφίον, but before this point the narrator introduces so much material which is new to the reader that he has to repeat the subject. U 21 should therefore be regarded as a partly parenthetical item,[64] which, together with U 22—24, explains why the steward spoke as he did. U 21—24, as essential information prior to a speech, most closely resembles vv. 1—2 and v. 6.

We are not informed how the water in the Jewish purification vessels became wine. There is not even a mention of a word of power spoken by Jesus. Indeed Jn shows little interest in *how* the miracles occurred, 5:8f; 6:19, 21; 9:6f; 11:43f.[65] All we can say is that which *before* was water is wine *now*, 2:9, he who *before* was blind *now* sees, 9:13, 17, 18.[66] The miracle itself remains hidden. According to our text only the servants knew of it.

[63] Smitmans 1966, p. 279, regards vv. 9f only as a verification of the reality and quality of the miracle. Similarly in Barrett and Schnackenburg, Comm., ad loc. Note that the verification in ch. 9 is a part of a theological reasoning and that the verification in ch. 6 also describes the function of the disciples (see below, 3.4.6). In the same way 2:9f may have more than one function.

[64] None of the other "notes" in Jn has this form. Cf., however, 19:38; 1:12b—13 and 1:41, and also 4:25; 5:2; 7:50; 11:16.

[65] Not that Jesus wishes to help without being noticed, as Büchsel, Comm., ad loc., suggests. Bultmann, Comm., ad loc., states that this is a feature of the genre (miracle stories), but the Johannine texts, as we now have them, scarcely belong to this genre. See the evangelist's comment in v. 11 and 2.2, U 27—31 and 2.4.5.

[66] Abbott 1906, p. 78 paraphrases: "Now when he tasted the water— /I say water, but/ it had become wine..." and adds: "This brief and parenthetic statement of the first of Christ's miracles—in which the reader is let into the secret in two words ('become wine') while the master of the feast talks, outside the secret, in twenty ('Every man—until now') is highly characteristic of the Fourth Gospel".

U 22 $\kappa\alpha\grave{\iota}$ οὐκ ᾔδει πόθεν ἐστίν

He did not know where it came from.

U 22 continues to prepare and explain the last speech of the text (U 26), in the framework of parenthesis.[67] The steward did not know where the wine came from. Since the idea of *knowing where someone/something comes from* (γινώσκειν / εἰδέναι πόθεν ἐστίν) plays a leading role in Jn (1:48; 3:8; 4:11; 6:5; 7:27, 28; 8:14; 9:29f; 19:9) and *to know* may be used as almost synonymous with *to believe*, e.g. 17:8 and 14:7, 10, a number of scholars have asked whether or not U 22—23 should be interpreted on the basis of this Johannine usage.[68] The Samaritan woman does not know *where* Jesus will *get* "living water", 4:11, the disciple does not know *where* the bread will *come from*, 6:5. Nicodemus cannot understand where the Spirit *comes from*, 3:8. The passages in 7:27f; 8:14; 9:29f and 19:9, discuss where Jesus *comes from*. The wording of 9:28ff is especially pointed. The man answered "Why, this is a marvel. You do not know where he *comes from*, and yet he opened my eyes... If this man were not *from God*, he could do nothing".[69]

The crucial question of where Jesus or his gifts come from is an essential element in the whole "theology of mission" in Jn. Its central importance emerges from the fact that belief can be determined as to content by the clause ὅτι σύ με ἀπέστειλας and paralleled by ἔγνωσαν ἀληθῶς ὅτι παρὰ σοῦ ἐξῆλθον, 17:8; cf. 17:3. A true disciple of Jesus knows where Jesus/Jesus' gifts come from.[70]

The phrase ᾔδει πόθεν ἐστίν is therefore a further example of expressions which in the Gospel in general have a central theological meaning. Provided no compelling reasons are adduced to regard 2:9 as the only exception, it is natural to allow general Johannine usage to determine the interpretation in this case.

U 23 οἱ δὲ διάκονοι ᾔδεισαν

The servants knew it.

The servants can testify that a miracle took place and who performed it,[71] as can the man born blind in ch. 9, the chronic invalid in ch. 5, or ὁ βασιλικός in 4:46ff. They are all witnesses of Jesus' acts after they obeyed his words. The contrast with the steward is striking—comparisons of this kind are very common in Jn, e.g. 1:8, 12, 14, 17, 19ff; 2:21, 25; 3:12; 4:12 etc. The conclusions drawn from U 22 may allow of the view that the evangelist wishes to suggest their realization that the wine/Jesus came "from above", 3:3,

---

[67] U 21 may be non-parenthetical, but not U 22—25. These are generally described as parentheses, Bultmann, Schnackenburg, Comm., ad loc. For such notes in John on knowing and not knowing, see 20:9; 12:16; 13:28f; 8:27; 6:64; 13:11, in 6:6 a comparison between two persons.

[68] See the survey in Smitmans 1966, p. 27, who mentions Hoskyns, Bultmann, Schnackenburg, Schmidt, Mollat, Noetzel and Leroy as supporters of a specific Johannine usage in U 22.

[69] Ἡμεῖς οὐκ οἴδατε πόθεν ἐστιν ... εἰ μὴ ἦν οὗτος παρὰ θεοῦ. We have the same question in the following monologue about the good shepherd, 10:1ff. The shepherd of the sheep is the one who came the right way, 10:2f. See Olsson ²1973, pp. 258f.

[70] This knowledge is given by the revelation of Jesus and his work, 1:31, 33; 9:1ff; 17:4, 6, 8.

[71] Early Latin translations add: *et videntes factum mirabantur* (a, b and r), *quae vinum factum est* (e), *quia de aqua vinum factum est* (1).

6—8.[72] Yet unlike chs. 4 and 9 there is no mention that they believed.[73] Our text attributes belief only to the disciples, v. 11. Prior to this statement the reader encounters a series of "witnesses" to Jesus: *Jesus' mother* informs the servants that Jesus is the person they must obey, *the steward* affirms that Jesus' wine was excellent, *the servants* who obeyed Jesus throughout can bear witness to where the wine came from. It is clear that all except the steward express some form of belief in Jesus. The disciples have complete faith, based on the revelation of Jesus' *doxa*, v. 11. I shall try do describe the attitude of the servants and Jesus' mother later.[74]

U 24 οἱ ἠντληκότες τὸ ὕδωρ
They had drawn the water.

The reader must have assumed the action in U 24 from the foregoing text, whether it refers to the drawing from the vessels or from the spring.[75] This unit gives no new information but emphasizes a fact already known, and makes it quite clear that the steward was not present when it was drawn.[76] It is an appositional phrase to διάκονοι and constitutes the fourth part of the parenthesis in v. 9 which prepares for the speech.

The appositional phrase evidently explains the servants' knowledge of where the wine comes from. It is noteworthy that the text says ὕδωρ throughout and not οἶνος. The servants had drawn the water, not the wine.[77] This, coupled with our previous comments on ἀντλεῖν, may be adduced as reasons for a transferred meaning on a par with, for example, Is 12:3 (ἀντλήσετε ὕδωρ ... ἐκ τῶν πηγῶν τοῦ σωτηρίου). The wine in the vessels is the water Jesus gives, 4:7ff; 7:37ff; 9:7 and 19:34. This is "the Jesus water" which proved on tasting to be the "good wine".[78]

U 25 φωνεῖ τὸν νυμφίον ὁ ἀρχιτρίκλινος
The steward calls the bridegroom.

The repetition of the subject depends on the long parenthetical insertion in v. 9 and is hardly intended to emphasize the steward.[79] The verb φωνεῖν, here with a personal ob-

---

[72] Thus Kreyenbühl, Comm., vol. 1, p. 588.

[73] Bultmann, Hoskyns, Bouyer and Wilkens describe the servants as believers, according to Smitmans 1966, p. 27.

[74] See below, 2.3.5 and 2.4.4.

[75] The wording of v. 8 indicates a drawing from the stone vessels, a symbolic interpretation implies a drawing in general or a drawing from the well (that is from Jesus). Cf. the drawing of water in Jn 4.

[76] Nothing in the text marks a distinction between those servants who had drawn the water and those who had not (the other servants of the house), against Abbott 1906, pp. 42f.

[77] The servants are "the drawers of water". Cf. the use of ἀντλητῆρες about the two testaments of the Bible in Epiphanius, Panarion seu adversus lxxx haereses, 66.85.10 (GCS, vol. 3, p. 128).

[78] For the function of the servants, see below, 2.4.4.

[79] Against Abbott 1906, pp. 450f, in spite of his Johannine parallels. The frequent explanation that the repetition depends on different sources is of little help for the interpretation of the text as we now have it.

ject, used in the sense of "call for, summon",[80] seems to imply that the bridegroom was not in the immediate vicinity. It is not Jesus who proclaims the miracle but the steward of the feast.[81] The bridegroom is introduced without explanation; his presence is assumed, which is natural in the context. There is no confirmation in contemporary sources that the bridegroom was normally responsible for providing wine at his wedding. Yet only if this was the case would the steward's comment have a significance in the account worthy of its place in the total composition.

The metaphor of the bridegroom (ὁ νυμφίος) is frequently used in the OT and Late Judaism of Yahweh and his covenant with Israel but, according to Joachim Jeremias, we have no Jewish evidence that it was applied to the Messiah.[82] But in NT texts ὁ νυμφίος refers to Christ, 2 Cor 11:2; Eph 5:22f; Mk 2:19f (par.); Mt 25:1ff; Rev 19:7, 9; 21:2, 9; 22:17, often in contexts dealing with Christ's Church on earth. There is a similar metaphor in Jn 3:29.[83] The bridegroom in our text therefore could be an allusion to Christ.

U 26 καὶ λέγει αὐτῷ
a.   πᾶς ἄνθρωπος πρῶτον τὸν καλὸν οἶνον τίθησιν, καὶ ὅταν μεθυσθῶσιν τὸν ἐλάσσω
b.   σὺ τετήρηκας τὸν καλὸν οἶνον ἕως ἄρτι

He says to him: "Every man serves the good wine first and when men have drunk freely, then the poor wine. You have kept the good wine until now."

If we ignore the comment in v. 11,[84] the narrative of the miracle of the wine at Cana ends with a speech, the sixth and longest in the text.[85] It is to a high degree built up of contrasts and contains a general statement and an application of some kind.

This literary form is typical of Jn. He tends to repeat *speeches* with or without comment, 1:15, 29, 30; 3:7, 28; 4:10, 17; 5:11, 12; 6:36, 41, 42; 7:36; 8:22, 24, 33, 48, 52; 9:11, 41; 10:36; 11:40; 13:13, 33; 14:9; 16:17, 18; 18:6, 8; 19:21; 21:23.[86] Many

[80] Synonymous to καλεῖν, προσκαλέσθαι in Lk 16:2; 19:15; Acts 9:41; 10:7; Jn 4:16; 9:18, 24. The text does not read φωνήσας εἶπεν or similar expressions. For further examples see Bauer, s.v., and O. Betz in ThWNT, vol. 9, p. 296.

[81] "Ein wesentliches Merkmal seines Handelns", Schlatter, Comm., ad loc. A similar feature in 9:1ff with φωνεῖν in v. 18 and v. 24.

[82] J. Jeremias in ThWNT, vol. 4, pp. 1094f.

[83] See below, 3.2.2. "As it stands it is an allegory, in which Jesus is the bridegroom and the Baptist is the best man", Lindars, Comm., ad loc. Lindars would here see a parable of Jesus, which has been transferred to John the Baptist, Lindars 1969—70, pp. 324ff.

[84] On the relation between v. 10 and v. 11, see below, 2.3.1.

[85] The speeches of Johannine text generally become longer and longer and dialogues become monologues. See below, 3.3.1 and 3.4.1. The closing speeches normally have an essential function, but many commentators ignore v. 10 in their interpretation of the Cana narrative, with or without "source critical" motivations. According to the ordinary method of composition v. 10 should be the climax of the narrative, Meyer 1967, p. 193. Cf., for example, v. 20 in 2:13ff. The device of ending with a direct speech may indicate a didactic interest on the part of the narrator. Cf. the composition of the Book of Jonah and Kreyenbühl, Comm., vol. 2, p. 483.

[86] The Johannine use of "notes", see below, 4.2.

speeches are thus given special emphasis. They become links in a process of interpretation and reflection, in which individual words and expressions at times acquire different meaning according to the context. This is particularly evident in the words about Jesus' "going away".[87]

The use of *meshalim* of various types is akin to this literary form. They may be *proverbs*, such as 4:35, 37, *short parables*, such as 3:8, 29; 5:19f; 8:35; 16:21, "*Bildreden*", 10:1ff; 15:1ff, *short idioms*, 9:24, or *general statements*, 2:10; 3:6, 27; 6:63a; 7:4, 18a; 9:4; 12:35; 13:10, 16; 15:13, 20. It is not easy to delimit the various forms of *meshalim*. The general statements are almost always incorporated into an argument where the apparently self-evident general rule, often culled from everyday life, is an essential part of the evidence.[88] In U 26 the general statement in U 26a is applied in U 26b to the situation described.

The generally worded, somewhat proverbial rule[89] in U 26a says: one usually offers one's guests the better wine first and then, when they have drunk freely—and their judgement is clouded—the less good. There is no confirmation of such a custom in contemporary sources,[90] "but it is the type of shrewd practice that is common to human nature".[91] The application is based on a comparison: πᾶς ἄνθρωπος - σύ.[92] The bridegroom has not followed the custom but has reversed it.[93] The steward here seems to be wholly unaware of the supply of wine, of the shortage or of the drawing of water. He merely states that the wine is excellent (καλός)[94] and that the bridegroom's actions are not those of ordinary men.[95]

[87] See Leroy 1968, passim.

[88] On the relations between sons, slaves and masters, 13:16; 15:15,20, on religious and legal circumstances, 7:49, 51, 52; 8:17; 9:31; on *sarx — pneuma* 3:8; 6:63a, and, as in U 26, on general human conditions, 7:4,18a; 13:10; 3:27.

[89] Note the phrase πᾶς ἄνθρωπος, the use of the present tense (τίθησιν) and ὅταν with the aorist (iterative action, Turner, p. 113).

[90] See Schnackenburg, Comm., ad loc., and the literature he mentions. The customs seem to have been the opposite. Lindars 1969—70, pp. 318ff, suggests that v. 10, like Jn 3:29, was originally a parable of Jesus, which is very difficult to verify or contradict. Bultmann, Comm., ad loc., quotes Bauer: "möglich aber auch, dass die Regel 'ad hoc im Interesse der Wundertat gebildet ist' (Br.)".

[91] Brown, Comm., ad loc.

[92] Note also the use of καλόν, which may have a comparative or superlative meaning, Moule, p. 97, Turner, p. 31, and Black [3]1967, p. 117. The comparison mentioned above suggests a comparative meaning. Σύ marks emphasis, Turner, p. 37.

[93] This feature of the text is made the basis of the interpretation in Meyer 1967. The wine is regarded as "a comprehensive symbol" of salvation and the words of the steward become a parallel to, for example, Heb 4:6; 11:39f; Rom 11:11ff, 25ff (Why has God kept the salvation until now?). The message of the text is a reaction against Hellenistic cosmogonies and salvation doctrines in which the good always comes first. However, Meyer has not succeeded in explaining all the parts of the text.

[94] A comparative sense of καλός is possible—see note 92 above—but considering the parallel expressions in Lk 5:39; Mk 2:22 (about the new wine); Jn 10:11,14 (about the good shepherd) and Jn 10:32f (about Jesus' works) I here preferred the translation "good, excellent".

[95] Note the many contrasts (comparisons) in this speech: every man—you, the good wine—the

The steward's words have often been described as "eine humorvolle Bemerkung", "half playful", "a bit of peasant humour".[96] At the same time there is a certain similarity to the Jews' objections, for example in 7:35; 8:22, and indeed to the feature usually described as "Johannine irony": the opponents of Jesus are given to making statements about him that are derogatory, sarcastic, incredulous, or, at least, inadequate in the sense they intend. However, by way of irony these statements are often true or more meaningful in a sense they do not realise.[97] U 26 may be a special form of this irony where the more profound meaning is to be found in a symbolic significance of the terms *bridegroom* and *good wine*. The steward sees only the outward, human side of the occurrence and is slightly humorous about the customs at feasts. The narrator and everyone who, like him, knows who Jesus is, see a deeper meaning: Jesus has now brought from his store the *good* wine, superior to the old.[98] By his action the new age has begun. The reasons which may here be adduced for such a reading are Jn's use of speeches and *meshalim* illustrated above, the "ironic" feature of his style and the possibilities of allusion inherent in νυμφίος, ἀρχιτρίκλινος, οἶνος and καλός.[99]

U 27 ταύτην ἐποίησεν . . . ὁ Ἰησοῦς ἐν Κανά
This Jesus did at Cana.

This unit brings us to the last part of our text, which consists of v. 11 (= U 27–31). This verse is separated by structure and content from the preceding ones. It takes the form of a parenthetical comment and thus reveals something of the narrator's view of the events he describes. Even a first reading makes it clear that v. 11 leads in to the Gospel in general and its account of what Jesus did (ἐποίησεν), his signs (τὰ σημεῖα), his work of revelation (ἐφανέρωσεν), his glorification (ἡ δόξα) and the belief in him (ἐπίστευσαν εἰς αὐτόν).

Verse 11 is thus an integral part of the Gospel as a whole and constitutes a special link between the Cana narrative and a Johannine context. A discussion of its various parts would necessitate extensive analyses of basic features of the Johannine presentation of Jesus (of ἔργα, σημεῖα, φανεροῦν, δόξα and πιστεύειν εἰς). Such analyses are not possible in the framework of this book. The following points seem to be the most important for further analysis. The combination in v. 11 of related concepts peculiar to Jn made it difficult to analyse the various segments (units) separately, but I have chosen to divide up the text as before. This has the advantage that questions of the relations between the different units come out clearly and demand answers.

The introductory deictic adjective ταύτην directs the attention back to the preceding account and combines it into a single unit. Many "comments" in Jn begin in this way.[1]

---

poor wine, first–then. This use of comparisons is typical of Jn, marked by such words as καθώς, πρῶτον, μείζων, τάχιον, ὑπέρ, μᾶλλον, πρότερον. See also de Dinechin 1970.

[96] See Schnackenburg, Westcott and Sanders-Mastin, respectively, Comm., ad loc. Westcott adds: "The last clause seems to be one of those unconscious prophecies in which words spoken in recognition of a present act reveal the far deeper truth of which it is a sign".

[97] See above, 2.2, U 18, and the literature mentioned there in note 55.

[98] "The new faith is better than the old", Barrett, Comm., ad loc.

[99] For further discussion, see 2.4.2 and 2.4.4.

[1] See below, 4.2, note 26.

The remarks usually concern what someone *said*, 6:6, 59; 7:39; 8:20; 9:22f; 10:6; 11:51, but they may refer to something that *happened*, 1:28; 4:54; 19:36; and cf. 12:16; 13:28; 21:14 and 12:37 (τοσαῦτα... σημεῖα) and 20:30f (πολλὰ μὲν οὖν καὶ ἄλλα σημεῖα... ταῦτα δὲ...), especially *what Jesus said and did*. In two passages, 8:20 and 10:6, the pronoun is followed by a noun and there with the article according to normal Greek usage (ταῦτα τὰ ῥήματα, ταύτην τὴν παροιμίαν). In 2:11 and 4:54 the article is missing. Ordinary Greek grammar suggests that the substantive should here be read predicatively: Jesus did this in Cana as the beginning of the signs ... as the second sign.[2] These two passages in their entirety read:

ταύτην ἐποίησεν ἀρχὴν τῶν σημείων ἐν Κανὰ τῆς Γαλιλαίας, 2:11.

τοῦτο δὲ πάλιν δεύτερον σημεῖον ἐποίησεν ὁ Ἰησοῦς ἐλθὼν ἐκ τῆς Ἰουδαίας εἰς

τὴν Γαλιλαίαν, 4:54.

There are a number of variants of 2:11. The text given here has the best support and is probably the original. The addition of the article before ἀρχήν and changes in the word order may be explained as different ways of normalizing the text. The reading of the original hand in p66 (ταύτην πρώτην ἀρχὴν ἐποίησεν) and in Codex Sinaiticus (πρώτην after Γαλιλαίας) creates greater problems.[3] In certain contexts πρῶτος and ἀρχή may be entirely synonymous, in the sense of "first".[4] The latter word, however, has a far wider range of meaning[5] and from the point of view of the Greek is definitely less common as an ordinal. If, as Fortna maintains,[6] an earlier source had τοῦτο πρῶτον, as in 4:54, an amendment to ἀρχήν must mean that this word is used in a sense somewhat different from πρῶτος. If ἀρχήν alone was original, which is likely, an addition of πρώτην shows that there was a need to specify the meaning of the word (or perhaps bring it into agreement with 4:54). Even in this case it is probable that the change was prompted by other senses of ἀρχή than the purely temporal. The variant πρώτην therefore may well be regarded as an indication that ἀρχή in 2:11 should not be read as wholly synonymous with πρῶτος.[7]

Jn 2:11 and 4:54, quoted above, are evidently related to each other. They state three facts:

[2] Turner, p. 192: "the omission of the art. is possible where conceivably the noun is regarded as a predicate of the pronoun". Cf. Pr 8:22: κύριος ἔκτισέν με ἀρχὴν ὁδῶν αὐτοῦ ἔργα αὐτοῦ, Abbott 1906, pp. 287f, Meyer, Holtzmann, Bauer and Schulz, Comm., ad 4:54, and Riedl 1963, p. 268.

[3] See Fortna 1970, p. 35, and, for a discussion of the variant in p66, Fee 1968, pp. 15f, 60, 62, 74f. He characterizes πρώτην as "probably an early corruption due to a misunderstanding—or right understanding—of αρχην" (p. 75).

[4] See, for example, LXX Ex 12:2 and Dt 21:17.

[5] See Liddell-Scott, s.v., Moulton-Milligan, p. 81 ("The double meaning, answering to ἄρχειν and ἄρχεσθαι severally, can be freely paralleled. ... Ἀρχή 'beginning, foundation' may be illustrated by ..."), and K. Delling in ThWNT, vol. 1, pp. 477ff.

[5] Fortna 1970, p. 36. By changing the text to ταύτην πρώτην ἀρχὴν τῶν σημείων the evangelist wished to stress that the first sign was "the chief one of all" and to give "the Cana pericope unique symbolic importance". This redundant expression has later on been eliminated by scribes in different ways.

[7] For further discussion, see 2.4.4.

1. The important point is what Jesus *did* (ἐποίησεν), his ἔργον.[8] Both narratives, however, contain no real description of Jesus' acts, except in the form of "evidence" from individuals who were not present at the meeting with Jesus (the steward, the slaves). The only "actions" explicitly attributed to Jesus in the text are verbal, Jesus' sayings in 2:4, 7, 8; 4:48, 50 (λέγει, εἶπεν). Jesus' words in 2:7f and 4:50 coincide to some extent with the miraculous event but this is not manifest until a situation when Jesus is no longer present. The fact that Jesus is the agent of the miracle is realized by those who heard and obeyed his word (= "believed his word", 4:50). This time-lag and involvement of "new" individuals in the account of Jesus' ἔργον allow of a certain perspective on what happened and who did it, and may perhaps be connected with the narrator's way of regarding Jesus' ἔργα as σημεῖα. The narrator can use the wording of Jesus' speeches, the words and acts of other individuals, comments, and his composition in general to state or suggest a deeper meaning in what Jesus did.

2. Jesus did it *in Cana after he had left Judea and gone to Galilee.* This emerges clearly from 1:28f, 43; 2:1, 11; 3:22f; 4:3, 43, 45, 46, 47, 54.[9] The location at Cana runs through the entire narrative (ἀκούσας, 4:47, καταβαίνειν, vv. 47, 49, 51, ἐχθές v. 52). The wording of v. 46 (πάλιν, ὅπου ἐποίησεν τὸ ὕδωρ οἶνον) and v. 54 (δὲ πάλιν, δεύτερον) shows that the narrator is primarily interested in linking the later event with the previous one. Moreover the similarity of composition of the two Cana narratives has often been pointed out.[10] This striking association emphasizes the central importance of the first account and its focus at Cana.[11]

3. What Jesus did is described as a *sign* (σημεῖον; see U 29). According to the conclusion in 20:30f, the Gospel is primarily a collection of Jesus' signs. The first two of these are special. They are marked as the first and the second sign at Cana, which Jesus did after he "migrated" from Judea to Galilee.[12]

The comparison with 4:54 thus confirms that in U 27 the narrator is focusing on what Jesus *did* and is anxious to locate it in *Cana.* Judging by U 27 Jesus' ἔργον is the object of the account, that which the narrator wishes to describe, that which may be the subject of his reflections and comments. It gives us reason to further investigate what Jn says of Jesus' act(s).

According to Jn both Jesus' *acts* and his *words* are part of the work (τὸ ἔργον) which God gave him to do and both form part of his revelation, 17:4; 4:34; 14:10; 8:28.[13] Jesus'

---

[8] This word is not used in our text but occurs frequently in Jn as a designation of Jesus' acts. See below, note 13.

[9] See above, 2.2, U 3. On these "migrations" to Galilee, see also below, 3.2.3.

[10] See Holtzmann and Brown, Comm., ad loc.

[11] There is no interest of "Fernheilung" in the text as it now stands, Schnackenburg, Comm., ad loc., Schnider-Stenger 1971, pp. 79ff.

[12] See below, 3.2.3.

[13] Jesus' *words* and his *acts* belong together in Jn. This is especially marked by the use of ἔργα. This word and ῥήματα are sometimes used as parallels, 14:10; cf. 8:28; 15:22, 24; 17:4, 8, 14. This does not imply that Jesus' erga are his words, as Wilkens 1969, pp. 83ff, strongly asserts with reference to Bultmann. His sharp distinction between σημεῖα(in "Erzählungsstoff") and ἔργα (in "die Reden") does not help us to understand the text as it now stands. The literary unity of Jn and the evidence of a near connection between Jesus' acts and words in the NT contradicts his

sayings take up a large part of the many monologues and dialogues in Jn but this does not mean that Jesus' acts are of lesser importance. In the confrontation between Jesus and "the world", Jesus' acts are assigned such a central role that the statements and the speeches function rather as comments and expositions of what Jesus did, and especially of his suffering and death on the cross.[14]

Jesus performed *many miracles and signs*, especially in *Jerusalem*. This is impressed on the reader again and again, 2:23; 3:2; 4:45, 54; 6:2; 7:3f; 10:25, 32, 38; 11:47; 12:37; 15:24; 20:30f; (21:25) and cf. 5:17ff; 9:16 and 14:11f. Yet we are seldom told which acts these were or how they were carried out. The evangelist generally confines himself to the results of the signs, the consequences and the implications, the many discussions about them, 5:16ff; 6:28ff; 7:21ff; 9:8ff; 10:24ff, sometimes incorporated in the description of the actual event, 11:1ff. This form of presentation is most prominent in the case of the chief act in that last week in Jerusalem. A long introduction, chs. 13—17, and a special composition for the passion and resurrection narratives tell the reader far more about what the evangelist regards as the real meaning and the consequences of what happened in Jerusalem than actually occurred. It seems beyond dispute therefore that the narrator is more interested in "discussing", commenting on, and explaining Jesus' ἔργα than in describing them. The reader is given only a very limited selection of signs (20:30f), so few that—apart from the events of the final week—we can list them here: the miracle of the wine, the cleansing of the Temple, the curing of a dying boy, of a chronic invalid and of a man born blind, the feeding of the 5 000 (with the walking on the water) and the raising of a dead man. All these are interpreted by long monologues or inserted dialogues, except for the first two, the miracles at Cana. Yet there is no reason to assume that the evangelist's main interest was different when he described them than when he expounded the others. The primary function of Jesus' ἔργα is, according to John, "one of symbolism".[15]

Jn describes Jesus' works with the words ἔργα and σημεῖα. Ἔργα, which in the Synoptic Gospels is used only twice of Jesus' works, refers in the LXX mainly to God's saving acts when he made Israel a people for his own possessing.[16] Indeed the very wording confers a divinity on Jesus' works. The Gospel says many times that Jesus' ἔργα are God's saving activity in the world, 4:34; 5:17ff; 8:28f; 9:3; 10:25. Therefore Jesus' acts and his "work of mission" in the world bear witness to God, to the union of Father and Son, 5:19ff; 10:38, to Jesus' identity, 9:16, 33; 10:21.[17] Man is faced with a choice between belief or unbelief, judgement or life, 2:11; 4:45, 53; 6:30; 10:38f; 12:37ff; 20 30f. Thus for Jn Jesus' ἔργα have an important part to play in revealing to mankind who Jesus is.

Jesus' earthly works apparently constitute a phase in the redeeming activity of the Father and the Son, works summed up in τὸ ἔργον in 4:34 and 17:4, and also in τὸ πο-

theory of the origin of Jn. Jesus' *erga* includes both Jesus' *acts* and his *words*. On Jesus' *erga* in Jn, see Nicol 1972, pp. 116ff, and the literature he mentions.

[4] The concentration on Jesus' death at Golgotha is rightly stressed by Wilkens 1969, passim.

[15] Brown, Comm., pp. 525ff.

[16] See, for example, Ex 32:10; Ps 66:5; 77:12; Dt 3:24 (var.); 11:3 (var.) and Acts 7:22. See also Brown's excellent excursus on Jesus' signs and works in his commentary, pp. 525ff.

[17] On this divine aspect of Jesus' *erga*, see Wilkens 1969, pp. 86ff.

τήριον in 18:11; cf. 19:28–30. The phase comes to an end with Jesus' "elevation", his death on the cross, 19:30. Nevertheless Jn also refers to works which are greater than these (μείζονα τούτων), 14:12 and 5:20. In 14:12 they are apparently associated with Jesus going to the Father (ὅτι ἐγὼ πρὸς τὸν πατέρα πορεύομαι), i.e. to the time *after* Jesus' earthly works. They are done by Jesus' disciples but, at the same time, according to vv. 13f, by Jesus himself. *He* will do (ποιήσω) what they ask in his name. The context in 5:20ff indicates that the "greater" works are to give *life* and to pronounce *judgement*, functions which naturally belong to Jesus' continued work after he has gone to the Father, notwithstanding that they are anticipated in different ways in his work on earth. God's work of salvation, his work of mission through the Son is for Jn a single whole, where God is the main subject, but this work is clearly differentiated into *two phases,* the time before and the time after Jesus' "glorification", 7:39; 12:16; 2:22.[18] Jesus' *ergon* in Jn is therefore described not only as God's *ergon* but also as the disciples'. They have the same mission, 17:18; 20:21, the same commandments, 15:10ff, the same sanctification, 17:17, 19, the same service, 13:1ff; 12:26. There are features in Jn indicating that these two phases in Jesus' *ergon* can be projected into each other.[19]

Accordingly the Johannine views of Jesus' works are in agreement with the emphasis in U 27 and the whole of v. 11 on what Jesus did. They suggest that the narrator saw in the event at Cana a manifestation of God's work of salvation, possibly in both its phases. Even the absence of an actual description of what Jesus did agrees with the Johannine method of presenting Jesus' ἔργα. Jesus' works do not merge into the background because they are of lesser importance. On the contrary, seen in their full range and as a whole, they are, according to the evangelist, of such crucial significance that their real meaning and consequences must be brought out in speeches, comments and discussions.

U 28 τῆς Γαλιλαίας

Cana is in Galilee.
See U 3 above.

U 29 ἀρχὴν τῶν σημείων

This is the beginning of the signs.
When analysing U 27 I found it most natural to regard ἀρχὴν τῶν σημείων as an adjunct to ταύτην. I also suggested a reason why ἀρχήν may express something more than is meant by πρῶτον σημεῖον, which would be a parallel to Jn 4:54.[20] The most obvious explanation of the wording should be sought in the wider range of meaning contained in ἀρχή, of both *initium* and *principum.*[21]

[18] On the two phases of Jesus' *erga,* see the extended analysis in Thüsing [2]1970. His results are summarized on pp. 201ff and 311ff.

[19] See Thüsing [2]1970, for example p. 204: "Die Darstellungsweise des Evangeliums, die beide Stadien vielfach ineinanderprojiziert, unterstreicht die Einheit des als Entfaltung eines Keimes gesehenen zusammenhängenden Heilswerkes", and also pp. 33, 56, 105, 176ff, 267ff. Cf. Cullmann [2]1950 and 1966, pp. 176ff, 232ff, Haenchen 1962–63, p. 214, Mussner 1965, pp. 38ff, 42ff, Hahn 1972, p. 140.

[20] See above, 2.2, U 27.

[21] See Riedl 1963, pp. 266ff, van der Loos 1965, p. 615, and the survey in Smitmans 1966, pp. 28f.

The Johannine Gospel in general and 4:54 in particular make it clear that the miracle of the wine is the *first* sign at Cana in Galilee but also presumably "a primary sign", somehow representative of "the creative and transforming work of Jesus".[22] "ein grundlegendes Zeichen" which may perhaps incorporate "die ganze Kreuzesherrlichkeit Jesu, nämlich die 'Stunde' der Passion".[23] Apart from the wording the place of the Cana narrative in the Johannine composition and its vital importance favour a wider sense of *principium* in ἀρχή. The author of Jn 2:1—4:54 seems to have been far from interested in simply listing Jesus' signs.[24]

The concept σημεῖον in Jn has been the object of a long series of investigations, although no agreement has been reached on its meaning.[25] The difficulties are primarily concerned with the type of symbolism implied in Jn's use of words. The background of the word seems to be roughly the same as that of ἔργα, i.e. the description of God's saving works in Exodus.[26] Σημεῖον also attributes a divine aspect of salvation to Jesus' works. The word has several meanings in Jn but is most often used of Jesus' miracles. Five of the miracles described by the evangelist are designated σημεῖα, 2:11; 4:54; 6:14; 9:16 and 12:18. All of them reveal a miraculous feature and bring men face to face with a decision: belief or unbelief, ζωή or κρίσις. This emanates from their revealing character, 2:11; 11:4; 6:35, 48, 51; 8:12 (to 9:1ff) and 11:25. The narrative in 5:1ff also has these qualities although it is not described as σημεῖον but only as ἔργον 7:21; 5:20, 36. The character of the "signs" in general could be summarized in Brown's words: "John presents the miracles as a work of revelation which is intimately connected with salvation. In the OT story of the Exodus the physical deliverance accomplished by God's work on behalf of His people is in primary focus (a deliverance with spiritual overtones, of course). In John the reference to spiritual deliverance is primary, and the symbolic element is stronger . . . there is little emphasis on the material results of the miracle and great emphasis on the spiritual symbolism".[27] This feature is also characteristic of the Johannine miracles in contrast to the synoptic accounts.

Σημεῖον occurs, unlike ἔργον, almost exclusively in narrative sections and could there be counted among the interpretative elements.[28] Most scholars are agreed that the evangelist uses the term to indicate that what he is describing is a "sign" in a *qualitative* sense: it has a more profound, transferred, spiritual meaning. The texts have two or more

---

[22] Barrett, Comm., ad loc., quoting Isocrates, Panegyr. 38, as a linguistic parallel: ἀλλ' ἀρχὴν μὲν ταύτην ἐποιήσατο τῶν εὐεργεσιῶν, τροφὴν τοῖς δεομένοις εὑρεῖν.

[23] Wilkens 1958, pp. 40f, cf. Abbott 1906, pp. 287f, referring to Origen: προηγούμενον σημείων.

[24] For further discussion, see below, 2.4.4.

[25] See the surveys in Schnackenburg, Comm., pp. 344ff, and Brown, Comm., pp. 525ff, and the literature mentioned there, and also the dissertation of Hofbeck from 1966, Wilkens 1969, pp. 27ff, and Wead 1970, pp. 12ff. On recent literature, see Nicol 1972, pp. 139ff.

[26] K.H. Rengstorf in ThWNT, vol. 7, pp. 255f, Schnackenburg, Comm., p. 355, and especially Brown, Comm., pp. 528f.

[27] Brown, Comm., p. 529.

[28] "Ein theologisches Interpretament", K.H. Rengstorf in ThWNT, vol. 7, p. 246, "ein bewusst gewählter, sinnerfüllter theologischer Begriff des Evangelisten", Schnackenburg, Comm., p. 344.

levels. Jesus' works have the nature *both* of events *and* of symbols.[29] It is more difficult to determine whether σημεῖον also means "sign" in a *temporal* sense, i.e. if that which Jesus does in a specific situation also *points forward* to that which is the result of Jesus' work as a whole. It has been suggested that there is a special sign period in Jn, chs. 2—12, called by Brown "The Book of Signs". Jesus' "hour" and his glorification are described in ch. 13 onwards, "The Book of Glory".[30] This means that the signs seem to belong to a preparatory period in Jesus' earthly activity. The theory that σημεῖον points forward is also supported by the two phase aspect of Jesus' work which seems to exist in Jn, by the use of σημαίνειν of future events, 12:33; 18:32; 21:19, and by a possible background in the symbolic actions of the prophets and in the synoptic miracles which are signs of the coming Kingdom of God.[31] The gifts of Jesus which appear to flash by in the Johannine miracles will be bestowed together with the Spirit which, according to 7:39, came after Jesus was glorified. This impels me to follow Thüsing, Brown and other scholars in seeing Jesus' signs as pointing forward.[32] Events taking place before the "hour" of Jesus also reveal a part of what will happen when that "hour" is come.

This understanding of σημεῖον may have far-reaching consequences for the interpretation of the Cana narrative: the evangelist may see in this a *symbolic presentation* of God's saving work of revelation through his Son, and a *prophecy* of something in Jesus' work which can only be understood after his "glorification", rooted in an *historical event* of some kind. Such conclusions must be treated with caution at this stage, however, as the above preliminary summary of the *semeion* concept in Jn should be complemented with a detailed analysis of each *semeion* text. Even if the conclusions are correct, our analysis of the *semeion* concept would not allow us to decide exactly what the Cana narrative is a sign of, but only to establish a symbolic, Christological and forward-looking framework for the interpretation of what happened at Cana.

U 30 καὶ ἐφανέρωσεν τὴν δόξαν αὐτοῦ

He revealed his glory.

This unit gives explicit expression to the revealing character of what—according to the narrator—happened at Cana and, like U 27 and U 29, emphasizes the divine aspect of Jesus actions. By its characterization and focus on Jesus' person and work, the statement could tell us the point of the text,[33] but a greater clarification of the meaning shows how

---

[29]Schnackenburg, Comm., p. 356, explains "die eigentümliche Verbindung des Ereignishaften und des Symbolhaften in der joh. Darstellung" by referring to the double background of the concept σημεῖον: the saving works in Exodus and the symbolic acts of the prophets. Wead tries to reduce the symbolic character of the signs but without convincing reasons, Wead 1970, pp. 27ff.

[30] Brown, Comm., pp. cxxxviiiff.

[31] Schnackenburg, Comm., pp. 355f, mentions this background but wishes to reduce "die vorausweisende Bedeutung" of the signs!

[32] Thüsing ²1970, pp. 228, 267ff, 320ff, and Brown, Comm., p. 530. Brown summarizes: "Thus, the miracle is a sign, not only qualitatively (a material action pointing toward a spiritual reality), but also temporally (what happens before *the hour* prophesying what will happen after the hour has come)". This prophetic element, according to Brown, is what allows the Johannine narrative of the miracle "to bear so often a secondary sacramental significance".

[33] Thus Schnackenburg, Comm., p. 341: "Das Wichtigste ist ihm /dem Evangelist/ die

difficult it is to use it as a simple key to the interpretation of the text as a whole.

Jn often refers to Jesus' "glory" (δόξα) and his "glorification" (δοξασϑῆναι). [34] The wording of U 30 (with Jesus as subject and his *doxa* as object), however, has no direct parallels in the Johannine writings. [35] The verb, characteristic of Jn, is here used in the sense of "make manifest, reveal, make visible". [36] The equivalent Hebrew and Aramaic verb ( ) is often used in the Targums when the revelation at Sinai is described, for example of Ex 19:9 "See I will reveal myself (מתגלי) to you in the cloud of glory (בצבא דענן יקרא)", [37] and 19:11 "On the third day the glory of Yahweh's *shekinah*(דיי שכינתא)(איקר will be revealed(תתגלי)". [38] Both the verb "to reveal oneself" and the concept "glory" (δόξα, יקרא)occur in a striking fashion in the Sinai texts and in the Cana narrative, a fact which is noted here because I have already made several references to Ex 19—24. [39] According to the Johannine use of φανεροῦν, it is *Jesus*, 1:31; 7:4; 21:1, 14, *Jesus' doxa*, 2:11, *God's erga*, 9:3; 3:21, and *God's Name*, 17:6, which are revealed. This revelation primarily concerns "the people whom the Father has given to the Son", 17:6. It is quite clear that in the time after Jesus' "hour" Jn expects Jesus to reveal himself only to "the disciples", 14:12ff; 21:1, 14. Certain formulations seem to assume a similar limitation also as regards Jesus' activity on earth, at any rate if it is considered in the perspective of the "hour", 17:6ff; 7:4; 1:31. [40] There is no statement in Jn to the effect that Jesus "revealed himself" to mankind without limitations. It seems appropriate, therefore, to interpret U 30 as meaning that Jesus revealed himself

---

Herrlichkeitsoffenbarung Jesu (V 11), und jede Deutung, die sich von dieser *christologischen* Sicht entfernt, führt vom Zentrum ab". See also Brown, Comm., ad loc.

[34] See 1:14; 2:11; 8:50; 12:41; 17:5, 22, 24 (the noun) and 7:39; 8:54; 11:4; 12:16, 23; 13:31f; 16:14; 17:1, 5, 10 (the verb). These passages are analysed in Thüsing [2]1970, pp. 41ff. See also Nicol 1972, pp. 119ff.

[35] Compare, however, the statements of Jesus' earthly *doxa*, 1:14; 11:4, 40, and also 14:18ff, a promise of a future revelation to the disciples alone (ἐμφανίσω αὐτῷ ἐμαυτόν). The phrase ἐμφάνισόν μοι σεαυτόν is parallel to δεῖξόν μοι τὴν σεαυτοῦ δόξαν in Ex 33:13,18 (about God's revelation to Moses at Sinai). The wording of U 30 may depend on the Sinai screen in the text; see below, 2.4.3.

[36] Jn 1:31; 2:11; 3:21; 7:4; 9:3; 17:6; 21:1, 14; cf. 1 Jn 1:2; 2:19, 28; 3:2, 5, 8; 4:9. The verb is rare outside NT, Schnackenburg and Barrett, Comm., ad loc., and R. Bultmann - D. Lührmann in ThWNT, vol. 9, pp. 4ff.

[37] Quoting Targ. Pseudo-Jonathan. Text with the variants of the other Targums in Potin 1971, vol. 2, p. 18. All Targums hava a form of גלה for MT בא (LXX: παραγίνομαι). For further evidence of the use of "reveal" in Sinai texts, see Potin 1971, vol. 1, pp. 233ff. He begins his examination with the words: "Il est significatif que le mot le plus employé dans ces textes théophaniques est le verbe *se révéler*".

[38] Quoting Codex Neophiti I. Text and variants in Potin, vol. 2, p. 21. All Targums have a form of גלה for MT ירד (LXX: καταβήσεται).

[39] For further discussion, see below, 2.4.3. An examination of the "ascent" and "descent" in the Sinai theophany and the Jewish speculations of them would here be of interest with regard to the specific Johannine terms καταβαίνειν and ἀναβαίνειν. Cf. Meeks 1967, pp. 156ff, 205ff, 241ff, 295ff.

[40] "Israel" in 1:31 refers primarily to the "true" Israel, not to Israel as a whole. See above, 2.2, U 5, and the literature mentioned there in note 70.

primarily to his disciples, τοῖς μαθηταῖς αὐτοῦ, as 21:1, 14 says. While others saw what happened, for them it was not a manifestation of Jesus' *doxa*. According to Jn 11:40, to see God's *doxa* in Jesus' works presupposes faith. The disciples in our text have a kind of faith according to 1:35−51, where v. 50 says that Nathanael *believed* because of Jesus' words.[41]

Jesus' doxa is always associated in Jn with *God's doxa*. This agrees with the Jewish usage, where "glory" (Hebr. בבד, Aram. יקרא, Gk. δόξα) is especially characteristic of God. "In the OT the *glory* of God implies a visible and powerful manifestation of God to men. In the Targums 'glory' also became a surrogate, like *memra* and *shekinah,* for the visible presence of God among men." God's *doxa* "is a *visible* manifestation of His majesty in *acts of power*". Both these elements are present in Jesus. "He represents the visible divine presence exercising itself in mighty acts."[42] According to Schnackenburg Jesus' *doxa* is in our text "zunächst seine schöpferische göttliche Macht, die ihm eigene göttliche δύναμις " at the same time as it preserves the union of "Lichtglanz" and "Wirkmacht" which are characteristic of the expression in the OT.[43] In a Jewish environment, therefore, it is natural to associate Jesus' *doxa* with the "glory" which is characteristic of God.

This is also in agreement with the evangelist's own words. "We have beheld his glory, glory as of the only Son from the Father" (δόξαν ὡς μονογενοῦς παρὰ πατρός), 1:14. From the Father the Son received the glory he possesses and mediates to others (ἣν δέδωκάς μοι), 17:22; cf. vv. 4ff, 8. He who sees Jesus' *doxa* in his works, at the same time sees God's *doxa*, 11:4, 40; 5:17; 14:10.[44] So when U 30 says that Jesus revealed *his* glory it is also a revelation of God's glory. The union of the Father and the Son underlies it.

Another of Jn's characteristics is his association of Jesus' glorification (δοξασθῆναι) with the "hour" of Jesus, 12:23, 28; 13:31f; 17:1f.[45] Jesus possessed *doxa* during his pre-existence, 17:5, during his earthly life, 1:14, but it is manifested above all in his elevation, 17:1ff, 24. The evangelist may even speak as if Jesus was not glorified until his death, 7:39. This leads to the question whether the manifestation of *doxa* in, for example, 2:1−11 was only partial, or an anticipation of the total experience of the disciples, including the *doxa* of the risen Lord.[46]

Jesus' *doxa* seems to cover all "ages". At the same time Jesus' "hour" is a kind of time limit in the manifestation of Jesus' *doxa*, in the same way as in Jesus' *ergon*.[47] The use of

[41] On revelation only to those who believe, see Schmidt 1921, p. 37, Wead 1970, p. 20, and the survey in Smitmans 1966, pp. 30f. On the relation between seeing and believing, see the comment below on U 31.

[42] Brown, Comm., pp. 34, 503.

[43] Schnackenburg, Comm., ad loc.

[44] "The glory of Jesus is the glory of God himself. Where Jesus is active, God is also at work, and where Jesus manifests his glory, the glory of God is also to be seen", Caird 1968−69, p. 272. Similarly in Brown, Comm., pp. 751ff, and Thüsing ²1970, passim.

[45] See the summary in Thüsing ²1970, pp. 240f, and the comments on these passages in Caird 1968−69 and in Brown, Comm.

[46] Barrett, Comm., ad loc., prefers the first alternative ("in all signs, a partial and preliminary manifestation was granted that the disciples might believe").

[47] See above, 2.2, U 27.

tenses in 12:28 (καὶ ἐδόξασα καὶ πάλιν δοξάσω) and in 13:31f (ἐδοξάσθη ... ἐδοξάσθη ... δοξάσει ... δοξάσει) marks two phases or periods in Jesus' glorification, although it is not entirely clear what these phases cover. However it seems most natural to follow Thüsing, Brown and Caird in interpreting the aorist as referring to Jesus' earthly ministry as a whole, and the future to the work of the risen Christ, when he draws "all" to him, 12:32.[48] Jesus "is glorified" according to 17:10, 17ff, 22f in his disciples, and God's *doxa* is manifested in the Son even after his death when the Son does what the disciples ask in his name, 14:13.[49] These two passages in chs. 17 and 14 show that the *doxa* of the Father and the Son is manifested both during Jesus' earthly life and in the age of the risen Lord, both in the κατάβασις of the Son and his ἀνάβασις, to use Johannine terminology. The manifestations during the first phase are represented as rather exceptional, and given only in the form of "signs", 2:11; 11:4, 40, whereas they are concentrated on the hour of elevation and the period thereafter, when Jesus goes to the Father and returns to the disciples in the form of the Paraclete. So when U 30 says that Jesus revealed his glory to the disciples there is some doubt as to whether the narrator is thinking of an occurrence during Jesus' earthly life, or of something which also incorporates the glorification of the "hour" and the *doxa* manifestation of the risen Christ in the age of the Church. The nearby statements in 2:17, 22 and the general description of the disciples in Jn indicate that the narrator is thinking of both phases, possibly with greater emphasis on the latter. It is not the very event at Cana as an isolated occurrence but that which it symbolizes, the deeper meaning so to speak, which really reveals Jesus' *doxa*. The disciples first comprehended the reality of the event after Jesus' death in the light of his glorification and ascension. The alternative of regarding v. 11 "as being part of the capsulizing of the training of the disciples where their whole career, including their sight of the glory of the resurrected Jesus, is foreshadowed", as Brown states, is to be preferred.[50] As in the representation of Jesus' *erga* and in the designation of the *doxa* of the Son/Father, Jn combines the two phases. The object of the revelation in both phases is the same: the name of the Father, and both stages have a similar structure.[51] The accent should be placed on the later stage. "Das, was in der ὥρα geschieht, und das, was von ihr ausgeht, wird als das Eigentliche, Entscheidende dargestellt, auf das alles Vorhergehende hingeordnet ist."[52] As in the case of U 27 and U 29, U 30 leads into very comprehensive total aspects of Jn

[48] Thüsing [2]1970, pp. 45ff, 101ff, 193ff, 311ff, Brown, Comm., pp. 475ff, 609ff, Caird 1968–69, pp. 272f. In Jn 13–20, according to Caird, Jesus is no longer talking about his own individual, isolated life with the Father, but about the manifestation of glory of the Son/Father "in the corporate life of the church". The individual manhood of Jesus becomes corporate and inclusive.

[49] To the second phase belong, for example, the bearing of fruit, 12:24; 15:8, 16, –see below, 3.4.6–the giving of whatever they ask in Jesus' name, 14:12f; 15:16f, the love of the brothers, the persecutions, the work of the Paraclete, 15:12ff. See Thüsing [2]1970, pp. 101ff.

[50] Brown, Comm., ad loc. Brown himself arrives at more than one interpretation by setting the Cana narrative in different contexts and situations.

[51] See Thüsing [2]1970, pp. 201ff.

[52] Thüsing [2]1970, p. 241. *Doxa* in Jn must be interpreted from both a theology of incarnation and a theology of glorification, pp. 320ff. "Bei einem theologischen Denker wie dem vierten Evangelisten wäre es eigenartig und von vornherein kaum wahrscheinlich, dass die irdische Doxa (2,11) nichts mit der 'Stunde' zugeordneten 'Verherrlichung' zu tun haben sollte", p. 325.

which I have not been able to analyse in their entirety. The preliminary results here must be combined with a text-linguistic analysis, and only then may they be regarded as sufficiently verified. They emphasize the above comment that v. 11 relates the Cana narrative to the Gospel in general in a special way: by its connecting function and by its content, it is an invaluable help for any interpretation of the narrative as a whole.

U 31 $\kappa\alpha\grave{\iota}\,\grave{\epsilon}\pi\acute{\iota}\sigma\tau\epsilon\upsilon\sigma\alpha\nu\,\epsilon\grave{\iota}\varsigma\,\alpha\grave{\upsilon}\tau\grave{o}\nu\,o\grave{\iota}\,\mu\alpha\vartheta\eta\tau\alpha\grave{\iota}\,\alpha\grave{\upsilon}\tau o\tilde{\upsilon}$
His disciples believed in him.

We encounter a dominant Johannine concept in the last unit in our text: *to believe* ($\pi\iota\sigma$-$\tau\epsilon\acute{\upsilon}\epsilon\iota\nu$).[53] The phrase $\pi\iota\sigma\tau\epsilon\acute{\upsilon}\epsilon\iota\nu\,\epsilon\grave{\iota}\varsigma$ is characteristic of Jn, followed by a personal object, almost always Jesus, sometimes the name of Jesus or of God.[54] This is the most common construction of $\pi\iota\sigma\tau\epsilon\acute{\upsilon}\epsilon\iota\nu$ in Jn and, with a few exceptions, designates the perfect, saving faith.[55] Schnackenburg, who made a special study of the Johannine concept of faith[56] sees in v. 11 a disciple's belief which "prinzipiell (oder wenigstens potentiell) den vollen christologischen Glauben in sich schliesst".[57] Belief, in Jn, involves "an active commitment to a person, and, in particular to Jesus", an acceptance of him and what he claims to be, a handing over of oneself to him, a willingness to follow all his commandments.[58] This personal commitment to ($\epsilon\grave{\iota}\varsigma$) Jesus Christ was summarized by Schnackenburg as "ein entschiedenes Anhangen Jesu, Ausharren bei ihm, auch wenn es gilt, das $\sigma\kappa\acute{\alpha}\nu\delta\alpha\lambda o\nu$ seiner Rede zu überwinden (vgl 6,60f 66), Bleiben in seinem Wort (8,31) und nicht zuletzt offenes Bekenntnis zu ihm (vgl 9,28—38; 19,38)".[59]

Belief in the Johannine sense is very closely associated with *hearing, seeing* and *knowing.*[60] Belief is sparked by Jesus' *word* in the wide sense as it is heard in the OT, 5:39ff; 12:37ff, in John the Baptist, 1:7, 15, 19ff, 29ff; 3:25ff; 10:40ff, in the earthly Jesus, 1:50; 4:7ff etc., in those who believe, 12:17ff, through the Spirit, 14:26; 15:26; 16:8, 13ff and through the disciples, 15:20, 27; 17:20. This shows belief to be "wesenmässig als Antwort oder als Ent-sprechung auf das Wort oder den Spruch der Aussage Gottes in Jesus hin".[61] To believe is primarily to hear, 1:37; 10:3f, a comprehen-

[53] 98 times in Jn, and always as verb (11 times in Mt, 14 in Mk and 9 in Lk). We find a similar dominance in Paul. See the excursus of belief in Schnackenburg, Comm., pp. 508ff.

[54] 36 times in Jn, 3 times in 1 Jn and only 8 times in the other books of NT. There are no good parallels in the Greek literature, including LXX. The Hebrew construction ‏בְ הֶאֱמִין‎ is sometimes referred to. This phrase occurs also in Ex 19 -24 when the Lord reveals himself to Moses that the people may hear His words and believe Moses for ever (‏וְגַם־בְךָ יַאֲמִינוּ‎, 19:9). See below, 2.4.3.

[55] Brown, Comm., pp. 512f. Exceptions: 2:23f and 12:42f.

[56] His dissertation from 1937, mentioned in his commentary, p. 509, note 2.

[57] Schnackenburg, Comm., ad loc. But it is not a "Vollblick des Glaubens". Referring to Jn 14:5,8; 16:12,17f,25,29ff he adds: "der Evangelist will sagen, dass ihr Glaube durch das Kanazeichen einen wesentlichen Impuls erfahren hat: er ist inhaltlich und innerlich in ihnen gewachsen". The main reason for this "reduction" of Schnackenburg must be his view of the text as in some way an historical, biographical narrative.

[58] Brown, Comm., p 513.

[59] Schnackenburg, Comm., p. 516.

[60] See especially Schlier 1964. On seeing and believing, see Cullmann 1950 and Hahn 1972.

[61] Schlier 1964, p. 280. Compare what has been said about obedience in Jn above, 2.2, U 10.

sive, concentrated hearing which receives, keeps and obeys, 12:47f; 17:6, a hearing which reveals the hearer, 8:47; 18:37. The hearing may precede or be simultaneous with belief, 4:42; 6:45, and both concepts may apparently be used wholly in parallel, 10:25ff; 8:46f; 12:46f. The same can be said of *seeing* and *believing*.[62] For Jn *seeing* is an integral part of *believing*, because "the word" became flesh and is revealed in works, *erga*. This brings to the fore the difficult problems of how U 31 is related to U 30 (i.e. the connection between the revelation of Jesus' *doxa* and the disciples' belief) and how the unit is to be linked with the earlier presentation of Jesus' disciples in 1:35—51. This section ends by noting that Nathanael *believes* because Jesus *said* something ($\H{o}\tau\iota\ \H{\epsilon}\iota\pi o\nu \ldots \pi\iota\sigma\tau\epsilon\acute{\upsilon}\epsilon\iota\varsigma$)[63] and by mentioning the promise that he (and the disciples) will *see* greater things ($\mu\epsilon\acute{\iota}\zeta\omega$ $\tau o\acute{\upsilon}\tau\omega\nu\ \H{o}\psi\H{\eta}$). When will this promise be fulfilled? How is our text related to the statement in 1:51? These questions call for *a short excursus on Jn 1:51*.

The promise to the disciples in 1:51 is so remarkable in form, and in its place at the beginning of the Gospel, that it is natural to expect a concrete fulfilment later on. Yet the disciples are vouchsafed no visions of angels in Jn. The statement in 1:51, probably a traditional *logion* applied and incorporated when the section 1:19—2:21 was composed,[64] presumably has a transferred meaning in its present context. In the attempts to interpret it scholars have often, and rightly, referred to Jacob's dream at Bethel and the Jewish expositions of the story, especially of Gen 28:12f.[65] But the Jewish material, primarily as it is preserved in Gen R 68—69 and the Targums, gives rise to many kinds of comparison.[66] Since the *logion* seems to have been incorporated during the composition of the material in general and motifs from the Sinai theophany evidently played a part in it,[67] I wish to draw attention here to the connection between 1:51 and Sinai.[68]

According to one of the interpretations of Gen 28:12 in Gen R 68, Jacob's dream should be understood on the basis of what happened at Sinai. Wünsches' translation of this text reads: "Nach den Rabbinen geht der Traum auf den Sinai. Die Leiter d.i. der Sinai, auf die Erde gestellt vergl. Ex. 19,17, deren Spitze bis zum Himmel reichte vergl.

[62] See Schlier 1964, p. 283, and the following analysis.

[63] Most commentators, including Brown and Schnackenburg, interpret the sentence as a question but without conclusive reasons. Jn 9:35; 16:31 and especially 20:29 favour a statement. See Zahn and Barrett, Comm., ad loc.

[64] Note the change of the quotation formula and the number, the loose connection with the context, similarities to Mt 26:64; 16:27f, and the stylistic properties of the verse. See Brown, Comm., pp. 38f, Schulz, Comm., pp. 43, 92, and Meeks 1972, p. 50.

[65] See, besides the commentaries, the literature mentioned in Lentzen-Deis, 1970, pp. 115ff and Meeks 1972, pp. 50f.

[66] Some scholars stress the interpretation of בו as "on him", referring to Jacob, and arrive at the parallels of Jesus = the Son of Man = Jacob = Israel (as corporate) or at the parallel of the heavenly and earthly Jacob = the heavenly and earthly Son of Man, whom the disciples see in Jesus. Others start from the note in the Jewish material that the *shekinah* of God was on the ladder, or that Bethel was the "gate of heaven", or that the rock at Bethel was the first stone created by God, etc. See the survey in Brown, Comm., ad loc.

[67] See below, 2.4.3.

[68] The Sinai material is regarded as relevant parallels by Serra 1971, pp. 22ff. Cf. Potin 1971, pp. 316f. The Bethel event and the Sinai events have many common themes and it is, therefore, not surprising that they are linked together in the Jewish expositions.

Deut. 4,11. Oder: Die Leiter d.i. der Sinai, denn die Buchstaben der zwei Wörter סלם Leiter und סיני Sinai sind sich in der Zahl gleich, *und die Engel Gottes* vergl. Ps. 68,18. Und wir haben gelernt, dass die Propheten Engel heissen s. Hagg. 1,13, und die Engel Gottes d.i. Mose and Aaron stiegen hinauf und herab vergl. Ex. 19,3, *und der Ewige stand oben* vergl. das V. 20".[69] The Rabbinic argument that *the ladder* corresponds to *Sinai* seems clear enough from the text quoted. Moreover we know from the Targums to Ps 68 and Hag 1 that these Biblical texts were interpreted in categories from the Sinai theophany[70] and the presence of angels at the revelation at Sinai is confirmed in early texts, for instance Dt 33:2(LXX); Gal 3:19; Acts 7:38; Heb 2:2f.[71] The statement in Jn 1:51, with its special concepts, can therefore very well have been chosen and incorporated in the present context because it could be interpreted on the basis of the Sinai theophany, although the wording comes mainly from Gen 28:12.[72] The narrator would then have understood v. 51 from the relationship Jesus - Son of Man - the ladder - Sinai as a prophecy of a future event concerning Jesus as a kind of equivalent of the manifestation at Sinai.

Serra, who adduced the Sinai theophany as material for the interpretation of Jn 1:51,[73] goes a step further in citing texts in which Sinai is equated with the fathers of Israel,[74] and draws the conclusion that Jesus is also regarded in the context of 1:51 as the new Israel. "Cristo e la nuova scala di Giacobbe, il nuovo Sinai, il nuovo Israele."[75] This exposition is in harmony with the interpretation of the promise in 1:51 as including both the earthly and the glorified Jesus, and with my total interpretation of the Cana narrative,[76] but it is difficult to support this solely on the rather disparate passages quoted by Serra. Jewish concepts of Sinai as the fathers of Israel may perhaps have made it easier for the narrator to use v. 51 of both phases in Jesus' work.

Whichever comparison we prefer, among the many possibilities offered by the Jewish material—Jesus as Jacob, as Sinai, as the fathers of Israel, as God's *Shekinah*, as God's Temple etc.—there is a common core: being the Son of Man Jesus is described in Jn 1:51 as *the place of God's doxa (shekinah, memra).*[77] The disciples are given the promise that in the future they will see God, his revelation and his work, in the Son of Man, or in Johannine terminology, they will be allowed to "see" that the Father and the Son are one.

---

[69] Aug. Wünsche in Bibliotheca Rabbinica, vol. 2, p. 332.

[70] See Potin 1971, vol. 1 passim.

[71] See also Pseudo-Philo XI.5, and Targ. Pseudo-Jonathan to Dt 33:2.

[72] Cf. Potin 1971, vol. 1, p. 317: "Cette citation de Gn 28 a perdu son sens primitif dans le contexte évangélique". His motivation is: 1. the angles do not ascend and descend upon Nathanael (i.e. the new Israel), 2. Gen R 68,18 does not explain Jn 1:51, and 3. This verse can be regarded as a general theophany text, in which it is natural to find angels.

[73] See above, note 68.

[74] Referring to Ex R 15,4; 28,2, and to TJ I ad Gen 49:25 and Dt 33:15. The Sinai texts may also indicate such an interpretation: LXX, as Mekilta, has in Ex 19:18 "all people" for MT "the mountain". Cf. 1 Cor 10:4; Cant R ad 2:14 (Simon's translation, pp. 130f).

[75] Serra 1971, p. 28.

[76] See below, 2.4.2.

[77] See Brown, Comm., p. 91: Jesus as Son of Man is "the locus of divine glory, the point of contact between heaven and earth".

75

Most scholars find the fulfilment of this promise in the account of the miracle of the wine at Cana which follows, or in Jesus' "signs" in general.[78] Some authors hold that the reference is not at all "to a particular object of vision, to a σημεῖον, or to an object of vision *quâ* object, but to a particular subjective faculty of the seer, which enables him to perceive—one might be tempted to add: permanently, and with increasing clearness—the δόξα of Christ: the union of the celestial with the terrestrial".[79] The alternative which emerges in this quotation from Odeberg would hardly do justice to the connection existing between *seeing* and *believing* in the Johannine writings. "Christlicher Glaube hat es nach dem Johannesevangelium mit einem konkreten Akt des Schauens zu tun, weil es um das konkrete, im irdischen Bereich manifest gewordene und insofern auch schaubare Heil Gottes geht."[80] This "Konkretheit der Heilsverwirklichung" in Jn as we now possess it, and the comments above on Jesus' erga and Jesus' doxa, indicate that in Jn 1:50f we presumably have a promise referring *both* to Jesus in his activity on earth (Jesus' signs) *and* the glorified and ascended Son of Man, i.e. the work of God in Jesus in its widest sense, which also includes the works of the disciples. The disciples will be allowed to "see" the union of the Father, the Son, and those whom the Father gave to the Son. This interpretation would seem to imply a certain inclusive meaning of the Son of Man in 1:51, referring to both the Son and those who believe in the Son, but this aspect of the Son of Man concept need not thereby apply to all the passages where the term occurs.[81] By reason of what is here adduced I find it most appropriate, for the time being, to hold fast to a more open interpretation which includes both phases in Jesus' *ergon,* and thereby the whole work of God's mission as it is described in Jn. Such an understanding of the promise in Jn 1:50 is in close harmony with the connections with the Sinai theophany mentioned above and the perspective it gives for the text in its entirety: the creation of a new covenant, a new Israel.[82]

To return to U 31, the connection between U 30 and U 31 is generally interpreted as a simple relation of the type: *since* the disciples saw Jesus' *doxa*—as was promised in 1:51—in the miracle at Cana, they placed, or were strengthened in, their faith in Jesus.[83] The existence of a connection between these two units is quite evident but the internal relation is difficult to describe logically. *Seeing* and *believing* are always correlated with each other in Jn: sometimes the seeing comes first, 11:45, sometimes it comes after, 11:40, sometimes the terms are used in parallel, 6:40; 12:44f; 14:8f. Yet they can hardly be inserted into the development process of belief.[84] In 4:46ff we encounter three stages: the man *believes* Jesus' words, he *sees* what has happened, and he *realizes* and *believes.* These stages should hardly be interpreted as three consecutive phases in the beginning

---

[78] See also the latest commentaries of Schnackenburg and Brown.

[79] Odeberg 1929, p. 37. He refers to Jn 14:9f, 13,19.

[80] Hahn 1972, p. 129; cf. pp. 139f. See also Cullmann 1950 and 1966, pp. 176ff, and Mussner 1965.

[81] Against Odeberg 1929, p. 40 and passim, who interprets 1:51 as referring only to "a spiritual experience" in the believers. On Cairds' interpretation, see above 2.2. U 30, note 48.

[82] See below, 2.4.2 and 2.4.3.

[83] See the survey in Smitmans 1966, pp. 29ff.

[84] See the analysis in Schlier 1964 and Hahn 1972 and compare Schottroff 1970, pp. 251ff, and Schnider-Stenger 1971, pp. 82ff.

and growth of an individual belief, but rather as expressions of the necessary elements of faith according to Jn. There is always a reciprocal relationship between an actual seeing and belief. The two elements are also interwoven in the introductory description of Jesus' disciples in 1:35—2:11. The statement in U 31 on the disciples' belief should therefore be regarded as a kind of conclusion of the description of their faith in the introductory "constitutive" week in Jn. It includes the elements which, according to what was said above, are parts of belief. In this sense their belief is represented in 2:11 as "ein Vollglauben". After his analysis of *seeing* and *believing* in Jn, Hahn comes to the conclusion "dass das rechte 'Sehen' auf den 'Glauben' angewiesen ist, dass aber der Glaube nicht Glaube an Jesus Christus wäre, wenn es nicht einen ganz konkreten Anhalt in der Geschichte hätte".[85] According to Hahn this bond with "the earthly" embraces both the historical Jesus and the concrete "Heilsvollendung" which is in the present for the reader, in and with the hour of Jesus, a doubleness which we previously found to apply also to the Johannine account of Jesus' *erga* and Jesus' *doxa*. U 30—31 seems therefore to mark a union of seeing and believing in the disciples' acceptance of Jesus as "he whom the Father sent". I would prefer to interpret 2:11 from a fusion in time and space, made by the narrator, of an event during Jesus' earthly life with the situation after the hour of Jesus when it was quite clear that God's work in the Son and his followers involved a "new Israel". The disciples' belief in Jesus in 2:11 replaces the covenant which once came into being through God's revelation through Moses at Sinai and the faith of the people of Israel in Moses.[86]

The last verse in our text thus proves to give rise to many preliminary statements concerning the interpretation of the text as a whole. This confirms the verse's strongly interpretative function. Before I take up the question of "the message of the text" the textual features which bind it together into a whole must be analysed, namely "the structure of the text".

2.3 The Structure of the Text

After the now complete division of the text into different statement units and their analysis, it should be possible to determine the structure of the text by describing the varying relationships existing between the different units: how is U 1 related to U 2, possibly U 3, U 4 etc., U 2 to U 3 etc., U 4 to U 5 etc. throughout the text.[1] The result should be a plan of how the lesser elements depend on each other, how they form larger units, which in their turn have a certain relationship to each other etc. Bearing in mind the rather complicated structure of the text and the purpose of the investigation, however, I prefer to analyse some features woven into the text, which bind it into a unit. I therefore choose the most important

[85] Hahn 1972, pp. 139f.
[86] See below, 2.4.
[1] E.A. Nida has used a similar method on a text from The Times, see above, 1.2, note 84.

qualities which are generally considered to be characteristic of a discourse: terminal features, spatial, temporal, logical relations, the role of the participants, the information flow and the point of view.[2]

2.3.1. Terminal Features[3]

Their *content* gives vv. 1—2 the nature of an introduction. They present the setting of the event (γάμος ἐγένετο) and both time (τῇ ἡμέρᾳ τῇ τρίτῃ) and place (ἐν Κανὰ τῆς Γαλιλαίας) are precisely stated. In addition, they introduce the persons whose presence cannot be directly assumed from the setting: Jesus' mother, Jesus and Jesus' disciples. Of these only Jesus is mentioned by name. The others are referred to by their relationship to him: this, together with many other features, indicates that he is the central figure. So far as *form* is concerned, this section is bound together above all by the words γάμος - ἐκεῖ - εἰς γάμον. The expression καὶ . . . ἐγένετο also seems to contribute formally to the terminal nature of these verses.[4]

The ending of the text is more complicated. Verse 11 evidently binds vv. 1—10 together and characterizes them as a unit.[5] Nevertheless v. 11 is in fact not a part of the text in the same way as the introductory verses but stands on a level above the text, as do the many "comments" in Jn.[6] If we are looking for terminal features in the usual sense we should therefore consider v. 10. There, however, we find completely different persons from those introduced at the beginning, unless we allow the bridegroom to stand for Jesus. Moreover the words have a more general form than the framework given at the beginning. The verse may act as a confirmation of the miracle—cf. 4:51—53; 6:12; 9:8f, 18—23—but even if this is the case a continuation of some kind is expected, an explicit statement about the reaction of those present, about Jesus, Jesus' mother or Jesus' disciples who were introduced at the beginning. The character of the verse as the conclusion of the entire narrative must therefore be designated as weak. If v. 10 is regarded as a comment interpreting what happened[7] then in terms of function it approaches v. 11.

Some of the features we expected in v. 10 are, however, to be found in v. 11. This has several links with the introduction: it focuses on Jesus as the central figure, reiterates the site of the event and again mentions Jesus' disciples, who

---

[2] On the purpose of my investigation and the "universals of the discourse" I just mentioned, see ch. 1.

[3] On terminal features, see above, 1.2, Longacre 1968, pp. 5f and Dressler 1972, pp. 57ff. ("Textanfang - Textschluss").

[4] See above, 2.2, U 2.

[5] The function of v. 11 has already been discussed to some extent above, 2.2, U 27—31.

[6] See below, 4.2.

[7] The verse as a kind of Johannine irony; see 2.2, U 26.

play no part in the narrative as a whole. The verse also describes the reaction of a number of those present. Thus we find that the verse which concludes the actual account, v. 10, has slight terminal features, but may act as a kind of comment on what took place, while the verse which makes explicit comments on the event, v. 11, also has a terminal character.

Since the disciples somehow provide a framework for our text it is of interest to note their role here as well.[8] They appear primarily as spectators. That which takes place is a *sign* (σημεῖον), which Jesus does *in the presence of the disciples;* cf. 20:30: ἐνώπιον τῶν μαθητῶν αὐτοῦ. At the same time as they are part of the event they stand outside, looking on. This role links our text both with 1:35—51 and the exhortation to *see* (1:39, 46) and the promise of being allowed to *see* more, 1:50f (μείζω τούτων ὄψῃ, ὄψεσθε), and also with 2:17, 21f, where the disciples *remember* (ἐμνήσθησαν), understanding things after Jesus has arisen from the dead, 2:22 (ὅτε οὖν ἠγέρθη ἐκ νεκρῶν). [9] The disciples' double role corresponds to a duality in v. 11: it partly concludes and is thus part of our text, and partly comments, thereby becoming part of a later comprehensive view of what happened. The two functions could perhaps be combined by the Johannine concepts *disciple, sign* and *seeing: the disciples* are present during the event and thus *see* all that happens, but at the same time they are receivers of the *sign* and *see* afresh later from a total perspective, sometimes noted in the text itself, e.g. 2:21f; 12:16.

2.3.2 Spatial Features

The precise information on place in vv. 1 and 11 is striking. It belongs to a wider spatial or geographical scheme which I analysed above.[10] In the light of the whole of Jn this scheme may have some "ecclesial" associations. The point of interest here is the spatial relationship between the various units in the text. Normally they play an important role in narrative texts since they place the event in a spatial framework and hold a narrative together.[11]

The data on place in the text are very vague: καὶ ἦν . . . ἐκεῖ, v. 1, and ἦσαν δὲ ἐκεῖ . . . κείμεναι, v. 6. These phrases introduce material necessary for what immediately follows.[12] The spatial relations seem to be of minor importance. There is no information as to where the vessels were, or from where the servants fetched the large quantity of water. The steward is assumed to be in a different place from both the servants (οὐκ ᾔδει πόθεν ἐστίν) and the bridegroom (φωνεῖ). He rebukes the groom for keeping (τετήρηκας) the good wine till the last. Indeed the

[8] Cf. 2.2, U 6, and 2.3.5.
[9] See below, 4.2.
[10] See 2.2, U 3 and below, 3.2.3.
[11] See, for example, Nida-Taber 1969, pp. 131f, Longacre 1968, pp. 3ff.
[12] See above, 2.2, U 4 and U 11.

minor stages of the event are not related to each other in terms of space but seem to a great extent separate:

1. Jesus' mother talks with her son.
2. Jesus' mother orders the servants to obey Jesus.
3. Jesus commands the servants and they obey.
4. The servants give some wine to the steward and he tastes it.
5. The steward rebukes the bridegroom.

There is no mention of the disciples' presence at the different "scenes" but it is implied by what was said above.

The spatial relations in our text are therefore very vague. The narrator was evidently not interested in describing a sequence of events in a specific setting. The various elements almost seem to take place on a stage with the disciples—and the reader—as spectators. The necessary description of the scene is given in the first two verses and in v, 6, and the reaction of the spectators in v. 11.[13]

2.3.3 Logical Features

The logical relations between the individual events are highly implicit, and are syntactically marked only in v. 3 (gen.abs.) and v. 9 ($\dot\omega\varsigma\,\delta\acute\epsilon$), unless these markings are to be interpreted as purely temporal. The shortage mentioned in v. 3 sets in motion a course of events which are piled on top of one another. If we regard them as links in a chain of events which really happened we have a sequence of relationships of the type reason-result: A results in B, A + B leads to C etc. The logical relations are less vague in the "commentary" sections: *Since* the servants drew the water they knew whence it came. The reverse is true of the steward: *since* he did not draw the water (or was not present when it was done) he did not know whence it came. Here a certain parallel with v. 11 presents itself: *since* the disciples in faith saw Jesus' *doxa* (that of which Jesus' action was a sign) they believed. The logical connection in this verse, however, is of a more complicated nature.[14]

The logical relations are clearer in the speeches: *if* Jesus says A, *then* you must do A, v. 5. Draw the water/the wine *in order to* taste/test it, v. 8. Contrasts in v. 10: ordinary men serve ... you kept, first ... then, good ... bad. The difficulties arise in Jesus' first speech, v. 4. It consists, as we saw, of three parts:

A $\tau\acute\iota\,\dot\epsilon\mu o\grave\iota\,\kappa a\grave\iota\,\sigma o\acute\iota$

B $\gamma\acute\upsilon\nu a\iota$

C $o\ddot\upsilon\pi\omega\,\ddot\eta\kappa\epsilon\iota\,\dot\eta\,\ddot\omega\rho a\,\mu o\upsilon$

The logical relations between A, B and C are highly dependent on the content of

[13] This "dramatic" character of the Cana narrative is reminiscent of the longer dramatic texts in Jn. chs. 4; 9; 11 and 18:28ff, and also 1:19ff, 20:1ff, and 21:1ff. See Windisch 1923 and below, ch. 3.

[14] See above, 2.2, U 31.

the parts. The negative meaning of A and the sequence of the clauses may be interpreted as a sign that C in some way justifies or explains A. The problem is whether, for similar reasons, B too is to provide justification. If this is the case B should be understood as a contrasting characterization of ἡ μήτηρ τοῦ Ἰησοῦ.[15] This meaning cannot be excluded as both B and C may provide an explanation of A.

Such a logical pattern, which is very difficult to verify, makes a drastic choice between the various alternative interpretations of A, B and C, and presupposes the following reading: To his mother's indirect request for wine Jesus' answer is negative (= A) on the ground that she is a human being (γυνή) without understanding of Jesus' work (= B). Jesus' words imply that he is not referring to wine in the usual sense but to the saving gifts he will give to mankind on his Father's orders. Even with this transferred meaning he cannot now grant her request. For his hour has not yet come (= C). The first motivation would then concern the literal meaning of the request for wine, the second a transferred meaning of the same statement. These logical relations are, however, so vague and implicit that they can hardly provide the basis for any interpretation of the text. The same can be said of all logical relations in our text. Nevertheless I wish to make two further comments.

In the speech now analysed and in v. 9 there is the same logical relation: *since* Jesus' hour has not yet come, he cannot grant the request for wine, and *since* the servants had drawn the water they knew whence the wine came. I tried to show above that νῦν in v. 8 denotes that Jesus' "hour" has come and that the miracle has occurred: now there is wine in the vessels.[16] If we appose these facts we have a chain of involvement: Jesus' "hour" → wine → drawing → realization. This pattern cannot be used as a basis for any interpretation either but perhaps, especially as the drawing is here a result of obedience to Jesus' word, it may be a reason why "drawing water" in the text expresses experience of Jesus and his gifts.[17]

A second point of interest is the association of Jesus with his mother concerning the servants' action. In 1:35—51 the disciples receive Jesus in three stages, so to speak: John the Baptist (his witness), Jesus himself and future experience.[18] We find a similar pattern with regard to the servants; Jesus' mother, Jesus himself and the testing of the wine. In any case it is striking that both Jesus and his mother give them instructions.

The question of whether these observations are relevant for the interpretation

[15] See the different interpretations of γύναι above, 2.2, U 9b.
[16] 2.2, U 18.
[17] Cf. above, 2.2, U 18 and U 24, and below 2.3.5 and 2.4.4, and the use of such verbs as "see", "hear", "know", "drink", "eat", etc. in Jn.
[18] See above, 2.2, U 6 and U 31.

of the text in its entirety must be discussed in a wider context. All we can say is that the logical relations in our text are extremely vague and implicit, without any clear function in the structure of the text.

2.3.4 Temporal Features

As often occurs in Jn the timing of the event is precisely stated ($\tau\tilde{\eta}$ $\dot{\eta}\mu\dot{\epsilon}\rho\alpha$ $\tau\tilde{\eta}$ $\tau\rho\dot{\iota}\tau\eta$).[19] Judging by the wording of the text all the events take place on one day (the third day) in the following sequence:[20]

E 1 The wedding—at which Jesus' mother was present ($\tilde{\eta}\nu$)—begins ($\dot{\epsilon}\gamma\dot{\epsilon}\nu\epsilon\tau o$).

E 2 Jesus and his disciples are invited ($\dot{\epsilon}\kappa\lambda\dot{\eta}\vartheta\eta$).

E 3 The wine fails ($\dot{\upsilon}\sigma\tau\epsilon\rho\dot{\eta}\sigma\alpha\nu\tau o\varsigma$).

E 4 Jesus' mother speaks to Jesus ($\lambda\dot{\epsilon}\gamma\epsilon\iota$).

E 5 Jesus speaks to her ($\lambda\dot{\epsilon}\gamma\epsilon\iota$).

E 6 Jesus' mother speaks to the servants ($\lambda\dot{\epsilon}\gamma\epsilon\iota$).

E 7 Jesus speaks to the servants ($\lambda\dot{\epsilon}\gamma\epsilon\iota$).

E 8 The servants fill the vessels—which were standing ($\tilde{\eta}\sigma\alpha\nu$) there—with water ($\dot{\epsilon}\gamma\dot{\epsilon}\mu\iota\sigma\alpha\nu$).

E 9 The water in the vessels becomes wine ($\gamma\epsilon\gamma\epsilon\nu\eta\mu\dot{\epsilon}\nu o\nu$).

E 10 Jesus speaks to the servants ($\lambda\dot{\epsilon}\gamma\epsilon\iota$).

E 11 The servants draw water/wine ($\dot{\eta}\nu\tau\lambda\eta\kappa\dot{o}\tau\epsilon\varsigma$).[21]

E 12 The servants take the water/wine to the steward ($\dot{\eta}\nu\epsilon\gamma\kappa\alpha\nu$).

E 13 The steward tastes the water/the wine ($\dot{\epsilon}\gamma\epsilon\dot{\upsilon}\sigma\alpha\tau o$).

E 14 The steward summons the bridegroom ($\varphi\omega\nu\epsilon\tilde{\iota}$).

E 15 The steward speaks to him ($\lambda\dot{\epsilon}\gamma\epsilon\iota$).

This sequence of event units is parallel to the order of the text. As a rule main clause follows main clause, joined by $\kappa\alpha\dot{\iota}$, $\delta\dot{\epsilon}$ or without any conjunction. Only in the case of E 3 (gen.abs.) and E 13 ($\dot{\omega}\varsigma$-clause) are syntactical constructions used to show the temporal sequence. There are, however, two exceptions to this parallelism: E 9 and E 11. There the perfect tense is used.[22] This use has the effect that the event described with this tense appears later, or recurs in the account, and is thus given special emphasis. This may be explained from narrative technique alone—a means of dramatizing and avoiding monotony—or as a deliberate or unconscious feature of the text, giving perspective to the entire account. The reader/hearer is forced to think back and confirm what he previously deduced (the

---

[19] On the larger temporal scheme in which our text is set, see above, 2.2, U 1.

[20] The relations between E 1, E 2 and E 3 are vague. The aorist ($\dot{\epsilon}\kappa\lambda\dot{\eta}\vartheta\eta$) may sometimes replace the pluperfect, Bl.-Debr., § 347,2.

[21] The drawing of the servants is also implied by $\varphi\dot{\epsilon}\rho\epsilon\iota\nu$.

[22] Otherwise the present tense is consistently used for verbal "acts", the aorist for non-verbal, and the imperfect for specific descriptive units. Similarly in the speeches. On pres. imper. of $\varphi\dot{\epsilon}\rho\epsilon\iota\nu$, see Turner, p. 75.

drawing), or to correct his impression by introducing yet another element into the event which he had not formerly taken into account (the miracle of the wine), a process which presumably reinforces these events in thought and gives cause for reflection. These two phenomena, E 9 and E 11, are linked to the statement that the servants *knew* whence the water/the wine came but the steward did not. Thus the temporal structure links *the miracle, the drawing,* and *the realization,* an indication that the sentence καὶ οὐκ ᾔδει ... τὸ ὕδωρ, v. 9, should be regarded as a reflective comment on the entire narrative at the same time as it prepares for the steward's statement in v. 10.

The temporal aspects are more marked in the speeches:
S 1 They have no wine (ἔχουσιν).
S 2 ... My hour has not yet come (οὔπω ἥκει ἡ ὥρα μου).
S 3 Do (ποιήσατε) whatever he tells you (λέγῃ).
S 4 Fill the vessels with water (γεμίσατε).
S 5 Now draw some out (ἀντλήσατε νῦν) and take it to the steward (φέρετε).
S 6 Every man serves the good wine first (πρῶτον ... τίθησιν) and when (καὶ ὅταν) men have drunk freely, then the poor wine. You have kept the good wine until now (τετήρηκας ἕως ἄρτι).

Most of these speeches have temporal parallels in the scheme of events: S 1 = E 3, S 4 = E 8, S 5 = E 11–12 and S 3 includes E 7–8 and 10–12. This contributes to the cohesion and shows the integration of the speeches with the series of events as such. This leaves Jesus' first speech and the steward's words, which are more independent. They are dominated by temporal references: οὔπω ἥκει ἡ ὥρα μου, πρῶτον ... καὶ ὅταν, τετήρηκας ἕως ἄρτι. The vital issue is whether these references and the series of events—especially the elements which are common to the speech scheme—are to be regarded as illustrating each other (a large temporal scheme) or as separate schemata, loosely related to each other. The very arrangement in texts necessitates the setting of the content in a temporal order of some kind. The way of marking time in our text indicates, however, that the temporal aspects are of importance. A temporal scheme predominates: **first** that, **then** that. This is most strongly marked in S 6: first the better wine, then the less good, an order which is contrasted by that of the bridegroom: first the bad wine, and then the good. This order of events in v. 10 links up with the rest of the account by means of the last clause in S 6, especially the words ἕως ἄρτι. This *now* (ἄρτι) in the text, with its secondary meaning of *not before now*, brings to the reader's notice two other points of time in the text, νῦν in S 5, and in particular ἡ ὥρα μου in S 2. Jesus' first speech brings his "hour" into focus. The text says implicitly that *first* Jesus' "hour" must come, *then* he can intervene in the situation, or possibly his intervention may coincide with the coming of his "hour". The temporal adverb νῦν in S 5 implies that the miracle has taken place.[23] Jesus'

[23] See the discussion above, 2.2, U 18.

"hour" has come. The wine is there. (This circumstance coincides with the bridegroom's production of the good wine.) The three elements of time mentioned, $\dot{\eta}$ $\dot{\omega}\rho a$ $\mu o \upsilon$, $\nu \tilde{\upsilon} \nu$ and $\ddot{a}\rho \tau \iota$ belong together: they should either be regarded as one and the same moment or, more probably, so understood that *first* the "hour" of Jesus, *then* the wine is there, the drawing, the bringing ($\nu \tilde{\upsilon} \nu$, $\ddot{a}\rho \tau \iota$). The time before the "hour" is characterized by the shortage of wine, or by bad wine, and by more or less empty stone vessels, the water from which was for the purification of the Jews, the time *after* the "hour" by wine in plenty, good wine, full vessels, drawing, tasting and the bringing of the good wine which had been saved for this occasion. Thus we have two main phases with "the hour of Jesus" as a kind of dividing line, a temporal structure found throughout the composition of the Gospel as a whole, and recurring in Jn in a long series of sayings on Jesus and the disciples.[24] In the text Jesus' mother appears only during the first phase, but the second is anticipated by her instructions to the servants. These are present during both phases and are represented as those who know how the miracle occurred. The steward and the bridegroom are only active during the last phase.

All that happens in the text seems therefore to revolve round the "hour", mentioned in Jesus' first speech, the equivalent of which in the course of events is the filling of the vessels and the miracle itself. In a wider Johannine context the "hour" includes the heart of Jesus' work on earth, which culminated during the last week, and especially on the sixth day on Golgotha. The temporal pattern in the text may therefore be said to extend over the whole of Jesus' work, both in the time before and the time after his glorification.

The earlier analysis showed that the spatial and logical relations play a subordinate part in the constitution of our text. The situation is different as regards the temporal relations. The timing of the speeches, and the connection between them and the occurrence in general mark a dominating temporal structure with $\dot{\eta}$ $\dot{\omega}\rho a$ $\tau o \tilde{\upsilon}$ $\text{'}I \eta \sigma o \tilde{\upsilon}$ in the centre. This striking temporal pattern—it should be noted that it appears just in the speeches—must reasonably be assigned a function when we endeavour to give an adequate and comprehensive interpretation of the Cana narrative.

2.3.5 The Roles of the Participants
The references to persons often play a very important part in narrative texts.[25] If we survey the different units in our text we find:

---

[24] The same temporal structure characterizes Jesus' *erga* and Jesus' *doxa* in Jn; see above, 2.2, U 27 and U 30. Corresponding to the Gospel as a whole, we have the same vagueness in the narrative: it is difficult to determine the "hour" but there is a time *before* and a time *after*.

[25] See Longacre 1968, pp. 13f, Nida-Taber 1969, pp. 153f, Dressler 1972, pp. 42ff. The references to persons contribute very much to the cohesion of the text and may reveal how the narrator looks on the *dramatis personae* and the events in which they take part.

U 4 . . . ἡ μήτηρ τοῦ Ἰησοῦ
U 5 . . . ὁ Ἰησοῦς
U 6 . . . οἱ μαθηταὶ αὐτοῦ
U 8 . . . ἡ μήτηρ τοῦ Ἰησοῦ . . . αὐτόν . . . αὐτόν . . . -σω
U 9 . . . αὐτῇ ὁ Ἰησοῦς . . . ἐμοί . . . σοί, γύναι . . . μου
U 10 . . . ἡ μήτηρ αὐτοῦ τοῖς διακόνοις . . . -ῃ ὑμῖν . . . -ατε
U 14 . . . τῶν Ἰουδαίων
U 16 . . . αὐτοῖς ὁ Ἰησοῦς . . . -τε
U 17 . . . -ν
U 18 . . . -ει αὐτοῖς . . . -τε . . . -τε . . . τῷ ἀρχιτρικλίνῳ
U 19 . . . οἱ δέ
U 20 . . . ὁ ἀρχιτρίκλινος
U 22 . . . -ει
U 23 . . . οἱ διάκονοι
U 24 . . . οἱ ἠντληκότες
U 25 . . . τὸν νυμφίον ὁ ἀρχιτρίκλινος
U 26 . . . -ει αὐτῷ· πᾶς ἄνθρωπος . . . -σω . . . σύ
U 27 . . . ὁ Ἰησοῦς
U 30 . . . -εν . . . αὐτοῦ
U 31 . . . αὐτὸν οἱ μαθηταὶ αὐτοῦ

The usual number of persons (or groups of persons) in Jesus narratives is two or three.[26] In Jn we sometimes encounter more but, considering the Johannine texts, and especially if we take its length into account, the Cana narrative has a remarkably large number: Jesus (mentioned 17 times), the servants (12), Jesus' mother (6), the steward of the feast (5), the bridegroom (3), the disciples (2), the Jews (1) and also general references in U 8 and U 26. If we ignore the final verse as comment, the servants are mentioned as often as Jesus, which gives them a major role in the text. Otherwise these references confirm Jesus' central role. He appears in 11 of the 20 units and is the only person to be repeatedly mentioned in the genitive: Jesus' mother, Jesus' disciples, Jesus' *doxa*, Jesus' hour.[27]

The form of the references provides certain information on the *dramatis personae* and divides up the text as a whole. *Jesus' mother* is designated by a pronoun only in U 9, which links U 8 and U 9.[28] The form of ἡ μήτηρ τοῦ Ἰησοῦ —and its repeated use—creates an allusive openness in the expression. Γύναι in U 9 may mean that the reference is not to Jesus' mother in the usual sense, but to her representative role in the text.[29] *The servants* are introduced as something known in U 10 and the use of the pronoun in U 16 brings these units together. Διάκονοι, like οἱ ἠντληκότες τὸ ὕδωρ may have certain associations.[30] *The steward* is also introduced as known by a somewhat obscure term asserting his superior status at the wedding. The repetition of ἀρχιτρίκλινος in U 25 indicates

[26] Bultmann [7]1967, pp. 335ff.
[27] Cf. "the purification of the Jews" in U 14.
[28] A pronominal reference would not be unnatural in U 10.
[29] See above, 2.2, U 4 and U 9b.
[30] See above, 2.2, U 10, U 18 and U 24.

that part of the material between U 20 and U 25 is parenthetical. If we also include the words *Jesus' disciples* and *the bridegroom*,[31] it must be admitted that the references open the way to an unusally large number of allusions. Moreover, the personal references give us the first division of the text: vv. 1—2, 3—4, 5—8, 9—10 and v. 11, with v. 6 and parts of v. 9 as parentheses.

The various *dramatis personae* appear on the scene in a certain order, only to be left off stage later: Jesus' mother, Jesus, the servants, the steward, the bridegroom. The disciples are in a sense "the audience". The action they witness is noteworthy in that the personages first presented, i.e. Jesus' mother, Jesus (and the disciples themselves) are not present at the conclusion but are replaced by two (three) others: the steward, the bridegroom (and the servants). This feature of the text brings us to the problem of how the various individuals are linked or contrasted in the events which the text describes.

The relations between the speeches are perhaps the easiest to establish. We have four "conversations:[32]

1. Jesus' mother — Jesus, vv. 3—4.
2. Jesus' mother — the servants, v. 5.
3. Jesus — the servants, vv. 7—8.
4. The steward — the bridegroom, vv. 9—10.

Both the content and the form of vv. 5—8 link the middle two conversations.[33] The other two have a number of features in common: a certain lack of insight and understanding between the parties, the time aspect of the actions of the one party, possibly a contrast with human ways of thought and action. Both are concerned with the serving of wine, in the latter case of good wine. The common features in the introductory and concluding speeches suggest comparisons between Jesus' mother in her first speech (abbreviated to Jesus' mother A) and the steward, and between Jesus and the bridegroom. Together with the explicit comparison in v. 9, we have three pairs of contrasts: Jesus' mother A — Jesus, the steward — the bridegroom and the steward — the servants, a grouping of individuals which may be connected with the narrator's total view of his material.

This personal "pattern" in the text is not excluded by the fact that the individuals mentioned also have a "natural" function in the chain of events encountered in vv. 3—10. If the events are to progress, certain actions are needed with certain persons as agents. Jesus' mother's first speech presents the situation to Jesus and prepares for his reaction. This occurs in v. 4, dominated by the reference to Jesus' "hour". This first exchange concentrates attention on Jesus and the prevailing situation. We are directed to consider ἡ ὥρα τοῦ Ἰησοῦ at the same time as Jesus' attitude remains mysterious and not fully described. New

---

[31] On "the disciples" and "the bridegroom" in Jn, see above, 2.2, U 6 and U 25.

[32] Only the first "conversation" is a real exchange of speeches. The other speeches only provoke non-verbal "answers".

[33] See above, 2.2, U 10.

acts are expected in the chain of events. The second speech by Jesus' mother again focuses attention on Jesus, at the same time as the servants enter the scene. The situation itself is linked the more strongly with what Jesus may be expected to do. Then comes Jesus' "work" in vv. 7—8, which specially involves the servants. They carry out Jesus' commands and the action continues. Nevertheless what Jesus has in fact done is not clear until the steward comes on the scene. He is needed in the action as an expert and responsible individual who states that the liquid is wine, and good wine at that. He confirms the miracle without knowing it. One of the main personages at the wedding, the bridegroom, provides his "audience". The final statement changes the shortage mentioned at the beginning into its opposite. The tension is at an end.

The individuals in the text therefore act as necessary agents in the events which together constitute the action: *situation A is changed to situation B as a result of Jesus' intervention (Jesus' work), when his "hour" is come.* Nevertheless this macrostructure may be made up of other events and other agents than those in our text, and the question arises why the narrator chose just these. The selection of events is very great and the way of referring to the agents is unusually rich in allusions. The narrator's choice depends on a number of factors, particularly the "material" at his disposal and what it includes. His total view of the events described and the message he wishes to transmit to his readers also influences his choice. In the latter case the formation of the text would seem to be to a great extent involuntary. The events described, and their sequence in the text, give us certain groupings and these may or may not be related to the message as a whole. Attention will therefore be drawn to further individual groupings in our text.

Jesus' mother, Jesus and Jesus' disciples are presented to the reader in the introduction as the *dramatis personae*, a triad with Jesus in the centre, the others being designated by their relationship to him. The reader undoubtedly expects the text to deal with these three, but Jesus' mother is not present at the end and the disciples are mentioned only in a comment on the narrative. At the end the reader finds instead three other people, *the servants, the steward and the bridegroom.* They are not presented but are implied from the situation and introduced as something known. If we confine ourselves to vv. 1—10, the story of Jesus' mother, Jesus and Jesus' disciples is changed into an account of these three characters at the wedding. We also find that *Jesus' mother, the servants and the steward* relieve each other. They are associated with the arrangement of the party and are responsible for it. Jesus' mother turns to the servants, they go to the steward. All somehow bear witness by word or action to Jesus or what he caused to happen. *Jesus' mother A* and *the steward* begin and end, reasoning κατὰ ἄνθρωπον, if we select the one interpretation of γύναι, and this in contrast to Jesus/the bridegroom. *Jesus' mother B* (her second speech) and *the servants* meet in the middle. Somehow they "believe" in Jesus. Jesus' mother exhorts the servants to obey her son and they hear and do what he says. By their obedience to him, and at the same time to his mother, they become "the drawers of water" in the narrative who know whence the water/the wine came. Both of them are close to Jesus and his "work", unlike the steward, who is represented as wholly unaware of what has happened, although he indirectly confirms the miracle. *Jesus* and *the bridegroom* have a great deal in common, including the fact that they produced wine—according to the servants and to the steward—yet in a temporal sequence which does not seem to fit in with Jesus' mother A or the steward.

Other groupings of the individuals mentioned in the text are possible but these seem to me to be unquestionably the most prominent, namely:

Jesus' mother, Jesus, Jesus' disciples.
The servants, the steward, the bridegroom.
Jesus' mother, the servants, the steward.
Jesus' mother A, the steward.
Jesus' mother B, the servants.
Jesus, the bridegroom.

Later on I will show that these combinations, like the form of the references, have some connection with the author's total view of the events reported and with the message he is seeking to convey.[34]

2.3.6 The Information Flow

A text may be analysed on the basis of the information it gives the reader. Considering textual analysis from the point of view of communication brings to the fore the whole problem of understanding the text, at the same time as it directs attention to textual qualities important for communication. Here I propose, without carrying out a full scale analysis, to discuss some related aspects of the information flow in our text.[35] I am concerned with references to the same piece of information (anaphora, cross-reference), joining of old and new information (theme—rheme, topic—comment) and distribution and focusing of information such as the question of foreground - background, plus some remarks on expected and unexpected information.

Scholars working on language and text research have concentrated on the problem of the means used in the text to refer back to something already men-

---

[34] See below, 2.4.4.

[35] Theoretical and practical work on textual analysis, based on the information the text gives the reader, has been done only in recent years, and we have no perfect methods for such an analysis. Therefore I take up only some aspects. My material is also very limited and not suited for methodological considerations. On the questions of the information flow of a text, see Halliday 1967, 1968, Wonderly 1968, pp. 183ff, Palek 1968, Longacre 1968 passim (ground—figure), Kirkwood 1969, Dahl 1969 (with a summary of the Russian literature on the subject), Chafe 1970, pp. 210ff, Brinker 1971, pp. 223ff, Fries 1971, pp. 225ff, and Dressler 1972, pp. 55ff. On more general problems, see Gleason 1965, pp. 329ff, 418ff.

tioned.[36] I showed above how the spatial, temporal and personal references bind the text together and divide it up.[37] I would here add the reiteration of *the water vessels* and of *the water* in the text. In v. 6 the reader is told of some water containers (ὑδρίαι) which were standing there. Later the text refers to them by τὰς ὑδρίας and αὐτάς in v. 7. The use of the article in Jesus' first speech to the servants indicates that information about the water vessels has already been given in v. 6.[38] The usage is similar concerning the water, first presented in v. 7 (ὕδατος), implied in vv. 7b and 8 and then mentioned in v. 9, τὸ ὕδωρ . . . τὸ ὕδωρ. The water is intimately connected with Jesus and what he does in the narrative. At his command the servants filled the vessels with water, at his command they drew water from the vessels for tasting. These references emphasize a definite interest on the part of the narrator in the "material" which is, so to speak, included in Jesus' miracle (the Jewish purification vessels, water). Jesus' act in the text, if we ignore his first speech, consists solely of events concerning this "material". Since v. 11 focuses on what Jesus does, this fact must be regarded as significant when interpreting the text.

The word ταύτην in v. 11, referring to all the information given so far, is essential for the interpretation. It denotes that v. 11 provides information on the Cana occurrence as a whole. In this perspective, only Jesus and the relationship between him and his disciples are of interest to the narrator.

The references mentioned here always mark *old information*. They refer to something mentioned previously or a fact already known. A message may be thought to consist of two parts: that already known and the new facts which the sender wishes to convey. The information flow in a text is to a great extent characterized by how these two "parts" are joined together. As a rule a sentence is governed mainly by the new information it is intended to convey.[39]

In the narrative of the wedding at Cana we notice that *the wine*, v. 3, *the servants*, v. 5, *the steward*, v. 8, and *the bridegroom*, v. 9, are introduced into the text without explanation. They are marked as old information, assuredly because they are assumed to be known by means of the situation given at the beginning. The wedding framework, therefore, is present in the entire text, although we have

---

[36] See especially Palek 1968, pp. 11ff, Brinker 1971, pp. 223ff. Textual analysis, according to Harweg, is essentially an analysis of different kinds of reference. On semantic recurrence, see Cummings-Herum-Lybbert 1971.

[37] See above, 2.3.1—2.3.4.

[38] Jesus' act is thus linked to the vessels, and by the vessels related to the Jewish purifications. See above, 2.2, U 11—15.

[39] In grammatical works these two parts have been called *topic* and *comment;* see Lyons 1968, pp. 334ff, and Dahl 1969, p. 5. From the Prague School we have the terms *theme* and *rheme;* see Daneš 1970 and Fries 1971, pp. 225ff, and the literature mentioned in these articles. For a more theoretical discussion of this distinction, see Chafe 1970, pp. 210ff, who uses the words *old* and *new information*. He analyses only the smallest semantic units of the language.

difficulty in finding parallels to what we are told in our existing knowledge of weddings at that period. This marking of old information seems to be one of the reasons why we feel a certain unevenness in the information flow between vv. 2 and 3.[40] The short introductory phrase in v. 3 is, like vv. 1—2, a description of a situation, and its content is reiterated in the first speech of Jesus' mother. Since texts. by our present standards, should not contain such repetitions, we are inclined to differentiate by saying that the contracted sentence indicates that the wine ran out, or that the speech is regarded as an exhortation by Jesus' mother. In any case v. 3 is a difficult unit from the point of view of the information flow.

The item in v. 3, however, is indispensable for the sequence of events. Verses 1—2 give us the basic data of the text: γάμος ἐγένετο, which is supplemented with information on time, place and a number of the persons involved. The next piece of information essential for the course of events comes later in the contracted sentence in v. 3: there was no wine at this wedding. It seems important to the narrator that Jesus' mother should tell Jesus of the shortage. The tension thereby introduced into the narrative underlies the information given mostly in the speeches and is not relieved until the steward says in v. 10: "But you have kept the good wine until now". The reader was told this earlier, in the parenthetical data in v. 9, in the same way as he learned about the vessels used. Finally in v. 11 we are given information about the content of the first two parts, vv. 1—2 and 3—10. If we consider the information flow in the text as a whole we have a coherent unit in vv. 3—10. The item in v. 3a proclaims the situation (the lack of wine) which in the text is changed to the reverse (wine) and even more (good wine) by the events described. Nevertheless the brevity of this introductory description of the situation is remarkable, as is the form of the information on the altered situation in vv. 9—10.

Only Jesus himself, his disciples, the timing, and perhaps Galilee in v. 1, are mentioned as old information from the events narrated in ch. 1.[41] The reader has also encountered the Jews, v. 6, in 1:19ff: we there find a similar distance between them and John the Baptist as we have in v. 6 between them and the narrator. This old information is reiterated in a special way in v. 11: this reinforces the impression that vv. 3—10 are the central new information unit, and that this unit should be seen from the message the author is seeking to convey in the wider context.

The quantitative distribution, and the focus of the information, in the text are difficult to establish, partly because these features of the flow so strongly depend

---

[40] Note the variant readings in v. 3, mentioned above, 2.2, U 7. The renderings of the quotation formula in v. 5 and v. 7 in some Old Latin translations may also be explained by the marking of the old information in these passages. See above, 2.2, U 10 and U 16.

[41] If we take ἡ ὥρα and ἡ δόξα in a specific Johannine sense they may also be regarded as old information. The readers already know what the "hour" of Jesus and the *doxa* of Jesus are.

on the reader's expectations and experience. If we consider the manner of presentation, *the persons* and *the speeches* stand out, while *the description of the situation* fades into the background. The narrative itself even concludes with direct speech. Together these parts of the text describe for the reader an underlying fact which, according to v. 11, is the most important. If we consider the information given to the reader, we must admit that it is often extremely scanty, especially at the beginning and at the end. There is a striking expansion in vv. 6 and 9 (and v. 11). The servants also play a major part, vv. 7f. It would be possible to make drastic reductions in the central chain of events in vv. 3—10: for example, "Jesus said: 'Fill the vessels standing there with water and then let the steward taste it'. They did so and when the steward tasted it—he did not know whence it came—he said ..." Why must the vessels be described in such detail? Why must the text say that the servants knew where the water came from? The text we now possess is interested in both Jesus' act and the role of the servants. This interest has a parallel in v. 11, which focuses Jesus' work and Jesus' disciples. The increase and concentration of the information flow in vv. 6—9 should, therefore, be explained by the remarkable comment on the entire occurrence in v. 11.

This reasoning brings us, to some extent, into the question of expected and unexpected information, thus involving the readers, then or now, consciously in the analysis. The reader's expectations depend to a considerable degree on his total concept of the text, including the question of the text type. Indeed many remarks by recent commentators express more of the exegete's expectation of the text than about the text itself and its first readers.[42] I will here only carry out the experiment of following the belief that the author wished to describe a part of Jesus' life and nothing more. We would be faced with "a simple narrative text".[43] Such expectations naturally suggest a number of questions:[44] When and how did Jesus arrive in Cana? Why was Jesus' mother present? When and where was Jesus invited? Who was getting married? Why had they no wine? How could Jesus' mother expect, or even demand, a miracle from Jesus when, according to v. 11, this was his first? Why is Jesus' answer so dismissive? What does the first speech really mean? Why this solemn, mysterious reference to the hour of Jesus? Why is there so much detail about the water vessels when the author is otherwise so reticent? And why so much wine? What did the guests say when they were given such a quantity? How could Jesus' mother give orders to the servants? Why was the steward not supervising the wedding and the activities of the servants? Did he not know that the wine had run out? What an odd rule he had for

---

[42] See, for example, Wellhausen 1908, Schwartz 1907, 1908, or Heitmüller, Comm.

[43] For a discussion of the text type, see below 2.4.1 and 2.4.5.

[44] On such questions, see, for example, Heitmüller, Loisy and Bauer, Comm., ad loc., and Strauss [4]1840, vol. 1, pp. 206ff. When Derrett 1970 wishes to describe what really happened when Jesus was in Cana he has to add a great deal of new information. At the same time he does not explain all the information we have in the text.

serving wine! We know from 1:35ff that the disciples believed in Jesus. Why then a new statement that they believed in him? Many questions of this kind could be put forward. Those suggested demonstrate that the narrator's intention was not primarily to give a description of an episode in Jesus' life. He constructed his text in such a way that the reader is obliged to describe it as other than "a simple narrative text". The selection, linking and focus of the information in the text is otherwise difficult to explain.

2.3.7 The Point of View

The narrative situation is probably the most elementary and characteristic of a narrative in its widest sense: *somebody tells something about something to somebody*.[45] This definition includes some important relationships which should not be neglected in an analysis of a narrative text, especially those between the narrator, what he narrates and the reader/hearer of the narrative. The concept *point of view* usually refers to the position adopted by the narrator in relation to what he describes, and those to whom he describes it, or in other words: the position from which the narrative is presented to the reader.[46] The fiction of the last two centuries reveals a highly sophisticated use of the possibilities inherent in the narrative situation; in literary analysis the concept *point of view* has therefore been subjected to far-reaching theoretical discussion and further development.[47] The narrative situation mentioned above will suffice for the present analysis, which concerns very old and very short texts with a complicated history.[48] It is possible to make a rough distinction between the situation when the narrator is describing what he wants to convey from an *external* point of view, so to speak, from that in which he allows the readers to see what is happening from the inside, from an *internal* point of view.[49] The external position tends to allow the narrator much greater freedom. He can use several means of conveying information, he can comment on the events he describes etc. At the same time he reveals himself more clearly in the text itself. *The Johannine presentation gives a good example of an external point of view.*[50]

[45] On the narrative situation, see Pelç 1971.

[46] See Björck [6]1970, pp. 9ff, Hägg 1971, pp. 112ff, and Uspensky 1972 and the literature mentioned there. The concept point of view is applicable to all kinds of art which has two planes (expression and content), according to Uspensky, and in his article he analyses both verbal and visual art.

[47] On the changes in novels, see Scholes-Kellog 1966, pp. 240ff, and on the theoretical discussions, see Hägg 1971, pp. 112ff, and the literature he mentions.

[48] Hägg 1971, pp. 112ff, has, with similar reservations, analysed early Greek novels with regard to the point of view and has in this way been able to describe some interesting features of early narrative art.

[49] See Uspensky 1972, pp. 6ff. The different positions are indicated by, for example, the psychological, verbal, temporal and spatial descriptions and by some "ideological" markers of the narrator.

[50] The anonymous character of the Gospel should be linked to this external point of view.

An analysis of a text's point of view should ideally cover an entire work, in our case the whole Gospel. The analysis presented here is therefore bound to be incomplete. In his thesis on the literary devices in Jn David W. Wead discusses this question, but without dealing with more theoretical aspects of the problems in a text such as Jn and without carrying out a complete analysis.[51] For the most part his observations provide an introduction to his analysis of the various stylistic features in Jn, although he himself emphasizes that they are of fundamental importance for the whole of his investigation. The result is not particularly surprising: the author of Jn has "a post resurrection point of view". He allows the reader to see the events from a later perspective and not from inside the situation at the time when they happened. The very prologue of the Gospel—an introduction and key to the text—establishes a perspective on the principal character in the book, which does not limit him to his earthly activity, and several remarks in the Gospel reveal a clearly post resurrection point of view.[52] This is also emphasized by the many explanations and amendments, for example in 1:28; 2:6; 4:9; 12:42f; 19:40; 2:22; 11:13; 7:39; 12:33; 13:11 and 21:23. Moreover the narrator takes the liberty of giving information independent of its timing, such as the item about Mary in 11:2; cf. 12:6; 18:14. "The writer stands beyond the resurrection and looks back upon the event. He emphasizes the inability of the apostles to understand the things that were happening in their true perspective at the time they happened (cf. Mark 8:17—18). It is only possible for us to come to know these things fully as we understand the resurrection and its significance."[53] This description should not be understood as meaning that only Jn is influenced by the resurrection and its interpretation. All the Gospels were written in the light of the resurrection and the existence of the Church.[54] Yet the point under discussion is *the manner of presentation* and here there is a difference between Jn and the Synoptic Gospels. The material in Jn is presented to the reader in a different way. The "hour" of Jesus and its consequences are the reality from which all the material is presented, and this is also incorporated in texts dealing with the period *before* the hour. The author's interest is by no means confined to the situations described, but also covers the situation in which he himself lives. The emphasis even seems to be placed on *the communication with the author's environment.*[55] Perhaps this emerges most clearly in the description of Jesus' disciples and Jesus' contemporaries on the whole: they do not understand everything, they do not see clearly, 6:52ff; 7:33ff; 13:7; 14:19; 16:29f. The full realization is not possible until after the "hour" of Jesus and his "elevation"; cf. 2:22; 12:16; 13:7; 20:9. So

[51] Wead 1970, pp. 1—11.
[52] Jn 2:17,22; 12:16; 20:9; see my analysis below, 4.2.
[53] Wead 1970, p. 5.
[54] Wead 1970 seems to me to reduce this fact and therefore arrives at "a basic difference" between Jn and the Synoptic Gospels.
[55] Cf. the analysis of Jn 4 below, especially of S 11 in 3.3.2 and S 4 in 3.4.2.

Jesus' earthly work does not come into its own until the post resurrection situation of the author and his readers.[56] In the Johannine presentation the narrator is standing at a distance from the events, at the same time as he possesses an insight and a knowledge which makes him a constantly present, although invisible, witness.[57]

My general remarks on the evangelist's point of view are confirmed by several features of the Cana narrative, such as the "dramatic" presentation with "scenes" and speeches, where the disciples are the audience, being both present and at a distance, or the interest shown by the author in the relationships between Jesus and his disciples, a relationship of current significance in his own time too. The formation of the speeches, the direct speech at the end of the narrative, the information given the reader in vv. 6, 9 and 11, and the parenthetical manner of its transmission are all features indicating that the emphasis is not laid on the communication that is contemporary with the events. In v. 6 the Jews and their customs are seen from outside and from a distance. All these textual features can be explained from the post resurrection point of view which seems characteristic of the whole Gospel. Thus the events which once occurred at Cana are presented to the readers from a position in the situation of the Church, which involves both author and reader in the narrative.[58] The main reason for this comprehensive aspect seems to be that this position gives the true meaning of Jesus' work(s).

2 4 The Message of the Text

2.4.1 Preliminary Remarks

The various statement units and the structural features have generally been treated separately up to this point. The result is a description of a series of characteristics in the text, several of which evidently may have different functions and form part of various total interpretations. In the following pages I shall discuss the text as a whole and try to combine the results in order to establish more accurately what the author was trying to say, namely his message, here called "the message of the text".

Since the idea of the general character of a text influences the selection and the structure of the elements which give it meaning, I shall first make a *rough estimate* of what type of text we are discussing in Jn 2:1—11. I postulated the somewhat vague designation "narrative" text and have found nothing which

---

[56] In the situation of the Paraclete; see below 4.3.

[57] Note in this connection the anonymous "witnesses" in Jn, 1:35ff; 18:15f; 13:24; 19:26; 20:2; 21:20, and also Nathanel in ch. 1. See below, 4.4.

[58] On the relation between the author and his readers, see below, 2.4.2.

prompts me to abandon it. The text consists of descriptions of events and situations, together with dialogues and isolated speeches.[1] Yet it is not what we would call "a simple narrative text", a report of an historical event, or an account in which the main emphasis consists in the actual description of what is happening. There is a long series of points at which the text does not give the information we would expect if this were the case.[2] The comment in v. 11 describes the occurrence as a σημεῖον and suggests that only a small group understood its meaning. There is a dearth of historical details. The relatively extensive information given on the purification vessels and the servants may have been included to illustrate the speeches and interpret the narrative. The speeches hold the centre position while the descriptions of situations tend to be in the nature of parentheses. Many elements of the text are strongly allusive. This enumeration of earlier observations[3] may suffice here to justify a *preliminary* designation of the Cana narrative as "*a symbolic narrative text*", i.e. a narrative which seeks to convey a message apart from the actual events described. Such a characterization is in agreement with the majority of modern exegetes. "Its meaning is to be found in its symbolism... The miracle itself is unimportant and all the interest lies in the symbolical possibilities of the event."[4] This rough distinction would exclude the possibility that the narrator's main interest was to describe "Jesus' positive attitude towards the natural human values of life"[5] or to represent him as the great wonder-worker.[6]

What then is the narrator trying to say? How many elements of the text have a transferred meaning? Does only the text as a whole have a symbolic meaning? These and similar questions on what "symbolical possibilities" are relevant from the narrator's own point of view appear to be the most difficult, and at the same time the most significant, for the determination of the message of the text and its character as a whole.[7] It is not difficult to discern a long series of characteristics in a text. The difficulties arise when we try to decide which textual features are

[1] Cf. the analysis of the macrosyntax of a text in Scherner 1970, pp. 55, 64ff.

[2] See above, 2.3.6.

[3] For these characteristic features of the text, see the analysis above, 2.2 and 2.3.

[4] Lindars, Comm., ad loc. He adds: "All critics recognize that some degree of symbolism is to be found in this story".

[5] Thus van der Loos 1965, p. 615; see above, 2.1.

[6] Thus, for example, Ceroke, Büchsel, Faulhaber and Michl. See above, 2.1.

[7] Compare the uncertainty on the symbolical possibilities in, for example, Lindars, Comm., ad loc.: "Inevitably there is some degree of allegorizing. In fact, once the search for allegorical detail is begun, the possibilities seem to be endless. The problem is to decide how much John really intended to imply". A moderate degree of symbolism is recommended. "The symbolical possibilities present an *embarras de richesses,* and the critic must tread warily". He sees himself being "within the bounds of the necessary (sic!) symbolism of the story" when he interprets the wedding as a standard symbol of the eschatological banquet and the *wine* symbolically from Mk 2:21f and no more. Why just his symbolism is that intended is not motivated.

psychologically relevant, which are intended to participate in a communication. Which do function? I could find no other solution than to look for the answers in a total interpretation of the text. Such an interpretation presumes knowledge not only of the text itself, but also of its linguistic context, its situation, and the author's "horizon".[8] I have illustrated the latter in part when, in the earlier analysis, I cited the Johannine parallel material and discussed the author's point of view. We know very little about the situation of the text, the great problem of the *Sitz im Leben* of the Gospel.[9] In the following discussion I wish to deal only with *the problem of the persons for whom the text was composed* and its relevance for the interpretation.

When we refer to the message of the text there are three points of interest: *1.* The message intended by the author, his intention. *2.* The message inherent in the text itself. *3.* The message which a specific reader hears in the text. An author usually intends to convey a single message. His text, on the other hand, is open to several interpretations, since the verbal form of his message involves an abstraction of what he wants to say and he cannot include all the information contained in his message when he "puts it into words". His text must be supplemented with a certain amount of extra information if it is to be understood aright. Only by a cooperation of the situational and linguistic context and by "merging horizons" can a text convey a message to the reader approaching that intended by the author.[10] When I here refer to "the message of the text" I mean—perhaps somewhat inappropriately—the meaning intended by the author, which may be said to coincide with what the "ideal reader" elicits from the text, the reader who really understands what the author is trying to convey.

[8] For further discussion of this communication model for interpreting texts, see Scherner 1971 and Brinkmann [2]1971, pp. 723ff, and his definitions of "Kontext", "Situation", "Redefolge" and "Horizont".

[9] See above, 1.1.

[10] See, besides Brinker 1971 and Faiss 1972, especially Scherner 1972, p. 53: "Da die Sprache qua Sprache immer schon abstrahiert, ist die Kodierung der Bedeutung dem Autor nicht in vollem Umfang möglich, so dass der Text infolge des hohen Allgemeinheitsgrades einen Spielraum für das Gemeinte erstellt, der zwar durch situative oder kontextuelle Bedingungen eingeschränkt, aber nicht völlig aufgehoben kann. . . . Dazu kommt die Unmöglichkeit, den 'Habitus' des Autors, d.h. seinen historischen und biographischen Determinanten, also seinen 'Horizont', völlig in den Text einzubringen. Alle diese Faktoren lassen nicht die vom Autor intendierte Bedeutung selbst in den Text eingehen, sondern nur den 'Sinn' als Bedeutungsrahmen, dessen Füllung vom Rezipienten zu leisten ist. Die 'Bedeutung' konstituiert sich dann auf Basis des 'Sinnes' durch das Zusammenspiel von Situation, Kontext und der Verschmelzung der Horizonte von Autor und Rezipient. An den damit gewonnenen methodologischen Vorteil einer möglichen Unterscheidung zwischen 'Autormeinung', 'Textmeinung' und 'Lesermeinung' sowie an die Beziehungen zum Husserlschen und Gadamerschen logichsen bzw. heuristichen Model kann hier nur erinnert werden. . . . Für unseren Gedankengang entscheidend ist hier, dass dem Text eine Offenheit zugesprochen wird, die der Leser für sich in die Eindeutigkeit zu überführen sucht". —On interpetation as a kind of supplementation procedure, see Christensen 1971.

Who then could be expected to understand the individual who wrote our narrative? Who are the readers who, according to the autor, were likely to comprehend the "symbolic" meaning of his account? This touches on the difficult problem of the purpose of Jn's Gospel, which cannot be discussed in its entirety here.[11] Yet some observations on the general character of the Gospel are of interest to the following work. We find in the Gospel a group of individuals possessing the same extensive insight as the narrator: the disciples *after* Jesus' resurrection, namely those who believe in Jesus. Thus they have the capacity to "merge the horizons". They are represented as those who comprehend, understand—or will understand—those who can bear witness to Jesus, 8:12—20, in contrast to the rest of mankind. Their insight comprehends everything the Gospel describes, its deeper meaning. In his dissertation in 1968, Herbert Leroy showed that the misunderstanding technique in Jn presupposes a Johannine "special language", which only the group of initiates understand, while the outsider interprets the words according to normal usage. Wayne A. Meeks has suggested, with good reasons, that we should regard the communicative function of the Gospel (the text) in approximately the same way as that of Jesus in Jn.[12] When I refer in what follows to the text's "symbolic" meaning, intended by the author, many features in the Gospel itself show that this was not manifest to many at the time it was written, but only to those in close contact with the evangelist. One may well ask if the Gospel was intended for people other than those possessing all the insight inherent in the Gospel as a whole. The author often seems to communicate with himself and fellow believers. In this sense the Gospel is "internalized". It is a book for "insiders".[13]

2.4.2 An Interpretation of the Text as a Whole

I shall here endeavour to establish what the author is trying to convey in his text,

[11] For an introduction, see Feine-Behm-Kümmel, pp. 157ff, and Wikenhauser-Schmid. pp. 342f.

[12] Meeks 1972, pp. 69f. "*The book functions for its readers in precisely the same way that the epiphany of its hero functions within its narratives and dialogues.* .... It is a book for insiders, for if one already belonged to the Johannine community, then we may presume that the manifold bits of tradition that have taken distinctive form in the Johannine circle would be familiar, the 'cross-references' in the book—so frequently anachronistic within the fictional sequence of events—would be immediately recognizable, the double entendre which produces mystified and stupid questions from the fictional dialogue partners (and from many modern commentators) would be acknowledged by a knowing and superior smile." Meeks calls the Gospel of Jn "an etiology of the Johannine group". I would not like to call it so—see below, ch. 5—but it seems to me that Meeks has shown that the Johannine text has *such a form* that it must be characterized as "a book for insiders", namely a similar result to that of Leroy 1968.

[13] On internalized language, see Vygotsky 1971—My view of the Gospel expressed here is essential for the following analysis, but I will not see it as proved until it is verified by a thorough text-linguistic analysis of the texts as such.

apart from the actual narrative, i.e. *the symbolic meaning of the text.* He describes one of Jesus' miracles. There is no indication in the text that he himself does not regard it as historically accurate. It is presented as an occurrence in Jesus' historical situation which is a sign of something else. I have already stated that the narrator does focus on the second, the symbolic, meaning. What is it then? The previous analyses suggested an abundance of interpretations.[14] Which are intended by the author? As I said, the only answer I could find was to first arrive at the central meaning of the text from such features as are particularly prominent and presumably help to convey the message. In general I consider that *the most probable, and therefore the correct, interpretation is that which assigns a communicative function to, or explains, the majority of the textual characteristics discerned, and is at the same time in harmony with what we know with some degree of certainty of the situational and linguistic context and the author's horizon.*[15] The central meaning intended by the author, thus established, enables us to determine the degree of symbolism in the individual details and to describe the type of text with which we are dealing in the Cana narrative.

First of all I shall present my findings on *the composition of the text.*[16] The use of references to individuals, to time, conjunctions, types of clause, terminal features etc. and the general presentation of the content provide a clear segmentation into the following sections: *a)* An introductory, general *description of the situation,* the chief item being γάμος ἐγένετο, and information on when and where the wedding took place and on the wedding guests whom the author wishes to introduce to the reader (vv. 1—2). *b)* A very brief, but vital, item *on the specific situation*—there was no wine for the wedding—with the consequent exchange between Jesus' mother and Jesus (vv. 3—4). *c) The instructions* of Jesus' mother and Jesus to the servants, with a *description* of the water vessels *inserted* before Jesus' first exhortation, v. 6, and *affirmative statements* that the servants did as they were told (vv. 5—8). *d)* The steward's *rebuke* to the bridegroom after he tasted the wine, also *incorporating information* on its origin and on the steward's unawareness—which, among other things, explains his words—and on the servants' insight (vv. 9—10). *e)* The author's *comment* on the event. The relationship between these five sections is indicated above in the survey of the statement units at the beginning of 2.2. The comment in v. 11 and the most deep-

---

[14] Note the quotation from Lindars above, note 7.

[15] It seems to me most natural to start from the premise that *a single message* dominated the author when he shaped his text. If the results of the textual analysis do not fit, then one may search for more than one message. Even if the author intended a single message the text may be open to more than one message; see above, note 10. —The total interpretation need not assign a communicative function to *all* the textual characteristics, depending on how language functions and how the text originated.

[16] What follows is a summary of my analyses in 2.2 and 2.3 with regard to the interpretation of the text as a whole. For discussions and references, see 2.2 and 2.3.

ly embedded parts of the text, v. 6 (= U 11–15) and v. 9 (= U 21–24) are of special interest for the interpretation.

The composition of our text allows the event to be, to a great extent, hidden from the reader's view. The text consists of short descriptions of the situation, speeches and parenthetical comments. This form of narrative offers many opportunities to the narrator of commenting on an event as he presents it, by means of the formation of speeches and descriptions, by a well controlled selection of information and by his own comments. For our interpretation, therefore, we should devote special attention to the situation itself, to the wording of the speeches and to the information given in vv. 6, 9, 11. If we consider the total composition, it reveals several features reminiscent of a play: a number of scenes in which characters come and go, the disciples being the audience. They see the action and also its deeper significance, the symbolic meaning of the text.

The author gives us explicit and useful guidance concerning his intention in his *commentary on the narrative* in v. 11. This concentrates, not on the situation or the speeches, but on Jesus' actions, described as a σημεῖον, even as an ἀρχὴ τῶν σημείων and as a revelation of Jesus' *doxa*. The earlier analysis showed how strongly v. 11 links the narrative with the whole Gospel and interprets it in its entirety. Above all it states that the subject of the narrative is *Jesus' ergon,* plus the effect it has on Jesus' disciples.[17] This work is represented as a sign, probably of something both in the present and in the future.[18] This character of a symbolic, prophetic event is reinforced by the statement that Jesus revealed his *doxa*. Jn in particular relates this revelation to the "hour" of Jesus and to God's saving acts through his emissary, Jesus Christ. According to the previous analysis, v. 11 would seem to show that the author sees in the Cana miracle something of God's saving acts in the work of Jesus, a work which in the Johannine view of Jesus' *erga* and Jesus' *doxa* includes a *before* and an *after,* although the location of the time limit is never quite clear. This divine occurrence culminates in the "hour" of Jesus. So when the author focuses on Jesus' action at Cana, seeing in it a symbolic meaning, bound up with Jesus' *doxa*, he is probably thinking of *Jesus' work in general,* his *ergon,* i.e. of God's revealing acts, his mission and his saving works in Jesus Christ, *covering the time before and after Jesus' hour.* In this context we should try to define the symbolic meaning of the text as a whole.[19]

The author's comment in v. 11 also directs attention to *the chain of events* in the narrative and the action in general. This emerges clearly from the text,

---

[17] Note that when the narrator comments on the text as a whole, he sees only Jesus and the disciples, i.e. the theme of 1:35ff.

[18] Nothing in the text indicates that the author regards the narrative as fiction. Cf. below, ch. 5.

[19] This frame for an interpretation approaches the Christological interpretation mentioned in 2.1, but I focus rather on the *work* of Jesus and his disciples. Jesus' work as a whole and its implications seems to be the theme of the text, not Christology.

although the method of presentation is surprising: situation A is changed to situation B by Jesus' action when his "hour" is at hand. The situation mentioned at the beginning (the lack of wine) is not only reversed (a supply of wine) but it is also apparent that there was *a large quantity* of wine and a *choice* wine at that! Since the macrostructure of the text is brought to the fore when the author comments on it, any attempt to evaluate the symbolic possibilities of the text ought first to deal with the elements most closely related to the chain of events, namely *wedding* and *wine*.[20] Nevertheless the most prominent feature is *the change in the situation associated with Jesus' "hour"*.

The author's comment and the course of events point indirectly to the "hour" of Jesus. I found that *the temporal relations,* unlike the spatial and logical, play an important part in our narrative. They have a special connection with the speeches which may be suspected to have an interpretative function. Together they provide a striking *temporal pattern* with *"the hour of Jesus"* in the centre. The closest equivalents to the "hour" in the course of events are (the filling of the vessels and) the miracle itself. The time *before* is characterized by lack of wine (possibly inferior wine), more or less empty vessels for Jewish purification rites, the time *after* by wine in abundance (good wine), full vessels, drawing of "water" and tasting of wine. This temporal structure links Jesus' action with his "hour" and draws attention to ἡ ὥρα μου in Jesus' first speech as an important key to the interpretation of the entire text.[21]

The meaning of *the first exchange* as a whole, however, is not completely sure. An analysis of the individual elements of the speeches, the Johannine parallels in 11:1ff. 4:46ff; 9:1ff; 3:1ff, and a general two-level thinking on Jn's part led me to interpret it as a shift marker, *altering horizon or perspective*. It seems most plausible to regard this as a typically Johannine way of beginning a narrative: the one party speaks and argues from ordinary human conditions which are described in a more polemic context as κατ' ὄψιν, 7:24, or κατὰ σάρκα 8:15, while Jesus reasons on a different level, which is always concerned with his work in general and the Father's acts of mission through the Son. This literary device on the part of the author would seem to be a means to elicit from the reader a right perspective on Jesus and who he is.[22] The change in perspective thus involves not only a deeper meaning in the narrative but also—as in v. 11—shows that it is concerned with Jesus Christ.

Both the time structure and the shift of horizon are primarily linked with the speeches. Of the information given in parenthetical form, we shall only mention

---

[20] Thus Lindars, Comm., ad loc., without explicit motivation. Wedding and wine, however, may be symbols for many things; see 2.2, U 2 and U 7. A determination of which elements have a symbolic meaning is not sufficient to establish the message of the text.

[21] This is stressed by many interpreters; see above 2.1 and 2.2, U 9c.

[22] We find the same purpose expressed in 20:30f.

v. 6 concerning *the water vessels for the Jewish purification rites,* since it does not seem at all necessary for the action.[23] The author, who is otherwise extremely sparing with details must have had a definite reason for drawing the reader's attention to the fact that they were Jewish purification vessels. All the details in v. 6 presumably emphasize the purification function. Thus Jesus' action is related to an essential element in the Judaism which is the background of Jn. At the same time we know that "good wine" may be a symbol of the new eschatological order which the Jews were expecting. The narrator's intention in v. 6 may be connected with his idea that Jesus' act introduces the new age. The old is replaced by what Jesus brings. This replacement motif is supported by the macrostructure of the text, by the information in v. 6 and, particularly, by the context in which Jesus and the consequences of his work replace the Jewish and the Samaritan religion.[24]

I wish to suggest the following *total interpretation,* derived from these *striking features of the author's way of narrating* what happened at Cana—they are all in harmony with his post resurrection point of view. In his account of Jesus' works at the beginning of his earthly activity, the evangelist considers *Jesus' saving acts in general.* Indeed the narrative deals with an isolated event in Jesus' life, but its real objective and theme is Jesus' *ergon* as a whole and its implications, i.e. according to the Gospel in general, God's saving acts in Jesus Christ, the union between the Father and the Son and its manifestation in the faith of the disciples. These acts culminated in *the "hour" of Jesus* but also cover the time *before* and the time *after* this "hour". All three periods are projected into the Cana narrative, giving us the same dominant structure in the account as in the rest of the Gospel. The essential point is that the *change* coincides with Jesus' "hour": the old "religion" is replaced by a new one. Since Jesus was the Messiah, the Son of God, 20:31, the ordinances and status of the people of God are changed and a "new" people of God emerges. The new, however, is not really new but a part of the old; it is the true people of God in all ages. There is here a continuity in God's saving acts. The narrator saw elements of this profound change in the wedding at Cana and this vision has formed his narrative in all its parts.

This interpretation from basic features of the text is in close harmony with the linguistic context: 1:19ff gives us a comprehensive picture of Jesus as the Messiah, the Son of God.[25] It also describes the relationship between the "old" and the "new". 1:35ff tell how Jesus gathers a group of people round him who confess him as King of "Israel", while 2:13ff relates how Jesus "replaces" and

[23] The information given in v. 9 (= U 21—24) is partly a preparation for the last speech of the text.

[24] This replacement motif is the key to the interpretation of the text according to some scholars; see above, 2.1.

[25] See especially Schnackenburg, Comm., ad loc., and his excursus on the names of Jesus in ch. 1, pp. 321ff.

"fulfils" the old order.[26] The interpretation also agrees with the rest of the Gospel, which deals to a high degree with the manner in which the true Israel is brought forth from the people of Israel.[27] It explains the text in its entirety and the many characteristics my analysis brought out previously. So I consider that this interpretation should provide the norm for the determination of the "symbolical possibilities" of the text and of its character (text type).[28]

2.4.3 The Sinai Screen in Jn 1:19—2:11 (22)

My proposed interpretation is verified and defined in greater detail by what I have called the Sinai screen in Jn 1:19—2:11.[29] By referring to Potin (1971) and Serra (1971) I previously indicated some agreements between our text and the Jewish interpretation of the events at Sinai (Ex 19—24).[30] These concerned the phrases τῇ ἡμέρᾳ τῇ τρίτῃ, ἐκλήθη, ὅ τι ἂν λέγῃ ὑμῖν ποιήσατε, ἐφανέρωσεν τὴν δόξαν αὐτοῦ and ἐπίστευσαν εἰς αὐτόν.[31] Here I shall return to these elements in the light of my total interpretation, adding the purification motif, the wedding setting, the symbol of the wine and the description of the disciples.

Potin and Serra make special mention of the counting of days in 1:19ff and the expression *on the third day*.[32] This timing is also given in the Hebrew text, Ex 19:10, 11, 16, appearing in the LXX with the same expression as we have in v. 1.[33] The text describes how on the first day of the third month after the Exodus

---

[26] See, for example, Dodd 1953, pp. 297ff, Brown, Comm., p. cxliii, and Lindars, Comm., pp. 133ff.

[27] For justification of this statement, see the arguments in Robinson 1959—60, Bowker 1964—65, Meeks 1972 and de Jonge 1972—73, and also below, ch. 5.

[28] My interpretation, with regard to those given in 2.1, is partly a combination of the Christological interpretation and the replacement motif interpretation, but it seems to exclude a specific "Messianic", sacramental or mariological interpretation. Note the reservations given above in note 19.

[29] I use "screen" and not "pattern" or "structure" or "motif" because of its *dynamic* character and its usefulness in an analysis of the semantic structure of a text and the postsemantic processes (see 1.2) behind a text. I obtained the concept from M. Furberg in Andersson-Furberg [2]1967, pp. 87f, who refers to the article "Metaphors" of Max Black, reprinted in *Models and Metaphors* (Ithaca N.Y. 1962), and M.C. Beardsley, *Aesthetics* (New York and Burlingame 1958), pp. 134—44. For the use of this term, see also below 3.5.2 and ch. 5.

[30] The date of the Jewish material is difficult to determine, but the Jewish exposition of the Sinai event mentioned is confirmed by different traditions, and seems to belong to NT times. See Serra 1971, pp. 30ff, and Potin 1971, vol. 1, pp. 201ff, and the passages quoted in the following examination. On the eschatological interpretation of the Sinai-Tradition in Qumran, see Betz 1967—68.

[31] See above, 2.2, U 1, U 10, U 30 and U 31.

[32] See above, 2.2, U 1.

[33] MT has יום השלישי with ל or ב, the Targums תליתאה יומא with some variations (see Potin 1971, vol. 2, pp. 21, 27). We have also a temporal marking in v. 15: in MT לשלשת ימים, in the Targ. לתלחא יומין (Potin 1971, vol. 2, p. 26), in LXX τρεῖς ἡμέρας.

from Egypt,[34] the Israelites arrive at Sinai and camp by the mountain. There God speaks with Moses, and through him tells the people of Israel: "... If you will obey my voice and keep my covenant, you shall be my own possession among all peoples ... You shall be to me a kingdom of priests and a holy nation" (19:5f). And they answer "together": "All that the Lord has spoken we will do" (19:8). God then tells Moses that he intends to show himself to the people and that they should make ready: "Consecrate them today and tomorrow, and let them wash their garments, and be ready by *the third day;* for on *the third day* the Lord will come down upon Mount Sinai in the sight of all the people" (19:10f).[35]

So *on the third* day God came down on Sinai—with fire and smoke, long trumpet blasts, thunder and lightning, and wrapped in darkness—and spoke with Moses. In such a way Israel receives the ten commandments, 20:1—21, the terms of the covenant and a list of ordinances, 20:22—23:33. Moses conveys these to the people and they again answer with one voice: "All the words which the Lord has spoken we will do" (24:3). Next morning Moses builds an altar and causes Israel to sacrifice to her God. When he has read the book of the covenant to them they reply for the third time, "All that the Lord has spoken we will do and obey" (24:7). Moses then took the sacrificial blood and sprinkled it on the people and said "Behold the blood of the covenant which the Lord has made with you in accordance with all these words". Moses and Aaron, Nadab and Abihu then climbed the mountain together with 70 of the elders of Israel and there "saw the God of Israel". When they had "beheld" God, they ate and drank (24:11). Later we find Moses alone on the mountain and "the glory of the Lord" was revealed to him and to all the Israelites (24:16f). He remained on the mountain for 40 days.

The time of these events, which made the Israelites God's people, is only partly defined in the Hebrew text. Four days are mentioned, 19:10f, 15f; 24:4. The "third" day stands in the centre. From the narrative, however, it is natural to imagine more days. Moreover in the Jewish tradition the chronology was later defined. The most complete counting of days, as mentioned above, is to be found in the Targum Pseudo-Jonathan: eight days, with the "third day" as the sixth.[36]

---

[34] The timing of the event in MT is vauge ("in the third month ... on that day"). The text was in Jewish tradition read as "on the first day of the third month" and connected with the feast of Weeks, which fell on the sixth day of the third month (i.e. on the day when the Law was given at Sinai), Str.-B., vol. 2, p. 601, M. Delcor in Dict. de la Bible, Suppl., vol. 7, col. 838ff, Noack 1968, pp. 93ff, and Potin 1971, vol. 1, pp. 119ff. This vagueness of MT may depend on the Jewish feast calender, Rylaarsdam, Comm., ad Ex 19:1, and Delcor, col. 866.

[35] The Targums present this as a *revelation* of the *doxa* of the Lord. See the texts quoted above, 2.2, U 30.

[36] On the date and character of Targ. Pseudo-Jonathan, see Levine 1971a, 1971b and Kupier 1970, 1971a, 1971b.

Mekilta also inserts the third day in a similar time table,[37] while we encounter two traditions in the Talmud: the giving of the law took place on either the sixth or the seventh day of the month.[38] This determination of the third day as the last in a scheme of six days is not confirmed in texts from the NT period,[39] but the material shows that the tradition is old.[40] So when Jn collects material on John the Baptist, the baptism of Jesus, the calling of the disciples and the wedding at Cana, and assigns them to an "introductory week" of six days, the last being described as "the third day", the possibility of relating this to the great week of preparation at Sinai immediately presents itself.[41] This association becomes the more probable when we find that even the selection and shaping of the material in Jn 1:19ff was influenced by Sinai concepts.[42] I consider that Jn, in his chronological pattern from the Sinai theophany in 1:19ff, was trying to show how the new covenant and its people came into being through Jesus and those belonging to him, an occurrence which is seen to culminate on the third day at the wedding at Cana, where Jesus revealed his *doxa* and the disciples believed in him.[43] The events narrated in 1:19ff are seen through a screen derived from the Sinai theophany.

Serra also assigns great significance to the *obedience* motif. It too appears in the Hebrew text but is strengthened in the Jewish tradition.[44] There Israel is represented as the only nation which was willing to accept God's terms and promised to *hear* and *obey* what God *said* and *commanded*.[45] Serra here sees an indirect identification between *Jesus' mother* in Jn 2 and the Israelites at Sinai.[46]

[37] Mek ad Ex 19:3 ("Dies ist der zweite Tag") and Mek ad Ex 19:10 ("*heute*, d.i. der 4. Tag. *Und morgen*, d.i. der 5. Tag. . . . *den dritten Tag*, d.i. der 6. Tag, an welchem die Thora gegeben wurde"; tr. by Winter-Wünsche).

[38] See, for example, b Shab 86b; 87a; b Yom 4b and b Taan 28b. See also Serra 1971, pp. 30f.

[39] It is not mentioned in, for example, Josephus or Philo, Serra 1971, p. 30.

[40] The same temporal scheme in PRE 41 and 46, in Friedlander's translation, p. 318: "On the sixth of Sivan the Holy One, blessed be He, was revealed unto Israel on Sinai", and p. 359: "Rabbi Elazar, son of 'Azariah, said: On Friday, on the 6th of the month, at the sixth hour of the day, Israel received the Commandments". For further discussion of the age of the traditions, see Serra 1971, pp. 30ff. He also interprets the notes of time in the Transfiguration pericope as referring to these days at Sinai ($\mu\epsilon\vartheta'$ $\dot{\eta}\mu\acute{\epsilon}\rho\alpha\varsigma$ $\ddot{\epsilon}\xi$, Mk 9:2; Mt 17:1; $\dot{\omega}\sigma\epsilon\grave{\iota}$ $\dot{\eta}\mu\acute{\epsilon}\rho\alpha\iota$ $\dot{o}\kappa\tau\acute{\omega}$ Lk 9:28), Serra 1971, pp. 30f.

[41] On the preparation at Sinai, see Mek ad Ex 19, which places the events of Ex 24:5—8, too, before the sixth day. See the following analysis and Potin 1971, vol. 1, pp. 203ff, especially p. 212, and Grassi 1972, p. 133.

[42] On the composition of Jn 1:19—51, see Muilenberg 1932.

[43] For another example of how "typology" has been chronology, see Jn 12—19 and its six-day-scheme; see above, 2.2, U 1 and U 9b, and Weise 1966.

[44] See above, 2.2, U 10.

[45] On the universal character of the Sinai revelation and on the determination to Israel, see Potin 1971, vol. 1, pp. 248ff.

[46] Serra 1971, pp. 20, 38f.

This does not wholly agree with the text, where it is *the servants* who hear and obey Jesus' instructions, and *the disciples* who believe in him. The servants' obedience has an excellent parallel in the Sinai material. The fact that the author is interested in them, and in his account refers to similarities between them and Jesus' disciples as they are described in Jn, is simply explained by the already mentioned Sinai screen, as is his concentration on the disciples in v. 11.

The fact that Jesus *revealed his glory* and that the disciples *believed* in him also has close parallels in the Sinai material which I need not discuss once more.[47] Serra would also see a parallel between Jesus and Moses in 2:2 (ἐκλήθη) and 2:12 (κατέβη) and Ex 19:20,25, partly to explain the cryptic transitional passage in 2:12.[48] It is difficult to find sufficiently cogent reasons for such an assumption. The disciples were invited as well as Jesus, 2:2, and the usage seems quite natural for a presentation of Jesus as a wedding guest. There is reason—to explain 2:12 and the item οὐ πολλὰς ἡμέρας —to see also 2:12—22 as a part of the material inserted under the Sinai screen. It would then stand for the seventh and eight days, Ex 24. The shifts in the material at Jn's disposal were so great that he could only link the events chronologically with the vague οὐ πολλὰς ἡμέρας. Several of the themes in Ex 24 and Jn 2:12—22 go together: sacrifice to atone for the sins of the people, the blood of the covenant, Jesus' death, God's *shekinah,* the eighth day as the day of resurrection etc. I leave open the question of the connection for the time being.

The *purification motif* may be cited as reason for an inclusion of 2:12—22 in the Sinai screen. We have seen how this permeates Jn, and not least Jn 1:19—2:22.[49] The purification of the people plays a fundamental role in the Jewish exposition of the events at Sinai. The starting-point is here in the Hebrew text, which refers to how the people consecrated themselves and washed their garments, 19:14f, and how Moses threw *blood* on the people and offered *sacrifice,* 24:5—8. According to the Targum exposition Moses' sacrifice was "un sacrifice d'expiation qui reconcilie Israël et son Dieu".[50] The Targums read in Ex 24:8 "he poured blood on the altar to expiate(לכפרא)for the people". In 24:11 they note that the people rejoiced that their "sacrificial gifts were graciously accepted" (דאתקבלו ברעוא).[51] In 19:14 they make a significant change to the effect that the people *made* their clothes *white* (וחוורו).[52] All their former

[47] See above, 2.2, U 30, and Serra 1971, pp. 20f.
[48] Serra 1971, pp. 17f.
[49] See above, 2.2, U 14.
[50] Potin 1971, vol. 1, p. 213. Potin has an extended analysis of the purification motif in the Sinai texts but does not connect it with Jn 1:19ff. Serra does not mention the purification theme. This motif plays an important role in the Qumran material, Betz 1967—68, pp. 93ff.
[51] For the variants in the Targums, see Potin, vol. 1, pp. 148f, 151f. The interpretation of Ex 24:5—8 as an expiational ritual is confirmed by Mek ad Ex 19:10ff and Philo, De Dec. 2. Cf. Mt 26:28 par. and Heb 9:19ff.
[52] MT: יכבסו, LXX: ἔπλυναν. This is the case in all Targums, also in Ex 19:10, according to

sins were forgiven and they became holy and perfect.[53]

Mekilta gives a similar picture of the Israelites at Sinai. Israel does *penance* (תשרבה) before the meeting with the Holy One,[54] and the *midrash* of 19:11 says that every Israelite had to be *baptized with water* (טבילה).[55] The whole of Israel was cleansed with water at Sinai. Despite all the difficulties this involves, the *midrash* also assigns the events described in Ex 24:4—8 (the sacrifices, the promises) to the fifth day, therefore to the week of preparation. Thus the giving of the Law on the sixth day is the absolutely decisive event in the Sinai cycle. Israel then met the Holy One and must then itself be holy. God purified the virgin Israel before he plighted his troth to her, in Ezekiel's words in 16:7ff. All her sins are forgiven: never again in the Jewish exposition is Israel regarded as so perfect and so pure as during the 40 days at Sinai. They were holy kings and priests, Ex 19:6.[56]

This pronounced purification motif in the Jewish material sheds new light on Jn 1:19ff and the central role of purification there.[57] John the Baptist with his *baptism with water* stands within the context of the old covenant, and only by revelation can he know of the new covenant to come: one who will *baptize in the Spirit*.[58] His function is to reveal to "Israel" the person who will baptize with the Spirit 1:31ff,[59] so his chief message is: "*Behold the Lamb of God who takes away the sin of the world*", 1:29,36.[60] This is the message which makes John's disciples into Jesus' disciples. Purification, liberation from sin, is essential—as it was once at Sinai—if a people of God is to be born.[61] In Jn's account it is there in

the texts in Potin 1971, vol. 2, pp. 20, 26. Similarly in Philo, De Dec 11. For further material on Israel's purification at Sinai, see Potin 1971, vol. 1, pp. 211ff.

[53] Compare the Targum presentation of Israel at Sinai as a people "of one heart" (Ex 19:2), of "a perfect heart" (בלבה שלמא 19:8). Similarly in Ex 24:3 and Hab 3:1.

[54] Mek ad 19:2.

[55] According to the translation of Winter-Wünsche: "Und sie sollen ihre Kleider waschen. Und woher entnehme ich, dass sie ein Tauchbad benötigten? Siehe, ich folgere: ... Es gibt kein Waschen der Kleider in der Thora, wobei ein Tauchbad nicht nötig wäre".

[56] See, for example, Mek ad Ex 19 and 20:18; PRE 41 (they were as angels); Cant R ad 4:7, b Shab 146a (no "craving" in their hearts); Potin 1971, vol. 1, pp. 211ff.

[57] And, perhaps, on the purification in Jn as a whole, see above 2.2, U 14, and below, 3.2.2.

[58] On water and spirit as symbols for the old and the new order, see Robinson 1966, pp. 20f.

[59] John the Baptist is the witness to the transition from the old to the new covenant. Cf. Nicodemus in ch. 3: he cannot accept this "transition". He does not understand that Israel must be born by *both* water *and* Spirit to "see" the Kingdom of God. Simon Peter, also, at first protests violently against a purification by Jesus, Jn 13:1ff.

[60] On the meaning of αἴρειν, see Rydbeck 1967, p. 163. Weise 1966, pp. 55ff, would explain 1:29 in this context by suggesting that John the Baptist said this on a Friday according Jn's temporal scheme in 1:19ff.

[61] This parallelism may be supported by the presentation of the people of God in Rev as clothed in "white garments", 3:4f, 18; 6:11; 7:9, as those who have "washed their robes and made them white in the blood of the Lamb", 7:14.

Jesus Christ. The revelation of Jesus as the Lamb of God[62] by John who baptized with water, therefore, has a natural place in 1:19ff, if we see the text from the Sinai screen. The Jewish purification vessels in our text have their full meaning. That which Jesus gives replaces the whole of the old purification process. Jesus' disciples, Jesus' own people, the people of his possessing, are in Jn cleansed by Jesus' death (blood), 13:1ff; 1 Jn 1:7,9,[63] and by Jesus' word (revelation), 15:2f; 17:14ff. So there must be a connection between the water which Jesus gives in 2:1—11, that which when tested proved to be "good wine", and Jesus' *blood* and *word*. The wine in our text would refer to the same reality as the word, the blood, the Spirit and other expressions in the Johannine writings, and cannot be bound to only one of them.[64]

In the quotation from Ezekiel, Israel at Sinai is represented as a virgin to whom the Lord plights his troth.[65] The Jewish tradition concerning the events at Sinai often mentions *the marriage of the Lord and Israel.*[66] It is not particularly far-fetched from a Sinai perspective to allow events at a village wedding—historical or imaginary—to carry a message of something which, according to the narrator, replaces the old wedding at Sinai. The author did not however use this element in *allegorical* fashion, so as to make Jesus consistently the bridegroom, and Jesus' mother or someone else the bride etc. It may be an allusive element for the initiated reader. Yet the essential point here is that the Sinai screen explains how material concerning a wedding could be incorporated into the Johannine week of introduction.[67]

There remain two features in the text where for various reasons the parallelism cannot be regarded as equally certain. The first concerns *the wine* in the text. This is usually interpreted eschatologically.[68] Yet in the light of the Sinai screen I

---

[62] On the revelation scheme in 1:29, 36, see de Goedt 1961—62.

[63] Cf. 19:34; the water and the blood from Jesus' side are evidence of his death and its implications.

[64] See below, 2.4.4.

[65] On the midrashic character of Ezek 16 (and its dependence on earlier material), see Bloch 1955. The theme of Israel as the bride of the Lord occurs several times in the OT: Hos 1—3; Jer 3:1ff; Ezek 23:1ff; also Is 1:21f; 62:5f. Cf. Knight 1959, pp. 177ff.

[66] On marriage terminology already in the MT, see Knight 1959, pp. 218ff. The Jewish material is extensive. See E. Stauffer in ThWNT, vol. 1, p. 652, Potin 1971, pp. 216f, also Ginzberg, vol. 3, p. 92, vol. 6, p. 36, and the Jewish exposition of SofS, Riedel 1898, Vulliaud 1925. "Toute l'exégèse rabbinique de Cantique chante également l'amour de Dieu pour son épouse Israël, et la perfection de l'amour de l'épouse aux jours du Sinaï", Potin 1971, p. 216.

[67] Note in this connection the role of Moses in some Sinai texts, for example, in PRE 41: he is presented as "best man" (שׁוֹשְׁבִין) who leads the bride (Israel) to the bridegroom (the Lord). Rabbinic material in Str.-B., vol. 1, pp. 45f, 500ff. John the Baptist describes himself in the same terms in Jn 3:29 (ὁ φίλος τοῦ νυμφίου), marking his relation to Jesus. He has a similar role in 1:35ff. On the function of John the Baptist, see also below, 3.2.2.

[68] See above, 2.1 and 2.2, U 7.

would see a connection with *the Law* which Israel received at Sinai—and all that the Law means to the Israelite.[69] The wine would stand as a symbol of the Law, especially when the events at Sinai are depicted under the guise of a wedding.[70] The *midrash* to the words "he brought me to the banqueting house" in SofS 2:4 reads: "Die Gemeinde Israel spricht: Gott brachte mich in den grossen Weinkeller, an den Sinai, und gab mir dort mein Panier, das Gesetz, die Gebote, die guten Werke, und ich nahm sie mit grosser Liebe an".[71] This *midrash* in its final state is thought to be quite late, but judging by the traditional interpretation of SofS the interpretation quoted above would seem quite old.[72] To emphasize the wine in an account whose more profound significance was somehow comparable with the events at Sinai must have appeared natural, and may perhaps have indicated or confirmed the deeper meaning for those close to the author.

The second feature concerns *the description of the disciples* in 1:35ff. As in Ex 19 we have a gathering of the people of God before the revelation. In both cases the fact that they will *see* God, and his glory, is emphasized.[73] The Johannine description is concentrated in the person of Nathanael, the *true Israelite* who, in contrast to the rest of Israel, confesses Jesus as *Israel's* king, Nathanal in whom there is *no guile,* like Israel once before God at Sinai.[74] The promise to Nathanael (= the disciples) in 1:51 may, as we saw, be interpreted from the Sinai theophany.[75] The very meagre, and somewhat cryptic, details in the description of Jesus' disciples in 1:35ff may thus be explained from the Sinai screen, although the parallelism is not as strong here, at least as regards expression.

The *comparative analysis* could be taken much further by a thorough analysis of 1:19ff, and of the whole of St John's Gospel, the rest of the Johannine writings and other books in the NT, and by a more extensive survey of the Jewish material.[76] Yet with the purpose of the investigation in mind I consider that my analysis will suffice. I consider it proven that we have a Sinai screen in 1:19ff, which gives us special help in understanding the obscure narrative of the miracle at Cana. The result is supported by religious history in the form of Meeks' extensive comparative study of the Christology of Jn, in which he convincingly shows that the texts on Jesus as prophet and king must be understood from the Sinai

[69] On the wine as a symbol for the Law, see the material in Str.-B., vol. 2, pp. 484, 614.
[70] The Jewish exposition of SofS, Vulliaud 1925, p. 62. See, for example, Cant R ad 1:2, 4, 9, 12; 2:1, 4, 14; 3:11; 4:4, 7; 5:1; 8:5.
[71] Cant R ad 2:4, Aug. Wünsche's translation in Bibliotheca Rabbinica, vol. 1, p. 59. We have the same concepts in Cant R ad 1:2 (p. 15; cf. p. 29).
[72] Riedel 1898, pp. 41ff.
[73] See above, 2.2, U 6 and U 30.
[74] See above, notes 52 and 55, and the presentation of the purification of Israel at Sinai.
[75] See above, 2.2, U 31.
[76] An analysis of Jn (and 1 Jn) from this Sinai perspective would be most interesting. —Cf. also 1 Fet. —Many central concepts in Jn seem to provoke an analysis from a covenantal setting. Cf. Brown, Comm., p. 753.

theophany as it was expounded in the evanglist's environment.[77] The Sinai screen explains the composition and many of the details of the introductory week in Jn. It confirms the total interpretation of the Cana narrative which I suggested above. The narrator saw in his material an equivalent of the events that once took place at Sinai, and this provides the best explanation of the way in which the present text was shaped and constructed.

2.4.4 Some Other Textual Features

The interpretation of the text here given and the Sinai screen just presented are based on, and explain, a large number of the features of the text, in particular its composition, the comment in v. 11, the temporal structure with $\dot{\eta} \, \omega \rho a$, the general structure of events, the speeches at the beginning, the item on the connection between the water vessels and the purification of the Jews, and the description of the water as $\dot{o} \, \kappa a \lambda \dot{o}\varsigma \, o\tilde{\iota}vo\varsigma$, the expression $\tau\tilde{\eta} \, \dot{\eta}\mu\acute{e}\rho a \, \tau\tilde{\eta} \, \tau\rho\acute{\iota}\tau\eta$, the wedding situation, the role of the wine in the action and the obedience motif.[78] Nevertheless, as the earlier analysis showed, there are other textual features and the question is whether they can be reconciled with my explanation of the message of the text. Without discussing each element anew I would answer this question in the affirmative. Indeed several features may be adduced in support of my interpretation. Whether all the features also have a communicative function and thus lead the reader to the real message of the text is uncertain. For those who were very close to the author and were already conversant with his material the majority of the textual features would have helped to convey the message. The entire text seems to be woven in one piece and wholly shaped from the symbolic meaning of the text. Finally I shall mention some elements illustrating this.

The *Galilean location* is one of the outstanding features of the text. The event took place $\dot{e}v \, Ka\nu\grave{a} \, \tau\tilde{\eta}\varsigma \, \Gamma a\lambda\iota\lambda a\acute{\iota}a\varsigma$, vv. 1 and 11. In Jn Galilee is primarily the place where people accept Jesus as the revealer and become his disciples. There the true people of God come into being.[79] When the evangelist sees in his narrative the growth of the people of the new covenant, it is easy to understand why he emphasizes the identification with Galilee. The attribute $\tau\tilde{\eta}\varsigma \, \Gamma a\lambda\iota\lambda a\acute{\iota}a\varsigma$, not only points out which Cana is meant, but also links the event with the "birthplace" of the new people of God in Jn.

There may well be in this geographical symbolism a special interest in the place-name *Cana*, even though the author does not give its meaning, as in Jn 9:7, and

[77] Meeks 1967, passim. See also Meeks 1972.

[78] See above, 2.4.2 and 2.4.3. The analysis of the information flow (2.3.6) also supports my interpretation as does the "openness" of the end of the text (2.3.1).

[79] See above, 2.2, U 3, and now also Díez Merino 1972 (Galilee as "terra christiana", the Galileans in Jn as "populus christianus"). For further discussion of Galilee contra Judea, see below, 3.2.3.

thus allow it to have a communicative function. The name Cana, meaning "ownership, possession" may suggest the people who were God's own possession, those whom the Son received from the Father, Jesus' "own".[80] The Sinai screen also actualises the meaning of Cana since the Sinai texts explicitly state that Israel became God's own *possession* at the wedding at Sinai, Ex 19:5.[81] Yet it is here difficult to find definite criteria. In any case a symbolic meaning of the place-name is certainly in accord with the message the author is trying to convey.[82]

The author also describes the event at Cana as ἀρχὴ τῶν σημείων. Previously I adduced reasons for understanding this phrase as somewhat more than a counting of Jesus' signs, roughly synonymous with πρῶτον σημεῖον. This suggestion is now supported by the total interpretation: the narrator regards the miracle at Cana as a basic element in Jesus' work: the act of the Son transforms the old covenant into a new covenant with its own people. The designation ἀρχή should therefore be seen as a deliberate wording, derived from the deeper meaning of the text. It suggests to the reader that the sign of Cana is of special weight, that a fundamental attribute of Jesus' work is here concealed. It is a primary sign, representing Jesus' work as a whole.

There remain the references to individuals and to roles, seen in the light of my comments on the message of the text. All the features of the description of *the servants* point in the same direction: they are described with the people of the new covenant in mind, in the following often called the new people of God. They have an important role in the narrative: they obey Jesus' mother, they hear and do what Jesus says, they are "the drawers of water", knowing "whence" the water/the wine came, and they are designated οἱ διάκονοι. All these attributes link them with the new people of God. The fact that the disciples have a similar function in the text as a whole, and especially in the context of 1:35ff, need not

---

[80] Note the combination "Nathanael of Cana in Galilee", 21:2.

[81] MT סְגֻלָּה, LXX: περιούσιος. All Targums have עַם חֲבִיבִין, in some versions with הֵיךְ סְגֻלָּה, Potin 1971, vol. 2, p. 13, by Potin (vol. 1, p. 47) translated "un peuple d'aimes (comme une propriété personelle)". Some have also the addition אָחֳרָן "another". Cf. Jub 16:17f. Mek ad Ex 15:16f describes the people of Israel as God's "possession" (קִנְיָן). Targ. Onkelos and Targ. Pseudo-Jonathan—like Peshitta—always translate סְגֻלָּה with חֲבִיבִין, Potin 1971, p. 52. Cf. 4 Ezra 5:27. Are there any connections between this description of God's people at Sinai and the presentation of Jesus' disciples, especially "the Beloved Disciple" in Jn, ὁ ἄλλος μαθητὴς ὃν ἐφίλει ὁ Ἰησοῦς 20:2, and similar expression in 13:23; (18:15f); 19:26; 21:7,20?

[82] It is worth noting that the evangelist in 9:7 does not start from a direct translation of the name of the pool, in Hebrew שִׁילֹחַ or שֶׁלַח, in Greek Σιλωάμ. He revocalizes the word or gives a free etymological interpretation. His interpretation of the name of the pool may have a background in Jewish expositions (of Gen 49:10 and Is 8:6)—like our text. See Brown and Schnackenburg, Comm., ad 9:7. On symbolism of names in OT, see Barr 1969. —A symbolic interpretation of Cana actualizes Hanhart's suggestion of a connection to Is 11:11 (Hanhart 1970, p. 43, note 3, referring to Jn 4:46ff). For a discussion of Is 11:11, see below, 3.4.6 and 3.5.

have prevented the narrator from describing the servants with the new people of God in mind, if he were unwilling to form an allegory in which every single element had one transferred meaning. The servants have a part to play in the total course of events, but at the same time we find them described in such a way as to suggest the symbolic meaning of the text, in which they may be said to represent the new people of God.

Thus the disciples and the servants are closest to Jesus. They are present before, during and after Jesus' "hour". What of Jesus' mother and the steward? They have a part to play in the event as a whole, but at the same time they may have a representative role. Let us first consider *the steward*. There are elements in his reaction which are reminiscent of Nicodemus in ch. 3, the Pharisees in ch. 9 and "the Jews" in general in Jn. They see the results of Jesus' acts, they admit "the miracles", but they cannot perceive Jesus' identity. Despite their deep insight their judgement is wrong. The description ἀρχιτρίκλινος indicates that his position was superior to that of the servants, as does the instruction that they take the water/the wine to him.[83] We find a similar attribute of "the Jews" in several passages in Jn, such as 1:19ff; 7:45ff; 9:13ff; 12:42 and 16:1ff.[84] The superior status is to be found in our text, but not the hostility. The steward is never confronted with Jesus, but only with the servants and the bridegroom. His act and his words follow Jesus' "hour" and concern the results of what Jesus did when his "hour" had come. He is explicitly compared with the servants and contrasted with them as regards the "knowledge whence". These features may be interpreted as if the narrator in him saw a kind of representative of the Judaism which rejected Jesus and his work, of that part of the old people of God which was not included in the new. He thinks κατὰ σάρκα. He does not understand God's work in the Son, because he is not born of water and the Spirit, of God himself. This role of representation cannot be said to be well worked out and strongly marked in the text but seems to be defensible from the chief message of the text and the features cited.

Jesus' mother is only active in the text before Jesus' "hour", in conversation with Jesus and with the servants. Formerly I found it difficult to reconcile her roles and therefore referred to Jesus' mother A and Jesus' mother B. The uncertainty in the interpretation of the first exchange of speeches is the main source of difficulty in explaining her function in the text. Her second speech, on the other hand, gives a clear picture, so I prefer to begin there. From what I said above, Jesus' mother cannot be said to represent the people of the new convenant, although she is very close to them.[85] Her function somehow *precedes* the new

---

[83] Compare the remarkable formulation in Mt 8:4 ὕπαγε σεαυτὸν δεῖξον τῷ ἱερεῖ... εἰς μαρτύριον αὐτοῖς and Hartman's analysis of the later phrase, Hartman 1963, pp. 62ff.

[84] Martyn 1968 describes the conflict in ch. 9 and ch. 5 as a conflict between believers of Jesus and Orthodox Jews of the evangelist's own time.

[85] See above, 2.2, U 4 and U 9b, 2.3.5 and 2.4.3. Against Brown, Comm., p. 109 ("we believe

covenant and Jesus' "hour" when, according to Jn, the Church was born. Reasoning from Jn as a whole and my earlier analysis, I would prefer to describe Jesus' mother as representing that part of the people of God which really is faithful to its tradition and its faith, those who believe in Moses and the Scriptures and are thereby the link between old and new. By her side stand, according to Jr, Abraham, 8:39ff, Moses and the Scriptures, 5:39, 45ff, Isaiah, 12:41 and John the Baptist, 1:29ff; 3:27ff. They all belong to the old covenant, but by obeying the God of this covenant they are witnesses to and for his Son, Jesus Christ. For God there is no separation between the old and the new. According to Jn, God made of those who were truly faithful to the old covenant a "new" people, a "new" Israel.[86] Judging by the second speech, the role of Jesus' mother approaches that of John the Baptist: they both bear witness to, and point to, him who God sent to baptize $\dot{\epsilon}\nu$ $\pi\nu\epsilon\dot{\upsilon}\mu\alpha\tau\iota$.[87] Such an interpretation explains the feature in the text that obedience to Jesus' mother is at the same time obedience to Jesus. Moreover, it can easily be combined with Jn's words about Jesus' mother at the end of the Gospel. Jesus' mother is there until the hour. Then she is given a son, the beloved disciple, the new people of God, of which she herself forms a part.[88]

The first exchange of speeches can also be explained in the light of this total view of Jesus' mother in the Cana narrative. Her words in v. 3 may be seen as a first testimony to Jesus, a way of introducing him in the delicate situation then prevailing. This testimony is however on a lower level: she asks Jesus somehow to produce wine for the wedding guests. Jesus' reply in v. 4 raises her request to another level, concerning the Son's mission from his Father. In John the Baptist this change is paralleled by the special revelation he must be given in order to perceive who Jesus is, and who sent him, 1:31, 33f. The change of perspective is expressed in strong terms, formally addressed to Jesus' mother. One may well ask whether Jesus' reply is also intended to cause a shift in the reader's perspective. If this is the case, the relevance of the speech to the definition of the role of Jesus' mother is reduced, and it is easier to arrive at an homogenous picture of her in the text: she is described on the basis of *the true Israel within the framework of the old covenant,* the Israel which by God's work in Christ is

that the Johannine stress is on Mary as a symbol of the church"). The tendency is, even in Catholic circles, away from a mariological interpretation of the Cana narrative, Collins 1972, p. 125.

[86] Cf. the analysis of Jn 4 below, 3.5.

[87] She is not *representing* John the Baptist and his people, as Müller 1967, pp. 100f, suggests in his consequently allegorical interpretation of the Cana narrative.

[88] She may be a representative of the true people of God *in all ages* as the woman in Rev 12, but in our text she has a marked "preparing" role.

transformed into the "new" Israel.[89] It is natural to make consistent use of the term ἡ μήτηρ τοῦ Ἰησοῦ in such a perspective.[90] Nevertheless, as in the case of the steward of the feast, this representative aspect of the mother of Jesus is not primary in the text. The picture would then have been much clearer. It is rather a consequence of the total aspect which I previously found to be the standard for the production of our text.

This survey shows that the personal groupings which my analysis brought out,[91] with some reservations concerning the division into Jesus' mother A and Jesus' mother B, depend on the symbolic meaning of the text. The characters are not only agents in the course of events laid down by the narrative, but they are also depicted to some extent in a representative fashion, so as to point to different sides of the message which the author saw in his material. The entire text is coloured by a single idea. This concerns both the choice of material and the manner of its presentation, and not only that which is sometimes called "the Johannine insertions".[92] This final survey of the textual features also emphasizes the accuracy of my interpretation. It gives a function to, and explains, all the features which I previously found to make up our text.

Which elements then are symbolic? This was one of the main questions before. In different ways, and to differing degrees, the following expressions in the text proved to be especially dependent on a symbolic meaning:[93] τῇ ἡμέρᾳ τῇ τρίτῃ, γάμος, Κανὰ τῆς Γαλιλαίας, ἡ μήτηρ τοῦ Ἰησοῦ, γύναι, ἡ ὥρα μου, οἱ διάκονοι, ὅ τι ἂν λέγῃ ὑμῖν ποιήσατε, λίθιναι, κατὰ τὸν καθαρισμὸν τῶν Ἰουδαίων, ἕως ἄνω, ἀντλήσατε, ἀρχιτρίκλινος, ἔγευσατο τὸ ὕδωρ, οὐκ ᾔδει / ᾔδεισαν πόθεν ἐστίν, οἱ ἠντληκότες τὸ ὕδωρ, νυμφίον, τὸν καλὸν οἶνον, ἀρχήν, σημείων, ἐφανέρωσεν, δόξαν, ἐπίστευσαν εἰς.

There is little point in describing all these elements as symbolic. They differ greatly in character. Some are formulated from the Sinai screen, others are dependent on Johannine usage and thought, still others are generally associated with the symbolic meaning of the text. Their communicative power varies greatly in its strength. I prefer, therefore, to describe the text *as a whole* as symbolic, while these *elements* which, together with other textual features, indicate, and to varying extents announce, the symbolic meaning should be seen as different

---

[89] Michaud 1962, 1963 relieves the tension in the text by referring v. 3 more to a historical plane and v. 4 to a theological plane of the Johannine narrative.

[90] The word of address γύναι is also given a function in such a reading of the text: as a part of a shift marker, as an indication of her representative role and as a reference to the *motif* of γυνή in Jn. The *motif* of γυνή may partly be combined with my interpretation but it is difficult to say how much of the OT background is to be found in the use of γύναι in 2:4.

[91] See above, 2.3.5.

[92] See source critical work on Jn, for example, Fortna 1970, pp. 29ff.

[93] I leave out such features of the text as cannot be delimited to single elements of the text.

kincs of allusion. What I have shown here is that the text contains many and different allusive elements.

2.4.5 The Question of Text Type

Now at last it is possible to define more accurately the character of the text. What are its characteristics? As yet the answer is brief and preliminary.

1. The impression of the symbolic nature of the text has been reinforced more and more in the course of the investigation. At the same time as the author describes an external happening, he is suggesting something else: he is seeking to convey a message of which the external events are a "sign". This "deeper" meaning of the text, the symbolic meaning, even dominates his thinking when he shapes his material. The entire text is coloured by its symbolic message. So I have every reason to hold fast to the earlier definition: *a symbolic narrative text*.

2. The text can *not* be described as an *allegory*.[94] There is no consistent identification of expressions in the text with a transferred meaning, but several elements, for instance, may represent the same thing.[95] The wedding motif, which I found essential to the text, is not developed into an allegory.[96] The representative aspect in the descriptions of individuals I found to be merely secondary in some cases.[97] In my opinion, this proves that the text is not an allegory. Indeed it rather resembles Johannine imagery ("Bildreden") in all its variety.[98]

3. In order to bring out the symbolic meaning the author—consciously or unconsciously—uses different means: apart from the selection of material and its general presentation, a large number of *allusions* of different kinds, most of them connected with a Sinai screen and the perspective of Jesus' *ergon* in general (with its Johannine vocabulary). Individual *elements* may have a "symbolic" function in the sense that, as well as being part of the whole, they point out features belonging to the symbolic meaning, which is the author's chief message. I found that the text contains many such allusive elements.

I will for the time being give a wholly preliminary definition of the text type: *a symbolic narrative text with many allusive elements*.[99]

[94] Allegory as defined by, for example, L. Goppelt in ³RGG, vol. 1, col. 239: "Eine Allegorie im strengen Sinn ist eine Darstellung, die in allen Einzelzügen bildlichen Sinn hat, eine metaphora continua". Cf. the descriptions in Jülicher ²1910, pp. 49ff, and Lausberg, ³1967, pp. 139f, and also in ThWNT, vol. 5, p. 742 (Fr. Hauck). On the allegorical method of Philo, see Christiansen 1969.

[95] Note, for example, the roles of the servants and the disciples, of Jesus and the bridegroom.

[96] The bride, for example, is not mentioned. In some way the servants and the disciples correspond to her! Cf. Jn 3:29, discussed below, 3.2.2.

[97] See the conclusions above, 2.4.4.

[98] Jn 10 and Jn 15. On the literary character of the discourse on the good shepherd, see Olsson, ²1973, pp. 256f.

[99] For further discussion of the type of text, see below, 3.5.2. and ch.5.

3

A "Dialogue" Text, Jn 4:1—42

3.1 Introduction

The analysis of the short Cana narrative indicated certain "dramatic" qualities in the text.[1] Nevertheless it contained only one exchange of speeches, that between Jesus' mother and Jesus in vv. 3f, consisting of two speeches which were not easy to relate to each other. It was not a dialogue. I have chosen the account of Jesus in Samaria, Jn 4:1—42, as my second main text for analysis because it is manifestly *dramatic* in character and contains one of the longest *dialogues* in the Gospel. As mentioned below, it belongs to another group of Johannine texts. The narrative also gives us a *longer* unit of coherent composition, suitable for the type of analysis used in the previous account.[2]

In his well-known article on Johannine narrative style in the Festschrift to Gunkel, Hans Windisch cites Jn 4:1—42 as one of the best examples of "die breit ausgeführten, dramatisch ausgestalteten Erzählungen" in Jn and illustrates his assertion by translating the text as a "drama" in seven scenes.[3] In this group of texts he also includes the account of the man born blind, 9:1—41, the report of the raising of Lazarus, 11:1—53, and the final scene at Lake Tiberias, 21:1—23. "Es gibt kein synoptisches Gespräch", he says of Jn 4, "dass so ausführlich verläuft, dass so viel seelsorgerliche Kunst aus der Seite Jesu verrät, den Charakter der Person, die Jesus gegenübersteht, so treffend zeichnet, und so viel religiöse Themata anschlägt. Ohne Analogie ist auch das Auftreten der Jünger ... Auch der Inhalt des Zeugnisses Jesu ist reichhaltiger ... Ebensowenig kennt die Synopse die Einzelbekehrung als Vorstufe einer Massenbekehrung."[4]

---

[1] Use of direct speech, division into "scenes", etc. See 2.3.1, 2.3.4 and 2.4.2.

[2] If we combined the Cana narrative with 1:19—51, we should also arrive at a longer unit of coherent composition. The unity of 1:19—2:11 has been shown by my previous analysis, —see especially 2.4.3—Windisch 1923, pp. 191ff and Muilenberg 1932, pp. 42ff.

[3] Windisch 1923, pp. 175, 178ff. We have the same form of translation in Thompson 1918 and the same result in Schmid 1929.

[4] Windisch 1923, p. 181. He calls this kind of narrative in Jn "die dramatisch ausgesponnene Novelle". "Sie dankt ihre Entstehung und Ausgestaltung einer unleugbar bei dem Evangelisten vorhandenen Freude am Erzählen sowie dem Interesse an einer möglichst eindrucksvollen Demonstration der Glauben wirkenden Kraft und Offenbarung des Christus", p. 186.

I shall discuss the question of whether or not Windisch's total interpretation of Jn 4 as a pastoral dialogue does the text justice *after* the analysis of the text.[5] In this context his words can provide a general description of a group of texts (Jn 4; 9; 11; 21), which not only diverges from the style of the synoptic narratives[6] but also holds a special place in Jn. The traces of literary activity are particularly obvious here, and the Samaria narrative has often been praised for its artistic qualities, for instance by Reymond E. Brown: the evangelist has taken the material at his disposal "and with his masterful sense of drama and the various techniques of stage setting . . . formed it into a superb theological scenario". Various "dramatic touches have been skilfully applied to make this one of the most vivid scenes in the Gospel and to give the magnificent doctrine of living water a perfect setting".[7] One may very well ask why the author allowed his artistic skill full reign just here.

The choice of Jn 4 also offers me an opportunity to discuss Johannine *dialogues*. This is not a dialogue discourse in the technical sense of the term, with affirmation—negation arguments, yes—no responses, or answers to question with *who, what, where, which, how* etc.[8] The Samaria story provides examples of narrative, of exposition and of dialogue. Taken as a whole it, like the Cana narrative, should be included among narrative texts, with the difference that the exchange of speeches dominates in Jn 4. Many Johannine texts are in the nature of dialogues: 3:1—27; 7:1—8: 59; 9:1—10: 21; 11:1—44; 18:28—19:27 etc., and one often speaks of a special Johannine dialogue pattern.[9] An analysis of the Samaria text could therefore contribute, not only to the classification of the longer literary texts I just mentioned, but also to the problem of the form and function of the Johannine dialogue.

Nevertheless a number of scholars have pointed out inconsistencies and contradictions (aporias) in the text and seriously questioned its compositional literary unity.[10] At the beginning of this century, Wellhausen and Schwartz, in

[5] "Ein seelsorgerliches Gespräch", Windisch 1923, p. 186. My interpretation is given below in 3.5.

[6] On the narrative technique of the Synoptics, see Bultmann [7]1967 (1921), pp. 335ff, and the comparisons in Albertz 1921, pp. 2ff, and Windisch 1923, pp. 174ff. Dodd 1954—55 deals with the dialogue form of the Synoptic Gospels in comparison with Jn.

[7] Brown, Comm., p. 176, and see, besides the commentaries, Schmid 1929, p. 153 ("ein kleines Kunstwerk"), Dodd 1953, p. 311 ("a highly wrought dramatic dialogue, with an appropriate narrative setting") and Bligh 1962, p. 329 ("one of the most skilfully written passages in the fourth gospel").

[8] Nida-Taber 1969, pp. 132f, Longacre 1968, pp. 160ff, Klammer 1973.

[9] See, besides the commentaries, Connick 1948, pp. 167ff, Dodd 1954—55, pp. 60ff, and Leroy 1968, passim.

[10] This applies more to the Samaria text than to the Cana narrative. The unity of the text is defenced by, for example, Thompson 1918, Windisch 1923, Schmid 1929, Dodd 1953, pp. 311ff, Roustang 1958, pp. 345ff, Schnackenburg and Brown, Comm., ad loc. On the "contradictions" of the text, see especially Fortna 1970, pp. 189ff.

particular, brought out such aporias in their analyses of the text and explained them by assuming a "Grundschrift", which was later supplemented with various kinds of addition.[11] In more recent years scholars have attempted to discern different literary strata in Jn 4.[12] Schenke arrived at four layers in his analysis.[13] At the bottom, so to speak, there is "eine in sich vollständig geschlossene, volkstümliche, wunderhafte Erzählung von der Begegnung Jesus mit einer Samaritanerin". Like the next layer it has a basic trend: to establish the relationship between Samaritan and Jewish religion from the Christian point of view. This narrative would have included vv. 5–7, 9ab, 16–19, 28–30, 40. In a Palestinian environment it would later have been rewritten as a typical Jewish Christian narrative with the addition of vv. 20–22, 23 (partly), which are assumed to derive from a "Topos palästinensisch-urchristlicher, eschatologisch ausgerichteter Kontroverstheologie", and of vv. 35–36a, probably "ein selbständig umlaufendes Logion synoptischen Typs". This produces a "fast völlig in sich verständlich" unit, "eine in ihrem Verlauf folgerichtige und unter einem Thema stehende Erzählung". The material, which was incorporated in a somewhat disguised form in the first layer, is here discussed from three points of view: a) a concrete case, vv. 5–7, 9, b) in theory, vv. 20–23 and c) the aspect of mission, vv. 35–36a. This narrative is the evangelist's "source". By joining vv. 1 (partly), 3f, 8, 10–15, 23 (partly), 24–27, 31–34, 36b, 39, 41f, he tried—as he does everywhere in his Gospel—to show that Jesus "die Leben schenkende Offenbarung bringt, die von den Menschen im Glauben ergriffen werden muss". Finally, there is a fourth layer consisting of some post-Johannine additions: vv. 1 (ἔγνω ὁ κύριος ὅτι), 2, 9c and 37f.

Schenke's conclusions are in general agreement with Bultmann's analysis from 1941, which nevertheless stops at three layers.[14] Bultmann considers that vv. 4–9, 16–19 are strongly contradictory to vv. 10–15, which reveal typically Johannine features (misunderstanding, revelation discourses). The section on right cult site, vv. 20–26, deals with the original theme on a higher level, while vv. 31–38 are concerned with something completely different, the task of mission and its realization. Bultmann asserts that v. 39, which also has features of Johannine style, is "unmöglich" after v. 30, and vv. 39f "konkurrieren unerträglich". Thus, according to Bultmann's commentary, the original text included vv. 5–7, 9ab, 16–19, 28–30 and 40 with some small changes. Verse 7 must

[11] Wellhausen 1908, pp. 20ff, regards vv. 1–3, 8, 27, 37f as later *additions* and interprets vv. 30ff as referring to the Samaritans. Schwartz 1908, pp. 504ff, brings out many more aporias in the text.
[12] Cf. Wilkens 1959, pp. 23ff, on the related text in Jn 11. He discerns three strata: an original tradition, "eine *johanneische* Grundgestalt" and the text as it now stands. These three layers are parts of a "*Verkündigungsgeschichte* der Perikope", pp. 28ff.
[13] Schenke 1968, pp. 159ff.
[14] Bultmann, Comm., ad loc. A reconstruction of Bultmann's text in Smith 1965, pp. 39f.

have been followed by a speech marking that Jesus was not concerned with the social barriers. Bultmann refers to a similar legend about Buddha.

Bultmann's work on source criticism has recently been discussed, primarily by Robert T. Fortna, who tried in his book in 1970 to reconstruct "the narrative source underlying the Fourth Gospel".[15] His conclusions concerning Jn 4 differ from Bultmann's only insofar as he would add vv. 25f and, with some hesitation, also the end of v. 42. "It is quite obvious", he says of our text, "that a simple narrative . . . has been expanded by the addition of several dialogues on themes which have only incidental ties to the story proper. . . . The dialogues John has introduced are readily identified, each with its own theme (vv. 10–15, 20–24, 31–38) . . . When these are removed, a coherent story, with only slight Johannine retouching, remains".[16]

We find in Luise Schottroff[17] an example of a source critical analysis which goes a step further than Bultmann. She distinguishes between vv. 5–7,9ab, a narrative of Jesus intended to counteract hatred between Jews and Samaritans—"Ausdruck einer innerjüdischen Argumentation"—and vv. 16–18 on how Jesus the *miracle-worker* meets a *woman*. These originally separate sections were later combined because they both have the form of a dialogue between Jesus and a woman. According to Schottroff, the great contradiction in principle in Jn 4 is between vv. 5–7, 9ab and vv. 10–15. The former section deals with "innerweltliche Probleme", and the latter with salvation in the Johannine sense, which, according to Schottroff's consistently dualistic interpretation, has nothing whatever to do with "innerweltliche Dinge".[18] This contradiction cannot be resolved. "Eine sachgemässe Aufnahme der alten Legende war dem Evangelisten nicht möglich . . . Die johanneische Heilskonzeption muss durch ihr negatives Verhältnis zur Welt das in der alten Jesuslegende berichtete Geschehen für irrelevant halten, ja für falsch".[19]

These literary critical analyses have been briefly reviewed here because they seem seriously to question the possibility of discussing the text as a whole, and thereby the method of analysis formerly applied to Jn 2:1–11.[20] There is no denying that the text contains certain irregularities, perhaps most marked in the introduction and in v. 39. These would tend to show that the text did not come

[15] Fortna 1970, pp. 189ff. His results have been accepted by many. See, for example, the surveys in Martyn 1970 and Robinson 1971 and also the recensions by Murphy-O'Connor 1970, Smith 1970 and Barrett 1971. For a critique of Fortna, see Lindars 1971, pp. 27ff.

[16] Fortna 1970, pp. 189f.

[17] Schottroff 1969, pp. 200ff.

[18] See also Schottroff 1970, pp. 228ff, and the critique of her position in Ruckstuhl 1972. Schottroff chooses the first alternative as the genuine Christian view, against Bultmann, which is typical of our own time.

[19] Schottroff 1969, p. 208.

[20] Bultmann, Comm., p. 127, calls Schmid's composition analysis from 1929 "keine kritische Analyse"!

into being in a single context but has a prehistory. The author who gave the narrative its present form had at his disposal different kinds of material, each with its own "history". At the same time there is much evidence of a close connection between the different phases in the history of the text. There is a kind of continuity, as confirmed by the three most recent great commentaries on Jn by Brown, Schnackenburg and Lindars.[21] Furthermore there are sufficient qualities in the text to bind it together into a unit, so that I feel justified in analysing the narrative as a whole.[22] How can the various "disparate" parts function in the whole? In what way do they function? What did the author who shaped the present text—possibly with certain minor editorial additions later—wish it to express? If we must apply aspects of literary criticism to every kind of textual analysis, that which here follows corresponds with what the analyses quoted usually call the evangelist's layer, the decisive final stage in the formation of the text and the situation it covers.

Even when the text as a whole is interpreted the opinions differ.[23] Unfortunately there is no comprehensive survey of interpretations concerning the Samaria narrative similar to that of Smitmans on Jn 2:1—11. The following pages contain a rough schematic draft with four models of interpretation: the historico-biographical, the symbolical (allegorical), the salvation-historical and sacramental, and the Christological (soteriological).

The purely *historico-biographical* view assumes that in Jn 4 we have an eye witness account of a single historical event in Jesus' life, in which an individual and her meeting with Jesus are in the centre. We can quote *Godet's* commentary from 1877 as an example. According to him the theme of Jn 4 is: "une âme toute terrestre se trouvant en contact avec une pensée céleste, qui travaille à l'élever jusqu' à son niveau".[24] The narrative is generally called "Jesus and the Samaritan Woman". We are able to follow the *woman's* development in the text: at first she has no awareness whatever of spiritual need; she then becomes more and more conscious of her situation; she tries for a while to conceal her misconduct but is finally compelled to yield and commit herself to Jesus and become his messenger.[25] This positive change is contrasted with the disciples' uncomprehending attitude to what is happening, although they are at the same time, at least according to Godet, the harvesters who wait to baptize the Samaritans who come

[21] Schnackenburg, Comm., pp. 46ff, Brown, Comm., pp. xxivff, and Lindars, Comm., pp. 46ff, complemented by Lindars 1971, pp. 27ff.

[22] For a justification of my method, see above ch. 1, and the results of my analysis, 3.5.

[23] The best illustration of this disagreement is perhaps the different interpretation of vv. 16—18. See below, 3.3.2, S. 7.

[24] Godet, Comm., vol. 2, p. 347. He is a good representative of this interpretation model giving a religious, psychological picture of the conversion of the woman which is coloured by his own time. Other representatives: Westcott, Sanders-Mastin and Morris, Comm., ad loc.

[25] Here following Godet, Comm., ad loc.

to Jesus. "The others" who have laboured, v. 38, refer to Jesus and the woman. The text thus becomes an account of conversion in which a woman of low morals becomes aware of her sin.[26] The dialogue becomes a pastoral talk—the emphasis is on the woman throughout—an example of how Jesus, with deep psychological insight, talks to a human being and brings her to an awareness and an admission of sin, so that she is converted and begins a new life.[27] The isolated historical event which the text describes may, as such, have a certain "typological" character: this happens when a person meets Jesus. Yet this interpretation model sees all the details and expressions in the text from a single situation: a meeting between Jesus and a woman at Jacob's well in Samaria, once in Jesus' earthly life. This also establishes that only the persons mentioned in the text may be included in the acts of communication which belong to the text. We have there a communication between Jesus—the woman, Jesus—the disciples, the woman—the people, and Jesus—the people. The interpretation of the text does not take into consideration its sender, i.e. the author, or its receiver, i.e. those for whom the author intended it. Or it is assumed that the author's only purpose was to reproduce in writing some acts of communication from Jesus' life. His text is then but slightly dependent on its receivers. It was written for all.

The following three interpretation models have an attribute in common: the writer and the reader of the text are to different degrees, and in different ways, included in the interpretation. This is most pronounced in the *symbolical (allegorical)* expositions, which may vary considerably in relation to each other.[28] Those who regard Jn as "eine Lehrschrift in Evangelienform" (*Holtzmann*), as "eine ausgesprochene, den Überlieferungsstoff frei und souverän gestaltende und behandelnde Lehrschrift" (*Heitmüller*) interpret the Gospel only symbolically as a metaphorical account of the spiritual and universal character of Christianity, with the core of the text in vv. 21—26 (freedom from time, space, nation and culture) or with a certain emphasis on the way of Christian mission.[29]

[26] See, for example, Weiss, Comm., ad loc., and the survey in Friedrich 1967, pp. 13ff.

[27] Windisch, 1923, pp. 181, 186f, Schmid 1929, pp. 154f. A presentation of this type of interpretation in Friedrich 1967, pp. 13ff. The theme of Jn 4, according to Roustang 1958, is given in the title of his paper: "Les moments de l'acte de foi et ses conditions de possibilité".

[28] The oldest commentaries on Jn 4, those of Heracleon and Origen, belong to this group of interpretations. See Janssens 1959, who shows how Heracleon, in her opinion a Valentinian Gnostic, interprets Jn 4 as an allegory referring to the meeting of a soul with God. The pericope of the Samaritan Woman was in early times read before Easter "und in unmittelbarer Weise für die Taufvorbereitung ausgewertet", combined with a reading of Num 20, Maertens 1967, p. 108.

[29] I quote here Holtzmann, Comm., p. 2, and Heitmüller, Comm., p. 14, respectively. Both of them are good representatives of this interpretation model. For a reference to older literature, see Holtzmann, Comm., pp. 11ff. The Johannine texts are regarded as "allegorische Anschauungsmittel für Glaubenswahrheiten", Holtzmann, Comm., p. 3. "Die Geschichte ist nur eine andere Form der Lehre. Alles Vergängliche, d.h. hier *alles Geschichtliche ist nur ein Gleichnis*", Heitmüller, Comm., p. 15. For a partly applied allegorical interpretation, see Loisy and Bauer, Comm., ad loc.

The Jesus speaking in the text is the author himself, and his words are addressed to the author's contemporaries: the different persons in the narrative are only literary devices to express certain ideas.[30] Here the theory of the situation of the text and the act of communication there included—with the author as sender and the readers as receivers—seems to be crucial for its interpretation.

According to *Kreyenbühl* we have in Jn 4 a regular religious dialogue in figurative form between a Jewish Gnostic (Justin) and a Christian Gnostic (Menander, besides the author of the Gospel; the Gospel is thought to have come into existence around 140 A.D.).[31] The first speech is a plea for instruction in the other's doctrine, the second expresses both surprise and satisfaction at this invitation, and in the third the Christian Gnostic asserts that only his doctrine gives true insight etc.

In his comparative investigation of Jn 1—12 from 1929, *Odeberg* has roughly the same idea of the text as a whole but with the difference that in Jn 4 he sees an encounter between an orthodox Samaritan circle, characterized by certain mystical speculations, and the Johannine concept of Christianity.[32] The bucket in v. 11 denotes training in mysticism and knowledge of mystical explanations of the Mosaic law, while the husband in vv. 16—18 is Yahweh, whom the woman still does not really know. Nevertheless, by her loyalty to her own tradition the woman receives a full knowledge of God and becomes one of Jesus' disciples: this is in contrast to the Jews, who do not follow Abraham, Moses and Isaiah, 8:53ff; 5:47 and 12:37ff.

According to *Leroy,* Jn 4 reveals a part of the history of the Johannine Church: the union of a circle of Christian Samaritans and the Johannine community.[33] The narrative justifies the integration of the Christian Samaritans with their traditions, at the same time as it provides a motive for the teaching of the Johannine community by tracing it back to Jesus himself. The faith, theology and language of the community are all an outflow of revelation through Jesus Christ. Since they regard themselves as the true Israel, the Jewish element in the text is emphasized, while the Samaritans are depreciated. The entire text is thought to have received its form in the baptismal instruction of the Johannine community.[34]

Both Odeberg's and Leroy's expositions allow the text to deal with Jesus and the Samaritans—and not specifically the Samaritan woman—and the encounter

---

[30] "Für die Personen, für die Szenen, für das Geschehene als *solches* hat er kein Interesse. ... Der *Lehrer* in dieser Lehrschrift ist der Form nach Jesus. Er lehrt durch sein Wort und durch sein Tun. In Wirklichkeit erteilt der Evangelist den Unterricht", Heitmüller, Comm., pp. 14f.

[31] Kreyenbühl, Comm., vol. 2, pp. 397ff. On the general character and purpose of Jn, see vol. 1, pp. 370ff.

[32] Odeberg 1929, pp. 149ff. His result has been partly confirmed by Meeks 1967. Cf. Meeks' references to Odeberg, pp. 10f and 301, note 1.

[33] Leroy 1968, p. 99.

[34] See Leroy 1968, pp. 88ff, 149ff, 178.

between the Christian revelation and Samaritan belief.[35]   *O. Cullmann* too interprets the end of the text as referring to the Samaria mission, but the most striking feature of his *salvation-historical and sacramental* exposition are the references to baptism and to the Eucharist he finds in Jn.[36] He tries to combine an historical with a symbolical interpretation but firmly denies that his exposition is allegorical.[37] This he does from his salvation-historical view of the NT: every Jesus event has certain concrete connections with God's acts *before* Jesus and his acts *after* Jesus, namely in the age of the Church. Therefore the Johannine texts, beyond all others, give us both eye witness evidence and a reminder prompted by the Spirit. The evangelist endeavoured to discern the deeper content of salvation history in the story of Jesus. We find in the text both history and interpretation (symbolism). The historical event contains "in sich selber ausser dem mit den Sinnen Wahrnehmbaren den Hinweis auf weitere Heilstatsachen".[38] Since the author wishes to describe the relationship between the Christ present in worship and the historical Jesus, his symbolism often refers to the two most important aspects of worship: baptism and the Eucharist. Jn 4:20—24, according to Cullmann, speak of Christ as the centre of all worship, while the mention of the Spirit and the water is a reference to baptism; vv. 31—34 may designate the Eucharist. Verses 35ff, on the other hand, bring to the fore another important side of the Church's life: her mission. The "others" who are mentioned in v. 38 refer to the Hellenistic missionaries who are described in Acts 8, and especially Philip.[39] Thus, according to Cullmann, the purpose of the narrative considered as a whole is, not only to describe an event in Jesus' life, but also to provide instruction in the fundamental principles of the life of Christ's Church, of worship and mission, a doubleness which he tried to establish by the many expressions in the text having two or more meanings. The purpose of the Gospel is to bring mankind to believe that (the historical) *Jesus* is the *Christ* (present in worship and in the now), 20:30f. The author and his readers play essential roles in this interpretation model too.

The increasingly common *Christological (soteriological)* interpretation is characterized by the text's focus on Christ. The essential point in Jn 4 is the picture of Jesus Christ there given. According to *Bultmann's* gnostic/dualistic exposition, the text shows him to us as the divine Revelation: how he searches out man's thirst for life, revealing him in his anguish, shows him God's miracles and

[35] There is a similar general view in Bauer and Strathmann, Comm., ad loc., and Gerhardsson 1964.
[36] Cullmann ²1950, pp. 39ff, and Cullmann 1966, pp. 232ff. For his total view of Jn see also his articles from 1948 and 1950.
[37] See, especially Cullmann ²1950, p. 52, and also Cullmann 1966, pp. 176ff.
[38] Cullmann ²1950, p. 56. A "historical" and a "symbolical" interpretation do not cancel out each other. Cullmann defends a *both—and*.
[39] Cullmann 1966, pp. 232ff.

brings him to a moment of decision: God or the world. Here the Revelation and the natural human needs are opposed. The acceptance of Revelation is "Entweltlichung". All earthly gifts are "scheinbare, unechte Güter ... und das natürliche Leben nur ein uneigentliches Leben ... Allein, was die göttliche Offenbarung schenkt, hat den Charakter des Eigentlichen, des Echten, des ἀληθινόν".[40] Verses 31ff tell of the heralds of the Revelation and of "Hörer erster und zweiter Hand". The temporal and spatial paradoxes at the end of the Samaria text show only that the preaching of the disciples is an eschatological phenomenon which has its own laws.

The latest large commentaries belong to this group of interpretations. *Schnackenburg* emphasizes Jesus' gradual revelation of himself in the text. As the Revealer, Jesus seeks to bring the woman to belief. He has a special insight, vv. 16—18, he can see into the future, v. 21, he is convinced of his union with the Father, v. 34.[41] At the same time there are certain features of special interest to the evangelist: the contrast with the Nicodemus narrative, 2:23ff, the universality of the revelation, 4:42, the Samaritan mission, 4:38, and the Christian worship, 4:20—24. *Brown* sets Jesus' revelation and its consequences in the centre but keeps the way open for several interpretations.[42] In *Lindars* the meaning as a whole is shifted even more toward the consequence of belief in Christ, in that he gives the theme of Jn 4 as the meaning of the new birth: of the kingdom of God, of eternal life, of Jesus as the replacement of the Law, of the Church's mission etc.[43] This gives variety to his interpretation but it is difficult to grasp the meaning, according to him, of the text as a whole. Lindars' difficulty in combining the two main parts of the text into a unit is especially apparent. His commentary again brings to the fore the question of whether there is an interpretation which fulfills the entire text, or whether it should be divided into different sections for explanation.

This rough division of the interpretations of Jn 4:1—42 as a whole may here serve as a general background to the analyses of the text and to the discussion of its message under point 3.5. Considering the length and complexity of the text in relation to the Cana narrative discussed above, I have here divided the analysis

---

[40] Bultmann, Comm., p. 133. A more consistently dualistic interpretation is given by Schottroff 1969, pp. 206ff, 1970, pp. 228ff.

[41] Schnackenburg, Comm., ad loc., argues against those who regard Jn 4 as Jesus' pastoral teaching to a woman.

[42] Brown, Comm., ad loc. His comment on the Samaria narrative is remarkably short. Besides his focus on Jesus' revelation and its consequences there are others: "there is a good *possibility* that a baptismal motif was intended" in Jn 4, p. 180. "In this scene John has given us the drama of a soul struggling to rise from the things of this world to belief in Jesus", p. 178; cf. p. 185. It is difficult to grasp Brown's interpretation of the text as a whole.

[43] Lindars, Comm., ad loc. Cf also Lindars 1971, p. 65: "Chapter 3 was concerned with the spiritual capacity to *receive* the eternal life which Jesus has come to give. Chapter 4 is concerned with the *nature* of this eternal life which the spiritual person may except to receive".

into three parts: the first deals with the actual course of events in the text (3.2), the second and the third with the two dialogues (3.3, 3.4). I felt that I could curtail somewhat the account of various possible interpretations of the smaller units of the text after the detailed survey in ch. 2, which makes my method clearer.

3.2 The Event Structure

3.2.1 A Survey of the Event Units (E 1—E 32)

In the following survey my sole purpose is to bring out the different event units existing in our text, some of them only implicit, and to comment on various points of language and content.[1] Later I shall discuss the relations between the different units. In order to clarify the account which follows they are listed as far as possible in the order in which they occur.

E 1. John baptizes and wins followers.
E 2. Jesus/Jesus' disciples baptize and win followers.
E 3. Jesus baptizes and wins more followers than John.
E 4. The Pharisees hear of this (i.e. E 3).
E 5. The Lord knows it (i.e. E 4).
E 6. Jesus leaves Judea.
E 7. Jesus returns again to Galilee.
E 8. Jesus has to pass through Samaria.
E 9. Jesus is tired by his journey.
E 10. Jesus comes to a town in Samaria.
E 11. Jesus stops outside the town at Jacob's well.
E 12. Jesus sits down beside the well.
E 13. Jesus' disciples go off to the town to buy food.
E 14. A woman of Samaria comes to the well to draw water.
E 15. Jesus talks with the woman.
E 16. Jesus' disciples buy food in the town.
E 17. Jesus' disciples return to the well.
E 18. Jesus' disciples marvel that he is talking to a woman.
E 19. None of the disciples asks Jesus:
    a) What do you seek?
    b) Of what are you talking with her?
E 20. The woman leaves her jar at the well.
E 21. The woman goes off to the town.
E 22. Jesus talks with his disciples.
E 23. The woman bears witness to the townspeople, saying:
    a) Come, see a man who told me all I have done.
    b) Can he be the Messiah?

---

[1] On various ways of segmenting the text, see above, 1.2, and the introduction of 2.2.

E 24. Many of the Samaritans from the town come to believe in Jesus.

E 25. The Samaritans go out to the town.

E 26. The Samaritans make their way to Jesus at the well.

E 27. The Samaritans come to Jesus.

E 28. The Samaritans ask Jesus to stay with them.

E 29. Jesus stays two days with the Samaritans.

E 30. Jesus talks to the Samaritans.

E 31. Many more Samaritans come to believe.

E 32. The Samaritans say to the woman:

    a) Now we no longer believe because of your words.

    b) We have heard Jesus for ourselves.

    c) We know that Jesus is indeed the Saviour of the world.

One is immediately tempted to compare this survey with the way in which the text presents the course of events. Nevertheless I shall do so below, when I analyse separately some special structural features binding the units together[2] and here make a few comments on details of value for the continued analysis.

E 1 follows implicitly from v. 1 and refers to 3:22ff. See 3.2.2. John has an important role in the Gospel, 1:6—8; 1:15; 1:19ff; 3:22ff; 5:31ff and 10:40ff. He is the great witness to Jesus.[3] While we know from some other sources that John had disciples,[4] yet it emerges clearly that his work was not directed toward the formation of an esoteric fellowship of the Qumran type. He did not wish to found a new covenant but within the framework of the old covenant to *prepare* the people of God for the coming judgement.[5] This also holds according to the account in Jn, with the changes resulting from his role as witness. The Baptist's task is to "reveal" Jesus to Israel, the people of God, 1:31. He is, so to speak, the last representative of the old covenant.

E 2 should perhaps be divided into two clauses on the basis of vv. 1f: Jesus' disciples baptized and Jesus won followers.[6] Since 3:22 states, without comment, that Jesus did baptize, scholars have given much thought to the nature of this baptism.[7] I need nct com-

---

[2] See below, 3.2.2, 3.2.3, 3.2.4 and 3.2.5, with a preliminary summary in 3.2.6.

[3] See, besides the commentaries, Schütz 1967, pp. 94ff, Wink 1968, pp. 87ff, Boice 1970, pp. 80ff, and Lentzen-Deis 1970, pp. 92ff.

[4] Mk 2:18 par.; 6:29; Mt 11:2; Lk 7:18f; 11:1; Jn 1:35, 37; 3:25; Acts 18:24ff and Pseudo-Clementine Recognitions, but our evidence on the sectarians of John the Baptist is very limited, Brown, Comm., pp. lxviiff.

[5] See especially Lentzen-Deis 1970, pp. 92ff. He describes the baptism of John as "ein ausserer Ritus, der an Gottes Heilveranstaltung Anteil gibt, insofern er die 'Umkehr', die tätige Abkehr von den Sünden und Hinwendung zu Gott, welche Früchte bringt, vollmächtigt bestätigt. Sie ist ausgerichtet auf das Kommen des 'Stärkeren' " (p. 94).

[6] The word μαϑηταί has here a more general sense. Cf. Jn 6:60f, 66; 7:3; 8:31; 9:27ff. "Darin kommt ein späterer Sprachgebrauch zum Vorschein (vgl. Apg), nach dem alle Gläubigen als μαϑηταί gelten", Schnackenburg, Comm., ad loc.

[7] Is this a baptism "with the Holy Spirit" or not? Is it the same as the Christian baptism? See especially Schwank, Comm., ad loc., and the examination of Jn 3:22ff in Léon-Dufour 1964. "Du

mit myself on this point here. As a rule v. 2 is explained as being a gloss.[8] Yet is this not an attempt to explain away the verse, as no function can be found for v. 2 in the given interpretation of the text as a whole? If a redactor did insert this item, why then did he not so do in 3:22? The opening verses of ch. 4 are heavily loaded even without v. 2. We can also note that there are many corrections in Jn, although not all can be explained as glosses.[9] The situation seems to me to be such that we should investigate whether or not v. 2 may have a function related to the text as a whole.

E 3 should in the Greek text be regarded as a direct quotation.[10] On comparisons between Jesus and John in Jn, see 2.2, U 3 and 3.2.2.

E 4 mentions the Pharisees. They are usually associated in Jn with Jerusalem, 1:24; 3:1; 7:32,47f; 9:13,15f,40; 11:46f, 57; 18:3, and are at the same time presented as the ruling authority, with the right to hold hearings and to pass judgement. They question John the Baptist, 1:24,[11] send officers to arrest Jesus, 7:32ff, cross-examine the man born blind and his parents, 9:13ff, and decide to put Jesus to death, 11:40ff. The ἄρχοντες mentioned as believers in 12:42 dare not acknowledge Jesus openly because of the Pharisees. The designation οἱ Φαρισαῖοι thus becomes almost synonymous with the Johannine term for the religious leaders of the Jewish people, οἱ Ἰουδαῖοι.[12] Such a usage is not found among the Synoptics and seems to reflect a later period than Jesus' own time.[13] This general presentation of the Pharisees in Jn should, in all reason, also affect the reading of v. 1. This implies that the leaders in Jerusalem cannot be expected to sit idle now, after John the Baptist has evidently gone north, that they hear of Jesus' successes. In 12:19 it is just the Pharisees who say ἴδε ὁ κόσμος ὀπίσω αὐτοῦ ἀπῆλθεν.[14] Information received had, according to Jn, led to intervention on other occasions, 7:32ff; 9:40ff; 11:45ff. So I can find no other interpretation of the statement in E 4 than as a threat to Jesus.

point de vue historique Jn tire de l'ombre une étape indispensable dans l'histoire du baptême chrétien. Si les disciples ont aussi rapidement baptisé dès le jour de la Pentecôte, c'est qu'ils avaient été initiés à ce geste par Jésus lui-même. ... En étant baptisés par Jésus, les disciples formaient la communauté eschatologique groupée autour de Celui qui devait venir", p. 309. There are, according to Léon-Dufour, three forms of baptism: the baptism of John, the baptism of Jesus and the Christian baptism. On the baptism of John and the baptism "in the name of Jesus", see Hartman 1971, pp. 139ff.

[8] With reference to the content of the verse and some linguistic features (καίτοι γε only here, Ἰησοῦς without article). See Comm., ad loc.

[9] See Abbott 1906, pp. 460ff.

[10] Direct speech is very often used in Jn, Abbott 1906, p. 466.

[1] "The Pharisees" in 1:24 is best taken as a further description of "the Jews" in 1:19. For arguments, see Lindars, Comm., ad loc.

[2] Compare, for example, 1:19 and 1:24; 9:13, 15f, 40 and 9:18; 9:22, and 12:42. Martyn 1968, pp. 18ff, 71ff, stresses that they are an authoritative Jewish group, the local *gerousia* in the mind of the evangelist (p. 72). 12:42 would then point to a schism within the *gerousia* itself. Schlatter, Comm., ad loc., mentions that οἱ Φαρισαῖοι in the Mishnah refers to the rabbinate as a closed, didactic and deciding instance.

[3] See H.F. Weiss in ThWNT, vol. 9, pp. 46f, and Lindars, Comm., p. 37.

[4] The reason for Jesus' departure from Judea seems therefore to be clear according to Jn (against Brown, Comm., ad loc. No Galilean Pharisees are mentioned in Jn). —Jn 12:19 has parallels in 3:26; 7:32ff and 11:48.

E 5 first presents us with a problem of textual criticism. Are we to read ὁ κύριος or ὁ Ἰησοῦς.[15] If we follow the external criteria we should probably choose the former.[16] The internal reasons are more difficult to weight. Generally Jn does not use the designation ὁ κύριος in narrative sections[17] but it occurs in two transitional passages, 6:23 and 11:2; we cannot there say that it was a later addition. Thus there are Johannine parallels for the use of ὁ κύριος in 4:1, and in sections of a similar character at that. A reading with ὁ Ἰησοῦς may have arisen from a harmonizing with what follows in vv. 1f and indeed with common Johannine usage.[18] It seems easier to me to explain how ὁ Ἰησοῦς arose from ὁ κύριος than *vice versa*. Therefore I prefer, although hesitantly, to read ὁ κύριος. This reading is also in harmony with a total view of the opening verses, which will be discussed in 3.2.3.

A further characteristic of some other transitional passages is that they refer to Jesus' omniscience, his full insight into present and future events, 2:24f; 6:15; 13:1,3; 18:4; 19:28. The recurring picture in the Gospel of Jesus as omniscient[19] makes it feasible to read in 4:1: "Now when the Lord *knew* . . .". Jesus, in full control of the situation, and by his own decision, chooses to avoid Jerusalem and Judea until his "hour" is come, 7:1ff, 30; 8:20, 59; 11:7ff; 13:1ff; 18:4; 19:28.[20]

E 6 begins the account of Jesus' wandering. Westcott and other scholars[21] have noted that the choice of verb in this clause (ἀφῆκεν) is somewhat unexpected. Καταλείπειν, for example Mt 4:13 and Heb 11:27, would have been more natural. There are few exact parallels.[22] The verb carries a sense of "to leave to itself, to abandon". With the reaction of "the Jews" in mind Jesus abandons Jerusalem and Judea, "his own home", 4:44,[23] and has the threat of death hanging over him throughout when he is there later in the Gospel, 5:16, 18; 7:1ff, 25, 30, 44; 8:20, 37, 40, 59; 10:31, 39f; 11:8, 53f. On Jesus' route see the commentary on E 8.

E 7. For ἀπῆλθεν cf. 6:1; 10:40; 11:54; 12:36. Jesus goes away. The verb here indicates an unfinished action: *started back to.*[24] On the pattern of his journeys and on Galilee in Jn see 2.2 and the discussion there of U 3 and below 3.2.3.

---

[15] Nestle-Aland (25th ed.) reads ὁ κύριος but notes in the apparatus that ὁ Ἰησοῦς may be the original reading. "The Greek New Testament" reads the latter, indicating the relative degree of certainty with the letter C (a considerable degree of doubt), Metzger 1971, pp. 205f.

[16] See the quotation of the evidence in "The Greek New Testament".

[17] The use in 20:20 and 21:12 may be explained from the specific context. See 20:18, 25, 28 and 21:7. Lk often uses ὁ κύριος as an integrated part of a narrative text.

[18] Against the arguments adduced by Metzger 1971, pp. 205f. The most natural beginning of the text is "when Jesus heard . . ." and this has caused the change of ὁ κύριος into ὁ Ἰησοῦς. The smoothing effect of ὁ κύριος (instead of ὁ Ἰησοῦς) must have been very slight in this clumsy text. The use of Ἰησοῦς in v. 1b depends on the direct speech of this clause.

[19] 1:48; 4:18ff; 5:6; 6:6, 61, 64; 16:19.

[20] Note especially the mention of Jesus' will in 1:43 and 7:1.

[21] See Morris, Comm., ad loc., and the literature he mentions. See also Barrett, Comm., ad loc.

[22] Schlatter, Comm., ad loc., refers only to one passage, Josephus, Ant II.335, with τὴν Αἴγυπτον as object. With other kinds of object, cf. Mt 4:11, 20, 22; Mk 11:16 and Jn 10:12.

[23] For further discussion, see my analysis of 4:44 below, 3.2.3.

[24] A complexive aorist, Bl.-Debr. § 332, Brown, Comm., ad loc.

E 8. Josephus notes that Galileans who had been to Jerusalem usually took the road through Samaria, Ant XX.118 (ἔθος ἦν τοῖς Γαλιλαίοις) and Bell II.232, and that this was necessary (ἔδει) if the traveller was in a hurry (Vita 269). The road over the mountain ridge of Judea and Samaria was the shortest way. This fact and the data in Josephus are usually taken as evidence that ἔδει in v. 4 cannot have any theological content.[25] This expression may perhaps imply a certain urgency, caused by the attitude of the Pharisees. Yet as the evangelist now presents Jesus' journeys, he is not coming from Jerusalem but probably from somewhere in the Jordan valley, 3:22ff; it is then more difficult to see why Jesus *had to* take the road through Samaria for reasons of geography or tradition.[26] The crucial point for the interpretation of E 8 is here, as in many other passages, the understanding of the geographical features as such in Jn.[27] The wording suggests a certain openness to a theological meaning if we consider it from the whole of Jn. Indeed the evangelist uses δεῖ repeatedly in contexts generally concerned with Jesus' saving mission *in toto*, 3:14; 9:4; 10:16; 12:34; 20:9. Cf. 3:30; 4:20,24.[28] If one can speak of a special Johannine usage in these passages, the wording of E 8 points to a transferred meaning, i.e. by reason of his task of mission from the Father, the Son must even take the road through Samaria.

E 9's wording is such as to provoke a number of questions. Does the item in v. 6 say only that Jesus *is tired* by the journey or is κοπιᾶν used in a more specialized sense, relating it to the meaning of the verb in v. 38.[29] Is any particular emphasis laid on *the journeying* itself? Does the perfect participle mark an earlier event? We have two main alternatives:[30] the text gives a picture of Jesus the traveller *or* a picture of the Son of God on his path of mission through the world. Is there a possibility of combining these alternatives? For the time being I shall stop at the translation given above. An interesting parallel from Josephus is discussed under 3.2.4.

E 10 again brings Jesus' route to the fore. Judging by the context, he did not enter the town. If he came by the main road from the south, in this context from the Jordan valley in the south, by way of Ephraim, he first reached Jacob's well at the foot of Mt. Gerizim. On the other hand, if he came direct down the valley of the Jordan he arrived first at Sychar, i.e. Askar, below Mt. Ebal, Jacob's well being another kilometre away.[31] The text gives no sure guidance on these points. See 3.2.3 on the location of the various places.

E 11. There is some doubt as to whether this unit should be included. I feel that it is implicit in v. 6. If we have Jesus come first to Sychar the unit should read: "Jesus goes to ...". On the location of the well, see 3.2.3.

---

[25] See, for example, Bultmann, Barrett and Schnackenburg, Comm., ad loc.

[26] On the roads from the Jordan Valley, See E 10 below and 3.2.3.

[27] On the total aspect of the opening verses, see below 3.2.3.

[28] See Abbott 1906, p. 217, and Schwank and Morris, Comm., ad loc. On δεῖ in the NT as an expression of "die Notwendigkeit des eschatologischen Geschehens", see W. Grundmann in ThWNT, vol. 2, pp. 21ff.

[29] See the comment on this verb below, 3.4.2, S 4.

[30] Compare Bultmann, Barrett and Schnackenburg, Comm., ad loc. (E 9 as a natural part of the description of the scene), Schwank and Morris, Comm., ad loc. (E 9 as stressing Jesus' human character) and Lightfoot, Comm., ad loc. (E 9 as a link with the Passion narrative).

[31] On the topography, see below 3.2.3.

E 12 has an interesting parallel in Josephus, based on Ex 2:15. See 3.2.4 and 3.2.7. The imperfect ἐκαθέζετο here has an aorist meaning.[32] Ἐπί means "by" and not "on".[33] The placing of οὕτως may give this word a certain emphasis. It is usually taken with the verb—although a placing before the finite verb would then be more natural as in Acts 20:11; 27:17—with the meaning "at once, right away, without more ado".[34] If the word is taken with the participle it tends to mean: tired as he was.

E 13 should naturally be understood as meaning that *all* the disciples left Jesus.[35] Verses 31ff show that their chief intent was to buy food for Jesus.[36] The fact that Jews, for reasons of ritual cleanliness, could only buy a very limited range of foods from Samaritans does not seem to be of current interest to the author, although he generally comments on the tension between the two religious groups.[37]

E 14. Ἀντλεῖν meaning "to draw from a spring", is used here in a more general sense.[38] Since the Jews often likened the Torah to a well or a spring, they were able to see a transferred meaning in "draw", namely "acquire knowledge, learn".[39] The scene in Jn 4 resembles that in Gen 24, Gen 29 and Ex 2. See 3.2.7. On the actual fetching of water, see 3.2.5.

E 15 is marked in many ways in the text. On the thirteen quotation formulae, see 3.3.1. Moreover the conversation is referred to in the dialogue itself (αἰτεῖς, v. 9, ὁ λέγων σοι, ᾔτησας, v. 10, εἶπες, εἴρηκας, vv. 17f, ὁ λαλῶν σοι, v. 26) and even later in the text (ἐλάλει, λαλεῖς, v. 27, εἶπεν, vv. 29, 39). This device and the length—vv. 7—26—mark that this first dialogue has a chief function in the text as a whole.

E 16 may well belong to the units which can be omitted in the given survey. It follows implicitly from vv. 8,31 and 33. I included it here having in mind the presentation of the two scene composition of the text. See 3.2.4.

E 17 brings us to v. 27. See further 3.2.4.

E 18. Commentators tend to place great emphasis on the fact that the text does not read μετὰ γυναικὸς Σαμαρίτιδος.[40] The problem of Jews and Samaritans would then no longer be part of the text. Yet it is obvious to the reader that the passage deals with the

---

[32] Bl.-Debr. § 101, s.v., and Bauer, s.v. Cf. Jn 6:3; 11:20.

[33] In those days the wells had no well rings, Schwank, Comm., ad loc. Cf. the variant reading in p[66] (επι τη γη). We have the same construction in Ex 2:15 and in Josephus' repetition of this passage. See 3.2.4. On the dative instead of the genitive, see Jn 5:2, Bl.-Debr. § 235,1.

[34] See, for example, Bultmann, Barrett, Schnackenburg and Brown, Comm., ad loc.

[35] The suggestion that somebody stayed at the well only expresses a wish for a witness to describe the events. See, for example, Godet, Comm., ad loc., and the first interpretation model mentioned in 3.1.

[36] Τροφαί means "nourishment, food". The plural corresponds to both Greek and Jewish usage, Bultmann, Comm., ad loc.

[37] See v. 9c and the analysis of this comment below, 3.2.5. On the rules dealing with the acceptance of food from Samaritans, see Str.-B., vol. 1, pp. 541f. The Jews could only buy "certain dry food-stuffs", Daube 1956, p. 374.

[38] See above, 2.2, U 18, and below 3.3.2, S 1.

[39] On the figurative use of water as Torah, see Str.-B., vol. 2, pp. 433ff, and below, 3.3.6. Cf., for example, the rendering of Is 12:3 in the Targum: "Ihr werdet neue Lehre mit Freude annehmen von den auserwählten Gerechten" (tr. by Billerbeck).

[40] See, for example, Bultmann and Schnackenburg, Comm., ad loc.

dialogue carried on in vv. 7—26, and the disciples must in the situation described have been fully aware that this was a Samaritan woman. Nevertheless the point of greatest interest to the narrator here is to describe the reaction of the disciples to *this* dialogue, which was actually a conversation between Jesus and a representative of the Samaritans. See further 3.2.5.

E 19. On reasons for this rendering of v. 27b, see 3.2.5.

E 20 gives one of the very few details in the course of events, a detail which has through the history of exegesis acquired widely different meanings. See 3.2.5.

E 21, taken with E 23, suggests that the author believes the woman to come from Sychar.

E 22 is denoted by the quotation formulae in vv. 31—38. See 3.4.1.

E 23. Verse 39, μαρτυρούσης, explicitly states that this refers to an *act of witness* by the woman. This is essential as μαρτυρεῖν in Jn has a very special function.[41] Ἄνθρωπος is often used of Jesus in this Gospel, 5:12; 8:40; 9:11, 24; 10:33; 11:47, 50; 18:14, 17, 29; 19:5. Μήτι does not always expect an wholly negative answer, so I have here given the end of the woman's speech as an hesitant question.[42] The question may be worded from the point of view of the people,[43] in which case an expected negative answer would be a more natural reading. The question recurs in different forms throughout the Gospel.[44] The woman's words to the people point particularly to a part of the dialogue, namely vv. 16—18, which, judging by the exegetical history, may be assigned many different functions.[45]

E 24. Jn never uses the construction πολλοί τῶν ... but on the other hand πολλοί + verb + genitive or ἐκ -construction, 6:60; 12:11; 19:20. Cf. 7:44. On πιστεύειν εἰς, see U 31 in 2.2.

E 25 may also include the woman. Cf. vv. 41f. Concerning the combination ἐξῆλθον – ἤρχοντο – ἦλθον, which we have in E 25—27, Abbott refers to the related phrases in 11:29—32 and 20:3f, and draws the conclusion that the imperfect here prepares for "some important action".[46]

E 26. The use of the imperfect here depends on the two scene composition. See 3.2.4.

---

[41] The frequent use of μαρτυρεῖν (47 times in the Johannine corpus, 30 times in the rest of NT) and μαρτυρία (30 and 7 times respectively), and the diversity of contexts and associations in which these two words occur, point to the conclusion that Jn has reflected long and perceptively on the idea of witness in connection with the work of Jesus. All of the testimony in the Gospel—with the possible exception of Christ's own testimony—deals with the essential nature and meaning of Jesus Christ. It is a religious witness, involving the presentation, verification and acknowledgement of the claims of Jesus Christ. For John the witness of Jesus is *revelation,* and the witnesses who cluster round it are expressions of certain aspects of revelation. See Boice 1970, especially pp. 24ff, and the literature he quotes. On the woman as a witness, see the further discussions in 3.2.5, 3.3.4 and 3.5.

[42] A negative answer is expected in Jn 8:22 and 18:35, but compare Jn 7:26 and see Bl.-Debr. § 427,2.

[43] Thus Bultmann, Comm., ad loc.

[44] See the comments on S 12 in 3.3.2.

[45] See the survey of interpretations below, 3.3.2, S 7.

[46] Abbott 1906, p. 338.

This is therefore hardly a matter of a graphic imperfect showing how the people came slowly, carefully and hesitantly.[47]

E 28. In contrast to the Jews, the Samaritans do not here seem to be repelled by the Revealer's origin. Cf. 6:42; 7:27, 41f, 52. There is a striking contrast to 2:18, 20; 4:1—3, 44; 6:30f, 41, 52. Nor do they react as does the woman in vv. 7 and 9. Ἐρωτᾶν here has the meaning usual in the Koine, "to request" (= αἰτεῖν).[48] The use of μένειν, one of the typically Johannine terms, is natural in the situation here but this does not mean that it must be theologically colourless.[49]

E 30 is somewhat problematic. The text only mentions τὸν λόγον αὐτοῦ, v. 41, and in v. 42 ἀκηκόαμεν has no object. Is this wording deliberate? The nominalization and the absence of an object creates a vagueness in the account, which makes it possible here to consider the *word of revelation* in all its breadth, and not only what Jesus once said to some Samaritans.[50] For the time being I render this phrase in v. 41 from the situation in the text.

E 31 is parallel to E 24, but there πιστεύειν is absolute, without a prepositional phrase or dative construction. Cf. 4:53 and see the material on U 31 in 2.2.

E 32 should for reasons of content and form be regarded as *a confession.* The expression is typically Johannine. On οὗτός ἐστιν ἀληθῶς, see the identical wording in 6:14 and 7:40. Cf. 7:25. We meet οἴδαμεν in many other confessions and assurances, 3:2, 11; 9:31; 16:30; 21:24 and 1 Jn 3:2, 14; 5:15, 18, 19, 20. Ὁ σωτήρ τοῦ κόσμου appears in the NT only here and in 1 Jn 4:14, but has many contentual parallels in the Johannine literature, Jn 1:29; 3:16f; 6:35, 51; 1 Jn 2:2; 4:9. Ἀκηκόαμεν also recalls the repeated use found in the introduction to 1 Jn, vv. 1, 3 and 5. Thus the Samaritans speak a clearly Johannine language. The word order τὴν σὴν λαλιάν gives σήν a certain emphasis by Johannine usage.[51] Bearing in mind the usage in Jn 8:43 it is difficult to maintain any essential difference between λαλιά and λόγος. Possibly λαλιά places heavier emphasis on the outward human speech, while λόγος stands for the whole of Jesus' revelation of himself, for the whole of his meassage.[52] The variation in the choice of words would then

---

[47] Against Westcott and Schwank, Comm., ad loc.

[48] See also 4:31,47 and 19:38. Barrett and Schwank, Comm., ad loc. state that Jesus only goes to non-Jews by request, Jn 12:20—22; Mk 7:24—30.

[49] Cf., for example, the use of μένειν in 1:38. The verb is used 68 times in the Johannine corpus and 50 times in the rest of the NT. See Brown, Comm., pp. 510ff, Borig 1967, pp. 199ff, and Heise 1967, pp. 44ff.

[50] Note the use of ἀκηκόαμεν in v. 42 and the comment on E 32 below. "Die Bemerkung gehört zur Theologie der Offenbarung und des 'Wortes' Jesu, die der Evanglist in seinem ganzen Buch entwickelt", Schnackenburg, Comm., ad loc. The "word" has a divine origin, 7:16; 12:49; 14:10; 17:6, 8, 14, 17, and is received only by "the children of God", 8:47; 18:37; 14:17. It gives eternal life and spirit, 6:63, 68. Morris, Comm., ad loc., refers to Mk 2:2. The "word" is the message of Jesus as a whole.

[51] Cf. 5:47; 7:8,16; 8:51 and see Abbott 1906, p. 67, and Kilpatrick 1960, p. 173.

[52] See the comment above on E 30. There seems to be a similar difference in Jn 8:43 "Why do you not understand *what I say?* It is because you cannot bear to listen to *my message*". See also Schnackenburg, Comm., ad loc.: "Ein grundsätzlicher Gegensatz zwischen der Verkündigung durch andere und Jesu eigenem, ihn unmittelbar bezeugendem Wort, zwichen Autoritätsglauben

link up with the previous designation of the woman's words as an act of witness[53] and with the possible nuance of a revelation saying present in ὁ λόγος. Yet there seems to be no derogatory sense in λαλιά.

The closing words of the narrative (ὁ σωτήρ τοῦ κόσμου), which echo after its end, call for further comment. In NT times the title σωτήρ had a rich and varied usage and it is difficult to decide what may be relevant parallel material to Jn 4:42.[54] In the NT itself, the title is of surprisingly rare occurrence, apart from the pastoral epistles and 2 Pet.[55] The point of greatest interest to us here is the possible meaning inherent in these closing words in a Johannine setting.

According to Jn, God's work of salvation through Jesus Christ is directed to *the world,* 1:29; 3:16f; 4:42; 6:33, 51; 8:12; 9:5; 12:47 and 16:8. The purpose is clear: ἵνα σωθῇ ὁ κόσμος δι' αὐτοῦ, 3:17; 12:47. The work of redemption concerns not only those who believe but the entire world, 1 Jn 2:2. When in 4:42 we find "Saviour of *the world*" it is not new in the Johannine context. God's work of salvation concerned the world.[56]

According to Jn, this work of salvation is connected with the sin of the world. John the Baptist says: "Behold the Lamb of God which takes away the sin of the world, ὁ αἴρων τὴν ἁμαρτίαν τοῦ κόσμου, 1:29. Jesus was revealed ἵνα τὰς ἁμαρτίας ἄρῃ, 1 Jn 3:5.[57] The central words on God's work of salvation in Jn 3:16ff have a very close parallel in 1 Jn 4:9f;[58] it says there that God sent his Son as a sacrifice for our sins, ἱλασμὸν περὶ τῶν ἁμαρτιῶν ἡμῶν; cf. 1 Jn 2:2. Immediately thereafter, in 1 Jn 4:14, comes the epithet "Saviour of the world", the only parallel we have to the expression in 4:42. Thus in the Johannine environment the idea of Jesus as "Saviour" is connected with his work of redemption, with purification from sin. This is not peculiar to John. We find the same thought in other places in the NT, such as Tit 2:13; Acts 5:31 and Mt 1:21. Cullmann summarises: "Wir befinden uns also hier deutlich im Bereich jüdisch-christlichen Denkens: Christus ist *Soter*, weil er uns von der Sünde erlöst hat".[59] The Samaritans' final

---

und einem Glauben, der selber seinen Gegenstand erfasst, ist vom Evangelisten nicht beabsichtigt".

[53] Note the variant reading μαρτυριαν in Codex Sinaiticus, Codex Bezae and three Old Latin manuscripts (b, l, r). Codex Vaticanus and p[75] read λαλιαν σου.

[54] See the survey by W. Foerster in ThWNT, vol. 7, pp. 1004ff, and the literature he mentions. The title has very often been used in Christianity and it there tends to have a very general sense which makes an examination more difficult.

[55] Lk 1:47; 2:11; Acts 5:31; 13:23; Phil 3:20; Eph 5:23; Jn 4:42; 1 Jn 4:14; Jude 25, ten times in the Pastoral Epistles and five times in 2 Pet. See W. Foerster in ThWNT, vol. 7, pp. 1004ff, and G. Fohrer in the same handbook, p. 1013, and the literature mentioned there. The word is not an ordinary name for the Messiah.

[56] The same picture of God's work of salvation is found in, for example, the Book of Isaiah. See, for example, chs. 43 and 49, and below, the excursus on the mission in Jn, 3.4.6. Lindars, Comm., ad loc., refers to Is 43:3 (God as Saviour in the Exodus) and adds: "It is as the agent of a new Exodus that it might be applied to Jesus".

[57] See also 1 Jn 1:7 "the blood of Jesus his Son cleanses us from all sin (ἀπὸ πάσης ἁμαρτίας)".

[58] Common themes: the love of God, God sends his Son, the purpose of this mission. See Schnackenburg, Comm., ad loc.

[59] Cullmann 1963, p. 250, referring mostly to non-Johannine passages on Jesus as "Saviour". On a Jewish background of σωτήρ in the NT, see also Betz 1963a, pp. 29f. God is described as

confession is thus connected with the important problem of *purification* in Jn. By means of Jesus and his works the old purification ordinances are superseded. He is "the Saviour of the world", "the Lamb of God who takes away the sin of the world". There seems to be no marked universalism in the closing words of the Samaria narrative.[60]

3.3.2 Terminal Features

The Samaria text has a definite conclusion, vv. 39—42. Points previously made in the text are reiterated and linked together, and the whole narrative culminates in the Samaritans' final confession in v. 42. Ἐκ τῆς πόλεως ἐκείνης, v. 39, refers back to v. 5 (and also to vv. 8, 28, 30), the designation of the people as Samaritans, τῶν Σαμαριτῶν, v. 39, οἱ Σαμαρῖται, v. 40, to v. 5 (and also to vv. 4, 7, 9), Jesus' stay among the Samaritans, ἔμεινεν ἐκεῖ, v. 40, to v. 6. With a reference to the stay in Samaria the journey continues in v. 43. Both the woman's conversation with the people, vv. 28f, and Jesus' dialogue with the woman, vv. 7—26, are referred to in the closing verses, διὰ τὸν λόγον τῆς γυναικός, v. 39, διὰ τὴν σὴν λαλιάν, v. 42, and εἶπέν μοι, v. 39. On the other hand, there is no mention of Jesus' disciples and his dialogues with them. We can even remove vv. 8, 27 and 31—38 and still find vv. 39—42 to be a natural ending. Verse 42 summarizes both vv. 39—41 and the whole text: the first part of the speech refers back to v. 39, the second to vv. 40f and the words οἴδαμεν ὅτι οὗτός ἐστιν conclude a main theme in the text which begins in v. 10: εἰ ἤδεις τὴν δωρεὰν τοῦ θεοῦ καὶ τίς ἐστιν ὁ λέγων . . . [1] These last words resound as a final chorus in a drama, with *Jesus*, the *Samaritan woman* and the *Samaritans of Sychar* in the leading roles.[2]

The end of the text is thus markedly terminal in character. It binds vv. 5—42 together into a unit. Only one theme extends outside this text: different individuals' *belief* in Jesus. The fact that *many* in Samaria come to believe also links up with the text prior to vv. 5—42,[3] but there it is more difficult to delimit

"Saviour" in the OT, especially in Ps and Is (Cullmann[3]1963, p. 246, with examples), and the use of the word in Lk and the Pastoral Epistles supports the view that a description of God has been transferred to Jesus.

[60] Note the use of "world" in Jn 1:29 ("the sin of *the world*") without any universalistic emphasis (not the contrast "the Jews" and "the rest of the mankind"). Being the Saviour of Israel Jesus becomes the Saviour of the world. See below, 3.4.6. Many commentators see in v. 42 a reference to the Gentile (*contra* Jewish) mission of the Church, for example, Schnackenburg and Lindars. Comm., ad loc.

[1] See the characterizations of Jesus in vv. 12, 19, 25, 26, and also the question in v. 29.

[2] See Dodd 1953, p. 311, and the comparisons with Greek drama in Bruns 1969, pp. 43ff (with references).

[3] There is also a link with 4:43ff, but note the difference: in vv. 39—42 we have *the word of the witness* and *the word of Jesus*, in vv. 43ff the theme of *the sign of Jesus* and *the word of Jesus*. In the former passage Jesus' word is a word of revelation and teaching, in the latter a specific saying of Jesus. For further discussion of vv. 39—42, see below, 3.2.5. We encounter different reactions to Jesus in 2:23ff; 3:22ff and 4:43ff.

the text. What is the character and function of the first verses in Jn 4?

The introduction, clumsy in form,[4] places Jesus in transit through Samaria, διέρχεσθαι διὰ τῆς Σαμαρείας, v. 4. His destination is Galilee, v. 3. Even if v. 4 serves as a transition between vv. 1—3 and vv. 5—6, I wish to relate it to the presentation of the great journey framework reading: ὡς οὖν ἔγνω ὁ κύριος . . . ἀφῆκεν . . . καὶ ἀπῆλθεν . . . ἔδει δὲ αὐτὸν διέρχεσθαι διὰ τῆς Σαμαρείας.

Verses 5—6 later describe the situation prevailing throughout the narrative: Jesus at Jacob's well, in the field Jacob gave his son Joseph, near the town of Sychar in Samaria.[5] In a way we have a *double* opening of the text, *two settings,* vv. 1—4 and vv. 5—6. The latter is absolutely necessary for the narrative, and is clearly in the nature of an introduction: the chief character is placed in a specific setting, the site is described and the time is given. The text could have begun at v. 5, approximately as 3:22: μετὰ ταῦτα ἦλθεν ὁ Ἰησοῦς [καὶ οἱ μαθηταὶ αὐτοῦ] εἰς . . . Nevertheless, as it now stands, this beginning has itself a kind of introduction in vv. 1—4. The item κεκοπιακὼς ἐκ τῆς ὁδοιπορίας in v. 6 refers to what is said in this introduction, and τῆς Σαμαρείας in v. 5 links with corresponding phrases in v. 4, ἔρχεται, v. 5, ἐκαθέζετο, v. 6, with the earlier verbs of movement. The two introductions are interwoven to some extent.

The junctions between the first four verses and vv. 5—42 are otherwise very weak. We are reminded that Jesus' disciples are present and working with Jesus, v. 2; cf. 3:22; 4:8, 27, 31—38. Jesus is here said to win many disciples, as at the end, vv. 39—42. The baptism may be connected with the water in vv. 7—15.[6] Otherwise vv. 1—4 seem to be most closely connected with 3:22ff and 4:43ff. Nevertheless it is essential to establish the function of the first verses before the text as a whole can be interpreted. What is the connection between the author's intention in vv. 5—42 and his words in the text near these verses?

The connection between 4:1—4 and *4:43ff* is discussed primarily in section 3.2.3. Here I shall note only that Jesus' journey is given a special explanation in 4:44,[7] which makes it difficult to regard the information on the journey as mere conjunctions of pericopes. Indeed formulations in 4:1—4 may be interpreted as if Jesus' journey from Judea to Galilee through Samaria is a necessary part of his divine task of salvation.[8] If this is the case, the stay in Samaria is presented as a part of God's salvation plan, which Jesus in his obedience here realizes. The

---

[4] Linguistically "eine Ungeheuerlichkeit", Schwartz 1908, p. 119. The same judgement in Wellhausen 1908, p. 20, and in later commentaries. Many transitional passages in Jn have a specific linguistic character which has sometimes caused problems in the transmission of the text. See for example, 2:12, 23—25; 4:43—45; 6:22—24; 13:1—3.

[5] On the situation described in vv. 5—6, see below, 3.2.3.

[6] Note also the possible theme of Jesus' omniscience in v. 1 and in vv. 16—18, 29 and 39. See the comment on E 5 above, 3.2.1.

[7] See also 4:1 and the reason mentioned there.

[8] On the "theological" character of the journey, see below 3.2.3.

opening verses would then give a perspective of "salvation history" to the Samaria text.[9]

The connection with *3:22—36* may appropriately be investigated here. While the opening verses may perhaps be transitional rather than terminal in character and tend to introduce 4:1—54, I include them in the Samaria text mainly because of their association with vv. 5—6 and the new beginning there expressed in contrast with the preceding verses.[10] At the same time as the deepest rooted clause in the introduction Ἰησοῦς πλείονας μαθητὰς ποιεῖ καὶ βαπτίζει ἢ Ἰωάννης [11] and the comment on it in v. 2, καίτοι γε Ἰησοῦς αὐτὸς οὐκ ἐβάπτιζεν ἀλλ' οἱ μαϑηταὶ αὐτοῦ clearly refer to, and presuppose, 3:22ff, the mention of the Pharisees is something new, being the main justification of the journey in the text.[12] The possible function of these introductory verses here depends on how we interpret 3:22—36.

This section is one of the less coherent scenes in the Gospel. The course of events is described only in fragments and it is often difficult to see how the different pieces fit together.[13] Under these circumstances the more over-riding structure should reveal something of the author's intention. The text begins by presenting Jesus and John as baptizing at the same time. Jesus is staying with his disciples[14] in the countryside of Judea, presumably near the Jordan, possibly in the vicinity of John's old place of baptism, 1:28; 10:40. John himself seems to have gone off up north to Samaria, or perhaps to the Decapolis area.[15] Thus both of them are baptizing and winning followers but in separate places. People come

[9] See the comments on E 5, E 6 and E 8 above (3.2.1) and 3.2.3.

[10] Ὡς οὖν often has an introductory character; see 2.2, U 20. The beginning of ch. 4 cannot be regarded as the conclusion of what precedes.

[11] This clause seems to be in direct speech, a quotation of what people said (the present tense, Ἰησοῦς and not ὁ κύριος as before), Abbott 1906, p. 466.

[12] Note, however, μετὰ Ἰουδαίου in 3:25, and see the comment on E 4 above (3.2.1).

[13] The solutions offered by literary criticism are many. See, for example, the discussion in Brown, Comm., ad loc.

[14] It is noted twice in v. 22 that the disciples are with Jesus. Cf. 4:2. They are mentioned here for the first time after 1:35ff; 2:12—if we disregard the comments in 2:17,21—and we meet them again in 4:2, 8, 27, 31—38 and then in ch. 6.

[15] It is difficult to identify *Aenon near Salim* with certainty. Verse 26 suggests that John the Baptist was staying on the western side of Jordan and the note in v. 23 (there was much water) may indicate that he was not baptizing in the Jordan. The most probable site of Salim is 7 km east-southeast of Shechem, Brown, Comm., ad loc. (referring to W.F. Albright) and Boismard 1973, pp. 219ff (referring to Gen 23:18 (LXX) and Jub 30:1). Aenon—the modern Ainun 14 km northeast of the modern Salim—would then be in the heart of Samaritan territory. Boismard 1973, p. 223, summarizes: "La localisation de Aenon et de Salem en plein coeur de la Samarie, non seulement est favorisée par les données toponymiques samaritaines, mais encore est exigée par la logique interne et la théologie des récits johanniques: l'activité baptismale de Jean à Aenon (*Jn*, III,23) sert de préface à l'entretien de Jésus avec la Samaritaine (*Jn*, IV,4 ss.)." Jesus succeeds John not only in Judea but also in Samaria. Jesus "increases", John "decreases", 3:30.

to both, but definitely more to Jesus, πάντες ἔρχονται πρὸς αὐτόν, vv. 23, 26. This is the background to John the Baptist's words in vv. 27—30, the last we hear from him in the Gospel. The whole of the first part of the text points forward to these verses. The theme is as always regarding John in the Gospel: a comparison between him and Jesus.[16] The closing words give the theme which sums up the whole: ἐκεῖνον δεῖ αὐξάνειν, ἐμὲ δὲ ἐλαττοῦσθαι, v. 30. Then follows a more general remark in vv. 31—36, comparable with the many comments made by the author of the Gospel.[17] The summarizing theme mentioned above has to give way to a more general theme: the question of how individuals receive him whom God sent. Here too the closing words summarize the content of the text by mentioning the alternatives: ὁ πιστεύων—ὁ δὲ ἀπειθῶν, v. 36. The over-riding theme in 3:22—36 therefore is *how people flock to Jesus and become his disciples*,[18] πάντες ἔρχονται πρὸς αὐτόν, v. 26.[19] Jesus "increases". However, at the same time, this means that John the Baptist, according to Jn the chief witness among the Jews to Jesus' identity, must "decrease". The different parts of the text must be understood from this total aspect.

The dispute between a Jew and John's disciples concerning purification, καθαρισμός, v. 25, may not at first sight seem justified in this context, as suggested by the conjectures on the text. Why not merely a mention of the fact that when John's disciples learned that Jesus baptized more than John—cf. 4:1—they came to him and said? However, after what was said above, it is easy to associate with 1:19—2:22 and the function of purification there, especially mentioned in 2:6.[20] 1:19ff and 3:22ff may be seen as parallels at many points: the

[16] See 1:8 (οὐκ . . . ἀλλά); 1:15 (ὀπίσω μου . . . ἔμπροσθέν μου . . . πρῶτός μου); 1:19ff (the different names of Jesus); 1:33 (ἐν ὕδατι . . . ἐν πνεύματι); 3:29 (the bridegroom—the bridegroom's friend) and 5:35f; 10:41. The contrast between Jesus and John characterizes all that is said of the Baptist in Jn.

[17] Verses 31—36 comment on both ch. 3 and ch. 4. Schnackenburg, Comm., ad loc., places them before 3:13ff, and Brown, Comm., ad loc., compares them with 3:11—21 and 12:44—50. The marking of Jesus as the speaker in 12:44ff does not imply, as Brown suggests, that vv. 31—36 are an isolated discourse of Jesus without a quotation formula, attached to the scenes of ch. 3 as an interpretation of these scenes. Schnackenburg rightly notes that "die Alternative 'Offenbarungsrede Christi' oder 'kerygmatische Rede des Evangelisten'" are false (p. 394) and characterizes vv. 31—36 as "Rückblick auf das einmalige grosse Geschehen, von dem er berichtet, und Hinblick auf die Menschen, für die er schreibt, Geschichtsdeutung aund gegenwärtige Anrede, Zeugnis und Kerygma", as a part of "das johanneische Kerygma" (p. 393). These verses would then reveal the "horizon" of the narrator and be of special interest for the interpretation of ch. 4 as we now have it.

[18] This seems to be the theme of the whole beginning of the Gospel, 1:19—2:11 and 2:1—4:54. See my interpretation of 2:1—11 above in 2.4 and the interpretation of 4:1—42 below in 3.5.

[19] See also 11:48 (πάντες πιστεύσουσιν εἰς αὐτόν) and 12:19 (ἴδε ὁ κόσμος ὀπίσω αὐτοῦ ἀπῆλθεν). John came "that *all* might believe through him", 1:7. Note also the word of Jesus in 12:32: πάντας ἑλκύσω πρὸς ἐμαυτόν and see below, 3.4.6.

[20] See the comment on U 14 above (2.2) and the function of purification in the Sinai screen, 2.4.3.

triad of the Jews (the Pharisees),[21] John, and Jesus, the programme of the journey from the Jordan in Judea to Cana in Galilee, the theme of how Jesus receives disciples etc. The item on the large quantity of water in v. 23 also favours a connection, if it brings to the fore the baptism of John as a baptism in water.[22] In contrast to the Synoptic writers, Jn does not describe the baptism of John as other than a baptism $\dot{\epsilon}v\ \ddot{v}\delta\alpha\tau\iota$, 1:26, 31, 33, and as having a single purpose: to reveal Jesus to "Israel", the "true" people of God, 1:31.[23] The evangelist seems only to understand his baptism as a Jewish purification rite of the old order. Thus the question on purification naturally belongs to the theme of how the old merges into the new.

John's reply contains first a general clause, v. 27, which is later explained in vv. 28–30.[24] This rule may be given several interpretations according to the context in which it stands.[25] If we start from the context sketched above, the meaning seems to be as follows: Nobody can come to Jesus unless God gives him to Jesus. Since it is a reply to an implicit quesiton about Jesus (v. 26), v. 27 should be interpreted as referring to him. The total perspective rejects 6:35 and 19:11 as parallels, in favour of 6:37: $\pi\tilde{\alpha}v\ \ddot{o}\ \delta\iota\delta\omega\sigma\acute{\omega}\nu\ \mu\omega\iota\ \acute{o}\ \pi\alpha\tau\grave{\eta}\rho\ \pi\rho\grave{o}\varsigma\ \dot{\epsilon}\mu\grave{\epsilon}\ \ddot{\eta}\xi\epsilon\iota.$ The disciples as gift of God recur in several places in the Gospel. Cf. 17:2, 9, 11, 24; 10:29; 6:39 and perhaps even 3:35.[26] *God has given to Jesus all the people who come to him*—this is John's answer. For Jesus is $\acute{o}\ X\rho\iota\sigma\tau\acute{o}\varsigma$, he whom God sent. God had also sent John, but only to *go before*, to *bear witness*, v. 28. John is שושבין (the "best man"), Jesus is the bridegroom, v. 29. His task is only to bring the bride to the groom.[27] The bride in this context is the people who by baptism and by acceptance of Jesus' message, v. 33, come to Jesus. We have the same theme as in 1:19ff: Jesus being who he is, certain people gather round him. The people of the new covenant appears. John has the joy of being involved in this process when he reveals Jesus to "Israel". The joy is perfected just in the events narrated in the text, v. 29b. The old era is over, the eschatological age is beginning.

The evangelist's comment in vv. 31–36 refers to both Jn 3 and Jn 4.[28] The

---

[21] Note the variant reading 'Ιουδαίων in 3:25. There is no reason to hazard conjectures on the text. On the connection between "the Jews" and "the Pharisees" in Jn, see 3.2.1, E 4.

[22] On the difference between the baptism of John and the baptism of Jesus, see the literature mentioned above (3.2.1), note 7, and Schütz 1967, pp. 94ff, Wink 1968, pp. 87ff, Lentzen-Deis 1970, pp. 92ff, and Barth 1973, pp. 130ff.

[23] See above, 3.2.1, E 1, and Pancaro 1969–70, pp. 123ff.

[24] A common literary form in Jn; see 2.2, U 26.

[25] Referring to *John*, to *Jesus* or to *the believer*. See the surveys in Brown, Comm., ad loc.

[26] See also above, 2.2, U 6, and below, 3.3.2, S 3.

[27] This corresponds to the picture of John in 1:19ff. See above, 2.4.3. The Hebrew שושבין corresponds only partly to the English "best man". In our culture it usually is the father of the bride who brings the bride to the groom.

[28] Compare 3:31 and 3:6, 3:31 and 3:12, 3:32 and 2:23ff (especially 3:11 and cf. also 1:5, 10f),

emphasis on *the word, the testimony* and *the Spirit* in these verses is new in relation to the previous illustration of how the people gather round Jesus.[29] God stands as the sole source behind the events occurring around Jesus, the Messiah, him whom God sent, vv. 31—35. This is an outflow of God's love, v. 35. The continued analysis will show that there are many bonds linking this comment with the dialogues in Jn 4.[30] A consideration of the course of events gives us a common denominator: people come to Jesus, believe in him and become his disciples. This is most striking in 3:22—30; 4:1f and 4:39—42. Here the beginning and end of the Samaria text are tied together. This is one reason to include also the opening verses in chap. 4 in the Samaria text and, at least for the present, to hold open the possibility that the perspectives we saw in 3:22—4:4 and 4:43ff are relevant to the interpretation of the Samaria narrative.

Summary: The text has a striking conclusion, which binds vv. 5—42 together. In this conclusion we encounter only Jesus, the woman and the Samaritans, not Jesus' disciples. The introduction to the text is more complicated. Verses 5—6 are clearly terminal in character, while vv. 1—4 have a more transitional nature, which casts doubt on whether they should be included in the text. The first verses are particularly related to the context, 3:22ff and 4:43ff, and give a special perspective to the Samaria narrative: the old order with its water and purifications is disappearing and a new is coming into being through Jesus who is the Messiah, the one sent by God. To him alone has God entrusted the Spirit. Now a large throng of people gathers round Jesus, those who are baptized by Jesus' disciples, those who accept Jesus' testimony, those whom God gives to Jesus. As in 1:19ff we have an image of how the people of the new covenant is born from that of the old. John acts as "best man" at this wedding of bride and groom. He decreases while Jesus increases. The rest of the analyses will show whether this perspective is relevant to the interpretation of the Samaria narrative. Here I may say that the remarkable conclusion of the text, vv. 39—42, not only refers to vv. 5ff but also to the opening verses with their connection with 3:22ff.

3.2.3 Spatial Features

The analysis of the spatial features in the text must chiefly deal with the journeying pattern in vv. 5—42, the account of the two main sites (the town of Sychar and Jacob's well) and the "migration" from Judea to Galilee.

3:33 and 3:20ff (cf. 1:11ff), 3:34b and 3:5. On the connections with ch. 4, see the following analysis, 3.3.4, 3.4.4 and 3.5.

[29] Note, however, the *voice* of the bridegroom and the *listening* friend in v. 29.

[30] This concerns especially vv. 33—35, on those who receive Jesus' testimony, on the word of Jesus as the word of God, on the Spirit, on God who gives and on the relation between the Father and the Son.

The survey of the event units above under 3.2.1 shows a highly monotonous course: people *travel* and people *talk* to each other.[1] The various expressions for movement and rest come thick and fast: ἀφῆκεν, ἀπῆλθεν, v. 3, διέρχεσθαι, v. 4, ἔρχεται, v. 5, τῆς ὁδοιπορίας, ἐκαθέζετο, v. 6, ἔρχεται, v. 7, ἀπεληλύθεισαν, v. 8, ἦλθαν, v. 27, ἀπῆλθεν, v. 28, δεῦτε, v. 29, ἐξῆλθον, ἤρχοντο, v. 30, ἦλθον, μεῖναι, ἔμεινεν, v: 40. We also encounter verbs of movement in the dialogue: διέρχωμαι v. 15, ὕπαγε, ἐλθέ, v. 16, and with a somewhat different usage ἔρχεται, ἔλθῃ of the Messiah in v. 25.[2] The majority of these verbs have spatial adjuncts,[3] which gives a clear pattern in vv. 5—42: The first dialogue at the well (Jesus and the woman) takes place while the disciples go to the town and back, and the second (Jesus and the disciples) during the woman's, and later also the Samaritans', comings and goings. Thus we have a well defined *two scene composition,* which we recognize from other places in the Gospel. The well is the main scene, but the events taking place there are accompanied by action in the background, on the road between the two places or in the town. See further the discussion of this technique of composition under point 3.2.4.[4]

The description of *the two main sites in vv. 5f* seems to emphasize that the well is at the centre.[5] What does the text say of these places and what do we otherwise know about them?

The text itself gives a surprising amount of information, explicitly or implicitly, on the external features of the site of the events.

1. Jacob gave his son Joseph a field, v. 5.[6] This statement is based on a tradition combining information given in Gen 33:19; 48:22 and Jos 24:32. According to Gen 33:19, Jacob comes to Shechem and camps on a piece of land (LXX μερὶς τοῦ ἀγροῦ) which he later buys from the sons of Hamor[7] and dedicates with an altar to El-Elohe-Israel. At the end of his life, when Jacob blesses his sons, he gives Joseph (LXX δίδωμί σοι) a special ridge (MT שְׁכֶם, LXX Σίκιμα),[8] which he had taken from the Amorites by the sword. Joseph's bones are buried, according to Jos 24:32 (ἐν τῇ μερίδι τοῦ ἀγροῦ, οὗ ἐκτήσατο Ιακωβ παρὰ

---

[1] Disregarding E 1—5 we arrive at the following result: 15 of 27 units on movement and rest, 6 on verbal "acts", 2 on people believing and only 5 other units.

[2] Ἔρχεται is also used on ὥρα in v. 21 and εἰσεληλύθατε on the disciples' co-operation in the work in v. 38.

[3] To the town of Sychar in vv. 5, 7, 28, 30, 39, to Jacob's well in v. 6 (v. 40) and through πρὸς αὐτόν in v. 30 and v. 40. More references to space in the dialogues: vv. 11, 12, 13, 15, 20, 21.

[4] Johannine parallels to this technique are mentioned there.

[5] It is not said that the field (the well) was near the town, but that the town was near the field in which the well was.

[6] Χωρίον means "field", Mt 26:36; Acts 1:18. The method of localizing the places in vv. 5f indicates that χωρίον does not refer to a large area. Cf. the use of the word in the ingress of Ig Rom.

[7] Hamor, prince of Shechem, Gen 34:2; Jos 24:32 and Jg 9:28.

[8] Some Rabbinic sources support the reference to Shechem in Gen 48:22. See Str.-B., vol. 2, pp. 432f.

τῶν Ἀμορραίων τῶν κατοικούντων ἐν Σικιμοις), on the piece of land which Jacob bought according to Gen 33:19—which was evidently thought to be the same place as this ridge. Moreover the text says: ". . . it became an inheritance of the descendants of Joseph" (LXX   καὶ ἔδωκεν αὐτὴν Ιωσηφ ἐν μερίδι).
Stephen's speech in Acts implies that all the patriarchs were buried at Shechem, 7:15f.[9] In later times Joseph's grave at Shechem became a holy place.[10] Indeed the area all round Shechem was an ancient cult site, Gen 12:6f; 33:18ff; 35:4; Jos 24:26,32; Dt 11:29; Jg 9:6,37. For the Samaritans it was the centre of their religion.[11]

2. Jacob gave the well in the field to his son Joseph. This follows reasonably from the information in vv. 5f.[12] The well, here called Jacob's well, came with the field he received from Jacob, πηγὴ τοῦ Ἰακώβ.[13] This is generally identified as the Jacob's well of today at the foot of Mt. Gerizim, 32 m deep, with fresh running spring water and with two openings where water can be drawn with the necessary equipment.[14] However, the well is not mentioned in the OT or in Jewish or Samaritan literature, which may seem surprising in view of its central role in the Samaria narrative.[15] On the well see further the excursus, The Well in Jewish Tradition, 3.2.7.

3. Jacob gave the well[16] to the Samaritans. This is expressly stated in v. 12, ὃς ἔδωκεν ἡμῖν τὸ φρέαρ.   This suggests a connection between Jacob's son Joseph and the Samaritans, v. 5 and v. 12; this is strengthened by the presentation of Jacob as the ancestor of the Samaritans, τοῦ πατρὸς ἡμῶν Ἰακώβ, v. 12.[17] Thus,

[9] This has been taken as an indication of th Samaritan background of Stephen's speech, Spiro 1967 p. 286, Scharlemann 1968, pp. 12ff. Acts 7:15f, according to both Schenke 1968, p. 168, and Kippenberg 1971, p. 112, is evidence of that Jacob was believed to be buried at Shechem. In the OT, Josephus and Rabbinic sources, Jacob's tomb is at Hebron, Str.-B., vol. 2, p. 676.

[10] Schenke 1968, pp. 174ff.

[11] See the following investigation.

[12] Ἐκεῖ refers to χωρίον. This is the most plausible solution. Thus Jerome (in quo), against Eusebius (ἐν ᾗ), according to Schenke 1968, pp. 166f.

[13] The omission of the article does not imply the meaning "a well of Jacob" but the expression is regarded as a geographical name, Bl.-Debr. § 261,1.

[14] Schnackenburg, Comm., ad loc. There seems to be no doubt of the identification of this well. See, besides the commentaries, Schenke 1968 and the literature he mentions.

[15] Str.-B., vol. 2, pp. 431f, refers to ‏סוכר‎ ‏עין‎ as a possible parallel, translated "Quelle von Sykhar"; Sychar is in Talmudic literature the same as Askar. Only two passages are mentioned: M Men X.2 and p Shek 5.48[d].19. But Askar has many wells, Schnackenburg, Comm., ad loc.—‏עין‎ ‏יעקב‎ is mentioned in Dt 33:28 but this passage is not linked to Jacob's well in Shechem in the early versions (LXX, Vulg., the Samaritan Pentateuch or Targum, the Aramaic Targums).

[16] On the change of πηγή to φρέαρ, see 3.2.7.

[17] Barrett, Comm., ad loc., notes that it is not usual outside the NT to call one of the patriarch πατήρ. See, however, Mek ad Ex 14:15 and especially the Targums, for example, TJ I and TJ II ad Gen 28:10. TJ II has "our father Jacob" seven times in a very short passage. The different texts in Lentzen-Deis 1970, pp. 217ff.

according to the text, the Samaritans are the descendants of Jacob, descendants of Joseph etc. This belief is confirmed by other sources. Josephus says of the Samaritans: . . . ἐκ τῶν Ἰωσήπου γενεαλογοῦντες αὐτοὺς ἐκγόνων Ἐφραίμου καὶ Μανασσοῦ.[18] Rabbi Meir says, according to Pesiqta 11 (Pes K), that the Samaritans call Jacob their father, and Jacob, and in particular Joseph, hold a preeminent position in the Samaritan sources.[19] The description of the site in vv. 5f, therefore, brings to the fore the Samaritans' claim to be descended from Jacob, the patriarch who has a special relationship to *the people* Israel, to the 12 tribes,[20] and who, at least in some Jewish circles, is represented as the real father of the true Israel. Jacob and his children are the people for God's possessing for all time to come.[21] According to Samaritan belief he is "the actual progenitor of the elect".[22] The description of the sites in vv. 5f not only gives a geographic placing of the events but also points to central religious traditions among the Samaritans. For them Joseph's field and the land there and in its vicinity became an equivalent to the Jews' Mamre at Hebron. This was their holy centre.[23]

4. Jacob, his sons and his sheep[24] used to drink from the well, v. 12. No text telling of this has been preserved. See however the excursus on the Well, 3.2.7.

5. The Samaritans were accustomed to drink from the well. This is implied by v. 7, v. 12 and v. 15, where the woman who is wont to go there, v. 15, is presented as γυνὴ ἐκ τῆς Σαμαρείας, v. 7, and the well is described as belonging

---

[18] Ant XI.341. The same in Ant IX.291: . . . ὡς ἐξ Ἰωσήπου φύντες καὶ τὴν ἀρχὴν ἐκεῖθεν τῆς πρὸς αὐτοὺς ἔχοντες οἰκειότητος . . . This was a very natural claim since Samaria included most of the territories of Ephraim and Manasseh, Jos 16f. These two tribes may have the name "Joseph", Gen 49:22ff; Jg 1:22ff, also Jos 16:4. The tribe of Ephraim was the most important and "Ephraim" often stands for the Northern Kingdom, Is 9:8; 11:13; 17:3; 28:1,3; Hos 4:17; 5:3,11; 9:3; 12:1 etc.

[19] On the Rabbinic material, see Schlatter, Comm., ad loc., and Ginzberg, vol. 6, p. 361. On the Samaritan material, see Bowman 1950, p. 242 ("proudly and defiantly it is asserted that they are Joseph's sons"), p. 247, MacDonald 1964, index s.v. *Jacob* and *Joseph*, especially pp. 227 and 448, Meeks 1967, pp. 227ff, and Kippenberg 1971, pp. 111f, 199, 203, 226, 250ff. Kippenberg has a whole chapter on Joseph. Note the position of Joseph in Stephen's speech (Acts 7), Scharlemann 1968, pp. 39ff.

[20] See H. Odeberg in ThWNT, vol. 3, pp. 191f. He quotes b Shab 146a: "Drei Generationen hindurch schwand die Unreinheit nicht von unseren Vätern: Abraham zeugte Ismael, Isaak zeugte Esau, erst Jakob zeugte die zwölf Stämme, an denen kein Makel war".

[21] See A. Weiser in ³RGG, vol. 3, col. 520, and, for example, the Book of Jubilees, in which Jacob is presented as the true heir of Abraham, 1:28; 19:15ff; 22:10ff; 25:4ff; 33:21ff; 36:1ff. "The children of Jacob" is a parallel expression to "Israel", 1:28. Jacob and "his seed" are to be sanctified by God as a nation of His inheritance. God will cleanse them and renew the covenant with them, 22:10, 12, 14f, 29f.

[22] MacDonald 1964, p. 448.

[23] This has been especially stressed by Schenke 1968.

[24] "θρέμματα sind im Unterschied von den anderen Haustieren die Schafe", Schlatter, Comm., ad loc. Both Josephus (Ant II. 258, 263) and Philo (Vita Mosis I. 51, 53) use this word when describing Moses at the well of Midian (Ex 2:15ff). See below 3.2.5 and 3.2.7.

to the Samaritans, ἡμῶ, v. 12. Judging by the account that follows, the woman seems to live in Sychar and there have been conjectures as to why she did not go to one of the springs which lay nearer the town.[25] As the text now reads, the well emerges as belonging to all the Samaritans, not to be compared with any other spring, and the woman as a representative of the Samaritans.[26]

6. The well is deep, calling for equipment, gives ὕδωρ ζῶν, which nevertheless cannot slake the thirst forever, vv. 11, 13. The description of the well agrees with what we know of Jacob's well today. See further 3.2.7.

7. Near Joseph's field is the town of Sychar, v. 5. Some scholars previously identified Sychar with the now small town of Askar at the foot of Mt. Ebal, about 1 km north-east of Jacob's well, and Schenke seems to me to have clearly shown that this is true.[27] After Shechem's destruction by the Jews in 128 and 107 B.C., and before the erection of Neopolis was begun in 72 A.D., Askar appears to have been a rather large town, which seems to have taken Shechem's place, namely to have been *the* Samaritan religious and national centre. The town in our account would then be a centre for the Samaritans.

8. Near the well lies Mt. Gerizim. This is implied by the words ἐν τῷ ὄρει τούτῳ, vv. 20f,[28] i.e. the mountain was assumed to be so well known that it is not named at all. The readers of the text were also evidently expected to be well acquainted with the topography.[29] Mt. Gerizim's all over-shadowing place in Samaritan belief need not be expounded here.[30] All we can establish is that the mention of the mountain confirms what was said before; by means of the place description in the Samaria text and allusions to it, the site of the event is presented as the Samaritans' most holy place. The data on the topography of the text, which is presumed to be known to the reader, agree with what can now be established by archaeology, and also the traditions associated with it are confirmed by other sources, but with one exception: we have no material on Jacob's well. In the excursus in 3.2.7 I shall discuss material which may illustrate this.

Therefore: the spatial features in the text, their dominant position, their reference to Samaritan centres and their association with traditions about the

---

[25] See, for example, Godet and Lagrange, Comm., ad loc.

[26] See below, 3.2.5.

[27] Schenke 1968. This localization is preferred by Schnackenburg and Lindars, Comm., ad loc., Str.-B., vol. 2, p. 431, and Kippenberg 1971, p. 94. Brown, Comm., ad loc. reads Συχέμ instead of Συχάς. For a discussion of different possibilities, see Brown and Lindars, Comm. ad loc. Some would see a symbolic meaning in the name: Συχέμ has been altered to Συχάρ, which recalls the meanings "drunk" or "drunken" (from שכר). See, for example, Kreyenbühl 1905, pp. 395ff. Early literature mentioned in Holtzmann, Comm., ad loc.

[28] Cf. the same deictic constructions in v. 13 and v. 15.

[29] This textual feature need not contradict the comment in v. 9c. See below, 3.2.5.

[30] See most recently MacDonald 1964, pp. 327ff, and Kippenberg 1971, passim, and the literature they mention.

Samaritans, Jacob's sons, decisively focus on Samaria and the Samaritans in Jn 4.[31]

We are left with *the spatial notes in vv. 1—4*. Formerly I described the cyclic structure revealed by the geographical data in Jn, and in this connection I maintained that Galilee has in Jn certain "ecclesial" overtones.[32] The direction of movement was there *toward* Jerusalem. The events occurring in Jerusalem take up more and more space in the Gospel the further forward we come. The rejection of Jesus and the mortal danger to him is gradually intensified, and the happenings described in the Gospel culminate in the events of the "hour". These occupy more than half the Gospel chs. 12—20 (21), with ch. 11 as an introduction. The journeyings in this geographical pattern are regulated by the laws of the "hour".

The opposite direction of movement is dominant in Jn 4; away *from* Jerusalem. Nowhere else in the Gospel is so much attention devoted to spatial movement;[33] there is therefore reason to discuss the "geographical pattern" once more, and this also with the analysis of the Samaria text in mind. This says:

ὡς οὖν ἔγνω . . . ἀφῆκεν τὴν Ἰουδαίαν, 4:1, 3.
καὶ ἀπῆλθεν πάλιν εἰς τὴν Γαλιλαίαν, 4:3.
ἔδει δὲ αὐτὸν διέρχεσθαι διὰ τῆς Σαμαρείας, 4:4.
μετὰ δὲ τὰς δύο ἡμέρας ἐξῆλθεν[34] ἐκεῖθεν εἰς τὴν Γαλιλαίαν. αὐτὸς γὰρ
 Ἰησοῦς . . . 4:43f.
ὅτε οὖν ἦλθεν εἰς τὴν Γαλιλαίαν, 4:45.
ἦλθεν οὖν πάλιν εἰς τὴν Κανὰ τῆς Γαλιλαίας, 4:46.
Ἰησοῦς ἥκει ἐκ τῆς Ἰουδαίας εἰς τὴν Γαλιλαίαν, 4:47.
(πάλιν δεύτερον) . . . ἐλθὼν ἐκ τῆς Ἰουδαίας εἰς τὴν Γαλιλαίαν, 4:54.

Jn 4 must in any case be said to contain an almost too obvious marking of Jesus' travels. Why these repetitions? If they are intended to act only as conjunctions—and there is no doubt that they have this function—why then must the junction be so compact? The way in which the present text is constructed indicates that these textual features contain something more. Yet it is difficult to comprehend what this may be.[35] Three points may be established for a start:

1. The text constantly reiterates that the journey goes *from* Judea *to* Galilee *through* Samaria, 4:3f, 43, 47, 54, and if we also include ch. 3, from *Jerusalem in Judea* to *Cana in Galilee,* 2:23ff; 3:22; 4:46.

[31] From the topographical features in Jn, Kundsin 1925, pp. 27ff, concludes that Jn 4 is a cult legend which presents *opera ecclesiae* as *opera Jesu.* See below, 3.5.
[32] See above, 2.2, U 3, and 2.4.4.
[33] Note however the introduction to chs. 7—10.
[34] That ἐξῆλθεν . . . εἰς is an unnatural expression is proved by variant readings (καὶ ἀπῆλθεν or καὶ ἦλθεν), mentioned in the apparatus of Nestle-Aland.
[35] Cf. Brown's words on 4:43—45 ("a notorious crux") and his survey of different interpretations, Comm., ad loc.

143

2. The journey is presented as a repetition, $\pi\acute{\alpha}\lambda\iota\nu$, 4:3, 46, 54; cf. $\delta\epsilon\acute{\upsilon}\tau\epsilon\rho\upsilon\nu$ $\sigma\eta\mu\epsilon\tilde{\iota}\upsilon\nu$, 4:54. It is the *second* journey from Judea to Galilee.[36]

3. The journey is justified partly by 4:44 ($\gamma\acute{\alpha}\rho$), partly by 4:1 ($\dot{\omega}\varsigma$ $\upsilon\tilde{\upsilon}\nu$). These justifications are of course of special interest.

The chief reason why Jesus withdraws to Galilee is to be found in 4:44. This verse was subjected to detailed analysis by Johannes Willemse; he came to the conclusion that $\dot{\eta}$ $\iota\delta\acute{\iota}\alpha$ $\pi\alpha\tau\rho\acute{\iota}\varsigma$ refers to Judea and Jerusalem.[37]

According to common usage, $\gamma\acute{\alpha}\rho$ at the beginning of the verse marks that what follows explains what precedes.[38] Furthermore vv. 5—42 are a parenthesis in the journey from Judea to Galilee, a *passing through*.[39] Thus 4:43ff links up with 4:1—4. There the reason for the journey is evidently a threat from the Pharisees.[40] The Jews' unwillingness to accept Jesus, 2:23ff, becomes, later in the Gospel, the stronger by the contrast with the Samaritans in 4:5—42. Thus the context preceding the passage indicates that $\dot{\eta}$ $\pi\alpha\tau\rho\acute{\iota}\varsigma$ is Judea and Jerusalem.

That which follows v. 44 gives further support for this belief. For even if the Galileans' acceptance of Jesus in 4:45 is not intended to convey much more than the related item on the Jews in Jerusalem in 2:23ff, in Jn 4 it leads to a true and perfect belief in Jesus in 4:46ff, and this in contrast to the development in 2:23ff.[41] In Galilee, according to the author, Jesus is properly received at Cana.[42]

To see Judea and Jerusalem as Jesus' $\pi\alpha\tau\rho\acute{\iota}\varsigma$ also agrees with the Gospel as a whole. When God's son came into the world he came primarily to *Judea, Jerusalem* and *the Temple,* his Father's house, 2:16. His divine work of salvation was concentrated there, "when the hour was come".[43] $\Pi\alpha\tau\rho\acute{\iota}\varsigma$ may mean "native land", "native town" or "father's house" (German: Vaterland, Vaterstadt or

---

[36] Jn 2:11 and 4:54 have been analysed above, 2.2, U 27.

[37] Willemse 1964—65. See also Meeks 1967, pp. 39ff, and the discussions in the commentaries of Schnackenburg, Brown and Lindars. Schnackenburg, referring to Origen, Barrett, Dodd, Feuillet and others, resolutely takes sides against this interpretation, Lindars takes sides with it. Brown regards v. 44 as an addition by the redactor. On the arguments see the following examination.

[38] The opposite in Schnackenburg and Brown, Comm. ad loc.: v. 44 explains v. 45. If v. 44 is an addition and mainly explains v. 45 as Brown suggests, why has the redactor not added v. 44 *after* v. 45?

[39] See above 3.2.2. Judea is the main point of departure, not Samaria; against Brown, Comm., ad loc.

[40] See above, 3.2.1, E 4.

[41] Note the same phenomenon in ch. 6 (vv. 14, 22ff, *contra* vv. 60ff)

[42] See above 2.2, U 3, and 2.4.4.

[43] Jn's constant emphasis of Jesus' Galilean origin, 1:45f; 6:42; 7:3, 41, 52; 18:5, 7; 19:19, need not contradict this, as Schnackenburg and Brown, Comm., ad loc., assert. We have here two different aspects of Jesus' life. Lindars, Comm., ad loc., rightly notes that Jn 4:44 must be regarded "from the point of view of the history of salvation (cf. Sir 24.8—12)".

Vaterhaus).[44] In v. 44 its primary reference must be to Jerusalem where "the Jews" and "the Pharisees", in the Johannine sense, had their headquarters. This interpretation is in harmony with the words of the prologue, 1:10f. "Lorsqu'il vient dans le Temple, il vient 'chez lui' ($\epsilon\grave{\iota}\varsigma$ $\tau\grave{\alpha}$ $\check{\iota}\delta\iota\alpha$, 1:11). Car c'est Dieu qui est son 'propre Père' ($\pi\alpha\tau\grave{\eta}\rho$ $\check{\iota}\delta\iota\sigma\varsigma$, 5:18) et c'est le Temple qui est la 'maison de son Père' ($\grave{o}$ $o\check{\iota}\kappa\sigma\varsigma$ $\tau\sigma\tilde{\upsilon}$ $\pi\alpha\tau\rho\acute{o}\varsigma$ $\mu\sigma\upsilon$, 2:16)".[45] The context in which v. 44 is set, the verse's own wording and its relationship to the Gospel in general seem to me to demand that it be interpreted as referring to Judea and above all, to Jerusalem.

The interpretation of 4:44 is the more vital as it colours the entire programme of the journey in ch. 4. If the above interpretation is correct—and in my opinion the reasons adduced are convincing—Jesus' journeys are seen from the viewpoint that he is *the Son of God,* come into the world to save the world. The journeys are seen as important parts of his saving work on earth. The wording of the second justification, Jn 4:1—4, also favours such a *divine* aspect of the journeys, although in less decisive terms. Jn 4:1—4 may be read as follows: Our Lord ($\grave{o}$ $\kappa\acute{\upsilon}\rho\iota\sigma\varsigma$) in his omniscience sees the situation ($\check{\epsilon}\gamma\nu\omega$), he leaves ($\grave{\alpha}\varphi\tilde{\eta}\kappa\epsilon\nu$) Judea of his own volition and must ($\check{\epsilon}\delta\epsilon\iota$) then, in accordance with God's salvation plan, pass through Samaria. This realization of God's will tires Jesus ($\kappa\epsilon\kappa\sigma\pi\iota\alpha\kappa\grave{\omega}\varsigma$ $\grave{\epsilon}\kappa$ $\tau\tilde{\eta}\varsigma$ $\grave{o}\delta\sigma\iota\pi\sigma\rho\acute{\iota}\alpha\varsigma$).[46] The whole of Jn 4 should then be considered from a specific aspect: *how the Son performs his work on earth,* work which is of the Father and justified by his redeeming will.

If the journeys are now considered from the point of view of Jesus' $\check{\epsilon}\rho\gamma\sigma\nu$,[47] and we have already found reason to speak of *two phases* in Jesus' work of salvation,[48] with the "hour" of Jesus as the critical point in time, the question arises whether we have anything similar in Jn 4. On occasion, scholars have wondered whether the Samaria narrative describes the *opera Jesu* or the *opera ecclesiae.* In the analysis of the Cana miracle we found that the two phases were projected, so to speak, into each other, and that they could be regarded as fused in an account of the *opera Christi.*[49] Phase 2 shed a light of revelation on phase 1 and gave the co-ordinating total aspect of the events narrated from phase 1. Does Jn 4 contain anything similar?

---

[44] See the material adduced by Willemse 1964—65, pp. 359ff, especially 2 Macc 13:14 on the *Temple,* the *town* and the *native land.* On other features of v. 44 which confirm his interpretation, see pp. 358ff.

[45] Willemse 1964—65, p. 364. This interpretation of 1:10f, however, is not necessary for the interpretation of 4:44 given here.

[46] On the details of vv. 1—4, see above 3.2.1, E 5—9, Among modern commentaries only Schwank gives a "divine" and a "human" reading of these verses.

[47] On the *ergon* perspective in the text, see especially the analysis of vv. 31—38 below (3.4) and the summary in 3.5.

[48] See above 2.2, U 27—31, and my interpretation of the Cana narrative (2.4.2).

[49] See 2.4.2.

To answer this question we must take the whole text into account.[50] However, there is interesting parallel material which should be mentioned in this context, namely two earlier "emigrations" from Jerusalem in Judea.

A number of personal designations in Jn have always caused difficulties because of their ambiguity. These include οἱ Φαρισαῖοι, οἱ Ἰουδαῖοι, Ἰσραήλ and λαός.[51] We find the first two in our text. The commentary on E 4 above (3.2.1) gives material showing that οἱ Φαρισαῖοι in Jn tends to reflect a later period, i.e. the narrator's own situation, although the term also referred to Jesus' own time. The Pharisees are in a number of cases set on a par with the Johannine concept of οἱ Ἰουδαῖοι, namely a general usage in Jn of those who regarded Jerusalem as centre of their religion, and thus in particular the leaders of the cult there, the priests.[52] Οἱ Ἰουδαῖοι as a special term in Jn is clearly oriented to Judea—Jerusalem—the priesthood, and this in contrast to Ἰσραήλ and λαός, which denote the people of God, the children of God scattered throughout the world.[53] The conclusion therefrom that οἱ Ἰουδαῖοι only denotes those who live in Judea[54] constitutes negligence of the manifest religious and sacerdotal sense of the word. It suggests rather the use of Judah in the Damascus Document. *Judah* is there "Bezeichnung des offiziellen, im Jerusalem sesshaften Priestertums", *Ephraim* a symbol of the sect, CD VII. 10—21a.[55] "Ephraim" was once part of "Judah" but was compelled to emigrate to "Damascus". There the new covenant was concluded, CD VIII.12ff; XIV.1f; XX.22; VI.3ff; VIII.21. The new people of God are those cursed by Israel, שבי ישראל, IV.2; VI.5; VIII.6,[56] those who left the land of Judah and settled in the country of Damascus, היוצאים מארץ יהודה ויגורו בארץ דמשק VI.5.

Gerhard Kippenberg has recently shown that there are several parallels between the rise of the Samaritan cult and that at Qumran.[57] As far as Samaria is concerned, old conflicts derive from the time when Israel was divided into two kingdoms. Kippenberg describes the Gerizim cult as "die Folge einer Verdrängung von Priestern, die sich nordisraelitischen Traditionen verbunden fühlten".[58] The question of the *whole* of Israel—Judea, Samaria and Galilee—is also topical in Jn 4, but at this stage of the analysis it is difficult to determine

---

[50] See below, 3.5.

[51] Note also ἡ μήτηρ τοῦ Ἰησοῦ, ὁ μαθητὴς ὃν ἠγάπα ὁ Ἰησοῦς, ἀρχιτρίκλινος, βασιλικός.

[52] Buchanan 1968, pp. 162ff, gives an historical survey of the interpretation of οἱ Ἰουδαῖοι in Jn.

[53] See above, 2.2, U 6 and U 30, and Pancaro 1969—70, pp. 123ff.

[54] Thus Buchanan 1968, pp. 158ff, 172f.

[55] van der Woude 1957, pp. 46, 23, 219ff. See also CD IV.11; XIVf.

[56] For a justification of this translation, see van der Woude 1957, p. 11. "Israel" is used in CD for the people as such, consisting of two houses, Ephraim and Judah, VII.12f, but rather often for the people who apostatized, I.3,14; III.14; IV.1, 13, 16; V.19; VI.1; VII.18; XVI.3; XX.16,23.

[57] Kippenberg 1971, especially pp. 33ff.

[58] Kippenberg 1971, p. 59.

whether the pattern of the journeys from Judea to Galilee has any relevance to concrete events after "the hour of Jesus", i.e. in the history of the early Church, and whether the "Johannine community" had to emigrate in the same way as mentioned above. The course of events underlying the accounts in Acts naturally come to mind. Nevertheless I must leave these questions open for the time being.

Therefore: It is possible to interpret the itinerary in Jn 4 merely as a journey which Jesus either did make or could have made *or* as part of the wanderings of God's Son on earth as he performs his Father's work of salvation—I previously suggested the existence of this "divine" aspect of the journey information in Jn 4—*or* as a section from the earliest Christian history, a migration from Jerusalem through Samaria to Galilee because of persecution in Jerusalem *or* a combination of all three aspects. The second aspect in particular, Jesus' *ergon,* may incorporate the first and the third. Yet this analysis of the spatial features has established with certainty the two scene composition of the text and the strong focus on Samaria and the Samaritans.

3.2.4 Temporal Features

First of all we must state that the temporal markings in the text strongly emphasize the *two scene composition* already mentioned. The narrative provides two parallel courses of events, which change scenes in the middle:

Jesus arrives at the well.

The woman comes to the well to draw *water*.	The disciples go to the town to buy *food*.
Jesus talks with the woman (on drinking).	(The disciples buy food). The disciples return to the well (with *food*) and are astounded by the conversation.
The woman leaves the well without her jar (*water*). The woman goes to the town. The woman bears witness to the townspeople. Many come to believe in Jesus. They go out to Jesus at the well.	**Jesus talks with his disciples (on eating).**

All gather at the well.

Apart from the order of the sentences in the text, this temporal pattern is created by the use of tenses and the temporal phrases in vv. 8, 27, 30 and 31.

Verses 7—30 are held together by what the woman does. Verses 8 and 27 are inserted into this passage, both preparing for vv. 31—38.[1] By placing the information concerning the disciples *after* the statement in v. 7 the reader is, so to speak, faced with what is happening—has happened—*behind the scenes*.[2] From v. 8 onwards, he has to expect two courses of events. Verse 8 tells him *that* the disciples are with Jesus, a fact obviously assumed throughout the Gospel after 1:19—2:12, *that* they have already left the well ($\dot{\alpha}\pi\epsilon\lambda\eta\lambda\dot{\upsilon}\vartheta\epsilon\iota\sigma\alpha\nu$), and *that* they will surely reappear later in the narrative with what food they were able to obtain. They return just as the dialogue is coming to an end, v. 27 ($\dot{\epsilon}\pi\grave{\iota}\ \tauo\dot{\upsilon}\tau\omega$,[3] the use of the imperfects $\dot{\epsilon}\vartheta\alpha\dot{\upsilon}\mu\alpha\zeta o\nu$, $\dot{\epsilon}\lambda\dot{\alpha}\lambda\epsilon\iota$, the content of the verse). Verse 27, its position and its content, makes it quite clear that in the text the disciples are confronted with the meeting between Jesus and the woman and with their conversation, vv. 7—26. We have their reaction in v. 27.[4] Otherwise no mention is made of events behind the scenes when the parallelism begins.

In the latter part of the text, from v. 28 onwards, the two courses of events are more detailed.[5] The woman's activity in the town is described and concludes with the departure of the people (imperfect $\ddot{\eta}\rho\chi o\nu\tau o$)[6] to Jesus. Like v. 8, v. 30 indicates that those mentioned in the verse will probably reappear on stage. While this is in progress on stage behind them, $\dot{\epsilon}\nu\ \tau\tilde{\omega}\ \mu\epsilon\tau\alpha\xi\dot{\upsilon}$, a confrontation between Jesus and his disciples takes place ($\ddot{\eta}\rho\dot{\omega}\tau\omega\nu$, $\epsilon\ddot{\iota}\pi\epsilon\nu$, $\ddot{\epsilon}\lambda\epsilon\gamma o\nu$, $\lambda\dot{\epsilon}\gamma\epsilon\iota$). This dialogue clearly plays on the events going on in the background.[7]

These temporal notes in vv. 8, 27, 30 and 31 show how well planned the literary composition is.[8] I find it difficult to regard this only as evidence that the author is a skilful narrator who can use scanty material to link up elements which he otherwise interprets differently.[9] It is reasonable to assume that the man who wrote this text saw a connection between its different parts. In any case this

---

[1] Note the use of $o\ddot{\upsilon}\nu$ in v. 9 and v. 28, which sometimes occurs after parenthetical passages; see 2:16—18; 3:23—25.

[2] A similar use of the pluperfect in 7:30; 8:20; 11:13 and also 1:24. In parenthetical passages, 3:24; 9:22; 11:19, 30, 57. See Abbott 1906, pp. 348f.

[3] 'E$\pi\grave{\iota}$ $\tauo\dot{\upsilon}\tau\omega$ has a nuance of "in the meantime" (German "während-dessen") and some manuscripts read $\dot{\epsilon}\nu\ \tau\tilde{\omega}\ \lambda\alpha\lambda\tilde{\eta}\sigma\alpha\iota$, Bultmann and Schnackenburg, Comm., ad loc.

[4] See below, 3.2.5.

[5] The use of $\mu\epsilon\tau\alpha\xi\dot{\upsilon}$ as an adverb is very rare. See Barrett, Comm., ad loc, and also Abbott 1906, pp. 511f. Its position at the beginning of the clause gives it a certain emphasis.

[6] A similar use of $\ddot{\epsilon}\rho\chi\epsilon\sigma\vartheta\alpha\iota$ (aorist + imperfect + aorist) in 11:29—32; cf. 20:3f.

[7] See below, 3.4 and the summary in 3.5.

[8] The same literary device is used in Jn 7—8 (see Dodd 1953, p. 347) and specially in Jn 18:28—19:16, also 18:12—27. Note "the 'sandwich' constructions" in Mk 5:21—43; 11:12—21.

[9] Thus Leroy 1968, p. 148, on the latter part of the Samaria text: "Man wird aber aus diesen mehr oberflächlichen Entsprechungen nicht mehr ersehen, als dass der Evangelist ein geschickter Erzähler ist".

possibility, must be tested first, when we attempt to interpret the text as we now have it.

The order in the text in general, if we ignore the complicated insertion of clauses in the introduction, runs parallel with the course of events,[10] yet with one startling exception: v. 39, after the dialogue with the disciples, contains the first mention of the fact that the Samaritans came to believe in Jesus when they heard the woman's testimony. In the sequence of events, this would reasonably come before the statement in v. 30. Οὐκέτι in v. 42 refers to the length of time between the two occasions. It is difficult to find an explanation for this here.[11]

There are another two interesting temporal notes in the structure of events; ὥρα ἦν ὡς ἕκτη in v. 6, δύο ἡμέρας in v. 40.[12] The latter is repeated in the transitional phrase in v. 43, μετὰ δὲ τὰς δύο ἡμέρας. Although we have many parallels to such introductory constructions with μετά, we have no formal equivalent of 4:43.[13] The repetition would seem then to indicate that the author laid some emphasis on this detail in a narrative which is otherwise not at all rich in detail.[14] The wording of 4:43 underlines the view that the journey through Samaria was only a *passing through* and seeks to assert that the stay there was short.[15] There are possible associations of different kinds, but they cannot be established in any other way than by various aspects of the text as a whole.[16] The wording as such does not offer us many clues.

The statement of time in v. 6, ὥρα ἦν ὡς ἕκτη, says that Jesus came to Jacob's well *around noon*.[17] There is controversy as to whether this also has associations

---

[10] See the survey above, 3.2.1. Κεκοπιακώς in v. 6 may also be regarded as information *post eventum*.

[11] For further analysis of vv. 39—42, see below, 3.2.5 and 3.5.

[12] I have already noted πάλιν (v. 3) above, 3.2.3. On the use of ὡς οὖν in v. 1 and v. 40, see above 2.2, U 20.

[13] Jn 2:12; 3:22; 5:1; 6:1; 7:1; (11:7,11); 19:28,38; 20:26; 21:1. With the exception of 20:26 (μεθ' ἡμέρας ὀκτώ) all these phrases have τοῦτο or ταῦτα. Following this usage 4:43 would begin μετὰ τοῦτο / ταῦτα ἐξῆλθεν . . .

[14] Except for the description of the site in vv. 5f. See above 3.2.3.

[15] Commentators generally refer to Jn 11:6 (ἔμεινεν... δύο ἡμέρας), but in this context "two days" marks a considerable delay (Lazarus dies, 11:12f.).

[16] There are many possibilities. The temporal phrase in 11:6 is linked with Lazarus' death, which is to some extent a parallel to Jesus' death, and "a little while" (μικρόν) is an important theological concept in Jn, referring to Jesus' death and resurrection. "Two days" therefore may allude to the "hour" of Jesus, which has influenced other narratives in Jn (see above, 2.2, 9a and 2.3.4). The Samaritans' belief because of Jesus' word would not then come until *after* the "hour" of Jesus. —There may be some connection with the "third day" in 2:1 and its reference to the Sinai event. The text as it now stands seems to set the second Cana event on the third day, at the seventh hour (4:43,52). According to PRE 46 Israel received the commandments at Sinai "on Friday, on the 6th of the month, at the sixth hour of the day".

[17] Not at 6 p.m., as Walker 1960, p. 69f, suggests. His view that Jn is using the modern—the Roman—reckoning of hours does not solve the problems of the temporal markings in Jn, especially not Jn 19:14. See, besides the commentaries, Bruns 1966—67.

in any particular quarter. We know that Jn devotes an unusual amount of space to temporal notes[18] and that some of these may well have definite associative functions.[19] The possibility of a symbolic use in 4:6, therefore, should not be excluded.[20]

The commentators usually state that this is not the usual or the natural time for fetching water,[21] but that it is appropriate for rest and refreshment. The note on time has a natural place in the narrative, as an explanation of Jesus' exhaustion and thirst.[22] The fact that this is the case need not mean, however, that 4:6 can have no associative function.[23] Finally, therefore, I shall here mention three possible connections, although I cannot commit myself to any one of them. As we saw above, the view of the text as a whole tends to decide whether or not such associative features may be said to exist in the text.[24]

Perhaps the most common symbolic explanation is that we find in Bruns: the revelation emerges into full daylight in Jn 4.[25] It was, so to speak, high noon. We have the opposite in 13:30 and 3:2. Jesus' earthly time runs parallel with the time of revelation.[26]

R.H. Lightfoot, in his commentary, linked Jn 4 with the Passion narrative: Jesus' weariness, 4:6; 19:1f, his thirst, 4:7; 19:28, his completion of his Father's work, 4:34; 19:30.[27] The temporal note in 4:6 is then associated with the identical wording in 19:14. The time refers to Jesus' death. Such a shade of meaning could be supported by the other two statements of time in Jn 4, vv. 40 and 52, with their possible connection with the "hour" of Jesus.

Perhaps Ex 2:15—22 offers the most interesting parallel.[28] This passage tells

---

[18] 1:39; 4:6,52; 19:14 (reckoning of hours), 3:2; 13:30; 18:28; 19:39; 20:1,19; 21:3f (part of day or night), 1:29,35,43; 2:1,12, 19f; 4:40, 43,52; 6:22; 7:14,37; 11:6,17; 12:1 etc. (reckoning of days). Note also 5:9; 9:14; 20:1,19,26 (day of week), 2:13; 5:1; 6:4; 7:2 etc. (Jewish feasts) and 10:22 (season).

[19] See, for example, 1:19ff (six days), 13:30 (night) and 19:14 (the sixth hour). See above 2.2, U 1.

[20] Bruns 1966—67 interprets all markings of hours in Jn symbolically, but changes 1:39 to "the sixth hour" as in Codex Alexandrinus.

[21] Morris, Comm., ad loc., refers to Ex 2:15ff in Josephus' version (Ant II.257ff quoted below) as evidence that the custom was not really uncommon, but the situation there is very specific.

[22] Thus Bultmann, Barrett, Schnackenburg and Lindars, Comm., ad loc.

[23] The introductory verses may be read from the point of view of the history of salvation. See above 3.2.3.

[24] See especially 2.4.

[25] Bruns 1966—67, pp, 287f. He interprets 19:14 in the same way.

[26] Cf. Bultmann, Comm., p. 368, on Jn 13:30.

[27] Lightfoot, Comm., p. 122. Jn may "be recalling of set purpose incidents which point to the Passion, wherein man's salvation was wrought out", Morris, Comm., p. 255, referring to the phrase "the Saviour of the world" in 4:42.

[28] Kreyenbühl, Comm., vol. 2, p. 397 adduced Josephus, version of this event (Ant II.254ff), referring to Max Krenkel, and this passage has then been quoted in many commentaries.

how Moses fled from Pharaoh and came to the land of the Midianites, where he camped by the well (LXX: ἐκάθισεν ἐπὶ τοῦ φρέατος). Judging by vv. 17f the seven daughters of the Midianite priests were accustomed to come daily to the well to water their father's sheep; they came in the morning in order, if possible, to avoid the shepherds.[29] When on this occasion they were hindered by the shepherds Moses intervened to help them.[30] Josephus gives the following account of the scene:[31]

εἴς τε πόλιν[32] Μαδιανὴν ἀφικόμενος . . .
καθεσθεὶς ἐπί τινος φρέατος
ἐκ τοῦ κόπου καὶ τῆς ταλαιπωρίας ἠρέμει[33]
μεσημβρίας οὔσης
οὐ πόρρω τῆς πόλεως

If we add the item that Moses is presented on his journey as without food (ἄπορος τροφῆς) and that the word θρέμματα which does not otherwise occur in Biblical Greek, is to be found in Jn 4 and in Josephus' account, we have no choice but be struck by the startling similarities.[34] Yet how could just Josephus' version influence Jn 4? I could not confirm the details with which we are here concerned in other sources of the same text. Josephus' version can hardly be regarded other than as an embroidery of the Biblical text. Then was the situation in Ex 2 so similar to that in Jn 4 that the description of the scene was influenced by the Moses narrative?

Previously we were able to establish that the statements in 4:5ff correspond with the topography of the site (the town, the well) and that the journey here described concerns a wider context. These two circumstances may explain the description in Jn 4 apart from one detail: the timing. The Hebrew text of Ex 2 indicates that Moses reached the well in the morning, and Josephus' information is

Kreyenbühl wishes to show that in ch. 4 Jn is shaping a typical well scene, but the situation in Ex 2:15ff is too specific to be good evidence of typical well scenes (watering of sheep in a specific situation).

[29] The text is so read by Philo, Vita Mosis I.50ff, Josephus, Ant II.254ff, Ex R 1,32.

[30] He watered their sheep (LXX: τὰ πρόβατα, but Josephus and Philo τὰ θρέμματα as in Jn 4:12. See Ant II.258,263 and Vita Mosis I.51,53).

[31] Ant II.257. Parallels to Jn 4 are underlined.

[32] MT, LXX and Targ. all have the land of Midian. There is a place Madyan on the east of the gulf of Akabah but the context requires a site west of the gulf. See the note in Thackeray's translation of Josephus, vol. 4, pp. 276f. Josephus' description of the scene as a town with its well and the text in Ex 2:18—20 imply that the well was near to the town.

[33] Josephus has already said that Moses fled across the desert (διὰ τῆς ἐρήμου), where he was without provisions (ἄπορος . . . τροφῆς), "proudly confident of his powers of endurance", Ant II.256 (tr. by Thackeray).

[34] I could not find the details of Josephus' account in other sources. The Targums are very close to the Hebrew text. Ex R 1,32 notes that the daughters used to arrive "early" and come home "last". —The Biblical text mentions also "food" as does Jn 4, v. 20.

a way of presenting a fact already implicit in the event. Does the Moses scene in any way underlie Jn 4? This could explain the unusual timing, which the evangelist in his turn expressed in the same way as in 19:14, perhaps thus acquiring a further association. The question depends above all on whether Ex 2:15 is in any way relevant to our text. In the excursus on the Well (3.2.7) I shall show that the Moses scene forms part of a wider context, which may be related to the Samaria text.

3.2.5 Some Other Features

The text contains other features of interest for the analysis; I found it most practical to discuss them in a single context: logical relations (which are more pronounced only in vv. 39—42), forms of personal reference and the presentation of the *dramatis personae,* what they do and how they are brought together. I shall discuss the different characters in turn.

Jesus, unlike the others, is present in most of the event units, which is natural as he is the protagonist.[1] As the agent in the different event units, he is generally referred to as ὁ Ἰησοῦς, or merely by means of the verb ending, with the exception of v. 1, where I found reason to accept the reading ὁ κύριος.[2] Later, when we discuss the dialogues, we shall see that there he has many designations; in connection with the analysis of these I shall return to the words ἄνθρωπος and ὁ Χριστός in v. 29 and ὁ σωτὴρ τοῦ κόσμου in v. 42.[3] Thus, regarding the course of events, ὁ κύριος in v. 1 is the only term to attract attention. I showed above that the opening verses may be regarded from a special perspective, which is connected with Jesus as the Son of God.[4] In this context ὁ κύριος, which is encountered particularly in Jn 4, is explicable.

Jesus' actions are easy to describe: he *comes, stays, speaks* (and goes).[5] If we include v. 1 we also learn that Jesus *wins disciples.* Yet he does not baptize; his disciples do that, v. 2. This picture is undoubtedly reminiscent of that of the prologue: the Word itself came into the world, sojourned here, some received him, 1:9ff.

The woman is the first to meet this Jesus, v. 7. She is presented as γυνὴ ἐκ τῆς

---

[1] See the survey above, 3.2.1. In 23 of 32 unites Jesus is explicitly mentioned as agent, goal or in some other "role". Of the other 9 units, two are implicit (E 1 and E 16), one is closely linked to Jesus (E 31; cf. E 24) and the rest (E 13, 14, 17, 20, 21, 25) concern movements, two of which have *Jesus'* disciples as agents. The Samaritans occur in 10, the woman in 8 and the disciples in 6 units. This does not include the references in the two dialogues.

[2] See 3.2.1, E 5.

[3] See below 3.3.2, S 12, and above 3.2.1, E 23 and E 32.

[4] See 3.2.3.

[5] Verse 1 also mentions the insight of the Lord.

Σαμαρείας,[6] not as γυνὴ ἐκ τῆς πόλεως —cf. v. 39—or γυνὴ ἐκ τῆς Συχάρ, or indeed just γυνή. This startling presentation is later emphasized three times over in v. 9, in the quotation formula ἡ γυνὴ ἡ Σαμαρῖτις, in the speech, γυναικὸς Σαμαρίτιδος and in the comment, Σαμαρίταις. This beginning should be interpreted as meaning that the woman in some way stands for the Samaritans. She is a "daughter of Samaria". Later on she will be designated only as γυνή.[7]

Her *dialogue with Jesus* takes up more than half the narrative, being assigned a function in the text as a whole.[8] Thus the most important action is connected with her. Moreover we also learn that she *talks with the people of Sychar*, although this dialogue is only denoted in the text by two speeches, one from each side, v. 29 and v. 42.[9] Indeed both parties bear witness to Jesus.[10] The contrast in content should be noted: The woman says μήτι οὗτός ἐστιν ὁ Χριστός;[11] the townspeople confess οἴδαμεν ὅτι οὗτός ἐστιν ἀληθῶς ὁ σωτὴρ τοῦ κόσμου. Whether or not the woman came to believe may remain a moot point. So may the content of her possible faith. Yet one point is sure: the author who gave our text its present form is not primarily interested in *her* belief in Jesus but in that of the Samaritans. They are the first to be described as believing, at the end of the text, vv. 39, 41 and 42.[12]

Apart from these verbal "acts", the text notes that the woman *comes* and *goes*.[13] In the former case, the text says that she comes to fetch water, ἀντλῆσαι ὕδωρ, v. 7. As we saw above, the verb means roughly "to draw water from a spring".[14] The verb may also be read as an expression denoting "to acquire knowledge, to learn from some-one".[15] The fact that she takes a jar (ὑδρία) with her to the well is presumed self-evident in the contemporary environment. It is also highly probable that if Jesus asked the woman for some water, she would have given him her full jar from which to drink, as we read in Gen 24:14ff.[16]

---

[6] Cf. ἦν δὲ ἄνθρωπος ἐκ τῶν Φαρισαίων, 3:1, and Λάζαρος ἀπὸ Βηθανίας, 11:1. Σαμαρεία in NT always refers to the region of Samaria, not to the town.

[7] This applies also to v. 39 and v. 42. Γυνή is always used when the woman is agent (except in vv. 28b and 28c).

[8] On the references to the dialogue, see above 3.2.1, E 15.

[9] Note the change of tense: λέγει in v. 28 and ἔλεγον in v. 42.

[10] On the character of these speeches, see above 3.2.1, E 23 and E 32.

[11] She does not say: οἶδα ὅτι οὗτός ἐστιν Χριστός. The first part of her speech points to both vv. 16—18 and v. 25 (εἶπέν μοι πάντα) and v. 26 (Jesus' self-revelation). Therefore it implies a kind of belief in Jesus as the Messiah. On the character of her question, see above 3.2.1, E 23.

[12] The linguistic expressions imply a complete belief in Jesus as in 3:36 and 4:50,53. See above 2.2, U 31.

[13] E 14 and E 21 and implicitly in E 25—27.

[14] 2.2, U 17. Jesus has no vessel with which to draw the water (ἄντλημα), v. 11.

[15] See above, 3.2.1, E 14.

[16] Abraham's servant arrives at the well at the time when women go out to draw water (ἀντλῆσαι ὕδωρ, v. 13). It is assumed that they have jars and the servant is to say: ἐπίκλινον τὴν

When the jar is mentioned later in v. 28 the reference conveys no new information. Its presence was implicit from the beginning. This verse says that the woman *left her jar* at the well. This is the only detail in the description of the woman in the sequence of events. The details being few, it is perhaps not so unexpected that just this passage has given rise to such different interpretations.[17]

The most interesting material has been adduced by David Daube, who links up the details with v. 9c: οὐ γὰρ συγχρῶνται Ἰουδαῖοι Σαμαρίταις.[18] *The regulations for ritual cleanliness* for the Jews when dealing with the Samaritans, were tightened up on Pharisaic lines in the middle of the first century. A regulation from 65 or 66 A.D. says that "the daughters of the Samaritans are menstruants from their cradle", M Nid IV.1. Thus it was out of the question for a Jew to use a drinking vessel belonging to a Samaritan woman.[19] Daube also seeks to prove that the verb συγχρᾶσθαι is not confirmed in NT times in the traditional meaning "to be on friendly terms with". He explains the absence of v. 9c from several MSS.[20] by assuming that the evangelist's comment was unintelligible to some copyists, since they were not aware of this meaning of the verb. He suggests the translation: "Jews do not use—*scil.* vessels—together with Samaritans", allowing the dative in the phrase to be governed by the σύν of the verb and understanding an object. The fact that the woman leaves her jar at the well means, in his view, that she places it there at Jesus' disposal "to use it for getting water and drinking". According to Daube, this is part of the original point of the narrative, which seems to have become incomprehensible to Christian readers at an early date.

On the whole I find Daube's careful analysis convincing, although it met

---

ὑδρίαν σου, ἵνα πίω v. 14. Later the jar is explicitly mentioned, vv. 15, 16, 17, 18, 20, 43, 46. The situation is very clear, Rebekah lets down her jar from her shoulder and gives the stranger a drink, vv. 18,46.

[17] Many follow Chrysostom and the thought behind a variant reading in Codex Koridethi (τρεχουσα): the detail depicts the haste of the woman, her enthusiasm, her eagerness to spread the news. Schnackenburg, Schwank, Comm., ad loc. The abandoned jar meant, according to Godet and Lindars, Comm., ad loc., that she would certainly return. She left it so that Jesus could drink, Barrett, Comm., ad loc. The jar is a symbol of earthly things, Schwank, Comm., ad loc. Now she is filled by the Spirit and does not need anything earthly. "This detail seems to be John's way of emphasizing that such a jar would be useless for the type of living water that Jesus has interested her in", Brown, Comm., ad loc. The waterpot has the same function as the vessels in 2:6 and the multitude of water in 3:23, Kreyenbühl, Comm., vol. 2, p. 423.

[18] Daube 1956, pp. 373ff (first published in *Journ. of Bibl. Lit.* 69 (1950), pp. 137ff). I report his results in the following.

[19] The waterpot was of clay and had probably been in contact with her spittle, which was contaminating in a very high degree, M Kel I.1ff, Tos Shab I.14.

[20] Verse 9c is missing in, for example, Codex Sinaiticus, Codex Bezae and some Old Latin MSS (a, b, d, e, j). Metzger 1971, p. 206, suggests that the omission is accidental, or may "reflect scribal opinion that the statement is not literally exact and therefore should be deleted." The second alternative assumes that the verb means "to be on friendly terms with"!

strong opposition.[21] This primarily concerned his philological arguments.[22] Now the linguistic parallel material to συγχρᾶσθαι is extremely scanty, not least as regards the grammatical construction we find in the Samaria text.[23] Under such circumstances the context is of great significance. The linguistic material quoted by Daube and Hall seems to me to show that the meaning "to use something together with some one" is fully possible, if not the only alternative.[24] The material on contemporary customs included in Daube's paper is obviously relevant to the Samaria text.[25] His reasoning from textual criticism is also plausible. In addition to the material quoted by Daube there is the emphasis laid by Jn on *the purification*[26] and the importance of ritual cleanliness in the Jewish/Samaritan conflict.[27] It would also seem feasible to find an interpretation of v. 9c in association with the speech on which it comments. This evidently concerns a request for water, namely, in the contemporary environment, a loan of a woman's water jar. All this favours the interpretation: *the Jews do not use things together with the Samaritans in order to avoid being made unclean.*[28] Above all, the question of cultic and ritual cleanliness seems to me to be inherent in the evangelist's comment.

The interpretation of this remark in the text may seem highly peripheral, but the history of its interpretation shows that it often affected the interpretation of the text as a whole, not least because of conclusions drawn concerning the readers of the text.[29] The interpretation here given need not, however, be associated with the item in v. 28, although it is a possibility. If we consider the structure of the text, v. 28a refers back to v. 7 and the words ἀντλῆσαι ὕδωρ.[30] The item concerning the

---

[21] Barrett, Brown and Morris, Comm., ad loc., accept Daube's result, but Schnackenburg, Lindars, Comm., ad loc., and Hall 1971—72 firmly contradict him, saying that the verb has no object and that the meaning "to have commercial dealings with" is attested for the early second century.

[22] See especially Hall 1971—72. Lindars' main reason—that Gentiles must have understood this explanation—presupposes that the text was written for Gentile readers, which is in no way proved. See above, 2.4.1, and below, ch. 5, and the discussion there of the readers of the Gospel.

[23] The chief argument against Daube in Hall 1971—72 (there is no clear case where the dative after συγχρᾶσθαι depends on σύν) is contradicted by the Johannine use of συνσταυροῦσθαι in 19:32 (συσταυρωθέντος αὐτῷ) where σύν clearly governs αὐτῷ. Note that both Mt 27:44 and Mk 15:32 have σὺν αὐτῷ. See also the use of verbs with σύν in Jn 6:22; 11:33 and 18:15.

[24] As there is no proof that the verb is a technical term in regulations for ritual cleanliness I read an implicit τι in v. 9c.

[25] This is also acknowledged by Schnackenburg, Lindars and Hall.

[26] See above 2.2, U 14, 2.4.3, and on Jn 3:25 see above, 3.2.2.

[27] Kippenberg 1971, pp. 85ff.

[28] Note the translation in Brown, Comm., ad loc.: "use nothing in common". The formulation in v. 9c is somewhat general. The traditional rendering is to some extent contradicted by v. 8, which implies that the disciples have commercial dealings with the Samaritans.

[29] If my interpretation is correct, for example, the readers are assumed to be conversant with the situation. Cf. what is said of the readers in 2.4.1 and ch. 5.

[30] Verse 15 indicates that the woman used to go to the well to fetch water.

jar may indeed chiefly mark *the change in the woman's activity*. In the first part of the text, she is the Samaritan woman, drawing water from Jacob's well, while in the second, from v. 28, she is the Samaritan woman bearing witness to the Samaritans about Jesus.[31]

We do not often encounter *Jesus' disciples*[32] in the sequence of events, but much is said about them. According to the introductory verses *they baptize people* (E 2). In the narrative itself they *go* into town to *buy food* and then *return*, evidently after achieving their purpose (E 13, 16, 17). They *are astounded* at Jesus' dialogue with the woman but do not ask him what he seeks or of what he speaks to her (E 18, 19). Above all they *receive teaching* from Jesus in vv. 31—38 (E 22).[33] The only ones of these units to present problems are those in v. 27: What underlies the disciples' astonishment? Is the first question supposed to be addressed to the woman?[34] What is the purpose of the second question: the cause of, the actual content of, or the meaning of Jesus' dialogue with the woman?

The information in v. 27 is usually read on the basis of some known facts from Jesus' time: a rabbi shall not speak with women. This is why the disciples are astonished. From reverence for Jesus, however, they do not interrupt the dialogue or criticize Jesus. A disciple may not question his master's actions.[35] If we read the text from Jn as a whole, the picture becomes slightly different.[36] Unlike the Synoptics, Jn does not describe people's reaction of astonishment or admiration when faced with Jesus.[37] The only verb he uses for "to astonish" is $\vartheta\alpha\nu\mu\acute{\alpha}\zeta\epsilon\omega$ which has a definitely negative ring. It expresses the scandal prompted by Jesus, it marks individuals' lack of insight into what is happening, their gross misunderstanding. According to Jn, a disciple of Jesus should not "be astonished".[38] The first saying in v. 27 clearly prepares the way for the dialogue to follow, in which the disciples are presented as wholly lacking in insight into what was going on around them.[39] The second is linked with the first by an ap-

---

[31] The waterpot and the drawing of water could to some extent be symbols of her old life, or of her old religion. On water as referring to the old order, see 1:19ff; 2,6; 3:5 (?); 3:22, and the comments on these passages in 2.2, U 14 and U 16, and in 3.2.2.

[32] On the referential forms, see below 3.4.1.

[33] On the revelation character of this dialogue, see below 3.4.

[34] Thus Bernard, Comm., ad loc., Foster 1940—41 and some translations.

[35] See Comm., ad loc., especially Schnackenburg and the material he mentions. The narrator focuses here on the reaction of the disciples to the dialogue with the *Samaritan* woman. See above, 3.2.1, E 18.

[36] The interpretation depends very much on which aspect is chosen: a reading from the reality behind the text bound to the historical situation of Jesus *or* a reading from the Johannine text and the reality the narrator wishes to communicate, for example, the reality of Jesus' work as a whole bound to both the time of Jesus and the time of the disciples.

[37] An account of the material by G. Bertram i ThWNT, vol. 3, p. 40.

[38] Jn uses the verb six times: 3:7; 4:27; 5:20,28; 7:15,21. On its mainly negative meaning, see Abbott 1905, p. 161, and G. Bertram in ThWNT, vol. 3, p. 40. Cf. $\vartheta\alpha\nu\mu\alpha\sigma\tau\acute{o}\nu$ in 9:30.

[39] See below, 3.4.

parently adversative μέντοι.[40] The reading which comes to mind runs: the disciples merely stood astonished, they understood nothing, and nevertheless none of them (οὐδείς) asked a question. In contrast to θαυμάζειν the questioning in Jn is a positive element. It is an attribute of a disciple to ask questions, to be led to the truth, 13:25, 37; 14:5, 8, 22.[41] Later in 16:5ff the questioning is linked with the whole problem of revelation in Jn. The time for questions is said to be limited: "On that day" they will no longer need to question, says Jesus, 16:19, 30.[42] So the fact that in the Samaria narrative they ask no questions must in a Johannine context be regarded as something negative.[43]

This context means that both questions must be addressed to Jesus [44] The first one runs "What do you seek?" and is evidently answered in v. 34, where Jesus says that he is doing the work of the Father, of him who seeks (ζητεῖ) true worshippers, v. 23. In Jn 7:14ff Jesus' sayings and teaching are presented as a seeking of the *doxa* of the Father. The second runs "Of what are you talking with her?[45] What are you telling her and what does it mean?" The disciples should have put these questions and asked for an explanation of the dialogue. But now they just stand there in silence. The explanation will emerge, however, on the next encounter between the disciples and Jesus, vv. 31ff.[46]

The Samaritans enter the scene very late but they totally dominate its close.[47] The issue here is the relationship between *Jesus and the Samaritans*.[48] The people, in v. 28 τοῖς ἀνθρώποις, are presented in vv. 39f as Samaritans (τῶν Σαμαριτῶν, οἱ Σαμαρῖται), although this is hardly necessary with regard to the flow of information in the text.[49] Their actions are concerned just with Jesus. If we consider the statements in the text from their point of view we arrive at the following units:

[40] The word has a certain emphasis in Jn: 7:13; 12:42; 20:5; 21:4.

[41] See Leroy 1968, pp. 178f. Also in 1:38,48 and 21:12,21f we have questions from the disciples.

[42] For an analysis of Jn 16, see below 4.3.

[43] Note that they do not ask any questions of *Jesus* in the dialogue either, vv. 31–38.

[44] There are no indications of a change of persons in the two questions and therefore it would be natural to take them as addressed to the same person. Double questions are common in Jn (14 times). The formulations as such offer no help: ζητεῖν is used of persons who seek of Jesus, 1:38; 6:24,26; 7:1, 11, 34, 36; 8:21; 13:33; 18:4, 7, 8; 20:15, but also with Jesus as agent, for example, 7:14ff. Τί may mean both "what", 1:38, etc., and "why", 7:19. Kreyenbühl, Comm., vol. 2, p. 422, renders the verb with "streiten", referring to 3:25.

[45] For a justification of this rendering, see, besides the context, the construction λαλεῖν (τι) μετά τινος in Jn 14:30 (9:37; Rev 1:12; 4:1; 10:8; 17:1; 21:9, 15), the Johannine usage of λαλεῖν with the accusative and τί meaning "what". The Syriac and the Latin versions have "what". The parallel with the first τί suggests "what". See also Jn 16:16ff.

[46] See below, 3.4.

[47] They occur in all units from E 23 to E 32, mostly as agents.

[48] Note the disciples' total absence at the close of the text.

[49] Ἐκ δὲ τῆς πόλεως ἐκείνης would be enough in v. 39.

They *hear* what the woman says about Jesus (implicit in vv. 28, 39, 42).
They *come to believe* in Jesus, v. 39.
They *leave* the town, v. 30.
They *go out* to Jesus, v. 30.
They *come* to Jesus, v. 40.
They *ask Jesus to stay* with them, v. 40.
They *listen to* Jesus, vv. 41, 42.
They *believe*, vv. 41, 42.
They *confess* to the woman, v. 42.[50]

These units are now placed in a certain logical and temporal relationship to each other, which, however, is not entirely clear. The connections are denoted, above all, by πολλοί – πολλῷ πλείους in v. 39 and v. 41, by the verb πιστεύειν in v. 39, v. 41 and v. 42, by διὰ τὸν λόγον, διὰ τὴν σὴν λαλιάν in v. 39, v. 41 and v. 42, and by οὐκέτι in v. 42. The comparisons made are thus marked in many ways in the text and must belong to that which the author emphasizes. We may describe the relation as follows:[51]

1. Οὐκέτι in v. 42, and indeed the parallel status of the event units—especially *to hear* and *to believe*—clearly show that this is a temporal comparison. We have in the text two points in time, let us call them *point A* and *point B*.

2. The first clause of the speech in v. 42 shows that *A* is the time *when the Samaritans came to believe in Jesus because of the woman's testimony*. Thus it corresponds with the account in vv. 28—30 and v. 39. *B* is the time *when the Samaritans believed because of Jesus' words*. This then corresponds to the content of v. 40 and, especially, v. 41.

3. These two happenings, separate in time, are compared in a way by the words πολλοί – πολλῷ πλείους in v. 39 and v. 41. This is the point at which difficulties arise, with v. 41 in mind. There the speakers are evidently the "many more" from the later occasion, but they identify themselves at the same time with those who believed on the first occasion. Logically this does not fit in since the two groups are said to be of different sizes. The text does not even say that they partly coincide. Yet if v. 42 is to have any meaning, the speakers there must be those who believed at *A* and those who believed at *B*. What then does this comparison show? Only that Jesus' words reached a wider audience? Or does it refer to a different belief so that, for instance, the first belief is made more profound on the second occasion?

---

[50] On their speech as a confession, see above, 3.2.1, E 32.

[51] Walker 1966 has performed an excellent analysis of some details in vv. 39—42 but he starts from a wrong premise: the text concerns "Jüngerwort und Herrenwort"—as is mentioned in the title of his article—"Glaube aus erster und zweiter Hand". He rightly criticizes Bultmann but took over this premise from him.

4. There is no clear statement in the text that there is a *qualitative* difference in the belief on the two occasions. The wording would rather suggest that on both occasions the belief was complete.[52] Thus it seems to be a question of a *change in basis of belief* from one occasion to another.[53] At first the belief was based on *the woman's testimony*, then on *Jesus' words*. Here we find no designation of the contrast "Jüngerwort und Herrenwort" or "Glaube aus zweiter - Glaube aus erster Hand"[54] but rather the comparison of "Zeugenwort" and "Jesuswort". On the first occasion, the belief is based on the testimony to Jesus, on the second on Jesus' own words. The one *relieves* the other without any appraisal to speak of.

This seems to me to be the structure of the contents existing in vv. 39—42, with their connection with vv. 28—30. How this is to be explained and interpreted is another problem. The role of the testimony may suggest a comparison with John the Baptist, the great witness in Jn, he who reveals Jesus to "Israel", the children of God throughout the world.[55] Indeed his testimony is mentioned in the context, 3:27ff. Moreover, when the bridegroom's voice is heard he stands there rejoicing. He disappears but Jesus gathers crowds of people round him. And it was for this gathering of God's children that he was sent to earth to witness of Jesus.[56]

3.2.6 Preliminary Summary

If after these analyses we divide the Greek text into smaller units and partly arrange it according to semantic relations, its appearance is as shown on the following page.[57] The relations between the different parts are not, however, as simple as the survey would suggest. I showed in section 3.2.2 that the text has, so to speak, a double introduction: vv. 5—6 and vv. 39—42 may be regarded as terminal sections in the text, but at the same time there are bonds between the end and vv. 1—4 and a clear junction of these verses with vv. 5—6. The text is thus integrated in a wider context, 3:22—4:54. Previously I noted the transitional character of the introductory verses, but I tried at the same time to hold the way open for an integration of these verses with vv. 5—42, simply because they have certain terminal features. There is even a doubleness in the body of the text: vv. 8, 27 and 31—38 are linked in several ways, as are vv. 7, 9—26 and 28—30. The one

[52] On the expressions for "believe", see above 2.2, U 31. Λαλιά and λόγος are discussed below in 3.2.1, E 32.

[53] Note the repetition of διά plus the accusative. The witness of the woman and the word of Jesus are the foundation of their belief, rather than the means by which they come to believe.

[54] These expressions are from Bultmann, Comm., ad loc. and are used also by Walker 1966, who sometimes also uses "Zeugenwort".

[55] On John the Baptist in Jn, see above 3.2.1, E 1 and 3.2.2.

[56] I have previously (2.4.4) compared the mother of Jesus and John the Baptist. The revelation to the woman in vv. 7—26 may correspond to the revelation to John in 1:31ff.

[57] Only a few semantic relations can be marked in this two-dimensional survey. The lines which begin at A are semantically coordinated, the lines beginning at B are semantically subordinated to the previous A-line, the C-line semantically subordinated to previous B-line, etc.

A B C   D

1   Ὡς οὖν ἔγνω ὁ κύριος
        ὅτι ἤκουσαν οἱ Φαρισαῖοι
           ὅτι Ἰησοῦς πλείονας μαθητὰς ποιεῖ καὶ βαπτίζει ἢ Ἰωάννης
2   καίτοι γε Ἰησοῦς αὐτὸς οὐκ ἐβάπτιζεν ἀλλ' οἱ μαθηταὶ αὐτοῦ
3 ἀφῆκεν τὴν Ἰουδαίαν
    καὶ ἀπῆλθεν πάλιν εἰς τὴν Γαλιλαίαν.
4   ἔδει δὲ αὐτὸν διέρχεσθαι διὰ τῆς Σαμαρείας.
5 ἔρχεται οὖν εἰς πόλιν τῆς Σαμαρείας
      λεγομένην Συχὰρ
      πλησίον τοῦ χωρίου
         ὃ ἔδωκεν Ἰακὼβ τῷ Ἰωσὴφ τῷ υἱῷ αὐτοῦ.
6   ἦν δὲ ἐκεῖ πηγὴ τοῦ Ἰακώβ.
  ὁ οὖν Ἰησοῦς . . . ἐκαθέζετο οὕτως ἐπὶ τῇ πηγῇ.
      κεκοπιακὼς ἐκ τῆς ὁδοιπορίας
      ὥρα ἦν ὡς ἕκτη.
7 ἔρχεται γυνὴ ἐκ τῆς Σαμαρείας ἀντλῆσαι ὕδωρ.
7a—26   dialogue one.
    (οἱ γὰρ μαθηταὶ αὐτοῦ ἀπεληλύθεισαν εἰς τὴν πόλιν, ἵνα τροφὰς ἀγοράσωσιν.)
    (οὐ γὰρ συγχρῶνται Ἰουδαῖοι Σαμαρίταις.)
27 καὶ ἐπὶ τούτῳ ἦλθαν οἱ μαθηταὶ αὐτοῦ
    καὶ ἐθαύμαζον
      ὅτι μετὰ γυναικὸς ἐλάλει·
    οὐδεὶς μέντοι εἶπεν,
      τί ζητεῖς; ἤ, τί λαλεῖς μετ' αὐτῆς;
28 ἀφῆκεν οὖν τὴν ὑδρίαν αὐτῆς ἡ γυνὴ
    καὶ ἀπῆλθεν εἰς τὴν πόλιν
    καὶ λέγει τοῖς ἀνθρώποις,
29   δεῦτε ἴδετε ἄνθρωπον ὃς εἶπέν μοι πάντα ὅσα ἐποίησα·
    μήτι οὗτός ἐστιν ὁ Χριστός;
30 ἐξῆλθον ἐκ τῆς πόλεως
    καὶ ἤρχοντο πρὸς αὐτόν.
31—38   dialogue two.
39 ἐκ δὲ τῆς πόλεως ἐκείνης πολλοὶ ἐπίστευσαν εἰς αὐτὸν τῶν Σαμαριτῶν

      | διὰ τὸν λόγον τῆς γυναικὸς |

        μαρτυρούσης
          ὅτι εἶπέν μοι πάντα ὅσα ἐποίησα.
40   ὡς οὖν ἦλθον πρὸς αὐτὸν οἱ Σαμαρῖται,
  ἠρώτων αὐτὸν
      μεῖναι παρ' αὐτοῖς·
    καὶ ἔμεινεν ἐκεῖ δύο ἡμέρας.
41 καὶ πολλῷ πλείους ἐπίστευσαν

      | διὰ τὸν λόγον αὐτοῦ, |

42 τῇ τε γυναικὶ ἔλεγον
      ὅτι οὐκέτι . . . πιστεύομεν

      | διὰ τὴν σὴν λαλιὰν |

      αὐτοὶ γὰρ ἀκηκόαμεν,
      καὶ οἴδαμεν
        ὅτι οὗτός ἐστιν ἀληθῶς ὁ σωτὴρ τοῦ κόσμου.

series of events concerns Jesus and his disciples, the other Jesus and the Samaritan woman. The latter is continued in vv. 39—42 but not the former. Thus there are certain tensions between the different parts of the text, which do not emerge from the survey below.

The results of my analysis of the event structure in Jn 4:1—42 may be summarized preliminarily under three points.

A. The text reveals a complete *two scene composition,* marked chiefly by spatial and temporal features in the text (see 3.2.3, 3.2.4). This literary device explains some of the tensions just mentioned between the different parts of the text. The narrative contains two parallel series of events, which change scenes in the middle (3.2.4). Thus various linguistic devices are used to describe events on the main scene, i.e. with Jesus at Jacob's well, and events behind the scenes, in the town and in the field between the two places. The two series are interwoven, especially in the second half of the text. To regard this only as a literary device binding different kinds of traditions together seems to me to conflict with the careful way in which the composition is achieved. It points to a unity in the text, especially in vv. 5—42, and clearly suggests that the different parts, and in particular the two main parts, should somehow be considered from a common angle.

B. The event structure emphatically focuses on *Jesus and the Samaritans* in the text. The events narrated take place at the Samaritans' holy centre at Gerizim, at Sychar (Askar), in Joseph's field, at Jacob's well (3.2.3). Important Samaritan traditions emerge in the description of the external scene: the claim to be sons of Jacob, sons of Joseph, i.e. rightful heirs of the old Israel. The site of the event is depicted in detail, the other places prove to be Samaritan centres and significant Samaritan traditions are linked with them; all this at the beginning of the text directs the attention to the Samaritans. So also does the presentation of the woman in v. 7 and the beginning of the first dialogue (3.2.3). Moreover, at the end the Samaritans dominate completely (3.2.5). Theirs is the confession which concludes the narrative. They are the only people explicitly said to believe in Jesus. Thus if we consider the structure of events by itself, the main theme of the text becomes one alone: Jesus and the Samaritans.

C. At several points in the analysis I have indicated features in the text which may here be summarized under an *ergon* perspective in the text, i.e. the reality which underlies and shapes the text is God's work of salvation (*ergon*) through his Son, a work which also includes a "new" people of God. This aspect is most evident in the introductory verses and their connection with 3:22ff and 4:43ff. The information on the journeys in Jn 4 gives glimpses of the way of mission of God's Son through the world (3.2.3). He came to his own but his own received him not. The picture of Jesus given in the text is that already found in the prologue: the Word came into the world, sojourned here a while, some accepted him (3.2.5). The question in 3:22ff concerns Jesus' right to gather people round him (3.2.2). John's answer is clear: God gives these people to Jesus. Jesus increases, he himself decreases. The people of the new covenant is being born from that of the old. John's role is to be "best man" at the wedding which here takes place. This means that the perspective in 3:22ff is similar to that in 1:19ff. The parallels are many.

In this perspective the text deals with Jesus' ἔργον in a wider sense, with Jesus' divine task of salvation which was given him by the Father and which covers the time both before and after his "hour". The temporal items in v. 6 and v. 40 should perhaps be seen in this context.[58] I must return to the question of the extent to which this perspective is relevant to the Samaria text in its entirety after my analysis of the dialogues. With this *ergon* aspect I wish only to summarize what was said in the analyses about the introductory verses, about the picture of Jesus in the event structure, about the journey framework of our narrative and about the connection with 3:22ff.

3.2.7 Excursus I. The Well in Jewish Tradition

I noted previously that we appear to have no Samaritan material which illustrates Jacob's well in our text.[1] This is the more astonishing as we can refer to a rich material concerning other features in the text, both as regards the event structure (for example, on Gerizim, Sychar, Jacob's sons) and the first dialogue (for instance, on the worship on this mountain and on the Messiah who will reveal all things).[2] Jacob's well is nevertheless the central place in the text, and the first dialogue makes several references to it. The theme *water* in Jesus' talk with the woman may perhaps be a sufficient explanation for the inclusion of Jacob's well in the dialogue, but there are a number of features in the text, the description of the spring as a "well" in vv. 11f, the verb ἅλλεσθαι in v. 14[3] and the superior perspective of God's gift in v. 10,[4] prompting me to here discuss the Jewish tradition concerning the Well. In a paper published in 1963, Annie Jaubert collected material on this tradition with just Jn 4 in mind. At the same time, Roger Le Déaut independently refers *en passant* to this material, as does José Ramón Díaz, when he quotes the Codex Neofiti on Gen 28:10 to explain Jn 4:15.[5]

---

[58] The pattern of change in basis of belief (vv. 39—42; see 3.2.5) may also be connected with this *ergon* and its reference to the history of salvation.

[1] In 3.2.3.

[2] See above, 3.2.3 and the summary in 3.2.6, B, and below, 3.3.5, B.

[3] This verb has not yet been satisfactorily explained. See below, 3.3.2, S 5.

[4] See below, 3.3.2, S 3. We may also add the use of θρέμματα in v. 12. See 3.2.4.

[5] Le Déaut 1964, pp. 217f; cf. Le Déaut 1965, p. 55, Ramón Díaz 1963, pp. 76f (according to Nickels 1967, p. 54, in a Spanish version from 1962). For literature on this tradition, see the following notes.

However, no one has included the material in an analysis of the Samaria text as a whole.

Normally πηγή means a spring, φρέαρ a well and λάκκος a cistern.[5] In 4:6 πηγή is twice used of Jacob's well, while 4:11f has φρέαρ.[7] Some scholars explain this variation by saying that the evangelist is here using material from different sources,[8] or that one of the usages is in a later addition.[9] Others point out that the two words are at times used in parallel, as in Gen 24, which has πηγή in vv. 13, 16, 29, 30, 42, 43, 45, but φρέαρ in vv. 11 and 20.[10] Gen 21:19; 26:19 and SofS 4:15 also refer to φρέαρ ὕδατος ζῶντος.[11] The two words in Jn 4 are then regarded only as stylistic variants, having the same meaning. The LXX usage is of interest here, however. While πηγή is used to translate many Hebrew words, φρέαρ is closely linked with באר.[12] Indeed a Jewish tradition, contemporaneous with the NT, concerning a supernatural well which accompanied the Israelites on their journey through the desert (Num 21:16—18) is also linked with באר, the Well. Moreover it has associations with Moses in Ex 2:15 and with the patriarchs in Gen 21; 26; 29. The alternation of expressions in vv. 6, 11f may therefore suggest that the narrator is here thinking of this traditions.

Water is not often mentioned in the narrative of the desert journey, but there is one event—or several events—concerned with water associated with Israel's murmuring against Moses: God gives the Israelites water from the cliff after Moses strikes it with his staff, Ex 17:1—7; Num 20:1—13, referred to in Num 20:24; 27:14 and 33:14. This happened at Massa and Meriba.[13] We have a related narrative for the stopping places at Mara (and Elim): the bitter water became fresh from the tree which Moses was given by God, Ex 15:22—27; Num 33:14. There is otherwise hardly any mention of water,[14] except in "the Well Song" in Num 21:16—18. The tradition of the Well seems to originate from this somewhat cryptic text.

The Massoretic text of Num 21:16—20 is usually translated as follows:[15]

---

[6] See the material adduced by W. Michaelis in ThWNT, vol. 6, pp. 112ff.

[7] The use of πηγή in v. 14 may depend on its transferred meaning. See W. Michaelis in ThWNT, vol. 6, pp. 113ff.

[8] See, for example, Fortna 1970, p. 190, note 3.

[9] See, for example, Wellhausen 1908, p. 22, and Schwartz 1908, p. 505.

[10] Zahn, Comm., ad loc. W. Michaelis in ThWNT, vol. 6, p. 114, refers also to a synonymous use in Josephus (Ant. I.246, 254, but not as synonymous in Ant VIII.154).

[11] This means that the well draws its water from a spring (it is not rain water).

[12] See, besides the Concordance, W. Michaelis in ThWNT, vol. 6, p. 113.

[13] This event is referred to many times and interpreted already in the OT: Dt 8:15; 32:13; Is 48:21; Neh 9:15; Job 29:6; Ps 78:16—20; 81:17; 105:41; 114:8.

[14] Only in connection with the Red Sea and in Num 21:22 and in some geographical names.

[15] Using the Revised Standard Version with parenthesis around words which have no direct correspondence in the Hebrew text. A thorough philological examination of the text and of early

> And from there (they continued) to Beer; that is the well of which the Lord said to Moses, "Gather the people together, and I will give them water". Then Israel sang this song: "Spring up, O well! — Sing to it! — the well which the princes dug, which the nobles of the people delved, with the sceptre and with their stabes". And from the wilderness (they went on) to Mattanah, and from Mattanah to Nahaliel, and from Nahaliel to Bamoth, and from Bamoth to the valley lying in the region of Moab by the top of Pisgah which looks down upon the desert.

The text then becomes a description of the wandering of the Israelites from camp to camp: from there to Beer, from the desert to Mattanah, from Mattanah to Nahaliel etc. There are, however, two comments on Beer, which means "well" in Hebrew, one being a reference to an occasion involving Moses, when God gave the people water, the other to a song about a well which "the princes" dug and "the nobles of the people" delved. Verse 18b is also usually translated after emendation: "and from Beer to Mattanah . . .".[16] The Masoretic text, however, literally reads: and from the desert Mattanah. Thus this text is not homogenous and contains several obscure expressions, such as "princes".[17] The Greek translators also encountered difficulties. Evidently LXX does not regard Beer as a proper name as it translates καὶ ἐκεῖθεν τὸ φρέαρ, v. 16, and καὶ ἀπὸ φρέατος εἰς, v. 18. The text describes the Israelites at "the well". The unusual expression "spring up, O well" (MT עֲלִי בְאֵר) was differently translated: τότε ᾖσεν Ισραηλ τὸ ᾆσμα τοῦτο ἐπὶ τοῦ φρέατος Ἐξάρχετε αὐτῷ . "The princes" becomes "the kings of the peoples" (βασιλεῖς ἐθνῶν) [18] and the following verse has an entirely new meaning (ἐν τῇ βασιλείᾳ αὐτῶν, ἐν τῷ κυριεῦσαι αὐτῶν). This shows that the obscurity of the Hebrew text provokes different interpretations.

The Targum not only understood Beer as meaning "well" but also continued to read the various proper names from their meaning in the Hebrew: Mattanah = "gift", Nahaliel = "God's rivers" and Bamoth = "heights". Even the Targum which paraphrases least, Targum Onkelos, reads as follows:[19]

> And from there was given to them the well, that is the well of which the Lord said to Moses, "Assemble the people, and I will give them water". Then Israel sang this song: "Spring up (סְקִי), O well", they sang to it, the well which the princes dug,

interpretations thereof would be of interest but must be excluded here. There are indications of interpretative features already in the MT. The Samaritan text is close to the MT (with "gather *to me*" in v. 16 and the cryptic form עֲלֹה at the beginning of the song).

[16] See the apparatus in Biblia Hebraica, 3. ed.

[17] The inconsistencies of the text may depend both on different sources and on early interpretations of the text.

[18] LXX evidently read עַל "at" and included the first two words of the song in the quotation formula. The Targums all read "spring up" (in their text סְקִי), a verb which frequently recurs in the tradition of the Well.

[19] The text in Sperper, vol. 1, p. 259. Targ. Onkelos may be a revision of the other Targums, Levine 1971a, 1971b, Kuiper 1971a, 1971b.

the nobles of the people delved with their rods. It was given to them from (in) the wilderness. And from (the time) that it was given them, it descended with them to the rivers, and from the rivers it sprang up (סלקא) with them to the height.

It is of special interest here to note the reading of "Mattanah" as gift.[20] *The Israelites received the well as a gift (from God)* and it accompanied them on their journey. This recurs in the other Targum versions.[21] The theme of the well is there extended further with new details, which can be confirmed in other Jewish literature.[22] I here quote Targum Pseudo-Jonathan:[23]

> And from there was given to them the living well, the well of which the Lord said to Moses: "Assemble the people, and I will give them water". Then, behold, Israel sang the thanksgiving of this song, at the time that the well which had been hidden was restored to them through the merit of Miriam: "Spring up (סוקי), O well, spring up, O well", they sang to it and it sprang up (סלקא); the well which the fathers of the world, Abraham, Isaac and Jacob, dug, the princes who were of old dug it, the chiefs of the people, Moses and Aaron, the scribes of Israel, found it with their rods; and from the desert it was given to them for a gift. And from (the time) that it was given them as a gift it again went up with them to the high mountains, and from the high mountains it went down with them to the hills surrounding all the camp of Israel, and giving them drink, every one at the door of his tent. And from the high mountains it descended with them to the lower hills, but was hidden from them on the borders of Moab.

There are in this version a number of features which recur in various forms in other Jewish literature. *1.* The Well is associated with the whole of *the wandering in the desert.* Even the Masoretic text clearly states that the well in Num 21 is the same as that which burst from the rock in Ex 17 and Num 20.[24] It is a kind of divine well, from which God, through Moses, gives the people water to drink. The text quoted (TJ I) mentions Moses, Aaron and Miriam: Moses and Aaron found the marvellous well with their staffs, and it was given to the Israelites for Miriam's sake. It is therefore sometimes described in the literature as "Miriam's well".[25] *2.* It is clear from what was said above that the Well was regarded as *a gift* to the Israelites, understood from God. This is reiterated in the text, in v. 18

[20] The Hebrew word used here means "gift" in, for example, Num 18:6.

[21] Codex Neofiti and TJ II are very close to each other, according to Grelot 1959, p. 271f, and somewhat shorter than TJ I which I quote below.

[22] See the following examination.

[23] I follow here Etheridge's translation to a great extent. Cf. Jaubert 1963, p. 66, and Grelot 1960, p. 224. "The living well" is attested only in TJ I, Grelot 1960, p. 224. The Aramaic text is given in the Walton Polyglote and in Ginsburger's edition.

[24] Note the similarities between Num 21:16; Ex 17:2, 5, and Num 20:8. In this context we have the rare expression "give to drink"; see below 3.3.2, S 1.

[25] See Str.-B., vol. 1, p. 186, and vol. 3, pp. 406ff, Le Déaut 1964, pp. 209ff, and the material mentioned there.

evidently from a translation of "Mattanah".[26] *3.* The Well yields an abundance of water, indeed it *"springs up"*.[27] It suffices to give water to all Israel, to the whole camp. It flows to the door of each tent. In the Dura Europos paintings this detail is shown by 12 streams springing from the well, apparently one for each tribe.[28] This overflowing well is thought to accompany the Israelites on their journey, uphill and downhill. Sometimes it is invisible but is again revealed. *4.* The Well did not only exist during the desert wandering. When *the patriarchs,* Abraham, Isaac and Jacob dug their wells, it was this divine Well which they found. They saw it at the beginning according to TJ II. And "the princes of the world, Sanhedrin, the seventy wise men who were appointed by name beheld it" (TJ II). Thus the Well is depicted as a resource available to the Israelites throughout their history. According to Pirqe Aboth V. 9, it was in existence even before the Creation.

Num 21:16—18, therefore, refers to a very special well: a divine gift which manifests itself in different ways in the history of the Israelites, the Well whose water springs up and overflows, the Well from which God gives his people water to drink. The background seems to be an exegesis of Beer and Mattanah in Num 21:16—18, a "targumic (not midrashic) explanation" according to Diez Macho.[29] The impacts of this tradition in the Jewish literature are many.[30] The most detailed are Num R 19, 25f and Tos Sukk III.11ff. Fresh details are added to those already described, certain things are stated succinctly, a phenomenon which we have already encountered in the Targum tradition. This concept of the Well can also be confirmed in NT times from 1 Cor and Pseudo-Philo (possibly also from Philo and the Damascus Document), although it is impossible to determine how rich in detail it then was.

In 1 Cor 10:4 Paul refers to the rock which accompanied the Israelites through the desert, i.e. the water-giving rock, the well which is mentioned in Ex 17, Num 20 and Num 21:16—18. He describes it as $\pi\nu\epsilon\nu\mu\alpha\tau\iota\kappa\acute{o}\varsigma$, which, according to Malina, here means "from above, from the beginning, pre-existent".[31] If this is the case, the supernatural desert well was regarded as early as Paul's time as something created before the Creation—as in Pirqe Aboth V. 9. In any case, this passage in Paul implies the idea of a divine well, which accompanied the Israelites during their wanderings in the desert. Immediately above (vv. 2f) he

[26] Le Déaut 1964, p. 217, note 2, notes a connection between the verb "give" and the water in the desert.

[27] The Aramaic word is סלק "aufsteigen" (Dalman, Lex., s.v.).

[28] See Riesenfeld 1947, pp. 42ff.

[29] Diez-Macho 1960, pp. 231f. Before him James in his translation of Pseudo-Philo (1917, pp. 105f), referring to Thackeray.

[30] See the material in Str.-B., vol. 3, pp. 406ff, and in Ginzberg, vol. 3, p. 53. For the literature on the translation, see especially Grelot 1959, Jaubert 1963 and Le Déaut 1964, pp. 209ff. When we meet Moses in early Christian art it is not the scenes of Ex 14—15 or Ex 19—24 but the scene of the water from the rock, Leroy 1954, p. 362.

[31] Malina 1968, pp. 98f.

mentions *the pillar of cloud* and *the manna*, both "gifts" from God during the desert journey.

Pseudo-Philo mentions the Well on several occasions:[32]

> Populum autem suum Dominus deduxit in heremum, et quadraginta annis pluit illis de celo *panem*, et *ortigometram* adduxit eis de mari; et *puteum* aque consequentis eduxit eis. In *columna* autem *nubis* per diem deducebat eos, et in *columna ignis* per noctem lucebat eis (X, 7).

> Et ibi ei mandavit multa, et ostendit ei lignum vite de quo abscidit et accepit et misit in Myrram, et dulcis facta est aqua Myrre. Et sequebatur eos Dominus in heremo quadraginta annis, et ascendit in montem cum eis et descendit in campos (XI, 15).

> Et hec sunt tria que dedit Deus populo suo propter tres homines, id est, *puteum* aque mirre propter Mariam, et *columpnam nubis* propter Aaron, et *manna* propter Moysen. Et finitis his tribus ablata sunt hec tria ab eis (XX, 8).

These quotations show that the well is regarded as a gift of God, like the manna, the quails, the pillar of cloud and the pillar of fire (X,7; XX,8). It is given to the Israelites for Miriam's sake (XX, 8) and is believed to accompany Israel throughout the desert journey, the 40 years (X,7; XI,15; XX,8). It is linked with Ex 15(XI, 15; XX,8), with Ex 17(X, 7) and with Num 21:19(XI, 15). The wording of the latter quotation presupposes the same reading of Num 21:19 as we found in the Targums, a confirmation that the tradition of the Well rests on a targumic explanation of Num 21:16—18.[33] By means of 1 Cor 10:4 and the quotations given here from Pseudo-Philo, this tradition is clearly associated with the 1st century A.D.

To some extent, the Damascus Document and Philo may be quoted as further proof of the age of the tradition. The interpretations of Num 21:16—18 in these texts, however, are highly specific and deeply rooted in their messages as a whole. CD VI.2—11 gives an allegorical interpretation, applying to the people of the new covenant which is mentioned in the Damascus Document.[34]

> But God remembered the covenant of the forefathers, and he raised from Aaron men of understanding and from Israel men of wisdom and he caused them to hear; and they digged the well . . .

Num 21:18 is then quoted, being expounded with the people of the new covenant and its history in mind: the well = the Law, the princes = those who emigrated to Damascus, the staff = one who studies the law etc. The point of interest here is that the image of the well is abruptly introduced into the text, that it is here

---

[32] Pseudo-Philo's Liber Antiquitatum Biblicarum, from the first century, one of "the oldest specimens of historical Haggada", according to G. Kisch in his edition of the text (pp. 17f). I here quote Kisch's text (my italics). For comments, especially on XI,15, see James' translation of these passages.

[33] Thus James in his translation, pp. 105f.

[34] For comments, see especially van der Woude 1957, pp. 67ff.

directly interpreted as the Law, which was regarded in Late Judaism as the true gift given by God during the years in the desert,[35] and that Num 21 is inserted into the theme of God's new covenant with his people. When the well is mentioned for the first time in CD III.16, it is said to give much water; XIX.34 speaks of a "well of living water" (באר מים החיים), evidently referring to the same well. In the Damascus Document this water is seen primarily as cleansing the people[36] and hallowing them that they may become the people of the new covenant. To those who hold fast to the Law God explains his will, he reveals that which is hidden so that they can dig a well with abundant water, with living water. The Well is seen as the Law, interpreted aright in the light of the new "revelation" and the context in which are the new people of God. A concept of the overflowing desert well may indeed have facilitated this interpretation of Num 21:16—18 in CD, but it cannot be said to be directly confirmed there. On the other hand there are other striking similarities to the Samaria text and the water symbolism there.[37]

Philo has a consistent interpretation of the wells in Gen—Dt: the well stands for ἡ σοφία, ἡ ἐπιστήμη. This also applies to Num 21:16—18.[38] For Philo the essential purpose is to search for Wisdom, to find it and to practice it. According to him, in Num 21 the Israelites found Wisdom and therefore they sing their song of joy. This is the last and highest of the three stages in the desert wandering. "The song is the song of initiation into Sophia, where Moses, as hierophant, now leads the people".[39] He also interprets the "rock" and "manna" of the desert journey as symbols of Wisdom.[40] The history of the patriarchs is similarly interpreted—the wells in Gen 14:7; 16:7ff; 21:25ff; 24; 26:15ff and 28:10f. Abraham, Isaac and Jacob are searchers after Wisdom, Rebecca is represented as the true teacher of Wisdom.[41] As in the Qumran material we have no direct confirmation of the concept of the Well mentioned above, but it is to some extent in accord with Philo's interpretation. Underlying all the wells there is something shared, something divine, and the well in the desert is linked with that of the patriarchs. The latter provides the transition to the Jewish material on the Well and Jacob.

As shown above, the Palestinian Targums of Num 21:16—18 interpret the "princes" in v. 18 as Abraham, Isaac and Jacob, "the fathers of the World" and as "the princes who were of old". The many wells in the history of the

[35] See Odeberg 1929, pp. 150ff, and below 3.4.6.
[36] Water and spirit are mentioned together as that which cleanses in 1QS IV.20—22. See above 2.2, U 14, and for the following van der Woude 1957, pp. 67ff, 186ff, and Braun 1966, pp. 114f.
[37] See below, 3.4.6.
[38] De Ebrit 112f, De Somn II.267—271.
[39] Goodenough 1935, p. 221f.
[40] See, for example, Quod Deter 115—118, Leg Alleg II.86.
[41] De Fuga 195—202, De Somn I.5ff, Quaest in Gen IV.191—195, De Post 130f.

patriarchs—cf. especially Gen 21; 26; 29—are thus linked with the desert well. In the Jewish literature this link is strongest concerning *Jacob*.

Gen 29:1—10 relates how this patriarch comes fleeing to a strange land and in a "field" sees a "well" used for watering "sheep". There was a large stone on the mouth of the well which had to be removed every time the shepherds watered the sheep. Then Rachel comes to the well with her father's sheep—it was evidently at midday, v. 7—and Jacob rolled away the stone and watered them. He is invited to her father's house and stays there with his uncle Laban; the story tells how he herds Laban's sheep, and how he too gets wives, sons and sheep, Gen. 30. This is the main context in which we meet Jacob in the Bible as shepherd and a well in the Jacob narrative. If we are seeking a well from which "our father Jacob" drank, "he himself and his sons and his sheep" (Jn 4:12), Haran's well comes first to mind. According to Gen 30:35 it was Jacob's sons who herded *his* sheep.

This story of Jacob at Haran's well is so shaped in the Jewish literature that the well possesses attributes similar to those of "Miriam's well": it springs up and overflows for Jacob's sake. The Targums—Codex Neofiti, TJ I and TJ II—to Gen 28:10 refer to five "signs" (נסין), which "our father Jacob" (אבונן יעקב) did when he went from Beersheba to Haran:

> And the fifth sign: when our father Jacob raised the stone from above the mouth of the well, the well overflowed and sprang up (וסליקת) to its mouth and was overflowing for twenty years, all the days that he dwelt in Haran.[42]

When the event is described again in the Targums to Gen 29 this miracle emerges in the wording of v. 10 and v. 12:

> He rolled the stone with one of his arms from the mouth of the well; and the well uprose, and the water sprang up (סליקו) to the top of it; and he watered the sheep of Laban, his mother's brother; and it uprose for twenty years. ... how the stone had been removed, and how the well had upflowed and sprung up (סליקת) to the brink.[43]

Jacob's presence produces an abundance of water, and after he has served seven years for Rachel Laban consults his people on what to do to keep Jacob:

> Behold, seven years since Jacob came to us the wells have not failed and the watered places are multiplied ... (29:22).[44]

They decide to give him Leah instead of Rachel. When Jacob finally leaves Haran the following comment is made in 31:22

> But after Jacob had gone, the shepherds went to the well, but found no water; and they waited three days, if that it might (again) overflow; but it overflowed not; and

---

[42] Thus Codex Neofiti (tr. by McNamara in Díez-Macho's edition, vol. 1, p. 572). TJ I counts this sign as the fourth, TJ II is very close to Codex Neofiti.

[43] TJ I and TJ II. Codex Neofiti does not have this passage. I follow here and in the two following quotations Etheridge's translation.

[44] TJ I, TJ II and Codex Neofiti with small differences.

then they came to Laban on the third day, and he knew that Jacob had fled; because through his rightousness it had flowed twenty years.[45]

Thus Haran's well gives water in a supernatural manner. because of Jacob, in the same way as does the desert well for Miriam's sake. There is, however, no explicit comparison with Miriam's well in the Targums. On the other hand, PRE 35 refers to a well which accompanied the patriarchs, and especially Jacob:

> Rabbi Aqiba said: Every place where our forefathers went, the well went in front of them. . . . And it is written about Jerusalem, 'And it shall come to pass in that day, that living waters shall go out from Jerusalem' (Zech xiv. 8). This refers to the well which will arise in Jerusalem in the future and will water all its surroundings. Because they found (the well) seven times, he called it Shiba'ah (seven). Jacob was seventy-seven years old when he went forth from his father's house, and the well went before him.[46]

The text thus describes a wandering well, common to Abraham, Isaac and Jacob. It went before Jacob to Haran and also appears in Gen 29. This makes the resemblances to the desert well even more striking. Indeed in Gen R 70,8f we have an explicit parity with the desert well. Wünsche translates: "Das ist der Brunnen, welcher die Israeliten in der Wüste begleitete".[47] The three herds in Gen 29 are interpreted as Moses, Aaron and Miriam, from the well which produces water for all in the camp. The Well is also interpreted here as meaning Zion, the holy place of the great feasts, where the people gather to be hallowed by the Spirit, a link with Zech 14:8—as in PRE 35—and Ezek 47, which is essential with Jn's water symbolism in mind.[48]

Thus we have a rich material on Jacob and the Well:[49] Haran's well is a springing, overflowing well because of Jacob who, like other patriarchs and the desert generation, was accompanied on his wanderings by a supernatural well. Yet how old are these traditions? We know from the Book of Jubilees that Jacob held pride of place in certain Jewish speculations, and that he is linked with the question of a new covenant[50] and with the Well of the Oath (Beersheba), Jub 16:11ff; 18:17ff; 22:1ff; 24:13ff; 36:12ff; 44:1ff. Furthermore we know that the idea of the Well already existed during the first century, if not earlier. An early formulation of the account of Jacob at Haran's well is therefore not improbable, but I have discovered no unequivocal evidence of its early age—unless Jn 4 should be counted as such.

[45] Thus TJ I. TJ II has almost the same, also Neofiti which omits the last clause.

[46] Friedlander's translation, p. 263. The words "seven times" refer to the passage here omitted: Abraham dug *three* times and Isaac dug *four* times (Gen 26). PRE 36 (p. 268) mentions Haran's well in terms similar to the Targums quoted above.

[47] Simon's translation: "this alludes to the well". See also Gen R 66,3.

[48] See below, 3.3.6.

[49] More Jewish material is mentioned in Ginzberg, vol. 5, p. 293.

[50] See above 3.2.3, note 21.

Before I sum up this excursus in relation to Jn 4, I shall also refer to Ex R 1,32 and a few other Jewish sources, which discern the Well theme also in Ex 2:15f; there Moses, fleeing as Jacob once did, comes to the well at Midian, helps some women to water their sheep—evidently at high noon—and wins one of them for his wife.[51] Ex R 1,32, which, like PRE 36, here compares Moses, (Isaac) and Jacob, says that Moses watered the sheep as "Jacob had done for Rachel . . . He only drew out one bucketful and with this watered all the flock there assembled, for the water was blessed at his hands".[52] The way in which Moses waters the sheep later convinces Jethro that Moses is descended from Jacob. There is little evidence of this tradition,[53] but it is easily explained by the many similarities between Gen 29 and Ex 2.

No simple conclusions concerning the relationship between Jn 4 and the beliefs about the Well which I have described here can be drawn, at least not at this stage of the analysis. Nevertheless I shall attempt a summary. We have seen that the tradition grew up gradually. The extant material from the period of the NT seems to me to prove that during the evangelist's lifetime, there was in Judaism a belief concerning *a supernatural well which accompanied the Israelites throughout the desert journey,* manifested above all in the narratives in Ex 15, Ex 17 and Num 20. Through this well God gives his *people water to drink.* Like the manna and the quails, the well is a *gift of God.* Num 21:16—18, with the song of *the well which springs up,* is also important to this tradition. According to the reading of the Targums[54] this is an abundant, overflowing well, which is manifest at different points in Israel's history. It is not improbable that this belief concerning the overflowing divine well in the evangelist's time also referred to the patriarchs' wells, and especially *Jacob at Haran's well,* but this cannot be directly confirmed by material from NT times. The Jewish tradition also applies it to *Moses at Midian's well.* Philo has interpreted these wells allegorically as a symbol of *Wisdom.* The usage in the Damascus Document, in which the well in Num 21:18 is interpreted as *the Law,* is also allegorical. The context in CD is of interest: the founding of *the new covenant* by those who emigrated to Damascus. This gives us a certain *eschatological perspective* of the Well in Num 21, which is confirmed in other sources by a combination with the water which will flow from Jerusalem, Zech 14:8; Ezek 47 etc. I shall later return to this point in the excursus on the water symbolism in Jn, section 3.4.6.

[51] On this narrative in Josephus and Philo, see above 3.2.4.

[52] Quoted from Simon's translation, p. 41.

[53] See Ginzberg, vol. 2, pp. 289—92. Raschi has the comparison with Jacob and refers to Tanchuma: "er erkannte an ihm, dass er zu den Nachkommen Jaakobs gehörte, weil das Wasser ihm entgegen emporstieg" (Raschi on Ex 2:20). On Moses in early Christian art, see Leroy 1954, p. 362.

[54] The interpretation of Num 21:16—18 in the Targum depends on a targumic explanation of the names Beer and Mattana. See above, note 29.

Le Déaut wonders whether or not the beliefs concerning the supernatural well at Haran have been applied to Sychar's well via the designation "Jacob's well".[55] But it seems rather probable that a well in Joseph's field, in the Samaritans' most holy place, would be called Jacob's well[56] and the spring is first named as $\pi\eta\gamma\grave{\eta}$ $\tau o\tilde{v}$ 'Ιακώβ and not consistently as "Jacob's well". Yet even if the name is historically correct, it may for Jesus and/or the narrator bring to the fore Haran's well, and the idea of the Well which in Jewish literature was closely connected with Jacob.[57] The central place in the Samaria narrative may, therefore, be regarded in some sense as a gateway to the theme of the Well.

Jn 4, Gen 29 and Ex 2:15ff have a great deal in common, even if we confine ourselves to the Bible texts: a man in flight comes to a well, where he stops/settles; it was high noon; women come to the well, dialogue with the stranger, the women go home and tell the news, the stranger is invited to stay and he sojourns for a while.[58] In the whole of Jn we see that Jesus and Moses are apposed, and in the Samaria text Jesus and Jacob are contrasted.[59] Kreyenbühl interprets the similarities as meaning that we here have an wholly fictional composition of sections from well narratives in the OT. Nevertheless, they are too general for this to be the case. Yet I find some kind of influence from Gen 29 and Ex 2 to be probable.

The existence of many features common to this tradition of the well and to Jn 4 is evident. This applies especially to the reference to *God's gift*, the discussion of *the water from the well* and the water given by Jesus, and the image of the *well which springs up*, but also more general connections; the words "Gather the people and I shall give them water to drink", the fact that the Well gives water to the whole of Israel, that the Well is connected with the new covenant, with Wisdom, with the Law interpreted aright.[60]There is also the eschatological perspective which I shall discuss below under point 3.4.6. Among these many features there is one in particular where I am bound to say that direct influence by the tradition of the Well is the best explanation so far proposed. This concerns the image of "a fountain of water springing up ($\dot{\alpha}\lambda\lambda o\mu\acute{\epsilon}\nu o\nu$)".[61] Therefore, I find no alternative but to believe that the tradition of the Well was present in the environment in

[55] Le Déaut 1964, p. 217.

[55] On the topography of the text, see above 3.2.3.

[57] I have not found any evidence that the Samaritans linked Jacob's well with the well of Haran.

[58] That the stranger marries the woman he meets has no correspondence in Jn 4, but compare the perspective in 3:22—30, especially 3:29, analysed above, 3.2.2. This perspective is stressed by Boismard 1973, pp. 223ff.

[59] See below, 3.3.2, S 3.

[60] On these themes, see the analyses below, 3.3.2, S 3, 4 and 5, 3.3.6 and 3.4.6.

[6] The use of "fountain" and not "well" seems to depend on the figurative use and the connection with "eternal life". The phrase "a fountain of living water" is often used. See below, 3.4.6. On different explanations of the verb in this text, see below 3.3.2, S 5.

which the Samaria text was written, and that it affected its composition. The preliminary results of the analysis in ch. 2 impel me to suggest that, even at this stage, the Well be regarded as part of the screen, which influenced the shaping of Jn 4, but the entire text should be analysed before any further conclusions are drawn. See further the final summary in 3.5.

3.3 The Dialogue Structure of vv. 7–26

The first dialogue in our text is, with its 13 speeches, one of the longest in the Gospel.[1] The Johannine dialogues are usually made up of 5–7 speeches.[2] The following section gives a survey of the quotation formulae (3.3.1); the individual speeches, their form and content, are discussed separately (3.3.2); the reasoning underlying the dialogue (3.3.3) and its connection with the context (3.3.4) is analysed, before finally I give a preliminary summary of the first dialogue in the Samaria text.

3.3.1 The Quotation Formulae

If we take out the speeches themselves and the two explanatory sentences in v. 8 and v. 9, the following remains of the first dialogue section:

1. λέγει αὐτῇ ὁ Ἰησοῦς, v. 7.
2. λέγει οὖν αὐτῷ ἡ γυνὴ ἡ Σαμαρῖτις, v. 9.
3. ἀπεκρίθη Ἰησοῦς καὶ εἶπεν αὐτῇ, v. 10.
4. λέγει αὐτῷ ἡ γυνή, v. 11.[3]
5. ἀπεκρίθη Ἰησοῦς καὶ εἶπεν αὐτῇ, v. 13.
6. λέγει πρὸς αὐτὸν ἡ γυνή, v. 15.
7. λέγει αὐτῇ, v. 16.[4]
8. ἀπεκρίθη ἡ γυνὴ καὶ εἶπεν αὐτῷ, v. 17.
9. λέγει αὐτῇ ὁ Ἰησοῦς, v. 17.
10. λέγει αὐτῷ ἡ γυνή, v. 19.
11. λέγει αὐτῇ ὁ Ἰησοῦς, v. 21.
12. λέγει αὐτῷ ἡ γυνή, v. 25.
13. λέγει αὐτῇ ὁ Ἰησοῦς, v. 26.

[1] Only Jn 18:28–19:16, if we take this as one unit, is longer (27 speeches; but three "persons" at two different stages). Jn 8:31–59 has thirteen speeches, 13:31–14:31 ten, 21:15–18 nine, 6:25–36 and 9:8–12 eight speeches.

[2] See, for example, 1:47–51; 7:45–52; 8:12–19; 11:21–27; 3:2–10; 7:15–29; 8:21–29; 20:15–18; 1:20–23; 9:24–34; 11:7–16 and 13:6–20.

[3] Ἡ γυνή may belong to the original text. It is omitted in p⁷⁵, B and syrˢ, but Codex Sinaiticus prima manus reads ἐκείνη, which supports the view that we originally had no explicit subject. Cf. 21:15ff.

[4] Several MSS have here as in the other quotation formulae ὁ Ἰησοῦς but it is omitted in the best MSS, for example, p⁶⁶, p⁷⁵, B and C (prima manus).

The common denominator of these formulae is that they all begin with a finite verb and have no conjunctive particle.[5] In 10 out of 13 we have the formulation λέγει + object (+ subject), which must be regarded as typical of Jn.[6] We find the shortest phrase at the beginning of the second part of the dialogue, vv. 16—26. The longer formulation ἀπεκρίθη . . . καὶ εἶπεν, which we have in nos. 3, 5 and 8, is also characteristic of Jn. We encounter this quotation formula 30 times in Jn, at the same time as it is wholly lacking in the other Gospels and Acts.[7] It is easiest to explain this formula, which is hardly Greek, as an interference phenomenon, either by direct influence from the וַיַּעַן . . . וַיֹּאמֶר of the Hebrew, or from literature affected by Hebrew, primarily the Septuagint, where ἀπεκρίθη καὶ εἶπεν and ἀποκριθεὶς εἶπεν often translate the Hebrew formulation in question.[8] The question is whether the double occurrence of finite verbs gives a certain weight to the expression,[9] or whether in Jn's environment it is only a stylistic variant of the other forms of quotation formula. A review of the passages in Jn where ἀπεκρίθη καὶ εἶπεν occurs gives no unequivocal answer, although there is some justification for Abbott's assertion that the phrase "introduces elementary doctrine or explanation of misunderstanding".[10] In our text it is difficult to find reliable explanations of the alternation of the quotation formulae. Nos. 3 and 5 may denote a certain weight in the following speeches, both of which concern "the misunderstanding" in the first speech.[11] In v. 17 the longer formula introduces the shortest speech in the dialogue, to which great significance is nevertheless attached by Jesus' saying in vv. 17f.[12]

[5] Except no. 2, which has οὖν (v. 9), but this quotation formula is preceded by a long parenthetical sentence, v. 8. See above 3.2.4 and 3.2.6. Οὖν is used very often in quotation formulae in Jn: 1:22; 2:18,20; 4:33, 48, 52; 5:10,19; 6:28, 30, 32, 34, 53, 67 etc. The Synoptic Gospels do not have this usage.

[6] See, for example, λέγει in 1:36ff; 11:23ff; 13:6ff, 31ff; 20:13ff; 21:3ff, 15ff (here λέγει nine times!). Lk has always a connective and very often εἶπεν, Mk has a syndeton only in 8:19 and 10:29, disregarding ἔφη, Mt has rather often asyndeton by λέγειν in the present tense, mostly in the discussions in chs. 19—22. —Λέγειν usually has the dative, sometimes πρός plus the accusative. See Kilpatrick 1960, pp. 176f. The two constructions often occur in LXX.

[7] See however Mk 7:28 ἡ δὲ ἀπεκρίθη καὶ λέγει αὐτῷ. On the phrase as a Johannine characteristic, see Ruckstuhl 1951, pp. 197f, 201, 204, 208ff. The Synoptics very often have ἀποκριθεὶς plus finite verb.

[8] Thus F. Büchsel in ThWNT, vol. 3, pp. 946f. "Die Urform der Wendung ist augenscheinlich die parataktische, die wie das hebräische וַיֹּאמֶר . . . וַיַּעַן zwei verba finita hat, dh die joh: ἀπεκρίθη καὶ εἶπεν" (p. 946). We have the same stylistic feature in 1 Macc, Tob, Enoch, 3 Baruch, 4 Ezra and Ass Mos. See Dalman 1898, p. 19. Ἀποκρίνεσθαι in these phrases does not always mean "answer" but sometimes only "speak up". The meaning "answer" is highly predominant in Jn, Topel 1971, pp. 214f.

[9] Cf. the double ἀμήν in Jn, the repetitions in 1:20 and twofold variation in Jn, analysed by Morris 1969, pp. 293ff.

[10] Abbott 1906, p. 454.

[11] The longer formula is, however, not used before the longest speech, vv. 21—24.

[12] See below, 3.3.2, S 7, and 3.3.5.

Thus the quotation formulae in vv. 7–26 are typically Johannine. This applies to ἀπεκρίθη ... καὶ εἶπεν, which the evangelist chose instead of the more Greek ἀποκριθεὶς εἶπεν, the use of asyndeton, the use of the present tense of λέγειν and οὖν in v. 9. These belong to the more formal parts of the dialogue, which the author presumably has in common with the language environment in which the text took shape. So if one seeks parallel material to the Johannine dialogues, great weight should be given to these formulae. The little which has been quoted here may well suggest a Jewish environment, or one in which the influence from Hebrew language structure consciously or unconsciously affected the choice between the two forms found in the LXX.[13]

3.3.2 The Speeches (S 1–S 13)

In the analysis which follows, I shall discuss a number of questions concerning the language, form and content of the speeches and give a preliminary version of their message.[1] The Greek reads:

S 1 Δός μοι πεῖν.

S 2 Πῶς σὺ Ἰουδαῖος ὢν παρ' ἐμοῦ πεῖν αἰτεῖς γυναικὸς Σαμαρίτιδος οὔσης;

S 3 Εἰ ᾔδεις τὴν δωρεὰν τοῦ θεοῦ καὶ τίς ἐστιν ὁ λέγων σοι, Δός μοι πεῖν, σὺ ἂν ᾔτησας αὐτὸν καὶ ἔδωκεν ἄν σοι ὕδωρ ζῶν.

S 4 Κύριε, οὔτε ἄντλημα ἔχεις καὶ τὸ φρέαρ ἐστὶν βαθύ· πόθεν οὖν ἔχεις τὸ ὕδωρ τὸ ζῶν; μὴ σὺ μείζων εἶ τοῦ πατρὸς ἡμῶν Ἰακώβ, ὃς ἔδωκεν ἡμῖν τὸ φρέαρ καὶ αὐτὸς ἐξ αὐτοῦ ἔπιεν καὶ οἱ υἱοὶ αὐτοῦ καὶ τὰ θρέμματα αὐτοῦ;

S 5 Πᾶς ὁ πίνων ἐκ τοῦ ὕδατος τούτου διψήσει πάλιν· ὃς δ' ἂν πίῃ ἐκ τοῦ ὕδατος οὗ ἐγὼ δώσω αὐτῷ, οὐ μὴ διψήσει εἰς τὸν αἰῶνα, ἀλλὰ τὸ ὕδωρ ὃ δώσω αὐτῷ γενήσεται ἐν αὐτῷ πηγὴ ὕδατος ἁλλομένου εἰς αἰώνιον.

S 6 Κύριε, δός μοι τοῦτο τὸ ὕδωρ, ἵνα μὴ διψῶ μηδὲ διέρχωμαι ἐνθάδε ἀντλεῖν.

S 7 Ὕπαγε φώνησον τὸν ἄνδρα σου καὶ ἐλθὲ ἐνθάδε.

S 8 Οὐκ ἔχω ἄνδρα.

S 9 Καλῶς εἶπες ὅτι Ἄνδρα οὐκ ἔχω· πέντε γὰρ ἄνδρας ἔσχες, καὶ νῦν ὃν ἔχεις οὐκ ἔστιν σου ἀνήρ· τοῦτο ἀληθὲς εἴρηκας.

S 10 Κύριε, θεωρῶ ὅτι προφήτης εἶ σύ· πατέρες ἡμῶν ἐν τῷ ὄρει τούτῳ προσεκύνησαν· καὶ ὑμεῖς λέγετε ὅτι ἐν Ἱεροσολύμοις ἐστὶν ὁ τόπος ὅπου προσκυνεῖν δεῖ.

S 11 Πίστευέ μοι, γύναι, ὅτι ἔρχεται ὥρα ὅτε οὔτε ἐν τῷ ὄρει τούτῳ οὔτε ἐν Ἱεροσολύμοις προσκυνήσετε τῷ πατρί· ὑμεῖς προσκυνεῖτε ὃ οὐκ οἴδατε· ἡμεῖς προσκυνοῦμεν ὃ οἴδαμεν, ὅτι ἡ σωτηρία ἐκ τῶν Ἰουδαίων ἐστίν. ἀλλὰ ἔρχεται ὥρα· καὶ νῦν ἐστιν, ὅτε οἱ ἀληθινοὶ προσκυνηταὶ προσκυνήσουσιν τῷ πατρὶ ἐν πνεύματι καὶ ἀληθείᾳ· καὶ γὰρ ὁ πατὴρ τοιούτους ζητεῖ προσκυνοῦντας αὐτόν. πνεῦμα ὁ θεός, καὶ τοὺς προσκυνοῦντας αὐτὸν ἐν πνεύματι καὶ ἀληθείᾳ δεῖ προσκυνεῖν.

---

[13] On the Jewish situation of Jn, see ch. 5.

[1] Cf. the presentation of my analysis in 1.2 and the work described in 2.2 and 3.2.1.

S 12 Οἶδα ὅτι Μεσσίας ἔρχεται, ὁ λεγόμενος Χριστός· ὅταν ἔλθῃ ἐκεῖνος,
      ἀναγγελεῖ ἡμῖν ἅπαντα.
S 13 Ἐγώ εἰμι, ὁ λαλῶν σοι.

The translation below of these speeches is very literal, with the discussion of their
form and message in mind. The arrangement of each individual speech is linked
with the description of its form in the original.

S I
Give me to drink!
It is difficult to say whether this speech has the usual, natural form of a request
for water. Should one translate "give me to drink", which can hardly be
described as natural in the situation, or "give me a little water", which comes
closer to the common "may I have some water", or even the latter. Of the three I
am inclined to choose the first, from the form of the original. The view on the
character of the text as a whole, which I cannot discuss here, is important to the
choice of translation. S 1, as it now stands, gives two words which are important
for the dialogue to follow (S 1–S 6), perhaps the two most important, διδόναι
and πίνειν.[2] The construction with the infinitive is by no means remarkable.[3] It is
often found with φάγειν, Mk 6:37 (par.); Mt 25:35, 42, and further Mk 5:43; Jn
6:31, 52; Rev 2:7, in LXX for example Ex 16:8, 15; Num 11:18, 21. According
to Headlam δοῦναι πιεῖν is also "a very common phrase".[4] In the situation
described in Jn 4, however, it is not the only possibility. LXX, for instance, in
similar situations uses only πότισόν με (δὴ) μικρὸν ὕδωρ, Gen 24:17, 43, 45; Jg
4:19. In LXX and NT "to give someone water to drink" is expressed by ποτίζειν
τινά (ὕδωρ). However, there is one interesting exception: *in texts describing how
God gave his people water in the desert* δοῦναι ὕδωρ (πίνειν) *is almost always
used.* The combination δοῦναι and πίνειν is only found in Ex 17:2 (δὸς ἡμῖν
ὕδωρ, ἵνα πίωμεν) and in Num 21:16 (καὶ δώσω αὐτοῖς ὕδωρ πιεῖν), i.e. in the
perhaps most central texts on the Well. For examples of the phrase without
πίνειν, see Num 20:8; Neh 9:20 (LXX 2 Esd 19:20); Wis 11:4, 7 and Is 43:20.[5]

[2] See below, 3.3.3, C.
[3] Turner, p. 135.
[4] Headlam 1922, pp. 55f. In a medical receipt from the first century (Pap. Oxyr. 1088) δίδου
πεῖ is used as parallel to δὸς πεῖν and πιέτωι, in both cases with μετά: "give to drink with".
[5] Is 43:20 concerns the future salvation of Israel: God will give His chosen people to drink. He
will pour water, he will pour His Spirit on Jacob's descendants, 44:3. The phrase ὕδωρ διδόναι is

This seems to me to indicate that even the first speech "Give me to drink" is shaped not only by the situation described but also with the speeches which follow, and maybe also the theme of the Well, in mind.[6] Another alternative gives the reading "to drink" = "to receive instruction".[7] Jesus' first words would then be an invitation to a lesson. Whichever interpretation is followed, Jesus' action would have somewhat surprised a Samaritan woman.

S 2

How can you, a Jew,

ask a drink of me, a Samaritan woman?

This speech, to which the participial constructions give a certain symmetry, provides us with information on the parties of the dialogue (*you* are a Jew, *I* am a Samaritan woman),[8] and asks a thoughtful question concerning this information (how *then* is it possible that . . .). This combination of hesitant question and supplementary justification is characteristic of many $\pi\tilde{\omega}\varsigma$-clauses in Jn.[9] The question here, as in 3:4 and 3:9, concerns what Jesus has just said. The woman objects[10] and her reasons are evidently, according to the narrator, of a religious nature, or at least partly so. His remark in v. 9c, which I previously interpreted from the question of purification in Jn, would suggest this.[11]

S 3

If you knew God's gift,

and who it is who says to you: Give me to drink,

you would ask him,

and he would give you living water.

Externally this speech has a certain chiastic form, by means of the semantic com-

rare. See, besides Jn 4, Hos 2:5 (LXX 2:7), Is 30:20, Jer 9:1 (LXX 8:23). On the Well in the desert, see 3.2.7.

[6] See above, 3.2.7.

[7] See below, 3.3.6.

[8] The text does not tell us how the woman recognized that Jesus was a Jew.

[9] This applies to more than half of the Johannine $\pi\tilde{\omega}\varsigma$-clauses. The supplementary information may be given by constructions with participles as here (3:4; 5:44; 7:15), by statements (8:33; 12:34; 14:9) by rhetorical questions (6:42; 9:19) or by $\epsilon\iota$-clauses (3:12; 5:47). In all these cases the $\pi\tilde{\omega}\varsigma$-clause expresses more a negation of a certain possibility—"how is it then possible that"—than a true question. See Bauer, s.v., 1.b. Jn 4:9 has parallels in 3:4,9 (Nicodemus does not understand); 8:33; 12:34 (the Jews do not understand) and 14:5,9 (the disciples do not understand).

[10] $\Pi\alpha\rho'$ $\dot{\epsilon}\mu o\tilde{\upsilon}$ may emphasize that the woman is the agent in the giving act. The infinitive $\pi\epsilon\tilde{\iota}\nu$ functions as the accusative in the phrase $\alpha\dot{\iota}\tau\epsilon\tilde{\iota}\nu$ $\tau\iota$ $\pi\alpha\rho\dot{\alpha}$ $\tau\iota\nu o\varsigma$ "request something from someone". For this meaning compare 1 Jn 5:15; Mt 20:20 and in LXX, for example Ps 2:8 ($\alpha\dot{\iota}\tau\eta\sigma\alpha\iota$ $\pi\alpha\rho'$ $\dot{\epsilon}$-$\mu o\tilde{\upsilon}, \kappa\alpha\dot{\iota}\delta\dot{\omega}\sigma\omega\sigma o\iota$). Abbott 1906, p. viii, links $\pi\alpha\rho'$ $\dot{\epsilon}\mu o\tilde{\upsilon}$ to $\pi\epsilon\tilde{\iota}\nu$ and translates "askest drink of me".

[11] It is not only a social reason. See above 3.2.5.

ponents "*give*" in the outer clauses and "*ask*" in the inner two.[12] But semantically this parallelism is disturbed by the double implication: "if you knew, then you would ask him" and "if you asked him, then he would give you". The first part of the speech is also overloaded. In a natural dialogue situation one could well imagine a reduction to "If you knew who *I* am, *you* would instead ask me and I would . . .".[13] Yet now, in addition to this, the concept ἡ δωρεὰ τοῦ θεοῦ and the mcre general designation ὁ λέγων σοι[14] are inserted—a change from the first to the third person. Both these expressions are thus well marked in the speech. Then fol ows the designation of the water as ὕδωρ ζῶν.

The word δωρεά is used primarily of divine gifts,[15] in the NT of the Spirit, Acts 2:38; 8:20; 10:45; 11:17, of righteousness, Rom 5:17, and of salvation in general, 2 Cor 9:15; Eph 3:7; 4:7; Heb 6:4. "In δωρεά liegt im NT immer die Grade Gottes".[16] To the Jews, the gift of God was, above all, the Law.[17] The usage in our text may be influenced by Johannine thought.[18] Indeed Jn very frequently uses διδόναι in a religious sense, especially in the description of God.[19] The dominating aspect is just that *the Father gives,* partly to the Son, partly to mankind. The initiative is His, it was He who sent the Son;[20] Jesus did not come of his own accord, 7:28; 8:42. The Son himself is God's gift to mankind, 3:16; 6:32f, as is "the second Paraclete", 14:16. God once gave mankind the Law, now, through the Son, He gives "His words", 17:8; 12:49; also 3:34; 7:16; 8:26; 12:50; 14:24; 17:14, "His name", 17:11f, "His glory", 17:22,24. God once gave men "manna", now He gives "the true bread", 6:31f. Above all, the verb *to give* is used in the description of the relationship between the Father and the Son. The Father, as stated, gives to the Son "His words", "His name", "His glory" and in addition "works", 5:36; 17:4; 4:34; 9:3; 10:32,[21] "men", 6:37,39; 17:2, 6, 9, 24; 18:9,[22] the power to pass judgement and give life, 5:22, 26, 27, the Spirit, 3:34, yes everything He has given to the Son, 3:35; 13:3; 17:2,7. This relationship can also be expressed by the words "the Father *loves* the Son", 3:35; 10:17f;

[2] Schnackenburg, Comm., ad loc.

[3] Σύ is emphasized, Bl.-Debr. § 277,1, Turner, p. 37. Also Abbott 1906, p. 296.

[4] A form of εἰμί and participle is usual in Jn: 5:31f, 45; 6:33,63; 8:50f,54; 14:21. See Abbott 1906, p. 63.

[5] See Bultmann, Comm., ad loc., and the material he mentions.

[6] F. Büchsel in ThWNT, vol. 2, p. 169.

[7] See Odeberg 1929, pp. 150ff, and below 3.3.6. On the Well as a gift of God, see above 3.2.7.

[8] Vanhoye 1960 and Pinto de Oliveira 1965 give an extended analysis of "to give" in Jn but no. of the related "gift".

[9] The verb has a religious flavour in more than sixty passages, and in more than thirty God is the agent (Jesus 17 times, Moses 5 times and Jacob 2 times). A comparison between Jesus and Moses (and Jesus and Jacob) is manifest. See the analysis below.

[0] See below, 3.4.2, S 4.

[1] Note also 18:11 (a cup), and 14:31; 12:49 (a commandment).

[2] See above 2.2, U 6 and 3.2.2.

17:24–26. The whole of Jesus' work is a manifestation of God's will, 4:34, 10:18, a part of the Father's love, 10:17. But at the same time as Jesus is bidden to realize God's works, the Father performs them Himself, 14:10; 9:3f; 10:32,37.[23] God is the chief agent, the primary agent[24] and this the evangelist expressed in the concept that *the Father gives.*

The idea of God's giving is therefore central in Jn. The whole of God's work of salvation may be summed up in a giving by God to the Son and to mankind. The combination in S 3 of "God's gift" and "who it is who speaks to you" is therefore very natural in a Johannine context. Jesus himself is God's gift and the gifts he brings are part of God. On the gift of living water, see the Excursus 3.3.6. Other gifts of Jesus in Jn are bread and eternal life, 6:27, 33f, 51f, peace, 14:27, a new commandment, 13:34, his glory, 17:22, the power to become children of God, 1:12, and all that the disciples ask. With Jn 6 as starting point, the water which Jesus gives in ch. 4 is regarded as an expression of salvation and eternal life.

Concerning the gifts of God and of Jesus, we should note that we have in Jn a contrast between what God gives through *Moses,* and what He gives through *Jesus,* 1:17; 7:19ff; cf. 3:14; 6:32f; 5:47; 1:45.[25] The Law, the Manna and the Copper Serpent are associated with Moses. Each of these gifts has an equivalent in that which God gives through Jesus. In every case Jesus' gift is superior, namely eternal life.[26] This pattern in Jn indicates that we have a similar instance in Jn 4: God's gift through *Jacob,* namely the Well,[27] and that which God gives through *Jesus.*

The wording ὁ λέγων σοι would also seem to allude to a basic feature in Jn: Jesus as the Word, he who speaks. The idea of *the speaking God,* which permeates the entire Gospel, hardly needs confirmation here. In contrast to, for example, τίς ἐγώ εἰμι,[28] the present wording in a Johannine context confers a clear aspect of revelation on Jesus' action at the well.

S 3 marks a double re-orientation in relation to the foregoing. It is made clear that really the woman should ask Jesus for water and not *vice versa.* Moreover the dialogue is led away from water in the ordinary sense to water in a transferred sense by the ambiguous ὕδωρ ζῶν. The first speech, which is here repeated in S 3, thus acquires a meaning which was not given in the neutral and open wordings in S 1. There is a reference to the water which God gives.

---

[23] On Jesus' *erga,* see above 2.2, U 27.

[24] This is a dominant aspect in the Passion narrative in Jn, Vanhoye 1960, pp. 395ff.

[25] See the excellent analysis by Meeks 1967, pp. 287ff.

[26] Note the formulation in 6:49 and 3:15.

[27] See above, 3.2.7.

[28] Note the question with τίς concerning Jesus in Jn: 5:12f; 8:25; 9:36; 12:34 and 21:12.

S 4

Lord,
you have nothing to draw the water with,
and the well is deep.
Where will you get the living water?
Surely you are no greater than our father Jacob,
who gave us the well
and who used to drink from it, he himself, his sons and his sheep.

We have in this speech a mixture of questions and explanatory new information similar to that in S 2, arranged symmetrically with the two questions in the middle. With the different information units in a more logical sequence, the speech could read: "Lord,[29] this well is deep and you have nothing to draw the water with.[30] Where then will you get the living water (of which you speak)? Our father Jacob gave us this well. He himself used to drink from it, he and his sons and his sheep. You cannot be superior to Jacob?".

Even in this case we are faced with typically Johannine questions. *Where* Jesus is *from,* and where his gifts (works) come from is, as we saw in my first analysis, a key question in the Gospel.[31] Many of the μή-questions are part of the same theme.[32] We have a striking parallel to our text in 8:53: μὴ σὺ μείζων εἶ τοῦ πατρὸς ἡμῶν Ἀβραάμ, ὅστις ἀπέθανεν; which is also incorporated in a longer speech. Moreover, the later part of S 4 is "a perfect example of Johannine irony",[33] i.e. Jesus' companion speaks, indirectly and unwittingly, the truth about Jesus: he is greater than Jacob, the father of the Samaritans. This stylistic feature, the parallel in 8:53 and the types of question are a strong indication that we are here faced with the author's own language.

Jacob's central role in Samaritan belief, Jacob's well, the choice of the words φρέαρ and θρέμματα have already been treated above in sections 3.2.3, 3.2.4 and 3.2.7. The comparison, implicit in the text, of Jacob and Jesus is rendered ex-

---

[29] Κύριε, used in S 4, S 6, S 10, is a usual form of address in Jn which need not be Christological, 4:49; 5:7; 6:34, 68 etc. The usage implies a certain reverence, Schnackenburg, Comm., ad loc., an increasing respect, Brown, Comm., ad loc. It is difficult to give evidence of this.

[30] The first two clauses are connected by οὔτε . . . καί, a very rare construction. See, besides the commentaries, Bl.-Debr. § 445,3 and Turner, p. 340. Cf. 3 Jn 10 and Jn 5:37f. This connection seems to be stronger than a simple οὔτε. The logical relation is only semantically marked. — Ἄντλημα has the general meaning "implement for drawing water". See Liddell-Scott and Bauer, s.v.

[31] See 2.2, U 22. The construction with ἔχειν only here and in Mt 13:27. The questions as a rule have copula or ἔρχομαι.

[32] Jn has 18 such questions (15 in the section of the Jews, chs. 3—10), Mk only 1, Mt 4 and Lk 7.

[33] Brown, Comm., ad loc. See above 2.2, U 26. The same "irony" in the μή-clauses in 7:35f and 8:53. Cf. 7:41.

plicit in S 4 by μεῖζων.[34] Insofar as Jacob and his well here stand for the Samaritan tradition, the woman's mistake is not as serious as in, for example, the parallel speech in the Nicodemus dialogue, 3:4. Only if we assert that the woman is referring solely to ordinary water (from any well whatsoever), do we find the same crass "materialistic" objection as in ch. 3. The fact that the text often refers to Samaritan material, as do the speeches,[35] is a confirmation that the woman, at the same time as she, in her lack of insight, misunderstands Jesus, brings Samaritan belief face to face with the knowledge which Jesus brings.

S 5

Every one who drinks this water will become thirsty again,
but he who is to drink of the water which I shall give will never again thirst.
No, the water which I shall give will become in him a fountain of water,
springing up to eternal life.

The first part of the speech consists of two parallel clauses, related to each other by an adversative δέ. A repeated drinking (ὁ πίνων) and a returning thirst (πάλιν) are contrasted with a single draught (πίῃ) and a thirst slaked for ever (εἰς τὸν αἰῶνα). [36] The latter element has an interesting parallel in 6:35 καὶ ὁ πιστεύων εἰς ἐμὲ οὐ μὴ διψήσει πώποτε. The words which follow are introduced by an ἀλλά which here hardly has an adversative meaning but rather marks a reinforcement and justification of what was just said.[37] We find such a use of ἀλλά particularly often in the Johannine writings, both after expressions of negation, such as in Jn 5:24,41f; 6:39; 7:28; 8:12,28; 10:18; 12:49; 13:10; 1 Jn 5:16, and after positive clauses in Jn 16:2,4; 15:21.[38] There is an example of the former here in S 5, and of the latter in S 11.[39]

In the reinforcing supplement in S 5, image and fact are mingled in the Johannine way.[40] The image is a spring whose water streams forth or, if we define it from the description of the Well under 3.2.7, a well whose water constantly

---

[34] On comparisons in Jn, see above 2.2, U 23.

[35] See 3.2.6, B, and 3.3.5, B.

[36] On the change of tense, see Barrett, Morris and Lindars, Comm., ad loc. The double negation and the future tense express here "emphatic denial", Turner, p. 97. The change of conditional participles and conditional clauses in parallelisms is not rare in the NT. Of 74 conditional constructions in Jn 60 have participles. See Beyer, pp. 230ff, 210, 212.

[37] Cf. Bl.-Debr. § 448,6 (ἀλλά = "und nicht nur dies, sondern auch", "ein Hinzukommendes stark einführend") and Turner, p. 329f ("introducing a strong addition: . . . , yes, indeed"). They refer to 2 Cor 7:11; 1 Cor 3:2; Jn 16:2; Phil 1:18. See also Abbott 1906, pp. 97ff.

[38] Note also Jn 10:8. None of those who came before Jesus were the good shepherd, for the sheep did not heed them. See Olsson ²1973, pp. 252ff.

[39] See the analysis of the structure of S 11 below, 3.3.3, A.

[40] As in Jn 10:1−18, especially 10:9f, and Jn 15:1−17. Also 1 Jn 3:9. See Borig 1967, passim, and Olsson ²1973, pp. 256f.

springs up. The meaning of ἁλλομένου is not entirely clear. The verb is normally used of rapid movement by living beings, for example of the lame in Is 35:6 (LXX); Acts 3:8; 14:10, and then means "leap, spring".[41] It is seldom used of inanimate things: our text is the only *locus* where "water" is the subject.[42] Commentaries refer on occasions to the LXX, where the verb is used several times of the Spirit of the Lord which came upon people.[43] Here, however, a construction with ἐπί is always used.[44] Wis 18:15 says that God's "all-powerful word leaped (ἥλατο) from heaven ... into the midst of the doomed land". Yet none of these passages are good parallels to our text. This lack of linguistic material justifies us in giving special consideration to the possible background of the image in Jewish concepts of the overflowing Well.[45]

To this image are later linked the words εἰς ζωὴν αἰώνιον, whose relation to the preceding is not entirely clear. We find a related use of this prepositional phrase in Jn 4:36; 6:27 and 12:25. An wholly temporal interpretation would give the phrase the same meaning as εἰς τὸν αἰῶνα, which is hardly plausible.[46] A comparison with the closest parallel, 6:27, gives the meaning "which results in /leads to/ gives eternal life".[47] In both these passages, the prepositional phrase "interprets" the image used—the water, the bread—by a literal expression. Both images may be related to the gift which God gave during the journey through the desert.[48] On the water symbolism and the relationship to Jn 7:37f, see 3.3.6.

S 6

Lord,
give me this water
that I need not thirst
and come here to draw water.

By her reply the woman admits that Jesus' water is better than Jacob's. She is prepared to abandon Jacob's well, if she receives the water which slakes all

[41] See the examples mentioned in Liddell-Scott, Moulton-Milligan and Bauer, s.v.

[42] Liddell-Scott, s.v., gives as examples "arrow", "sound" and words for parts of body, Bauer, s.v., refers to the Latin *salire*.

[43] See, for example, Brown and Schnackenburg, Comm., ad loc. In LXX: Jg 14:6,19; 15:14; 1 Sam 10:10(MT: צלח "be strong, effective, powerful", Targ.: שׁרה "dwell"). The verb is also used in 1 Sam 10:2; Job 6:10; 41:17; Wis 5:21; 18:15 and Is 35:6.

[44] Note ἐφάλλεσθαι ἐπί in 1 Sam 10:6; 11:6; 16:13.

[45] See above, 3.2.7.

[46] Ζωὴ αἰώνιος occurs 17 times in Jn—only 8 times in the Synoptics—and has always a qualitative meaning: eternal life.

[47] See Barrett, Schnackenburg and Brown, Comm., ad Jn 6:27. The material adduced by Bultmann, Comm., ad loc., is not relevant.

[48] See above, 3.3.2, S 3.

thirst.[49] Thus the woman has partly understood Jesus' will: she asks Jesus for water, she sets a positive value on his water, she believes it can slake thirst for evermore. But at the same time there is evidently a misunderstanding almost as grave as in Jn 3:9 and 6:34. There is in the latter a striking parallel to S 6 (κύριε, πάντοτε δός ἡμῖν τὸν ἄρτον τοῦτον), which becomes the more important in that the two chapters have the same dialogue pattern.[50] Like the Jews, the woman is apparently thinking in material terms, often marked in translations by wordings such as "so that I may not thirst again and *need/have to* come here to draw water". There is some doubt, however, as to the degree to which this feature of the text should be emphasized. It should be weighed with the implied willingness with which the woman will abandon Jacob's well to which she was previously loyal. The last two clauses in S 6 are semantically parallel: "so that I need not thirst, nor come here to draw water".

S 7
Go and call your man
and (then) come here.

"Go home and fetch your husband and then come here to me" may be a natural reading of S 7 in the light of the situation described in the text. So general a meaning of φώνησον is not improbable,[51] but the verb usually has a sense of "call, summon, call by name".[52] It is difficult to determine whether this sense is present here. The other two verbs in S 7 clearly indicate that the woman is to leave Jesus and then return. To insert "call" or "summon" in this context creates certain difficulties. Perhaps the first two verbs should be read as a unit,[53] with the meaning "fetch". The semotactic tension could also be explained as an interference phenomenon: the Greek verb which is here almost synonymous with καλεῖν, is coloured directly or indirectly by the Hebrew and Aramaic קרא ,

---

[49] 'Αντλεῖν is used absolutely, as שאב in Gen 24:11. Cf. Ex 2:16f, 19 and Jn 2:8. Μηδέ functions as a normal conjunction after a negative clause, Bl.-Debr. § 445. Cf. Jn 14:27; 14:17 (οὐδέ), and in dependent clauses Mt 10:14; Mk 6:11; Lk 16:26.

[50] Compare 4:9 and 6:25, 4:13 and 6:27, 4:11f and 6:30f, 4:14 and 6:32f, 4:15 and 6:34. See Brown, Comm., ad loc.

[51] See, for example, Tob 5:8 (var.); Mk 10:49a, and also Jn 9:18,24, and the comment on U 25 above (2.2).

[52] See, for example, Mk 15:35ff; Mt 27:47; Jn 10:3. The verb is rare in LXX. O. Betz in ThWNT, vol. 9, p. 295, gives the meaning "rufen, beim Namen rufen", when a person is the object. Cf. Jn 12:17 and 11:43, and also Jn 1:48; 11:28.

[53] On ὕπαγε plus imperative, see Turner, p. 342, Bauer, s.v., 2.

[54] O. Betz in ThWNT, vol. 9, p. 296. Φωνεῖν has in LXX many equivalents in MT but for the most part קרא.

which has a very wide range of meaning.[55] It is often used with, for instance, God as object: "summon/invoke God".[56] If we allow a Semitic usage and Biblical concepts of God as a "husband"[57] to influence our reading of τὸν ἄνδρα σου it is possible to imagine God as object in S 7 too. The question is whether we here have, according to the narrator, a *double entendre*: "go and fetch your husband"—as the woman understood it—and "go and invoke your Lord"—as Jesus meant it.

The part of the dialogue containing S 7 and the two following speeches have ·given the exegetes the greatest problems. The readings thereof are many. Some scholars understand them as meaning that Jesus' gift was not for the woman alone, but also for her family. What was the good of the woman's thirst being slaked if the family for whom she fetched water became thirsty?[58] The three speeches are read, perhaps by most scholars, as a kind of "leading" of the woman: her newly aroused faith is tested,[59] she is made receptive to the revelation and thus brought to belief,[60] or her conscience is awakened. By the revelation of her "loose living" she is led to a true sense of guilt and awareness of sin.[61] Other scholars read these verses as a section on Samaritan belief in God,[62] while the majority of more recent commentaries in one way or another assume that their function is to reveal Jesus' omniscience.[63] According to Bultmann, the evangelist here wishes to show how the reality of man's being is revealed: anxiety, confusion and chaos. By learning to know herself, the woman encounters God.[64] Some of the exegetes' reasons for their different interpretations are given below. The main criteria must be sought in an understanding of the message and character of the text as a whole. S 7 does not provide us with many clues, except perhaps the ambiguity mentioned above. The wording of S 7, in any case, betrays a certain openness to the meaning "invoke your Lord". Nothing more can be said here. Like S 1 it is neutral in itself.

---

[55] "Call, give a name to, invoke, summon, proclaim, call on, appeal to, invite, recite", Holladay, Lex., s.v.

[56] See the Concordance. LXX has in this context usually ἐπικαλεῖν but also κράξειν (LXX Ps 16:6; 85:7, 87:10), βοᾶν (Is 12:4; 58:9; Jon 2:3) and καλεῖν (Ex 34:5; Is 41:25).

[57] Brown, Comm., ad loc., Boismard 1973, pp. 225f. See Hos 2:2 (LXX 2:4); 2:7(9); 2:16(18).

[58] Westcott and Moe, Comm., ad loc.

[59] Westcott, Comm., ad loc.

[60] Schnackenburg, Comm., ad loc.

[61] Tholuck, Weiss, Moe and Hoskyns, Comm., ad loc. See also above, 3.1.

[62] Such an allusion according to Hengstenberg, Kreyenbühl, Hoskyns, Barrett, Strathmann Comm., ad loc., Strauss [4]1840, vol. 1, p. 546, Odeberg 1929, pp. 179f and Dodd 1953, p. 313.

[63] This view is mentioned in, for example, Tholuck and Weiss, Comm., ad loc., and stressed by Bultmann—Jesus as θεῖος ἄνθρωπος—Barrett, Wikenhauser and Schnackenburg, Comm., ad loc.

[64] Bultmann, Comm. ad loc.

S 8
I have no man

The phrase τὸν ἄνδρα σου in S 7 implies that the woman has a man. She now denies this in S 8, which is the shortest speech in the dialogue. Her reply may mean "I am not married", or, more generally, "I have no man".[65] Most scholars interpret it as an attempt on the part of the woman to somehow evade the issue.[66]

S 9
You are right in saying: I have no man.
For you (once) had five men
and indeed, the man whom you now have is not yours.
This you said truly.

S 9 is symmetrically constructed: a justification in the middle and parallel assurances at the beginning and the end. The terminal clauses make it quite clear that Jesus lays heavy emphasis on the woman's speech,[67] at the same time as he seems to interpret it: the woman has a man but she still has no man. Repetition of, and comments on, speeches are common in Jn.[68] In this case the comment is hard to comprehend. We can establish that Jesus changes the word order in the woman's speech and in the phrase ἄνδρα σου. Moreover the comment is introduced by γάρ, it lays the emphasis on πέντε ἄνδρας and marks a temporal contrast. The dominant position of ἄνδρα and ἄνδρας unquestionably attracts attention to the word "man". She has a man, but what is meant by "man"? The most natural rendering of the temporal notes would be "you had five men before/once; the one you have now ...", accordingly a comparison between *then*

---

[65] Bauer, s.v., 2. Note the expression "to have God", "to have the Father and the Son", 2 Jn 9, 1 Jn 2:23, Jn 8:41. "Man kann Gott glauben, von ihm reden, man kan sich einbilden, ihn zu kennen, und kann ihn trotzdem 'nicht haben'; dh man erreicht ihn nicht mit dem Gebet, man wird seiner Segnungen, seiner Vergebung und ewigen Gnade nicht teilhaftig, man hat keine lebendige persönliche Gemeinschaft mit ihm", H. Hanse in ThWNT, vol. 2, p.823. The expression is rare in Greek literature and may have its background in the relation of possession between God and his people in the OT. See the material mentioned by Hanse, pp. 822ff.

[66] See, for example, Brown, Morris and Lindars, Comm., ad loc. The woman, according to Brown, "gives an ambiguous and even deceptive answer in instinctive reaction against moral probing" (p. 177). "The woman simply tells a white lie" (Lindars).

[67] She has spoken the truth, which is stressed by the first and the last clause. On καλῶς plus a verb of saying, see Mt 15:7; Mk 7:6; 12:28,32; Lk 6:26; 20:39; Jn 8:48;13:13; Acts 28:25, and Bultmann, Comm., pp. 225, 362. On ἀληθές, see Bauer, Comm., ad loc., Bl.-Debr. § 243. Kilpatrick 1960, p. 174, takes ἀληθές as the main predicative and translates: "This which you have said is true". Note the use of ἀληθῶς in 1:47. In both cases there seems to be a reference to the meaning which Jesus gives the speech (the "truth" as Jesus understands it).

[68] See above, 2.2, U 26. Τοῦτο of the last clause refers to the speech of the woman, probably as Jesus understands it and has just explained it.

and *now*.[69] The man she has now is not hers.[70] This is usually understood in terms of marital categories: the woman is not properly married to the man she now has. She has previously been married to five men. Now she is living in sin with the sixth.[71] According to Lindars, the number is exaggerated to illustrate her scandalous way of life by Jewish standards.[72] The life of the individual woman thus lies at the centre of the interpretation. Her evil deeds (sins) are revealed and Jesus shows himself as the Saviour of those rejected by society.

Certain minor features in the text, together with the misunderstanding technique in Jn, point toward a different conclusion. The speech revolves round the concept "man". The word may be used in Biblical material, especially in Hosea, as a designation of God.[73] Let us assume that the change in word order suggests another meaning of $\ddot{a}\nu\delta\rho a$ than that intended by the woman. As is many other passages in Jn, the explanation on Jesus' part relates to a special meaning of an expression previously used. As Jesus would understand her words, the woman has admitted that really she has no God. The five men in his explanation then refer to the earlier Samaritan cult,[74] while her current man stands for the contemporary religious conditions in Samaria. The reasons adduced against such a reading of the text, summarized by Schnackenburg, are not convincing.[75] A transferred meaning is favoured by the weight Jesus ascribes to the woman's words, by the focus on $\dot{a}\nu\dot{\eta}\rho$ in the word order and repetition, the temporal contrast $\check{e}\sigma\chi\epsilon\varsigma$ - $\kappa a\dot{\iota}$ $\nu\tilde{\nu}\nu$ [76] and by the contemporary concept of God as a husband. The natural comparison with Jn 1:47 also points in this direction. Jesus' omniscience there includes his seeing of Nathanael sitting under a fig tree, a detail which surely has a transferred meaning.[77] We have a detail in our text too: the woman once had five men and the man she now has is not hers. It is somewhat surprising that the woman then says that Jesus told her *all*, vv. 29,39. This wording is clearly linked with S 12, giving a religious aspect to what Jesus said. Yet our view of the text as a whole will finally decide how we interpret S 9. The

---

[69] See below, 3.3.3, B.

[70] Emphasized by Schlatter, Comm., ad loc.

[71] See also the most recent commentaries by Schnackenburg, Brown, Morris and Lindars.

[72] Lindars, Comm., ad loc. A person who had married more than three times was considered reprehensible among the Jews. See the material mentioned in Schnackenburg, Comm., ad loc.

[73] Hos 2:2,7,16 (LXX 2:4,9,18). See also above, 2.2, U 2.

[74] 2 Kg 17:24ff tells of *five* "nations" who were brought to Samaria from Assyria. A priest taught them how they should fear the Lord but they made gods of their own. Seven gods are mentioned but in his history Josephus (Ant IX.288) mentions *five gods:* $\check{e}\kappa a\sigma\tau o\iota$ $\kappa a\tau\grave{a}$ $\check{e}\vartheta\nu o\varsigma$ $\check{\iota}\delta\iota o\nu$ $\vartheta\epsilon\grave{o}\nu$ $\epsilon\dot{\iota}\varsigma$ $\tau\grave{\eta}\nu$ $\Sigma a\mu\acute{a}\rho\epsilon\iota a\nu$ $\kappa o\mu\acute{\iota}\sigma a\nu\tau\epsilon\varsigma$ $(\pi\acute{e}\nu\tau\epsilon$ δ' $\check{\eta}\sigma a\nu)$.

[75] Schnackenburg, Comm., ad loc. The mention of seven gods in 2 Kg is not conclusive (cf. Josephus), nor is the fact that the text pictures the life of an individual woman.

[76] See below, 3.3.3, B.

[77] See above, 2.2, U 6, and note the use of $\dot{a}\lambda\eta\vartheta\tilde{\omega}\varsigma$ mentioned above in note 67.

earlier reading of what is called an *historical contra* an *allegorical* interpretation is of little help here.[78]

S 10

Lord,
I see that you are a prophet.
Our fathers worshipped on this mountain,
but you say that in Jerusalem is the place where men ought to worship.

The woman here formulates—for the first and last time in the dialogue—a belief in Jesus (προφήτης εἶ σύ).[79] In this context she later refers to the most central element of Samaritan and Jewish faith, at least among priests: the temple cult on Gerizim and Zion, respectively. The image of "the prophet" as one having special understanding of people, and an ability to reveal them was common at that time, Lk 7:39; 1 Cor 14:24.[80] In a Johannine and a Samaritan context προφήτης, with or without the article,[81] leads to concepts of a "prophet like Moses", who is to come, Dt 18.[82] The characteristic of this prophet will be that he is sent by God and that he speaks the words which God places in his mouth. De Jonge has shown that in Jn προφήτης like βασιλεύς and Χριστός are not the most suitable nor final titles for Jesus. They are interpreted and supplemented by the central titles "Son of God" and "Son of Man".[83] Yet they are essential for the Johannine presentation of Jesus. Our text evidently places the main emphasis on the prophet's function of revealing, while the close parallel in 9:17 concentrates on the question of whether he is a true prophet, sent by God.[84] From the Samaritan point of view, it is natural to expect that a true prophet of God will reveal the right as regards the very heart of the conflict between Samaritans and Jews: which is the legitimate cult site, Gerizim or Jerusalem? The words ὁ τόπος,[85] προσκυνεῖν[86] and the use of the aorist in S 10[87] show that the woman's words

[78] For further discussion, see below 3.5.
[79] Θεωρεῖν is close to πιστεύειν, Jn 12:44ff, Sabugal 1972, p. 217.
[80] Schnackenburg, Comm., ad loc.
[81] With article 1:21,25; 6:14; 7:40,52 (p⁶⁶), without article 4:19, 7:52 and 9:17. All these passages concern a true prophet and from this it is a short step to *the* prophet, Meeks 1967, pp. 32ff, de Jonge 1973, p. 170.
[82] See the excellent monograph of Meeks (1967) and Coppens 1973. On the eschatological expectations of the Samaritans, see also Kippenberg 1971, pp. 276ff, 306ff, and the comments below (3.3.2) to S 12.
[83] de Jonge 1973, rightly correcting Meeks on this point.
[84] See below, 3.3.2, S 12, and on Jn 9, de Jonge 1973, pp. 170ff.
[85] The word refers to the Temple in 11:48. The expression is regarded as a specifically Samaritan word, Spiro 1967, pp. 286f.
[86] The verb is a technical term on cultic worship and is used in 12:20, referring to the pilgrimages to Jerusalem. See Bultmann, Comm., ad loc., and H. Greeven in ThWNT, vol. 6, pp. 759ff.
[87] See below, 3.3.3, B.

refer to the *Temple cult on Gerizim* and at Jerusalem. Where is the true Temple of God on earth? The woman, therefore, is thinking of the period of the Temple, namely from the end of the fourth century to the year 129/8 B.C. when John Hyrcanus destroyed the Gerizim Temple.[88] "Our fathers" are primarily the generations of the Samaritan Temple.[89] The Jews who "are quoted" ($\dot{\upsilon}\mu\epsilon\tilde{\iota}\varsigma$ $\lambda\epsilon\gamma\epsilon\tau\epsilon$)[90] presumably lived before the destruction of the Jerusalem Temple. In this situation, the main problem in the speech seems to be: has *a true prophet, who is a Jew* besides, any relevance for those who hope for a future restoration of the cult on Gerizim.[91] Oddly enough the different attitudes are only stated. No direct question is posed.

S 11

Woman, believe me,
the time is coming
when neither on this mountain nor in Jerusalem will you worship the Father.
You worship what you do not know,
we worship what we know,
for salvation comes from the Jews.
But the hour is coming, and now is,
when true worshippers will worship the Father in spirit and truth,
for such worshippers the Father seeks.
God is Spirit.
Those who worship him must worship in spirit and truth.

The structure of this speech, the longest in the dialogue, is analysed in detail below in section 3.3.3, A. Here I shall only comment on the first clause and the phrases $\dot{\epsilon}\nu$ $\pi\nu\epsilon\dot{\upsilon}\mu\alpha\tau\iota$ $\kappa\alpha\iota$ $\dot{\alpha}\lambda\eta\vartheta\epsilon\dot{\iota}\alpha$ and $\pi\nu\epsilon\tilde{\upsilon}\mu\alpha$ $\dot{o}$ $\vartheta\epsilon\acute{o}\varsigma$.[92]

The words of introduction are here used as are $\dot{\alpha}\mu\dot{\eta}\nu$ $\dot{\alpha}\mu\dot{\eta}\nu$ $\lambda\acute{\epsilon}\gamma\omega$ $\dot{\upsilon}\mu\tilde{\iota}\nu$ in the close parallel in 5:25, and thus mean roughly "Woman, I assure you".[93] The long explanatory speech is thus given special weight. Its latter part is dominated by the words "worship in spirit and truth".

[88] See the recent analysis by Kippenberg 1971, pp. 48ff.

[89] Morris, Comm., ad loc., refers to journeys of the Patriarchs in the area of Shechem.

[90] Similar references in vv. 9, 10, 17f, 26, 29, 35, 37, 39; see above, 2.2, U 26.

[91] On the eschatological expectations connected with Gerizim, see MacDonald 1964, pp. 359ff, Kippenberg 1971, pp. 113ff. On the restoration of the cult on Gerizim, see Josephus, Ant XVIII.85, commented on in MacDonald 1964, p. 365, and Kippenberg 1971, pp. 113ff, For further material, see below 3.3.2, S 12.

[92] On the "Father" as "Gott, wie ihn Jesus offenbart" and on the "salvation" as a primary reference to the Messiah, see Schnackenburg, Comm., ad loc.

[93] Note also $\pi\iota\sigma\tau\epsilon\dot{\upsilon}\epsilon\iota\nu$ "entrust, be convinced of" in 2:24 and 9:18.

Two lines of interpretation of this phrase run through its entire history.[94] The one, which Petri calls the "spiritualising", interprets πνεῦμα as *the spiritual element in man,* as contrasted with the physical, the other, the "objective", on the other hand, as *the Spirit,* the Spirit which God gives through Jesus Christ. In a Johannine context the latter is to be preferred. The text does not say "man is spirit"[95] but "God is spirit", nor does it mention only "in spirit" but "in spirit and truth".

Both πνεῦμα and ἀλήθεια in Jn have a content which here calls for the translation "worship in the sphere of the Spirit and the Truth"; the two concepts are very closely related.[96] Πνεῦμα, which by its position carries the emphasis in S 11, has an OT background and describes God's life-giving and creative activity among men.[97] This activity is in Jn especially related to His Son, Jesus Christ, who will baptize in the Spirit and mediate the Spirit, 1:33; 6:63; 7:39; 19:30; 20:22. Ἀλήθεια stands for the reality revealed by Christ, "das Offenbarungsgeschehen in Jesus Christus".[98] Both these concepts are related to Jesus' work: "Jesus is the truth (xiv 6) in the sense that he reveals God's truth to men (viii 45, xviii 37); the Spirit is the Spirit of Jesus and is the Spirit of truth (xiv 17, xv 26), who is to guide men in the truth". So says Raymond Brown.[99] I shall go on to interpret πνεῦμα ὁ θεός by quoting his excellent summary: "This is not an essential definition of God, but a description of God's dealing with men; it means that God is Spirit toward men because He gives the Spirit (xiv 16) which begets them anew. There are two other such descriptions in the Johannine writings: 'God is light' (1 Jn i 5), and 'God is love' (1 Jn iv 8). These two refer to the God who acts; God gives the world His Son, the *light* of the world (iii 19, viii 12, ix 5), as a sign of His *love* (iii 16)".[1]

Thus Jesus' words in S 11 deal in the highest degree with himself and his work, although he is not explicitly mentioned. Only those who have received the Spirit can worship the Father aright and the Spirit comes as a result of Jesus' glorification, 7:39; 16:7; 19:30; 20:22.

[94] See the detailed survey of interpretation in Petri 1946, 1956. As representatives of the first line he mentions, for example, Heracleon, (Chrysostom), Augustine, Erasmus, Calvin, Bernard, Odeberg, and to some extent also H. Holtzmann, Loisy, Zahn, Lagrange, Schlatter and Büchsel, of the second line, for example, Origen (Chrysostom), Luther, B. Weiss, Bultmann and Cullmann.

[95] This would be a typical Gnostic reading. See Heracleon's interpretation, Petri 1946, pp. 50ff.

[96] Note similar combinations in Jn 1:14,17; 14:6, 1 Jn 3:18 and 2 Jn 3.

[97] See, besides the commentaries, E. Schweizer in ThWNT, vol. 6, pp. 436ff, Rawlinson 1932–33, Schlier 1963. Dodd 1953, pp. 213ff, prefers a Hellenistic background.

[98] See the excursus in Brown, Comm., pp. 499ff, and Schnackenburg, Comm., vol. 2, pp. 265ff. The quotation is from Schnackenburg, p. 279.

[99] Brown, Comm., ad loc., a good representative of the "objective" interpretation.

[1] Brown, Comm., ad loc.

S 12

I know that the Messiah (this means Christ) is coming.
When he comes he will proclaim all things to us.

S 12, like earlier speeches, shows a Johannine turn of phrase: οἶδα, Μεσσίας, ὁ
λεγόμενος, ἀναγγέλλειν.[2] The woman here expresses a more general article of
belief in the same way as Martha in 11:24.[3] The Aramaic form Μεσσίας is only
to be found in Jn 1:41 and here in the NT writings, both times with a Greek explanation.[4] The phrase ὁ λεγόμενος has exact parallels in 11:16; 20:24 and
21:2.[5] The verb ἀναγγέλλειν is of special interest. In both profane and Biblical
literature it has a religious use in the sense "to proclaim, to reveal something to
someone", perhaps most obvious in the Psalter, Deutero-Isaiah and Jn, cf. Is
45:19b ἐγώ εἰμι ἐγώ εἰμι κύριος λαλῶν δικαιοσύνην καὶ ἀναγγέλλων
ἀλήθειαν.[6] The same verb is used of the revealing function of the Paraclete,
16:13—15.[7] Thus the woman expects a future Saviour, who will give the full
revelation. This description, the only one in the text, agrees closely with what
we know of Samaritan eschatology in NT times and even with the portrayal of
Jesus in Jn.

Earlier, in S 10, the woman referred to a basic eschatological theme which, according to information in, for example, Josephus, Ant XVIII.85ff; LXX Gen
35:4; Pseudo-Philo XXV,10 and 2 Macc 2:4—8, can be linked with the time
before the New Testament. The Samaritans held that *Miškān*, God's habitation,
had once been set up on Gerizim by Moses, but that it had later been hidden
there at the beginning of the era of divine disfavour. Yet they expected that
Miškān would be there once more at some time in the future, in the period of the
divine favour.[8] The Gerizim Temple was destroyed in 129/8 B.C., as stated, and

[2] For justification, see Sabugal 1972, pp. 219f.
[3] p⁶⁶ and p⁷⁵ and some other MSS read also οἶδαμεν which Schwank, Comm., ad loc., regards
as the original reading. The plural form is, however, best explained as a harmonization with the
context. Schwank describes S 12 as a suitable *credo* of the OT congregation.
[4] Μεσσίας occurs with and without the article in the same meaning, Sabugal 1972, pp. 46, 208.
The absence of the article here does not imply that the original name was Taheb, as Bultmann,
Comm., ad loc., suggests, referring to H. Odeberg.
[5] Jn often explains Semitic words. See below, 4.2.
[6] See the material adduced by J. Schniewind in ThWNT,vol. 1, pp. 56ff, and Sabugal 1972, pp.
219ff. Note the parallel use of λαλῶν and ἀναγγέλλων in this passage and in S 12—13.
[7] The almost literal correspondence with 16:13 is remarkable. See below, 4.3.
[8] Kippenberg 1971, ch. 9, gives the texts on *Miškān* and a thorough analysis of them. He traces
these traditions to the foundation of the Samaritan cult. "Jene Wanderbewegung Jerusalemer Prie-
ster nach Sichem vom Ende des 4. Jh. v. Chr. an könnte als das erste Lebenszeichen dieser Überlieferung gewertet werden. Ehemalige Aaroniten des früheren Nordreiches sehen in dem Abbruch
aller Beziehungen zu Nordisrael und seinen heiligen Stätten einen Abfall von Jahve. Eine neue Zeit
des Wohlgefallens Jahves wird durch die Neukonstituierung Israels in Sichem angebahnt. Hier
stand einst der *Miškān* — hier wird er wieder stehen", p. 253.

the Samaritans seem to have expected this eschatological manifestation on the mountain since then. There would seem to be no doubt that we have in these beliefs the background to the woman's reference to the Gerizim cult in S 10. She had thereby introduced into the dialogue one of the main features in Samaritan eschatology.

In S 10 these expectations are combined with *the question of Jesus as prophet,* which brings to the fore the second basic feature of Samaritan eschatology at that time, the expectation of a prophet such as Moses. In his detailed examination of the early Samaritan material, Kippenberg seeks to keep separate these two traditions on *Miškān* and *the Prophet,*[9] but Jn 4 seems to me to suggest that they belonged together in the evangelist's time. As a rule, commentators on S 10 and S 12 refer to concepts of *Taheb,* a figure in Samaritan sources specially characterized by his restoration of the true cult.[10] Kippenberg's investigation, however, sheds a different light on *Taheb.*[11] There is now no agreement on the Taheb concepts among the experts.[12] For my analysis here I need not refer to *Taheb,* the material on the Prophet will suffice.

As far as we know, the title *Messiah* was not used by the Samaritans. Accordingly it was placed in the woman's mouth.[13] In S 12 it gains its meaning from the description in the last clause: he will reveal all things to the Samaritans. We know from   4QTest 1–8; 1QS IX.9–11; 1 Macc 4:46; 14:41; Acts 3:22; 7:37, PsClem Rec I, 54 and the Samaritan Pentateuch's version of Ex 20:21b that Dt 18:15ff played an important part in the eschatological expectations in different Palestinian circles around the beginning of our era. This applies not least to Samaritan belief.[14] In Dt 18 the Lord says: προφήτην ἀναστήσω αὐτοῖς ἐκ τῶν ἀδελφῶν αὐτῶν ὥσπερ σὲ καὶ δώσω τὸ ῥῆμά μου ἐν τῷ στόματι αὐτοῦ, καὶ λαλήσει αὐτοῖς καθότι ἂν ἐντείλωμαι αὐτῷ (v. 18). In this connection the Prophet is in the above-mentioned sources also represented as the teacher, the interpreter of the law, he who has insight into all things. According to Kippenberg the task of the Prophet is one alone "in allen uns bekannten Zeugnissen", namely

[9] Kippenberg 1971, p. 236.

[10] See also the recent commentaries of Schnackenburg and Brown, and also MacDonald 1964, p. 365, and Sabugal 1972, pp. 222f.

[11] Kippenberg 1971, ch. 11. "Der Taheb ist ja nichts anderes als der Inbegriff derהבהצי der Umkehrenden" (p. 305). "Joh 4, 25 hat mit dem Taheb nichts zu tun" (p. 303). Later on Taheb became an expected saviour figure.

[12] See the literature mentioned in de Jonge 1972–73, p. 269.

[13] de Jonge 1972–73, p. 268, and the literature he mentions. On Μεσσίας-Χριστός in Jn, see the extended analysis of Sabugal 1972. Both he and de Jonge 1973 rightly stress that the Messiah in Jn must be interpreted from the experiences of the evangelist, especially from his concept of Jesus as ὁ υἱὸς τοῦ θεοῦ. Cf. note 17 below.

[14] See Meeks 1967, p. 217ff, Kippenberg 1971, ch. 12. These interpretations seem to be "censored" in Rabbinic sources, which interpret Dt 18 as referring to Jeremiah, Kippenberg 1971, pp. 306f.

"Verkündigung".[15] Several in Samaria also seem to have claimed to be this prophet during the first century, such as Dositheus, who evidently won many followers.[16] In S 12 the woman expresses her (and the Samaritans') belief in the Prophet who will speak "the words of God" and reveal all things. She confesses her Samaritan faith, but not her belief in Jesus.

S 13

I am,

I who speak to you.

In S 12 the woman confessed her faith in a revealer to come. In S 13 Jesus replies in terms clearly indicating his work of revelation. In the Gospel in general, Jesus appears as the great revealer, he who knows all and proclaims what is to happen.[17] Here Jesus does not say "he who speaks *with* you" but "he who speaks *to* you".[18] From Jesus' side the dialogue is not so much a conversation but a discourse to the woman, a "revelation discourse" in dialogue form. The change from the earlier ὁ λέγων σοι (which refers to previous speeches) in S 3 to ὁ λαλῶν σοι (which refers to the entire dialogue) may also be explained by the more strongly emphasized aspect of revelation in S 13.[19]

The latter part of S 13 thus has a form which attracts attention to Jesus as revealer. The same applies the more to the first two words in the speech. Ἐγώ εἰμι is in Jn "eine gewollte, zu einer vielsagenden Formel gewordene, theologisch bedeutsame Redeweise".[20] The words are sometimes complemented with a metaphor, 6:35, 48, 51; 8:12; 10:7, 9, 11, 14; 11:25; 14:6; 15:1, 5, sometimes they stand without epithet, 6:20; 8:24, 28, 58; 13:19; 18:5, 6, 8. Both Brown and Schnackenburg give convincing evidence—and they are today supported by many other scholars—that the background to the absolute use of ἐγώ εἰμι should be sought in "the OT and Palestinian Judaism".[21] "Jesus is presented as speaking

---

[5] Kippenberg 1971, p. 326.

[6] Kippenberg 1971, pp. 128ff, 316ff.

[7] See, for example, Jn 13:19; 18:4; 14:29; 16:4. This also applies to the use of Χριστός in Jn. "La función salvífica que caracteriza al Χριστός joanneo es la de revelar", Sabugal 1972, p. 445. In this function he is connected with the Paraclete; see below, 4.3.

[8] Λαλεῖν plus the dative: 6:63; 8:25,40; 9:29; 10:6; 12:29; 14:25; 15:3,11,22; 16:1,4,25,33; 18:20f; 19:10.

[9] Λαλεῖν is often used in revelation contexts. On the use in LXX see above, note 6, and Dt 18 on the Prophet (9 times in Dt 18:18—22).

[20] Schnackenburg, Comm., vol. 2, p. 59. On this formula, see Schnackenburg's extensive excursus (pp. 59—70) and the literature he mentions on pp. 59f, and also Brown's short appendix, Comm., pp. 533ff.

[21] Brown, Comm., p. 535ff. Cf. Schnackenburg, Comm., vol. 2, pp. 64ff, referring to H. Zimmermann. "Das absolute ἐγώ εἰμι ist die atl. Offenbarungsformel, die über die LXX im Munde Jesu zur ntl. Offenbarungsformel wird" (p. 63.)

in the same manner in which Yahweh speaks in Deutero-Isaiah".[22] "Jesus ist Gottes eschatologischer Offenbarer, in welchem sich Gott selbst zur Sprache bringt. Seine Selbstoffenbarung aber ist, wie schon die atl. Stellen zeigen, ... Heilsoffenbarung für die an ihn Glaubenden".[23] The same background should reasonably be attributed to the remaining use of the formula in Jn. Yet it is difficult to determine the extent to which the absolute use is glimpsed. The formula is also used with a participle as substantive, 4:26 and 8:18, and with a prepositional phrase, 8:23.[24] The continuation of the verse in our speech and the connection with S 12 make it most natural to read "I am he of whom you speak, he who will reveal all things, I who am here now and speak to you".[25] S 13 is *an unveiled self-revelation* by Jesus of such a nature that one can hardly speak of a gradual self-revelation in the text. S 13 is an absolute peak. The formulation of S 13 gives a strongly revelatory quality to Jesus' words, as judged by Johannine usage, not least to the first two words, even if they are not here used as a divine title.

3.3.3 The Junction of the Speeches

Apart from the quotation formulae, the individual speeches contain many elements which bind the dialogue in vv. 7—26 together into a unit. I shall here analyse this conjunction by discussing the references to persons, the spatial and temporal features, the most important concepts, the distribution of information and finally, to sum up, the composition in its entirety with its links of form and content.[1]

A. The references to persons[2] in the dialogue are primarily concerned with Jesus and the woman, but also the Jews and the Samaritans, the woman's men, the Messiah and God and a general reference in the third person ("every one"). In the text they are distributed as follows:

S 1 Jesus — the woman
S 2 Jesus — the woman (as Jew — Samaritan)
S 3 Jesus — the woman — God
S 4 Jesus — the Samaritans (we, Jacob, sons of Jacob)

[22] Brown, Comm., p. 537.

[23] Schnackenburg, Comm., vol. 2, p. 69.

[24] The use in 9:9 and 18:35 does not refer to Jesus.

[25] Jesus here accepts the title of Messiah but it has its content from the latter part of S 12, de Jonge 1972—73, p. 268.

[1] A different method is possible: to divide up the speeches into semantic components and then describe the relations between these. This more systematic analysis would make the description complicated and scarcely give more reliable results. On analysis of conversations, see Schegloff 1968, Pike-Lowe 1970 and Poythress 1973.

[2] I add the predicative descriptions of persons to the personal references.

S 5 Jesus — every one
S 6 Jesus — the woman
S 7 The woman — her man
S 8 The woman — her man
S 9 The woman — her men
S 10 Jesus — the woman — the Jews — the Samaritans
S 11 Jesus — the woman — the Jews — the Samaritans — God — every one
S 12 The woman — the Samaritans — the Messiah
S 13 Jesus — the woman

In that Jesus and the woman talk together in vv. 7—26, they are present, at least implicitly, in all the speeches.[3] Yet they are not mentioned in all. Jesus is not included in S 7 — S 9 or S 12,[4] while the woman appears in all but the generally worded S 5.[5] Indeed there are far more references to the woman and the Samaritans than to Jesus and the Jews.[6] This suggests that the dialogue not only deals with Jesus and his identity, not only with how Jesus gradually reveals himself, but also in the extreme with the Samaritans.

We find speeches involving just Jesus and the woman only at the beginning, S 1 — S 2, in the middle, S 6, and at the end, S 13. Considering the personal references, the first six speeches are far simpler and unequivocal than the remaining seven. Jesus appears in all six (S 1 — S 6), as does the woman, although in S 4 she is included among the Samaritans and in S 5 is, so to speak, hidden in a highly general formulation. The gradual extension of the reference in S 1 — S 5 makes it easier to include in S 5 the readers for whom the text is intended. Then S 6 again links the dialogue with only Jesus and the woman. Four of the speeches in S 7 — S 13 deal with the woman and the Samaritans, S 7 — S 9 and S 12. Even here we find an extension of the reference in S 10 — S 11, with a conclusion in S 13, which, like S 6, concerns only Jesus and the woman. The extension of the number of persons is here greater than in the first part and S 11 includes all the persons mentioned in the dialogue, excepting Jacob and his sons and the woman's men. Yet here the references are by no means as simple as the above survey would suggest. The problems are most acute in the determination of the content of $\dot{v}\mu\epsilon\tilde{\iota}\varsigma$ and $\dot{\eta}\mu\epsilon\tilde{\iota}\varsigma$ in v. 22.[7]

[3] Every speech presupposes a statement such as "X informs, exhorts, asks ... Y".
[4] S 12 mentions the Messiah, which the readers take as referring to Jesus.
[5] Πᾶς ὁ πίνων κτλ. in S 5 refers mainly to the woman and the Samaritans, i.e. those who used to drink from Jacobs' well. The woman would then be included in all speeches.
[6] That applies both to the number of speeches and to the number of references. Jesus and the Jews are referred to 27 times, the woman and the Samaritans 40 times.
[7] The problem is generally formulated as an alternative: does ἡμεῖς refer to the Jews as τῶν Ἰουδαίων in the following clause, *or* does it refer to the believers as in Jn 3:11? See Comm., ad loc. The problem is often solved by different theories of additions to the text.

At the beginning of S 10 the woman speaks of herself and of Jesus. She then mentions the Samaritans' fathers and the Jews in general, οἱ πατέρες ἡμῶν and λέγετε.[8] The use of δεῖ at the end of the speech gives a general reference: only in Jerusalem is it possible to offer true worship. The following comment on Jesus' part (S 11) is long, concluding with an expression which evidently discusses the ending mentioned in S 10: *those who* worship God must (δεῖ) do so in spirit and truth. Thus the text mentions three opinions: that of the Samaritans in v. 20, of the Jews in v. 20 and of Jesus in v. 24. This last belief is expounded, commented on and justified in vv. 21—24, which I must here analyse in more detail to be able to define the references.

S 11 consists of two more or less parallel sections, both of which begin with ἔρχεται ὥρα .[9] The introductory ἀλλά in v. 23 marks repetition, reinforcement, explanation and should not be understood adversatively.[10] What is said in the first section is partly repeated in the second, with a certain emphasis, being extended and explained. If we consider the content of the text we can divide it up as follows:

21 aa ἔρχεται ὥρα

ab ὅτε οὔτε ἐν τῷ ὄρει τούτῳ οὔτε ἐν Ἰεροσολύμοις προσκυνήσετε τῷ πατρί.

22 ac ὑμεῖς προσκυνεῖτε ὃ οὐκ οἴδατε.

ad ἡμεῖς προσκυνοῦμεν ὃ οἴδαμεν,

ae ὅτι ἡ σωτηρία ἐκ τῶν Ἰουδαίων ἐστίν.

23 ba ἀλλὰ ἔρχεται ὥρα, καὶ νῦν ἐστιν,

bb ὅτε οἱ ἀληθινοὶ προσκυνηταὶ προσκυνήσουσιν τῷ πατρὶ ἐν πνεύματι καὶ ἀληθείᾳ.

bc καὶ γὰρ ὁ πατὴρ τοιούτους ζητεῖ τοὺς προσκυνοῦντας αὐτόν.

24 bd πνεῦμα ὁ θεός,

be καὶ τοὺς προσκυνοῦντας αὐτὸν ἐν πνεύματι καὶ ἀληθείᾳ δεῖ προσκυνεῖν.

First of all we may note the wording in *ab*. Jesus does not say ὅτε οὔτε ἐν τῷ ὄρει τούτῳ προσκυνήσετε οὔτε ἐν Ἰεροσολύμοις[11] which would be a direct answer to the indirect question in S 10. *His reply points to* τῷ πατρί *at the end of the clause.* Here is the emphasis in *ab*. In fact, this clause makes two points: in

---

[8] The main characteristic of these Jews is their claim to the Jerusalemite cult.

[9] On the first words of S 11, see above 3.3.2, S 11. Schnackenburg, Comm., ad loc., notes that v. 22 is a "Zwischenbemerkung".

[10] See above, 3.3.2, S 11. An adversative meaning of ἀλλά is one of Schnackenburg's main reasons for referring ἡμεῖς to the Jews and no others, Comm., ad loc.

[11] Note the formulation of Jn 9:3, the single passage in Jn which has οὔτε - οὔτε as coordinating two parts of speech.

fut**ure** you will *worship the Father,* and it will *not be on Gerizim or at Jerusalem.*
The word ὁ πατήρ of God is repeated several times, although we have ὁ θεός in
vv. 10 and 24. The wording is unexpected, and could only be explained from
Johannine usage. Therefore, the expression ὁ πατήρ here describes *God as Jesus
has revealed Him.*[12] The formulation of *ab* prepares the way for the following explanation of Jesus' identity and the question of *truth* and *true insight* which are
there mentioned.[13] The worship of which Jesus speaks in S 11 thus seems to
presume his work of revelation, which, according to Jn, is not completed until
after Jesus' "hour".[14] The content of the ὅτε-clauses is then pointing forward to a
time after Jesus' death and glorification.

The temporal markings in the speech also point forward to this moment in
time. The phrase ἔρχεται ὥρα ὅτε with the future, 4:21, 23; 5:25; 16:25, is
always used in Jn to denote what will happen with Jesus' "hour".[15] Only the ὅτε-
clauses in S 11 have the future, while the clauses which follow are in the present.[16]
These present clauses may be related to the two times which are at issue in the
text, to the time of the speaker (Jesus), from which the prediction was made *or* to
the time when the prediction is realized. One is immediately tempted to find these
two points in time marked in the phrase ἔρχεται ὥρα, καὶ νῦν ἐστιν, where the
first is based on Jesus' situation, the second on the author's.[17] We would then
have in S 11 a kind of co-projection of the time *before* Jesus' "hour" and the time
after Jesus' "hour", a textual attribute which I previously found characteristic of
other parts of the Gospel too.[18]

That which follows the ὅτε-clause in the second part is clearly marked as a
justification and explanation (καὶ γάρ). Two reasons are given, formulated in *bc*
and *bd-be.* Notwithstanding that the latter two clauses are co-ordinated by syntax, it is most natural to read them as semantically subordinate: "since God is
Spirit, ... men must worship Him ...", when we here accept them as a justification of *bb.* We have a similar marking (ὅτι) in *ae,* but not in *ac-ad.*[19] The seman-

[12] A reference to the father of *mankind,* Schwank and Morris, Comm., ad loc., is very improbable. A Johannine sense is especially necessary in the second ὅτε-clause. Schnackenburg,
Comm., ad loc., takes the Johannine sense for granted ("Gott, wie ihn Jesus offenbart")'

[13] See especially the material adduced by Schnackenburg and Lindars. Comm., ad loc. Ὁ
πατήρ is typical of Jn but we have also ὁ θεός in speeches of Jesus, 4:10, 24; 5:42, 44; 6:46;
8:40. 42; 11:4,22,40.

[14] See especially Jn 16:25, commented on below, 4.3.

[15] Similarly in 5:28 (with ἐν ᾗ) and 16:2,32 (with ἵνα). To this future time belong the true worship of the Father, 4:21,23, resurrection and life, 5:25,28, persecutions and killing of the disciples,
16:2, the complete revelation, 16:25, and the scattering of the disciples, 16:32.

[16] Προσκυνεῖτε, (οἴδατε), προσκυνοῦμεν, (οἴδαμεν), ἐστίν, ζητεῖ, δεῖ.

[17] Only 5:25 has the same expression. Cf. 16:32 ἔρχεται ὥρα καὶ ἐλήλυθεν.

[18] See 2.2, U 27 and U 29, and the interpretation of 2:1—11 in 2.4.2.

[19] *ac* and *ad,* like *bd* and *be* belong together, but these two pairs of clauses are introduced asyndetically. The logical relations to the context must be derived from their position and their content.

tic relations in the section *ac-ae*, however, are more difficult to determine. The clauses *ac* and *ad* are strongly adversative, with identical elements, and form a unit. Both their construction (προσκυνεῖν + object) and the weight attributed to the unexpected τῷ πατρί in *ab* justify the assumption that these clauses are a kind of comment on προσκυνήσετε τῷ πατρί in *ab*.[20] The Samaritans do not now know God as Jesus has revealed Him.[21] They do not know "the Father" and therefore they worship ὃ οὐκ οἴδατε. This may apply both to the woman and the Samaritans in Jesus' time, and to readers who do not believe in Jesus,[22] in other words both the points in time mentioned. Considering the comments on S 11 just given I feel justified in interpreting ἡμεῖς in v. 22 as referring to the author and to those who believe in Jesus as he does. Through the Paraclete they have the full revelation, they have been brought to the whole truth and therefore now worship ὃ οἴδαμεν.[23] We would then have the same usage here as in 3:11. My chief reason then is not the portrayal of the Jews in Jn—because it is difficult to imagine that Jesus in Jn would say of the Jews that they worship what they know[24]—but the structure and content of the entire speech in the light of Johannine usage.[25] Thus we have a joint view in S 11, a co-projection of the time of Jesus and the time of the evangelist, not only as regards the references to time but also concerning those to persons.

The remaining ὅτι-clause in v. 22 may also be plausibly explained, if it is regarded as a comment by the evangelist,[26] not referring to *ac-ad* but to *ab,* and above all to the Samaritans' share in the true worship of the Father. Οἱ Ἰουδαῖοι is here used in a neutral sense,[27] and the comment confers an aspect of "salvation history" on the event mentioned in *ab*: from the Jew Jesus and the Jews who received him as the Messiah, the Son of God, comes salvation to the Samaritans

[20] The similarities to *bc—be* also suggest this logical relation.

[21] Ὃ οὐκ οἴδατε replaces τῷ πατρί. To know the Father through the Son is a main theme in Jn. See, for example, 7:27ff; 8:19,55; 14:7ff; 15:15; 16:3 and 17:3.

[22] If this is right, it implies that Jn 4 is shaped with regard to Samaritans who lived in the evangelist's own time. See below, ch. 5.

[23] Cf. Lindars, Comm., ad loc., who describes v. 22 as "a reflection of the actual position of Christianity", and of early commentaries, those by Loisy, Bauer, and Bultmann, and Odeberg 1929, pp. 170f. Brown, Comm., ad loc., rejects this interpretation very briefly, only referring to a specific view of the type of text.

[24] Bultmann, Comm., ad loc., asserts that ἡμεῖς as the Jews is quite impossible with regard to 5:37; 9:19, and Schnackenburg's argumentation is chiefly intended to contradict Bultmann on this point.

[25] Many interpretative sections in Jn concern the question of insight and lack of insight. See below, 4.1 and 4.2. This is also an important theme in Jn 4. See 3.3.3, C.

[26] On γάρ-clauses as the evangelist's remarks, see below, 4.2. Ὅτι-clauses with the same function do not occur, but compare 7:22, 9:8, 3:23, which confirm the parenthetical character of the ὅτι-clause in v. 22.

[27] See the material adduced by Schnackenburg, Comm., ad loc.

and the whole world.[28] God bound His world-wide work of salvation to Jerusalem, whose Temple Jesus calls "my Father's house", Jn 2:16, and where the events of the "hour" later took place, Jn 13—20, and not to Gerizim.[29]

The references to persons also give a pattern of contrasts in the dialogue as a whole: between Jesus and the woman in S 2 — S 3, between Jesus and Jacob in S 4, between Jews and Samaritans in S 2,[30] S 10—S 11, and, in the most general form, between those who drink from Jacob's well and those who are to drink of Jesus' water in S 5, between those who have insight and those who lack it, and between true and false worshippers in S 11. The woman is placed in the tension field between these two poles.

The differing expressions of the references have been discussed above in various contexts.[31] With the junction in mind, scholars have often referred to the series of descriptions of Jesus in the dialogue: Ἰουδαῖος in S 2, μείζων τοῦ πατρὸς ἡμῶν Ἰακώβ in S 4, προφήτης in S 10, indirectly Μεσσίας, Χριστός in S 12,[32] and finally ἐγώ εἰμι in S 13. A more definite link is provided by the expressions ὁ λέγων σοι – ὁ λαλῶν σοι in S 3 and S 13, describing Jesus' revealing function in the dialogue and clearly associated with the woman's expectations of the Messiah according to S 12. S 3 also introduces God and His activity into the dialogue by τὴν δωρεὰν τοῦ θεοῦ and in S 11 we have the same form of reference with πνεῦμα as predicate, which focuses on His activity among men.[33] As I have already mentioned, this activity is bound by the use of the Johannine ὁ πατήρ, three times in S 11, to him who sent Jesus Christ, the only one who knows the Father and can make Him known to others. Thus the way of referring to God and the activity aspect in S 3 and S 11 may be regarded as a connecting link in the dialogue.

Therefore: The analysis of the references to persons has proved a close connection between S 1 — S 6, a contrast throughout which found its most general form in S 5 and S 11, in S 11 with an obvious inclusion of the author and those who believe as he does, a connection link by the limitation to Jesus and the woman in S 1 — S 2, S 6 and S 13, a special shift from the woman to the Samaritans and an emphasis on them in the text (which poses the question of whether or not the Samaritans' religion is also somehow mentioned in S 7 — S 9)

---

[28] On the mission in Jn, see 3.4.6.

[29] On the eschatological role of Gerizim, see above 3.3.2, S 10 and S 12.

[30] The contrast is also stressed by the comment on this speech. See above 3.2.5.

[31] See above 3.2.3 (τοῦ πατρὸς ἡμῶν Ἰακώβ and οἱ υἱοὶ αὐτοῦ), 3.2.5 (Ἰουδαῖος and γυναικὸς Σαμαρίτιδος), 3.3.2, S 4 (κύριε), S 10 (προφήτης), S 12 (Μεσσίας and Χριστός) and S 13 (ἐγώ εἰμι).

[32] See my comment on S 12 above (3.3.2).

[33] See above, 3.3.2, S 11 and below 3.3.4, B.

and a marking of the revelation aspect.[34] All this holds the entire dialogue together, especially S 1 – S 6 and S 10 – S 13. The references to persons say little of S 7 – S 9, perhaps only that ἀνήρ, derived from בעל and from Jewish ideas of the relation between Yahweh and Israel, may refer both to husband and to God.[35]

B. *The temporal and spatial features* were discussed already in connection with the analysis of S 11, where I drew the conclusion that we had in the dialogue a certain co-projection of time and space. Remaining *spatial features* may be combined in a discussion of the phrases of movement in S 6 – S 7, of the different markings of direction in the text and of the ἐν -phrases in S 10 – S 11.

The only explicit conjunction in the transition between the two parts of the dialogue is διέρχωμαι ἐνθάδε in S 6 and ἐλθὲ ἐνθάδε in S 7. In the first case we are concerned with Jacob's well, previously referred to as τὸ φρέαρ twice in S 4, and as τοῦ ὕδατος τούτου in S 5.[36] In the latter case, however, Jesus is meant.[37] The closing words in S 6 refer to v. 7 andἀντλῆσαι ὕδωρ;this gives us an inclusion of vv. 7–15 concerning the woman who came with her jar to Jacob's well to fetch water. In S 7 and what follows, the woman will come with her husband to Jesus at the well.[38] The first part of the dialogue is greatly concerned with *the woman's (the Samaritans') water,* the second with *the woman's man and the God of the Samaritans.*[39] Jesus' exhortation in S 7 is partly picked up in the events narrated in vv. 28ff.

The word ἐνθάδε in S 6 and S 7 also brings out different trends in the text. The first part of the dialogue is concerned in various ways with the problem of *whence* (πόθεν):[40] the water *from* the Samaritan woman, παρ᾽ ἐμοῦ in S 2. *from* the Samaritans' well, ἐκ in S 4 and S 5, *from* Jesus, ἐκ in S 5. These expressions correspond to phrases about water *for* Jesus, μοί in S 1 and S 3, *for* the woman, σοί in S 3, μοί in S 6, *for* everyone who desires, it, αὐτῷ in S 5.[41] There are no equivalents to these many markers of direction from S 1 – S 6 in the latter part of the dialogue, with two interesting exceptions: salvation will come *from* (ἐκ) the

---

[34] The revelation aspect is marked by such forms of reference as ὁ λέγων σοι, ὁ λαλῶν σοι, προφήτης, ὁ πατήρ and ἐγώ εἰμι. Note the description of the Messiah in S 12.

[35] See Brown, Comm., ad loc.

[36] Note the deictic use of τό and τούτου.

[37] The words can be paraphrased: "come to me and I will give you my water". Jesus' water is referred to as τὸ ὕδωρ ὃ δώσω twice in S 5 and as τοῦτο τὸ ὕδωρ in S 6.

[38] S 7 as introducing the second part has many similarities to S 1 (Jesus exhorts the woman to do something, and her act is connected with Jesus by μοι in S 1 and ἐνθάδε in S 7).

[39] This parity suggests a transferred meaning in S 7–9, but such an interpretation has not here been adduced as a reason for it. The parity is confirmed by the formulation of vv. 7, 15 and 16.

[40] The word is explicitly mentioned in v. 11.

[41] Everyone who drinks of Jesus' water is given a fountain of water ἐν αὐτῷ, S 5.

Jews, v. 22—cf. water from the Samaritans above—and the Messiah will give them ($ἡμῖν$) knowledge of all things.

Instead of *whence* ($πόθεν$), we find in the later part of the dialogue the question *where* ($ποῦ$).[42] Twice we find $ἐν τῷ ὄρει τούτῳ$, twice $ἐν Ἱεροσολύμοις$, twice $ἐν πνεύματι καὶ ἀληθείᾳ$; all these $ἐν$ -phrases are concentrated in S 10 — S 11. The nearness to each other and the related constructions mean that the spatial nature of the first two phrases influences the reading of the third, and render less probable a theory of an adverbial use expressing manner.[43] God is not worshipped as the Father everywhere, not on Gerizim, not in Jerusalem, but wherever God Himself so pleased, in the sphere of the Spirit and the Truth, i.e. in the framework of the Revelation in and through Christ. This aspect gives rise to serious doubt as to a common interpretation of S 10 — S 11 as expressing *the universalism* and *freedom from* all limitation[44] of the true worship. The emphasis is on the *bond with* "the Spirit" and "the Truth". This in turn may imply universalism and freedom.

The *temporal features* are most evident and most complicated in the already analysed speech S 11. The mixture there of future and present is part of the projection of the author's time into that of Jesus.[45] The futural feature, however,—i.e. a starting point in the time of Jesus—dominates the dialogue as whole through S 5, where we only have the future: $διψήσει$ twice, $δώσω$ twice, and $γενήσεται$. The futural phrase $ἔρχεται ὥρα$ in S 11 reappears in S 12 in the words $ἔρχεται$ $Μεσσίας$: moreover the clause $ὅταν ἔλθῃ$ and the verb $ἀναγγελεῖ$ are manifestly pointing forward. Both Jesus and the woman are in S 11 — S 12 looking forward to something in the future, which is changed into the now by S 13.

S 11 is not the only passage in which we find an explicit temporal contrast.[46] Some scholars would read $πᾶς ὁ πίνω$ as a repeated drinking, but $ὃς δ' ἂν πίῃ$ as "a single draught". The marking by tense is not very strong, however, possibly "he who drinks"—"he who slakes his thirst".[47] Moreover, the text says that whoever drinks the woman's water will become thirsty again ($πάλιν$) while everyone who is permitted to drink Jesus' water will never again ($εἰς τὸν αἰῶνα$) thirst. The drinking, the origin of the water and the effect of the water are contrasted in S 5.

In S 9 too we have a temporal comparison, marked by the use of tense and the word $νῦν$. The position of $νῦν$ even seems to give a certain emphasis to the dis-

[42] A question with $ποῦ$ is not explicitly given but note the phrase $ὁ τόπος ὅπου$ in v. 20.

[43] On the different interpretations of this phrase, see above 3.3.2, S 11.

[44] See the allegorical or symbolical interpretation of Jn 4 at the turn of the last century, mentioned above in 3.1.

[45] See 3.3.3, A.

[46] Note, besides the comparisons mentioned in the following analysis, a certain implicit contrast in S 6—7: "*no longer* be thirsty and come to the well" *contra* "go *first* home and...".

[47] See above 3.3.2, S 5.

tinction between a *then* and a *now*. The aorist ἔσχες normally has an ingressive meaning, namely "obtained, received, got", but may be constative and mean "possessed".[48] With the comparison in mind I would translate "You once had five men, and the one you now have is not yours". The same tense used in the next speech (προσεκύνησαν) may give some guidance. The woman does not there mention anything contemporary. She does not say: ἡμεῖς προσκυνοῦμεν ἐν τῷ ὄρει τούτῳ · ὑμεῖς δὲ λέγετε .. The present tense in the latter would suggest such a formulation. The woman refers to the Samaritans' *earlier* religious practices on Gerizim and not to her *present* situation.[49] If we compare S 9 and S 10 concerning the temporal features, we find here an indication that the reference to her five men in S 9 also deals with the earlier history of Samaria.[50] We would then find the same characteristics at the beginning of both parts of the dialogue: the first speech is neutral, the woman understands it from her situation and from her earthly existence, while Jesus, on the other hand shows that he has in mind something religious and spiritual, the relationship to God.

The aorists ἔσχες and προσεκύνησαν may therefore be regarded as connecting links between S 9 and S 10. The temporal features otherwise have no great conjunctive function. S 5, S 11 and S 12 are connected by their futural character. Otherwise the temporal markings' chief function is to provide certain contrasts within the speeches, in S 5, S 9 and S 11, which point to a given moment in the past, in the present and in the future.[51]

C. *The most important semantic areas*, if we ignore the references to persons, may be distinguished by the words *water, give* and *know*. We encounter them together already in S 3: If you *knew* the *gift* of God . . . *give* you living *water*. The differing expressions for the areas *water* and *give* combine S 1 — S 6 into an indissoluble unit,[52] while the theme of knowledge pervades the entire dialogue, and primarily its last part. The first two areas are clearly marked in the short introductory speech δός μοι πεῖν, a phrase which reappears word for word in S 3, and in a somewhat altered form in S 6. In the short passage S 1 — S 6, we have in different forms ὕδωρ seven times, πίνειν six, διψᾶν three, φρέαρ twice, πηγή, ἄντλημα and ἀντλεῖν once, and the words are scattered throughout the six speeches. The first part simply deals with water in different senses, especially with *giving* water and *drinking* (receiving) water. When water is first mentioned explicitly in S 3, it is qualified, as in the other six cases. Apart from its description as

---

[48] Barrett, Comm., ad loc. The form of the verb has caused difficulties for grammarians which may depend on different views of S 7—9 as a whole.

[49] See also above, 3.3.2, S 10.

[50] On the "allegorical" interpretation of S 7—9, see above 3.2.2, S 7.

[51] Note also προσεκύνησαν and λέγετε in S 10.

[52] This unity is strengthened by the fact that S 7 and the following speeches do not have these semantic areas.

the water which Jacob gave and as that which Jesus will give, it is called ὕδωρ ζῶν in S 3, τὸ ὕδωρ τὸ ζῶν in S 4, and πηγὴ ὕδατος ἁλλομένου εἰς ζωὴν αἰώνιον in S 5.[53] The indefinite form in the first *locus* carries a *double entendre:* fresh running water, or water which gives life in a transferred meaning.[54] In the well known Johannine turn of phrase,[55] this technique of *double entendre* is so used that the following speech deals with the former meaning and the one after that with water which gives eternal life. In the concluding speech, S 6, the woman has realized that the point at issue is not ordinary water and she is prepared to abandon her jar, which she needed for Jacob's well. She begs for this special water, but without full insight into what it is. In the following speeches there is no further mention of water, but there are two indications of a connection with the ideas expressed in the second part of the dialogue: ζωὴ αἰώνιος links up with ἡ σωτηρία in v. 22, and the water as ἡ δωρεὰ τοῦ θεοῦ with πνεῦμα ὁ θεός in v. 24. Moreover, the water in S 1 — S 6 is connected with the second part of the dialogue by the common theme of insight, not least perhaps by the woman's confession in S 12 of the Messiah, who will give to the Samaritans knowledge of all things (ἀναγγελεῖ ἡμῖν ἅπαντα).

The verb ἀναγγελεῖ in S 12 is also the only term in S 7 — S 13 which can naturally be associated with the frequently occurring διδόναι in S 1 — S 6.[56] All the speeches there, except S 2,[57] contain expressions concerned with *giving:* δός in S 1, S 3 and S 6, δωρεάν in S 3, ἔδωκεν in S 3 and S 4, δώσω twice in S 5, thus eight times in all. The agent of the giving varies: the woman, Jesus, Jacob and God. The predominant aspect, according to S 3, is clearly *the gift of God.* To this is linked *Jesus'* gift, which in S 4 is contrasted with *Jacob's* gift. Jesus' gift is both in the future and in the present. Compared with Jacob, it lies in the future, and compared with the woman, as she understands the situation, it is in the present. Thus the first part of the dialogue becomes a discussion of the gift of God and of living water or the water God gives.

The semantic area of *knowledge* is primarily marked by the words ᾔδεις in S 3, θεωρῶ in S 10, ὃ οὐκ οἴδατε, ὃ οἴδαμεν in S 11, οἶδα in S 12, and, to some extent, the revelation formula ἐγώ εἰμι in S 13. The latter speech (ἐγώ εἰμι, ὁ λαλῶν σοι) apparently corresponds with Jesus' words in S 3 εἰ ᾔδεις . . . τίς ἐστιν ὁ λέγων σοι. The question of knowledge and insight must therefore be described as a connecting theme, running all through the dialogue. The main point at

---

[53] On these expressions, see 3.3.2, S 5, and 3.3.6.

[54] See 3.3.6.

[55] See especially Cullmann 1966, pp. 176ff, and Leroy 1968.

[56] The relation of possession, especially marked in S 7—9, is a very general link running through the entire dialogue.

[57] Giving is implicit in S 2, marked by παρ' ἐμοῦ πεῖν αἰτεῖς.

issue is the woman's insight, or perhaps her lack of it.[58] She begins with questions: $\pi\hat{\omega}\varsigma$ in S 2, $\pi\acute{o}\vartheta\epsilon\nu$ and $\mu\acute{\eta}$ in S 4. In these three cases the questions also refer to a certain insight on the woman's part, to her knowledge of the relationship between Jews and Samaritans, of the Samaritan's well and of the Samaritans' father, Jacob. No direct questions are asked however in the latter part of the dialogue. There the woman only states certain facts about herself and about the Samaritans: she has no husband, her fathers worshipped on Gerizim, she knows that the Messiah will come and will proclaim all things to the Samaritans. Her final speech rings like a Samaritan confession of faith.[59] Jesus counters these questions and assertions in different ways. In S 3 he states clearly that she lacks understanding of God's gift and of him who speaks to her. She does not know how to answer. In S 9, on the other hand, he sees a true saying in her speech: $\kappa\alpha\lambda\hat{\omega}\varsigma\ \epsilon\hat{\iota}\pi\epsilon\varsigma$, $\tau o\hat{\upsilon}\tau o\ \mathring{\alpha}\lambda\eta\vartheta\grave{\epsilon}\varsigma\ \epsilon\check{\iota}\rho\eta\kappa\alpha\varsigma$. It would be much easier to understand these sayings on Jesus' part, if the woman's relation to God were under discussion. Jesus would then understand the woman's words as a confession that she had no God to worship. She cannot invoke her God, for she, as well as the Samaritans, worships an unknown God, $\mathring{o}$ o$\mathring{\upsilon}\kappa$ o$\mathring{\iota}\delta\alpha\tau\epsilon$. Their lack of insight is self-evident and is particularly emphasized in S 11. The formulations $\tau\hat{\omega}\ \pi\alpha\tau\rho\acute{\iota}$, $\mathring{o}$ o$\mathring{\upsilon}\kappa$ o$\mathring{\iota}\delta\alpha\tau\epsilon$, $\mathring{\epsilon}\nu\ \pi\nu\epsilon\acute{\upsilon}\mu\alpha\tau\iota$ $\kappa\alpha\grave{\iota}\ \mathring{\alpha}\lambda\eta\vartheta\epsilon\acute{\iota}\alpha$ all express, in the Johannine turn of phrase, that the woman is in need of revelation. When she finally confesses her belief in the Messiah, Jesus openly confirms that he is the one for whom she waits, he who will reveal ($\mathring{\alpha}\nu\alpha\gamma\gamma\epsilon\lambda\epsilon\hat{\iota}$) all things to her and the Samaritans. The woman's reaction to this revelation comes only in the form of her witness in vv. 28ff. The dialogue ends with a clear self-revelation of Jesus.

The three predominant semantic areas in the text thus join the dialogue together, especially the theme of knowledge. The terms for *water* and *giving* in particular bind together the first part, but there are several features in the text which give us reason to see a continuation of these two themes in the mention of $\mathring{\eta}\ \sigma\omega\tau\eta\rho\acute{\iota}\alpha$, $\pi\nu\epsilon\hat{\upsilon}\mu\alpha$, $\mathring{\alpha}\lambda\acute{\eta}\vartheta\epsilon\iota\alpha$ and $\mathring{\alpha}\nu\alpha\gamma\gamma\epsilon\lambda\epsilon\hat{\iota}\ \mathring{\eta}\mu\hat{\iota}\nu\ \mathring{\alpha}\pi\alpha\nu\tau\alpha$ in the last speeches of the dialogue.

D. The quantitative distribution of information between various speeches can hardly be measured. A rough estimate gives the length of the speeches, here measured in words: 3, 11, 25, 42, 41 and 13 in the first part, 8, 3, 21, 26, 72, 13 and 5 in the second part. S 4 and 5 and S 10 and 11 are the most extensive in their respective parts. The speeches gradually expand and may be fairly long sections, such as S 11, a phenomenon we recognize from other "dialogue" texts in Jn.[60] We would have a somewhat better understanding of the information flow if we

---

[58] Note that almost all of the expressions mentioned have the woman (or the Samaritans) as agent.

[59] I have compared with Martha's saying in 11:24 above, 3.3.2, S 12.

[60] See, for example, 3:1ff, 4:31ff; 6:25ff; 8:21ff; 9:1ff.

noted all markings of the different semantic components contained in each speech, and established whether they occur in the immediately preceding and following speeches.[61] If we also consider the distribution in the various speeches, we reach the following result: the woman provides the most striking increase in information in the central speeches of the two dialogue sections, S 4 and S 10, and Jesus' speeches are connected more closely with those of the woman than *vice versa*. This is especially true of the symmetrically distributed S 3 and S 5, S 9 and S 11. This result corresponds to some of the observations made above. Although Jesus opens both series, the woman presents the new material, the questions, the admissions, which Jesus then "answers" and comments on. From this basic feature of the text, and the contents of the "questions" and the "answers", I would tend to consider the dialogue as a meeting between the divine revelation in Christ and the Samaritan faith, personified by the woman.

E. The composition of the entire dialogue[62] can now be described with the addition of a few further observations. They are primarily concerned with the speeches in general. If we omit the justifying or introductory material, what the woman says may be reduced as follows:

S 2   How can *you* ask me for a drink?
S 4   Where do *you* get running water?
      Are *you* perhaps greater than Jacob?
S 6   Give me of *your* water!
S 8   I have no husband.
S 10 I see that *you* are a prophet.
      You say that men must worship in Jerusalem.
S 12 I know that the Messiah will come.

Thus we first have three *questions* to and about Jesus and a plea to him for his water.[63] Then follow four *assertions,* only one of which explicitly concerns Jesus. The frequently suggested interpretation of S 12 as an expression of the woman's belief in Jesus can hardly be justified by the wording of the speech.[64] It would

---

[61] Such a method has been proposed by J.N. Winburne for an analysis of the sequence of sentences in a discourse. See his analysis of Lincoln's Gettysburg Address, published in 1964. In my analysis of Jn 4:7–26 I have counted the markings of Jesus, the woman, to give, to drink, the Jews, the Samaritans, to request, to know, God, to say, water, life etc. Interrogative words and relation words of different kinds have been excluded.

[62] The composition has been analysed before, expecially by Schmid 1929 and Roustang 1958. Brown, Comm., ad loc., reproduces Roustang's result and Schnackenburg, Comm., ad loc., pays little attention to the formation of the dialogue as a whole.

[63] Σύ is emphasized in S 2 and S 4, τοῦτο in S 6.

[64] The text is read, not only as a *gradual* self-revelation of Jesus, but also as a narrative concerning an individual who *gradually* comes to believe in Jesus, with a climax in S 12.

seem rather to express the Samaritan community's belief in, and expectation of, a saviour who will reveal all things to them.[65] The woman is present throughout, with her questions, her plea and her confessions within the framework of the old covenant, and it is the revelation in S 13 which first opens her eyes to Jesus' true identity, insofar as any such assertion may be made about the woman. Her actions and her witness later in vv. 28ff are directed rather toward influencing the Samaritans than to expressing her belief in Jesus.

We can reduce Jesus' speeches in a similar way:

S 1   Give me to drink!
S 3   If you knew ... you would ask me for water.
S 5   Everyone who drinks of this water ...
        Everyone who drinks of the water I shall give ...
S 7   Go, call your husband and come here!
S 9   You are right in saying you have no husband.
S 11 Woman believe me ... true worshippers will worship the Father in spirit and truth.
S 13 I am (the man of whom you speak).

I have already commented several times on the fact that S 1, S 3 and S 5 are closely connected, as are S 7 and S 9. Here I wish to point out the similarities existing between S 1 and S 7, between S 3 and S 9, and between S 5 and S 11.

Both S 1 and S 7 are exhortations to the woman to take a certain course of action. In both cases her action is related to Jesus ($\mu o\iota$, $\dot{\epsilon}v\vartheta\dot{\alpha}\delta\epsilon$), and applies in the first instance to *her water,* and in the second to *her man.* The action the woman is challenged to take is never actually performed. Jesus' words in the following speeches, in S 3 and S 9 respectively, show that the exhortations are only "apparent". Jesus does not seem inclined to accept any water, but rather to give it. In the second instance he evidently did not expect the woman to return to him with her husband, but possibly to worship the Father. The continuation of the dialogue concerns her and the Samaritans' relationship to God.. The continued conversation in both the first and the second parts of the dialogue may therefore be said to justify the belief that there is a *double entendre* already inherent in the introductory neutral speeches (S 1 and S 7). Jesus intends a dialogue concerning his work of salvation, while the woman understands his words in concrete terms from the situation. There may perhaps also be a direct indication of Jesus' work in S 1. Just as $\dot{\epsilon}\sigma\vartheta\dot{\iota}\epsilon\iota v$ is later used in the second dialogue as an expression signifying *to perform God's work of salvation,* a similar meaning may be read into $\pi\epsilon\tilde{\iota}v$ in S 1. Such a reading is supported by the description of Jesus' work of salvation as a drink in Jn 18:11 and 19:28f.

Both S 3 and S 9 deal with the woman's "insight". They comment on her answers in S 2 and S 8 respectively. In S 3 we have a clear change from a literal

[65] See 3.3.2, S 12.

meaning of the phrase *give me to drink* to a transferred meaning. Jesus begins to speak of different kinds of water. There are, as shown above, many points in favour of a similar understanding of S 9: Jesus' words about the woman's "insight", the weight he assigns to her confession, the emphasis on ἄνδρα in Jesus' repetition of her words, the very comment thereon and probably even the parallel between ἔσχες in S 9 and προσεκύνησαν in S 10.[66] Jesus is here thinking of the woman's relationship to God. This is, as stated above, in excellent agreement with the continuation of the dialogue. So even if in S 1 — S 3 and S 7 — S 9 Jesus is speaking of external, earthly things, he is, according to the evangelist, aiming primarily at questions concerning his mission, in our text at the Samaritans' relationship to the God he reveals.

S 5 and S 11 have previously been associated because of their general form of reference, their use of the future, their strong contrast, their place in the information flow and the words ζωὴν αἰώνιον and ἡ σωτηρία. Even these Jesus' sayings reveal striking parallel features. On the one hand, they mention *drinking from Jacob's well, worshipping on Gerizim and in Jerusalem, being without understanding;* and on the other, *drinking of Jesus' water, worshipping the Father in spirit and truth, having understanding.* These qualities in Jesus' speeches meant that I find therein a clear parallel between S 1 and S 7, S 3 and S 9 and S 5 and S 11, which together with the distribution of information in the text, the reference conditions etc. justify us in regarding S 1 — S 6 and S 7 — S 13 as parallel, at least to some extent.

The points made in section 3.3.3 concerning the junction of the speeches may be summarized in a description of *the composition of the dialogue.* We arrive at the following scheme:

S 1	S 7
S 2	S 8
S 3	S 9
S 4	S 10
S 5	S 11
S 6	S 12
	S 13

The results are in general agreement with those of Roustang.[67] The parallelising of the two main parts and the division of the last speeches is new. The reasons given are also more numerous and more explicit. Finally, summaries may be given of the junction of S 1 — S 6, S 7 — S 13 and of the entire dialogue.

---

[66] On these features of the speeches, see above 3.3.2.

[67] See Roustang 1958, pp. 345ff. The literary analysis of Roustang is, however, a part of his presentation of a very abstract pattern in vv. 7—26: "position de l'apparence" in vv. 7—10, "nega-

S 1 – S 6 is a very well composed unit in the text we now have. In view of the length of the speeches, the information therein and references to persons, it gradually expands, reaching a peak in S 4 and S 5, only to then be reduced in S 6 to the relation between Jesus and the woman. The plea in S 6 clearly refers back to S 3 and S 1. In contrast to S 7 – S 13, this first part of the dialogue has both simpler and more homogeneous references to persons. It deals with *water* and *giving*, with the question *whence,* and is dominated by questions and exhortations on the part of the woman. We have here a very strong junction of speeches. At the same time we note a division after the third speech. S 1 – S 3 are concerned with the *plea* for water[68] and *drinking,* while S 4–S 6 rather analyse the problem of the kind of drinking. As regards the distribution of information, S 3 is, as stated, linked with S 2 and S 5 with S 4. Thus we have two series of speeches in the first part: Jesus – the woman – Jesus and the woman – Jesus – the woman. The last speech, S 6, not only refers back to S 1 – S 3 but also, by its closing words, to the situation of the dialogue as given in v. 7 (ἀντλῆσαι ὕδωρ).[69] After the first six speeches, therefore, the action is, so to speak, returned to the starting point, with the difference that the woman is now prepared to abandon Jacob's well and receive water elsewhere.

The second part of the dialogue, S 7 – S 13, seems to be more loosely joined together, at least on a first reading. We first have *S 7 – S 9,* which deals only with the woman and her men. S 8 is repeated, with a change in the word order, in S 9, and the information there given links S 9 with S 8. I just pointed out certain parallels between S 1 – S 3 and S 7 – S 9. Then follows *S 10 – S 11* on ὁ τόπος ὅπου προσκυνεῖν δεῖ. We find a strong junction between the two parts mentioned in S 7 – S 13 (S 7 – S 9 and S 10 – S 11) only if we interpret S 9 as referring to the woman and her relationship with God, with a connection between ἔσχες in S 9 and προσεκύνησαν in S 10. S 10 and S 11 must be regarded as closely connected by their content, the construction with δεῖ and ἐν and the information flow. The futural aspect with ἔρχεται and the theme of insight provide a link with *S 12 – S 13,* where Jesus' words appear to be answering the woman's speech. This is so strong that there is cause to consider whether S 10 – S 13 should be regarded as a unit like S 7 – S 9. If we consider S 7 – S 13 as a whole—in contrast to S 1 – S 6 we have here only assertions by the woman —we find an extension of application and information similar to that in S 1 – S 6, and if we interpret S 7 – S 9 as referring to the woman's (the Samaritans') relationship with

---

tion de l'apparence" in vv. 11–15, "exclusion de l'apparence" in vv. 16–18 and "position de la vérité" in vv. 19–26. He entirely disregards the "material" of the speeches and the Samaritan milieu. Schmid 1929 divides the text into three parts, vv. 7b–15, vv. 16–19 and vv. 20–26, disregarding the clear twofold division of the text.

[68] Note the repetition of S 1 in S 3.

[69] Note ἀντλῆσαι in v. 7, ἄντλημα in v. 11 and ἀντλεῖν in v. 15.

God, we find that this part of the dialogue is, in terms of content, also a very coherent unit.

The features which bind the entire dialogue together are of different kinds. All the speeches deal with the woman and the Samaritans,[70] we have throughout a contrasting of different persons and things, and Jesus is repeatedly described in various ways. The speeches are confined to Jesus and the woman in S 1 – S 2, S 6 and S 13. In and between these speeches we have the theme of *insight*, especially in S 3, S 10, S 11 and S 12. Among the more limited conjunctions we may mention the words *come here* in S 6 and S 7, ὁ θεός and the description of him in S 3 and S 11, the direction *from* in S 1 – S 6 and S 11 and the connection between *giving* in S 1 – S 6 and *proclaiming* in S 12. There is therefore good reason to regard the dialogue as a unit and try to interpret it as such.[71]

3.3.4 The Dialogue and Its Context

The dialogue now analysed has features connecting it with the Samaria text as a whole and with the context thereof.[1] I shall summarise them under four points:

A. Both the dialogue and the event structure of the text are focused on *Jesus and the Samaritans*.[2] The Samaritan material occupies a surprisingly large part of the dialogue. The whole of the first part, and especially S 4, is concerned with the well which the Samaritans were given by Jacob; S 10 deals with the Temple cult on Gerizim and the concept of *Miškān*, S 12 with the Samaritans' expectation of a prophet like Moses who will reveal all things to them.[3] Moreover, Jesus' words in S 9 seem to play on the earlier history of the Samaritans. Thus the dialogue is also concerned with Jesus and the Samaritans, not only Jesus and the woman. She is depicted several times as the Samaritans' mouthpiece[4] and must be regarded as representative of the people of Samaria as a whole. On this point, accordingly, the dialogue and the text immediately surrounding it give the same testimony.

B. That which I described above as *the ergon aspect* of the text[5] also appears in the dialogue. Behind many formulations lies concealed Jesus' work in its entirety, covering both the time before and the time after his "hour". Through Jesus Christ, God reveals Himself and carries out His work of redemption. This

[70] Implicitly also in S 5.
[71] See below 3.3.5 and 3.5.1.
[1] The relation to the second dialogue is discussed in 3.4.4.
[2] On the event structure, see above, 3.2.6, B.
[3] See above 3.3.2, S 10 and S 12, and 3.2.7.
[4] See especially S 4, S 10 and S 12.
[5] See 3.2.6, C.

emerges from expressions such as "the gift of God", "he who speaks to you". "worship the Father in spirit and truth", "I am".[6] Jesus is the eschatological revealer and things previously existent, such as the gift the Samaritans received from Jacob and the Temple cult on Gerizim and on Zion fade before his works. This is given a more historical aspect in S 11, which says that God's redemption will come from the Jews (not from the Samaritans!) and which applies also to individuals from the evangelist's own time. The wide temporal aspect of Jesus' work shines through. We have a co-projection in time and space of Jesus' situation and that of the evangelist, namely the time before and the time after Jesus' "hour". This quality is also present in the dialogue, although Jesus' situation (the futural feature) predominates.

C. The dialogue ends with an unveiled self-revelation of Jesus. *The woman's reaction* is shown only in the form of her action in vv. 28ff. She there presents Jesus as he who εἶπέν μοι πάντα ὅσα ἐποίησα at the same time as she asks the question whether Jesus is Χριστός. This title has in S 12 a special meaning which brings out the revelation aspect, with its probable background in the concept of a future prophet like Moses.[7] The above-mentioned wording of her testimony therefore refers back not only to S 7 — S 9 but perhaps most to S 12 — S 13. By her words she brings the Samaritans face to face with the question of whether this man at Jacob's well is the prophet whom they await. She herself, in her dialogue with Jesus, encountered the revelation, with an absolute peak in S 13. In the light of Jesus' words there, the detail which Jesus previously revealed in S 9 stands for *the whole* of her (and of the Samaritans') life. Her reaction is unequivocal: after she has *heard* Jesus, she *bears witness* to him and *reveals* him to her countrymen. In this role she closely resembles John the Baptist in Jn, most recently depicted in 3:22ff.

D. With this latter point we have arrived at *the relationship between the dialogue and that which precedes the Samaria text*. At several points I have compared the speeches with the Nicodemus dialogue in ch. 3. We there find a dialogue pattern similar to that in our chapter.[8] Nevertheless there is also an interesting difference. In that the woman brings out Samaritan material to so great an extent in the dialogue, the portrayal of her is not as negative as is that of Nicodemus in ch. 3. The contrast becomes greater when we consider her reaction after the dialogue. The crass "materialistic" meaning of Nicodemus' speeches reappears in a modified form in the woman's words.

The connection between the dialogue and 3:22ff, and especially 3:31—36, is

---

[6] See 3.3.2, S 3, S 11 and S 13, and 3.3.3, A.
[7] See 3.3.2, S 10, S 12 and S 13.
[8] Compare, for example, 3:3 and 4:10, 3:4 and 4:11f, 3:5ff and 4:13ff.

the most interesting. In the latter passage we have a comment by the evangelist which reveals his thoughts (horizon) just before the Samaria text.[9] Jesus is there depicted as the Revealer, in terms which recall the mention above of "the prophet like Moses". Jesus is said to come from above, from heaven, from God, v. 31, sent by God, v. 34. Like the bridegroom in v. 29, he *speaks*; he *testifies* to what he has seen and heard with God, v. 32. Τὰ ῥήματα τοῦ θεοῦ λαλεῖ, v. 34.[10] The explanation of these acts of salvation lies in God's own work: God *gives* (δίδω-σω) to the Son the Spirit (τὸ πνεῦμα) in abundance, He *loves* the Son and *has given* (δέδωκεν) him all things, vv. 34f.[11] The Son, and only the Son, can therefore give *eternal life* to those who receive his testimony, v. 36. Those who so do confirm that God is the true God, v. 33.

The picture conveyed by this comment on the part of the evangelist is the same as that which, in a more implicit form, lies hidden behind the introductory words in ch. 4 and which emerges distinctly in the first dialogue in our text.[12] The structure of the Samaria narrative should therefore have some connection with the text immediately preceding it. On the other hand, I found no interesting link between the dialogue with the woman and that which follows the Samaria text.[13]

3.3.5 Preliminary Summary

Before analysing the second dialogue, it may be appropriate to give a brief summary:

A. Jesus is represented in the dialogue primarily as *the Revealer* who, like the prophet whom the Samaritans expected, will reveal all things (3.3.2, S 1, 9, 10, 11 and especially 12 and 13; 3.3.4, D). Thus the dialogue is not so much a conversation *with* the woman as a discourse *to* her, in which she raises, by point after point, essential features of the situation and belief of the Samaritans (3.3.2, S 2, 4, 10 and 12).

B. The Samaritans and their traditions occupy a large proportion of the dialogue, by means of the talk of Jacob and his sons (3.3.2, S 4, 3.2.3), of the

---

[9] See my analysis above, 3.3.2.

[10] Note the similar expression in Dt 18:18 and what is said above on the Prophet, 3.3.2, S 10, S 12 and S 13.

[11] Γάρ in the second clause of v. 34 suggests that the two main clauses of the verse are not semantically parallel, with the Son as subject in both of them. The context prefers God as the agent of δίδωσιν, likewise the parallel use of "give" and "love" in Jn. See above 3.2.2, S 3. The Prophet will be given the Holy Spirit according to TJ I ad Dt 18:18, Lentzen-Deis 1970, p. 246. Note the similarity between the Targum text and Jn 1:32f (the Spirit remained on him).

[12] Note especially these features of the dialogue: the gift of God in S 3, the question of who is who speaks to the woman, in S 3, the spirit in S 11 and the description of the Messiah in S 12–13.

[13] There are some formal or general connections: Jesus as a prophet, 4:49, Jesus gives life, 4:49,51,53, some believe in Jesus, 4:48, 53.

Temple cult on Gerizim and *Miškān* (3.3.2, S 10 and 12), of the *Prophet* who will reveal all things (3.3.2, S 10 and 12) and of the Samaritans' earlier history (3.3.2, S 9, 3.3.3, E). The representative role played by the woman in the presentation of the Samaritan faith, together with various more or less strong reasons which I mentioned above (3.3.2, S 9, 3.3.3, A, B and E), render it highly probable that in S 9 the author intended a play on the Samaritans' former religious conditions. Samaritans and Jews (3.3.2, S 2, 10 and 11), Samaritans (we, our fathers, Jacob, Jacob's sons) and "Christians" (we, Jesus Christ, the narrator and those who. with him, believe in Christ) are contrasted with each other (3.3.2, S 4, 5, 6 and 11). Thus the dialogue deals not only with how Jesus (gradually) reveals himself but rather with the meeting between Jesus and the Samaritans.

C. The dialogue has *a characteristic Johannine form* throughout. This applies to the quotation formulae, which indicate a Jewish environment (3.3.1). Parts of the speeches recur at other points in the Gospel (see, for example, 3.3.2, S 4 and 6). We find questions with $\pi\tilde{\omega}\varsigma, \pi\acute{o}\vartheta\epsilon\nu$ and $\mu\acute{\eta}$ (3.3.2, S 2 and 4) and in all the speeches a long series of Johannine constructions and expressions (especially 3.3.2, S 3, 5, 11 and 13). We can establish a mixture of facts and images (3.3.2, S 5), "Johannine irony" (3.3.2, S 4 and 8), ambiguous words (3.3.2, S 1, 3 and 7) and a consistent misunderstanding technique. The entire dialogue is permeated by an unmistakeable Johannine style. The composition in general is Johannine too. Earlier acclaim of the literary qualities of the text is confirmed by the above analysis. The structure of the text is very well made. By means of the references to persons, temporal and spatial features, distribution of information and the most important concepts in the text, we have a division into two parts, which I tried to survey above in 3.3.3, E. The first part consists of S 1 — S 3 and S 4 — S 6, the second of S 7 -- S 9, S 10 — S 11 and S 12 — S 13. The form of the first speeches in these two sections, S 1 and S 7, is such as to allow of more than one meaning (3.3.2, S 1 and 7, 3.3.3, E). They may be understood from an ordinary usage of natural phenomena — such as the woman according to S 2 and S 8—but also from a rather specialized linguistic context of Jesus' work of salvation—thus Jesus in S 3 and S 9. This beginning of the two parts is followed by the beliefs concerning *the Well* in S 4 — S 6, Gerizim and *Miškān* in S 10 — S 11 and *the expected Prophet* in S 12 — S 13. The revelation on Jesus' part, which is opposed to these Samaritan beliefs, is first the water Jesus gives, then the worship of the Father in spirit and truth and lastly Jesus himself. This special Johannine composition of the dialogue must be related to the message of the text as a whole, and should not be regarded as a manifestation of a "naïve" narrative technique.

D. The possible *double entendre* in S 1 and S 7 is connected with what I previously called *the ergon aspect* of the events narrated in the text. Only he who relates the speeches to Jesus' redeeming work *in toto* understands them aright.

This also emerges from the temporal and personal references in the text. The dialogue takes place in Jesus' time, but simultaneously the evangelist's situation is glimpsed in certain formulations (3.3.3, A). We have a double exposure in time and space. Ἔρχεται ὥρα, καὶ νῦν ἐστιν, S 11. The actual reference in several terms, for example in "the gift of God", "worship the Father in spirit and truth" is the reality which followed upon Jesus' "hour". Yet it is somehow depicted as present, even in the time before. A number of parties are involved in the dialogue:

Jesus — the woman
Christ — the Samaritans
The narrator and those who, like him, possess insight — those who lack this insight

Nevertheless it is not always easy to decide which of these three parties carries the stress. From the point of view of the author, they seem to be very closely connected. I shall return to this problem in chs. 4 and 5.

E. A preliminary attempt to define the theme of the dialogue would perhaps run: *The divine revelation in Christ encounters Samaritan belief.* The reality behind the text, which explains the many characteristics brought out in the above analysis, is not the relationship between Jesus and a single person, or between Jesus and mankind in general. It is the relationship between Jesus Christ and the Samaritans which is of interest to the narrator. This is the object of the narrative. The woman represents the Samaritans and much of what she says is Samaritan belief. In the dialogue she meets God's revelation through Jesus and his words. The result of this encounter is described in the text following the dialogue. This could be described as a Christological or a soteriological interpretation, in which the symbolic character of the text is emphasized and the entire text is seen in the light of Jesus' *ergon*. The usual understanding of the dialogue as a pastoral discourse, on the other hand, does not explain a long series of qualities in the text we now have. See further 3.5.

3.3.6 Excursus II. "Living Water" in Jn.
As I showed above, water plays an important part in Jn, not least in Jn 4,[1] so that it is perhaps appropriate here to carry out a detailed analysis of the water symbolism in the Gospel and in contemporary sources. So far as I know, no such analysis exists.[2] However, the comparative material is very extensive, and an analysis thereof calls for a thorough methodological discussion of the use of

[1] See 2.2, U 16 and 3.3.3, C.
[2] A general survey in ThWNT, vol. 8, pp. 313ff (L. Goppelt). See also Odeberg 1929, pp. 149ff, and Stemberger 1970, pp. 149 ff. On "living water", see Daniélou 1958.

metaphors in general.[3] Thus a survey of the water symbolism would break the bounds of my investigation. Here I shall confine myself to the essentials, to an analysis of the transferred use of water in Jn 4 and 7:37—39, the two passages in Jn—and in the entire NT for that matter—where the term "living water" appears.[4]

The expression "living water" ($\H{v}\delta\omega\rho\ \zeta\tilde{\omega}\nu$) usually carries the meaning "runing fresh spring water", for instance in Gen 26:19 and SofS 4:15 ($\varphi\rho\epsilon\alpha\rho\ \H{v}\delta\alpha\tau o\varsigma\ \zeta\tilde{\omega}\nu\tau o\varsigma$) and in regulations on ritual purification, Lev 14:5, 6, 50, 51, 52 etc.[5] In Jer 2:13, God is likened to a "spring of living water" ($\pi\eta\gamma\dot{\eta}\ \H{v}\delta\alpha\tau o\varsigma\ \zeta\omega\tilde{\eta}\varsigma$), in Him is "the source of life" ($\pi\eta\gamma\dot{\eta}\ \zeta\omega\tilde{\eta}\varsigma$), according to Ps 36:10. "Living water" will, on the Day of the Lord, flow from Jerusalem and water the surrounding country in summer as in winter, Zech 14:8 ($\grave{\epsilon}\xi\epsilon\lambda\epsilon\acute{v}\sigma\epsilon\tau\alpha\iota\ \H{v}\delta\omega\rho\ \zeta\tilde{\omega}\nu\ \grave{\epsilon}\xi\ I\epsilon\rho o\upsilon\sigma\alpha\lambda\eta\mu$), a prophecy which should be seen in the context of the eschatological expectations of a land of paradise, Is 30:23ff; Ezek 47:1ff; Joel 3:18; Zech 13:1. Here the water is not only fresh, running water, but something which gives life wherever it flows, Ezek 47:1ff. Even the OT usage seems to suggest a double meaning of "running" and "life-giving" water.

In Jn 4 first of all we find this *double entendre: running spring water* in v. 11, and a *water which results in eternal life* in v. 14. The expression "living water" is related to "water of life" in Rev 7:17; 21:6; 22:1, 17, where the water stands rather for life itself, for the final redemption.[6] Here the bond with Ezek 47 and Zech 14:8 is fully visible.

Nevertheless this rather superficial contrast is not sufficient to explain the metaphorical use in Jn 4. There we find many other data, all of which could apparently be covered by another contrast in the text, that between *Jesus' water* and *Jacob's well,* or in a wider sense, between the revelation of Christ and the Samaritan faith.[7] The water which Jesus gives is something he *shall give* ($\delta\acute{\omega}\sigma\omega$ twice in v. 14). It is here difficult to find any other temporal reference than that in the futural sayings in vv. 21ff, namely that Jesus will give his "water" when his "hour" is come.[8] The chiastic form in v. 10 may possibly be interpreted as meaning that Jesus' gift is, at the same time, seen as a gift of God.[9] This could refer us to the Spirit.[10] The first part of the dialogue goes on to say that Jesus' water will be a "portable" fountain of flowing water for whoever drinks it, an inner posses-

[3] On the methodological problems, see Black 1962, Pelç 1971a, pp. 142ff, and Stolt 1974 (in press).

[4] Note the related "the water of life" in Rev 7:17, 21:6, 22:1, 17.

[5] Running water is the best water for purification, M Mik, passim. See above 2.2, U 14. The fountain of life is mentioned in Pr 10:11; 13:14; 14:27; 16:22; 18:4; Sir 21:13. See also Freed 1965, p. 29.

[6] See L. Goppelt in ThWNT, vol. 8, p. 325.

[7] See above 3.3.5, E.

[8] See above 3.3.3, A and B.

[9] Thus Schnackenburg, Comm., ad loc.

[10] The expression $\delta\omega\rho\epsilon\acute{\alpha}$ almost always refers to the Spirit in the NT. See above 3.3.2, S 3.

sion similar to $\zeta\omega\dot{\eta}$, $\lambda\acute{o}\gamma o\varsigma$, $\grave{\alpha}\lambda\dot{\eta}\vartheta\epsilon\iota\alpha$ and $\pi\nu\epsilon\tilde{\nu}\mu\alpha$ $\tau\tilde{\eta}\varsigma$ $\grave{\alpha}\lambda\eta\vartheta\epsilon\acute{\iota}\alpha\varsigma$ elsewhere in Jn, and $\chi\rho\acute{\iota}\sigma\mu\alpha$ and $\sigma\pi\acute{\epsilon}\rho\mu\alpha$ in 1 Jn.[11] Most of these expressions are concerned with *the Revelation* through Jesus Christ, and the full and true insight it gives to the believer.[12] In the later part of the dialogue, Jesus' gift is also a revelation of all things, vv. 25f. Jesus' promise in the first part is *water which will spring up to eternal life* and (implicit) in the second part *a revelation which allows of true worship and bestows salvation*, vv. 22ff.[13] Such a worship presupposes "spirit and truth" ($\pi\nu\epsilon\tilde{\nu}\mu\alpha$ $\kappa\alpha\dot{\iota}$ $\grave{\alpha}\lambda\dot{\eta}\vartheta\epsilon\iota\alpha$), which affords us a common alternative for the interpretation of "water" in Jn 4: *The Spirit* or *the Revelation*. Nevertheless these concepts must be incorporated in the wider contrast mentioned above (Jesus — Jacob) and related to the explicit statement that Jesus' water is something which he will give. "Water" in Jn 4 then refers primarily to *something which will come with Jesus' "hour"* and to *something which can give eternal life and salvation* to the Samaritans—in contrast with Jacob's well.

In the choice between the Spirit and the Revelation, the reader is generally referred to a certain comparative material.[14] However, this can hardly decide the issue. This may support both the interpretations and it is difficult to decide which parallel material is relevant. Water as a symbol of *true revelation, doctrine, knowledge, wisdom,* i.e. in a Jewish context *the Law* interpreted and applied aright, appears mainly in the Wisdom literature, for instance, Pr 13:14; 18:4; Sir 15:1ff; 24:21ff; Wis 7:25; Is 55:1ff, and in Rabbinic literature such as Sifre Deut 11,22, Pirque Aboth VI.1f, but also in many other sources, including Enoch 48:1; 49; 96:6; CD XIX.34; III.16; VI.4ff; 1QH IV.11; Od Sal 6:8ff; 11:5ff; 30:1ff; 38:15.[15] We must admit that this is the most common metaphorical use of "water" in the material which may be regarded as relevant to Jn 4. It also appears in the Targum's presentation of Is 12:3 and 55:1:[16]

MT	Targ.
With joy you will draw water from the wells of salvation, 12:3.	And ye shall receive new instruction with joy from the chosen of righteousness.
Ho, every one who thirsts, come to the waters; and he who has no money come, buy and eat! Come, buy wine and milk without money and without price, 55:1.	Ho, every one that wishes to learn, let him come, and learn, and he that hath no money; come ye, and hear, and learn; come, hear, and learn, without price and without money, instruction that is better than wine and milk.

---

[11] See Schnackenburg, Comm., p. 466.
[12] See the contexts of these expressions and on $\grave{\alpha}\lambda\dot{\eta}\vartheta\epsilon\iota\alpha$ as a term of revelation, Ibuki 1972.
[13] On the junction of the two parts of the first dialogue, see above 3.3.3, B and C.
[14] See, for example, Bultmann, Barrett, Schnackenburg, Brown and Lindars, Comm., ad loc.
[15] See Odeberg 1929, pp. 153ff, and the material in Str.-B., vol. 2, pp. 435f.
[16] I here quote Stenning's translation. Is 12:3 has also been interpreted as referring to the Spirit. See Str.-B., vol. 2, p. 434.

Yet water is also used as an image of *the spirit of God.* Such a usage exists already in the OT expression "pour out my spirit", Is 32:15; 44:3; Joel 2:28f (MT 3:1f) and is given in more detail in, for example, Ezek 36:25—27:[17]

> I will sprinkle *clean water* upon you, and you shall be clean from all your un-
> cleannesses, and from all your idols I will cleanse you. A new heart I will give you,
> and *a new spirit I will put within you;* and I will take out of your flesh the heart of
> stone and give you a heart of flesh. And I will *put my spirit within you,* and cause
> you to walk in my statutes and be careful to observe my ordinances.

The function of the water and the Spirit here is primarily to *purify.* When God gathers in His scattered children, v. 24, and restores Israel, they must be cleansed from sin, so that Israel can once more become the people of God and the Lord can be their God, v. 28. But the Spirit also makes it possible for Israel to *obey God's commandments.* The Lord's covenant of old with Israel at Sinai again becomes a reality. It is worth noting that when Jer 31:33f speaks of this new covenant in terms similar to those in Ezek 36, he mentions *the law,* and not the Spirit:

> I will *put my law within them,* and I will write it upon their hearts; and I will be
> their God, and they shall be my people. And no longer shall each man teach his
> neighbour and each his brother, saying, 'Know the Lord', for they shall all know
> me, from the least of them to the greatest, says the Lord; for I will forgive their in-
> iquity, and I will remember their sin no more.

This new covenant in Ezek and Jer involves both an outflow of *the spirit* of God and a true *revelation* of God. Both ideas express a new and close contact with God, which naturally calls for *purification and forgiveness of sins.* In the Qumran material, these elements are combined in the metaphor "water". I have already mentioned instances in which water is a symbol of the Law interpreted and understood aright. In 1QS IV.21 water is used of the spirit:[18]

> He will cleanse him of all wicked deeds by means of *a holy spirit;* like *purifying
> waters* He will sprinkle upon him *the spirit of truth.*

These examples serve to show that comparative material may be adduced as arguments for both the interpretations, and further, that it may be difficult to separate the two possibilities. Spirit and revelation are one, to some extent, even in the comparative material

Indeed the Gospel itself gives an interpretation of the expression "living water" in Jn 7:37—39.

---

[17] Further material in Str.-B., vol. 2, pp. 434f.

[18] Note the expression "the spirit of truth", which also occurs in Jn 14:17; 15:26. See 4.3. In the Qumran material the purification has a very important role, Braun 1966, pp. 114ff.

If anyone thirst, let him come to me
and let him drink who believes in me.
As the Scripture says,
'From within him shall flow rivers of living water'.
(Here he was referring to the Spirit which those who came to believe in him were
to receive. For there was as yet no Spirit since Jesus had not been glorified.)[19]

Brown and Schnackenburg offer an excellent survey of the problems in this
controversial text, plus a detailed analysis and well thought out interpretation of
the text as a whole.[20] For the details, I refer the reader to their convincing
arguments. I concentrate here on the expression "living water" and the interpretation given in the following parenthesis.

Jesus emerges in the context as the Teacher *par préference,* as the Revealer
and the Prophet, 7:14ff, 28, 35, 37, 40, 46, 52; 8:20. He is the one whom the
Father sent to reveal His "teaching" ($\delta\iota\delta\alpha\chi\acute{\eta}$). No-one has ever spoken as Jesus
speaks, 7:46. In such an environment, Jesus' invitation in vv. 37f is most naturally
read as referring to his *revelation.* To drink is to come to him and accept his
teaching. This view is supported by the motifs from the Wisdom literature, which
appear in this text.[21] "Living water" in v. 38 would then refer to Jesus' revelation.

This interpretation presupposes that $\alpha\dot{\upsilon}\tau o\tilde{\upsilon}$ in v. 38 refers to Jesus: water will
flow from Jesus' heart. The words $\pi\iota\nu\acute{\epsilon}\tau\omega\ \dot{o}\ \pi\iota\sigma\tau\epsilon\acute{\upsilon}\omega\nu\ \epsilon\dot{\iota}\varsigma\ \dot{\epsilon}\mu\acute{\epsilon}$ then become an
obvious parallel to $\lambda\alpha\mu\beta\acute{\alpha}\nu\epsilon\iota\nu\ o\dot{\iota}\ \pi\iota\sigma\tau\epsilon\acute{\upsilon}\sigma\alpha\nu\tau\epsilon\varsigma\ \epsilon\dot{\iota}\varsigma\ \alpha\dot{\upsilon}\tau\acute{o}\nu.$ If we consider v. 38 in
its present context and in the light of Jn as a whole, it seems clear to me that
Jesus is the spring. He it is who gives the Spirit, 19:30; 20:22. Such sayings as Jn
4:10, 14a; 6:35 and 19:34 point to Jesus as the giver of water.[22] The OT
background of the quotations from Scripture also favour this interpretation. While
it is difficult to establish beyond doubt,[23] a twinfold origin seems to me most
probable after the detailed debate in *Revue Biblique* 1958—1963 between M.E.
Boismard and P. Grelot.[24] Certain features of the Scriptural quotation bring out
ideas of *the Temple spring,* with such texts as Zech 14:8 and Ezek 47.[25] As mentioned above, these underlie Rev 22. Other features of the text tend to find
parallels in the material concerning *the Well,* primarily in the formulations in Ps

[19] Brown's translation, which is confirmed by his extended analysis, corresponds to a great extent to Schnackenburg's interpretation, Comm., ad loc.

[20] Comm., ad loc. There is an extensive literature on these verses. See, besides the material mentioned in Brown and Schnackenburg, Comm., ad loc., the literature I mention in the following
notes and Malatesta 1967, pp. 96ff.

[21] See Brown, Comm., ad loc.

[22] For further arguments, see Brown and Schnackenburg, Comm., ad loc.

[23] See the many possibilities in Freed 1965, pp. 21ff, who, however, does not adduce material
on the Well!

[24] Boismard 1958, Grelot 1959, Boismard 1959, Audet 1959, Grelot 1960 and Grelot 1963.
Both Brown and Schnackenburg, Comm., ad loc., suggest a twofold background.

[25] On this background, see also Daniélou 1964.

78:15f and 105:40f.[26] In Jn, Jesus "takes the place", so to speak, of both the Well and the Manna (ch. 6). These texts are combined even in Jewish sources,[27] and there are several examples in Jn of joint quotations and concepts.[28] The expression "living water", like "the harvest" in vv. 35ff, would then be an image of *the new eschatological age*—n.b. ῥεύσουσιν and the reference given this term by v. 39. The new element enters in on Jesus' death—n.b. ἐκ τῆς κοιλίας αὐτοῦ. With his resurrection the new Temple comes into existence, 2:19ff, and the life-giving and redeeming water can begin to spring forth. He, the glorified Christ, is "the living Well"—cf. 1 Cor 10:4—, which offers life-giving water to all the new people of God.

After these references to *Jesus' revelation* and *the new age of salvation* (the Temple spring and the Well) as the meaning of the metaphor of "living water", it is perhaps somewhat surprising to read the evangelist's comment in v. 39, where he expressly interprets "living water" as referring to *the Spirit*. He there makes more explicit mention of Jesus' "hour" (ἐδοξάσθη). Its immediate consequence will be the gift of the Spirit to those who believe in Jesus: then "the living water" will spring up, so that every believer may drink.

In order to understand this comment, we must comprehend the phrase οὔπω ἦν πνεῦμα. This implies the two phases in Jesus' *ergon*, which we previously discussed. The "Spirit" did not exist before the "hour". The evangelist must here be thinking of the Paraclete, who can only come after Jesus' death, chs. 14—16.[29] This Paraclete, called "the Holy Spirit" and "the Spirit of truth", is very intimately related to the revelation of Christ—as I shall show in 4.3—and his function is to teach and guide the disciples and bring them into the revelation which was given with Jesus. This activity by the Spirit is essential, according to Jn, if the revelation of Christ is to reach men. Thus in a Johannine context, a revelation without the Spirit and a Spirit without integration in the revelation of Jesus are unthinkable. So, in 7:39, when the evangelist interprets "living water" as meaning the Spirit, the Revelation is there present. By his quotation from the Scriptures in 7:38, Jn is referring to the new eschatological situation, when the revelation of Christ by the action of the Spirit will reach men and give them life. The revelation becomes present with the Spirit, and, in a sense, only with the Spirit. Therefore the interpretation referring to the Spirit is natural despite the revelation theme manifest in the context.

After this review of Jn 4, the comparative material and Jn 7:37—39, it is quite clear that the alternative of the Spirit *or* the revelation is an erroneous starting

---

[26] Especially stressed by Boismard 1958. On the Well, see above 3.2.7.

[27] See above 3.2.7 and especially Tos Sukk III. 3—18, quoted in Str.-B., vol. 3, pp. 406f, and analysed by Grelot 1963, pp. 45ff.

[28] Examples in Brown, Comm., ad loc.

[29] See my analysis below, 4.3.

point for the interpretation of "water" in the Samaria text.[30] Like other exegetes, I have previously assumed that there must be a definite reference in the "(living) water". The problem is whether this too is a mistaken starting point. The text itself, as shown above, offered us many alternatives: there is a use of the *double entendre* in "living water" and a metaphorical account which is best explained by the concepts about the Well. Perhaps the evangelist shapes his material into a narrative, in which the various sayings concerning water fit the narrative as such and the message he wished to convey. In the latter case, he then alludes to the concepts of the Well described above, the water of life, and also the eschatological rivers from the Temple at Jerusalem. Thus the water in the text would include *Revelation (Truth)* and *Spirit,* which give salvation and eternal life. According to section 4.3 below, the revelation of Christ and the Spirit are interdependent, and salvation and eternal life are part of the Spirit and the Truth. I find it difficult to discern criteria which could allow of a choice between these alternatives. One stands out, however: not until the coming of the Spirit (the Paraclete) could the divine revelation in Christ give life and salvation to those who believed in Jesus. This could be understood as meaning that the Spirit is primary in Jn 4. But at the same time, Jn 14—16 shows that the Spirit is wholly attributed to the revelation by Jesus Christ. Thus we are brought back to the bond between spirit and revelation and the reality of the salvation there involved in the time of the Paraclete. I regard it as impossible to define the expression "living water" with greater precision.

3.4 The Dialogue Structure of vv. 31—38

In St John's Gospel Jesus speaks most with his disciples. This is particularly true of the latter part.[1] The discourse in our text is one of the longest among the sporadic dialogues before Jesus' "hour".[2] As such it resembles the long farewell discourse, 13—16. The disciples are often assumed to be listening even when Jesus speaks with other persons.[3] As Jesus' partners in the dialogues we elsewhere encounter the Jews, especially in chs. 7—10, and a number of private persons.[4]

---

[30] Brown, Comm., ad loc., and Ibuki 1972, pp. 315ff, also refer to both the Spirit and Jesus' revelation.

  [1] See Jn 13—16 and 20—21.

  [2] I.e. chs. 1—12. Cf. 1:35—39; 1:47—51; 6:5—10; 6:67—70; 9:2—5 and 11:7—16.

  [3] See above, 2.3.1 and 2.3.2.

  [4] Jesus speaks with his disciples 20 times, with the Jews 13 and with individuals 11 times. Other "conversations" are also presented, for example, between John the Baptist and representatives of the Jews, between different groups among the people and between different disciples.

The dialogues between Jesus and his disciples deal almost invariably with the events of the "hour" and its implications, 11:7ff; 13—16; 20—21. The form of reference we have for the disciples in 4:31—38, i.e. οἱ μαθηταί, which diverges in our text from the earlier οἱ μαθηταί αὐτοῦ, vv. 2, 8, 27, is found almost exclusively in such contexts.[5] This could be interpreted as an indication of a special post-resurrection point of view in 4:31—38. However, the change in the form of reference could be a coincidence or, in v. 31 for example, be due to an already mentioned pronoun.

3.4.1 Dialogue or Monologue

The quotation formulae in this section in no way display the same homogenous Johannine form as in the earlier dialogue. They run:

1. ἐν τῷ μεταξὺ ἠρώτων αὐτὸν οἱ μαθηταί λέγοντες, v. 31.
2. ὁ δὲ εἶπεν αὐτοῖς, v. 32.
3. ἔλεγον οὖν οἱ μαθηταί πρὸς ἀλλήλους, v. 33.
4. λέγει αὐτοῖς ὁ Ἰησοῦς, v. 34.

Only the last formula is typically Johannine.[6] The second one occurs very frequently in the Synoptic Gospels, but only rarely in Jn.[7] The first has only one close parallel in the Gospel, Jn 12:21.[8] We are left with the third formula which, I believe, should be interpreted from a similar passage in Jn, namely 16:16ff.[9]

The reactions of those present to what Jesus says and does are sometimes represented as an internal dialogue backstage so to speak, not least in Jn.[10] They often involve persons who do not believe in Jesus. We meet Jesus' disciples only twice in such a situation, in 4:33 and 16:17f. The quotation formulae in the latter passage take the form: εἶπαν οὖν ἐκ τῶν μαθητῶν αὐτοῦ πρὸς ἀλλήλους . . . ἔλεγον, οὖν . . . ἔγνω Ἰησοῦς ὅτι ἤθελον αὐτὸν ἐρωτᾶν, καί εἶπεν αὐτοῖς. Here is evidently a teaching situation, in which the disciples' lack of insight (τί ἐστιν τοῦτο ὃ λέγει ἡμῖν; repeated twice, οὐκ οἴδαμεν τί λαλεῖ) is amended by that which Jesus says and reveals. Νῦν οἴδαμεν ὅτι οἶδας πάντα is the disciples' reaction in v. 30. Jesus reveals all things to his disciples by means of the Paraclete's

[5] See Jn 11:7, 8, 12, 54 (all without pronoun); 12:16; 13:5, 22(αὐτοῦ only in v. 23); 20:10, 18, 19, 20 (αὐτοῦ) only in v. 26, and as variant in v. 30); 21:1, 4, 12, 14 (αὐτοῦ only in v. 2). The longer form with the pronoun is used in the rest of Jn.

[6] See above 3.3.1.

[7] Jn 1:38, 9:15, 17; 18:7; 20:25; 21:6.

[8] The formula in these two passages introduces a plea and an exhortation. See 3.2.1, E 28. It introduces a question in 1:19,21,25; 5:12, 9:2, (15), 19.

[9] Both ἔλεγον and οὖν are characteristic of Jn. See 3.3.1 and Abbott 1906, pp. 340f.

[10] See for example, Mk 2:6ff; 4:41; 8:16f; Jn 3:25ff; 6:41ff,52,60f; 7:11ff,25,32,40ff; 9:8ff; 11:56f, and 12:19.

interpretation of all that Jesus once said and did.[11] Have we the same situation in Jn 4:31—38? The quotation formula in v. 33 would so indicate. In any case this is a characteristic *teaching situation*—or perhaps rather a revelation situation. Jesus' words and the action to which they refer are interpreted. Later I shall discuss whether this may be placed on a par with the Paraclete's work of revelation according to Jn.[12]

The quotation formula in v. 33 marks that there is no direct dialogue between Jesus and his disciples. The very long speech in vv. 34—38 reduces this section's character as dialogue. As in many other passages in Jn we have a transition from dialogue to monologue.[13] Thus to a higher degree than previously we can describe the text as *a "revelation discourse" on Jesus' part*. As we shall see, the first three speeches merely provide an introduction to Jesus' teaching and interpretive words in vv. 34—38.[14]

3.4.2 The Speeches (S 1—S 4)

The second dialogue in our text, vv. 31—38, is thus somewhat different in character from the first. This also influences what follows. More information will be given in this section, especially on the dominant, long, speech in vv. 34—38, while the analysis of the junction of the speeches will be fairly brief. In the following pages I shall give the Greek text of each speech, the last speech being divided into three parts, and then discuss its linguistic expression, form and content.

S 1

'Ραββί, φάγε.

After the description of the situation in vv. 5f and the mention in v. 8 of the disciples' departure for the town, it is natural to read this opening speech as a plea to Jesus by the disciples that he will now eat the food which they have procured. Like the beginning of vv. 7—15 and vv. 16—25, this is in the imperative form: δός, ὕπαγε φώνησον and φάγε. Its function is, as we shall see, the same here as in those passages: the theme here set, *eating,* is then differentiated so that it is seen partly in the light of the concrete situation described in the text and partly in the light of Jesus' task of mission as a whole.[1]

The disciples here address Jesus as *Rabbi*. Jesus is so addressed by disciples in 1:38, 49; 4:31; 9:2 and 11:8—see also 11:28 and 13:13f—and by Nicodemus in 3:2.[2] This Greek transliteration of the Semitic word is found in the early Chris-

---

[11] For an analysis of 16:16ff, see below 4.3. In ch. 16 we have a kind of *reinterpretation* of what Jesus said, Brown, Comm., ad loc.

[12] See below 4.3.

[13] Jn 3:1f f; 6:25f f; 8:21f f; 9:1f f. See also above 3.3.3,D.

[14] They are part of the "teaching method" which Jn uses, Lindars, Comm., ad loc.

[1] On the function of S 1 and S 7, see 3.3.3, E and 3.3.5,

[2] John the Baptist is also addressed as Rabbi in Jn 3:26, in a teaching situation.

tian literature only in the Gospels and there mostly in Jn,[3] according to E. Lohse "ein Zeichen dafür, dass die palästinische Tradition zurücktrat und die Bezeichnung Jesu als Lehrer neben den anderen christologischen Titeln nur eine geringe Rolle spielte".[4] In the environment of the time the word was used both as a general courtesy title and by a pupil addressing his teacher.[5] The latter is the case in Jn. Jesus is there represented as the Teacher *par préférence,* so it is easy to understand why the evangelist uses the title *Rabbi.*[6] When he uses the word for the first time, 1:38, he gives the translation διδάσκαλε. The same applies to *Rabbouni* in 20:16. Nicodemus presents Jesus as a teacher from God (οἴδαμεν ὅτι ἀπὸ θεοῦ ἐλήλυθας διδάσκαλος), *a teacher sent by God,* who in the dialogue to follow is contrasted with Israel's teacher *par préférence,* 3:10. In the Gospel as a whole, this picture of Jesus as a teacher is evidently connected with ideas of the Prophet who is to come.[7] In our text the title *Rabbi* probably marks a teaching and revelation situation.

S 2

ἐγὼ βρῶσιν ἔχω φαγεῖν ἣν ὑμεῖς οὐκ οἴδατε.

Jesus does not only answer τροφάς/βρῶμα/προσφάγιον ἔχω,[8] with or without a relative clause, marking that the disciples are not really aware of the situation. The occurrence of pronouns ἐγώ – ὑμεῖς suggests to us a tension between Jesus and the disciples. Apparently Jesus has his *own* bread and does not need that *of the disciples.* Moreover the ordinary word for food is not used. Βρῶσις may indeed be synonymous with βρῶμα on occasion but tends rather to be used more generally of the act of eating.[9] In the other passages in Jn where the word appears (6:27 and 6:55) it has a transferred meaning: the food which gives eternal life, the bread of God, the revelation of Jesus, Jesus himself.[10] Βρῶσις in S 2 may be read as synonymous with βρῶμα, which may perhaps be the most natural reading, but we must at the same time establish that it has a further and more open character by means of its aspect of activity, and its figurative use in Jn, which may depend on the function of the speech as a whole.

[3] 4 times in Mt and 3 times in Mk. Διδάσκαλε is used 12 times in Lk, 10 times in Mk and 6 times in Mt but never as a form of address in Jn.

[4] E. Lohse in ThWNT, vol. 6, p. 966.

[5] See the material mentioned in ThWNT, vol. 6, pp. 962ff.

[6] Miranda 1972, p. 320, and the literature he mentions there.

[7] See above 3.3.2, S 10 and S 12, and also Jn 9:28–33.

[8] Jn uses these words for "food" in 4:8,34 and 21:5.

[9] On this meaning see, for example, 1 Cor 8:4; 2 Cor 9:10 and the phrase εἰς βρῶσιν frequent in LXX. Further examples in Bauer, s.v.

[10] There is a close connection between 4:32 and 6:27, according to Leroy 1968, pp. 150ff. The expression βρῶσιν φαγεῖν belongs to "die Sondersprache der johanneischen Gemeinde" and denotes "die Offenbarung Gottes in Jesus" *ex parte hominis* in 6:27 and "der Offenbarungsauftrag des sendenden Gottes" *ex parte Jesu* in 4:32.

The construction τι ἔχειν + infinitive also confers a certain openness. The first clause in S 2 may mean "I have my own food, I do not need yours".[11] Evidently the disciples so understood it. Yet the above construction usually has a modal nuance: "to have something one can/will/must do", Lk 7:40, 42; 12:50; Acts 23:17ff, etc.[12] When the phrase is used in Jn 8:26 and 16:12—see also 2 Jn 12 and 3 Jn 13—it obviously has a modal meaning. Thus we can read the first clause in S 2 as meaning "I have something/food which I must eat". This meaning is in better agreement with what Jesus then says in vv. 34ff and presumably exercised the strongest influence on S 2. "Food to eat" has even here a clear transferred meaning.[13]

The second clause in S 2 has many parallels in Jn: 3:11; 4:10; 4:22; 7:29; 8:14f; 19:34f.[14] The disciples need teaching and revelation. At the same time, the relative clause marks that the food here in question is not ordinary food, but is part of the "spiritual reality". In the Gospel in general we have the same picture of the disciples in 13:7 (on the meaning of the washing of the feet), in 14:5 (on Jesus "going to the Father") and in 16:18 (on the question of "a little time"). The disciples do not posses full insight into Jesus' *work,* especially its "completion" in the events of the "hour". We see from the continuation in vv. 34ff that we have the same state of affairs here: they are not aware of the work shared by the Father and the Son.

The wording of S 2 thus suggests that Jesus is thinking of an eating in the transferred sense, at the same time as his words can also be understood literally. The ambiguity is obvious: "I have my own food to eat which you do not know of" or "I have food which I must eat; you do not know it". The food which nourishes Jesus is on another plane, "in der Sphäre seines gottgegebenen Berufs".[15] Therefore, S 2 marks a shift in perspective, a marking which is especially apparent to those who are conversant with the Gospel as a whole.

S 3

μή τις ἤνεγκεν αὐτῷ φαγεῖν;

There is no change in perspective among the disciples in the text.[16] Thinking of food in the ordinary sense they ask each other: Has anyone brought him food?[17]

[11] The infinitive is regarded as an explanatory addition to βρῶσιν.

[12] Further examples in Bauer, s.v. Bl.-Debr. § 392,2 refers to Pseudo-Clement.

[13] Schnackenburg, Comm., ad loc., gives also examples of "to eat" as "to leave oneself to the will of God".

[14] Odeberg 1929, pp. 167f.

[15] J. Behm in ThWNT, vol. 1, pp. 640ff.

[16] We have a similar misunderstanding in Jn 14:8 and 16:17f, 30.

[17] The infinitive may be regarded as an accusative. See, for example, Mk 6:37 par.; Mt 25:35,42; Mk 5:43, Turner, p. 135. Cf. πεῖν in S 1, commented on above, 3.3.2. Φέρειν plus φαγεῖν are used in Gen 27:4 and 2 Sam 17:29, with βρώματα in 1 Chr 12:41. The formulation of S 3 clearly shows that they are thinking of βρῶμα in the ordinary sense.

They themselves are obviously prepared to give a negative answer. Yet the reverse is the truth if we consider the whole in the right perspective; Someone has given Jesus food to eat. Who? S 3 is thus an example of the same kind of "Johannine irony" as S 4 in the first dialogue.[18] The initiated reader knows that Jesus has received food to eat, in a transferred sense, and can give the right answer to the question asked in S 3.

S 4

This speech, vv. 34–38, is one of the most obscure texts in Jn.[19] It contains central Johannine themes, but does not possess the same homogeneous Johannine form as the Samaria text in general.[20] This may be a sign of a more varied prehistory than other parts of Jn. In order to interpret the text, "the literary critics" have gone to very great lengths as regards dividing it up into various independent fragments.[21] Commentators often fix on certain parts of the text, assigning them a meaning in a context which they themselves make up from ideas on how the text came into existence.[22] Preconceived ideas of the nature of the text, whether, for example, it is "parabolic" or "allegorical", have played an important part in the history of its interpretation.[23] Because of the purpose of my investigation I am, in the following pages, interested primarily in seeing the speech as a whole, set in the context we now have. For practical reasons, I shall divide it into three parts. Even a re-reading of S 4 confirms that it consists of three sections: v. 34, vv. 35f and vv. 37f.

S 4a

a. ἐμὸν βρῶμά ἐστιν
b. ἵνα ποιῶ τὸ θέλημα τοῦ πέμψαντός με
c. καὶ τελειώσω αὐτοῦ τὸ ἔργον.

The first part of the last speech—of the last words Jesus speaks in the Samaria text—is, according to Schnackenburg "schon stilistisch-rhythmisch (3 Zeilen) als Offenbarungswort geprägt".[24] It has *a single theme:* the relation between the Father and the Son, especially the work they share.

For the first time in the Gospel, we have here the typical Johannine phrase, ὁ

[18] See above, 3.3.2, S 4.

[19] See the surveys of interpretations in Schwartz 1908, pp. 507f, Thüsing ²1970, pp. 56f, and Schnackenburg, Comm., ad loc. Note the contradictory statements in the interpretations of this text in, for example, Schnackenburg and Brown, Comm., ad loc.

[20] Dodd 1963, pp. 391ff, lays excessive stress on its non-Johannine character. On its Johannine content, see my analysis here, on its Johannine form, see Bultmann. Comm., ad loc.

[21] Schwartz 1908, pp. 507ff, Wellhausen 1908, pp. 21f.

[22] This applies especially to Dodd 1963, pp. 391ff.

[23] See, for example, Barrett and Brown, Comm., ad loc.

[24] Schnackenburg, Comm., ad loc.

πέμψας με of God,[25] spoken by Jesus. The epithet is in Jn almost a proper name, but is occasionally supplemented by (ὁ) πατήρ, 5:23; 6:37, 44; 8:16, 18; 12:49 and 14:24, although never by (ὁ) θεός. Thus we are wholly justified in here referring to Jesus' relationship to *the Father*. This formula brings God to the fore as He who reveals Himself to mankind. He is *the one who sends*. At the same time it directs attention to him who speaks (μέ), i.e. Jesus. He is *the one sent by God*, and by no other. He is "der einzige und einzigartige Offenbarer Gottes".[26] The wording τοῦ πέμψαντός με instead of, for example, τοῦ θεοῦ[27] accordingly points to Jesus' work as an act of God's revelation.

The mission from the Father is here described as Jesus' food.[28] S 4a thereby answers the indirect question in S 3 on whether anyone had given Jesus food, at the same time as it explicitly says that the dialogue deals with food in the transferred sense. Just as the Father gave Jesus *a cup to drink* (18:11; 19:28f), He also gave him *food to eat*. Both refer to Jesus' ἔργον, and perhaps especially to its completion when Jesus' "hour" had come. The Father gave him his "work", 17:4; 5:36. The whole of his activity may be seen as a gift from God.[29] The Father *sends, gives, loves, acts*, all these expressions in Jn are intended to emphasize that God is the primary agent in the work of salvation which the Gospel describes. Moreover, S 4a states that the point at issue is the mission from *the Father*, the will of *the Father*, the work of *the Father*—note the position of αὐτοῦ —at the same time as the speech is to explain Jesus' words and actions.

Thus Jesus realizes God's will, plan and work (θέλημα,[30] ἔργον). He performs not his own will but the Father's, 6:38. He "lives through the Father", 6:57, receives his food from Him. In S 4a Jesus' work is described in two clauses: ποιῶ τὸ θέλημα τοῦ πέμψαντός με and τελειώσω αὐτοῦ τὸ ἔργον.[31] Are these clauses completely synonymous? The change of tense and meaning in the latter verb would say not.[32] The first formulation is the more general: Jesus carries out

---

[25] We have the phrase 23 times in Jn. See the survey in Miranda 1972, pp. 29f. Literature: Haenchen 1962—63 and the extensive monograph of Miranda 1972.

[26] Miranda 1972, p. 31. In his summary (p. 129) Miranda stresses that the different expressions on the missions of Jesus are "Epiphanie — bzw. Offenbarungstermini".

[27] Thus, for example, Mk 3:35. Mt generally has τοῦ πατρός μου, Jn τοῦ πέμψαντός με in 4:34; 5:30; 6:38,39, and τοῦ πατρός μου in 6:40.

[28] The predicate precedes the subject as in 1:1 and 4:24, Abbott 1906, pp. 68f. Ἵνα is explanatory as often in the Johannine corpus.

[29] On Jesus' "work", see above 2.2, U 27, on his work as a gift from God, 3.3.2, S 3.

[30] God's will (θέλημα) is in Jn especially bound to his mission work, G. Schrenk in ThWNT, vol, 3, pp. 55f.

[31] The present tense (ποιῶ) is to be preferred on internal criteria in spite of the strong external evidence of ποιήσω. See Jn 17:3 and 1 Jn 5:20, which also have present tense, and Schnackenburg, Comm., ad loc.

[32] Τελειοῦν "complete, bring to an end", Schnackenburg, Comm., ad loc., and the material he mentions. This meaning is stressed by Dodd 1953, p. 316.

the will of the Father,[33] while the second directs attention to the actual completion of the Father's mission, i.e. Jesus' death and glorification, 13:1; 17:4; 19:30.[34] As in 17:4 ἔργον here covers the whole of Jesus' mission, which in Jn may be seen concentrated in the events of the "hour". Thus 4a refers to *Jesus' work in its entirety* and has to a great extent a *post-resurrectional perspective*.[35]

Therefore: S 4a must be described as typically Johannine, both in content and in form. It deals with the relationship between the Father and the Son, particularly the close and indissoluble bond between their activities. Jesus lives *in* and *by* realizing the will of God. Jesus' work is God's work. The disciples are told of Jesus' ἔργον in all its range when they stand questioning the events at Jacob's well. Τελειώσω αὐτοῦ τὸ ἔργον confers a post-resurrectional aspect on Jesus' teaching, unless the verb is interpreted as futural. Like Jesus' "cup", 18:11; 19:28f, therefore, Jesus' "food" seems to be connected particularly with the completion of the mission on Jesus' death and glorification. Yet the main aspect in S 4a is how *the Father and the Son work*.

S 4b

a   οὐχ ὑμεῖς λέγετε
    aa   ὅτι ἔτι τετράμηνός ἐστιν καὶ ὁ θερισμὸς ἔρχεται;
b   ἰδοὺ λέγω ὑμῖν,
    ba   ἐπάρατε τοὺς ὀφθαλμοὺς ὑμῶν
    bb   καὶ θεάσασθε τὰς χώρας
    bc   ὅτι λευκαί εἰσιν πρὸς θερισμόν.
    bd   ἤδη ὁ θερίζων μισθὸν λαμβάνει
    be   καὶ συνάγει καρπὸν εἰς ζωὴν αἰώνιον,
    bf   ἵνα ὁ σπείρων ὁμοῦ χαίρῃ καὶ ὁ θερίζων.

S 4b, taken as a whole, has a form often found in Jn: a general clause with following application.[36] The first part opens with the words "you are accustomed to say" (clause *a*),[37] the second part with "but I say to you" (clause *b*).[38] These

[33] "Das immerwährende Tun", Weiss, Comm., ad loc., "das gegenwärtige Tun", Schnackenburg, Comm., ad loc.

[34] The aorist as "der einmahlige Akt des Vollendens", Bauer, Comm., ad loc. The same in Thüsing ²1970, p. 51. Τελειώσω may be future tense, Bl.-Debr. § 369,3, Jn 7:3; 15:8; 17:2; 5:20. Abbott 1906, p. 123. This would imply a temporal contrast (I now do . . . I shall bring to an end), but it is hazardous to assume this from temporal markings by tense in a ἵνα-clause.

[35] For further analysis, see Thüsing ²1970, pp. 51ff. He shows "dass das Wort τελειοῦν auf den Abschluss des irdischen Wirkens hindeutet, also auf den Kreuzestod bzw. die Erhöhung".

[36] See above, 2.2, U 26, and 3.2.2.

[37] Literally "Do you not say". Rhetorical questions with οὐ in Jn always refer to something already known, Schnackenburg, Comm., ad loc. The formulation here is similar to Rabbinic usage, Bultmann, Comm., ad loc.

[38] Literally "Behold, I say to you", but ἰδού has here as in Jn 16:32, an adversative meaning, Abbott 1906, p. 199. This phrase too is Semitic, Bultmann, Comm., ad loc. Ἰδού also gives Jesus' explanation a certain emphasis, Pryke 1967—68.

words again bring out the revelation situation, with its tension between the disciples, who do not possess insight, and Jesus, who can reveal all things.[39] The teaching Jesus gives his disciples is the heart of the text, while the primary function of the first two clauses (a and aa) is to introduce and form the transition.

The general clause aa should be described as a proverb or a saying, even if it is not confirmed by other sources. Its form is concise and rhythmical, with mainly Semitic parallels.[40] The background is the agrarian conditions in Palestine: the sowing ends in mid-December and the harvest begins in mid-April.[41] Thus when the seed was sown one could say: Four months to the harvest. This saying as a proverb could have several meanings depending on context. Bultmann gives two examples: an exhortation to patience "Eile mit Weile", and an expression of delay "Morgen, morgen; nur nicht heute".[42] In our text the words have a double function: to introduce *the image of harvest* and to express a *futural aspect* of that to which the harvest refers.[43] To counter this idea on the part of the disciples, Jesus asserts a *present aspect* at the same time as, in Johannine fashion, he comments on, and explains, what is taking place, by enlarging on the image.

The first two clauses, ba and bb, are a double exhortation to the disciples to really *see* what is happening around them.[44] Indeed their attention is directed to something absolutely definite, to "the fields" (τὰς χώρας, which by its proleptic position receives special emphasis).[45] According to the text, something is happening just then in the field: *after the testimony of the woman, Samaritans come to Jesus.* This seems to be the subject of Jesus' teaching to his disciples. He not only says ὁ θερισμὸς ἐλήλυθει or a similar expression, but refers explicitly to the fields where the Samaritans are now on their way out to him at the well. This event is likened to a harvest. Thus the situation is not that assumed from the proverb in clause aa, i.e. the end of the sowing, but *the beginning of the harvest* (λευκαὶ πρὸς θερισμόν).[46] This the disciples must realize and understand. The

---

[39] This contrast explains the use of ὑμεῖς.

[40] See the parallels mentioned in Abbott 1906, pp. 189f, and Bauer, Bultmann and Barrett, Comm., ad loc.

[41] Str.-B., vol. 2, pp. 439f. The Gezer calendar also has four months between sowing and harvest, Brown, Comm., ad loc.

[42] Bultmann, Comm., ad loc.

[43] On the image of harvest, see below 3.4.6.

[44] Ἐπαίρειν τοὺς ὀφθαλμούς, which has a Semitic flavour according to Bultmann and Schnackenburg, Comm., ad loc., is also used in Jn 6:5; 11:41 and 17:1. It is "a spiritual act" according to Abbott 1906, pp. 457f, and also Bauer, Comm., ad loc., referring to Chrysostom. The phrase is used in a central text on the gathering in of the people of God, mentioned below 3.4.6.— Θεᾶσθαι may be used of both physical and spiritual seeing, Bauer, s.v.

[45] Bl.-Debr. § 476, Barrett, Comm., ad loc., against Abbott 1906, p. 160.

[46] The clause bc, however, does not imply that the harvest is already reaped but that the harvest may immediately begin. Note the temporal change in the following clauses.

first three clauses, *ba—bc*, tell the disciples both that the harvest is at hand, and that the Samaritans are included.[47]

The meaning of the three remaining clauses, *bd—bf*, is more difficult to discern, partly because of uncertainty as to the text type involved. Have we here only an embellishment of the image of the harvest, or should the text be read as "eine Bildrede" in which fact dominates over image? If the latter is true, what is involved and how much does the element of fact dominate?

First of all *bd* again establishes the presentual aspect: already now ($\mathring{\eta}\delta\eta$)[48] the harvester is at work. The harvest is not merely at hand. The reaping has commenced. The image of the harvest is developed further by a focus on $\dot{o}\ \vartheta\epsilon\rho i\zeta\omega\nu$ and not, as earlier, on $\dot{o}\ \vartheta\epsilon\rho\iota\sigma\mu\dot{o}\varsigma$ and $\tau\dot{\alpha}\varsigma\ \chi\dot{\omega}\rho\alpha\varsigma$. In all three clauses, *bd—bf*, "the reaper" is the subject, in the last one together with "the sower". These words in the singular may indeed be interpreted collectively as reapers and sowers but it is more natural to first test an individual reference by associating them with the "harvest" in the fields. In this context Jesus appears as the reaper. The fact that Samaritans come *to him* is seen as an act of reaping in which *Jesus* brings in the harvest. At the beginning of the speech, in S 4a, just *Jesus' activity* is the theme. Therefore it seems appropriate to interpret $\dot{o}\ \vartheta\epsilon\rho i\zeta\omega\nu$ as referring to Jesus. The reading of the clauses only as an embellishment of "die im Gang befindliche Ernte und die Freude des Erntenden"[49] creates several difficulties. The phrase $\epsilon i\varsigma$ $\zeta\omega\mathring{\eta}\nu\ \alpha i\dot{\omega}\nu\iota o\nu$ marks that the meaning is not always metaphorical. Both $\sigma\upsilon\nu\dot{\alpha}$-$\gamma\epsilon\iota\nu$ and $\kappa\alpha\rho\pi\dot{o}\varsigma$ are in Jn pregnant mission terms with the associations this involves in a Johannine linguistic context.[50] The first clause, *bd*, is also surprising by its position and by its content, if the text is read as a parable. If these clauses were only an embellishment of the image of harvest, would not the natural expression be "he who sowed now reaps his harvest; he now receives reward for his effort". Even the last clause, *bf*, is best read as a metaphorical saying of *the joint work of two persons*. For v. 37 clearly indicates that there were two parties, not just one, for example Jesus. The word $\dot{o}\mu o\tilde{\upsilon}$ means "together, shared" rather than "at the same time".[51] And we then have a clear link with what was said in S 4a.[52]

In my view these features of the text mean that the last three clauses in S 4b

---

[47] An interpretation of the harvest as referring to the Samaritans is very common. See, for example, Bultmann, Barrett, Schnackenburg, Brown, Schulz, Morris and Lindars, Comm., ad loc.

[48] Textual evidence and Johannine usage suggest that $\mathring{\eta}\delta\eta$ belongs to *bd*, Barrett, Schnackenburg, Comm., ad loc. This word has a strong nuance of "now", Jn 15:3; 19:28; 9:22.

[49] Schnackenburg, Comm., ad loc., but later he interprets *bd-bf* as referring to the Father and the Son.

[50] See below, 3.4.6.

[51] See the material in Abbott 1906, p. 233, and Schnackenburg, Comm., ad loc. The Greek word corresponds to כְּאֶחָד in Ezra 2:64 and יַחַד in Job 34:29.

[52] See the excellent argumentation in Schnackenburg, Comm., ad loc. (the latter part of his exposition), and before him Thüsing [2]1970, pp. 53ff.

must be read as "eine Bildrede", as a metaphorical account in which fact prevails over image yet without destroying it. Certain elements are taken from the given image but these are used in formulations which are made primarily up of the factual content which the author sees in his clauses. That which Jesus said of himself in v. 34, he here expresses metaphorically, applying it to the existing situation. As in v. 34 Jesus' work is the theme, namely the act of the reaper, but the Father too, the sower, is included. The harvest is a traditional eschatological image of how God will one day intervene to redeem His people and judge the world, an image which is used in Mt 9:37 f and Lk 10:2 of the mission.[53] It shows in S 4 b that the work of the Father and the Son, to which it refers, is an eschatological event. The reaper, namely Jesus, now receives his "wages" (from the Father), which in a Johannine context means that God gives people to Jesus.[54] The form of expression in *bd* therefore seems dependent both on the image of harvest and on Johannine ideas of Jesus' work. The same can be said of the following clause *be*. Jesus is now gathering in the harvest, i.e. people, in Jn 4 Samaritans. The great gathering in of God's scattered people has begun. Καρπός may at the same time be an allusion to the mission term "to bear fruit" in Jn.[55] As in v. 14, the phrase εἰς ζωὴν αἰώνιον is difficult to relate to the foregoing, but seems to "interpret" the image of "gathering in fruit": Jesus' gathering of mankind is a giving of eternal life.[56] Since the expression "to gather in the fruit" is understood from its transferred meaning, the transition to a concrete account is easy.

This work of gathering is not bound up with Jesus alone. According to the last clause, *bf,* the Father is also present. Both rejoice in this season of harvest, a shared joy. Even in the clause *bd* God seems to be present implicitly as agent—He who gives the wages—and in *bc* Jesus works in a manner which in the OT sayings is ascribed to God: gathering in God's scattered people. The joy which is mentioned here is indeed linked with the image of harvest, but also with the Johannine account of the situation which arose with Jesus, especially with the situation after Jesus' "hour".[57]

To sum up: S 4b says that the eschatological season of harvest is at hand.

[53] See below, 3.4.6.

[54] Μισθὸν λαμβάνειν does not seem to be a common harvest expression. The only parallel in LXX, Pr 11:21, has a transferred meaning. A reference to μισθωτός is not suggested by the context; against Abbott 1906, pp. 189f. On God as the one who gives wages, see H. Preisker in ThWNT, vol. 4, p. 701, and on how God gives Jesus people. see above 3.3.2, S 3 and 3.2.2.

[55] For an interpretation of this expression in Jn, see below 3.4.6.

[55] See above, 3.3.2, S 5. Weiss, Comm., ad loc., interprets the phrase entirely spatially, and the evangelist may be thinking in two spheres: through the gathering in, people are transferred from the sphere of death to the sphere of life, Jn 5:24. A reference to Tos Peah 4:18 (Brown, Comm., ad loc.) seems to me irrelevant.

[57] Is 9:2, Ps 126:5f. On "joy" in Jn, see the material in ThWNT, vol. 9, pp. 301f (H. Conzelmann).

"These verses embody the theme of realized eschatology".[58] With Jesus the great gathering in has begun. In the text it is he who reaps and gathers, but behind him, as was stated explicitly in S 4a, stands the Father. In fact it is the Father who gives Jesus his "harvest": He was the sower. Now He gives people to Jesus. Therefore, there are two parties to the event which takes place at Jacob's well, when Samaritans come to Jesus after the woman's testimony: the Father and the Son. Both rejoice at what occurs. As shown by the excursus on The Mission in Jn (3.4.6), this account best fits the situation after Jesus' "hour". Jesus would then in S 4b be speaking primarily of his "work" after his glorification—of the mission—when he, like the grain of wheat, has been laid in the earth and died in order later to bear "much fruit". In this mission situation of the Church there would be two persons at work in Samaria: the Father and the Son.

S 4c

a   ἐν γὰρ τούτῳ ὁ λόγος ἐστὶν ἀληθινὸς

aa   ὅτι ἄλλος ἐστὶν ὁ σπείρων καὶ ἄλλος ὁ θερίζων.

b   ἐγὼ ἀπέστειλα ὑμᾶς θερίζειν ὃ οὐχ ὑμεῖς κεκοπιάκατε·

c   ἄλλοι κεκοπιάκασιν, καὶ ὑμεῖς εἰς τὸν κόπον αὐτῶν εἰσεληλύθατε.

In form this last part of the speech resembles the earlier S 4b, although we do not find the same formal characteristics. First comes a general clause *aa* (with an introduction in *a*), which is then applied to the existing situation in *b* and *c*. One difference is that the opening clause *a* binds the saying *aa* to both the preceding and the following clauses. The natural reading would take γάρ as a junction with the immediately preceding clause.[59] And ἐν τούτῳ refers both back and forward. —The relationships are here marked! The text does not only read οὗτος ὁ λόγος ἀληθινός ἐστιν ὅτι . . .—The prepositional phrase "always looks back" in Jn, according to Abbott,[60] but an analysis of the passages where it occurs shows that a double reference is the more usual.[61] The phrase both refers to something just stated and directs attention forward to its repetition, with or without addition of new information, 9:30; 13:35; 15:8. The first clause in S 4c has such a double reference. It gives a reason for the statement just made, for *bf* in S 4b, and introduces *aa*. The first two clauses *a* and *aa* are therefore not only an introductory transition to what follows—as are *a* and *aa* in S 4b—but also a conclusion of

---

[58] Brown, Comm., ad loc., who *in some parts* allows this aspect to determine his interpretation.

[59] This corresponds to Johannine usage. Γάρ is very seldom used in Jn, almost only in his own comments. See below, 4.2, and Abbott 1906, pp. 101ff.

[60] Abbott 1906, pp. 290f.

[61] Only one clear exception: Jn 16:30. We have the phrase 12 times in 1 Jn, referring backwards or forwards, or both backwards and forwards. See Haas-Jonge-Swellengrebel, Comm., ad 1 Jn 2:3,4,5; 3:10,16,19,24; 4:2,9,10,13,17; 5:2.

what precedes. Both this and what then follows in *b* and *c* "confirm" the general rule given.[62]

It seems that a link with S 4b would also partly explain the form of this general rule. The "word" (ὁ λόγος) expresses a "common reflection of many ancient peoples".[63] Attempts have been made to find parallels in the Ras Shamra texts,[64] in the OT[65] and in Greek literature.[66] Yet none of these have the same form as *aa*. The closest parallel to the Johannine text is to be found in the Greek proverbs, such as ἄλλοι μὲν σπείρουσιν, ἄλλοι δ᾽ ἀμήσονται and ἄλλοι κάμον, ἄλλοι δ᾽ ὤναντο. Constructions with ἄλλος—ἄλλος in the sense of "one—another" are not uncommon in Greek proverbs.[67] The Johannine text has a related wording, but not ἄλλοι—ἄλλοι which would fit the application in *b* and *c*, nor finite forms of σπείρειν and θερίζειν, nor the normal μέν—δέ in a contrast. Jn uses parataxis, singular constructions with copula and the expressions which appear just before in S 4b, in clause *bf*, namely ὁ σπείρων and ὁ θερίζων. In form the clauses in *aa* resemble the formulation in 5:32 (ἄλλος ἐστὶν ὁ μαρτυρῶν περὶ ἐμοῦ), which does not seem to be a common construction.[68] "The proverb" in Jn 4:37, therefore, has a clearly Johannine tinge[69] and it is likely that this is a Johannine formulation—influenced by the immediate context—of a common aphorism in the world of the time. There is one who sows and one who reaps.

Thus the proverb has a double function. Justifying the preceding statement, the "quoted" saying emphasizes that there are here *two* parties involved, according to my interpretation of S 4b of *the Father* and *the Son,* who are named and related to each other in S 4a. The one sows, the other reaps, metaphorically speaking. But this is a shared task. When the proverb is later applied in what follows, there is an obvious shift. Now the parties involved are no longer the Father and the Son but "*the disciples*" and "*others*".[70] This shift in the reference would not be so great in Jn's view. When the text previously mentioned Jesus as the reaper, this in the situation after Jesus' "hour" also means the disciples.

---

[62] On the meaning of ἀληθινός and textual problems in *a*, see Schnackenburg, Comm., ad loc. Λόγος may have the meaning "proverb" here. See Liddel-Scott, s.v., VII, 2.

[63] Brown, Comm., ad loc.

[64] Watson 1970.

[65] Mic 6:15; Dt 20:6; 28:30; Job 31:8. See Brown, Comm., ad loc.

[66] See especially Bauer and Barrett, Comm., ad loc.

[67] See Corpus Paroem. Graec, vol 1, pp. 7,25,184,205,382, vol. 2, pp. 6,97f,272,275, and Abbott 1906, p. 613. On ἄλλος - ἄλλος meaning "one ... another", see Liddell-Scott, s.v.

[68] Jn uses ἄλλος very often (34 times), mostly in comparisons where the second part has already been mentioned (for example, ἐγώ-ἄλλος, σύ-ἄλλος, ὑμεῖς-ἄλλος). Only Jn 5:32 is a direct correspondence to our text. I have not found any other parallel anywhere.

[69] The construction copula + definite article + participle is also frequent in Jn, 5:32,45; 6:33,63 etc. See Abbott 1906, pp. 59ff.

[70] A collective and generic meaning of ὁ σπείρων and ὁ θερίζων is quite possible, Bl.-Debr., § 252, 263.

Indeed according to Jn, Jesus continues his work through that of the disciples. Jesus' mission merges into the mission of the disciples.[71] In S 4c we have a clearly post-resurrectional point of view, marked by the tense of *b* and *c*. Jn does not mention any sending out of the disciples before 20:21 (and 17:18), but presents Jesus as working alone during his life on earth, 5:17, 19; 7:3; 9:4; 10:25, 32, 37; 14:10.[72] From the point of view of the narrator, S 4c is a backward look at the work of the disciples, i.e. Jesus' continued work through his disciples.

The disciples take over Jesus' work and become reapers: ἐγὼ ἀπέστειλα ὑμᾶς θερίζειν. They are involved in the same eschatological work as Jesus. They share in the joy of harvest. In the text they stand out in strong contrast to others who have laboured and toiled *before* them (ἄλλοι κεκοπιάκασιν – εἰς τὸν κόπον αὐτῶν εἰσεληλύθατε). This is actually stated twice over, both in *b* and in more detail in *c*.

There is a strong contrast between the disciples' *reaping* (θερίζειν) and the *wearisome* toil (κοπιᾶν) of the others. The verb κοπιᾶν is often used in the sense of "be tired, grow weary, work hard, toil".[73] An often quoted paper by von Harnack from 1928 asserts that Paul made this verb and its noun into a technical term for the Christian work of mission and toil in the parish. He felt that Paul followed this linguistic usage "im Hinblick auf die schwere Handarbeit, die er leistete und die ihm mit seinem Missionswerk sozusagen zusammenfloss".[74] von Harnack explains the later disappearance of these expressions—they occur very rarely in later Christian literature—from the change in the value set on the work in the Christian parish: it could no longer be compared with the wearisome slave labour.

This Pauline usage—its background can hardly be regarded as explained by von Harnack's reference to Paul's hard work as a tent-maker[75]—is sometimes thought to have influenced the wording of Jn 4:37f to the extent that we have here a technical term for the efforts of the early Christian missionaries.[76] Yet this is by no means self-evident. I here omit the general problem of the relationship between Paul and Jn and confine myself to an internal reading of S 4c. There κοπιᾶν is contrasted with θερίζειν and closely parallel to σπείρειν. The language there suggests that κοπιᾶν is used of "ploughing, sowing, tilling the

---

[71] See above, 2.2, U 27, and below 3.4.6.

[72] See Schnackenburg, Comm., ad loc.

[73] See the material in Liddell-Scott, s.v., the use of the verb in LXX and also F. Hauck in ThWNT, vol. 3, pp. 827f.

[74] v. Harnack 1928, p. 5.

[75] As δοῦλοι the word κόπος/κοπιᾶν may have a background in the OT and Jewish usage. The Christian work may have been regarded as κόπος while waiting for the parousia. See the following analysis.

[76] See, for example, F. Hauck in ThWNT, vol. 3, p. 829, and Schnackenburg, Comm., ad loc.

soil", i.e. as an antonym to θερίζειν.[77] The disciples' joy in the harvest is then paralleled by the laborious toil of "the others" in the sowing.

The OT use of κόπος and κοπιᾶν is also of interest here, not least because if the Pauline usage mentioned above was strongly influenced by Jewish usage, this may explain why it later dropped out of use. In the OT κόπος is regarded as particularly characteristic of the existing situation (this age), which will pass away when the Lord restores Israel, Is 33:24, 40:31. F. Hauck sums up, although without applying his findings to NT usage: "Der Mensch ist zu Mühsal geboren, so wie umgekehrt die Vögel zum Emporfliegen Hi 5,7. So wird κόπος Terminus der alttestamentlichen Leidensfrömmigkeit. Es malt die *Lebens-* und *Leidensmühsal,* die dem Menschen, bes dem Frommen in der Welt zubestimmt ist und aus der Gott errettet. ... Dementsprechend wird κοπ- auch wichtiger Gegensatzbegriff für die eschatologische Hoffnung. Mühsal der Gegenwart und erquickende Ruhe der Heilszeit (ἀνάπαυσις) treten einander gegenüber".[78] In the NT this usage appears—as Hauck says—in Mt 11:28f. The old order with its law and its onerous commandments is there contrasted with Jesus' easy yoke and his "rest". This could also provide a background to our text. The new order, which came with Jesus, and was of crucial significance only after his death and glorification, is here described as a work of harvest, full of *joy,* while the work before Jesus "hour" is characterized by κόπος. Jn 4 would not then depend on Pauline usage. All in all, a reference to κοπιᾶν as an antonym to θερίζειν would be a sufficient explanation of the usage in our text.

If κοπιᾶν should here be read as a parallel to σπείρειν we have to some extent defined the significance of ἄλλοι in 4:38—formerly God was the sower—and if we see κόπος as marking the time *before* God's eschatological intervention, we have also defined the activity of "the others" in terms of time. The suggested interpretations here are particularly numerous: ἄλλοι denotes Jesus, Jesus and the Father, the Prophets, John the Baptist, the Samaritan woman, the Early Christian missionaries, the Hellenists mentioned in Acts 8, etc.[79] It is very difficult to determine to what ἄλλοι refers. The interpretation of the text as a whole, with its connections with the idea of what text type we have in Jn 4, must here provide the most telling argument (see 3.5). I give here a very tentative solution.

S 4a deals with the Father and Jesus and the work they share. Jesus is described in S 4b as ὁ θερίζων and the Father as ὁ σπείρων and their joint effort is further presented, but in terms of metaphor. The image of the harvest continues

[77] See, for example, Jos 24:13; Sir 6:19; Is 65:21ff; 2 Tim 2:6, also Test Iss 3:5 and v. Harnack 1928, p. 5.

[78] F. Hauck in ThWNT, vol. 3, pp. 827f. On the "rest" in the new eschatological age, see also Riesenfeld 1947, pp. 206ff, and Riesenfeld 1959, and the literature he mentions.

[79] See the surveys in Schnackenburg and Brown, Comm., ad loc., and in Thüsing ²1970, pp. 56f

in S 4c but there is here a shift in reference from the Father and the Son to "others" and to "the disciples". This gives us the following pattern.

The *Father* who has sent Jesus   *Jesus* who has sent the disciples
"others"   "the disciples"
"to toil (to sow), to labour"   "to reap" (joy)

The "others" would then be a general reference to those who take part in God's work before the final harvest, in the text primarily the woman who bears witness to Jesus (and John the Baptist in 3:22ff). Since the time limit is actually at the "hour" of Jesus, one could also assign the *earthly* Jesus to the throng of those "sent", who worked before the great harvest, namely within the framework of the old covenant of God.[80] The woman was faithful to God's earlier work among the Samaritans and becomes a witness to the "Messiah" now that he has finally arrived. The parallel with John the Baptist is near at hand. If this is true then the text deals with *how genuine Samaritan faith naturally merges into a true belief in Christ after a meeting with the historical and glorified Jesus.* I shall return to this hypothesis[81] under point 3.4.5 and in the summary of the entire text, 3.5.

3.4.3 The Junction of the Speeches

The analysis of how the different speeches in the second "dialogue" are joined together cannot reach the same dimensions as that of the first dialogue (3.3.3). The following section is to some extent a summary of the comments I made under 3.4.2. We have here only four speeches, the last being pre-eminent by its length and its content. The dialogue, as we saw, becomes almost a monologue, in which Jesus gives detailed teaching to his disciples. The "revelation character" we found already in the quotation formulae recurs in the speeches: Jesus as Rabbi, S 1, the contrast Jesus—the disciples, S 2 and S 4, the disciples' lack of insight (οὐκ οἴδατε), S 2, the μή-question in S 3 and the phrases οὐχ ὑμεῖς λέγετε, ἰδοὺ λέγω ὑμῖν, ἐν γὰρ τούτῳ ὁ λόγος ἐστὶν ἀληθινός in S 4. The theme *Jesus teaches his disciples* pervades all the speeches and binds them together to a unit. Since the spatial and temporal features[1] in this case do not yield anything of interest, I shall concentrate my continued analysis on another recurring theme, namely *eating — reaping* and on a discussion of *the personal references.*

It is easy to establish that S 1, S 2, S 3 and S 4a all deal with *eating*, that this eating is explained without metaphors in S 4a and that the text following in S 4b and S 4c is concerned with *reaping*. Φαγεῖν and βρῶμα (βρῶσις)—corresponding

---

[80] Note the picture of Jesus in 4:5f.

[81] A similar hypothesis was put forward by H. Odeberg in his comparative investigation from 1929, p. 190, but without argumentation. So far as I know, nobody has taken up this hypothesis.

[1] The temporal relations are very important in S 4, most explicitly marked by ἔτι- ἤδη. See above the comments on S 4b and S 4c.

tc πεῖν and ὕδωρ in the first dialogue—frequently recur in S 1 – S 4a, as do the words derived from θερις-, σπειρ- and κοπ- in S 4b – S 4c. This abundant use of *eat* and *reap* (including *sow*) in the two halves of the dialogue, and, furthermore, in transferred senses, like the interpretation given in the transition between them in S 4a, necessarily poses the question of the connection between these two "images".

Both *the food* and *the harvest* refer to something mentioned earlier, the harvest through τὰς χώρας to the Samaritans who are on the way to Jesus, the food to that which the disciples were to buy in the town, v. 8. "Eating" is first used in its usual sense, but later with a transferred meaning. We find the same kind of shift in perspective in S 1 – S 4 as in vv. 7ff and vv. 16ff. In his speech Jesus aims at a teaching on his mission from the Father, on the *ergon* which he has been given to do. This is particularly clear in this last dialogue and there in the last speech of Jesus, which is also his last words in the text. In a Johannine context βρῶμα in S 4a must refer to Jesus' earthly ministry, which is characterized, according to Jn, by obedience to the will of the Father and by completion of the work of the Father.[2] Jesus has βρῶσιν φαγεῖν, S 2, for the Father has given him βρῶμα φαγεῖν, S 3, namely ἔργον ἵνα ποιήσῃ, S 4a; cf. Jn 17:4. The very concept "to complete" in this context brings us to the events of the "hour" and in Jn 5:36 a similar formulation is used of the acts which Jesus will perform after the "hour".[3] Jesus' "food" in our text then tends to cover *the whole* of Jesus' task of salvation and all that is implicit therein. We thus find ourselves on the dividing line between Jesus' earthly ministry and his work as the glorified one, namely in the very perspective of the "hour" with its look backwards and forwards.

This temporal perspective is essential, since the use of *the harvest image* creates a certain shift in time—with a corresponding shift in reference to persons. The disciples first assert that the harvest is *in the future*, then Jesus corrects them, saying that the harvest *is at hand*, and finally we discover that the harvest *is in full swing*.[4] Previously in the dialogue we learned that the Father gave Jesus "food to eat", but now we see that Jesus the reaper has a harvest to bring in. He receives "wages" and "fruit". I stated earlier from the context, coupled with Johannine ideas, that the text here must refer to the people who come to Jesus, namely Samaritans.[5] There is now in Jn a perspective which includes both Jesus' food" and "Jesus' harvest", namely *Jesus' erga*, which may in one sense be described as *God's erga*—something which the Father gives the Son—and in another sense *the erga of the disciples*.[6] The agents of this work are the Father, the Son and those whom the Father gave the Son. An *ergon* perspective therefore

---

[2] See above, 3.4.2, S 4a.
[3] On Jn 5:36, see above 2.2, U 27 and 29, and Thüsing [2]1970, p. 54.
[4] See my analysis of S 4b above (3.4.2).
[5] See 3.4.2, S 4b, 3.4.5 and 3.4.6.
[6] See 2.2, U 27 and U 29, 3.4.2, S 4a.

seems to provide the best explanation of the use of *to eat* and *to reap* in the dialogue now analysed. The narrator is primarily interested in *the "hour" and its consequences*. The metaphor of "Jesus' food" is explained mainly in terms of Jesus' "hour", S 4a, while with the traditional eschatological image of the harvest, Jesus—in our text apparently the glorified Jesus[7]—teaches on the consequences of the "hour" for the Samaritans. God's work, Jesus' work and the disciples' work are seen in one and the same perspective with the "hour" in the centre, which includes the two phases of Jesus' *ergon*.

The analysis of *the personal references* should refer primarily to the determination of the reference in ὁ ϑερίζων, ὁ σπείρων and ἄλλοι.[8] The text gives us the following data:

S 1	Jesus	('Ραββί, -ε)
S 2	Jesus	(ἐγώ)
	the disciples	(ὑμεῖς)
S 3	someone	(τίς)
	Jesus	(αὐτῷ)
S 4a	Jesus	(ἐμόν, -ω, μέ, -ω)
	The Father	(τοῦ πέμψαντος, αὐτοῦ)
S 4b	the disciples	(ὑμεῖς, ὑμῶ, -τε, ὑμῶν, -ϑε)
	Jesus	(-ω)
	x	(ὁ ϑερίζων, -ει, ὁ ϑερίζων)
	y	(ὁ σπείρων)
S 4c	y¹	(ἄλλος, ὁ σπείρων)
	x¹	(ἄλλος, ὁ ϑερίζων)
	Jesus	(ἐγώ)
	the disciples	(ὑμᾶς, ὑμεῖς, ὑμεῖς)
	z	(ἄλλοι, αὐτῶν)

Thus the text makes explicit mention of *three* "persons": the *Father, Jesus* and *the disciples*. The Samaritans are included implicitly under τὰς χώρας (μισϑόν, καρπόν)[9] and there is also a series of references to unknown entities, x, y, z, etc. Opinions can hardly be divided about the first part of the text, S 1 — S 4a. There *Jesus*, mentioned eight times, is teaching his *disciples*, mentioned only in S 2, concerning *his* "food", i.e. *his* "work", and must then refer to *the Father*. The indefinite τίς in S 3—here the disciples were perhaps thinking of the woman whom they saw at the well—acquires its true meaning from S 4a: it is the Father who had given Jesus food. This expresses Jesus' close affinity to the Father. The primary agent is God, who sent Jesus and gave him a task to perform and com-

---

[7] Cf. the function of the Paraclete, analysed below 4.3.

[8] The hypothesis which I put forward above (3.4.2, S 4b and S 4c) can here be tested with regard to the personal references.

[9] This derives from the context. See above 3.4.2, S 4b.

plete. *The first part of the text, therefore, focuses on Jesus and the Father in their shared activity.*

In S 4b we first recall the teaching situation by means of the many references to the disciples and by the contrast between Jesus and the disciples.—We find the same thing in S 2.—At the same time the attention is directed to the Samaritans who are on their way to Jesus, those who, according to the text to follow, believed in Jesus because of the woman's testimony. Since *Jesus'* activity was previously the centre of attention—Jesus "eats", works, completes—and v. 36 can hardly be read only as an embellishment of the harvest, then $\grave{o}$ $\vartheta\epsilon\rho\acute{\iota}\zeta\omega\nu$ must here refer to *Jesus*.[10] Jesus would then continue his teaching on his *ergon*. The fact that the disciples are reapers in v. 38 may be adduced against this theory[11] only on condition that the text is a severely restricted allegory. The fact that the reaper (=Jesus) here *receives* "wages" is well balanced by his receipt previously of "food", and both this and his "gathering of fruit" are appropriate for Jesus in a Johannine light. *There can hardly be any question that x = Jesus in our text.*

Some scholars would set y = x = Jesus.[12] Yet this is countered, as I said above, by the facts that another party, namely the Father, seems to be included implicitly in $\mu\iota\sigma\vartheta\grave{o}\nu$ $\lambda\alpha\mu\beta\acute{\alpha}\nu\epsilon\iota$, that there is mention of the shared joy of x and y, that the text previously directed attention to two parties, i.e. the Father and Jesus, and that the motivation in S 4c — n.b. $\gamma\acute{\alpha}\rho$ — clearly differentiates between x and y. Therefore we must here, as in S 4a, have *both the Father and Jesus*. The text now under discussion, S 1 — S 4b, may thus be read from one and the same theme: Jesus' *ergon*, which is primarily a work of the Father. The Father sows, Jesus reaps. S 4b says that both are now rejoicing when the harvest is gathered in. Nevertheless there is a temporal shift in the text, resulting from the change in image from *food* to a *harvest* now in progress.[13] S 4b is primarily concerned with the situation after Jesus' "hour", the season of the great harvest and joy according to Jn. Indeed this change also involves a change in the reference to Jesus, from the "earthly" Jesus to the "glorified" Jesus, a shift which does not seem unnatural in Jn.[14]

Thus, in terms of the personal references, the text so far dealt with *Jesus* and *the Father*, their joint work, with *the disciples* as receivers of teaching concerning this work, and with *the Samaritans* in the background as a kind of material, i.e. four "persons". In S 4c we have five "persons" and the question involves their relationship to those already mentioned.

If S 4c is to be a justification of the comment immediately preceding, y^1 must equal y and x^1 equal x. Yet at the same time, we find in the continued application

---

[10] See also the arguments above in 3.4.2, S 4b.

[11] Thus, for example, Brown, Comm., ad loc.

[12] Thus, for example, Barrett, Comm., ad loc.

[13] See the analysis of S 4 above and of the image of harvest below, 3.4.6.

in S 4c that x^1 = the disciples and y^1 = z. This means, firstly, a change from a singular to a plural reference. Furthermore the disciples are involved in the subject of the teaching and are not, as previously, merely receivers thereof. Even if the object previously was *Jesus'* work, it is now *the disciples'* work. The transition from Jesus to the disciples is, as I said before (3.4.2, S 4c), easy to understand in the light of the temporal shift, which previously took place.

We still face the problem of determining to what ἄλλοι refers, and thereby one of the meanings of y^1.—We have already established that y^1 = the Father in its backward reference.—The idea in Jn that Jesus' work merges, so to speak, into that of the disciples suggests that ἄλλοι be read as a reference to Jesus (z = x), but this is refuted by the fact that the plural form is used, like the earlier designation of Jesus as he who reaps—not he who labours with the sowing. The plural form is sometimes explained by allowing ἄλλοι to refer both to Jesus and the Father, the two persons left once the diciples have been mentioned.[15] The fact that the disciples join in *their* work also fits the Johannine account, but the formulation of the text contradicts this reading.[16] The word κοπιᾶν does not fit God as subject, and Jesus was previously associated with the joyous work of harvest. At the same time, we must state that ἄλλοι seems in some way to be associated with God, partly by y^1, partly by the verbs which are used in the text (σπείρειν, κοπιᾶν). Under these circumstances, it seems most natural to hold fast to the clear division into two parts, which we previously found in the text, namely the theme of the work of *Jesus* and of *the Father*. In S 4c there is a shift concerning both parties: from Jesus to the disciples and from the Father (God) to *those who took part in God's work of sowing,* namely in God's work towards the decisive "hour", which meant that God's work of harvest could begin.[17] This reading is suggested by the reference in y^1, the use of the verb κοπιᾶν and even the connection thus created with the Samaritans implicit in the text. Only the Samaria text in its entirety can determine in more detail who are these assistants of God. It is self-evident that they must be related to the Samaritans. The first to be considered is the woman of Samaria, who, in the text, "brings" the Samaritans to Jesus.[18] Through her, the history and faith of the Samaritan people also come into contact with Jesus. It is difficult to say whether the earthly Jesus is also included here—with meetings between him and the Samaritans before the disciples begin "to harvest the Samaritans"; according to 4:6, Jesus is κεκοπιακώς. Yet at this point in the analysis we may say: ἄλλοι in S 4c refers to "those sent" by the

---

[14] See below, 4.3.

[15] Thus especially Thüsing ²1970, p. 54, notwithstanding that the Samaria text concerns the Samaritans.

[16] See above 2.2, U 27 and U 29.

[17] See the excursus on mission in Jn below, 3.4.6.

[18] See above, 3.3.6.

Father, who toiled and laboured among the Samaritans within the framework of the old covenant, i.e. before the "hour" of Jesus and the wholly altered situation which thereby arose in God's work of salvation.

Summary: the four speeches in S 1 — S 4 are bound together by the theme of Jesus' *ergon*, which incorporates the work of both the Father and the disciples. It covers the time before and the time after Jesus' "hour", which corresponds in the text to a shift both in the temporal aspect and in the personal references—and also in a transition from the image of *food* to that of *harvest*. The text merges into a teaching on the *disciples'* work of harvest in the land of Samaria, namely how Jesus' disciples bring Samaritans to a true faith in Jesus Christ. In this situation they are evidently to remember that "God" worked among the Samaritans before them. Their work of harvest was preceded by God's work of sowing. The fact that the disciples must be told of this emerges very strongly in the entire text.

3.4.4 The Dialogue and Its Context

In the foregoing account, I have had reason, on several occasions, to refer to the Samaria text in general, which is natural in view of the position of vv. 31—38 late in the text. This applies, for example, to the very dialogue form, with its similarities to vv. 7ff and vv. 16ff (3.3.3, E), the question of food, prepared by v. 8, the reference to what is happening in "the fields"—see v. 30 and vv. 39ff—and even "the others" in v. 38, who are presented by, among others, the woman, vv. 28ff, and perhaps also Jesus' "weariness" in v. 6. I would here add, in particular, the revelation character of the text, the *ergon* perspective and the idea that Jesus is given followers.

Already in the first dialogue (see 3.3.5, A), the reader was shown the picture, strongly defined in vv. 31—38, of *Jesus* as *the Revealer*—see 3.4.5. There the woman was in need of true insight, while here it is the disciples. The picture of them as lacking understanding and in need of teaching is prepared by v. 27. Faced with Jesus' conversation with the Samaritan woman they react only with "astonishment" and inability to ask questions (3.2.1, E 18, 3.2.5). The teaching in vv. 31—38 is concerned with the Samaritans (the harvest) and their relationship to the revelation of Christ.

The unifying theme in the second dialogue, however, is Jesus' *ergon* in all its range, explicitly stated in v. 34. This theme was glimpsed already in the event structure of the text (3.2.6), and through such concepts as "God's gift" and "worship the Father in spirit and truth" it was implicit in the first dialogue (3.3.4, 3.3.5, D). The comment preceding the Samaria text deals explicitly with Jesus' relationship with the Father, 3:33—35 (see 3.2.2 and 3.3.2, S3). The Father "has sent" the Son and "given" him all things. His "word" is God's word. As in the first dialogue, we have in connection with this *ergon* perspective a shift in the temporal aspect— ἔρχεται ὥρα, καὶ νῦν ἐστιν — and in the personal references

(3.3.5, D and 3.3.3, A respectively). The fact that Jesus' *ergon* is directly discussed in the closing dialogue binds together the whole Samaria text.

The dialogue is specially illuminated by its context through the words on *how Jesus is given people*, 3:26—30, 34; 4:1f, 30, 39ff, 43ff. I interpreted the image of the harvest as an expression of how mankind comes to Jesus and receives eternal life. The eschatological harvest and the great reaping has begun (see 3.4.5). The Father gives Jesus "wages" and "fruit", v. 36, namely followers, i.e., the Samaritans in the text. Thus vv. 31—38 are primarily a comment on *how Samaritans come to belief in Jesus*, and that in a situation after the "hour", when the disciples are carrying out Jesus' work ("the Samaria mission"). Such a context explains the obscure item in 4:1f: *Jesus wins people by baptism but the disciples do the baptizing.* Verse 2 would then mark a post-resurrectional view of the events narrated in the Samaria text.—I am now speaking of Jn 4:1—42 as a whole in the form we now have.—The opening verses refer to 3:22ff, in which the main theme is how Jesus is given followers (see 3.2.2 and 3.3.3, S 3). Πάντες ἔρχονται πρὸς αὐτόν, v. 26—cf. 4:30 and 4:39ff—and οὐ δύναται ἄνθρωπος λαμβάνειν οὐδὲ ἓν ἐὰν μὴ ᾖ δεδομένον αὐτῷ ἐκ τοῦ οὐρανοῦ —cf. μισθὸν λαμβάνει in v. 26—and indeed the theme of Jesus' bonds with the Father in vv. 31—38. Later 3:29 refers to how Jesus receives "his bride", and 3:30 to how Jesus "increases".—In this perspective the saying that John decreases evidently means that John's followers in Samaria become Jesus' followers.—3:34 assures that God "has given" Jesus "all things". The account of how the reaper gathers in his harvest, and his dependence on the sower, must therefore be regarded as well prepared in the context of the dialogue, and what has now been said may be seen as further support for my interpretation of vv. 31—38. 4:43ff continue the theme of how Jesus is given people: a man from the throng of *the Galileans* comes forward and professes total belief in Jesus. This is the second sign at *Cana*, similar to the first in the sense that in both "Jesus is given people" *in Galilee* through those who believe and do as he says—cf. 3:33 and 3:36. In Jn 4, where Jesus "must travel through *Samaria*", the emphasis lies on how Jesus, *after the "hour"*, receives *Samaritan* disciples, i.e. on the "Samaria mission", seen in the light of how a throng gathers round Jesus and forms the people of the new covenant (see 3.4.5).

3.4.5 Preliminary Summary

By referring to the following excursus on mission in Jn (3.4.6), I can now try to summarize the analysis of the second dialogue in the Samaria text.

A. By its last speech the dialogue tends to become a *monologue,* somewhat similar to "the revelation discourses" in Jn, for instance those in chs. 3, 5, 10 and 13—16 (3.4.1). Thus the text has a striking *revelation character*: Jesus, who can reveal all things, teaches his disciples, who lack understanding of Jesus' work. This emerges particularly in the quotation formulae (3.4.1), the title Rabbi in S 1, the formulation of S 2 and the beginning of S 4b and S 4c (3.4.3) and furthermore in the very misunderstanding technique in the text.

B. Thus the dialogue has *the same Johannine form as vv. 7ff and vv. 16ff* earlier in the text: the first speech has a neutral form, the second is ambiguous and may be read from an *ergon* aspect—the wording would tend to suggest such a reading—or from the concrete situation described in the text. So the disciples understand it in the third speech, thus revealing their total lack of insight. At the same time, there is some truth in their reaction, if it is set in the right context (Johannine irony). The last speech presents a detailed explanation, first without images, then with the help of concepts of the harvest. The shift in prespective is thereby completed: it is fully evident that Jesus is speaking of his mission from the Father.

C. The main theme of the dialogue is Jesus' *ergon* in all its range, with the change this involves in temporal aspect and in personal references (3.4.3.). The speeches deal with *food to eat* in the literal, and in a transferred sense. In S 4a "the food" is interpreted as Jesus' work, its performance and its completion, a task which Jesus received from the Father. With this image we find ourselves essentially in the situation before Jesus' "hour". Just as Jesus received a cup to drink, he also received food to eat. With S 4b and the image of the harvest there is a change of the temporal aspect from an ἔτι and an ἔρχεται to an ἤδη. The transition is related to that formulated in 4:23 ἔρχεται ὥρα, καὶ νῦν ἐστιν. The traditional eschatological image of the harvest best fits the situation after the "hour" (3.4.6), and the reasoning in S 4b and S 4c is most easily understood as a speech on phase 2 of Jesus' work (3.4.2). In v. 38 this post-resurrectional aspect is clearly marked by tense. I interpreted the image of the harvest from the theme of Jesus' *ergon*, as it is reported without metaphors in S 4a, with the changes resulting from the shift in time just mentioned. Such a reading does justice to the context and to the character of "Bildrede" inherent in S 4b and S 4c. For even if the text may be read as a description of the work of harvest, it is above all a figurative discourse in which the factual content occasionally predominates over the imaginary (3.4.2, S 4b). Thus I read vv. 35—38 as a metaphorical account of *the shared work of the Father and the Son in the perspective of the "hour"*. The eschatological harvest is now at hand. The reaper gathers in people, a harvest which he receives from the Sower, the Father. This connection gives rise to a common joy. In S 4c there is a clear shift in the personal references to *Jesus' disciples* and to *those of God's fellow workers who laboured in Samaria before the disciples*.

D. The people whom Jesus (and the disciples) gather in the dialogue are *Samaritans.* The reference to "the fields" and the context of the dialogue demand such an interpretation. This creates an essential limitation, both of the contextual theme of how Jesus is given people (3.4.4) and of the theme of Jesus' *ergon.* The dialogue concludes with a saying concerning the disciples' "mission to Samaria", but "mission" in this context must be understood in a Johannine sense as *a gathering of the people of God* who are scattered throughout the world (3.4.6). Jesus' *ergon* included, as we saw in the first text we analysed, the creation of a new people of God. By obedience to John the Baptist and the other witnesses about Jesus and Jesus' mother, the disciples and the servants in the Cana narrative arrive at a true understanding of Jesus. In the second dialogue of the Samaria text the disciples are told of *how the Samaritans are integrated into the new people of God.* Thus Jesus draws their attention to the existence of those who preceded them in the work among the Samaritans. The dialogue ends at this point, v. 38. The attitude to "the others who laboured earlier" is very positive. The background could be the Samaritans' participation in the old Israel, and thereby also in God's earlier gifts to His people, and in addition the promises of the union of Judah and Ephraim, when comes God's harvest and the gathering of the scattered Israel (3.4.6.) We would then have a certain parallel to how the true Israel received him whom God sent and became a "new" Israel (2.4). The *whole* of the old Israel, i.e. those who there were true to their faith, Jews and Samaritans alike, are part of the new and true Israel. The chief justification of such an hypothesis must lie, apart from in the interpretation of vv. 35—38 now given, in the Samaria text as a whole and its context, and further in the Johannine concepts of how the people of the new covenant came into existence, and thereby in the idea of mission in Jn. Therefore I refer to 3.4.6 (excursus on mission) and to 3.5, in which I consider the text as a whole and also discuss the interpretation of the woman's role and of the "others" mentioned in v. 38. The very fact that *Samaritans come to Jesus because of the woman's testimony* favours a connection between the woman and "the others". For the moment we may formulate the theme of the dialogue as follows: *Jesus' ergon means that Samaritans, a part of the old Israel, are incorporated in the people of the new convenant, (a union of "Judah" and "Ephraim").* The very role of the Father and of the "others" in the text indicates that the situation of the Samaritans *before* disciples' "work of harvest" when the "hour" is at hand is of great interest to the narrator.

3.4.6 Excursus III. Mission in Jn

A number of words in the second dialogue, primarily θερίζειν, συνάγειν and καρπός oblige me to discuss here what Jn says about the Christian mission. The whole of our text seems subordinate to a certain mission aspect: indeed vv. 35—38 have also been described as the most pregnant words of mission in the fourth Gospel.[1] However, the survey of the material must be very brief.[2]

Sowing and reaping were essential elements in the life of the inhabitants of the Near East, so were naturally used in religious imagery. Here we are primarily interested in *the harvest*.[3] In the OT, in Jewish writings and in the NT, harvest is an image of God's intervention in the world, which involves both salvation, blessing, joy, Is 27:12; Hos 6:11; Is 9:3; Ps 126:5f, and judgement, punishment, destruction, Joel 4:13; Is 18:5; 63:1ff. In 4 Ezra 4:28ff and 2 Baruch 70:2ff the eschatological age is depicted as a harvest by God and we find a similar use of the image in the NT, Mt 3:12; 13:30,39; Mk 4:29; Rev 14:14ff. This widely occurring idea, later also found in the Fathers of the Church,[4] makes it probable that harvest in the Johannine environment was a common image of God's eschatological intervention in the world. The positive use of this image is the more interesting for our text: when "the harvest" comes, God will redeem His people. The image of the harvest is linked in such contexts with pictures of how God will gather in His scattered people. Is 27:12f reads:[5]

> In that day from the river Euphrates to the Brook of Egypt the Lord will thresh out the grain (MTחבט LXX: συμφράξει), and you will be gathered one by one, O people of Israel. And in that day a great trumpet will be blown, and those who were lost in ... and those who were driven out to ... will come and worship the Lord on the holy mountain at Jerusalem (προσκυνήσουσιν τῷ κυρίῳ ἐπὶ τὸ ὄρος τὸ ἅγιον ἐν Ιερουσαλημ).

Israel will be healed when "the harvest" comes, Hos 6:10—7:1.

> In the house of Israel I have seen a horrible thing;
> Ephraim's harlotry is there, Israel is defiled.
> For you also, O Judah, a harvest is appointed.
> When I would restore the fortunes of my people,
> when I would heal Israel,
> the corruption of Ephraim es revealed,
> and the wicked deeds of Samaria.

---

[1] Fridrichsen 1937, p. 145.

[2] There is, as far as I know, no thorough analysis of the thought of mission in Jn. The article of Fridrichsen is very short. See, however, Ström 1944, Jeremias ²1959, Hofius 1967 and Pancaro 1969—70.

[3] For a survey and for literature, see A. Hermann and I. Opelt in RAC, vol. 6, col. 275—306.

[4] See I. Opelt in RAC, vol. 6, col. 294f.

[5] Especially this text and Is 11:11f (quoted below) seem to be the background of the 10th of the Eighteen Benedictions: "Sound the great trumpet for our freedom; lift up the ensign to gather our exiles, and gather from the four corners of the earth. Blessed art thou, O Lord, who gatherest the banished ones of thy people Israel", translated in Barrett 1956, p. 163, and in Str.-B., vol. 4, p. 212.

The harvest time of God, the uniting of the people, the gathering in of the scattered Israel are combined in the OT. In Mt 9:36—38—and its parallel in Lk 10—we probably have a similar combination. Both the texts are set in the context of mission, indeed Mt 9:35ff is the opening of a longer section on mission. The task in Mt concerns "the lost sheep of the house of Israel", 10:6, i.e. in the light of Ezek 34 "tout le peuple d'Israël, qui est comparé à des brebis dispersées dans les collines".[6] When the people are described in 9:36, the allusion is probably to Num 27:17, and we have a related image: the scattered sheep need a shepherd who can gather and lead them, as Joshua once led the people of God. Pierre Bonnard says of this text: "c'est précisément parce que l'Israël de Dieu est dispersé que la moisson est grande".[7] Indeed Jesus says in this context: "The harvest is plentiful, but the labourers are few; pray therefore the Lord of the harvest to send out labourers into his harvest". When this saying is read in Lk 10:2 it is usually taken as referring to the *Gentile* mission, an interpretation which is anything but self-evident. The number 70 (72) in the Lucan text certainly confers a universal aspect on the mission there described. But why must it only apply to the Gentiles? When "the peoples" are gathered in the Lucan writings (in Acts 2) they are all Jews. The number 70 may be related to the people of Israel.[8] And Jacob Jervell has shown that the mission in Lk and Acts is to a great extent governed by the idea of a new people of God: the Church is the restored Israel even in Luke.[9] Therefore there appears to be no great difference between Mt and Lk on this point. Schnackenburg says of these two passages in the Gospels: "Die Mission wird zu einem eschatologischen Geschehen: Jesus sammelt das Gottesvolk, um es in Gottes Reich zu führen, und er sendet seine Jünger aus, dass sie bei diesem Werk helfen bzw. es fortführen".[10] Those NT passages, in which the image of the harvest comes closest to that in Jn 4, connect together harvest and gathering of God's people, a usage evidently also found in Is 27:12f.

Many texts in OT, Late Judaism and Rabbinism, refer to how God will gather ($\sigma\upsilon\nu\acute{\alpha}\gamma\epsilon\iota\nu$) His scattered people.[11] The idea must have been popular in all camps. Here I shall only quote some *loca* which are particularly linked with Jn 4. Is 11:11—13 mentions the relationship between Jews and Samaritans:

[6] Bonnard, Comm., ad Mt 10:5.
[7] Bonnard, Comm., ad Mt 9:36.
[8] Metzger 1958—59.
[9] Jervell 1972 pp. 41ff, 75ff, 95.
[10] Schnackenburg, Comm., ad Jn 4:36.
[11] See Is 11:12; 27:12; Mic 4:6; 7:11f; Jer 23:3; Ezek 11:17; 20:34; 28:25; 34:12f,16; Sir 36:13; 2 Macc 1:27; Pss Sol 8:34; 11:3; 17:19, 28, 50, etc. Literature: Str.-B., vol. 4, pp 902ff, K.L. Schmidt in ThWNT, vol. 7, pp. 419ff and Riesenfeld 1956 and his analysis of Did 9:4.

> In that day the Lord will extend his hand yet a second time (MT: שֵׁנִית) to recover (MT: לִקְנוֹת)[12] the remnant which is left of his people, from . . .
> He will raise an ensign for the nations,
> and will assemble the outcasts of Israel,
> and gather the dispersed of Judah
> from the four corners of the earth.
> The jealousy of Ephraim shall depart,
> and those who harass Judah shall be cut off;
> Ephraim shall not be jealous of Judah,
> and Judah shall not harass Ephraim.

When God's harvest comes, and the gathering in of God's people begins, the hostility between Jews and Samaritans will cease.[13] This union of Judah and Ephraim is described in many other texts, such as Ezek 37:16—28; Jer 31:17—20 and Zech 10:6f.[14] *The Lord will gather, bring, cleanse, redeem and restore a people of God in a new covenant and then both Judah and Ephraim will be included.* Then the habitation of God will stand amid His people.[15] "*Lift up your eyes round about, and see; they all gather together, they come to you*", Is 60:4. The same exhortation is used here—as in Is 49 (v. 18), which is the chapter most often quoted in the Rabbinical literature on the gathering of the people[16]—as in Jn 4:35. This phrase, among others, the theme of Jews—Samaritans (Judah—Ephraim), the image of the harvest and the verb συνάγειν bind our text to accounts of *God's gathering of His scattered people,* when the eschatological age begins. The fact that this is an essential background of our text is confirmed by other passages in Jn, primarily 11:51f.

Jn 11:51f is a clearly defined comment on the part of the evangelist, giving us special insight into his way of thinking.[17] His comment concerns Caiaphas' words   συμφέρει ὑμῖν ἵνα εἷς ἄνθρωπος ἀποθάνῃ ὑπὲρ τοῦ λαοῦ καὶ μὴ ὅλον τὸ ἔθνος ἀπόληται, 11:50, which he understands as a prophetic saying with a profound meaning. His explanation reads: . . . ἐπροφήτευσεν ὅτι ἔμελλεν Ἰησοῦς ἀποθνῄσκειν ὑπὲρ τοῦ ἔθνους, καὶ οὐχ ὑπὲρ τοῦ ἔθνους μόνον ἀλλ' ἵνα   καὶ τὰ τέκνα τοῦ θεοῦ   τὰ διεσκορπισμένα συναγάγῃ εἰς ἕν, 11:51f. It is clear that the vocabulary in the last clause is taken from the account of the gathering in of

---

[12] See above, 2.2, U 3.

[13] Jews and Samaritans are mentioned in the context, for example, in 9:21. There are many connections between Is 9—12 and Jn 3:31—4:54. See, for example, Is 9:1,3; 11:1ff, 11ff, 12:3.

[14] Cf. Mic 2:12; Jer 23:3; 4 Ezra 13:12f, 40—48; Pss Sol 17:28,50; 2 Baruch 77f; Sir 48:10. Further Jewish material in ThWNT, vol. 9, pp. 243f(C. Maurer).

[15] Ezek 37:26ff. The presence of God and his Temple is mentioned several times in these texts. See, for example, Is 27:13; 2 Macc 2:18 and texts on the pilgrimage to Zion, Is 2:3; 60:6, Zech 14:15.

[16] See Str.-B., vol. 4, pp. 902ff.

[17] On the remarks of the narrator, see below 4.1 and 4.2.

God's people.[18] Yet in what way does the evangelist use it? S. Pancaro has shown that Jn here, as in many other passages "plays" with different meanings of words.[19]

In the LXX and the NT λαός is almost always used as a description of Israel, the people of God, while ἔθνος is especially reserved for the Gentile nations.[20] These two words are of very rare occurrence in Jn, except in 11:48—52 only in 18:14 (a repetition of 11:49) and in 18:35. In this last passage and in 11:48 ἔθνος evidently means "the Jewish nation". The great danger, according to Caiaphas, was that the Romans would come and take τὸν τόπον καὶ τὸ ἔθνος. If Jesus were killed—as he seemed to think—the Jews would keep "the place" and "the entire nation" would be preserved. Here we again encounter the "Johannine irony". The reality turned out to be different, which is evident if the clause is considered in the right perspective. Jesus' death resulted in the destruction of "the Temple", 2:13ff; 4:19ff, and a radical change in the status of the Jewish people, discussed mainly in chs. 5—12.

The evangelist allows Caiaphas to use both ὁ λαός and τὸ ἔθνος. When he again quotes him in 18:14 ὁ λαός is also used, but in the commentary in 11:51 we find τὸ ἔθνος where ὁ λαός was previously used. Evidently this, according to the evangelist, is the prophetic feature of Caiaphas' words. He said ὑπὲρ τοῦ λαοῦ, i.e. according to the usage in the LXX and the NT "for the people of God". In fact Jesus died for the benefit of the people of God, 1:29; 6:51; 17:19; 10:11,15; 15:13. Caiaphas is thinking of Israel as God's people, i.e. the nation of Israel, while the evangelist sees in his words the true and new people of God. "At this point the Jews have ceased to be a people and have become a nation like any other nation",[21] in the eyes of the evangelist. In a sense, Jesus did die for the Jewish people, but only insofar as he died for the people of God. This is explained in v. 52. Jesus died in order that the scattered children of God should be gathered into a unit. The expression τὰ τέκνα τοῦ θεοῦ here refers to the same persons as τοῦ λαοῦ previously.[22] Both terms may be used in a double sense: λαός = "the Jews" or "the (new) people of God", and τὰ τέκνα τοῦ θεοῦ = "the Jews of the Dispersion" or "those who believe in Jesus, both Jews and non-Jews from the whole world". Pancaro sums up: "The word λαός is used in a pregnant sense which tends to identify the Christian community with the 'People of God'. The 'children of God', mentioned in John xi 52, are . . . neither the Gentiles nor the Jews of the dispersion as such, but rather: all those (whether Jew of Gentile) who

---

[18] On διασκορπίζειν see K.L. Schmidt in ThWNT, vol. 2, pp. 98ff, Riesenfeld 1956, pp. 142ff, and O. Michel in ThWNT, vol. 7, pp. 419ff.

[19] Pancaro 1969—70, pp. 120ff.

[20] See the examination by Pancaro 1969—70, pp. 116ff.

[21] Pancaro 1969—70, p. 121, quoting Westcott.

[22] I take καί with the verb, as in Jn 12:9.

would be united into this new People by the death of Christ".[23] Thus the evangelist uses the image of the gathering in of Israel transferred to the new Israel.[24] In his comment he is interested in the "change of people", in the fact that the people of God are no longer the Jews, but "all who believe in the name of Jesus", 1:12, all those who "received him". These are to be found throughout the world and now through Jesus' death they are gathered into a unit. We have the same image in Jn 10, but there in terms of sheep and a flock. The narrative and the comments in Jn 9—10 describe how a flock gathered round Jesus. Some of "*his* sheep" come from "this sheepfold", i.e. from Jerusalem-centered Judaism, others from elsewhere, such as the Gerizim faithful.[25] Jn 10 does not refer to *two* flocks, but to sheep from different folds who are united in a single flock.[26] The old ideas of Israel are here transferred, as in 11:51f, to the new people of God as a whole. There is indeed a continuity with the old but the break with the nation of Israel is final.

The image of how God's children are gathered into a unit (a new people of God) may also be glimpsed behind the words in Jn 6:12f; 19:23f and 17:21, and behind the Johannine concept of how Jesus is given followers.[27] Almost all these Bible passages associate the gathering with the death of Jesus. "When I am lifted up from the earth, I will *draw all men* to myself", says Jesus in Jn 12:32. "All men" is here the same as "the children of God" in 11:52. Thus the gathering of the scattered Israel is depicted as a consequence of the glorification of Jesus (of Jesus' "hour"). Jn 21 should also be read in this perspective; the disciples draw in the net—the same verb as in 12:32—which had within it all sorts of fish, 153 of them.[28] Thus we have arrived at a keyword of mission in Jn, namely Jesus' saying in 12:24, which particularly illustrates the word καρπός in our text.[29]

When in Jn 12:12ff the people go out bearing palm branches to welcome Jesus

[23] Pancaro 1969—70, p. 129. The same interpretation in Schnackenburg, Comm., vol. 2, p. 452: "'Kinder Gottes' sind hier die zum Christusglauben Berufenen und Erwählten, die sich durch ihr Hinzukommen zur Gemeinde Jesu dann auch als solche erweisen ... Das Bild der einen Kirche aus Juden und Heiden steigt auf". Brown, Comm., p. 443, on the other hand mentions "the gathering of the Gentiles and their union with Israel".

[24] Cf. "Israel" in Jn which includes all believers. See above, 2.2, U 6, and Pancaro 1969—70, pp. 123ff.

[25] Note *Ephraim* in 11:49—54, which may be an allusion to the Samaritans. See above, 3.2.3.

[26] There is only *one* flock in Jn 10. Against Jeremias ²1959: "Die verstreute Herde der Völker wird durch Gottes Hirten auf dem Zion mit der Herde des Gottesvolkes vereint" (p. 55) and Hofius 1967: "die Sammlung der Heiden zur Herde Israels" (p. 289).

[27] See Braun 1962—63 and also above 2.2, U 6, 3.2.2, 3.3.2, S 3 and 3.4.4. Jn 6 links up with Jn 11:51, Meeks 1967, pp. 91ff.

[28] The figure 153 may have a universal meaning. See Brown, Comm., ad loc.

[29] This passage may be said to be the main text of Åke V. Ström's dissertation from 1944. He gives a survey of different interpretations on pp. 404ff and an analysis on pp. 411ff.

who has just been anointed for his burial, and greet him as "Israel's" king, this provokes a comment by the Pharisees: ἴδε ὁ κόσμος ὀπίσω αὐτοῦ ἀπῆλθεν, v. 19.[30] This is an excellent transition to the scene with "the Greeks"—evidently proselytes faithful to Jerusalem—who wished to "see Jesus", 12:20–36. For the evangelist this picture of how "Greeks" come to Jesus evidently had so strong a theological meaning that he goes over completely to various sayings of Jesus, without concluding the scene.[31]

Jesus' first reaction is a reference to the "hour": ἐλήλυθεν ἡ ὥρα, v. 23. Those who were "to worship" in Jerusalem apparently may not "see Jesus" until Jesus has died and risen again ("been glorified"),[32] which, according to Jn 2:13ff, for example, would mean that a new Temple had come into being. Then Jesus says: ἐὰν μὴ ὁ κόκκος τοῦ σίτου πεσὼν εἰς τὴν γῆν ἀποθάνῃ, αὐτὸς μόνος μένει· ἐὰν δὲ ἀποθάνῃ, πολὺν καρπὸν φέρει,12:24. "Jesu Tod ist notwendig, um reiche Missionsfrucht einzubringen",[33] yes if the mission is to come into existence at all and the gathering of the scattered people of God begin. Κἀγὼ ἐὰν ὑψωθῶ ἐκ τῆς γῆς, πάντας ἑλκύσω πρὸς ἐμαυτόν, v. 32. Unless the grain of wheat dies, it will bear no fruit at all. The saying about the grain of wheat means that from Jesus' death will come the new people of God, the union of God's scattered children, the gathering of the flock, 12:24,32; 11:51f; 10:16ff, and further 7:35; 17:21; 19:23f. For Jn that Jesus "bears fruit" is mission, as is the fact that he "gathers in fruit", "receives wages" 4:36. The last passage then corresponds with sayings such as Jn 6:44, where it is the Father who "draws" those who come to Jesus. Jesus' disciples (the true people of God) are a gift from God.[34]

Apart from 12:24 and 4:36, the word καρπός only occurs in Jn in the figurative discourse on the vine and the branches, 15:2, 4, 5, 8, 16. The phrase is here always the same as in 12:24 (καρπὸν φέρειν). Borig tried to prove that the expression here "to bear fruit" cannot in any passage mean "Missionsfrucht" but only "religiös-sittlicher Tat", yet he does so by strongly asserting the idea of the people of God. In ch. 15 "geht es um das *neue Bundesvolk*, um seine Wesensstruktur und um sein Grundgesetz". To "bear fruit" is "die treue Bewährung als Bundesvolk".[35] Thus he has in fact also said that the mission is included in this text since, as we saw, it is very closely related to the idea of the people of God in Jn. The wording of 15:16 with its clear reference to 15:7f, and with

---

[30] The note is similar to that in Jn 4:1; see 3.2.2. Jn 12:19; 7:35f and 11:51f, according to Bultmann, Comm., ad Jn 12:19, are unconscious prophecies of Jesus as "the Saviour of the world".

[31] Brown, Comm., ad loc.

[32] Ström 1944, p. 412, gives the section the headline "Jesus dies to gather the scattered children of God".

[33] Schnackenburg, Comm., ad loc. For further analysis of this verse, I refer to the latest commentaries.

[34] See below 3.4.4 and the references there.

[35] Borig 1967, pp. 237ff. The quotations are from p. 246.

such parallels as 14:13; 17:22; 12:28 and 13:31f, means that we must see here a saying which also covers *Jesus' continued mission through his disciples*. I cannot analyse the text here but must refer to the arguments in Thüsing, Brown and Lindars.[36] The continuation in 15:18ff shows that the reference is to the disciples' mission in a Jewish environment.

Thus the mission in Jn is the work of the Father, the Son and the disciples, which also emerges clearly in Jn 17.[37] All three parties are involved in "the drawing", 6:44; 12:32 and 21:6, 11. This is also suggested in 15:16:

> And I appointed *you* to go and bear fruit—fruit that will remain—so that *the Father* will give you whatever you ask Him in *my* name.

In the related phrase in 14:13 it is *Jesus* who does that which *they* ask and *the Father* is glorified in the Son.

Summary: The mission in Jn may be best described as the gathering of the people of God, who are dispersed throughout the world. Here we do not have the usual question of Gentile mission, but in that some received Jesus as the Messiah, the Son of God, the people of the new covenant existed and had already according to the promises in the OT, a universal character. The mission is a result of Jesus' death, and thus possible only when Jesus is glorified. Then begins the gathering in of "God's scattered children", the calling and uniting of Jesus' "own sheep" into a flock. Jesus as reaper (the disciples) "receives wages" and "gathers fruit". The harvest motif and the gathering of the Israel of the dispersion are mentioned together in the OT and seem to be present together in Mt and Lk too. Several passages in the OT texts refer to a union of Judah and Ephraim, when God's gathering begins. The dissension and the hatred which existed between these two parts of the old people of Israel will vanish. Since the thought of the people of God is so stronlgy characteristic of the idea of mission in Jn, it is by no means improbable that this image of the union of Judah and Ephraim influenced his account of the gathering of the new people of God. As regards the rise of this people of God, Jn is zealous to emphasize the continuity: the new Israel is born from the old, the *new* Israel is the *true* Israel, which has existed through all ages. A genuine and true belief within the framwork of the old covenant merges naturally into a belief in Jesus as the Messiah, the Son of God.[38] The question is whether Jn envisaged a similar fusion, when Samaritans were integrated into the new people of God.

[36] Thüsing [2]1970, pp. 111ff, Brown and Lindars, Comm., ad loc.
[37] See Olsson [2]1973, pp. 260ff.
[38] See above, 2.4.4.

3.5 The Message of the Text

This section need not be extensive. I have already (2.4.1, 2.4.2) described what I mean by the message of the text, and how this can be established by textual and non-textual criteria. Moreover, in sections 3.2.6, 3.3.5 and 3.4.5 I gave preliminary summaries of my subsidiary analyses of Jn 4, and in excursus discussed concepts having some claim to relevance for the interpretation of the Samaria text, those on The Well with Springing Water in 3.2.7, on The Living Water in 3.3.6, on The Harvest and the Gathering In of the Scattered Israel in 3.4.6.

The same themes recur to a great extent in the three summaries: a characteristic Johannine form in the composition and the dialogue technique, the central role of the Samaritans, and what I have called the *ergon* aspect in the text. Any interpretation of the Samaria narrative as a whole must do justice to such textual characteristics as the well constructed literary form which binds the text into a unit, and there especially the relationship between the two dialogues in the text, the strongly positive interest devoted to the Samaritans in the text (topography, doctrine, history, belief in Jesus) and the aspects which emerge from the opening verses and the context (on how Jesus wins disciples, on the relationship between John the Baptist and Jesus, on the Samaritans and the Galileans *contra* "the Jews") and from such concepts as "the gift of God", "to worship the Father in spirit and truth", "to do the will of Him who sent me and to accomplish His work" and "to receive wages and gather fruit for eternal life". As in 2.4, I first determine the general character of the text and then decide on its message (3.5.1), and finally again return to the question of text type (3.5.2).

3.5.1 An Interpretation of the Text as a Whole

It is possible to read Jn 4:1—42 psychologically and biographically as a continuous narrative of an event in Jesus' earthly ministry. This applies not least to the meeting between Jesus and the woman at the well. The various speeches can then be understood as a pastoral dialogue, which displays Jesus' psychological perception, or they may, for example, be regarded as a part of a more commonplace conversation, in which, at first, the woman does not seem really to take the stranger seriously, but is making fun of him. Her request for water is only a way of showing that he does not possess the miraculous water of which he speaks. When her private life is disclosed, her tone becomes more serious and she begins to touch on religious matters. The stranger reveals his identity and, in shock, she then leaves her jar and her errand to tell the news to her acquaintances.

Thus the incident narrated carries the stamp of probability, although the second series of events, with the disciples and Jesus, does not appear to be equally true to life, nor does the conclusion of the narrative, on how the Samaritans came to belief in Jesus (see 3.2.5). At the same time, there are features in the text which give a different impression. The narrative is strongly stylized throughout, wholly coloured by the Johannine style (3.2.6, A, 3.3.5, C and 3.4.5, A and B). Even the Samaritans speak in "Johannine" terms (3.2.1, E 32). The two scene composition is well constructed and the misunderstanding technique is used three times (vv. 7ff, 16ff and 31ff). This sophisticated literary design of the narrative at least brings up the question of whether or not the narrator had other intentions than that of reproducing an event from Jesus' lifetime. The picture of Jesus is reduced to some basic traits, which may be interpreted from the prologue in Jn. Jesus/the Word came, stayed a while, spoke (revealed the Father) and won disciples (3.2.5). The geographical data and the formulations in the opening verses are best explained from some aspects of the history of salvation (3.2.3). "The woman from Samaria" acts as a mouthpiece for Samaritan faith, a circumstance which partly sets her apart from reality, and the text refers to Samaritan conditions in a way which makes the Samaritans and their faith an essential theme of the text (3.2.6, B, 3.3.5, B and 3.4.5, D). The speeches also reflect a shift of the situation from Jesus' time to that of the evangelist (temporal and personal references, 3.3.2, S 11, and 3.4.2, S 4), as do a series of terms belonging to the time after Jesus' "hour" (the gift of God, worship the Father in spirit and truth, the harvest etc., 3 3.2, S 3 and S 11, 3.3.5, D, 3.4.5, C and 3.4.6). Certain expressions also bring out special concepts of the Well in Israel's earlier history (3.2.7), of the gathering in of the scattered people of God (3.4.6) or of the Living Water, which will flow from the Temple in the eschatological age (3.3.6). These references to more than one situation, to Johannine ideas and formulations and to OT texts in Jewish interpretation suggest that here, as in the Cana narrative, we have *a symbolic narrative text*—with two dialogues—i.e. a narrative which seeks to pass on a message which is above and beyond the events described (see 2.4). We have *two levels* in the text, a narrative level and a "symbolical" level; the latter appears to have shaped the text as a whole The question then arises of what is the real object of the narrative. What is the author trying to say in his account of Jesus, the woman, the disciples and the Samaritans?

It is natural to assume that a text in Jn deals *with Jesus Christ*, as he is presented at the beginning and at the end of the Gospel (1:1—18; 20:30f). This general assumption may also be made concerning the Samaria narrative. It has a Christological theme, *sensu lato*, as the majority of recent commentaries maintain (see 3.1). Yet at once I wish to define this theme more precisely: the Samaria text deals *with Jesus' ergon*, i.e. Jesus' work in all its scope, covering both the time before and the time after Jesus' "hour", and bound to the work of God and of the disciples (see 2.2, U 27, U 29 and 2.4.2). The accuracy of this assessment emerges in several features of the text. The disciples are represented as unable to understand the events described (see 3.2.5 and 3.4.1). Jesus then reveals to them what is happening, vv. 31—38, referring in the first place to the *ergon* entrusted to him, v. 34. It is in fact the Father's work but realized and completed by the Son. He "eats the food" the Father has given him. The completion of this work involves the events of the "hour" and its consequences: Jesus' *ergon* in v. 34 thus includes both the time before Jesus' "hour" and the "hour" itself (3.4.2,S4,3,4,5,C). Indeed the very text says that the subject of the narrative is Jesus' *ergon*. The variation in the temporal and personal references in the longest speech in the first and in the second dialogue confirm that this is the case (3.3.2, S 11, 3.4.2, S 4). The shared work of the Father and the Son is seen in the perspective of "the hour" and then includes also the narrator's own time. The text contains both an ἔτι and an ἤδη, both ἔρχεται ὥρα and καὶ νῦν ἐστιν, referring to the time before and after Jesus' "hour". The theme of Jesus' *ergon* is also manifested in the concepts already mentioned, such as "the gift of God", "worship the Father in spirit and truth", "revelation of all things", "gathering in of the harvest", etc. (3.3.2, S 3, S 11, S 12–13, 3.4.2, S 4). The very manner of describing Jesus' journeys in the text and in its context is also explained from an *ergon* perspective, which may indeed include an isolated journey in Jesus' lifetime, the wandering of the Divine Word through the world and also Christ's "path of mission", i.e. of those who believe in him (3.2.3, 3.2.6, C). It is difficult to say whether or not the temporal data, "at the sixth hour" and "two days" are part of this context (3.2.2). Nevertheless this apart, the *ergon* perspective explains a long series of peculiarities in the text.

The context confirms that the narrator has Jesus' *ergon* in mind. In 3:31—36 he displays Jesus as the Divine Revealer, as the Prophet who speaks the work of God, being filled with the Spirit, and shows that Jesus' *ergon* leads to his attraction of disciples. The latter emerges the more strongly in 3:22ff and 4:43ff. We find here the same theme as in the Cana narrative: Jesus' *ergon* includes the creation of a "new" people of God. The Father gives people to the Son, Jesus gains many disciples, the Prophet is accepted in Galilee. The bridegroom wins his bride and John the Baptist rejoices, 3:29f (3.2.2).

We may arrive at a more precise definition of the theme of the Samaria narrative by establishing that it deals *with Jesus' ergon and the Samaritans*. In all three summaries (3.2.6, 3.3.5, 3.4.5), I could establish that the Samaria text clearly focuses on Jesus and the Samaritans. I need not record here the many features in the context which confirm this theory: the detailed description of the site, the interest in Jacob and his sons, the fixation on God's gift and the well, the mention of the Temple cult (Miškan) and the prophet who will reveal all things, the *double entendre* in the expression "the five men", the portrayal of the woman as a representative of the Samaritans, the reaping of the harvest of Samaritans and the magnificent closing scene, when the Samaritans confess their belief in Jesus. From these qualities in the text, we must conclude that the narrator is not

thinking primarily of Jesus and a private individual(s) or of Christ the Revealer
and Mankind in general, but of Jesus and the Samaritans, of how the revelation
of Christ comes face to face with the Samaritan faith, of how Jesus' *ergon* means
that Samaritans flock to him and are incorporated in the new people of God.

To me, these more general formulations of the message of the text appear easy
to justify from the qualities of the text mentioned above. The Samaria text tells of
the role of the Samaritans in the birth of the people of the new covenant, in the
following often called the new people of God. *Jesus' ergon involves a revelation of
Christ to the Samaritans and an incorporation of the Samaritans in the new people of God.*

One aspect of this incorporation is clearly marked in the closing verses (3.2.5)
which, in a Johannine context, are best understood from 1:19ff (see 2.4). We
have a double incentive to the belief in Christ: first a testimony about Jesus, and
then a meeting with him. The woman is clearly portrayed in the text as a *witness*
(see 3.2.1, E 23), her role being similar to that of John the Baptist, Andrew and
Philip in 1:19ff. John the Baptist repudiates all "Messianic" titles, and points to
Jesus, Andrew bears witness that Jesus is the Messiah, Philip that Jesus is the one
described by Moses and the prophets. The woman also wonders whether Jesus is
the Messiah, in the sense attributed to the title in v. 25: he who will reveal all
things. Thus she associates Jesus with Samaritan belief, and presumably *denotes
the continuity between the old and the new*. In the dialogue, she has confessed her
Samaritan faith and Jesus faces her with his revelation, just when she admits her
belief in the "Messiah", vv. 25f. As a result she bears witness to the Samaritans
of Jesus as the Saviour whom they await (3.3.4, C). The Samaritans' belief
because of the woman's testimony is thus a belief that Jesus is he who, according
to their traditional faith, will come to proclaim all things and restore the true
worship. In this situation the attribute of being a true Samaritan means being one
who believes in Christ. Thus the woman's role in the text, according to the
narrator, appears to be to show, as receiver of the revelation of Christ, the continuity between the old and the new people of God. Jesus' *ergon* resulted in a *new*
people of God, but this people was at the same time the *genuine* and *true* Israel,
including both Judah and Ephraim, with whom God had made a covenant in ancient times. According to the narrator, the obedience to God in His old covenant
and the obedience to the revelation of Christ is one and the same for both Jews
and Samaritans, and his message in the text could be worded as follows: *Jesus'
ergon means that "true" Samaritans, on meeting the divine revelation in Jesus
Christ, are included in the new people of God.* Or we can divide up the message
into three points:

that Jesus' *ergon* involves a revelation of Christ to the Samaritans. (The
meeting between the Revelation and Samaritan belief is described primarily in the
first dialogue and is further mediated by the woman's testimony).

that "true" Samaritans, in the narrator's opinion, find in the revelation of Christ a fulfilment of their longing and their faith. (This is marked by the fact that they believe in Jesus because of the woman's testimony).

that Jesus' *ergon* means a gathering in of the new people of God, to which even Samaritans belong. (This is emphasized in the second dialogue and confirmed by the full confession in the concluding verse.)

According to the narrator, the disciples need instruction on these three points, especially the last. Judging by the composition of the text, the subject of Jesus' teaching in vv. 35—38 is indeed *the coming of the Samaritans to Jesus because of the woman's testimony.* Bearing in mind the transferred meaning of the text, it is difficult to read the passage except as meaning that the disciples object to the meeting between Jesus and the Samaritans, and wish to protest at the inclusion of the Samaritans in the new people of God. Their reason could, according to v. 35, be that the time is not yet ripe. As we saw, Jesus' words mean an emphasis on the fact that the final harvest and the gathering in of the scattered people of God is at hand (3.4.2, S 4). In the text, Jesus gathers Samaritans, and this is by the will of God. Indeed it is God who gives him this "wages".

Thus the justification for the participation of the Samaritans in the people of God is very strong. Perhaps the last verse of Jesus' teaching should also be read as evidence that it is God's will for Samaritans to be gathered in. The text reads: "I sent you to reap that for which you did not labour; others have laboured, and you have entered into their labour" (v. 38). This verse was omitted from my earlier attempts to determine the message of the text. My conclusions are not refuted by this verse but give no definite interpretation of the "others" who are mentioned here. It is not easy to arrive at a final opinion on this point. What I say here is an attempt to reiterate the alternatives in the light of my earlier conclusions, but the result does not possess the same degree of probability as the previous one.

The content of vv. 34—38 and its connection with the text in general may be discerned from the table on the following page. The temporal frame with Jesus' "hour" in the centre and the relationship between the work of the Father, the Son and the Spirit (the Paraclete) are given by the Gospel in general (see 2.2, U 9c, U 27 and U 29, 2.3.4, 3.3.2, S 3, 3.4.2, S 4a, 4.2 and 4.3). Then the possibility of interpreting the clearly defined temporal references from the dialogues in the text on the basis of Jesus' "hour" arises and is confirmed by the content of the speeches (see 3.3.2, S 5 and S 11, 3.3.3, A, 3.4.2, S 4, 3.4.5, C). The sowing and the labouring belong to the time before Jesus' "hour", the harvest and the rejoicing to the time after, as also suggested by the image used and the choice of words (3.4.2, S 4, 3.4.6). If we also wish to narrow down the relationship between Jesus' "food" and Jesus' "work of harvest", it is most natural to refer the former to the earthly Jesus and the latter to the glorified Christ (3.4.5, C, 3.4.6). Then come the

The time before	Jesus' "hour"	the time after

The Father   at work

     The Son   at work

              The Spirit at work

Sowing	*Reaping*
Labour	*Rejoicing*
(the earthly Jesus)	(the glorified Jesus)
Jesus'	Jesus receives wages,
food	gathers fruit
Others: "the woman"	The disciples
John the Baptist	
(the Hellenists)	
The old covenant	The new covenant
The "old" people of God	The "new" people of God
Jacob's well (the Well)	Jesus' "belly" (Jn 7:38)
	(Jesus' death, 19:30,34)
Running water	Life-giving water
Baptism in water	Baptism in the Spirit
Revelation through Moses	Revelation through Jesus
(the first Prophet	(the second Prophet)
To worship God on Gerizim	To worship the Father in spirit
(and in Jerusalem)	and truth
Hatred between Judah and	Union of Jews and Samaritans
Ephraim	
Dispersion on the people	Gathering in of the people
of God	of God

difficulties with the "others" in the text.

Indeed if we read v. 38 within its immediate context, which is the alternative to be tested first, only the woman appears. She may be said to be at work before the disciples: she bears witness to Jesus and leads the Samaritans to him. Previously she was designated as a representative of Samaritan faith in an encounter with the divine revelation in Christ (3.3.5). I have earlier interpreted her role in parallel with "the witnesses" in 1:19ff. If she is regarded as representative of the old people of God—in this case the Samaritan people—the verb "to labour" is appropriate. If the woman only is referred to as the "others", she should here be seen as symbolizing all God's labourers among the Samaritan people who worked before Jesus' "hour", i.e. within the framework of the old covenant. This is possible but difficult to prove. If we accept this reading of the text, v. 38 would provide further reason for the disciples to allow Samaritans to be incorporated in the new people of God. God has previously worked among them, and obedience to God in the Samaritan faith involves an obedience to the revelation of Christ.

If we read v. 38 from 3:22ff, which proved to have much in common with our text (see 3.2.2, 3.3.4, D and 3.4.4), John the Baptist (and possibly his disciples) emerge as those who worked before Jesus' disciples (Jesus and his disciples) in Samaria, at Aenon, near Salim (see 3.2.2).[39] The group of followers round John decreases while that round Jesus increases and this is, by John's testimony, the will and work of God. His task is merely to go before, as "best man" to lead the bride to the groom. Now when Jesus (Jesus' disciples) harvests people, he rejoices.

If we read v. 38 in the light of the *ergon* perspective, which clearly exists in our text, covering both the phases in Jesus' work, "others" may refer to Philip (and "Hellenists") who, according to Acts 8, worked before the Twelve in Samaria.[40] Indeed this chapter in Acts shows how Samaritans are integrated into the new people of God. In this case, the verb "to labour" is less appropriate, having been previously associated with the conditions within the framework of the old covenant. Yet the problem is whether this verse in Jn 4 carries but one reference. There appears to be reason to include "the woman", John the Baptist and Philip. Possibly the narrator had all three in mind. The problem is closely related to our definition of the character of the text. May an element have more than one function? We have several examples of such a circumstance. Since the immediate context points out God's worker among the Samaritans within the framework of the old covenant ("the woman"), the important introduction in 3:22ff speaks equally strongly in favour of John the Baptist and the *ergon* aspect pervading the text, with its inclusion of the history of the first Christians, indicates Philip, I suggest that all three are intended at the end of the text. The disciples were then taught not only that Samaritans are to be included in the new people of God but also that John the Baptist prepared the ground even in Samaria, and that the work of mission performed there by Philip (and "Hellenists") was a work of God before them.

This interpretation of Jn 4:1—42 is supported by my interpretation of the Cana narrative above (2.4.2). In both cases we have a general theme: *how the new people of God was born from the old* (see 2.4.2). In my analyses above, I noted many similarities between Jn 1:19—2:11 and 3:22—4:54: the pattern of journeys from Judea to Cana in Galilee, (3.2.3), the comparison between Jesus and John the Baptist (3.2.2), the theme of how Jesus is given people (3.2.2 , 3.2.6, C, 3.4.5, D),

---

[39] For this interpretation, see especially Robinson 1959 and Boismard 1973, pp. 227ff.
[40] For this interpretation, see especially Cullmann 1966, pp. 232ff.

purification and baptism in water *contra* worship of the Father in spirit and truth and acceptance of Jesus' water etc. Here I cannot refrain from referring once more to Is 11:11—13 (see 2.2 , U 3, 2.4.4):

> In that day the Lord will extend his hand yet *a second time* to *acquire* the remnant which is left of his people ... Ephraim shall not be jealous of Judah, and Judah shall not harass Ephraim.

The text is of vital importance, considering the concept of the gathering in of the scattered Israel, on which the idea of mission in Jn is based (see 3.4.6). According to Jn, the founding of the new people of God took place in 2:1—11, with the *first* miracle at *Cana*. By my interpretation of Jn 4:1—42, the gathering of the scattered Israel occurred on the *second* journey to *Cana* in Galilee. Jews and Samaritans are united in the harvest which began in and with Jesus' "hour". The question asks itself: Did Is 11:11 govern the structure of Jn 1:19—4:54?[41] The common theme of this part of Jn may be seen as justifying this theory, apart from the special reference to "a second time" and the use of the verb *qanah* "acquire, recover" in the Bible text. Nevertheless my analysis was only concerned with 2:1—11 and 4:1—42, not with 1:19—4:54.

3.5.2 The Question of Text Type

As I have just shown, the Samaria text as a whole has a message which is on a different level from the events narrated. These events and the speeches are part of a teaching on Jesus' *ergon* and its consequences. There are also a number of individual details which suggest a meaning other than that which is natural on the narrative level, or allude to special concepts such as: $\ddot{\epsilon}\gamma\nu\omega, \kappa\acute{\nu}\rho\iota\sigma\varsigma, \dot{\alpha}\varphi\tilde{\eta}\kappa\epsilon\nu,$ $\ddot{\epsilon}\delta\epsilon\iota, \kappa\epsilon\kappa\sigma\pi\iota\alpha\kappa\acute{\omega}\varsigma$ (?), $\ddot{\omega}\rho\alpha\ \tilde{\eta}\nu\ \dot{\omega}\varsigma\ \ddot{\epsilon}\kappa\tau\eta, \delta\acute{\sigma}\varsigma\ \mu\sigma\iota\ \pi\epsilon\tilde{\iota}\nu, \tau\dot{\eta}\nu\ \delta\omega\rho\epsilon\grave{\alpha}\nu\ \tau\sigma\tilde{\nu}\ \vartheta\epsilon\sigma\tilde{\nu}, \ddot{\upsilon}\delta\omega\rho$ $\zeta\tilde{\omega}\nu, \tau\grave{\sigma}\ \varphi\rho\acute{\epsilon}\alpha\rho, \pi\eta\gamma\grave{\eta}\ \ddot{\upsilon}\delta\alpha\tau\sigma\varsigma\ \dot{\alpha}\lambda\lambda\sigma\mu\acute{\epsilon}\nu\sigma\upsilon, \pi\acute{\epsilon}\nu\tau\epsilon\ \ddot{\alpha}\nu\delta\rho\alpha\varsigma, \pi\rho\sigma\sigma\kappa\upsilon\nu\acute{\eta}\sigma\epsilon\tau\epsilon\ \tau\tilde{\omega}\ \pi\alpha\tau\rho\acute{\iota},$ $\dot{\epsilon}\nu\ \pi\nu\epsilon\acute{\upsilon}\mu\alpha\tau\iota\ \kappa\alpha\grave{\iota}\ \dot{\alpha}\lambda\eta\vartheta\epsilon\acute{\iota}\alpha, \dot{\alpha}\nu\alpha\gamma\gamma\epsilon\lambda\epsilon\tilde{\iota}\ \ddot{\alpha}\pi\alpha\nu\tau\alpha, \dot{\epsilon}\gamma\acute{\omega}\ \epsilon\dot{\iota}\mu\iota, \dot{\epsilon}\vartheta\alpha\acute{\upsilon}\mu\alpha\zeta\sigma\nu, \beta\rho\tilde{\omega}\sigma\iota\nu, \tau\epsilon\lambda\epsilon\iota$ $\omega\sigma\omega\ \alpha\dot{\upsilon}\tau\sigma\tilde{\upsilon}\ \tau\grave{\sigma}\ \ddot{\epsilon}\rho\gamma\sigma\nu, \vartheta\epsilon\rho\iota\sigma\mu\acute{\sigma}\varsigma, \mu\iota\sigma\vartheta\grave{\sigma}\nu\ \lambda\alpha\mu\beta\acute{\alpha}\nu\epsilon\iota, \sigma\upsilon\nu\acute{\alpha}\gamma\epsilon\iota\ \kappa\alpha\rho\pi\acute{\sigma}\nu, \dot{\alpha}\kappa\eta\kappa\acute{\sigma}\alpha\mu\epsilon\nu,$ $\sigma\ddot{\iota}\delta\alpha\mu\epsilon\nu, \dot{\sigma}\ \sigma\omega\tau\dot{\eta}\rho\ \tau\sigma\tilde{\nu}\ \kappa\acute{\sigma}\sigma\mu\sigma\upsilon.$

Some of these phrases refer to specifically Johannine concepts and are then part of the total portrait of Jesus in the Gospel, which is most clearly visible in what I have called the *ergon* perspective. Others are reminiscent of the concept of the Well and the narratives in Gen 29 and Ex 2:15ff, while still others recall the harvest and the gathering in of the scattered Israel. In $\mu\iota\sigma\vartheta\grave{\sigma}\nu\ \lambda\alpha\mu\beta\acute{\alpha}\nu\epsilon\iota$ and $\sigma\upsilon\nu$-$\acute{\alpha}\gamma\epsilon\iota\ \kappa\alpha\rho\pi\acute{\sigma}\nu,$ for instance, in v. 36, there is a fusion of expressions on the narrative level (ordinary harvesting), on the concept of the gathering in of the scattered Israel and on the Johannine idea of "mission" as a consequence of

---

[41] "OT texts which are sometimes alluded to in a NT passage only as an isolated word or phrase may nonetheless figure decisively in the ordering and structuring of NT material of disparate origin and form", Miller 1971, p. 61.

Jesus' death (see 3.4.2, S 4b, 3.4.6). The various elements appear to be interwoven within one another, and, in general, the Samaria text may be described as sounding more like a simple narrative than the brief and cryptic Cana text. Yet it is possible to describe the two texts similarly as *a symbolic narrative with many allusive elements* (2.4.5) with the difference that we have embedded in Jn 4 two longer dialogues, and that the allusive elements, relatively speaking, are not as numerous. The latter difference and the, thereby, more continuous character of the Samaria narrative pose the question of whether or not it would be better to describe the text as *a strongly "screened" text,* i.e. in his account of a Jesus event the narrator is dependent on a complex of screens which, whether he was aware of it or not, influenced his choice of material, in that he adds certain details and arranges the whole into a continuous narrative. In Jn 4 several screens appear to be included in the screen which influenced the text as a whole: a basic *ergon* screen, which includes a total concept of Jesus and his work and makes it possible to oscillate between the time before and the time after Jesus' "hour", a *Well screen,* which is part of the concept of the Well (see 3.2.7) and explains the similarities to the scenes in Gen 29 and Ex 2:15ff, and finally even the idea of *the gathering in of the people of God.* Nevertheless the latter is not as clear as a screen in that this concept is at the same time part of the Johannine idea of mission. Such a description of the text type has the advantage that it better explains the simultaneously symbolic and narrative character of the text without needing to point out specific details as symbolic or allusive, a procedure which leads at times to the belief that in Jn we have allegories, in the common sense of the word. I shall return to the problem of text type in the last chapter.

4

The Interpretative Character of the Text and the Paraclete

The analyses of Jn 2:1—11 and 4:1—42 above show that several elements of the text have an interpretative function, i.e. at the same time as they are more or less natural links in the narrative itself, and in that which is narrated, they have a form and/or a content which, at least to the initiated reader, reveals a "more profound" meaning in the text, a meaning which I previously asserted (2.4 and 3.5) to be the most essential and that which created the structure of the text as a whole. Both texts possess what I have called the *ergon*-perspective: a section in Jesus' earthly life is seen and narrated in the context of Jesus' work as a whole, which includes both the time before and the time after Jesus' "hour". This general *ergon* screen, with the Johannine vocabulary which is related to it, is combined with other concepts which have also functioned more or less as screens, in Jn 2 primarily the Sinai screen, in Jn 4 Jewish traditions about the Well and the gathering in of the scattered Israel (2.4 and 3.5). I am thinking especially of the elements in the text which are connected with these "screens" when I refer to the interpretative character of the text.

4.1 Interpretative Elements in Jn

In saying that the text of Jn has a clear interpretative character I have already begun to answer one of the main questions I asked in the introduction. How are we to characterize Johannine text as such? In sections 2.4.5 and 3.5.2 I gave preliminary answers to this *question of text type*: I tried to characterize the first text as a symbolic narrative text with many allusive elements, a definition which I combined with another for the second text: a strongly "screened" text. I shall return to this problem in the last chapter.

To answer the question of the Johannine text type, I chose in this investigation to analyse two texts *in their entirety,* insofar as this is possible, and thereby to apply a number of insights we have into texts in general (1.2). There is a temptation to try another means: from the question of text type to analyse certain elements in Jn, occasionally remarkable in form, which have, or may have, an interpretative function. The earlier analysis indicated several such elements, for example the temporal references in 1:19ff, and particularly that in 2:1, possibly also the mention of places in this text, the parenthetical remark about the vessels in 2:6, the narrator's comment in 2:11, the longer section in 3:31—36 and a number of terms such as $\dot{\eta}$ ὥρα μου, σημεῖον, δόξα, ἡ δωρεὰ τοῦ θεοῦ, ἔργον. Only on one or two occasions, in connection with an interpretative element in the Cana narrative or the Samaria text, have I been able to analyse this in the entire Gospel. The following elements are worthy of a thorough examination, in the context of the problem of the Johannine type of text.

1. *Longer discourses,* for example 3:16—21 and 3:31—36. By describing these sections as "das johanneische Kerygma" and "Rückblick auf das einmalige grosse Geschehen, von dem er berichtet, und Hinblick auf die Menschen, für die er schreibt, Geschichtsdeutung und gegenwärtige Anrede, Zeugnis und Kerygma",[1] Schnackenburg has also admitted that in these sections we are particularly close to the author. In the interpretation of the Johannine texts, as we now have them, the insights into the narrator's "horizon" given by these "comments" must be of great importance, and I have also tried to use 3:31—36 to understand the Samaria text. The introduction to the entire Gospel, 1:1—18, and the teaching given in 5:19—47; 10:1—18; 12:44—50; 13:31—17:26 are of similar character. The longer discourses in chs. 6—8 are more in the nature of dialogue.

2. *The Johannine dialogues* with their special literary features: use of ambiguous words and phrases, "Johannine irony", shifts in perspective, the form of the speeches with alternating temporal and personal references etc.[2] "The misunderstanding technique" is very common in Jn.[3]

3. *Remarks by the author.* There are many such, clearly marked in the text, as emerges from the survey below (4.2). In these passages we know that the author is addressing his "readers", i.e. the text here is worded on the basis of the act of communication, contemporary with the author, or the acts of communication, if we assume a number of situations when these "notes" were written.

4. *Individual concrete details,* which at certain points may give the text a high degree of lucidity, but at the same time, by their form, quantity and distribution in the text, often bring about a striking ambiguity in the actual course of events.[4] This applies to certain chronological and topographical data,[5] and sometimes also to details of the description of the situation or of events. These parts of the text may function as a piece of the historical

---

[1] Schnackenburg, Comm., p. 393. Note on the same page: "Man kann sagen, dass in ihr die tragenden Aussagen des Joh Ev und der joh. Theologie zusammengedrängt sind".

[2] See my analysis of Jn 4 above, especially 3.3.2, S 3 and S 11, 3.3.3, E, 3.3.5, 3.4.2, S 2 and S 3, 3.4.3 and 3.4.5. There seem to be examples of this Johannine "dialogue technique" also in Jn 2:1—11, although we have no real dialogues there. See, for example, 2.2, U 9 and U 26.

[3] See 2:18—21; 3:4; 4:10—12, 15, 33f; 6:5—9, 14f, 41f, 52f; 7:27f, 35; 8:22f, 33f, 39f, 57; 11:24 and the analyses in Leroy 1968 and Wead 1970.

[4] Gyllenberg 1960, 1965 and 1967. Rissi 1967, p. 77, mentions "die auffallend grosse Zahl von konkretesten Einzelzügen, die den Evangelisten als den bestinformierten Zeugen der Geschehnisse erscheinen lassen, in Wahrheit aber alle Spuren historischer Unwahrscheinlichkeit an sich tragen." He refers to Fr. Overbeck who called this feature "unhistorischen Idealismus". A different view is expressed in Stauffer's article "Historische Elemente im vierten Evangelium" (1960).

[5] Cf. my comments above (2.2) on U 1, U 2, U 3 and U 9c, and my analyses in 2.3.4, 3.2.3 and 3.2.4.

reality which is described *or* merely as interpretative elements on the part of the author *or* have both functions, a possibility which is often forgotten in the Johannine analysis.[6]

5. *Certain words and concepts* from the Johannine vocabulary—the special Johannine language—perhaps primarily ambiguous expressions[7] and certain gnoseological terms.[8] By means of an analysis of these latter terms, and with the help of hermeneutic concepts from H.G. Gadamer, Franz Mussner tried to arrive at a description of the features typical of Johannine writing.[9] His results, which are also based on investigations by Thüsing and Blank,[10] have a great deal in common with my own conclusions in my analysis of the texts as a whole. According to Mussner we must in Jn assume a special way of seeing, "die johanneische Sehweise", which has influenced the formulation of the text. "Der johanneische Sehakt", he says, "ermöglicht einen kerygmatischen Transpositionsprozess", which covers both Jesus' words and Jesus' works. "Das epiphan verstandene Christusereignis wird bei Johannes im kerygmatischen Umsetzungsprozess zum 'epiphan' formulierten, evangelischen 'Zeugnis' ".[11] Just by the Johannine language "spricht Jesus so, dass das was sich in seinem Wort und Werk für den apostolischen Sehakt 'gezeigt' hat, für die Kirche bewahrt bleibt".[12] Yet one of the difficulties inherent in a separate analysis of Johannine vocabulary based on the problem of text type, however, is the integral character usually possessed by the Johannine terms in the Johannine account.

6. *Larger structures* in the text, for example the structure of 2:1–11, of 1:19–2:11, of 1:19–4:54, or of the whole Gospel. Here however it is still more difficult to find definite criteria in the analysis.[13] The many cross-references in Jn are well defined elements for an analysis of the structure of the Gospel as a whole.

An analysis of these linguistic elements, which are listed under points 1–6, elements understood *sensu lato,* would call for a number of separate investigations. Yet an analysis of the Cana narrative and the Samaria text, like the Johannine interpretation history,[14] already show that a determination of the meaning and function of these elements is essential for a final determination of the Johannine text type. The list here is primarily intended to suggest the interpretative character seemingly inherent in the whole of the Johannine text and not merely Jn 2:1–11 and 4:1–42.

[6] Examples of interesting details in 1:48; 2:1, 6, 9, 14f; 3:2, 23; 4:2, 5f; 6:4, 12f; 11:54; 12:1, 12f, etc. and especially in the Passion narrative, chs. 18–19.

[7] See Cullmann 1966, pp. 176ff ("Der johanneische Gebrauch doppeldeutiger Ausdrücke als Schlüssel zum Verständnis des vierten Evangeliums", an article published for the first time in 1948) and Wead 1970.

[8] Such words as ὁρᾶν, ϑεωρεῖν, ϑεᾶσϑαι, βλέπειν, ἀκούειν, γινώσκειν, οἰδέναι, μαρτυρεῖν, μιμνήσκεσϑαι, μνημονεύειν, ὑπομιμνήσκειν.

[9] "Die johanneische Sehweise und die Frage nach dem historischen Jesus" (Freiburg im Breisgau 1965). published in French 1969 (Queaestiones Disputatae, vol. 4).

[10] Thüsing ²1970 (the first edition 1960) and Blank 1964.

[11] Mussner 1965, pp. 80, 82.

[12] Mussner 1965, p. 83.

[13] On the structure of Jn as a whole, see the dissertation of Willemse (1965).

[14] See, besides the commentaries, Bacon 1910, pp. 332ff.

4.2 The Remarks of the Narrator

The elements most clearly marked by form in Jn, in which the evangelist himself is speaking are, apart from the prologue, the many remarks,[15] although we can find a series of phrases and sentences where it is difficult to decide whether they should be regarded as remarks or as an integral part of the narrative.[16] In the texts I have discussed, we encountered several obvious remarks.[17] Strangely enough, there is no special work on these "footnotes",[18] although such an investigation could provide valuable information on the structure of the Gospel, on the evangelist's "horizon" and on the situation(s) of the text. In what follows I shall discuss only a few "footnotes", which I regard as especially illuminating as regards the interpretative character of the text.

Remarks appear throughout the Gospel, but are extremely rare in speech sections, which may be considered an indication that the speeches themselves act as interpretative comments by the evangelist, for example 3:16—21, 31—36; 5:19—47; 12:44—50, although there are no formal markings to say that they are author's remarks. The content of these "footnotes" varies widely:[19] translations of words,[20] identification of individuals,[21] data of time, place and customs,[22] summarizing comments,[23] explanations of speeches and events[24] and longer theological expositions as in 12:37ff. There is no definite shape to them. Most usual are clauses with $\gamma\acute{\alpha}\rho$,[25] clauses beginning with $\tau\alpha\tilde{\upsilon}\tau\alpha$ ($\tau o\tilde{\upsilon}\tau o$)[26] and clauses with $\mathring{\eta}\nu$ as the verb.[27] Such expressions as "that the Scriptures/Jesus' words

[15] See 1:28, 38, 39, 40, 41, 42, 44; 2:11, 21f; 3:24; 4:2, 9c, 25, 54; 5:2; 6:1, 6, 39, 64, 71; 7:5, 39, 50; 8: (6), 20, 27; 9:7, 22ff; 10:6; 11:2, 5, 13, 16, 30, 51f; 12:6, 16, 21, 33, 37ff; 13:11, 28; 14:22; 18:2, 5, 9, 13f, 32, 40; 19:13, 17, 35, 36f, 38, 39; 20:9, 16, 24, 30f; 21:2, 14, 19, 20, 23, 24f.

[16] See, for example, 1:23, 24; 2:6, 9, 17, 25; 3:14, 23b; 4:44; 5:9; 6:4, 10, 31; 7:22, 38; 9:8, 14, etc.

[17] 2:11; 4:2, 9c, 54; 7:39; 11:51f and the parenthetical sections in 2:6, 9; 4:8, 45. See above 2.2, U 27, 3.2.5, 3.3.6 and 3.4.6.

[18] I could only find a short descriptive article by Tenney (1960).

[19] A classification by content in Tenney 1960, with a survey on p. 364.

[20] 1:38, 41, 42; 4:25; 9:7; 19:13, 17; 20:16.

[21] 7:50; 11:2; 18:10, 14, 40.

[22] 4:9; 6:4, 59; 7:2; 8:20; 9:14; 10:22f; 11:18, 30; 19:14, 31, 42. These remarks are often integrated in the narrative.

[23] 2:11; 4:54; 21:14.

[24] 2:9, 25; 4:2; 6:6, 23, 64, 71; 7:5, 39, 50; 11:2, 51; 12:6; 13:11; 19:36; 20:30f; 21:7, 8, 19.

[25] Negative clauses: 4:9; 7:5; 3:24; cf. 11:30; 20:9; 19:36f. Positive clauses: 5:4, 4:8(?).

[26] 1:28; 2:11; 4:54; 6:59; 8:20; 10:6; 12:16; 13:28f; 19:36f; 12:33; 21:19; 7:39; 6:6; 9:22f; 11:51f; 12:6.

[27] See, for example, 11:2; 1:44; 18:40; 21:7; 19:31; 18:13f. Many of these clauses are integrated in the narrative.

252

should be fulfilled",[28] "this he/they said",[29] "he/they knew/did not know",[30] "that is, in translation",[31] are repeated several times. Yet definite formulae for these notes cannot be said to exist. Thus we find that the remarks appear throughout the Gospel, that they deal with many different subjects and that they have no definite form.[32] Their function also, as in the case of the concrete details mentioned above (4.1), seems to vary in nature. This abundance and variety may depend to some extent on the fact that the Johannine text has a long prehistory, and that the notes were added on different occasions. I would, however, regard them primarily as an indication that the Johannine text as a whole has an interpretative character.

The remarks describing the disciples' understanding before and after Jesus' "hour" are of particular importance for the problem of the nature of the Johannine text: 2:21f; 12:16, and also 13:26 and 20:9.[33] 12:12ff tells how the people of Jerusalem go to meet Jesus with palm branches and cries of exultation and how Jesus then mounts a donkey according to Zech 9:9. The comment runs as follows:

> His disciples did not understand (ἔγνωσαν) this at first; but when Jesus was glorified (ἐδοξάσθη), then they remembered (ἐμνήσθησαν) that this had been written of him and that they had done this to him.[34]

The narrator here distinguishes between two periods of time, with Jesus' "hour" as the dividing line.[35] When the events narrated in 12:15f took place, the disciples—according to the narrator—did not understand their meaning. On this point, Jesus' glorification was necessary to allow even Jesus' closest followers to understand him. The understanding is described as a "remembering" (ἐμνήσθησαν), which concerned both *the Scriptures* and *what actually happened*.[36] This formulation refers to the activity of the Paraclete according to 15:26; 16:13f,[37] to the Spirit who was not present (οὐκ ἦν) during the first period, although he was in

---

[28] 19:28, 24b, 36f; 12:37ff; 15:25; 13:18b; 18:9, 32. The related clauses with καθώς may also have the character of remarks, 7:38; 1:23; 6:31; 12:14.

[29] 12:33; 21:19; 11:13; 12:6; 6:71; 7:39; 2:21f; 6:6; 11:51f; 9:22f.

[30] 12:16; 20:9; 13:28f; 6:64; 13:11; 10:6; 2:9.

[31] 1:42; 9:7; 1:38, 41; 20:16; 4:25; 11:16 (= 20:24; 21:2), 19:13, 17.

[32] This fact, like the difficulty of delimiting remarks from the text, indicate that the remarks are an integrated part of the Gospel.

[33] Cf. 6:5ff; 13:7; 16:25ff and passages on the Paraclete which I analyse below (4.3). The we-words in Jn (1:14, 16; 3:11; 4:22), and the many gnoseological terms mentioned above (note 8), may be related to these interpretative remarks.

[34] The agent in the last clause is probably the people.

[35] Cf. 12:23; 13:31f; 17:1ff. We have the same phrase in 7:39.

[36] The first ταῦτα refers to vv. 12—15, the second to vv. 14f, and the third to vv. 12f.

[37] See the analysis below, 4.3.

the second, 7:39. What understanding then did the disciples receive afterwards? In my opinion, the manner of telling and of quoting the Scriptures[38] gives an unequivocal answer to this question: they—like the narrator—see in this event a confirmation of Jesus' universal kingship. Like the crucifixion of the "King of the Jews"—with a *titulus* in the three languages of the day—and the trial before Pontus Pilate—with the discussion of Jesus' kingship—the actions of the people and of Jesus on "the entry" into Jerusalem bear witness to Jesus' true identity. In 12:12ff he is depicted as "a gift of life for people all over the earth, not a sign of rationalistic glory for Israel".[39] The event itself may be interpreted in rationalistic earthly categories, but a right understanding concerns Jesus as the King of Israel (ὁ βασιλεὺς τοῦ Ἰσραήλ, v. 13), namely the new people of God, consisting of believers from all over the world.[40] Here we have the same *double entendre* in Ἰσραήλ as in the word λαός in 11:51f.[41] This deeper meaning, which the disciples first achieved in the age of the Paraclete, must be described as that which decided the structure of the narrator's account of the event. R.E. Brown summarizes: "This narrative has in its order and details been heavily adapted to fit the writer's theological insight".[42] Thus the author's remark in 12:16, and his narrative in 12:12—15, shows: *1*. that the right perspective on this *Jesus event* was first given with Jesus' "glorification", i.e. based on what I previously designated in general as the *ergon*-aspect, *2*. that true understanding came by a "remembering" of certain texts from *the Scriptures* and of *what happened,* and *3*. that this understanding is that which *provided the structure of the evangelist's description* of the event and of the Scriptures.

This remark bears many similarities to the comment on the cleansing of the Temple in 2:13ff, especially if vv. 17 and 21f are combined:[43]

> His disciples remembered (ἐμνήσθησαν) that it was written: 'Zeal for thy house will consume me' (v. 17).

> But he spoke of the temple of his body. When therefore he was raised from the dead (ἠγέθη ἐκ νεκρῶν) his disciples remembered (ἐμνήσθησαν) that he had said this: and they believed the Scripture (τῇ γραφῇ) and the word which Jesus had spoken (τῷ λόγῳ, ὃν εἶπεν ὁ Ἰησοῦς).

[38] Note, for example, the mention of palm branches, the phrase εἰς ὑπάντησιν, the addition of καὶ ὁ βασιλεὺς τοῦ Ἰσραήλ, the setting of Jesus' mounting the donkey *after* the meeting with the people and the combination of Zeph 3:16 and Zech 9:9. See the excellent analysis in Brown, Comm., ad loc.

[39] Brown, Comm., ad loc., referring to the context of Zeph 3:16.

[40] Cf. Zeph 3:19f.

[41] See above, 3.4.6, and Pancaro 1969—70, pp. 123ff.

[42] Brown, Comm., ad loc. See the details mentioned above in note 38 and for further arguments, see Brown, Comm., ad loc.

[43] The similarities to 12:16 suggest that v. 17 and vv. 21f be read together. See also Abbott 1906, p. 2.

We have in this text the same periods of time, even if the wording is different,[44] and a similar reference to the Scriptures. The text should be read as meaning that after the Resurrection—when the Paraclete has come—the disciples came to understand aright the cleansing of the Temple, *inter alia* in the light of Ps 69:9,[45] and that τῇ γραφῇ in v. 22 then means "the scriptural passage", namely the *locus* Ps 69:9 just quoted.[46] In his zeal for his Father's house, i.e. from love for the Father, Jesus surrenders his life unto death, in order to resume it after a short period. Such an idea is clearly formulated in, for example, 10:17f. The tense of the Scriptural quotation is changed to the future to fit the context more closely, and the event itself is described, at least partly, from the later true understanding of it.[47] This agrees with 12:16. Nevertheless the emphasis on *what Jesus said* is new, namely his speech in v. 19 (ἔλεγεν, v. 21, ἔλεγεν, τῳ λόγῳ ὃν εἶπεν ὁ Ἰησοῦς, v. 22). On the event itself, which is also described in the other Gospels, the disciples "remember" what *the Scriptures* say (v. 17, mentioned in v. 22), and in addition *what Jesus said* (v. 19, referred to in vv. 21 and 22).[48] Taken together, these give the true understanding of the event, an understanding which the disciples did not possess when the event occurred but acquired afterwards, when Jesus had risen and conferred the Spirit.[49] The result is here the same as in 12:12−16, although in ch. 2 we have a reference to three things: *a Jesus event, a Scriptural passage* and *a Jesus saying*, and, by the reiteration of "remembered", also the Paraclete. However, these three things are more intricately interwoven in 2:13ff than the event and the Scriptural quotation (v. 15) in 12:12ff. Yet in both cases it is emphasized that the true understanding—which concerns Jesus' work as a whole—came with Jesus' resurrection and "glorification" (with the Paraclete) and we can clearly see how the later perspective shaped the text as a whole.

That the disciples understood—or will first understand—events and Jesus' sayings in a later perspective is mentioned in several passages in Jn: it is also suggested in the remarks in 13:28 on the words to Judas, and in 20:9 on the disciples' understanding of the Resurrection.[50] Considering St. John's narrative style it is most natural in the latter passage to allow the disciples as such to be the

---

[44] The verb ἐγείρειν is used just before, vv. 19f.

[45] Thus, for example, Brown, Comm., ad loc. As in his comments on 12:12ff, he refers to the context of the passage quoted in the text.

[46] The position of v. 17 may be explained by the connection with v. 16.

[47] Note the strong reaction of Jesus, the complete cleansing and the phrase "my Father's house" in v. 16.

[48] This saying of Jesus recalls Mk 14:58 par. and originally may not have been connected with the cleansing of the Temple. See Dodd 1963, pp. 89ff.

[49] This is implied by the word ἐμνήσθησαν, and what is said of the Paraclete in 15:26 and 16:12ff (see below, 4.3).

[50] Cf. also 20:14; 21:4; 6:6, 64; 7:39; (8:6); 11:13, and of other persons, 8:27(?); 10:6 and 11:51f.

agent. The understanding from the Scriptures that Jesus must rise again does not strike them until later. This makes the more surprising the datum in v. 8 that the Beloved Disciple "saw and believed" already on the Day of Resurrection *without* the witness of the Scriptures.

Summary: 1. In several of his remarks the author comments on the disciples' understanding of Jesus, his words and his deeds. *2.* These remarks state that the disciples did not receive the complete and real understanding until *after* Jesus' "hour", when Jesus had risen again, and been glorified and the Spirit had been given. The whole of Jesus' *ergon*—his work seen in the light of completion—then becomes a condition of understanding Jesus' words and works. *3.* The true insight is given by a *"remembering"* (*through the Paraclete*), and this applies to *the Jesus sayings, the Jesus events* and *the Scriptures* (various passages). *4.* This interpretative combination of event, saying and Scripture is constitutive for the composition of what the author wishes to say. In any case this applies with complete clarity in 2:13ff and 12:12ff. In the following section I shall show that this moulding, interpretative process is related to the activity of the Paraclete.

4.3 The Paraclete as the Interpreter

The use of the word μιμνήσκεσθαι and the reference to the two periods of time in 2:17, 21f and 12:16, gave me reason above to mention the Paraclete in Jn. He is explicitly mentioned in five texts, and described in terms of his relations with the Father, the Son, the disciples and the world, 14:16f; 14:25f; 15:26f; 16:7—11 and 16:12—15. In these passages the Paraclete is not an interpretative element in the text, but his interpretative function and the way in which it is described justify an analysis of the Paraclete in this context. It need not be extensive, since I can refer to a recently published article by Alois M. Kothgasser: "Die Lehr-, Erinnerungs-, Bezeugungs- und Einführungsfunktion des Johanneischen Geist-Parakleten gegenüber der Christus-Offenbarung".[51] He there gives a detailed, descriptive analysis of the relevant texts, and on most points I can summarize his results. In the following section I shall concentrate on the second and the fifth Paraclete sayings, 14:25f and 16:12—15, and in this context I shall also deal with the statements on Jesus' "figurative" and "plain" sayings (ἐν παροιμίαις, ἐν παρρησία) in 16:16—33, a text which should be discussed in connection with these Paraclete passages.[52]

---

[51] In *Salesianum* 33 (1971), pp. 557—598, and 34 (1972), pp. 3—51.

[52] The most important literature on the Paraclete is quoted in Kothgasser 1971, pp. 557f. For a general introduction, see especially Betz 1963, Brown 1966—67 and Johnston 1970, and, for the problems I discuss here, Sasse 1925, Mussner 1961, 1965, Schlier 1963, Blank 1964 and de la Potterie 1965.

If we combine the data on the Paraclete from the five texts, their essence could be stated under three points:[53] *1. The Paraclete comes from the Father and the Son* and is, so to speak, the continuation of their work on earth.[54] *2. The Paraclete comes to the disciples* and is present with (μετά), among (παρά) and in (ἐν) *them* for all eternity (εἰς τὸν αἰῶνα), after Jesus has left the earth and gone to the Father. The world cannot receive him, nor can it see or know him.[55] *3. The* primary function of the Paraclete is *to teach the disciples about "all things", to bring them into the full truth*[56] and further, to convince the world of sin, righteousness and judgement.[57] Since the coming and the function of the Paraclete are so strongly bound up with the disciples, it is probable that his work in relation to the world is expected to be carried on through them. Cf. 17:21ff. Thus the work of the Paraclete would, in all respects, be linked with the disciples.

This clearly marked interpretative and teaching *function* seems to be in conflict with the *title* held by the Paraclete, a problem which has often puzzled scholars.[58] In the extant texts, the Greek word παράκλητος —and its transcription in Hebrew and Aramaic—has a definitely legal, forensic meaning: "Anwalt, Beistand, Fürsprecher".[59] Regarding the survey in Betz *et al.,* the closest Hebrew equivalent seems to me to be מליץ, a word which can mean both "translator, interpreter, teacher" *and* "mediator, advocate, defender".[60] In the Qumran literature, this title is used of the right teacher and the true "revealer" of God's secrets as they are concealed in the Scriptures,[61] and in the Targum to Job 16:20 and 33:23 this word is given as פרקליטא.[62] Thus the Hebrew-speaker had a word which covered both the "kerygmatic" and the forensic aspect, and in the

---

[53] Excellent surveys in Brown 1966—67, pp. 115ff, Brown, Comm., p. 1135, and Kothgasser 1971, pp. 564ff.

[54] He comes forth from the Father, 15:26, the Father will give him at Jesus' request, 14:16, He will send him in Jesus' name, 14:26, Jesus will send him from the Father, 15:26; 16:7.

[55] Note especially 14:17 and the fact that the disciples almost always are the object for the work of the Paraclete.

[56] He will teach the disciples, 14:26, guide them into the truth, 16:13, declare to them what belongs to Jesus, 16:14, bear witness about Jesus, remind them, 14:26, speak to them, 16:13.

[57] This function is only mentioned in 16:8—11. To bear witness about Jesus, 15:26, may mean a public witnessing to the world, but rather an "inner" witnessing about Jesus to the disciples, which will strengthen their belief during the persecutions. Thus de la Potterie 1965, pp. 99ff, and Kothgasser 1972, p. 67.

[58] A survey of different solutions in Riesenfeld 1972, pp. 266f.

[59] See the lingusitic material in ThWNT, vol. 5, pp. 799ff (J. Behm), and in Betz 1963, pp. 137ff. Παράκλητος has been interpreted as "advocate", as "intercessor, mediator, spokesman", as "comforter, consoler" and as "preacher". See Brown, Comm., pp. 1136f.

[60] See, for example, Gen 42:23; Job 33:23; 16:20; 1QH II.13; XVIII.11.

[61] See Betz 1963, p. 139, Roloff 1968—69, pp. 145f, and the passages mentioned there.

[62] The texts in Johansson 1940, pp. 24ff. The context in Job is legal but at the same time it is said of the spokesman that he "declares to man what is right of him", 33:23. The texts are not preserved in 11QtgJob.

267

reading at worship of Job 33:23—where both aspects are in fact present—this was given as מליץ . Together with the Johannine dualism, this may explain the choice of the word παράκλητος in Jn.[63] This kerygmatic aspect emerges clearly in the other designation of the Paraclete, "the Spirit of truth", 14:17, 15:26, 16:13.[64] As the following pages show, the prime meaning of this expression is "the Spirit who mediates the Truth", i.e. the Revelation of Christ. The Paraclete, the Spirit of Truth, is the true translator and interpreter.

This interpretative function first emerges in *the second Paraclete text, 14:25f,* which is set in a context dealing with the disciples' understanding of the Father.[65] Jesus promises in v. 20 that "on that day" they will know (γνώσεσθε) that the Son is in the Father and they in the Son and the Son in them. If the disciples are to receive this understanding, Jesus must reveal himself to them, vv. 21f. Why then does he not reveal himself to the world? Jesus replies by referring to those who keep *Jesus' word* (τὸν λόγον μου, τοὺς λόγους μου,   14:23f), which is also *the word of the Father,* and to *the work of the Paraclete.* The text of 14:25f reads:

ταῦτα λελάληκα ὑμῖν παρ' ὑμῖν μένων· ὁ δὲ παράκλητος, τὸ πνεῦμα τὸ ἅγιον ὃ πέμψει ὁ πατὴρ ἐν τῷ ὀνόματί μου, ἐκεῖνος ὑμᾶς διδάξει πάντα καὶ ὑπομνήσει ὑμᾶς πάντα ἃ εἶπον ὑμῖν ἐγώ.

The situation of the farewell discourse, the immediate context, and the use of the perfect tense in v. 25 justify the belief that ταῦτα refers to the whole of Jesus' revelation activity. His thoughts—according to the narrator—now at the end of his earthly ministry deal with his teaching while he was with the disciples (παρ' ὑμῖν μένων), which is equivalent to the ὁ λόγος ὃν ἀκούετε mentioned just before, the word of revelation from the Father, vv. 23f, which he handed on to the disciples, 17:6—8, 14, 17. The introductory δέ in v. 26 denotes a certain distance between Jesus' earthly activity and that of the Paraclete. We have here the account of "deux grandes périodes dans l'économie de la révélation, la première étant constituée par sa propre parole, la seconde par l'enseignement de l'Esprit",[66] corresponding to the two phases in Jesus' *ergon,* which I described above.[67] The revelation which is mentioned in vv. 21f would then be the same as the teaching of the Spirit in v. 25.

[63] Note the reference to Pr 8:4ff in Riesenfeld 1972. "Consolation is described, in this context, as being identical with teaching: demonstrating what is right and refuting all that is wrong" (pp. 271f). - Betz' reason against מליץ as the background of παράκλητος (1963, p. 139) becomes invalid if the material in Job is adduced.

[64] Note also Jn 4:23f and 1 Jn 4:6; 5:6. See Kothgasser 1971, pp. 575ff.

[65] Note Philip's question already in 14:8.

[66] de la Potterie 1965, p. 90.

[67] See, for example, 2.2, U 27, U 29 and U 30, and the bibliographical references in these sections

268

The first thing said of the Paraclete is that he will *"teach them all things"*. Διδάξει and πάντα are apposed to the earlier words λελάληκα and ταῦτα. The eyes are turned both back and forward in the situation of "the hour". Διδάσκειν is a term of revelation in Jn,[68] and the question arises whether the Paraclete is described in the text as a Revealer side by side with Jesus. The answer depends on how we understand πάντα and the connection with the following clause: καὶ ὑπομνήσει ὑμᾶς πάντα ἃ εἶπον ὑμῖν ἐγώ.

The word ὑπομιμνήσκειν here, in Schlier's summary means "ein Vergegenwärtigen", "eine Auslegung" and "ein Erfahrenlassen".[69] Thus the Paraclete will realise all Jesus' sayings to the disciples,[70] he will interpret them in their situation and thus give rise to new insights and experiences. In principle this novelty is not new, since the Paraclete in all his "recalling" activity is bound by what Jesus had previously told the disciples.[71] Christ alone is *the* Revealer, with the definite article, while the Paraclete is the Teacher and Interpreter.[72] The reminder of the Paraclete concerns "all things", i.e. "das Christus-Ereignis" in its entirety, the work (*ergon*) which Jesus completes by his death and resurrection ("glorification"). Since the later clause in v. 26 on the Paraclete's activity binds the Paraclete so closely to Jesus, πάντα in the first clause should be delimited in an analogous fashion. Καὶ has an explanatory meaning.[73] Such a reading of v. 26 is confirmed by the more detailed text in 16:12—15.

The *fifth text on the Paraclete, 16:12—15*, directly follows the fourth, but should be regarded as an independent unit by reason of its content. The text runs:

ἔτι πολλὰ ἔχω ὑμῖν λέγειν, ἀλλ᾽ οὐ δύνασθε βαστάζειν ἄρτι· ὅταν δὲ ἔλθῃ ἐκεῖνος, τὸ πνεῦμα τῆς ἀληθείας, ὁδηγήσει ὑμᾶς ἐν τῇ ἀληθείᾳ πάσῃ · οὐ γὰρ λαλήσει ἀφ᾽ ἑαυτοῦ, ἀλλ᾽ ὅσα ἀκούσει λαλήσει, καὶ τὰ ἐρχόμενα ἀναγγελεῖ ὑμῖν. ἐκεῖνος ἐμὲ δοξάσει, ὅτι ἐκ τοῦ ἐμοῦ λήμψεται καὶ ἀναγγελεῖ ὑμῖν. πάντα ὅσα ἔχει ὁ πατὴρ ἐμά ἐστιν· διὰ τοῦτο εἶπον ὅτι ἐκ τοῦ ἐμοῦ λαμβάνει καὶ ἀναγγελεῖ ὑμῖν.

The temporal marking at the beginning[74] again recalls the two periods of time in Christ's work of revelation and redemption. Jesus has spoken to the disciples—all that underlies the situation of farewell— but he still has much (πολλά) to

---

[68] See, for example, 8:28; 7:14, 28, 35; 8:20. The context of 7:37ff is discussed above in 3.3.6, the title Rabbi in 3.4.2, S 1. For further material see Kothgasser 1971, p. 588f, especially 1 Jn 2:27.

[69] For justification, see Schlier 1963, p. 235, and Kothgasser 1971, pp. 590ff.

[70] The phrase "all that I have said to you" in v. 26 may include Jesus' work as a whole, his work of revelation. Cf. the meaning of ἔργον in Jn, 2.2, U 27.

[71] The words πάντα ἃ εἶπον ὑμῖν ἐγώ, with an emphatic ἐγώ at the end, correspond to the previous ταῦτα λελάληκα.

[72] Kothgasser 1971, p. 597.

[73] Thus Bultmann, Mussner, Zerwick according to Kothgasser 1971, p. 595.

[74] The words ἔτι, ἄρτι, ὅταν, the future tense.

say. This may seem to conflict with what Jesus says in 15:15. Yet πολλά here does not refer to new revelations on Jesus' part—that which he has already revealed is in itself the complete revelation—but to a deeper and better understanding of that which came with Christ. Jesus has said all things, but by reason of the disciples' inability to understand—and perhaps also because of the nature of the revelation—his words, so to speak, have not come home to the disciples. Judging by what follows, that which Jesus has not said is identical with that mediated by the Paraclete.

The main function of the Paraclete is here described in the words ὁδηγήσει ὑμᾶς ἐν τῇ ἀληθείᾳ πάσῃ. The Paraclete is to guide and lead the disciples into (and inside) the revelation of Christ in its entirety.[75] Here πάσῃ corresponds to the earlier πάντα, 14:26, and πολλά in 16:12. The fact that ἀλήθεια refers to the revelation of Christ is manifest from the use of the word in Jn, and in this context from v. 12 and from the following justification with γάρ. The Paraclete will call to mind what *Jesus* said, 14:26, bear witness to *Jesus*, 15:26, guide into *the Truth*, 16:13, glorify *Jesus*, 16:14, take what belongs to *Jesus*, 16:15. He is the true translator and interpreter: οὐ λαλήσει ἀφ᾽ ἑαυτοῦ, ἀλλ᾽ ὅσα ἀκούει λαλήσει, v. 13. This, of course, means new insights on the part of the disciples, but here, as in 14:25f, it is not described as new revelations from Jesus. The revelation is completed in and with Christ. The Paraclete leads into this revelation.

The continuation of the text is an explanation of this. Ἀναγγέλλειν/ἀπαγγέλλειν means not only "to narrate, to mediate, to pass on", but in prophetic and apocalyptic texts also "ein erklärendes Enthüllen eines vorliegenden Geheimnisses".[76] The expression τὰ ἐρχόμενα as object of this verb indicates the latter meaning. In my opinion, this object, the meaning of which is under dispute, should in its present context be taken on the basis of 14:20; 16:2, 4, 25, and interpreted as referring to phase 2 of Jesus' ergon,[77] which according to Jn is the eschatological era, and from the situation of the farewell speech, "the age to come". The Paraclete's interpretative and explanatory mediation of the revelation of Christ is finally brought back to the Father in v. 15 (the Paraclete - the Son - the Father). The revelation in its entirety is a work of the Father, the Son and the Paraclete.

The continuation in ch. 16, and especially the statement concerning Jesus' sayings in v. 25, should be read in connection with these texts about the Paraclete:[78]

[75] The verbs mean here "anleiten, hinführen, unterweisen, lehren", Kothgasser 1972, p. 27. For a discussion of the many details in these passages I must refer to Kothgasser's analysis (1972, pp. 19ff).

[76] Kothgasser 1972, p. 44, and the material he quotes. Cf. pp. 41f and above 3.3.2, S 12.

[77] Cf. 5:20, Kothgasser 1972, p. 43, interprets the expression as referring to "das was Jesus durch die Jünger in der Kraft des Geistes tun will".

[78] Note what is said in 3.4.1 on its revelationary character.

ταῦτα ἐν παροιμίαις λελάληκα ὑμῖν· ἔρχεται ὥρα ὅτε οὐκέτι ἐν παροιμίαις λαλήσω ὑμῖν ἀλλὰ παρρησίᾳ περὶ τοῦ πατρὸς ἀπαγγελῶ ὑμῖν.

In 14:25f we found that the Paraclete's work of teaching is contrasted with that of Jesus (saying, revelation) during his earthly ministry. The wording of 16:12f implies two periods in Jesus' teaching to his disciples. The disciples cannot understand in the first period that which Jesus says during the second. This second period is later placed on a par with the activity of the Paraclete. The Paraclete acts as a kind of translator, v. 13, and in fact it is Jesus who speaks through him.[79] Thus we have two phases in Jesus' revelation, corresponding to those we previously found in the case of Jesus' ergon and doxa.

16:25 also refers to the two periods in Jesus' revelation to his disciples: Jesus has spoken (λελάληκα) and he will speak (λαλήσω, ἀπαγγελῶ). Judging by the situation of the farewell discourse, the temporal references in chs. 14—17, and particularly in the immediate context, and that which I just said of Jesus and the Paraclete, it is most feasible to allow ταῦτα λελάληκα to refer to Jesus' earthly ministry, in analogy with the same phrase in 14:25, and the following clauses to the period after Jesus' "hour". For a more detailed analysis and explanation I must refer the reader to Brown and Rubio Morán.[80] This determination of the temporal references is essential, since it has an important consequence: the whole of Jesus' earthly work of revelation is designated παροιμία, i.e. it is seen as something mysterious and not wholly intelligible. Not until Jesus speaks through the Paraclete have we a discourse ἐν παρρησίᾳ, namely in terms which the disciples completely understand.[81] This reading of v. 25 agrees closely with my comments above (4.2) on the data in 2:17, 21f; 12:16 and that suggested by the remark in 7:39 (see 3.3.6). The eyes of the disciples were opened to Jesus' identity only after the coming of the Paraclete. As is clear from the farewell discourse and from the immediate context, 16:16ff, the meaning of Jesus' departure (death and resurrection) is the point at issue. On this point the mystery thickens and a discourse ἐν παρρησίᾳ is particularly necessary. When Jn defines the subject of this discourse as "the Father" (περὶ τοῦ πατρός), this is his way of expressing the same thought. The work of redemption, which culminates in Jesus' "glorification", is in the last resort the work of the Father.[82]

Thus Jesus' earthly ministry is seen as something mysterious. Not until after "the hour" are the secrets revealed. This change from παροιμίαι to a discourse ἐν παρρδσίᾳ must have left traces in an account of Jesus' life intended to promote

[79] Note the expressions ἔτι πολλὰ ἔχω ὑμῖν λέγειν, ὅσα ἀκούσει λαλήσει, πάντα ἃ εἶπεν ὑμῖν ἐγώ (14:26), ἐκ τοῦ ἐμοῦ λήμψεται / λαμβάνει.
[80] Brown, Comm., ad loc. and Rubio Morán 1972.
[81] Cf. Mk 8:32 (παρρησίᾳ) with 9:32 (ἠγνόουν).
[82] See above 2.2, U 27, and 3.3.2, S 11.

the belief in Jesus' true identity, 20:30f. Thus 16:25 is relevant to the problem of the Johannine text type.

Summary: 1. The revelation is seen as completed in and with Jesus' earthly work. *2.* The revelation does not, so to speak, come home to the disciples until Jesus is relieved by the Paraclete. *3.* The Paraclete's most important function is to bring the disciples into the revelation given with Christ, especially in Jesus' total, universal, work of salvation (*ergon*).[83] The new revelation of the Paraclete is not really new, but "vom Geist ausgelegte, eingeführte, vertiefte und von den Aposteln neu erkannte, neu verstandene Christusoffenbarung, und das in ihrer Totalität".[84] *4.* The Johannine message may thereby be regarded as—to borrow Kothgasser's words once more—"eine geist-gewirkte Gesamterinnerung, ein neues Einsehen, Verstehen und Erfahren der gesamten Christuswirklichkeit".[85] Several scholars have *en passant* noted that this should be seen as a constitutive element even for Jn *regarded as a text,* although without arriving at a description of the Johannine text type.[86] *5.* The events narrated in Jn were, according to 16:25, once something mysterious ($\pi\alpha\rho\omega\mu\acute{\iota}\alpha\iota$), but they are seen in the light of revelation from a view of Jesus' work as a whole as the work of the Father. The Gospel may therefore be regarded as a revelation of mysterious secrets. *6.* Considering the function of the Paraclete in Jn, and especially the statement in 16:25, a transition in the reference of the word Jesus from the earthly Jesus to the glorified Jesus—a co-projection of the two phases of Jesus' *ergon*—is very natural.

4.4 Excursus IV. The Beloved Disciple in Jn

The problem of the interpretative character of the text and the description of the Paraclete's translatory function justify a short excursus on the beloved disciple in Jn (abbreviated BD), although, for many readers, such an excursus may lead into a question of how the text came into existence and not of how the text is constituted. This figure has long been associated with the problem of the author of Jn.[87] The material on the BD was most recently collected and analysed in a paper

[84] Kothgasser 1972, p. 33. Kothgasser assumes that "the disciples" in Jn is the same as "the apostles", which is anything but self-evident. See below, 4.4.

[85] Kothgasser 1971, p. 593.

[86] See especially Cullmann 1966, pp. 176ff (first published in 1948), Schlier 1963, p. 235, note 11 Blank 1964, p. 268, Mussner 1965, pp. 79ff, and Kothgasser 1971, p. 593.

[87] See, for example, Feine-Behm-Kümmel, pp. 161ff, and Schnackenburg 1970, pp. 97ff.

by Jürgen Roloff,[88] in which he pays special attention to the parallels with the Teacher of Righteousness in the Qumran texts. Roloff rightly begins by stating that the earlier analysis was too closely linked with the problem of authorship and the alternative *either* an historical person *or* a totally symbolic figure.[89] His analysis deals primarily with the function of the BD in the Johannine text, a textual orientation which is in harmony with my interest here.

The BD is explicitly mentioned in five texts (13:23—26; 19:25, 27; 20:2—10; 21:1—14, 15—23) and it is feasible to see him in 19:34ff, while there is some doubt about the anonymous figure in 1:35—40 and 18:15f.[90] These passages assign a specific role to the BD. Firstly the BD is he who "sees and believes" *before Peter*, 20:8. A certain tension between the BD and Peter is apparent in the Gospel. At the Last Supper the BD is lying nearest Jesus and is "mediator" between Jesus and Peter, 13:23f.[91] He reaches the grave before Peter, 20:1ff, he is the first to recognize Jesus at Lake Tiberias, 21:1ff, and the relationship between him and Peter is discussed at the end of ch. 21.[92] Secondly the BD appears *in connection with some interpretative remarks* in Jn, especially 20:8, 19:35 and 21:23, which may be regarded as an indication that he is involved in the interpretation of the events narrated. Thirdly, the BD is *on particularly close terms with Jesus,* as emerges already from the name and the scene mentioned in 13:23f.[93] This special closeness to Jesus seems also to be the reason why he comes to understanding of Jesus' death and resurrection before all others and before the disciples are given such insight through the Scriptures, 20:8f.[94] Fourthly, his insight makes him a *special witness to Jesus,* and in particular to the true meaning of Jesus' death, 19:34ff. As Brown's excellent commentary on these verses

---

[88] Roloff 1968—69 with bibliographical references on p. 130. Thyen 1971, p. 343, refers to a work of one of his pupils, "Hans-Peter Otto, Funktion und Bedeutung des Lieblingsjüngers im Joh-Ev., die als Examensarbeit vorliegt und zur Dissertation ausgebaut werden soll", which I have not read. His thesis is, according to Thyen (p. 352) "dass der Verfasser des 21. Kapitels, eben der Redaktor unseres Evangeliums, in Kapitel 21 nicht eine im Evangelium schon vorgefundene *symbolische* Gestalt des 'Lieblingsjüngers' nachträglich historisiert und zur Figur des Evangelisten und Traditionsbewährsmannes seines Kreises gemacht hat. Er hat vielmehr diese in ihrer pseudonymen Anonymität schillernde Figur 'des Jüngers, den Jesus liebte' . . . selbst geschaffen. . . . Er will damit einmal dem verehrten 'Jünger' seines Kreises ein Denkmal errichten und zum anderen seinem Evangelium die Autorität des geliebten Augenzeugen verleihen".

[89] Roloff 1968—69, p. 130.

[90] "Die traditionsgeschichtliche Untersuchung der LJ-Stellen ergibt einen überraschend eindeutigen Befund. Sie weisen sich nämlich durchweg als *literarische Kompositionen* aus, hinter denen keine älteren Traditionen stehen", Roloff 1968—69, p. 133.

[91] He may also understand more of Jesus' words to Judas, 13:28f.

[92] On Peter in the Gospel of John, see Brown-Donfried-Reumann (eds.) 1973, pp. 129ff, on his relation to the BD, pp. 133ff.

[94] Note the use of "love" and "know" and "the commandment" in 10:15f, 17f; 14:15, 15:9f, and "friends" in 15:14f.

[94] Brown-Donfried-Reumann (eds.) 1973, pp. 137f.

shows, they may be regarded as a very extensive exposition on Jesus' death.[95] Roloff says of the BD in this context: "Er ist *Interpret* der vom Tode Jesu ausgehende Heilsbedeutung".[96] Thus the BD's function to some extent resembles that of the Paraclete.

The characteristic role of the BD in the text, together with his anonymity and special title, may be adduced as reasons why we here have merely a literary fiction. However, this is contradicted by the reference to the death of the BD in ch. 21, and also by the many comparisons with Peter. Moreover we have a parallel phenomenon in the Teacher of Righteousness at Qumran, who is now generally believed to be an historical figure, particularly associated with the founding of the sect, who is at the same time described in the texts as an ideal type, as the True Teacher.[97] He, like the BD, is regarded as the true interpreter, in his case of the Holy Scriptures, in that of the BD of the Jesus-phenomenon (and the Scriptures). "*Beide sind weder Offenbarer, noch Tradenten, sonder primär Interpreten und Exegeten*".[98] Roloff summarizes: "Der Lehrer ist für die Sekte zugleich individuelle historische Gestalt und idealer Repräsentant des Typus des rechten, weil auf der Seite Gottes stehenden Lehrers. Nicht anders steht es um den Lieblingsjünger ist für einen Kreis von Schülern zugleich eine geschichtliche Gestalt und die Verkörperung des Typs des wahren Jüngers, der Jesus aus einem unmittelbaren Verstehen heraus zu deuten vermag".[99]

Roloff's conclusions are convincing. They are perhaps most interesting in view of the situation in which our text was written but also for determination of the text type. Together with what I said above about the Paraclete and the author's remarks, they *emphasize the extensive and thorough interpretation process which underlies our text.* The Johannine text must somehow be regarded as a concrete manifestation of this process.

---

[95] Brown, Comm., ad loc, with references.
[96] Roloff 1968—69, p. 139.
[97] Roloff 1968—69, pp. 143ff, referring to the thorough examination of Gert Jeremias.
[98] Roloff 1968—69, p. 148.
[99] Roloff 1968—69, p. 150.

5

Epilogue

With the analyses above in chs. 2 and 3, I have completed the task laid down in the Introduction (1.1), of establishing the message of two Johannine texts from textual criteria, as far as is now possible, and of then describing their linguistic and literary character (text type), considering especially the so-called Johannine symbolism. Apart from the internal analysis of the text, with its description of various textual qualities, I have, in the question of the environment and situation of the text, assumed only that the Johannine language was subject to Semitic influence (see 1.2), with the limitation of the linguistic comparisons which this involves; moreover, prior to the interpretation of the first text (2.4.1), I have proposed the hypothesis that Jn is a book for the initiated, i.e. it is addressed primarily to those who are already conversant with its substance and its special linguistic form. The Johannine texts were written *in* a certain situation, but not necessarily *for* a certain situation.[1] This hypothesis was later confirmed by the two texts which I have analysed: their content and, above all, their form are in closer agreement with the theory that Jn was written for the believers, and primarily the Johannine community, than with the assertion that it is a mission pamphlet.[2] Indeed, the two texts are not characterized by an emphasis on the relation to the readers.[3] Nevertheless the conclusions should be regarded as preliminary until more of Jn's texts have been analysed, including also the Johannine discourses, and certain comparative studies have been carried out on the question of the type(s) of text here concerned.

The analysis of these two texts showed that their *message* is to a great extent the same: how the people of the new covenant, in the following often called the new people of God, is born from that of the old. In the *Cana narrative* the author is seeking to describe how Jesus' *ergon*, i.e. Jesus' work of salvation in all its range, covering both the time before and the time after Jesus' "hour", implies the creation of a new people of God (2.4.2). This he does by telling of the wedding at

---

[1] Thus de Jonge 1972–73, pp. 264f.

[2] On different opinions, see Feine-Behm-Kümmel, pp. 157f, and Riesenfeld 1965. It is perhaps necessary to distinguish between the purpose(s) of the Gospel as a whole and the purposes of the pericopes.

[3] The "Signalfunktion", to use Karl Bühlers terminology, is not very strong. The "Symbolfunktion" is predominant.

Cana in the light of Jewish concepts of what once happened at Sinai (2.4.3), and by using a vocabulary all his own, which is bound to an interpretation of Jesus' work in its entirety, including its consequences. The structure and themes of the opening week in Jn (1:19—2:11), culminating on the third (= the sixth) day at Cana, are dependent on a Sinai screen, in order to show how the new people of God is born from the old. As once at Sinai, a *purification* of the people is called for, a purification realized by the death of Jesus (the Lamb of God). The baptism in water is complemented with the baptism in the Spirit, the water in the Jewish purification vessels is transformed at Jesus' "hour" to "choice wine". As once at Sinai, *obédience* to God's revelation is also essential. In talking of this obedience the narrator evidently wishes to point out the connection between the old and the new.

The description of the relationship between John the Baptist and Jesus is one of the basic features of the opening week. The genesis of the new people of God is involved with these two figures. John is presented as the great witness to Jesus before the people of God (3.2.1, E 1). The first disciples come from among his followers, once they have heard his witness. John was sent by God, but he was not the light. He came to bear witness of the light, that "all" should believe in Jesus, 1:8f. These words in the prologue of St John's Gospel provide the structure for the presentation of John the Baptist in 1:19ff. With his baptism in water, he stands within the framework of the old covenant, showing how this merges into the new after the revelation of Jesus' identity. Andrew and Philip too, and perhaps also the mother of Jesus,[4] appear to have played a similar part: after their meeting with Jesus they bear witness about him to others. Andrew says that Jesus is the Messiah, Philip that Jesus is the One of whom Moses and the Prophets wrote, i.e. both link the new revelation with the old. The disciples in 1:35ff, and also the servants in the Cana narrative,[5] are obedient in a double sense: they believe the testimony concerning Jesus and they believe in Jesus himself. By this structure the narrator is presumably trying to show that the new people of God came into existence through obedience both to the Divine Revelation in the old covenant and to the Divine Revelation in Jesus Christ. It is worth noting that the latter revelation is presented as embracing two phases according to 1:50f,[6] which, from the role played by Jesus' "hour" and the Paraclete in Jn, should be interpreted as referring to the time before and the time after Jesus' "hour".[7] Thus in Jn 1:19ff we have two main stages in the coming into being of

[4] Her role in the Cana narrative is difficult to determine. I found (2.4.4) it most feasible to regard her as a parallel to John in his witnessing function, as the representative of the true Israel who merges into the people of the new covenant.

[5] Everything in the picture of the servants suggests such a role, parallel to the disciples, 2.4.4.

[6] See above, 2.2, U 6 and U 31.

[7] On Jesus' "hour" in Jn, see above 2.2, U 9c, U 27, U 29 and 2.3.4. On the Paraclete, see my analysis in 4.3.

the true people of God: the testimony about Jesus and the meeting with Jesus, the latter covering both the time before and the time after Jesus' "hour". In my opinion, the over-riding Sinai screen and the theme of the creation of the new covenant in the opening week call for an interpretation of the disciples' belief as described in the text, not as a faith gradually increasing during the life-time of private individuals, but as an expression of how the belief in Jesus as the Messiah, the Son of God, arose within Judaism and resulted in a new people of God, born of the old.[8]

In *the Samaria text,* the narrator is trying to show how Jesus' *ergon* means that even Samaritans are to be included in the new covenant, i.e. that the "new" Israel involves a union of Judah and Ephraim, a gathering in of the scattered Israel (3.5.1). Here we encounter a number of the themes from the opening week, especially if we begin the reading at 3:22ff: the question of purification, the baptism in water and the giving of the Spirit, the "emigration" from Judea to Galilee, with its destination at Cana, the description of the relationship between John the Baptist and Jesus, and the mention of the obedience to the revelation in Christ. Here John again emphasizes that he is only a witness, one who goes before, one who, like a "best man", rejoices when the bridegroom wins his bride. John's disciples become Jesus' disciples, the former decreases, the latter increases (3.2.2). The text emphasizes that the Samaritans *first* believe in the testimony concerning Jesus, *then* in Jesus' own words (3.2.5). Their belief in the revelation in Christ, which follows upon the "two days", however, does not here embrace two phases, as in 1:50f, one among several indications that the meeting with Jesus is here regarded as a meeting with Christ after Jesus' "hour".[9] Previously (3.5.1), I found the most probable interpretation of this structure in the text to be identical with that in 1:19ff: the obedience to the revelation in Christ is also an obedience to the revelation of God in the Samaritan religion. The Well was given to the Samaritans through Jacob, but the Spirit and the Truth came by Jesus Christ.[10] In both cases it is God's gift, God's will and God's work, 4:10, 24, 34, 36. The contrast with the old is there, but so is the continuity. *Every true Israelite, every true Samaritan, every true disciple of John the Baptist, confesses that Jesus is the Messiah, the Son of God, the King of Israel, the Saviour of the world,* 1:49; 3:28; 4:25, 29, 42.

These interpretations of the two texts, which combine several features of other

[8] On the belief in Jn, cf. above 2.2, U 31.

[9] See above 3.2.1, E 30. In the perspective mentioned here it is easy to find a connection between the two expressions "two days" and Jesus' "hour". See my discussion above, 3.2.4.

[10] Cf. Jn 1:17. I have explained the presentation of the well of Jacob in Jn 4 primarily by a Well screen, 3.2.7, 3.5, but by the contrast with the living water of Jesus, interpreted as referring to both the Revelation (Truth) and the Spirit, the water from Jacob's well also becomes a symbol of the Law, as in the Damascus Document (see 3.2.7 and 3.3.6). To the Samaritans the Law was the only source of revelation; see, for example, J. Jeremias in ThWNT, vol.7, pp. 89f.

interpretation models mentioned above in 2.1 and 3.1, must be regarded as results of the text-linguistic method I have applied. The general approach described in ch. 1 and the questions I have put to the texts require an extensive use of a textual (internal) analysis, and the application of some general linguistic conclusions on how texts are constituted and understood, and also my holistic method, seem to me to give more reliable results than many traditional methods.

My interpretations of the two texts may also be described as giving each other mutual support. In both the narratives we see how the "new" Israel came to be distinct from the "old",[11] an Israel which embraced both "Judah" and "Ephraim". Nevertheless, the latter is only expressed in the Samaria narrative, and there in the form of a teaching of the disciples (3.5.1). The confrontation underlying these texts would, therefore, not only include that between Judaism and Christianity, and that between Samaritanism and Christianity, but also reflect different ideas within the Church herself.[12] In any case this is a feasible interpretation of a strongly marked structural feature in Jn 4 (the teaching of the disciples), which is not present in 1:19ff, nor is it explained by the theme of the creation of the "new" Israel from the old (Judah and Ephraim). The role of the disciples in the text is fairly clear-cut: they receive teaching on something of which they are ignorant (4:32), the content of which includes three related things: that Jesus' *ergon* includes a revelation of Christ even for the Samaritans, that Jesus' *ergon* involves the gathering in of the scattered Israel, and that they themselves, in their work of harvest, have only to enter into the labour which others have done before them in Samaria. As mentioned above (3.5.1), the word "others" in 4:38 may refer both to those who laboured in the framework of the old covenant (represented by the woman as witness and by John the Baptist), or those who worked in the Samaria mission within the new covenant, before the apostles. The latter interpretation is in good agreement with the second account in the NT on how the Samaritans are incorporated in the new people of God, Acts 8, and is perhaps to be preferred, in the light of the *ergon* perspective.[13] If this is correct, it implies that the narrator himself in some way was connected with the circle round Stephen and Philip, a conclusion with far-reaching consequences for the concept of the origin and environment of the Gospel. However I must leave this question open.

The interpretation I have here given of 2:1—11 and 4:1—42 confers a special meaning and function on the entire section, 1:19—4:54, which may be noted, even though I have not analysed, for example, the Nicodemus narrative, and the

[11] This is the predominant theme of Jn, according to Bowker 1964—65, p. 407.

[12] Cf. de Jonge 1972—73, p. 264: "I differ from Schnackenburg and Meeks, in that I would put more emphasis on the fact that Johannine christology is developed not only in contrast with Jewish thinking but also with other christological views".

[13] A reference to Acts 8 for the interpretation of Jn 4 is found already in Strauss [4]1840, vol. 1, pp. 525ff, and especially in Cullmann 1953 and 1966, pp. 260ff. See above, 3.1, and below, the conclusion of ch. 5.

curing of the official's son.[14] We have in 1:19—2:11(22) an opening week, corresponding in some way to the last week in 12—20. By its theme of the new covenant (including a new people) and by the comments in 2:11 and 4:54 it is strongly linked to 3:22—4:54. We arrive at a long section at the beginning of the Gospel (1:19—4:54), which may function as a kind of second introduction, evidently in two parts, the emphasis being on the first and second signs at Cana. The Gospel as we now have it seems to have two introductions (1:1—18; 1:19—4:54), with a specific picture of Jesus and his work, which should, in all reason, have consequences for the interpretation of the Gospel in general.[15]

The linguistic and literary character of the two texts, *the text type,* may be similarly described, although for the Cana text (2.4.5) I suggested the definition: *a symbolic narrative text with many allusive elements,* while for the Samaria narrative (3.5.2) I preferred *a strongly "screened" text.* Thus there are quite clearly *two levels* in the Johannine text, a narrative level and a symbolic level, a conclusion of my investigation which agrees with many other scholars' descriptions of Jn.[16] The problems are primarily concerned with how one is to describe the relations between these two levels. I have shown on several points that they are intricately interwoven with each other, so that they can hardly be clearly distinguished as regards the individual parts of the text. The dialogues, for example, are necessary for the course of events in the narrative, being an integral part thereof, at the same time as they deal with essential themes in Johannine theology (3.3 and 3.4). The persons are included as necessary, and usually natural, agents in the course of events, but have at the same time a certain representative function (2.3.5, 2.4.4 and 3.5). The conclusion on this point coincides with the latest investigation of the signs in Jn, which speaks of "the surprising unity of event and meaning".[17]

One consequence of this unity is the impossibility of working out a scheme of simple relations between the two levels of the text. The Johannine texts should therefore *not be defined as allegories,* with their often well arranged relations between two distinctive levels, but should rather be compared with the typological way of thought,[18] to use terms frequently recurring in descriptions of

---

[14] Jn 2:23ff concern unbelief in Jerusalem of Judea, Jn 4:43ff concern belief in Kana in Galilee, the former connected with night, the latter with day and high noon. My interpretation of 2:1—11 and 4:1—42 gives a certain perspective, which may shed light on such expressions as "be born by water and spirit" (cf. above 2.4.3, note 59) and the unusual designation   in 4:46.

[15] Note the double prologue in Mt (1:1—2:23 and 3:1—4:11), analysed by Gerhardsson 1973, pp. 73ff.

[16] See, besides the commentaries, Dillon 1962, pp. 268, 274, Michaud 1962, 1963, Feuillet 1965, pp. 527ff, Martyn 1968, Hanhart 1970, pp. 22f, and Nicol 1972, pp. 106ff.

[17] Nicol 1972, p. 122. Cf. p. 107: "Literal meaning and deeper meaning cannot be clearly distinguished".

[18] Cf. Lausberg [3]1967, pp. 139ff, and L. Goppelt in [3]RGG, col. 239f, and their definitions of

Biblical text types. Such a rejection of allegory as a suitable epithet is also confirmed by the fact that the narrative level in the Johannine texts does not exist only for the sake of the symbolical level, but refers to something which *is interpreted* by the symbolical level. In ch. 4 I showed how the narrator regarded Jesus events and Jesus sayings from the time before the "hour" as something mysterious (ἐν παροιμίαις), which were revealed and explained after Jesus' "hour" by the interpretative and teaching activity of the Paraclete. I am of the opinion that an explanation of the relations between the two text levels in Jn cannot ignore the clear *interpretative character* of the texts and the interpretation process behind them, a process vouched for in the text in so many different ways.[19] In any case a part of the events narrated in the two texts which I have analysed may therefore, I think, be regarded as primary in relation to the symbolic level.[20]

The narratives on which the author comments in 12:16 and 2:17, 21f, where this interpretation is explicitly mentioned, refer to three things which should also be found in the Cana and Samaria narratives: *a.* Jesus events and Jesus sayings, *b.* a comprehensive aspect of what Jesus said and did, on the basis of Jesus' "hour", i.e. that which I included under the *ergon* aspect, and *c.* certain passages from the Scriptures (the OT as it was read and used in the milieu of the evangelist).[21] Thus I find it reasonable to assume that there are certain Jesus events and Jesus sayings also behind the Cana and the Samaria narratives, although it is very difficult to delimit them.[22] When the narrator reproduced, interpreted and applied these,[23] he was dependent on a double screen, an *ergon* screen and a Scripture screen. Through the *ergon* screen the entire narrative has been seen in the light of Jesus' "hour", i.e. from a specific concept of Jesus' work of salvation as a whole. This implies a certain vocabulary, which we recognize as the Johannine, and also includes certain experiences from the early history of the new covenant. Indeed, as I have often pointed out, Jesus' *ergon* includes both the time before and the time after Jesus' "hour" and is also, according to Jn, the

allegory. "Die Schriftdeutung des NT ist beherrscht von der typologischen Auswertung des AT; allegorische Deutungen erscheinen nur ganz am Rande", Goppelt, col. 240. "Verwandt mit der Allegorie ist die biblische *Typologie,* die historische Realitäten in eine typologische Korrespondenz bringt", Lausberg, p. 140.

[19] See above, ch. 4.

[20] For further discussion of the relation between the event and its interpretation, see Nicol 1972, pp. 106ff. The symbolism in Jn is an interpretation of the deeds of Jesus; his deeds are not only illustrations of the truths expressed in the symbolism.

[21] See above, 4.2 and 4.3.

[22] The existence of Synoptic parallels to Jn 2:13ff; 4:46ff(?); 6:1ff and 12:12ff supports such an assumption. For the Cana narrative, Williams 1967 refers to Lk 5:33—39, and Lindars 1969—70, pp. 318ff, describes 2:10 as an earlier parable of Jesus, which has been connected with a Jesus narrative of the same type as the infancy narratives. On Synoptic material behind Jn 4, see Dodd 1963, pp. 236ff, 391ff.

[23] This "interpretation" process surely belongs to a longer period.

work of the disciples.[24] Certain features of the text, therefore, refer to specific Johannine concepts, and to specific experiences in the history of the early Church. The co-projection, somewhat alien in our eyes, of the two phases is justified in Jn by, above all, the activity of the Paraclete. The revelation and the work of salvation are given with the earthly Jesus according to the evangelist, but they do not come home to men—and this also applies to Jesus' disciples according to Jn—until the time of the Paraclete by his mediation. He is the great exegete and interpreter of Jesus' words and actions (4.3).

The second screen, the Scripture screen, consists of Jewish (and Samaritan) concepts related to certain texts in the OT, in the Cana narrative, for example, of concepts of how the old people of God was born at the wedding once at Sinai (the Sinai screen), and in the Samaria narrative of the concepts of the Well, which God gave the Israelites (and the Samaritans) and of the gathering in of the scattered Israel and the union of Judah and Ephraim. Certain features in the two texts allude to these concepts, which seem to have specially influenced the structure of the narrative as a whole (the Sinai screen and the Well screen).[25] The narrator could then combine material from "the Jesus tradition", an *ergon* screen and various Scripture screens, into the lucid, and often dramatic, narrative which we now have in the extant text.

If I must choose, I would prefer the second description of the text type in the two texts: *a strongly "screened" text*. The screen concept offers some explanation of how the larger structures in the texts are bound to the symbolic meaning, and brings some order to the many allusive elements mentioned in the first description. Moreover, it may well be related to the interpretative character of the Johannine texts which must, in my opinion, be included in a determination of the relation between the two text levels. It should also be pointed out here that many details in the text are dependent on more than one screen (e.g. "the gift of God" in 4:10) and that such details may well be incorporated at the narrative level (e.g. "gathering in fruit" in 4:36). The description of the Johannine texts as strongly "screened" texts, therefore, is also highly compatible with the first characteristic feature, which I attributed to the two levels of the text, the unity between the narrative and the symbolic.

---

[24] See, for example, above 2.2, U 27 and U 29, 2.4.2, 3.2.6, 3.3.5 and 3.4.5.

[25] Note the summary statement in Miller's survey of the use of the OT in Targum, Midrash and the NT: "OT texts which are sometimes alluded to in a NT passage only as an isolated word or phrase may nonetheless figure decisively in the ordering and structuring of NT material of disparate origin and form. It is a fact that in recent studies interest in the application of Jewish exegesis has stressed its importance for questions of the structure and form of NT material and has seen this as being of greater import than the search for material parallels", Miller 1971, p. 61. How OT texts have influenced the composition of apocalyptic texts has been investigated in Hartman 1966, "the first serious attempt to focus on and clarify the use of OT texts in the formation of apocalyptic traditions", Miller 1971, p. 74.

It is selfevident that this type of text will only function in a context in which both the *ergon* screen and the Scripture screens are present for the receivers, and in this respect the Johannine texts resemble allegory: they were written with the "initiated" in mind, those who are already "in the know", and who are given deeper and clearer knowledge through the texts.[26] My conclusions as regards the character of the texts as a whole, therefore, confirm Leroy's thesis of a Johannine "Sondersprache", and Meeks' description of Jn as a book for insiders and, to some extent also, de Jonge's designation of Johannine theology as "a typical in-group theology".[27] The Johannine language is a language of initiates, the qualities of which cóuld be but little analysed in this investigation. They call for a number of subsidiary investigations. The fact that the texts have a strongly symbolic character renders them especially open to other meanings than the one which first determined their form in a specific situation, which was surely of significance when the Johannine texts began to be used in other contexts than the original small group, in Gnostic circles, or in Christian circles, where they were incorporated in the NT canon as a Gospel.[28]

This description of the Johannine text is based solely on a textual analysis of two passages, and should therefore be regarded rather as an hypothesis for further investigations of the Johannine text type(s). The remaining texts in Jn should be analysed in a similar fashion, and this internal analysis should be complemented by *comparative studies of texts other than Jn,* concerning the very question of text type and genre. In my opinion, the material which ought to be examined first is that which is at times called narrative midrash of implicit, internal or covert type,[29] known mainly perhaps from the more paraphrastic Targums, such as the Targum Pseudo-Jonathan, which I have already had occasion to quote several times.[30] The characteristic of these texts is that the interpretative material is wholly integrated with the Biblical text, to form a continuous narrative. The result is a completely rewritten Biblical narrative, sometimes called a paraphrase because of its relation to the written text of the Bible. There must be several types of text in this category of material but, as far as I know, there are

---

[26] The difference in this respect between the allegory and the parable is stressed by Pedersen 1972.

[27] Leroy 1968, especially pp. 21ff and 157ff, Meeks 1972, pp. 63f, and de Jonge 1972—73, p. 264.

[28] The symbolic meaning of the texts suggested by me may later have been changed to, for example, a sacramental meaning. On the rather common interpretation of Jn as referring to the sacraments, see the survey in Klos 1970.

[29] See Wright 1967, p. 58, Bowker 1969, pp. 85ff, Ellis 1969, p. 62, Levine 1971a, p. 89. As early as 1926 Fiebig points to Jewish literary forms as parallels to the Gospel narratives.

[30] For a characterization of Targum Pseudo-Jonathan, see Levine 1971a, pp. 89, 101ff, 1971b, pp 47ff. Bowker 1969, p. 85, mentions as good early examples of narrative midrashim Jub and Pseudo-Philo, and also PRE, Ellis 1969, pp. 63f, mentions 1QGenAp, Jub and Targ. Pseudo-Jon.

no investigations of narrative midrashim, regarding a description of their literary qualities.[31]

Research on the relationship between Targum, Midrash, the OT and the NT has increased considerably in recent years, as emerges from Merril P. Miller's excellent and comprehensive survey from 1971.[32] Regarding my conclusions, I wish here to make special mention of Lentzen-Deis' investigation of the pericope on Jesus' baptism in the Synoptic Gospels,[33] since it also includes the question of text type and emphasizes its importance for the understanding and interpretation of texts. He gives his conclusions as follows: "Der Taufbericht, die Mitteilung von Jesu Taufe mit der Deute-Vision, ist in ähnlicher Weise wie die Erklärung des Pentateuch in der Synagoge Haggada. Am besten fassen wir den Bericht als Unterweisung, Erklärung des "Lebens Jesu" (im weiten Sinn). 'Liturgisch' ist die Perikope dann nur in der Weise, wie die Erzählung vom Leben Jesu in das liturgische Leben dieser Gemeinde Eingang fand."[34] He concentrates the latter part of his investigation on "eine bestimmte Art der haggadischen Erweiterung in einigen Targumtexten", which he describes as "eine eigene literarische Gattung", called "Deute-Vision". "Es handelt sich um die literarische Gattung der 'Vision'. Hier liegt sie in einer Spezialisierung vor, die eine Deute-Funktion für im Bibeltext genannte Gestalten ausübt und davon geprägt ist".[35] In my view, Lentzen-Deis has shown that this literary form, which is not confirmed in, for example, the Greek or the Syrian translations of the OT, is relevant for the baptism narrative and has thereby bound the basic design of the baptism text to a specific environment, characterized not least by the tradition of the synagogue and "ältere biblische Erzählweise".[36] "Aus dem Judentum stammen die Einzelmotive, die Erzählgattung, die Art und die Prinzipien der 'Schriftverwendung' im Taufbericht".[37] This conclusion, which is in many respects comparable with my own, has, I think, the greater value in that Lentzen-Deis' method differs from mine. His work is based primarily on a comparative analysis of related texts, while I use an internal textual method. Evidently both the methods may lead to similar results, which gives further justification for complementary comparative studied regarding the determination of the Johannine text type(s).

A few scholars, such as K. Hanhart and M.-E. Boismard, have described

[31] Note, however, the general characterization in Levine 1971a and 1971b.
[32] An earlier bibliography in Nickels 1967 and extensive references also in Lentzen-Deis 1970, pp. 252ff. See also Hanhart 1970, Gerhardsson 1969, 1970, 1972–73, 1973, Le Déaut 1971, Grossfeld 1972 and Boismard 1973.
[33] "Die Taufe Jesu nach den Synoptikern. Literarkritische und gattungsgeschichtliche Untersuchungen". Frankfurt am Main 1970.
[34] Lentzen-Deis 1970, p. 277.
[35] Lentzen-Deis 1970, p. 200f.
[36] Lentzen-Deis 1970, p. 252.
[37] Lentzen-Deis 1970, p. 259.

Johannine text as midrashim. After stating in his analysis of Jn 1:35—4:54 that a two level approach is necessary for an understanding of Jn, K. Hanhart describes this section as "a *midrashic* comment" on episodes from Synoptic Gospels, which the evangelist chose because of their message.[38] Jn 4:1—42 is an "aggadah of John's own making", dependent on Acts 8,[39] while Jn 2:1—11 is an allegorical haggadah, based on synoptic material and Acts 2.[40] "John based the structure of i 35—iv 54 on characteristic themes from Mark, Matthew and Luke-Acts", and represents "a further development of the art of Gospel writing. . . . John wrote as it were a Gospel and Acts in one".[41] Thus the narrator in Jn starts from the Synoptic Gospels and Acts as given texts, which would mean that the book was not written until the end of the first century. The similarity to the Jewish midrashim thereby consists, not only in the narrative, interpretative character, but, above all, in the dependence on specific texts.

Boismard describes Jn 4 "comme un midrash chrétien qui reprend les données de *Gen.*, xxiv, 10ss. Il veut présenter la conversion de la Samarie comme un nouveau 'mariage' entre Dieu et son peuple, selon une façon de parler courante dans l' A.T.".[42] Thus the narrator would be building on OT texts. According to both these investigations, which were published during the course of my work, Jn would then be a midrash on specific texts, from the NT or the OT. According to my description of the Johannine text type, both an *ergon* screen "from the NT" and a Scripture screen "from the OT" are necessary, and these combine to give us a very close connection between tradition, interpretation, application and concepts related to the OT. All these are interwoven to yield narrative texts, evidently of a similar type to that found in narrative midrashim.

In this context the question arises whether or not we should for the creation of the Gospel material assume "a midrashic approach to the Gospel tradition",[43] already at the stage when it was not yet written down, or a haggadic way of telling of Jesus. A number of the Jews who believed in Jesus as "the Messiah" would, at a very early stage, have had the same attitude to Jesus events and Jesus sayings as to the Scriptures,[44] a fact which has occasionally resulted in an inter-

[38] Hanhart 1970, p. 23.
[39] Hanhart 1970, p. 33.
[40] Hanhart 1970, p. 38.
[41] Hanhart 1970, p. 46.
[42] Boismard 1973, p. 225. The similarities between Gen 24 and Jn 4 which he mentions are very general and link up with all the well scenes in Gen 24, Gen 29 and Ex 2:15ff. They are better explained by a Well screen.
[43] Miller 1971, p. 64.
[44] Note the way in which the "words" of Jesus are made functionally parallel to the Scriptures in Jn (18:9, 32; 2:22; 5:47). The mission of Jesus and of Moses—who gave the Law to the Jews, 7:19—are also described in the same way, Meeks 1967, pp. 289f. On the Johannine method of using "speeches", see above 2.2, U 26.

pretative paraphrase of the received tradition resembling the material mentioned above. Such an attitude would imply certain laws for the formation of the Jesus tradition, and also assume a definite relation between this tradition and the Scriptures. The narratives concerning Jesus are seen as tradition, interpretation of tradition and application, and are thus not something created wholly *de novo*. This theory was suggested in M.P. Miller's survey mentioned above.[45] With a reference to a study of the Parable of the Good Samaritan by Birger Gerhardsson Miller sums up by saying: "I am suggesting, however, that midrashic adaptations of the received tradition were more fundamental and far-reaching and that such adaptations were not transmitted on an explicit midrashic pattern of text and commentary, but were incorporated and merged with the received tradition. Such a process may occasionally have resulted in an interpretative paraphrase of the received tradition".[46] Naturally Miller's survey does not include any analysis of texts which could confirm this.

A number of the observations and conclusions in my textual investigation rouse my interest in Miller's suggestions: the actual text type as I described it, the strong influence of the OT material on the structure, the combination of several texts from the OT and Jewish (Samaritan) concepts in the screen, the close association of a total view of Jesus and the Scriptures, and indeed also the feature of *aporias* inherent in the Johannine texts, if designated otherwise than J have done. We should perhaps assume a far more comprehensive interpretation process in certain environments at the very beginning of the Gospel tradition, in which Jewish categories were the only ones, and the result was sometimes what we call symbolical texts. When the various pericopes were later included in the Gospel genre, a certain desymbolization took place, and the texts were read more as history and biography.[47]

This latter reasoning has diverted us somewhat from my investigation, but it should show that a textual analysis concerning the message and character of the text has several consequences for the description of the situation of the text and its prehistory. It is impossible wholly to separate internal and external, synchronic and diachronic criteria in the analysis of the text. Yet in the present situa-

---

[45] Miller 1971, pp. 62ff.

[46] Miller 1971, p. 63, note 1. That the Gospel tradition was not only carefully preserved but was so preserved precisely to form the object of intensive study and reapplication, and thus to give rise to a kind of midrashic activity is also stressed by Gerhardsson, for example in his thesis (1961), pp. 331ff, in Gerhardsson 1966 and in the articles he mentions in Gerhardsson 1972b, p. 26, note 1.

[47] See, for example, the different forms of the temptation narrative, analysed by Gerhardsson 1966, of the tradition of the baptism of Jesus, analysed in Lentzen-Deis 1970, or of the Synoptic apocalypse, analysed by Hartman 1966. Such an hypothesis is, as far as I know, not yet generally tested. The common view is that the symbolic interpretations of the traditions of Jesus come very late in the history of the Gospel tradition and then in the form of allegorical interpretations.

tion of research, I regard it as fruitful to start first of all from an internal textual analysis.[48]

Finally there is the temptation to discuss the many questions inherent in Jn, "das Rätsel des NT, historisch und literarisch, religionsgeschichtlich und theologisch",[49] and try to answer them in the light of my preliminary results, even before these are confirmed by further analyses of Johannine text and by comparative investigations. Nevertheless I shall restrain myself to mentioning only three problems, and those very briefly.

1. The environment of the text. I hardly need say that my analysis of the text supports one of the tendencies in the Johannine research of today: the texts in Jn are deeply rooted in a Jewish environment.[50] This is proved both by the content of the two texts and their forms as I have described it. The Gospel of St John is in many respects a settlement with the Jewish background of Christianity,[51] and could therefore be described as "the most Hebraic book in the New Testament, except perhaps the Apocalypse".[52] At that time, however, Judaism was a religion with many facets, so that the environment should be described in detail. My analysis seems to have brought out four fairly general delimitations, which are worth examining with regard to the environment of the text.

The first concerns Jewish worship, the *synagogue environment,* with its special language and use of the Scriptures, manifested in Targums and homilies. Jn is hardly a "gottesdienstliches Perikopenbuch",[53] but it uses material the form of which may be explained by a "Sitz im Leben" in Jewish worship and in a Christian form of worship derived from it.[54]

The second interesting problem is the trend which Janssen, in his book on different Jewish concepts of the people of God, calls the *"priestly"* in contrast to the more Rabbinical and the Apocalyptic model for the view of the people of God and its history.[55] It starts from priestly concepts, stressing "den Kultus und seine Bedeutung für das Land und die Welt".[56] Salvation as a present reality is emphasized, as is the demand for

---

[48] See the introduction above, ch. 1.

[49] Stauffer's characterization ([4]1948, p. 24).

[50] See, besides the commentaries, Robinson 1959—60, Mitton 1959—60, Bowker 1964—65 and the literature mentioned in the following notes. A general survey in Wind 1972.

[51] This has often been pointed out by Harald Riesenfeld, for example in Riesenfeld 1969, p. 420.

[52] Robinson 1959—60, p. 118, referring to J.B. Lightfoot.

[53] Thus, for example, Michaelis, p. 117.

[54] Stauffer [4]1948, p. 25, notes "die betont liturgische Stilgebung, Terminologie und Bilderwelt der drei Hauptschriften, die im NT unter dem Name des Apostels Johannes gehen", but explains this feature by suggesting that they are made *for liturgical use,* which may be questioned. Raney 1933 suggests a "Sitz im Leben" in Christian worship at the beginning of the second century. A synagogue environment for the formation of Johannine texts also points to the function of the *methurgeman.* See Stauffer 1963 and his references, and on the homiletic patterns in the synagogue, Borgen 1965 with the review by Aalen 1966.

[55] Janssen 1971, pp. 194ff.

[56] Janssen 1971, p. 195.

purification and the need for redemption.[57] The whole of Israel is seen as "ein Priestervolk inmitten der Völkerwelt ... Das Verständnis Israels als Priestervolk ist in sich sehr variabel. Eine Auffassung betont die Reinheit des Volkes. Dadurch kommt es zu einer starken Hervorhebung des Gegensatzes zu den Völkern, der soweit gehen kann, dass selbst die Unreinen Israels nicht mehr als zu Israel gehörig angesehen werden. Nur noch eine 'ecclesiola in ecclesia' stellt das wahre Israel dar. Es kann aber auch ebenso der Dienst für die Welt, der Opferdienst, als das Spezifikum Israels als Priestervolk heraus bestellt werden. Eine dritte Auffassung sieht den 'Priesterdienst' in dem beispielhaften Leben nach der Tora oder auch im Studium dieses Gesetzes sich verkörpern. Die priesterlichen Auffassungen haben eins gemeinsam, dass alle staatlichen Vorstellungen entweder verdrängt sind oder ganz von den priesterlichen usurpiert werden. Das kann soweit gehen, dass der Hohepriester königliche Funktionen übernimmt, aber die priesterlichen dabei die Hauptsache bleiben".[58] In my view the "universalistic" feature in Jn ("saviour of the world", etc.) and the emphasis on purification are above all worth investigating on the basis of the traditions here mentioned by Janssen.[59]

This "priestly" tradition brings us to the material from Qumran, and also to a *Samaritan environment* of a part of the Johannine material (third point).[60] Indeed, as early as 1929, Hugo Odeberg pointed out that Jn 4 reflects a controversy with Samaritans, who particularly devoted themselves to "mystical speculations and interpretations of the Tora".[61] The interest in a Samaritan background of Jn has greatly increased in recent years:[62] scholars cite a long series of individual features in the Gospel, which are best explained on the basis of Samaritan vocabulary and tradition.[63] I have maintained that the Samaria narrative tells how the Samaritans will be integrated in the new people of God, and that this teaching is presumably given by some one who has another view than most of the apostles (3.5.1). The Gospel strongly emphasizes that the disciples in the text need this teaching. Thus they seem to oppose the acceptance of the Samaritans. At the same time we can say that the narrator's knowledge of Samaritan topography and tradition is extensive, and that he is very favourably inclined to Samaritan belief, and to those who worked among the Samaritans before the disciples, notwithstanding that he holds steadfast to the view that salvation will come from the Jews. This interpretation applies to the text as we now have it, which must be described as typically Johannine in form. So there must be a connection between the narrator of Jn 4, the man generally called the evangelist and Samaritan religion, a connection which has not yet been clarified.

[57] Janssen 1971, pp. 195, 197, 198ff.

[58] Janssen 1971, p. 199.

[59] Note also the picture of Jesus as a priest in Jn, Wallis 1971, and the role of priests in the Gospel. Janssen mentions Sir (pp. 16ff), the Damascus Document (pp. 109ff), Johanan b. Zakkai (pp. 127ff) and Eliezer b. Hyrcanus (pp. 135ff) as representatives of the priestly concepts of the people of God.

[60] On the priestly character of the Qumran sect and the Samaritan community, see Kippenberg, 1971, passim.

[61] Odeberg 1929, p. 185.

[62] See Bowman 1958, 1967, MacDonald 1964, Spiro 1967, Meeks 1967, pp. 216ff, 313ff, Buchanan 1968, Scharlemann 1968, Freed 1968, 1970. For a survey on the Samaritans and the NT, see de Robert 1970 and Scobie 1972—73.

[63] See, for example, the eighteen points in Freed's summary from 1970.

This connection may be related to *the Hellenists in Acts* (fourth point), represented by such men as Stephen and Philip.[64] Indeed in Stephen's speech in Acts 7 there are several features which may be connected with Samaritan beliefs,[65] while his attitude to "the holy place and the law" has much in common with the same problems in Jn 1:19—4:54. My analysis, therefore, recalls Cullmann's thesis from 1958, that Jn developed among Christians who had previously been nonconformist Jews, i.e., according to him, the Hellenists in Acts, whereas the Synoptic tradition took shape among Christians who had been Orthodox Jews before their conversion.[66] Cullmann here sees a connection via "esoterisches Judentum — Johannes der Täufer — Hellenisten der Apostelgeschichte" with the Johannine community.[67] The details of how these links should be described have not yet been investigated. Indeed it would be of interest to examine Jn 1:19—4:54 and acts 2—8 regarding the fact that both these texts seem to describe the creation of the new people of God within the Jewish (and Samaritan) community.

2. The age of the text. I am here primarily thinking of the dating of the texts which we now have in 2:1—11 and 4:1—42, which seem to belong to the final stage of the Gospel. Many of those who assert that we have in Jn a text with two levels are accustomed to refer it to the end of the first century. The symbolical level is thought to have come into existence at a late stage in the history of the text.[68] But why late? We know that the Christians had total visions of Jesus at a very early date,[69] and that these could have been shaped in several ways, including midrash forms common in a Jewish setting.[70] The form of the texts I have analysed is most plausibly connected with a Jewish setting, especially that of the synagogue. Moreover the subject of the texts, on how the new people of God was born from the old and how it also included Samaritans, must have been of topical interest very early in Christian history.[71] What possible situations would call for the instruction of certain Christians on the justification of the Samaria mission? Unquestionably there are many indications of a situation similar to that underlying the first chapters in Acts. Nowadays there is a manifest tendency to set an earlier date on Jn.[72] I

---

[64] Probably there are connections between the Hellenists, the synagogal, the priestly and the Samaritan milieus I mentioned here.

[65] See especially Spiro 1967 and Scharlemann 1968. Scobie 1972—73, pp. 391ff, gives an excellent summary of the discussions on Acts 7 just now.

[66] A shorted version of the French original from 1958 was published in *NT Stud.* 5 (1968—69) and in *Exp. Times* 71 (1959—60). I here follow the German version in Cullmann 1966. pp. 260ff.

[67] Cullmann 1966, p. 289. The connections between Jn and "esoterisches Judentum" was pointed out very strongly by Odeberg 1929. In many ways my internal analysis of the texts seems to confirm results in Odeberg's extremely comparative investigation.

[68] See, for example, Martyn 1968, Hanhart 1970 and Nicol 1972.

[69] This is confirmed by, for example, the early baptismal praxis; see Hartman 1971.

[70] See Gerhardsson 1966 and his analysis of the *shema'*-theme in Mt (1966, 1967—68, 1969, 1972a, 1972b, 1972—73, 1973). The specific literary forms of this theme seem to me to belong to the early Christian era rather than to Jesus. The changes of the theme in the final edition of Mt and in Lk suggest an early date for this "midrashic" work. —For a general survey of midrash forms in the NT, see Miller 1971, pp. 55ff (with references).

[71] The question of the incorporation of the Samaritans in the new people of God seems to have been solved before Lk wrote his work, Jervell 1972, pp. 41ff, 113ff.

[72] See the survey in Cribbs 1970.

am of the opinion that in this context we should ask whether or not some Johannine texts to a great extent took form very early, perhaps even before the meeting of the apostles—which dealt with the problem of the Gentiles, not the Samaritans—in discussions and acts of worship in the synagogues of Jerusalem and Judea, and then in the stream of Christian "Hellenists" who had to leave Jerusalem in connection with the appearance and death of St. Stephen.[73] An arrangement in Gospel form may have emerged later. The problem of the so-called Johannine transformation process, when the Johannine material acquired its typical shape, and its dating is not yet solved.

3. *The prehistory of the text.* As regards the symbolic level, the two texts proved to be very well shaped into a unit, especially the Cana narrative (2.4). Thus it appears difficult to distinguish Johannine additions to them. Quoting his pupil, Hans-Peter Otto, Hartwig Thyen shows in the Festschrift to Kuhn that the person described by Bultmann as the "kirchlicher Redaktor" played a far more important part in the creation of Jn than Bultmann imagines. He wonders whether it "überhaupt noch sinnvoll ist, den Editor unseres Johannesevangeliums einen '*kirchlichen Redaktor*' zu nennen. . . . Wahrscheinlich nennte man ihn aber wohl zutreffender den 'vierten Evangelisten' und versuchte sein ganzes Buch—was immer es an Ungereimtheiten und literarischen Rätseln enthalten mag—als Autosemantikon für sich selber sprechen zu lassen".[74] The latter must be considered confirmed by my textual analyses. There is every justification for trying to interpret the Johannine texts as they now stand without necessarily involving their prehistory. There is a narrator behind the texts, who knew how to shape them in order to express the message he sought to convey.

Scholars concerned with Gospel research are interested in a situation other than that of the text (the final stage). I am here thinking of the situation of the "historical" Jesus. This has forced many scholars to dwell on situations between the two just mentioned, in order to use a traditio-historical method to establish what belongs to the "historical" Jesus and what is later additions. Such research as often concentrates on details and delimination of certain linguistic expressions, however, must be complemented by other lines of argument, if the historical probability of the portrait of Jesus, mediated by the texts, is to be established. Assuming that the interpretation of the texts, which I have proposed, is correct, what is the connection between their picture of Jesus and the "historical" Jesus? Which criteria and which lines of argument will suffice to answer this question? The homogeneity displayed by the two texts aggravates the usual reasoning from traditional history, and seems to me to require a complement in other types of arguments in the discussions on the problem of the "historical" Jesus.

---

[73] An investigation of such an hypothesis of an early formation of the Johannine traditions can link up with earlier suggestions of Jn as *a primitive gospel* by especially Burch 1928, pp. 211ff, Gardner-Smith 1938, Goodenough 1945 and Cribbs 1970 (with further references). Cribbs suggests as a tentative hypothesis that Jn "could be an interpretation of the life of Jesus written by a cultured Christian Jew of Judea during the late 50's or early 60's who addressed it to (1) non-Christian Jews . . . and (2) to certain Jewish Christian communities" (p. 55). Note, however, note 27 above and my discussion there of the Johannine texts as texts for initiates, and the probable connections with nonconformist Jews, Odeberg 1929, passim, and Cullmann 1966, pp. 260ff.

[74] Thyen 1971, p. 356. Doubts of the possibilities of being able to distinguish between tradition and redaction are expressed fairly frequently nowadays; see, for example, Simonsen 1972.

These three problem complexes (1—3 above) must be examined in a wider context than that of my investigation. Nevertheless I wish to reiterate that a textual analysis of the type I have here performed is necessary, and is perhaps the best way to find answers to many problems concerning the Fourth Gospel which are not yet solved.

Bibliography

(The works in A and B are referred to by author's name or by abbreviations given below, the works in C by author's name and Comm., the works in D by name and date.)

A. Texts and Translations

Novum Testamentum graece, ed. E. Nestle and K. Aland. Stuttgart ^{25}1963.
The Greek New Testament, ed. K. Aland, M. Black, C.M. Martini, B.M. Metzger, and A. Wikgren. Stuttgart ^{2}1968.
Synopsis Quattuor Evangeliorum..., ed. K. Aland. Stuttgart 1964.
Novum Testamentum Domini nostri Jesu Christi latine secundum editionem Sancti Hieronymi, ed. J. Wordsworth and H.J. White. Vol. 1. Oxford 1889—1898.
Itala. Das Neue Testament in altlateinischer Überlieferung, ed. A. Jülicher, et al. Vol. 4. Berlin 1963.

Biblia Hebraica, ed. R. Kittel, et al. Stuttgart ^{13}1962.
Septuaginta..., ed. A. Rahlfs. 2 Vols. Stuttgart ^{7}1962.
The Book of Wisdom. Ed. J. Reider (Jewish Apocryphal Literature, ed. S. Zeitlin et al.). New York 1957.
Targum Onkelos..., ed. A. Berliner. 2 Vols. Berlin 1884.
Neophyti 1.... Ed. A. Díez Macho. 3 Vols. Madrid-Barcelona 1968—1971.
Das Fragmententhargum, ed. M. Ginsburger. Berlin 1899.
Pseudo-Jonathan..., ed. M. Ginsburger. Berlin 1903.
The Bible in Aramaic, ed. A. Sperber. 3 Vols. Leiden 1959—1962.
The Targum of Isaiah, ed. J.F. Stenning. Oxford 1949.
SS. Biblia polyglotta, ed. B. Walton. 4 Vols. London 1657.
The Targums of Onkelos and Jonathan ben Uzziel on the Pentateuch; with the Fragments of the Jerusalem Targum. Trans. J.W. Etheridge. 2 Vols. London 1862—1865.

Der hebraïsche Pentateuch der Samaritaner. Ed. A. von Gall. 5 Vols. Giessen 1914—1918.
Das samaritanische Targum. Ed. A. Brüll. Frankfurt am Main 1875.

Die Mischna. Text, Übersetzung und ausführliche Erklärung..., ed. G. Beer, et al. Giessen 1912ff, Berlin 1956ff.
Mishnayoth, ed. P. Blackman. 6 Vols. New York ^{3}1965.
The Mishnah. Translated..., by H. Danby. Oxford 1933.
Tosephta, ed. M.S. Zuckermandel. Pasewalk, Trier 1879—1882.
The Tosefta..., ed. S. Lieberman. Iff. New York 5715—1955ff.

Die Tosefta; Text, Übersetzung, Erklärung. Ed. G. Kittel, et al. (Rabbinische Texte, I. Reihe). Stuttgart 1933ff.

Der babylonische Talmud . . . , ed. L. Goldschmidt. 9 Vols. Berlin, Leipzig, Haag 1897–1934.

The Babylonian Talmud . . . translated into English . . . , ed. I. Epstein. 35 Vols. London 1935–1948.

Le Talmud de Jérusalem traduit pour la première fois. Trans. M. Schwab. 11 Vols. Paris 1878–1890.

Mechilta, der älteste halachische und haggadische Commentar zum zweiten Buche Moses . . . , ed. I.H. Weiss. Wien 1865.

Mechilta, ed. H.S. Horovitz (Corpus tannaiticum 3:1:1). Frankfurt am Main 1928ff.

Mechilta. Ein tannaitischer Midrasch zu Exodus. Erstmalig ins Deutsche übersetzt und erläutert von J. Winter und Aug. Wünsche. Leipzig 1909.

Midrash Rabbah translated into English . . . , ed. H. Freedmann and M. Simon. 10 Vols. London 1939.

The Midrash on Psalms, trans. by W.G. Braude (Yale Judaica Series 13). 2 Vols. New Haven 1959.

Bibliotheca Rabbinica. Ed. Aug. Wünsche. 12 Vols. Leipzig 1880–1885.

Pirkê de Rabbi Eliezer. Translated . . . by G. Friedlander. London 1916.

Pseudo-Philo's Liber Antiquitatum Biblicarum. Ed. G. Kish (Publications in Mediaeval Studies 10). Notre Dame 1949.

The Biblical Antiquities of Philo. Trans. M.R. James (Translations of Early Documents, Series I, Palestinian Jewish Texts). London 1917.

Raschis Pentateuchkommentar. Vollständig ins Deutsche übertragen . . . von S. Bamberger. Frankfurt am Main [3]1935.

The Apocrypha and Pseudepigrapha of the Old Testament in English. Ed. R.H. Charles. 2 Vols. Oxford 1913.

The Greek Versions of the Testaments of the Twelve Patriarchs . . . , ed. R.H. Charles. Oxford 1908.

The Odes and Psalms of Solomon, ed. R. Harris and A. Mingana. 2 Vols. Manchester, London, New York . . . 1916–1920.

Die Texte aus Qumran, hebräisch und deutsch . . . , ed. E. Lohse. München 1964.

The Zadokite Documents . . . , ed. and trans. C. Rabin. Oxford [2]1958.

Josephus; With an English Translation. Ed. H.St.J. Thackeray and R. Marcus (Loeb Classical Library). 9 Vols. London 1926–1965.

Philo; With an English Translation. Ed. F.H. Colson and G.H. Whitaker (Loeb Classical Library). 12 Vols. London 1929–1964.

Neutestamentliche Apokryphen in deutscher Übersetzung. Ed. E. Hennecke. 3rd ed. by W. Schneemelcher. 2 Vols. Tübingen 1959–1964.

Die apostolischen Väter. Neubearbeitung der Funkschen Ausgabe. Ed. K. Bihlmeyer, W. Schneemelcher (Samml. ausgew. kirchen. u. dogmengesch. Quellenschr. II:1:1). Tübingen [2]1956.

Epiphanius (Griechische christliche Schriftsteller 25, 31, 37). 3 Vols. Leipzig 1915, 1922, 1933.

Corpus Hermeticum, ed. A.D. Nock and A.J. Festugière. 4 Vols. Paris 1945–1954.
Epictetus. The Discourses as Reported by Arrian, the Manual, and Fragments. Ed. and trans. W.A. Oldfather (Loeb Classical Library). 2 Vols. London 1926–1928.
Corpus Paroemiographorum Graecorum. Ed. E.L. Leutsch and F.G. Schneidewin. 2 Vols. Göttingen 1834–1851.
The Oxyrhynchus Papyri. Part VIII. Ed. A.S. Hunt (Egypt Exploration Fund. Graeco-Roman Branch). London 1911.

B. Works of Reference

Bauer, W., *Griechisch-deutsches Wörterbuch zu den Schriften des Neuen Testaments und der übrigen urchristlichen Literatur.* Berlin ⁵1958.
Beyer, Kl., *Semitische Syntax im Neuen Testament* I:1 (Stud. z. Umwelt des NT 1). Göttingen ²1968.
Blass, F., and A. Debrunner, *Grammatik des neutestamentlichen Griechisch.* Mit einem Ergänzungsheft von D. Tabachovitz. Göttingen ¹²1965. (abbreviated: Bl.-Debr.)
A Concordance to the Greek Testament according to the Texts of Westcott and Hort, Tischendorf, and the English Revisers. Ed. W.F. Moulton and A.S. Geden. Edinburgh 1957.
A Concordance to the Septuagint and the Other Greek Versions of the Old Testament . . . , ed. E. Hatch and H.A. Redpath. 2 Vols. Graz-Austria 1954.
Dalman, G.H., *Aramäisch-neuhebräisches Handwörterbuch zu Targum, Talmud und Midrasch.* Frankfurt am Main ²1922.
Dictionnaire de la Bible. Supplément, ed. L. Pirot, et al. Paris 1928ff.
Feine, P., and J. Behm, *Einleitung in das Neue Testament,* völlig neu bearbeitet von W.G. Kümmel. Heidelberg ¹³1964. (abbreviated: Feine-Behm-Kümmel)
Galling, K., *Biblisches Reallexikon* (Handbuch zum Alten Testament 1). Tübingen 1937.
Ginzberg, L., *The Legends of the Jews.* 7 Vols. Philadelphia 1909–1938.
Goodenough, E.R., *Jewish Symbols in the Greco-Roman Period* (Bollingen Series 37). 13 Vols. New York 1953–1968.
Holladay, W.L., *A Concise Hebrew and Aramaic Lexicon of the Old Testament.* Leiden 1971.
Krauss, S., *Talmudische Archäologie.* 3 Vols. Leipzig 1910–1912. (abbreviated: Krauss, Archäologie)
Krauss, S., *Griechische und Lateinische Lehnwörter im Talmud, Midrasch und Targum.* 2 Vols. Berlin 1898–1899. (abbreviated: Krauss, Lehnwörter)
Kühner, R., *Ausführliche Grammatik der Griechischen Sprache.* 2. Teil: Satzlehre. In neuer Bearbeitung besorgt von B. Gerth. 2 Vols. Hannover, Leipzig ³1898–1904. (abbreviated: Kühner-Gert)
Liddell, H.G., and R. Scott, *A Greek-English Lexicon.* New ed. rev. by H.S. Jones. Oxford 1961. (abbreviated: Liddell-Scott)

Mayser, E., *Grammatik der griechischen Papyri aus der Ptolemäerzeit.* 2 Vols. Berlin, Leipzig 1906—1934.

Michaelis, W., *Einleitung in das Neue Testament.* Bern [2]1954.

Morgenthaler, R., *Statistik des neutestamentlichen Wortschatzes.* Zürich 1958.

Moule, C.F.D., *An Idiom Book of New Testament Greek.* Cambridge [2]1960.

Moulton, J.H., and G. Milligan, *The Vocabulary of the Greek Testament Illustrated from the Papyri and Other Non-Literary Sources.* London 1914—1929.

Reallexikon für Antike und Christentum, ed. Th. Klauser. Stuttgart 1950ff. (abbreviated: RAC)

Die Religion in Geschichte und Gegenwart, ed. K. Galling. 7 Vols. Tübingen [3]1957—1965. (abbreviated: [3]RGG)

Strack, H.L., and P. Billerbeck, *Kommentar zum Neuen Testament aus Talmud und Midrasch.* 4 Vols. München 1922—1928. (abbreviated: Str.-B.)

Svenskt Bibliskt Uppslagsverk, ed. I. Engnell. 2 Vols. Stockholm [2]1962—1963. (abbreviated: [2]SBU)

Theologisches Wörterbuch zum Neuen Testament, ed. G. Kittel and G. Friedrich. Stuttgart 1933ff. (abbreviated: ThWNT)

Turner, N., *A Grammar of New Testament Greek* (by J.H. Moulton). Vol. 3. Syntax. Edinburgh 1963.

Wikenhauser, A., and J. Schmid, *Einleitung in das Neue Testament.* Freiburg im Breisgau [6]1973.

C. Commentaries

Barrett, C.K., *The Gospel according to St. John.* London 1955.

Bauer, W., *Das Johannesevangelium erklärt* (Handbuch zum Neuen Testament 6). Tübingen [3]1933.

Bernard, J.H., *A Critical and Exegetical Commentary on the Gospel of St. John* (International Critical Commentary 30). 2 Vols. Edinburg 1928.

Brown, Raymond E., *The Gospel according to John* (The Anchor Bible 29 and 29a). 2 Vols. New York 1966, 1970.

Bultmann, R., *Das Evangelium des Johannes* (Kritisch-exegetischer Kommentar über das Neue Testament II). Göttingen [19]1968 (= [10]1941). Ergänzungsheft 1957.

Büchsel, F., *Das Evangelium nach Johannes* (Das Neue Testament Deutsch 4). Göttingen [4]1948.

Godet, F., *Commentaire sur l'Evangile de Saint Jean.* 3 Vols. Paris, Neuchatel [2]1876—1877.

Heitmüller, W., *Das Johannes-Evangelium* (Die Schriften des Neuen Testaments 4). Göttingen [3]1918.

Hengstenberg, E.W., *Das Evangelium des heiligen Johannes.* 3 Vols. Berlin [2]1867—1870.

Holtzmann, H.J., *Evangelium, Briefe und Offenbarung des Johannes* (Hand-Commentar zum Neuen Testament 4). Dritte, neubearbeitete Auflage, besorgt von W. Bauer. Tübingen [3]1908.

Hoskyns, E., *The Fourth Gospel* edited by F.N. Davey. London [2]1947.

Kreyenbühl, J., *Das Evangelium der Wahrheit.* Neue Lösung der Johanneischen Frage. 2 Vols. Berlin 1900, 1905.

Larange, M.-J., *Évangile selon saint Jean* (Études bibliques). Paris [3]1927.

Lightfoot, R.H., *St. John's Gospel.* A Commentary with the Revised Version Texts. Ed. by C.G. Evans. London 1956.

Lindars, B., *The Gospel of John* (New Century Bible). London 1972.

Loisy, A., *Le quatrième évangile. Les épîtres dites de Jean.* Paris [2]1921.

Meyer, H.A.W., *Kritisch-exegetisches Handbuch über das Evangelium des Johannes* (Kritisch-exegetischer Kommentar über das Neue Testament II). Göttingen [5]1869.

Moe, O., *Johannesevangeliet,* Innledet og Fortolket. Oslo [2]1951.

Mollat, D., and F.-M. Braun, *L'Évangile et les épitres de Saint Jean* (La Sainte Bible). Paris [2]1960. (abbreviated: Mollat)

Morris, L., *Commentary on the Gospel of John* (The New International Commentary on the New Testament). Grand Rapids, Michigan 1971.

Sanders, J.N., *A Commentary on the Gospel according to St John.* Edited and completed by B.A. Mastin. (Black's New Testament Commentaries) 1968. (abbreviated: Sanders-Mastin)

Schlatter, A., *Der Evangelist Johannes.* Wie er spricht, denkt und glaubt. Ein Kommentar zum 4. Evangelium. Stuttgart 1930.

Schnackenburg, R., *Das Johannesevangelium* (Herders Theologischer Kommentar zum Neuen Testament IV:1−2). 2 Vols. Freiburg im Breisgau 1965, 1971.

Schulz, S., *Das Evangelium nach Johannes* (Das Neue Testament Deutsch 4). Göttingen [12]1972.

Schwank, B., *Das Johannesevangelium erläutert* (Kleinkommentare zur Heiligen Schrift 7/1). Vol. 1. Düsseldorf 1966.

Strathmann, H., *Das Evangelium nach Johannes* (Das Neue Testament Deutsch 4). Göttingen [10]1963.

Tholuck, A., *Commentar zum Evangelium Johannis.* Gotha [7]1857.

Vawter, B., The Gospel according to John, in *The Jerome Biblical Commentary,* ed. R.E. Brown, J.A. Fitzmyer, and R.E. Murphy, London 1968, Vol. 2, 414−466.

Weiss, B., *Das Johannes-Evangelium* (Kritisch-exegetischer Kommentar über das Neue Testament II). Göttingen [9]1902.

Westcott, B.F., *The Gospel according to St. John* [Reprint from the "Speaker's Commentary" 1880. Introd. by A. Fox]. London 1958.

Wikenhauser, A., *Das Evangelium nach Johannes* (Regensburger Neues Testament 4). Regensburg [2]1957.

Zahn, Th., *Das Evangelium des Johannes* (Kommentar zum Neuen Testament 4). Leipzig-Erlangen [5−6]1921.

Bonnard, P., *L'Évangile selon Saint Matthieu* (Commentaire du Nouveau Testament 1). Neuchâtel (Switzerland) 1963.

Haas, C., M. de Jonge, and J.L. Swellengrebel, *A Translator's Handbook on the Letters of John* (Helps for Translators 13). London 1972.

Michel, O., *Der Breif an die Hebräer* (Kritisch-exegetischer Kommentar über das Neue Testament 13). Göttingen [12]1966.

Rylaarsdam, J.C., *The Book of Exodus* (The Interpreter's Bible 1). New York, Nashville 1952.

Schmid, J., *Das Evangelium nach Lukas* (Regensburger Neues Testament 3). Regensburg ³1955.

Spicq, C., *L'Épitre aux Hébreux* (Études bibliques). Paris 1952—53.

Taylor, V., *The Gospel according to St. Mark.* London ²1966.

D. General Works

Aalen, Sverre, 1966. 'Opposisjonsinnlegg ved Peder Borgens disputas for den teologiske doktorgrad 11. juni 1966', *Norsk Teol. Tidskrift* 67, 243—260.

Abbott, Edvin A., 1905. *Johannine Vocabulary* (= Diatessarica 5). London.

— 1906 *Johannine Grammar* (= Diatessarica 6). London.

Aberle, Moritz v., 1868. 'Über den Darstellungscharacter des Johannesevangeliums', *Theol. Quartalschrift* 50, 11—29.

Albertz, Martin, 1921. *Die synoptischen Streitgespräche.* Ein Beitrag zur Formengeschichte des Urchristentums. Berlin.

Alonso Schökel, Luis, 1963. *Estudio de Poética Hebraea.* Barcelona.

Andersson, Jan, and Mats Furberg, ²1967. *Språk och påverkan.* Lund.

Aspelin, Kurt, and Bengt A. Lundberg (eds.) 1971. *Form och struktur.* Stockholm.

Audet, Jean-Paul, 1959. 'La soif, l'eau et la parole', *Rev. Bibl.* 66, 379—386.

Bacon, Benjamin Wisner, 1910. *The Fourth Gospel in Research and Debate.* New Haven.

Baird, J. Arthur, 1969. *Audience Criticism and the Historical Jesus.* Philadelphia, Penn.

Barr, James, 1969. 'The Symbolism of Names in the Old Testament', *Bull. J. Ryl. Libr.* 52, 11—29.

Barrett, C.K., 1956. *The New Testament Background: Selected Documents.* London.

— 1971. Review of R.T. Fortna, The Gospel of Signs, in *J. Theol. Stud.* 22, 571—574.

Barosse, T., 1959. 'The Seven Days of the New Creation in St. John's Gospel', *Cath. Bibl. Quart.* 21, 507—516.

Barth, Gerhard, 1973. 'Zwei vernachlässigte Gesichtspunkte zum Verständnis der Taufe im Neuen Testament', *Zschr. Theol. Kirche* 70, 137—161.

Batey, Richard A., 1971. *New Testament Nuptial Imagery.* Leyden.

Betz, Otto, 1963. *Der Paraklet.* Fürsprecher im häretischen Spätjudentum, im Johannesevangelium und in neugefundenen gnostischen Schriften (= Arb. z. Gesch. Spätjud. Urchrist. 2). Leyden.

— 1963a. 'Die Frage nach dem messianischen Bewusstsein Jesu', *Nov. Test.* 6, 20—48.

— 1967—68. 'The Eschatological Interpretation of the Sinai-Tradition in Qumran and in the New Testament', *Rev. Qumr.* 6, 89—108.

Björck, Staffan, ⁶1970. *Romanens formvärld.* Stockholm.

Black, Matthew, ³1967. *An Aramaic Approach to the Gospels and Acts.* Oxford.

Black, Max, 1962. *Models and Metaphors.* Ithaca, New York.

Blank, Josef, 1964. *Krisis.* Freiburg im Breisgau.

Bligh, John, 1962. 'Jesus in Samaria', *Heythr. Journ.* 3, 329—346.

Bloch, Renée, 1955. 'Ezéchiel XVI: exemple parfait du procédé midrashique dans la Bible', *Cah. Sion.* 9, 193–223.

Bode, Edward Lynn, 1970. *The First Easter Morning*. The Gospel Accounts of the Women's Visit to the Tomb of Jesus (= Anal. Bibl. 45). Rome.

Boice, James Montgomery, 1970. *Witness and Revelation in the Gospel of John*. Diss. Basel. Grand Rapids, Michigan.

Boismard, M.-É., 1956. *Du Baptême à Cana* (= Lect. Div. 18). Paris.

— 1958. 'De son ventre couleront des fleuves d'eau (Jo., VII,38)', *Rev. Bibl.* 65, 523–546.

— 1959. 'Les citations targumiques dans le quatrième Évangile', *Rev. Bibl.* 66, 374–378.

— 1973. 'Aenon, près de Salem (Jean, III, 23)', *Rev. Bibl.* 80, 218–229.

Borgen, Peter, 1965. *Bread from Heaven*. An Exegetical Study of the Concept of Manna in the Gospel of John and the Writings of Philo (= Suppl. Nov. Test. 10). Leiden.

Borig, Rainer, 1967. *Der wahre Weinstock*. Untersuchungen zu Jo 15, 1–10 (= Stud. z. A. u. N.T. 16). München.

Boulton, P.H., 1959. 'Διακονέω and its Cognates in the four Gospels', *Stud. Evang.* I, ed. K. Aland, et al. (= TU 73), Berlin, 415–422.

Bouttier, Michel, 1964. 'La notion de frères chez Saint Jean', *Rev. Hist. Phil. Rel.* 44, 179–190.

Bowker, J.W. (John), 1964–65. 'The Origin and Purpose of St. John's Gospel', *NT Stud.* 11, 398–408.

— 1969. *The Targums and Rabbinic Literature*. An Introduction to Jewish Interpretations of Scripture. Cambridge.

Bowman, John, 1950. 'The Exegesis of the Pentateuch among the Samaritans and among the Rabbis', *Oudtest. Stud.* 8, 230–262.

— 1958. 'The Fourth Gospel and the Samaritans', *Bull. J. Ryl. Libr.* 40, 298–308.

— 1967. *Samaritanische Probleme* (= Franz Delitzsch-Vorlesungen 1959). Stuttgart.

Bovon, François (ed.), 1971. *Analyse structurale et exégèse biblique*. Neuchâtel (Schwitzerland).

Braun, F.-M., ²1954. *La mère des fidèles*. Essai de theologie johannique. Tournai-Paris.

— 1962–63. 'Quatre 'signes' johanniques de l'unité chrétienne', *NT Stud.* 9, 147–155.

— 1970. 'Avoir soif et boir (Jn 4,10–14; 7,37–39)', *Mélanges bibliques en hommage au R.P. Béda Rigaux...* ed. A. Descamps and A. de Halleux, Gembloux, 247–258.

Braun, Herbert, 1966. *Qumran und das Neue Testament*. I. Tübingen.

Brinker, Klaus, 1971. 'Aufgaben und Methoden der Textlinguistik', *Wirkendes Wort* 21, 217–237.

Brinkmann, Hennig, ²1971. *Die Deutsche Sprache*. Düsseldorf.

Brown, Raymond E., 1966–67. 'The Paraclete in the Fourth Gospel', *NT Stud.* 13, 113–132.

Brown, R.E., K.P. Donfried and J. Reumann (eds.), 1973. *Peter in the New Testament*. Minneapolis.

Brown, Schuyler, 1964. 'From Burney to Black: The Fourth Gospel and the Aramaic Question', *Cath. Bibl. Quart.* 26, 323–339.

Bruns, J. Edgar, 1966–67. 'The Use of Time in the Fourth Gospel', *NT Stud.* 13, 285–290.

— 1969. *The Art and Thought of John*. New York.

Buchanan, George Wesley, 1968. 'The Samaritan Origin of the Gospel of John', *Religions in Antiquity*. Essays in Memory of Erwin Ramsdell Goodenough, ed. J. Neusner (= Suppl. Numen 14), Leiden, 149–175.

Bultmann, Rudolf, ⁷1967. *Die Geschichte der synoptischen Tradition*. Göttingen.

Burch, Vacher, 1928. *The Structure and Message of St. John's Gospel*. London.

Burney, C.F., 1922. *The Aramaic Origin of the Fourth Gospel*. Oxford.

Caird, G.B., 1968–69. 'The Glory of God in the Fourth Gospel: An Exercise in Biblical Semantics', *NT Stud.* 15, 265–277.

Ceroke, Christian P., 1959. 'The Problem of Ambiguity in John 2,4', *Cath. Bibl. Quart.* 21, 316–340.

Chabrol, C., and L. Marin (eds.), 1971. '*Sémiotique narrative: récits bibliques*', *Languages* 22, 3–130.

Chafe, Wallace L., 1970. *Meaning and the Structure of Language*. Chicago.

Charlier, J.-P., 1959. *Le signe de Cana*. Essai de théologie johannique (= Et. rel. 740). Paris.

Christensen, Erik M., 1971. *Verifikationsproblemet ved litteraturvidenskapelig meningsanalyse* (= Odense Univ. Stud. in Lit. 2). Odense.

Christiansen, Irmgard, 1969. *Die Technik der allegorischen Auslegungswissenschaft bei Philon von Alexandrien.* (= Beitr. Gesch. Bibl. Herm. 7) Tübingen.

Collins, R.F., 1972. 'Mary in the Fourth Gospel. A Decade of Johannine Studies', *Louv. Stud.* 3, 99–142.

Colwell, Ernest Cadman, 1931. *The Greek of the Fourth Gospel*. Chicago, Illinois.

Connick, C. Milo, 1948. 'The Dramatic Character of the Fourth Gospel', *J. Bibl. Lit.* 67, 159–169.

Coppens, J., 1973. 'Le prophète eschatologique. L'annonce de sa vennu. Les relectures', *Ephem. Theol. Lovan.* 49, 5–35.

Coreth, Emerich, 1969. *Grundfragen der Hermeneutik*. Ein philosophischer Beitrag (= Philosophie in Einzeldarstellungen 3). Freiburg i. Br., Basel, Wien.

Cribbs, F. Lamar, 1970. 'A Reassessment of the Date of Origin and the Destination of the Gospel of John', *J. Bibl. Lit.* 89, 38–55.

Cullmann, Oscar, 1948. 'Der johanneische Gebrauch doppeldeutiger Ausdrücke als Schlüssel zum Verständnis des vierten Evangeliums', *Theol. Zschr.* 4, 360–372. I use the revised German version in Cullmann 1966, pp. 176–186.

— 1950. 'Εἶδεν καὶ ἐπίστευσεν. La vie de Jésus, object de la "vue" et de la "foi" d'après le quatrième Evangile', *Aux sources de la tradition chrétienne*. Mélanges offerts à M. Maurice Goguel, Neuchâtel, 52–61.

— ²1950. *Urchristentum und Gottesdienst* (= Abh. z. Theol. A. u. N.T. 3). Zürich.

— 1953. 'La Samarie et les origines de la mission chrétienne. Qui sont les 'alloi' de Jean 4,38?', *Annuaire de l'Ecole Pratique des Hautes-Etudes,* 1953–54. Section des sciences religieuses, Paris, 3–12. I use the revised German version in Cullmann 1966. pp. 232–240.

— ²1963. *Die Christologie des Neuen Testaments*. Tübingen.

— 1966. *Vorträge und Aufsätze 1925–1962*. Tübingen-Zürich.

Cummings, D.W., John Herum and E.K. Lybbert, 1971. 'Semantic Recurrence and Rhetorical Form', *Language and Style* 4, 195–207.

Dahl, Östen, 1969. *Topic and Comment: A Study in Russian and General Transformational Grammar* (= Slavica Gothoburg. 4). Göteborg.

Dalman, Gustaf, 1898. *Die Worte Jesu.* Mit Berücksichtigung des nachkanonischen jüdischen Schrifttums und der aramäischen Sprache. I. Leipzig.

Daneš, František, 1970. 'Zur linguistischen Analyse der Textstruktur', *Folia Ling.* 4, 72—78.

Daniélou, Jean, 1958. 'Le symbolisme de l'eau vive', *Rev. Sci. Rel.* 32, 335—346.

— 1964. 'Joh. 7,38 et Ezéch. 47,1—11', *Stud. Evang.* II, ed. F.L. Cross (= TU 87), Berlin, 158—163.

Daube, David, 1956. 'Samaritan Woman', D. Daube, *The New Testament and Rabbinic Judaism* (Jordan Lectures 1952), London, 373—382 (first published in *J. Bibl. Lit.* 69 (1950), pp. 137ff).

Derrett, J. Duncan M., 1970. 'Water into Wine', J.D.M. Derrett, *Law in the New Testament,* London, 228—246. The article was first published in *Bibl. Zschr.* 7 (1963), pp. 80—97.

Díez Macho, A., 1960. 'The Recently Discovered Palestinian Targum: Its Antiquity and Relationship with the Other Targums', *Congress Volume Oxford 1959* (= Suppl. Vet. Test. 7), Leyden, 222—245.

Díez Merino, Luis, 1972. ' "Galilea" en el IV Evangelio', *Estud. Bíbl.* 31, 247—274.

Dijk, Teun A. van, 1972. *Some Aspects of Text Grammars.* A Study in Theoretical Linguistics and Poetics. (= Janua Ling. Ser. Mai. 63). The Hague, Paris.

Dijk, Teun A. van, Jens Jhwe, János S. Petöfi and Hannes Rieser, 1972. 'Two Text Grammatical Models. A Contribution to Formal Linguistics and the Theory of Narrative', *Foundations of Language* 8, 499—545.

Dillon, Richard J., 1962. 'Wisdom Tradition and Sacramental Retrospect in the Cana Account (Jn 2,1—11)', *Cath. Bibl. Quart.* 24, 268—296.

Dinechin, Olivier de, 1970. 'ΚΑΘΩΣ: La similitude dans l'evangile selon Saint Jean', *Rech. Sci. Rel.* 58, 195—236.

Dodd, C.H. 1953. *The Interpretation of the Fourth Gospel.* Cambridge.

— 1954—55. 'The Dialogue Form in the Gospels', *Bull. J. Ryl. Libr.* 37, 54—67.

— 1963. *Historical Tradition in the Fourth Gospel.* Cambridge.

Doty, William G., 1973. 'Linguistics and Biblical Criticism', *J. Am. Acad. Rel.* 41, 114—121.

Dressler, Wolfgang, 1972. *Einführung in die Textlinguistik.* Tübingen.

Ellis, E. Earle, 1969. 'Midrash, Targum and New Testament Quotations', *Neotestamentica et Semitica* (in hon. M. Black, ed. E.E. Ellis and M. Wilcox), Edinburg, 61—69

Faiss, Klaus, 1972. 'Übersetzung und Sprachwissenschaft — Eine Orientierung', *Int. Rev. Appl. Ling.* 10, 1—20.

Fee, Gordon D., 1968. *Papyrus Bodmer II (P 66):* Its Textual Relationships and Scribal Characteristics (= Studies and Documents 34). Salt Lake City.

— 1968—69. 'Codex Sinaiticus in the Gospel of John: A Contribution to Methodology in Establishing Textual Relationships', *NT Stud.* 15, 23—44.

Feuillet, André, 1962. *Études johanniques* (= Museum Lessianum. Section biblique 4). Paris.

— 1964. 'Les adieux du Christ à sa Mère (Jn 19,25—27) et la maternité spirituelle de

Marie'. *Nouv. Rev. Théol.* 86, 469—489.

— 1965. 'La signification fondamentale du premier miracle de Cana (Jo. 2, 1—11) et le symbolisme johannique', *Rev. Thom.* 65, 517—535.

— 1966. 'L'heure de la femme (Jn 16,21) et l'heure de la Mère de Jésus (Jn 19,25—27)', *Bibl.* 47, 169—184, 361—380, 557—573.

Fiebig, Paul, 1926. 'Der Erzählungsstil der Evangelien', *Angelos* 2, 39—43.

Fillmore, Charles J., 1968. 'The Case for Case', *Universals in Linguistic Theory*, ed. E. Bach and R.T. Harms, New York, 1—88.

Fortna, Robert Tomson, 1970. *The Gospel of Signs.* A Reconstruction of the Narrative Source Underlying the Fourth Gospel (≡ Soc. NT Stud. Monogr. Ser. 11) Cambridge.

— 1970a. 'Source and Redaction in the Fourth Gospel's Portrayal of Jesus' Signs', *J. Bibl. Lit.* 89, 151—166.

— 1973. 'From Christology to Soteriology. A Redaction-Critical Study of Salvation in the Fourth Gospel', *Interpr.* 27, 31—47.

Foster, John, 1940—41. 'What seekest Thou? John iv.27', *Exp. Times* 52, 37—38.

Freed, Edvin D., 1965. *Old Testament Quotations in the Gospel of John* (= Suppl. Nov. Test. 11). Leiden.

— 1968. 'Samaritan Influence in the Gospel of John', *Cath. Bibl. Quart.* 30, 580—587.

— 1970. 'Did John Write His Gospel Partly to Win Samaritan Converts?', *Nov. Test.* 12, 241—256.

Fridrichsen, Anton, 1937. 'Missionstanken i Fjärde evangeliet', *Svensk Exeg. Årsbok* 2, 137—148 (Also in Skr. utg. av Sv. Inst. för Miss.-forsk., 5, Uppsala 1954, 37—49).

Friedrich, Gerhard, 1967. *Wer ist Jesus?* Die Verkündigung des vierten Evangelisten, dargestellt an Joh 4, 4—42. Stuttgart.

Fries, Udo, 1971. 'Textlinguistik', *Lingusitik und Didaktik* 2, 219—234.

Gaechter, Paul, 1953. *Maria im Erdenleben.* Neutestamentliche Marienstudien. Innsbruck-Wien-München.

Galland, Corina, 1973. 'Introduction à la méthode de A.-J. Greimas', *Ét. Theol. Rel.* 48, 35—48.

Gardner-Smith, Percival, 1938. *St. John and the Synoptic Gospels.* Cambridge.

Gerhardsson, Birger, 1958. *The Good Samaritan — the Good Shepherd?* (= Coniect. Neotest. 16). Lund, Copenhagen.

— 1961. *Memory and Manuscript.* Oral Tradition and Written Transmission in Rabbinic Judaism and Early Christianity(= Acta Sem. Neot. Upsal. 22). Diss. Uppsala. Lund, Copenhagen.

— 1964. 'Joh 4:5—26, Joh 4:27—42', *Kommentar till evangelieboken*, 2 (SPT:s handböcker), Uppsala, 204—209.

— 1966. *The Testing of God's Son* (Matt 4:1—11 & par). An Analysis of an Early Christian Midrash (= Coniect. Bibl. NT Ser. 2:1). Lund.

— 1967—68. 'The Parable of the Sower and Its Interpretation', *NT Stud.* 14, 165—193.

— 1969. 'Jésus livré et abandonné', *Rev. Bibl.* 76, 206—227.

— 1970. 'Einige Bemerkungen zu Apg 4,32', *Stud. Theol.* 24, 142—149.

— 1972a. 'Geistiger Opferdienst nach Matth 6,1—6.16—21', *Neues Testament und Geschichte*, Festschrift für O. Cullmann, Zürich, 69—78.

- 1972b. 'Du Judéo-christianisme à Jésus par le Shema^e', *Rech. Sci. Rel.* 60, 23—36.
- 1972—73. 'The Seven Parables in Matthew XIII', *NT Stud.* 19, 16—37.
- 1973. 'Gottes Sohn als Diener Gottes. Messias, Agape und Himmelsherrschaft nach dem Matthäus-evangelium', *Stud. Theol.* 27, 73—106.

Gleason, H.A., 1965. *Linguistics and English Grammar,* New York.

Goedt, Michel de, 1961—62. 'Un schème de révélation dans le quatrième evangile', *NT Stud.* 8, 142—150.

Goodenough, Erwin R., 1935. *By Light, Light.* New Haven.
- 1945. 'John a Primitive Gospel', *J. Bibl. Lit.* 64, 145—182.

Grassi, J.A., 1972. 'The Wedding at Cana (John II,1—11): A Pentecostal Meditation', *Nov. Test.* 14, 131—136.

Greenwood, David, 1971. 'Rhetorical Criticism and Formgeschichte: Some Methodological Considerations', *J. Bibl. Lit.* 89, 418—426.

Greimas, Algirdas Julius, 1966. *Sémantique structurale.* Recherche de méthode. Paris.
- 1970. *Du sens.* Essais sémiotiques. Paris.
- 1971. 'Narrative Grammar: Units and Levels', *MLN* 86, 793—806.

Greimas, A.-J. (ed.), 1972. *Essais de sémiotique poétique.* Paris.

Grelot, Pierre, 1959. 'De son ventre couleront des fleuves d'eau', *Rev. Bibl.* 66, 369—374.
- 1960. 'A propos de Jean VII,38', *Rev. Bibl.* 67, 224—225.
- 1963. 'Jean, VII,38: Eau du rocher ou source du temple?', *Rev. Bibl.* 70, 43—51.

Grossfeld, Bernhard, 1972. *A Bibliography of Targum Literature* (= Bibliogr. Jud. 2). New York.

Guilding, Aileen, 1960. *The Fourth Gospel and Jewish Worship.* A Study of the Relation of St. John's Gospel to the Ancient Jewish Lectionary System. Oxford.

Gyllenberg, Rafael, 1960. 'Cykliska element i Johannesevangeliets uppbyggnad', *Teol. Tidskrift* 65, 309—315.
- 1965. 'Åskådlighet och brist på åskådlighet i Fjärde evangeliet', *Societas Scientiarum Fennica. Årsbok — Vuosikirja* 41 (1962—63). B. N:o 4, Helsingfors, 3—15.
- 1967. 'Anschauliches und Unanschauliches im vierten Evangelium', *Stud. Theol.* 21, 83—109.

Güttgemanns, Erhardt, ²1971. *Offene Fragen zur Formgeschichte des Evangeliums* (= Beitr. Evang. Theol. 14). München.

Haenchen, Ernst, 1962—63. 'Der Vater, der mich gesandt hat', *NT Stud.* 9, 208—216.

Hägg, Tomas, 1971. *Narrative Technique in Ancient Greek Romances.* Studies of Chariton, Xenophon Ephesius, and Achilles Tatius (= Skr. utg. av Svenska Inst. i Athen, 8°, VIII). Stockholm.

Hahn, Ferdinand, 1972. 'Sehen und Glauben im Johannesevangelium', *Neues Testament und Geschichte.* Historisches Geschehen und Deutung im Neuem Testament. Oscar Cullmann zum 70. Geburtstag, ed. H. Baltensweiler and B. Reicke, Zürich, Tübingen, 125—141.

Hall, D.R., 1971—72. 'The meaning of συγχράομαι in John 4,9', *Exp. Times* 83, 56—57.

Halliday, M.A.K., 1967, 1968. 'Notes on Transitivity and Themes in English', *J. of Linguistics* 3, 37—81, 199—244, and 4, 179—215.

Hanhart, K., 1970. 'The Structure of John i 35—iv 54', *Studies in John.* Presented to Professor Dr. J.N. Sevenster . . . (= Suppl. Nov. Test. 24) Leiden.

Harnack, Adolf v., 1928. ʿΚόπος (Κοπιᾶν, Οἱ Κοπιῶντες) im frühchristlichen Sprachgebrauch', *Zschr. Nt. Wiss.* 27, 1—10.

Hartman, Lars, 1963. *Testimonium linguae*. Participal Constructions in the Synoptic Gospels. A Linguistic Examination of Luke 21,13. (= Coniect. Neotest. 19). Lund, Copenhagen.

— 1966. *Prophecy Interpreted*. The Formation of Some Jewish Apocalyptic Texts and of the Eschatological Discourse Mark 13 par. (= Coniect. Bibl. NT Ser. 1). Diss. Uppsala. Lund.

— 1971. 'Dopet "till Jesu namn" och tidig kristologi', *Svensk Exeg. Årsbok* 36, 136—163.

— 1972. 'Scriptual Exegesis in the Gospel of St. Matthew and the Problem of Communication', *L'Évangile selon Matthieu* ... ed. M. Didier (= Bibl. Ephem. Theol. Lovan. 29), Gembloux, 131—152.

Hartmann, Peter, 1971. 'Texte als linguistisches Objekt', in Stempel (ed.) 1971, 9—29.

Headlam, Walter, 1922. *Herodas*. The Mimes and Fragments, ed. A.D. Knox. With notes by W. Headlam. Cambridge.

Heise, Jürgen, 1967. *Bleiben*. Menein in den Johanneischen Schriften (= Herm. Unters. zur Theol. 8), Tübingen.

Henriksen, Aage, 1971. 'Johannes-Evangeliet som novelle', A. Henriksen, *Gotisk tid*. Fire litterære afhandlinger, Haslev, 77—100.

Hirsch, E.D., Jr., 1967. *Validity in Interpretation*. New Haven and London.

Hofbeck, Sebald, 1966. *SEMEION*. Der Begriff des "Zeichens" im Johannesevangelium unter Berücksichtigung seiner Vorgeschichte (= Münsterschwarzacher Stud. 3). Münsterschwarzach.

Hofius, Otfried, 1967. 'Die Sammlung der Heiden zur Herde Israels (Joh 10,16; 11,51f)', *Zschr. Nt. Wiss.* 58, 289—291.

Howard, Wilbert Francis, 1931. *The Fourth Gospel in Recent Criticism and Interpretation*. London.

Ibuki, Yu, 1972. *Die Wahrheit im Johannesevangelium* (= Bonner Bibl. Beitr. 39). Bonn.

Ihwe, Jens (ed.), 1971. *Literaturwissenschaft und Linguistik*. Ergebnisse und Perspektiven. I—II. (= Ars poetica, Texte, Band 8). Frankfurt am Main.

Ihwe, Jens, 1972. *Linguistik in der Literaturwissenschaft*. Zur Entwicklung einer modernen Theorie der Literaturwissenschaft. München.

Janssen, Enno, 1971. *Das Gottesvolk und seine Geschichte*. Neukirchen-Vluyn.

Janssens de Varebeke, Albert, 1962. 'La structure des scènes du récit de la passion en Joh. XVIII—XIX', *Ephem. Theol. Lovan.* 38, 504—522.

Janssens, Yvonne, 1959. 'L'épisode de la Samaritaine chez Héracléon', *Sacra Pagina* (= Bibl. Ephem. Theol. Lovan. 12—13) 2, 77—85.

Jaubert, Annie, 1963. 'La symbolique du puits de Jacob. Jean 4,12', *L'Homme devant Dieu*. Mélanges offerts au Père Henri de Lubac. Vol. 1 (= Théologie 56), Aubier, 63—73.

Jeremias, Joachim, 1930. 'Die Berufung des Nathanael (Jo 1,45—51)', *Angelos* 3, 2—5.

— ²1959. *Jesu Verheissung für die Völker* (= Franz Delitzsch-Vorlesungen 1953). Stuttgart.

— 1971. 'Die Drei-Tage-Worte der Evangelien', *Tradition und Glaube*. Das frühe

Christentum in seiner Umwelt (Fs K.G. Kuhn), Göttingen, 221–229.

Jervell, Jacob, 1972. *Luke and the People of God*. A New Look at Luke-Acts. Minneapolis.

Jespersen, Otto, 1924. *The Philosophy of Grammar*. London.

Johansson, Nils, 1940. *Parakletoi*. Vorstellungen von Fürsprechern für die Menschen vor Gott in der alttestamentlichen Religion, im Spätjudentum und Urchristentum. Diss. Lund. Lund.

Johnson, Marshall D., 1969. *The Purpose of the Biblical Genealogies* (= Soc. NT Stud. Monogr. Ser. 8). Cambridge.

Johnston, George, 1970. *The Spirit-Paraclete in the Gospel of John* (= Soc. NT Stud. Monogr. Ser. 12). Cambridge.

Jonge, M. de, 1972–73. 'Jewish Expectations about the 'Messiah' according to the Fourth Gospel', *NT Stud*. 19, 246–270.

— 1973. 'Jesus as Prophet and King in the Fourth Gospel', *Ephem. Theol. Lovan.* 49, 160–177.

Jülicher, D. Adolf, ²1910. *Die Gleichnisreden Jesu*. I. Tübingen.

Käsemann, Ernst, 1966. *Jesu letzter Wille nach Johannes 17*. Tübingen.

Kieffer, René, 1968. *Au delà des recensions?* L'évolution de la tradition textuelle dans Jean VI,52–71 (= Coniect. Bibl. NT Ser. 3). Diss. Uppsala. Lund.

— 1972. *Essais de méthodologie néo-testamentaire* (= Coniect. Bibl. NT Ser. 4). Lund.

Kilpatrick, G.D., 1960. 'Some Notes on Johannine Usage', *The Bible Translator* 11, 173–177.

Kippenberg, Hans Gerhard, 1971. *Garizim und Synagoge*. Traditionsgeschichtliche Untersuchungen zur samaritanischen Religion der aramäischen Periode. Berlin.

Kirkwood, H.W., 1969. 'Aspects of Word Order and Its Communicative Function in English and German', *Journ. of Ling*. 5, 85–107.

Klammer, Thomas P., 1973. 'Foundations for a Theory of Dialogue Structure', *Poetics* 9, 27–64.

Klos, Herbert, 1970. *Die Sakramente im Johannesevangelium* (= Stuttg. Bibelst. 46). Stuttgart.

Knight, George A.F., 1959. *A Christian Theology of the Old Testament*. London.

Koch, Klaus, ²1967. *Was ist Formgeschichte?* Neue Wege der Bibelexegese. Neukirchen.

Kothgasser, Alois M., 1971,1972. 'Die Lehr-, Erinnerungs-, Bezeugungs- und Einführungsfunktion des johanneischen Geist-Parakleten gegenüber der Christus-Offenbarung', *Salesianum* 33, 557–598, and 34, 3–51.

Krafft, Eva, 1956. 'Die Personen des Johannesevangeliums', *Evang. Theol*. 16, 18–32.

Kuiper, Gerhard J., 1970. 'Targum Pseudo-Jonathan: A Study of Genesis 4:7–10,16', *Augustin*. 10, 533–570.

— 1971a. 'Targum Pseudo-Jonathan in Relation to the Remaining Pentateuchal Targumin at Exodus 20:1–18,25–26', *Augustin*. 11, 105–154.

— 1971b. 'The Pseudo-Jonathan Targum at Leviticus 22:27, 23:29,32', *Augustin*. 11, 389–408.

Kundsin, Karl, 1925. *Topologische Überlieferungsstoffe im Johannes-Evangelium* (= FRLANT 22). Göttingen.

— 1939. 'Character und Ursprung der johanneischen Reden', *Acta Univ. Latv*. I, 4, Riga, 185–293.

— 1954. 'Zur Diskussion über die Ego-eimi-Sprüche des Johannes-Evangeliums', *Charisteria I. Köpp,* Stockholm, 95—107.

Kysar, Robert, 1973. 'The Source Analysis of the Fourth Gospel—a Growing Consensus?', *Nov. Test.* 15, 134—152.

Lagerroth, Erland, 1974. 'Närstudium, funktionsanalys, tolkning', *Forskningsfält och metoder inom litteraturvetenskapen,* ed. L. Gustafsson, 2nd ed., Stockholm, 64—108.

Lambrecht, Jan, 1967. *Die Redaktion der Markus-Apokalypse.* Literarische Analyse und Strukturuntersuchung (= Anal. Bibl. 28). Rom.

Langendoen, D. Terence, 1970. *Essentials of English Grammar.* New York.

la Potterie, Ignace de, 1965. 'Le Paraclet', in I. de la Potterie and S. Lyonnet, *La vie selon l'Esprit* (= Unam Sanctam 55), Paris, 85—105.

— 1969. 'Structura primae partis Evangelii Johannis (capita III et IV)', *Verb. Dom.* 47, 130—140, and 'Dialogus Jesus cum Nicodemo', *Verb. Dom.* 47, 141—150.

Laurentin, René, 1957. *Structure et Théologie de Luc I—II* (Et. Bibl.). Paris.

Lausberg, Heinrich, 1960. *Handbuch der literarischen Rhetorik.* Eine Grundlegung der Literaturwissenschaft. I—II. München.

— ³1967. *Elemente der literarischen Rhetorik.* München.

Le Déaut, Roger, 1964. 'Miryam, soeur de Moïse, et Marie, mère du Messie', *Bibl.* 45, 198—219.

— 1965. *Liturgie juive et Nouveau Testament;* le témoignage des versions araméennes. Rome 1965.

— 1971. 'Un phénomène spontané de l'herméneutique juive ancienne: le "targumisme" ', *Bibl.* 52, 505—525.

Lentzen-Deis, Fritzleo, 1970. *Die Taufe Jesu nach den Synoptikern.* Literarkritische und gattungsgeschichtliche Untersuchungen (= Frankfurter Theol. Stud. 4). Frankfurt am Main.

Léon-Dufour, Xavier, 1964. ' "Et là, Jésus baptisait" (Jn 3,22)', *Mélanges Eugène Tisserant,* Vol. I, Rom, 295—309.

Leon-Dufour, Xavier (ed.), 1971. *Exégèse et Herméneutique* (By R. Barthes, et al.). Paris.

Lepschy, Giulio C., 1972. A *Survey of Structural Linguistics.* London.

Leroy, Herbert, 1968. *Rätsel und Missverständnis.* Ein Beitrag zur Formgeschichte des Johannesevangeliums (= Bonner Bibl. Beitr. 30). Bonn.

Leroy, Jules, 1954. 'Sur quelques images de Moïse dans la tradition juive et chrétienne', *Cah. Sion.* 8, 355—369.

Levine, Etan, 1971a. 'Some Characteristics of Pseudo-Jonathan Targum to Genesis', *Augustin.* 11, 89—103.

— 1971b. 'A Study of Targum Pseudo-Jonathan to Exodus', *Sefarad* 3, 27—48.

Lightfoot, Robert Henry, 1938. *Locality and Doctrine in the Gospels.* London.

Lindars, Barnabas, 1969—70. 'Two Parables in John', *NT Stud.* 16, 318—329.

— 1971. *Behind the Fourth Gospel.* London.

Lohfink, Norbert, 1961. 'Jona ging zur Stadt hinaus (Jon 4,5)', *Bibl. Zschr.* 5, 185—203.

— 1963. *Das Hauptgebot.* Eine Untersuchung literarischer Einleitungsfragen zu Dtn 5—11 (= Anal. Bibl. 20). Romae.

Lohmeyer, Ernst, 1936. *Galiläa und Jerusalem* (= FRLANT 34). Göttingen.

Longacre, Robert E., 1968. *Discourse, Paragraph, and Sentence Structure in Selected Philippine Languages*. Vol. 1. (= Summer Inst. of Ling. Publ. in Ling. and Related Fields 21). Santa Ana, Calif.

Loos, H. van der, 1965. *The Miracles of Jesus* (= Suppl. Nov. Test. 9). Leiden.

Louw, Johannes P., 1973. 'Discourse Analysis and the Greek New Testament', *The Bible Translator*, 24, 101–118.

Lu, Benjamin C.-Y. 'Turning Water Into Wine', *Rev. Univ. Ottawa* 42, 342–363.

Luz, Ulrich, 1971. 'Die Jünger im Matthäusevangelium', *Zschr. Nt. Wiss.* 62, 141–171.

Lyons, John, 1968. *Introduction to Theoretical Linguistics*. Cambridge.

Lyons, John (ed.), 1970. *New Horizons in Linguistics*. Harmondsworth.

MacDonald, John, 1964. *The Theology of the Samaritans*. London.

MacRay, George W., 1970. 'The Fourth Gospel and Religionsgeschichte', *Cath. Bibl. Quart.* 32, 13–24.

Madsen, Peter (ed.), 1970. *Strukturalisme*. En antologi. København.

Maertens, Thierry, 1967. 'Geschichte und Funktionen der drei grossen Perikopen', *Concil.* 3, 108–110.

Malatesta, Edward, 1967. *St. John's Gospel. 1920–1965* (= Anal. Bibl. 32). Rome.

— 1971. 'The Literary Structure of John 17', *Bibl.* 52, 190–214.

Malina, Bruce J., 1968. *The Palestinian Manna Tradition* (= Arb. z. Gesch. Spätjud. Urchrist. 7). Leiden.

Marin, L., 1971 *Sémiotique de la Passion*. Topiques et figures. (Coll. Bibliothèque de Sciences religieuses). Paris, Aubier-Montaigne.

Martyn, J. Louis, 1968. *History and Theology in the Fourth Gospel*. New York and Evanston.

— 1970. 'Source Criticism and Religionsgeschichte in the Fourth Gospel', *Perspective* 11, 247–73.

Meeks, Wayne A., 1967. *The Prophet-King*. Moses Traditions and the Johannine Christology (= Suppl. Nov. Test. 14). Leiden.

— 1972. 'The Man from Heaven in Johannine Sectarianism', *J. Bibl. Lit.* 91, 44–72.

Metzger, Bruce M., 1958–59. 'Seventy or Seventy-two Disciples?', *NT Stud.* 5, 299–306.

— ²1968. *The Text of the New Testament*. Its Transmission, Corruption, and Restoration. Oxford.

— 1971. *A Textual Commentary on the Greek New Testament*. London, New York.

Meyer, Paul W., 1967. 'John 2,10', *J. Bibl. Lit.* 86, 191–197.

Michaels, J. Ramsey, 1966–67. 'Nathanael Under the Fig Tree', *Exp. Times* 78, 182–183.

Michaud, Jean-Paul, 1962, 1963. 'Le Signe de Cana dans son contexte johannique', *Laval Théol. Phil.* 18, 239–285, and 19, 257–283.

Michl, Johannes, 1955. 'Bemerkungen zu Joh. 2,4', *Bibl.* 36, 492–509.

Miller, Merrill P., 1971. 'Targum, Midrash and the Use of the Old Testament in the New Testament', *J. for the Study of Jud.* 2, 29–82.

Miranda, Juan Peter, 1972. *Der Vater, der mich gesandt hat*. Religionsgeschichtliche Untersuchungen zu den johanneischen Sendungsformeln. Zugleich ein Beitrag zur johanneischen Christologie und Ekklesiologie (= Europäische Hochschulschriften Reihe XXIII. Theologie, Bd. 7). Diss. Tübingen. Bern, Frankfurt/M.

Mitton, C. Leslie, 1959—60. 'Modern Issues in Biblical Studies. The Provenance of the Fourth Gospel', *Exp. Times* 71, 337—340.

Moreno Jiménez, R., 1971. 'El discipulo de Jesucristo, según el evangelio de S. Juan', *Estud. Bíbl.* 30, 269—311.

Morris, Leon, 1969. *Studies in the Fourth Gospel.* Grand Rapids, Michigan.

Moule, C.F.D., 1954. 'A Note on 'Under the Fig Tree' in John 1,48—50', *J. Theol. Stud.* 5, 210—211.

Muilenburg, James, 1932. 'Literary Form in the Fourth Gospel', *J. Bibl. Lit.* 51, 40—53.

Murphy-O'Connor, J., 1970. Review of R.T. Fortna, The Gospel of Signs, in *Rev. Bibl.* 77, 603—606.

Mussner, Franz, 1961. 'Die johanneischen Parakletsprüche und die apostolische Tradition', *Bibl. Zschr.* N.F. 5, 56—70.

— 1965. *Die johannesiche Sehweise und die Frage nach dem historischen Jesus* (= Quaest. Disp. 28). Freiburg-Basel-Wien.

Müller, Ludolf, 1967. 'Die Hochzeit zu Kana', *Glaube Geist Geschichte.* Festschrift für Ernst Benz . . . , Leiden, 99—106.

Nicol, W., 1972. *The Sēmeia in the Fourth Gospel.* Tradition and Redaction (= Suppl. Nov. Test. 32). Leiden.

Nickels, Peter, 1967. *Targum and New Testament.* A Bibliography together with a New Testament Index (= Script. Pont. Inst. Bibl. 117). Rome.

Nida, Eugene A., 1964. *Toward a Science of Translating.* Leiden.

— 1969. 'Science of Translation', *Language* 45, 483—497.

— 1971. 'Semantic Components in Translation Theory', *Applications of Linguistics,* ed. G.E. Perren and J.L.M. Trim, Cambridge, 341—348.

— 1972a. 'Implications of Contemporary Linguistics for Biblical Scholarship', *J. Bibl. Lit.* 91, 73—89.

— 1972b. 'Linguistic Theories and Bible Translating', *The Bible Translator* 23, 301—308.

— 1972c. 'Communication and Translation', *The Bible Translator* 23, 309—316.

— Forthcomming. *Exploring Semantic Structures.*

Nida, Eugene A., and Charles R. Taber, 1969. *The Theory and Practice of Translation* (= Helps for Translators 8). Leiden.

Nielsen, Eduard, 1971. 'Literature and Structure', *Religion och Bibel* 30, 23—28.

Noack, Bent, 1968.'Pinsedagen', *Københavns universitets festskrift i anledning af Hans Majestæt Konges fødelsdag 11. mars 1968,* København, 5—159.

Odeberg, Hugo, 1929. *The Fourth Gospel.* Interpreted in Its Relation to Contemporaneous Religious Currents in Palestine and the Hellenistic-Oriental World. Uppsala and Stockholm. (Reprint: Amsterdam 1968.)

Oehler, Wilhelm, 1956. 'Typen oder allegorische Figuren im Johannesevangelium?', *Evang. Theol.* 16, 422—427.

Olsson, Birger, 1972—73. 'Rom 1:3f enligt Paulus', *Svensk Exeg. Årsbok* 27—28, 255—273.

— ²1973. 'Joh. 10:1—18, Joh. 17:1—20', *Ur Nya Testamentet,* ed. L. Hartman, Lund, 251—265.

Pak, Tae-Yong, 1972. 'Limits of Formalism in Discourse Analysis', *Linguistics* 77, 26—48.

Palek, Bohumil, 1968. *Cross-Reference.* A Study from Hyper-Syntax. (= Acta Univ. Carolinae. Phil. Monogr. 21). Prag.

Palmer, Humphrey, 1968. *The Logic of Gospel Criticism.* An account of the methods and arguments used by textual, documentary, source, and form critics of the New Testament. New York.

Pancaro, Severino, 1969—70. ' 'People of God' in St. John's Gospel', *NT Stud.* 16, 114—129.

Pedersen, Sigfred, 1972. 'Lignelse eller allegori. Eksegetisk-homiletiske overvejelser', *Svensk Teol. Kvartalskrift* 48, 63—68.

Pelç, Jerzy, 1971. 'On the Concept of Narration', *Semiotica* 3, 1—19.

— 1971a. *Studies in Functional Logical Semiotics of Natural Language.* (= Janua Ling. Ser. Min. 90). The Hague, Paris.

Perrin, Norman, 1972. 'Historical Criticism, Literary Criticism and Hermeneutics', *J. Rel.* 52, 361—375.

Petri, Sigurd, 1946. 'Tillbedjan i ande och sanning. En exegeshistorisk skiss till Joh. 4:19—24', *Svensk Exeg. Årsbok* 11, 47—76.

— 1956. 'Tillbedjan i tro. Den lutherska tolkningen av Joh. 4:21—24 från Luther till 1800-talets mitt', *Svensk Exeg. Årsbok* 21, 109—151.

Pike, Kenneth L., and Ivan Lowe, 1970. 'Pronominal Reference in English Conversation and Discourse — a Group Theoretical Treatment', *Folia Ling.* 3, 68—106.

Pike, Kenneth L., and Evelyn G. Pike, 1972. 'Seven Substitution Exercises for Studying the Structure of Discourse', *Linguistics* 94, 43—52.

Pinto de Oliveira, Carlos-Josaphat, 1965. 'Le verbe ΔΙΔΟΝΑΙ comme expression des rapports du Père et du Fils dans le IVe Évangile', *Rev. Sci. Phil. Théol.* 49, 81—103.

Potin, Jean, 1971. *La fête juive de la Pentecôte.* Études des textes liturgiques. I—II (= Lect. Div. 65). Paris.

Poythress, Vern, 1973. 'A Formalism for Describing Rules of Conversation', *Semiotica* 7, 285—299.

Pryke, E.J., 1967—68. 'ΙΔΕ and ΙΔΟΥ', *NT Stud.* 14, 418—424.

Quiévreux, François, 1953. 'La Structure Symbolique de l'Evangile de Saint Jean', *Rev. Hist. Phil. Rel.* 33, 123—165.

Räisänen, Heikki, 1969. *Die Mutter Jesu im Neuen Testament* (Annales academiae scientiarum fennicae. Ser B, 158). Helsinki.

Rawlinson, A.E.J., 1932—33. 'In Spirit and in Truth: An Exposition of St. John iv. 16—24', *Exp. Times* 44, 12—14.

Ramón Díaz, José, 1963. 'Palestinian Targum and New Testament', *Nov. Test.* 6, 75—80.

Raney, W.H., 1933. *The Relation of the Fourth Gospel to the Christian Cultus.* Tübingen.

Refoulé, François, 1973. 'Exegetiken ifrågasatt', *Svensk Teol. Kvartalskrift* 49, 103—116, 162—175.

Reiss, Katharina, 1971. 'Die Bedeutung von Texttyp und Textfunktion für den Übersetzungsprozess., *Ling. antverp.* 5, 137—147.

Richter, Wolfgang, 1970. 'Formgeschichte und Sprachwissenschaft', *Zschr. At. Wiss.* 88, 216—225.

— 1971. *Exegese als Literaturwissenschaft.* Göttingen.

Riedel, Wilhelm, 1898. *Die Auslegung des Hohenliedes in der jüdischen Gemeinde und der griechischen Kirche*. Leipzig.

Riedl, J., 1963. 'Der "Anfang" der Wunder Jesu (Jo 2,11a) und die johanneische Geschichtsschreibung', *In Verbo tuo*. Festschrift zum 50 jährigen Bestehen des Missionspriesterseminars St. Augustin bei Siegburg 1913—1963, Steyl, 259—27.

Riesenfeld, Harald, 1947. *Jésus transfiguré*. L'arrière-plan du récit évangélique de la transfiguration de Notre-Seigneur (= Acta Sem. Neot. Upsal. 16). Diss. Uppsala. Lund, Copenhagen.

— 1956. 'Das Brot von den Bergen. Zu Did. 9,4', *Eranos* 54, 142—150.

— 1959. 'Sabbat och Herrens dag i judendomen, Jesu förkunnelse och urkristendomen', *Religion och Bibel* 18, 52—70.

— 1965. 'Zu den johanneischen ἵνα-Sätzen', *Stud. Theol.* 19, 213—220.

— 1969. 'Nytestamentlig teologi', *En bok om Nya Testamentet*, ed. B. Gerhardsson, Lund, 357—455.

— 1972. 'A Probable Background to the Johannine Paraclete', *Ex orbe religionem* (= Suppl. Numen 21), vol. 1, Leiden, 266—274.

Rigaux, Beda, 1970. 'Die Jünger Jesu in Johannes 17', *Tüb. Theol. Quart.* 150, 202—213.

Ringgren, Helmer, 1961. *Tro och liv enligt Döda-havsrullarna*. Stockholm.

— 1971. 'Semantik och bibelteologi', *Religion och Bibel* 30, 37—40.

Rissi, Mathias, 1967. 'Die Hochzeit in Kana (Joh 2,1—11)', *Oikonomia*. Heilsgeschichte als Thema der Theologie. Oscar Cullmann zum 65. Geburtstag gewidmet, ed. F. Christ, Hamburg-Bergstadt, 76—92.

Robert, Philippe de, 1970. 'Les Samaritains et le Nouveau Testament', *Et. Theol. Rel.* 45, 179—184.

Robinson, D.W.B., 1966. 'Born of Water and Spirit: Does John 3:5 Refer to Baptism?', *Ref. Theol. Rev.* 25, 15—23.

Robinson, J.A.T., 1959. 'The "Others" of John 4,38. A Test of Exegetical Method', *Stud. Evang.* I, ed. K. Aland, et al. (= TU 73), 510—515.

—1959—60. 'The Destination and Purpose of St. John's Gospel', *NT Stud.* 6, 117—131.

Robinson, James M., 1970. 'On the Gattung of Mark (and John)', *Perspective* 11, 99—129.

— 1971. 'The Miracles Source of John', *J. Amer. Acad. Rel.* 39, 339—348.

Rohde, Joachim, 1966. *Die redaktionsgeschichtliche Methode*. Einführung und Sichtung des Forschungsstandes. Hamburg.

Roloff, Jürgen, 1968—69. 'Der johanneische "Lieblingsjünger" und der Lehrer der Gerechtigkeit', *NT Stud.* 15, 129—151.

Roustang, F., 1958. 'Les moments de l'acte de foi et ses conditions de possibilité', *Rech. Sci. Rel.* 46, 344—378.

Rubio Morán, Luis, 1972. 'Revelacion en enigmas y revelacion en claridad. Anális ex-egético de Jn 16,25', *Salmantiensis* 19, 107—144.

Ruckstuhl, Eugen, 1951. *Die literarische Einheit des Johannesevangeliums* (= Stud. Friburg. N. F. 3). Freiburg in der Schweiz.

— 1972. 'Das Johannesevangelium und die Gnosis', *Neues Testament und Geschichte*. Historisches Geschehen und Deutung im Neuen Testament. Oscar Cullmann zum 70. Geburtstag, ed. H. Baltensweiler, B. Reike, Zürich-Tübingen, 143—156.

303

Rydbeck, Lars, 1967. *Fachprosa, vermeintliche Volkssprache und Neues Testament.* Zur Beurteilung der sprachlichen Niveau-unterschiede im nachklassischen Griechisch (= Acta Univ. Upsal. St. Graeca Upsal. 5). Diss. Uppsala. Uppsala.

Sabugal, Santos, 1972. ΧΡΙΣΤΟΣ. In vestigación exegética sobre la cristología joannea. Barcelona.

Salgado, Jean-Marie, 1971. 'Reflexions en marge du T. V des "Acta" du congress de Santo-Domingo', *Marianum* 33, 42–84.

Sasse, Hermann, 1925. 'Der Paraklet im Johannesevangelium', *Zschr. Nt. Wiss.* 24, 260–277.

Sawyer, John F.A., 1972. *Semantics in Biblical Research* (= Stud. Bibl. Theol. 24). London.

Scharlemann, Martin H., 1968. *Stephen: A Singular Saint* (= Anal. Bibl. 34). Rome.

Schegloff, Emanuel A., 1968. 'Sequencing in Conversational Openings', *Amer. Anthrop.* 70, 1075–1095.

Schenk, Wolfgang, 1973. 'Die Aufgaben der Exegese und die Mittel der Linguistik', *Theol. Lit.-zeit.* 98, 882–894.

Schenke, Hans-Martin, 1968. 'Jakobsbrunnen–Josephsgrab– Sychar. Topographische Untersuchungen und Erwägungen in der Perspektive von Joh. 4, 5.6', *Zschr. d. Deut. Pal. Ver.* 84, 159–189.

Scherner, Maximilian, 1970. 'Makrosyntax und Textinterpretation', *Der Deutschunterricht* 22, 51–66.

– 1971. ' 'Code' oder 'Horizont' ', *Der Deutschunterricht* 23, 37–57.

– 1972. 'Text und Sinn. Zur linguistischen Basis der Analyse fiktionale Texte', *Der Deutschunterricht* 24, 51–68.

Schlatter, Adolf, 1902. *Die Sprache und Heimat des vierten Evangelisten* (= Beitr. Förd. Christ. Theol. 6:2). Gütersloh. (Also in K.H. Rengstorf (ed.), *Johannes und sein Evangelium,* (= Wege der Forsch. 82), Darmstadt, 28–201.)

Schlier, Heinrich, 1963. 'Zum Begriff des Geistes nach dem Johannesevangelium', *Neutestamentliche Aufsätze.* Festschrift für Prof. Josef Schmid . . . , ed. J. Blinzer, O. Kuss, F. Mussner, Regensburg, 233–239.

– 1964. 'Glauben, Erkennen, Lieben nach dem Johannesevangelium', H. Schlier, *Besinnung auf das Neue Testament.* Exegetische Aufsätze und Vorträge. II. Freiburg im Breisgau, 279–293.

Schmid, Lothar, 1929. 'Die Komposition der Samaria-Szene Joh. 4:1–42. Ein Beitrag zur Charakteristik des 4. Evangelisten als Schriftsteller', *Zschr. Nt. Wiss.* 28, 148–158.

Schmidt, Karl Ludwig, 1921. 'Der johanneische Charakter der Erzählung vom Hochzeitswunder in Kana', *Harnack-Ehrung.* Beiträge zur Kirchengeschichte ihrem Lehrer Adolf von Harnack zu seinem siebzigsten Geburtstage dargebracht von einer Reihe seiner Schüler, Leipzig, 32–43.

Schnackenburg, Rudolf, 1951. *Das erste Wunder Jesu.* Freiburg i. Br.

– 1970. 'Der Jünger, den Jesus liebte', *Evang.-Kath. Kom. NT Vorarb.* 2, Zürich, Einsiedeln, Köln, Neukirchen, 97–118.

Schnider, Franz, and Werner Stenger, 1971. *Johannes und die Synoptiker.* Vergleich ihrer Parallelen, (Biblische Handbibliothek 9). München.

— 1972. 'Beobachtungen zur Struktur der Emmausperikope (Lk 24,13—35)', *Bibl. Zschr.* 16, 94—114.

Scholes, Robert, and Robert Kellogg, 1966. *The Nature of Narrative.* New York.

Schottroff, Luise, 1969. 'Johannes 4,5—15 und die Konsequensen des johanneischen Dualismus', *Zschr. Nt. Wiss.* 60, 199—214.

— 1970. *Der Glaubende und die feindliche Welt.* Beobachtungen zum gnostischen Dualismus und seiner Bedeutung für Paulus und das Johannesevangelium (= Wiss. Mongr. A. u. N.T. 37). Neukirchen-Vluyn.

Schulz, Siegfried, 1957. *Untersuchungen zur Menschensohn-Christologie im Johannesevangelium.* Göttingen.

— 1960. *Komposition und Herkunf der Johanneischen Reden* (= Beitr. Wiss. A. u. N. T. 81). Stuttgart.

Schwartz, E., 1907, 1908. 'Aporien im vierten Evangelium', *Nachrichten von der Königlichen Gesellschaft der Wissenschaften zu Göttingen.* Phil.-hist. Klasse, Berlin, 1907, 342—372; 1908, 115—188, 497—560.

Schütz, Roland, 1967. *Johannes der Täufer* (= Abh. z. Theol. A. u. N. T. 50). Zürich/Stuttgart.

Scobie, Charles H.H., 1972—73. 'The Origins and Development of Samaritan Christianity', *NT Stud.* 19, 390—414.

Serra, Aristide M., 1971. 'Le tradizioni della teofania sinaitica nel Targum dello pseudo-Jonathan Es. 19.24 e in Giov. 1,19—2,12', *Marianum* 33, 1—39.

Sibinga, J. Smit, 1970. 'A Study in 1 John', *Studies in John.* Presented to Prof. Dr. J.N. Sevenster . . . (= Suppl. Nov. Test. 24), Leiden, 194—208.

— 1972. 'Eine literarische Technik im Matthäusevangelium', *L'Évangile selon Matthieu* . . . , ed. M. Didier (= Bibl. Ephem. Theol. Lovan. 29), Gembloux, 99—105.

Simonis, A.J., 1967. *Die Hirtenrede im Johannes-Evangelium.* (= Anal. Bibl. 29). Rom.

Simonsen, Hejne, 1972. 'Zur Frage der grundlegenden Problematik in form- und redaktionsgeschichtlicher Evangelienforschung', *Stud. Theol.* 27, 1—23.

Smith, Dwight Moody, Jr., 1965. *The Composition and Order of the Fourth Gospel.* Bultmann's literary theory (= Yale Publ. in Rel. 10). New Haven and London.

— 1970. Review of R.T. Fortna, The Gospel of Signs, in *J. Bibl. Lit.* 89, 498—501.

Smitmans, Adolf, 1966. *Das Weinwunder von Kana.* Die Auslegung von Jo 2,1—11 bei den Vätern und heute (= Beitr. z. Gesch. Bibl. Exeg. 6). Tübingen.

Spiro, Abram, 1967. 'Stephen's Samaritan Background', J. Munch, *The Acta of the Apostles* (= The Anchor Bible 31), New York, 285—300.

Stange, E., 1914. *Die Eigenart der johanneischen Produktion.* Dresden.

Stagg, F., 1972. 'The Abused Aorist', *J. Bibl. Lit.* 91, 222—231.

Stauffer, Ethelbert, [4]1948. *Die Theologie des Neuen Testaments.* Stuttgart.

— 1960. 'Historische Elemente im vierten Evangelium', *Bekenntnis zur Kirche.* Festgabe für Ernst Sommerlath zum 70. Geburststag, Berlin, 33—51.

— 1963. 'Der Methurgeman des Petrus', *Neutestamentliche Aufsätze.* Festschrift für Prof. Josef Schmid . . . , ed. J. Blinzer, O. Kuss, F. Mussner, Regensburg, 283—293.

Stein, Robert H., 1969. 'What is Redaktionsgeschichte?', *J. Bibl. Lit.* 88, 45—56.

Steinseifer, Bernd, 1971. 'Der Ort der Erscheinungen des Auferstandenen. Zur Frage alter galiläischer Ostertraditionen', *Zschr. Nt. Wiss.* 62, 232—265.

Stemberger, Günther, 1970. *La symbolique du bien et du mal selon saint Jean.* Paris.

Stempel, Wolf-Dieter (ed.), 1971. *Beiträge zur Textlinguistik* (= Int. Bibl. für Allg. Ling. 1). München.

Stendahl, Krister, 1960. 'Quis et unde? An Analysis of Mt 1—2', *Judentum Urchristentum Kirche.* Festschrift für Joachim Jeremias, ed. W. Eltester (= Beitr. Zschr. Nt. Wiss. 26), Berlin, 94—105.

Stolt, Birgit, 1970. *Docere, delectare* und *movere* bei Luther, in *Deutsche Vierteljahrsschrift für Literaturwissenschaft und Geistesgeschichte* 44, 433—474.

— 1974. *Wortkampf.* Frühneuhochdeutsche Beispiele zur rhetorischen Praxis (= Stockholmer germanistische Forschungen 13, = Respublica literaria 8). Frankfurt/Main.

Strauss, David Friedrich, [4]1840. *Das Leben Jesu kritisch bearbeitet.* I—II. Tübingen.

Ström, Åke V., 1944. *Vetekornet.* Studier över individ och kollektiv i Nya Testamentet med särskild hänsyn till Johannes-evangeliets teologi Joh. 12:20—33 (= Acta Sem. Neot. Upsal. 11). Diss. Uppsala. Stockholm.

Tabachovitz, David, 1956. *Die Septuaginta und das NT* (= Skr. utg. av Svenska Inst. i Athen, 8°, IV). Lund.

Tångberg, K. Arvid, 1973. 'Linguistics and Theology: An attempt to analyse and evaluate James Barr's argumentation in The *Semantics of Biblical Language* and *Biblical Words for Time', The Bible Translator* 24, 301—310.

Tenney, Merrill C., 1960. 'The Footnotes of John's Gospel', *Bibl. Sacra* 117, 350—364.

Theissen, Gerd, 1974. *Urchristliche Wundergeschichten* (= Stud. z. NT 8). Göttingen.

Thompson, J.M., 1918. 'An Experiment in Translation', *The Expositor (Ser. 8)* 16, 117—125.

Thyen, Hartwig, 1971. 'Johannes 13 und die "Kirchliche Redaktion" des vierten Evangeliums', *Tradition und Glaube.* Das frühe Christentum in seiner Umwelt (Fs. K.G. Kuhn), Göttingen, 343—356.

Thüsing, Wilhelm, [2]1970. *Die Erhöhung und Verherrlichung Jesu im Johannesevangelium* (= Ntl. Abh. 27:1—2). Münster. (1th ed. 1960).

Topel, L. John, 1971. 'A Note on the Methodology of Structural Analysis in Jn 2:23—3:21', *Cath. Bibl. Quart.* 33, 211—220.

Turner, Nigel, 1965. *Grammatical Insights into the New Testament.* Edinburgh.

Uspensky, B.A., 1972. 'Structural Isomorphism of Verbal and Visual Art', *Poetics* 5, 5—39.

Vanhoye, Albert, 1960. 'L'ævre du Christ, don du Père (Jn. 5,36 et 17,4)', *Rech. Sci. Rel.* 48, 377—419.

— 1963. *La structure litteraire de l'Epitre aux Hébreux* (= Stud. Neotest. 1). Paris, Bruges.

Vermes, Geza, 1961. *Scripture and Tradition in Judaism* (= Stud. Post-Bibl. 4). Leiden.

Vulliaud, Paul, 1925. *Le Cantique des Cantiques d'après la tradition juive.* Paris.

Vygotsky, Leo Semenovich, 1971. *Thought and Language.* Cambridge, Mass. (Russian Version 1934, 1th English Version 1962).

Walker, Norman, 1960. 'The Reckoning of Hours in the Fourth Gospel', *Nov. Test.* 4, 69—73.

Walker, Rolf, 1966. 'Jüngerwort und Herrenwort', *Zschr. Nt. Wiss.* 57, 49—54.

Wallis, Ethel E., 1971. 'Contrastive Plot Structures of the four Gospels', *Notes on Translation* No. 40, 3—16.

Watson, Wilfred G.E., 1970. 'Antecedents of a New Testament Proverb', *Vet. Test.* 20, 368—370.

Wead, David W., 1970. *The Literary Devices in John's Gospel* (= Theol. Diss. IV). Diss. Basel. Basel.

Weise, M., 1966. 'Passionswoche und Epiphaniewoche im Johannes-Evangelium. Ihre Bedeutung für Komposition und Konzeption des vierten Evangeliums', *Ker. u. Dogma* 12, 48—62.

Wellhausen, J., 1908. *Das Evangelium Johannis.* Berlin.

Wilder, Amos N., 1964. *Early Christian Rhetoric.* London.

Wilkens, Wilhelm, 1958. *Die Entstehungsgeschichte des vierten Evangeliums.* Diss. Basel. Zollikon.

— 1959. 'Die Erweckung des Lazarus', *Theol. Zschr.* 15, 22—39.

— 1969. *Zeichen und Werke.* Ein Beitrag zur Theologie des 4. Evangeliums in Erzählungs- und Redestoff (= Abh. z. Theol. A. u. N. T. 55). Zürich.

Willemse, Johannes, 1964—65. 'La patrie de Jesus selon Saint Jean IV.44', *NT Stud.* 11, 349—364.

— 1965. *Het vierde evangelie.* Een onderzoek naar zijn structur. Diss. Nijmegen. Hivrrsum-Antwerpen.

Williams, Francis E., 1967. 'Fourth Gospel and Synoptic Tradition. Two Johannine Passages', *J. Bibl. Lit.* 86, 311—319.

Winburne, John Newton, 1964. 'Sentence Sequence in Discourse', *Proceed. 9th Int. Congr. Ling.,* ed. H.G. Lunt, The Hague, 1094—1099.

Wind, A., 1972. 'Destination and Purpose of the Gospel of John', *Nov. Test.* 14, 26—69.

Windisch, Hans, 1923. 'Der Johanneische Erzählungsstil', EYXAPIΣTHRION. Studien zur Religion und Literatur des Alten und Neuen Testaments Herman Gunkel zum 60. Geburtstage, am 23. Mai 1922 darbegracht von seinen Schülern und Freunden (= FRLANT 19), Göttingen, 174—213.

Wink, Walter, 1968. *John the Baptist in the Gospel Tradition* (= Soc. NT Stuc. Monogr. Ser. 7). Cambridge.

Wonderly, William L., 1968. *Bible Translations for Popular Use* (= Helps for Translators 7). Ann Arbor, Michigan.

Woude, A.S., van der, 1957. *Die messianischen Vorstellungen der Gemeinde von Qumrân* (= St. Sem. Neerlandica 3). Assen.

Wright, Addison G., 1967. *The Literary Genre Midrash.* Staten Island, N.Y.

Yadin, Yigael, 1965. 'The Excavation of Massada — 1963/64. Preliminary Report', *Isr. Expl. Journ.* 15, 1—49.

— 1966. *Massada.* Herod's Fortress and the Zealot's Last Stand. London.

Index of Authors

(Commentaries, general works, articles in ThWNT, RGG, RAC and SBU)

Aalen 286

Abbott 3f, 23, 30, 45, 46, 48f, 54f, 57f, 60, 64, 68, 70, 126, 128, 130f, 135, 148, 150, 156, 177f, 181, 219, 224—230, 264.

v. Aberle 3

Albertz 116

Alonso-Schökel 2, 6

Andersson 102

Aspelin 8

Audet 216

Bacon 1, 261

Baird 7

Barr 2, 110

Barrett 3, 19, 21, 24, 34, 40, 45, 49—51, 55f, 58, 63, 68, 71, 74, 118, 127—129, 131, 140, 148, 150, 154f, 181f, 184, 201, 214, 223, 226f, 227, 230, 236f, 236, 242

Barosse 24

Barth 137

Batey 26

Bauer 33, 40, 50, 64, 91, 120, 122, 185, 197, 225, 226, 230

Beardsley 102

Bernard 24, 156

Behm 57, 222, 267

Bertram 156

Betz 61, 102, 105, 132, 183, 266—268

Beyer 45

Björck 92

Black, Mathew 62ff

Black, Max 102, 213

Blank 261, 266, 272

Bligh 116

Bloch 107

Bode 23

Boice 125, 130

Boismard 19, 24f, 43, 135, 172, 184, 216, 217

Bonnard 38, 243, 284

Borgen 286

Borig 131, 181, 247

Boulton 45

Bouttier 30

Bowker 102, 278, 282, 286

Bowman 141, 287

Bovon 2, 8, 32

Braun, F.-M. 19, 33, 41, 246

Braun, H. 168, 215

Brinker 10—12, 17, 88f, 96

Brinkman 11, 96

Brown, R.E. 2f, 5f, 23f, 31, 39, 40—42, 46, 49, 52, 55—57, 62, 65f, 66, 68—76, 102, 108, 110f, 116, 119, 123, 125—127, 129, 131, 135f, 142—144, 154f, 180, 182—186, 189, 191—193, 197, 199, 204, 214, 216—218, 220, 223, 226—230, 232, 236, 246—248, 264f, 266f, 271, 273f

Brown, S. 3

Bruns 3, 133, 149f

Buchanan 146, 287

Bultmann 19, 24, 27, 30f, 33f, 40, 42, 44, 48, 50, 55, 58f, 62, 70, 85, 116—118, 123, 128—130, 148, 150, 159, 178, 182, 184f, 187, 190, 197, 214, 223, 225—227, 247

Burch 289

Burney 3

Büchsel 58, 174, 178

Caird 71f, 76

Ceroke 45

Chabrol 8, 12

Chafe 13, 15f, 21, 88f

Charlier 40

Christensen 96

Christiansen 114

Collins 18, 20, 40, 42

Colwell 3

Connick 3, 116

Conzelmann 228

Coppens 187
Coreth 3, 17
Cribbs 288f
Cullmann 3, 20, 34, 67, 73, 76, 122, 132f,
    202, 255, 261, 272, 278, 288f
Cummings 15, 89

Dahl 88f
Dalman 174
Dares 88
Daniélou 212, 216
Daube 129, 154f
Delcor 103
Delling 64
Derrett 35f, 44, 91
Diez Macho 166
Diez Merino 109
van Dijk 5, 8—13, 15
Dillon 279
de Dinechin 63
Dodd 1, 19, 25, 34, 102, 116, 133, 148,
    184, 189, 223f, 265, 280
Donfried 273
Doty 2
Dressler 8, 10—13, 15—17, 78, 84, 88

Ellis 282

Faiss 12, 96
Fee 33, 64
Feuillet 1, 19, 30, 41f
Foerster 132
Fohrer 132
Fiebig 282
Fillmore 21
Fortna 3, 5, 64, 113, 116, 118, 163
Foster 156
Freed 213, 216, 287
Fridrichsen, 242
Friedrich 120
Fries 10, 88f
Furberg 102

Gaechter 36, 38, 41
Galland 8—10
Gardner-Smith 289

Gerhardsson 31f, 122, 279, 283, 285, 288
Gleason 14, 88
Godet 119, 129, 142, 154
de Goedt 31, 41
Goodenough 168, 289
Goppelt 114, 212f, 279f
Grassi 24, 104
Greenwood 2, 5, 7
Greeven 187
Greimas 8, 9
Grelot 165f, 216f
Grossfeld 283
Grundmann 128
Guilding 19, 52
Gutbrod 32
Gyllenberg 28, 260
Güttgemanns 1, 12

Haas 229
Haenchen 3, 67, 224
Hägg 92
Hahn 67, 73, 76f
Hall 155
Halliday 21, 88
Hanhart 19f, 27, 34, 45, 52, 56, 110, 279,
    283f, 288
Hanse 185
v. Harnack 231f
Hartman 2, 11, 126, 281, 285, 288
Hartmann 10
Hauch 114, 231f
Headlam 176
Heise 131
Heitmüller 91, 120f
Hengstenberg 184
Henriksen 2
Herrmann 242
Herrum 15, 89
Hirsch 7
Hofbeck 68
Hofius 242, 246
Holtzmann 26, 29f, 34, 48, 52, 56, 64f,
    120, 142
Hoskyns 40, 55, 184
Howard 1

Ibuki 214, 218
Ihwe 2, 8, 10

Janssen 286f
Janssens de Varebeke 6, 49
Janssens 120
Jaubert 165f
Jeremias 23, 26, 32, 49, 51, 61, 242, 246
    277
Jervell 243, 288
Jespersen 34
Johansson 267
Johnson 49
Johnston 266
de Jonge 102, 187, 191, 193, 229, 275,
    278, 282
Jülicher 114

Käsemann 3
Kellogg 92
Kieffer 1, 3, 33
Kilpatrick 131, 174, 185
Kippenberg 140—142, 146, 155, 187f,
    190—192, 287
Kirkwood 88
Klammer 116
Klos 282
Knight 26, 107
Koch 1
Kothgasser 266—270, 272
Krafft 4, 30
Kreyenbühl 49, 56, 60f, 121, 142, 150f,
    154, 157, 184
Kuiper 103, 164
Kundsin 3, 26f, 143
Kysar 3

Lagerroth 2f, 7f, 17
Lagrange 3, 33, 142
Lambrecht 6
Langendoen 21
la Potterie 6, 266—268
Laurentin 6
Lausberg 15, 114, 279f
Le Déaut 162, 165f, 172, 283

Lentzen-Deis 50f, 74, 125, 136, 140, 210,
    283, 285
Léon-Dufour 2, 8, 10, 125
Lepschy 10
Leroy, H. 3, 5, 39, 62, 97, 116, 121, 148,
    157, 202, 221, 260, 282
Leroy, J. 166, 171
Levine 103, 164, 282f
Lightfoot 29, 128, 150
Lindars 3, 6, 27, 61f, 95, 98, 100, 102,
    118f, 123, 126, 132f, 142, 144, 154f,
    181, 185f, 196f, 214, 220, 227, 248,
    280
Lohfink 6
Lohmeyer 29
Lohse 221
Loisy 91, 120, 197
Longacre 13, 78f, 84, 88, 116
van der Loos 20, 67, 95
Louw 4, 14, 16
Lowe 193
Lu 19
Lundberg 8
Luz 31
Lybbert 15, 89
Lührmann 70
Lyons 2, 89

MacDonald 141f, 188, 191, 287
MacRay 3
Madsen 8
Maertens 120
Malatesta 1, 3f, 6, 18, 36, 49, 216, 279,
    288
Maurer 244
Malina 166
Marin 8, 12
Martyn 3, 5, 111, 118, 126
Meeks 3, 29, 70, 74, 97, 102, 109, 121,
    141, 144, 179, 189, 191, 246, 282, 284,
    287
Metzger 33f, 45, 127, 154, 243
Meyer, H.A.W. 30, 48, 54, 64
Meyer, P. 61f
Meyer, R. 50
Michaels 32

Michaelis 163
Michaud 36, 38–41, 43, 45, 113, 279
Michel 57, 245
Michl 38, 40
Miller 256, 281, 284f, 288
Miranda 221, 224
Mitton 286
Moe 184
Mollat 24, 33
Moreno Jiménez 31
Morris 3, 119, 127f, 131, 150, 155, 181,
    185f, 188, 196, 227
Moule 32
Muilenburg 3, 7, 104, 115
Murphy-O'Connor 118
Mussner 67, 76, 261, 266, 272
Müller 112

Nicol 66, 68, 70, 279f, 288
Nickels 283
Nida 2, 13f, 21, 77, 79, 84, 116
Nielsen 2
Noack 25, 103

Odeberg 76, 121, 141, 168, 178, 184, 197,
    212, 214, 222, 233, 287–289
Oehler 4, 29
Oepke 40
Olsson 6, 59, 114, 181, 248
Opelt 242

Pak 13
Palek 88f
Palmer 1
Pancaro 31, 137, 146, 242, 245f, 264
Pedersen 282
Pelç 92, 213
Perrin 1
Petri 189
Pike, K.L. 13, 193
Pike, E.G. 13
Pinto de Oliveira 178
Potin 24, 70, 74f, 102–106, 110
Poythress 193
Preisker 228
Pryke 225

Quiévreux 49

Räisänen 20, 42
Rawlinson 189
Ramón Díaz 162
Raney 286
Refoulé 8
Rengstorf 19, 68
Rendtorff 50
Reumann 273
Reiss 13
Richter 2
Riedel 107f
Riedl 64, 67
Riesenfeld 3, 166, 232, 243, 245, 267f,
    275, 286
Rigaux 31
Ringgren 2, 50
Rissi 29, 39, 260
de Robert 287
Robinson, D.W.B. 54, 106
Robinson, J.A.T. 102, 255, 286
Robinson, J.M. 3, 118
Rohde 1, 5
Roloff 267, 273f
Roustang 116, 120, 204, 206
Rubio Morán 271
Ruckstuhl 3, 4, 118, 174
Rydbeck 106
Rylaarsdam 103

Sabugal 187, 190–192
Salgado 39
Sanders 44, 55, 63, 119
Sasse 266
Sawyer 2
Scharlemann 140f, 287f
Schegloff 193
Schenk 2
Schenke 117, 140–142
Scherner 7, 12, 95f
Schlatter 21, 26, 29, 48, 50, 57, 61, 126f,
    141, 186
Schlier 47, 73f, 76, 189, 266, 269, 272
Schmid, J. 38
Schmid, L. 115f, 118, 120, 204, 207

Schmidt, K.L. 23, 30, 55, 71, 243, 245
Schmidt, S.J. 10
Schnackenburg 2—4, 6, 18f, 25—27, 31, 33f, 36, 49, 52, 55f, 58f, 62f, 65, 68—71, 73f, 76, 101, 110, 116, 119, 123, 125, 128f, 131—133, 136, 140, 142, 144, 148, 150, 154—156, 178, 182, 184, 186, 187—189, 191—193, 195—197, 204, 213f, 216, 222—227, 230—232, 243, 246f, 260, 273
Schnider 8, 65, 76
Schniewind 190
Scholes 92
Schottroff 3, 76, 118, 123
Schrenk 47, 224
Schulz 3, 5, 42, 64, 74, 227
Schwank 31, 125, 128f, 131, 154, 190, 196
Schwartz 91, 117, 134, 163, 223
Schweizer 189
Schütz 125, 137
Scobie 287f
Serra 24f, 30, 46, 74f, 102, 104f
Sibinga 6, 49
Simonis 6,
Simonsen 289
Smith 117f
Smitmans 18—20, 24—27, 29, 33, 35, 40, 44—46, 52, ·54, 56, 58—60, 67, 71, 76
Spicq 57
Spiro 140, 187, 289f
Stählin 54f
Stange 3
Stagg 30
Stauffer 26, 48, 107, 260, 286
Stein 5
Steinseifer 29
Stemberger 1, 54, 212
Stempel 10
Stendahl 29
Stenger 8, 65, 76
Stolt 16, 213
Strathmann 20, 40, 48, 122, 184
Strauss 91, 184, 278
Ström 242, 246f
Swellengrebel 229

Tabachovitz 36
Taber 13, 21, 79, 84, 116
Tångberg 2
Taylor 33
Tenney 4, 262
Theissen 2
Tholuck 184
Thompson 3, 115f
Thyen 273, 289
Thüsing 44f, 67, 69, 70—72, 223, 225, 227, 232, 234, 237, 248, 261
Topel 6, 174
Turner 31

Uspensky 92

Vanhoye 6, 178f
Vawter 52
Vermes 51
Vulliaud 107f
Vygotsky 97

Walker, N. 149
Walker, R. 158f
Wallis 287
Watson 230
Wead 3f, 57, 68f, 71, 93, 260f
Weise 24, 104
Weiser 141
Weiss, B. 55, 120, 184, 225, 228
Weiss, H.F. 126
Wellhausen 3f, 31, 91, 117, 134, 163, 223
Westcott 24, 34, 40, 48, 55, 63, 119, 131, 184
Wikenhauser 184
Wilckens 33
Wilder 7
Wilkens 65f, 68, 117
Willemse 144f, 261
Williams 280
Winburne 204
Wind 286
Windisch 3, 5, 80, 115f, 120
Wink 49, 125, 137
Wonderly 13, 14, 88
van der Woude 146, 167f

Wright 282

Zahn 56, 74

Yadin 50, 53

Index of Passages

OLD TESTAMENT
Genesis
3:15 *41f*, 3:20 *41*, 4:1 *42*, 12:6f *140*, 14:7 *168*, 14:19 *26*, 16:7ff *168*, 21 *163 169*, 21:19 *163*, 21:25ff *168*, 24 *129 163 168 284*, 24:10ff *284*, 24:11 *163 183*, 24:13 *55 163*, 24:14ff *48 153*, 24:14,15 *154*, 24:16 *154 163*, 24:17 *154 176*, 24:18 *154*, 24:20 *48 55 154 163*, 24:29,30 *163*, 24:40 *55*, 24:42 *163*, 24:43 *48 154 163 176*, 24:45 *48 163 176*, 24:46 *48 154*, 26 *163 169f*, 26:15ff *168*, 26:19 *163 213*, 27:4 *222*, 27:35 *51*, 28:10f *168*, 28:12f *74*, 28:12 *75*, 29 *129 163 169f 256f 284*, 29:1−10 *169*, 29:7 *169*, 30 *169*, 30:35 *169*, 31:12 *23*, 33:18ff *140*, 33:19 *139f*, 34:2 *139*, 35:4 *140 190*, 41:55 *46 47*, 42:23 *267*, 48:22 *139*, 49:10 *110*, 49:22ff *141*.

Exodus
2:15ff *129 141 150f 171f 256f 284*, 2:15 *129 152 163*, 2:16f,19 *55 183*, 2:18−20 *151*, 12:2 *64*, 14−15 *166*, 15 *167*, 15:22−27 *163 165−167*, 17:2 *165 176*, 17:5 *165*, 19−24 *24f 46f 54 70 73 102 166*, 19:1 *103*, 19:3 *75*, 19:5f *103*, 19:5 *110*, 19:6 *106*, 19:6 *25 46 103*, 19:10f *103*, 19:10 *102*, 19:11 *25 102*, 19:14f *105*, 19:15f *103*, 19:16 *25 102*, 19:17 *74*, 19:20 *25 75 105*, 19:24 *25 30*, 19:25 *105*, 20:1−21 *103*, 20:22 −23:33 *103*, 24 *105*, 24:3 *25 103*, 24:4−8 *106*, 24:4 *103*, 24:5−8 *105*, 24:7 *46 103*, 24:11,16f *103*, 25:7ff *46f*, 32:10 *66*, 33:13,18 *70*, 34:5 *184*.

Leviticus
11:32ff *49*, 14:5,6,50,52 *213*.

Numbers
11:18,21 *176*, t118:6 *165*, 20 *120 165f*, 20:1−13 *163*, 20:8 *165 176*, 20:24 *163*, 21 *165 168*, 21:16−20 *163 166 167 168 171*, 21:16 *164f 176*, 21:18 *164 165 167 168 171*, 21:19 *167*, 21:22,27:14,33:14 *163*.

Deuteronomy
3:24 *66*, 4:11 *75*, 8:15 *163*, 11:3 *66*, 11:29 *140*, 18:15ff *187 191f*, 18:18−22 *192*, 18:18 *191 210*, 20:6 *230*, 21:17 *64*, 28:30 *230*, 32:6 *26*, 32:13 *163*, 33:2 *75*.

Joshua
16f *141*, 19:28 *27*, 22:24 *26 40*, 24:13 *232*, 24:26 *140*, 24:32 *139f*.

Judges
1:22ff *141*, 4:19 *176*, 7:16,19f *48*, 9:6 *140*, 9:28 *139*, 9:37 *140*, 11:12 *36 37*, 14:6,19,15:14 *182*, 16:28 *54*.

1 Samuel
10:2,6,10 11:6 16:13 *182*.

2 Samuel
16:10 *36f 40*, 17:29 *222*, 19:22 *36−38 40*.

1 Kings
7:26 *52*, 17:12,14,16 *48*, 17:18 *36−38 40*, 18:34 *48*, 19:4 *54*, 9:18f *36*, 9:22 *37*, 17:24ff *186*.

2 Kings
3:13 *36f*, 9:18f *36*, 9:22 *37*, 17:24ff *186*.

1 Chronicles
12:41 *222*.

2 Chronicles
4:5f *52*, 26:8 *54*, 35:21 *36f 40*.

Ezra
2:64 *227*.

Nehemiah
9:15 *163*, 9:20 *176*, 9:21 *33*.

Job
5 7 *232*, 6:10 *182*, 12:11 *57*, 16:20 *267*, 29:6 *163*, 31:8 *230*, 33:23 *267f*, 34:3 *57*, 34:29 *227*, 41:17 *182*.

Psalms
2:8 *177*, 12:2f *51*, 16:6 *184*, 17:1 *51*, 23:1 *33*, 32:2 *51*, 34:9 *57*, 36:10 *213*, 43:1, 52:5f *51*, 66:5 *66*, 68:1ff, 18 *75*, 69:9 *265*, 77:12 *66*, 78:15f *217*, 78:16—20, 81:17 *163*, 84:12 *33*, 85:7,10 *184*, 104:24 *26*, 105:40f *217*, 105:41 114:8 *163*, 126:5f *228 242*, 139:13 *26*.

Proverbs
8:4ff *268*, 8:22 *26 64*, 10:11 *213*, 11:21 *228*, 12:6 *51*, 13:14 *213f*, 14:27, 16:22 *213*, 18:4 *214*, 31:18 *57*,

Ecclesiastes
12:6 *48*,

Song of Solomon
4:15 *163 213*,

Isaiah
1:21f *107*, 2:3 *244*, 2:10 *54*, 8:6 *110*, 9:1 *244*, 9:2 *228*, 9:3 *242 244*, 9:8 *141*, 9:21 *244*, 11:1f *244*, 11:11—13 *243 256*, 11:11ff *244*, 11:11f *242*, 11:11 *26 110 256*, 11:12 *243*, 11:13 *141*, 12:3 *55 60 129 214 244*, 12:4 *184*, 17:3 *141*, 18:5 *242* 27:12f *242f*, 27:12 *242—244*, 28:1,3 *141* 29:17 *34*, 30:20 *177*, 30:23ff *213*, 32:15 *215*, 33:24 *232*, 35:6 *182*, 40:31 *232*, 41:25 *184*, 43 *132*, 43:3 *132*, 43:20 *176*, 44:1 *54*, 44:3 *215*, 45:19 *190*, 47:12 *54*, 48:21 *163*, 49 *132*, 49:18 *244*, 49:20ff *42*, 51:14 *33*, 53:9 *51*, 54:1 *42*, 54:4ff *26*, 55:1ff *214*, 58:9 *184*, 60:4,6 *244*, 62:4f *26*, 62:5f *107*, 63:1ff *242*, 65:21ff *232*, 66:7ff *42*,

Jeremiah
2:13 *213*, 2:18 *36*, 3:1ff *107*, 9:1 *177*, 18:11 *54*, 23:3 *243f*, 31:5 *34*, 31:17—20 *244*, 31:33f *215*, 33:13 *54*,

Ezekiel
11:17 *243*, 16 *107*, 16:7ff *106*, 20:34 *243*, 23:1ff *107*, 28:25, 34:1ff,12ff,16, 34:16 *243*, 36:1ff,24,25—27,28 *215*, 37:16ff,26ff *244*, 47:1ff *170f 213 216*,

Hosea
1—3 *107*, 2:2 *184 186*, 2:5 *177*, 2:7,16 *184 186*, 2:24 *34*, 4:17, 5:3,11 *141*, 6:10—7:1 *242*, 6:11 *242*, 9:3 *141*, 12:1 *51 141*, 14:9 *36*,

Joel
3:1f *215*, 3:18 *213*, 4:13 *242*, 4:18 *34*, 9:13 *34*,

Amos
9:13 *34*

Jonah
2:3 *184*, 4:5 *6*

Micah
2:12 *244*, 4:6 *243*, 6:15 *230*, 7:11f *243*,

Zephaniah
3:13,16,19f *264*,

Haggai
1:1ff,13 *75*,

Zechariah
9:9, 10:6f *264*, 13:1 *213*, 14:8 *170f 213 216*, 14:16 *244*,

OT Apocrypha and Pseudepigrapha

Tob 5:8 *183*

Wis 5:21 *182*, 7:25 *214*, 11:4, 11:7 *176*, 18:15 *182*,

Sir 6:19 *232*, 15:1ff, 21:13 *214*, 24:8ff *144* 24:21ff *214* 32:1 *56*,, 36:13 *243*, 36:19 *57*, 48:10 *244*

1 Macc 4:46, 14:41 *191*

2 Macc 1:27 *243*, 2:4—8 *190*, 2:18 *244*,, 13:14

Ps Sol 8:34, 11:3, 17:19 *243*, 17:28, 17:50 *243f*

Enoch 10:19 *34*, 48:1, 49:1ff, 96:6 *214*

Jub 1:28 *141*,, 16:1ff *170*, 16:17f *110*, 18:17ff *170*, 19:15ff *141*, 22:1ff *170*, 22:10ff *141*, 24:13ff *170*, 25:4ff, 33:21ff, 36:1ff *141*, 36:12ff, 44:1ff *170*

Test Iss 3:5 *232*

4 Ezra 4:28ff *242*, 5:27 *110*, 13:12f, 13:40—48 *244*

2 Baruch 29:5 *34* 70:2ff *242*, 77f *244*

SibOr II.31f, III.620ff, III.744f *34*

QUMRAN TEXTS

1QS IV.20—22 *168*, IV.21 *215*, IX.9—11 *191*

1QH II.13 *267*, IV.11 *214*, XVIII.11 *267*

4QTest 1—8 *191*

11QtgJob *267*

CD I.3,14, III.14 *146*, III.16 *168*, *214*, IV.1f, 11, 13, 16, V.19, VI. 1,5 *146*, VI.2ff *146*, *167*, *214* VII.10—21a, VII.12ff,18,

VIII.6, 12ff, 21 *146*, X.10b—13 *52*, XIVf, XIV.1f, XVI.3 *146*, XIX.34 *168*, *214*, XX.16, 22f *146*

JOSEPHUS

Ant I.246, 254 *163*, II.254ff *150f*, II.256 *151*, II.257ff *150*, II.257 *151*, II.258, II.-263 *141*, *151*, II.335 *127*, VI.194 *33*, VIII.154 *163*, IX.288 *186*, IX.291, XI.341 *141*, XV.70,200 *33*, XVIII.85ff *190*, XVIII.85 *188*

Bell II.232 *128*

Vita 269 *128*

PHILO

De Dec 2 *105* 11 *106*

De Ebrit 112f *168*

De Fuga 195—202 *168*

De Post 130f *168*

De Somn I.5ff, *168* II.267—271 *168*

Leg Alleg II.86 *168*

Quaest in Gen. IV.191—195 *168*

Vita Mosis I.51, 53 *141*, *151* I.50ff *151*

RABBINIC LITERATURE AND THE TARGUMS

M Men X.2 *140*

M Kel II.1ff *49*, *154* XI.1 *49*

M Mikw I.4,7, II.I—3, 5, 10, III.1f, V. 6
VIf *53*
VI.3,6—9 *52*

Pirqe Aboth V. 9 *166* VI.1f *214*

Tos Pea IV.18 *228*

Tos Shab. I.14 *154*

Tos Sukkah III.3—18*217*, III.11ff *166*

Tos B K VIII.8 *51*

Tos Men VIII.19 *51*

b Shab 86b, 87a *104*, 146a *106*, *141*
a622b **Erub** 46 *53*

b Pes 57a *51*, 109a *53*

b Yom 4a *104*, 31a *53*

B Taan 28b *104*

p Shek 5.48^d.19 *140*,

Mek ad Ex 14:15 *140*, 15:16f *110*, 19:1ff
104,*106*, 19:2 *106*, 19:3 *104*, 19:10ff *105*,
19:10 *104*, 19:11 *105*, 19:18 *75*, 20:18
106

Sifre ad Num 11:4 *57*

Sifre Dt 11,22 *214*

Pes K 11 *141*

Gen R 66,3 *170*, 68—69, 68:18 *74*, 70,8f
170

Ex R 1,32 *151,170f*, 15,4, 28.2 *75*

Num R 19:25f *166*

Cant R ad 1:2, 4, 9, 12, *2:1,4*, 100, 2:14
75,108, 3:11, 4:4,7, 5:1, 8:5 *108*

Midr Ps 32 § 2 *51*

PRE 35 *170*, 36 *170f*, 41 *104*, *106f*, 46
104

Pseudo-Philo X,7 *167*, XI,5 *75*, XI, 15,
XX,8 *167*, XXV,10 *190*

Raschi on Ex 2:20 *171*

Targ ad Gen 28:10 *140*, *162*, *169*, 29:10,
12, 22, 31:22, 49:25 *75*

Targ. ad Ex 2:15 *151*, 19:2 *106*, 19:5 *110*,
19:8 *46*, *105*, 19:9 *25*, *70*, 19:20 *102*, *105*
19:11 *25*, *70*, *102* 19:14 *105*, 19:15f *102*,
24:3 *46,106*, 24:8, 24:11 *105*

Targ. ad Num 21:16—18 *164f*

Targ. ad Dt. 33:2,15 *75*

Targ. ad Is 12:3 *169*,

Targ. ad Hab 3:1 *106*

NEW TESTAMENT

Matthew

1—2 *29 279*, 1:1—17 *49*, 1:21 *132*, 2:1 *27*,
3:1—4:11 *279*, 3:12 *242*, 4:11,13,20,22
127, 8:4 *56 111*, 8:6 *35*, 8:11 *26*, 8:29 *37
38*, 9:35—38 *243*, 9:37f *228*, 10:5,6 *243*,
10:14 *183*, 11:2 *125*, 11:28f *232*, 12:43ff
38, 13:27 *180*, 13:30,39 *242*, 15:2 *53*,
15:7 *185*, 15:28 *40*, 15:32 *35*, 16:9 *43*,
16:18 *32*, 16:21 *23*, 16:27f *74*, 17:1 *104*,
17:23 *23*, 19—22 *174*, 19:20 *33*, 20:19 *23*,
20:20 *177*, 21:11 *27*, 22:1—14 *46*, 22:2
26, 22:3f,8f *30*, 23:25f *50*, 25:1ff *61*,
25:1,5 *26*, 25:6 *25*, 25:35,42 *176 222*,
26:28 *105*, 26:36 *139*, 26:64 *74*, 27:42,43
54, 27:44 *155*, 27:47 *183*, 27:51 *54*,
27:62,64 *23*,

Mark

1:9 *27*, 1:24 *37 38*, 1:44 *56*, 2:2 *131*, 2:6ff
219, 2:18ff *19*, 2:18 *125*, 2:19f *26 61*,
2:21f *95*, 2:22 *34 62*, 3:35 *224*, 4:21 *44*,
4:29 *242*, 4:40 *43f*, 5:7 *37f*, 5:8 *46*,
5:21–43 *148*, 5:43 *176 222*, 6:1ff *27*, 6:11
183, 6:29 *125*, 6:37 *176 222*, 7:1ff *50*, 7:4
53, 7:6 *185*, 7:24–30 t2131, 7:28 *174*, 8:1
35, 8:16f *219*, 8:17f *44 93*, 8:17 *43*, 8:19
174, 8:21 *43*, 8:32 *271*, 9:2 *104*, 9:32 *271*,
9:35 *45*, 10:21 *33*, 10:29 *174*, 10:43 *45*,
10:49 *183*, 11:12 *23*, 11:16 *127*, 12:28,32
185, 14:58 *265*, 15:32 *54 155*,

Luke

1–2 *20*, 1:47, 2:11 *132*, 2:11 *132*, 2:29
55, 4:16ff,31ff *27*, 4:34 *37f*, 5:33–39 *280*,
5:39 *62*, 6:26 *185*, 7:18f *125*, 7:39 *30 187*,
7:40,42 *222*, 8:28 *37f*, 8:29 *46*, 8:31 *38*,
9:22 *23*, 9:28 *104*, 9:57–62 *16*, 10:2 *228*
243, 11:1 *125*, 12:36 *26*, 12:37 *45*, 12:50
222, 13:12 *40*, 14:7ff *30*, 16:2 *61*, 16:26
183, 17:8 *45*, 17:10 *46*, 17:14 *56*, 18:33
23, 19:15 *61*, 20:39 *185*, 22:27 *45*, 22:36
55, 24:7,46 *23*,

John

1–12 *121 218*, 1:19–4:54 *256 261 278f*
288, 2–12 *69*, 2–4 *19 52 68 136*,
3:22–4:54 *255 279*, 5–12 *245*, 7–9 *27*
116 148, 7–10 *143 218*, 9–10 *246*,
12–20 *143 279*, 12–19 *23 104*, 13–16
218f 239, 13–17 *66*, 13–20 *28 69 72 198*,
13:31–17:26 *260*, 14:17 *271*, 14–16
217f, 18–19 *57 261*, 20–21 *218f*,

Ch. 1

1:1ff *31f 101 250 260 279*, 1 *224*, 5 *137*,
6–8 *125*, 6 *25*, 7 *73 136*, 86f *276*, 8 *59*
136, 9ff *152*, 10f *26 137 145*, 11ff *28 138*,
11f *20*, 11 *145*, 12 *59 179 246*, 12b–13
58, 14ff *54*, 14 *25 59 70f 189 263*, 15 *61*
73 125 136, 16 *263*, 17 *19 25 59 179 189*
277, 19ff *18 23–25 28f 51f 54 59 73f 80*
90 101f 104–108 111 115 125 136–138

148 150 156 162 252 254–256 259 261
276–279, 19 *126 219*, 20–23 *173*, 20
174, 21 *187 219*, 22 *174*, 23 *262f*, 24
;2126 148 262, 25 *53 187 219*, 26 *53 137*,
28f *28 65*, 28 *28 53 64 93 135 262*, 29ff
51 73 112, 29 *51 61 106f 131–133 150*
245, 30 *61*, 31 *106 159*, 31 *53 59 70 112*
125 137, 32f *54 210*, 33f *112*, 33 *53 59*
136f 189, 35–4:54 *20 284*, 35ff *24 29 31f*
71 74 77 79 81 92 94 99 101 107f 110 135
218 273 276,35f *24*, 35 *24 28 31 125 150*,
36ff *174*, 36 *31 51 106f*, 37–39 *44*, 37 *73*
125, 38 *31 131 157 219–221 262f*, 39 *24*
44 79 159 262, 40 *262*, 41 *24 31 58 190*
262f, 42 *32 262f*, 43 *24 27f 44 ó5 127*
150, 44 *262*, 45ff *26*, 45f *27 144*, 45 *28 31*
179, 46 *29 44 79*, 47–51 *173 218*, 47 *24*
32 186, 48 *59 127 157 183 261*, 49 *31 220*
277, 50f *31 44 76 79 276f*, 50 *32 71 73 76*
51 *19 32 46 74–76*,

Ch. 2:

1–11 **18–114** *118f 136 196 256 259–261*
278f 284 288, 1 *150 259 261*, 3f *115*, 6
154 156 260–262, 8 *183*, 9 *261–263*, 10
280, 11f *29*, 11 *144 260 262 279*, 12–22
105, 12 *23 27f 30f 105 134f 149*, 13ff *44*
61 101 245 247 264–266 280, 13 *28 50*
150, 14f *51 261*, 16–18 *148*, 17 *51 72 79*
262 264–266 271 280, 18–21 *260*, 18
131 174, 19ff *44 217*, 19f *51 150 265*, 20
61 131 174, 21f *79 262–264 266 271 280*,
21 *59 265*, 22 *67 72 79 93 265 284*, 23ff
28 123 133f 137 143f 279, 23f *73*, 23 *28*
57 66, 24f *127*, 24 *27 188*, 25 *59 262*,

Ch. 3:

1ff *39 56 100 106 111 116 181 203*
220 239, 1 *50 56 126 153*, 2–10 *173*, 2f
39, 2 *66 131 150 220 261*, 3 *59 209*, 4 *177*
181 209 260, 5ff *209*, 5 *54 138 156*, 6–8
60, 6 *62 137*, 7 *61 156*, 8 *59 62*, 9 *177*
183, 10 *56 221*, 11–21 *136*, 11 *131 137*
194 197 222 263, 12 *59 137 177*, 13ff *136*,
14 *45 128 179 262*, 15 *179*, 16ff *132 260*,
16f *131f*, 16 *178 189*, 17 *132*, 19 *189*, 20ff

138, 21 *47 70*, 22ff *27—29 54 125 128 133—136 138 159 161f 172 209 233 239 251 255 277*, 22f *28 65*, 22 *23 26 53 125f 134f 143 149 156*, 23—25 *148*, 23 *30 53f 135—137 154 197 261f*, 24 *148 262*, 25ff *73 219*, 25 *25 51 125 135—137 157*, 26—30 *239*, 26 *28f 53 126 135—137 220 239*, 27ff *112 136 159*, 27 *62 137*, 28—30 *137*, 28 *61 137 277*, 29f *251*, 29 *26 61f 107 136f 172 210 239*, 30 *28 128 135f 239*, 31—36 *136f 209 251 260*, 31—35 *138*, 31 *137 210*, 32 *137 210*, 33—35 *138*, 33 *137f 210 239*, 34f *210*, 34 *54 138 178 210 239*, 35 *137f 178*, 36 *136 153 210 239*,

Ch. 4:1ff *34 54 60 67 80 93 112* **115—257** *259—261 277—280 284 287f*, 1 *53 57*, 2 *53 261f*, 3 *28 65*, 5f *261*, 6 *29 44 150*, 7ff *57 60 73*, 7 *55*, 8 *262*, 9 *29 50 93 262*, 10—12 *260*, 10 *61 277 281*, 11,12 *59*, 14 *54*, 15 *55 260*, 16 *61*, 17 *61*, 19ff *245*, 21 *40 44*, 22 *50 263*, 23f *268*, 23 *44*, 24 *277*, 25 *58 262f 277*, 27 *156*, 28 *48*, 29 *277*, 30 *29*, 32 *278*, 33f *260*, 33 *174*, 34 *47 65f 178f 277*, 35 *62*, 36 *277 281*, 37 *62*, 38 *278*, 39—42 *29*, 40 *28 57*, 42 *74 277*, 43—45 *133f 143 138 161 239 251*, 43f *143*, 43 *24 65 149f*, 44 *26—28 127 131 134 144f 262*, 45f *28*, 45 *28f 57 65f 143f 262*, 46ff *18 26 29f 35 44 59 76 100 110 144 280*, 46f *33f*, 46 *26—28 53 56 65 143f 279*, 47 *28 65 131 143*, 48 *65 174 210*, 49 *28 65 180 210*, 50 *29 39 65 153*, 51—53 *58 78*, 51 *28 65 210*, 52f *44*, 52 *65 149f 174*, 53 *39 66 131 153 210*, 54 *28 64—68 143f 262 279*,

Ch. 5:1ff *18 27 30 54 59 68 111 239*, 1 *23 26 28 50 149f*, 2 *53 58 129 262*, 3f *53*, 3 *48 4 53, 262*, 5 *29*, 6f *33*, 6 *48 127*, 7f *34*, 7 *53 180*, 8f *58*, 9 *150 262*, 10 *174*, 11 *61*, 12f *179*, 12 *61 130 219*, 16ff *66*, 16 *127*, 17ff *66*, 17 *71 231*, 18 *127 145*, 19ff *66 260*, 19f *62*, 19 *47 174 231*, 20ff *67*, 20

67f 156 225 270, 22 *178*, 23 *224*, 24 *47 181 228*, 25 *44 188 196*, 27 *47*, 28 *44 156 196*, 30 *47 224*, 31ff *125*, 31f *178*, 32 *230*, 35f *136*, 36 *68 178 224 234*, 37f *180*, 37 *197*, 38ff *46*, 39ff *73*, 39 *112*, 41f *181*, 42 *196*, 44 *177 196*, 45ff *46 112*, 45 *178 230*, 47 *121 131 177 179 284*,

Ch. 6:1ff *18 20 23 27 34 57f 135 179 217 246 280*, 1 *23 28 127 149 262*, 2 *29 66*, 4 *50 150 261f*, 5ff *218 260 263*, 5f *33*, 5 *59 226*, 6 *59 64 127 262f 265*, 10 *48 262*, 12—15 *58*, 12f *54 57 246 261*, 12 *57 78*, 13 *31*, 14f *260*, 14 *29 58 68 131 144 187*, 15 *58 127*, 16 *25 57*, 19 *28 58*, 20 *192*, 21 *28 58*, 22ff *29 134 144*, 22 *23 150 155*, 23 *127 262*, 24 *28f 157*, 25ff *173 203 220*, 25 *183*, 26 *157*, 27 *179 182f 221*, 28ff *66*, 28 *47 174*, 30f *131 183*, 30 *66 174*, 31f *178*, 31 *176 262f*, 32f *178f 183*, 32 *174*, 33f *179*, 33 *132 178 230*, 34 *174 180 183*, 35 *68 131 137 181 192 216*, 36 *61*, 37 *137 178 224*, 38 *47 224*, 39 *137 178 181 224 262*, 40 *76 224*, 41ff *219*, 41f *260*, 41 *61 131*, 42 *29f 61 131 144 177*, 44 *224 247f*, 45 *74*, 46 *196*, 48 *68 192*, 49,51f *179*, 51 *68 131f 192 245*, 52ff *33 93*, 52f *260*, 52 *131 176 219*, 53ff *57*, 53 *174*, 54ff *57*, 55 *221*, 57 *224*, 59 *64 262*, 60ff *31 144*, 60f *73 125 219*, 60 *130*, 61 *127*, 63 *131 178 189 192 230*, 63a *62*, 64 *59 127 262f 265*, 66 *29 73 125*, 67ff *29 218*, 67 *31 174*, 68 *131 180*, 69 *28*, 71 *262f*,

Ch. 7:1ff *127*, 1 *23 27f 127 149 157*, 2 *50 150 262*, 3f *66*, 3 *125 144 225 231*, 4 *62 70*, 5 *262*, 6ff *44*, 8 *44 131*, 9 *28*, 10 *57*, 11f *219*, 11 *157*, 13 *157*, 14ff *157 216*, 14 *150 269*, 15—29 *173*, 15 *156 177*, 16 *131 178*, 18a *62*, 19ff *179*, 19 *157 284*, 21ff *66*, 21 *68 156*, 22ff *262*, 22 *197 262*, 24 *100*, 25 *127 131 219*, 26 *130*, 27ff *197*, 27f *260*, 27 *59 131*, 28 *59 178 181 216 269*, 29 *222*, 30 *44f 127 148*, 31ff *28*, 32ff *126*, 32 *126 219*, 33ff *93*, 34 *157*, 35f *180*

247, 35 *57 63 216 247 260 269*, 36 *61 157*, 37—39 *213 215 217*, 37ff *60 269*, 37f *182 216*, 37 *53 57 150 216*, 38 *53f 216f 254 262f*, 39 *45 64 67 69f 93 189 217 262—265 271*, 40ff *219*, 40 *131 187 216*, 41ff *29*, 41f *131*, 41 *144 180*, 44 *127 130*, 45ff *111 173*, 46 *216*, 47f *126*, 49 *29 62*, 50 *58 262*, 51 *62*, 52 *29 62 131 144 187 216*,

Ch. 8:6 *262 265*, 7 *57*, 10 *40*, 12—19 *173*, 12 *68 132 181 189 192*, 14f *222*, 14 *45 59*, 15 *100*, 16 *224*, 17 *62*, 18 *193 224*, 19 *197*, 20 *44f 64 127 148 216 262 269*, 21ff *173 203 220*, 21 *45 157*, 22f *260*, 22 *57 61 63 130*, 23 *54 193*, 24 *61 192*, 25 *179 192*, 26 *178 222*, 27 *59 262 265*, 28f *47 66*, 28 *45 65 181 192 269*, 30ff *28*, 31—59 *173*, 31 *73 125*, 33f *260*, 33 *61 177*, 35 *62*, 37 *47 127*, 38ff *47*, 39ff *112*, 39f *260*, 40 *127 130 192 196*, 41 *45 185*, 42 *178 196*, 43 *47 131*, 45 *189*, 46f *74*, 47 *47 74 131*, 48 *29 61 185*, 50f *178*, 50 *70*, 51f *57*, 51 *131*, 52 *61*, 53ff *121*, 53 *180*, 54 *70 178*, 55 *197*, 57 *260*, 58 *192*, 59 *127*,

Ch. 9:1ff *18 29f 33 39 47 54 58—61 68 80 100 111 115f 187 203 220*, 2—5 *218*, 2 *39 219f*, 3f *179*, 3 *66 70 178 195*, 4 *62 128 231*, 5 *132 189*, 6f *58*, 7 *26 53 60 109f 262f*, 8ff *66 173 219*, 8f *78*, 8 *197 262*, 9 *193*, 11 *53 61 130*, 13ff *111 126*, 13 *58 126*, 14 *150 262*, 15f *126*, 15 *53 219*, 16 *66 68*, 17 *58 187 219*, 18—23 *78*, 18 *58 61 126 183 188*, 19 *177 197 219*, 22f *64 262f*, 22 *126 148 227*, 24—34 *173*, 24 *61f 130 183*, 27ff *125*, 28ff *59 73 221*, 29f *59*, 29— 30 *156 229*, 31 *47 62 131*, 33 *66*, 35 *74*, 36 *179*, 37 *157*, 40ff *126*, 40 *126*, 41 *61*,

Ch. 10:1ff *26 59 62 114 181 239 246 260*, 2f *59*, 3f *32 173*, 3 *47 183*, 6 *64 192 262f 265*, 7 *192*, 8,9f *181*, 9 *192*, 11 *42 62 192 245*, 12 *127*, 14 *62 192*, 15f *42 273*, 15 *245*, 16ff *247*, 16 *32 47 128*, 17f *42 178*

265 273, 17 *179*, 18 *179 181*, 19 *25*, 21 66, 22f *262*, 22 *25 150*, 24ff *66*, 25ff *74*, 25 *66 231*, 27 *47*, 29 *137*, 31 *127*, 32f *62*, 32 *66 178f 231*, 33 *130*, 36 *61*, 37 *179 231*, 38 *66*, 39f *127*, 40ff *73 125*, 40 *28 53 127 135*, 41 *136*,

Ch. 11:1ff *18 23 39 44 66 80 100 115 116 117 143*, 1 *153*, 2f *34f*, 2 *33 93 127 262*, 3f *39*, 3 *34*, 4 *68 70f 196*, 5 *262*, 6 *24 57 149f*, 7—16 *127 173 218f*, 7 *23 149 219*, 8 *127 219f*, 9 *44*, 11 *23 149*, 12—21 *148*, 12f *149*, 12 *219*, 13 *93 148 185 262f 265*, 16 *58 190 262f*, 17f *28*, 17 *24 150*, 18 *262*, 19 *148*, 20 *28*, 21—27 *173*, 22 *196*, 23ff *174*, 24 *190 260*, 25 *68 192*, 28 *183 220*, 29—32 *130 148*, 30 *28 148 262*, 32 *28*, 33 *155*, 38 *28*, 40ff *126*, 40 *61 70f 76 196*, 41 *65 226*, 43f *58*, 43 *183*, 45ff *29 126*, 45 *76*, 46f *126*, 47ff *42 57*, 47 *66 130* 48—52 *245*, 48 *126 136 187 245*, 49—54 *246*, 49f *57*, 49 *245*, 50 *130 244*, 51f *244 246f 262—265*, 51 *56 64 245f 262*, 52 *42 245f*, 53f *127*, 54 *28 127 219 261*, 55 *50f* 56f *219*, 57 *126 148*,

Ch. 12:1ff *23*, 1 *23f 28 150 261*, 2 *45*, 6 *93 262f*, 7 *23*, 9ff *29*, 9 *245*, 10 *57*, 11 *130*, 12—16 *265*, 12—15 *246 263—266 280*, 12f *261 263*, 12 *23f 28*, 13 *264*, 14f *263*, 15 *265*, 16 *59 64 67 70 79 219 262—266 271 280*, 17ff *73*, 17 *183*, 18 *68*, 19 *126 136 219 247*, 20—36 *247*, 20—22 *131*, 20 *187*, 21 *219 262*, 23—36 *46*, 23 *44f 70f 247 263*, 24 *72 246f*, 25 *182*, 26 *46 67*, 27 *44f 55*, 28 *45 71f 248*, 29 *192*, 31 *55*, 32 *45 72 136 246—248*, 33 *69 93 262f*, 34 *45 128 177 179*, 35 *62*, 36 *28 127*, 37ff *66 73 121 262f*, 37 *29 64 66*, 41 *70 112*, 42f *73 93*, 42 *28 111 126 157*, 44ff *136 187 260*, 44f *76*, 46f *74*, 47f *74*, 47 *132*, 49f *47*, 49 *131 178 181 224*, 50 *178*,

Ch. 13:1ff *51 54 67 106f 127*, 1—3 *134*, 1 *23 26f 44f 127 225*, 3 *27 45 127 178*, 5 *53*

219, 6ff *173f*, 6 *53*, 7 *23 93 222 263*, 8 *53*, 10 *53 62 181*, 11 *59 93 262f*, 12ff *46*, 12 *53*, 13f *220*, 13 *61*, 14 *53*, 16 *62*, 18 *27 263*, 19 *192*, 22 *219*, 23—26 *273*, 23f *273*, 23 *110 219*, 24 *94*, 25 *157*, 28f *59 262 273*, 28 *64 262f 265*, 30 *23 150*, 31ff *173f*, 31f *70—72 247 263*, 31 *45 55*, 33 *45 61 157*, 34 *47 179*, 35 *229*, 36 *45*, 37 *157*

Ch. 14:5 *73 157 177 222*, 6 *189 192*, 7ff *197*, 7 *59*, 8f *76*, 8 *73 157 222 268*, 9f *76*, 9 *61 177*, 10 *59 65 71 131 179 231*, 11f *66*, 12ff *70*, 12f *72*, 12,13f *67*, 13 *72 76 248*, 15 *47 273*, 16f *266*, 16 *178 189 267*, 17 *131 183 189 215 267f*, 18ff *70*, 19 *76 93*, 20 *268 270*, 211f *268*, 21 *47 178*, 22 *157 262*, 23f *268*, 24 *178 224*, 25f *266 268 270f*, 25 *192 268 271*, 26 *73 267—270*, 27 *179 183*, 29 *192*, 30 *157*, 31 *27 178*

Ch. 15:1ff *32 62 114 181 247*, 1 *192*, 2f *51 107*, 2 *247*, 3 *192*, *227*, 4 *247*, 5 *192 247*, 7f *247*, 8 *72 225 229 247*, 9f *273*, 10ff *67*, 10 *47*, 11 *192*, 12ff *72*, 12 *47*, 13 *62 245*, 14f *46 273*, 14 *47*, 15 *46 62 197 270*, 16f *72*, 16 *72 247f*, 18ff *248*, 20 *62 73*, 21 *181*, 22 *65 192*, 24 *65f*, 25 *263*, 26f *266*, 26 *73 189 215 265 267f 270*, 27 *73*

Ch. 16:1ff *111 157 220*, 1 *192*, 2 *44 181 196 270*, 3 *197*, 4 *44 181 192 270*, 5ff *157*, 5 *55*, 7—11 *266*, 7 *189 267*, 8—11 *267*, 8 *73 132*, 12—15 *266 269*, 12f *271*, 12 *73 222 270*, 13ff *73 190*, 13 *190 267f 270f*, 14 *70 267 270*, 15 *270*, 16ff *157 219f 266 271*, 17f *73 219 222*, 17 *61*, 18 *61 222*, 19 *127 157*, 21 *42 44 62*, 22ff *265*, 22 *55*, 25ff *263*, 25 *73 192 196 270—272*, 28 *45*, 29ff *73*, 29f *93*, 30 *131 157 222 229*, 31 *74*, 32 *44 196 225*, 33 *192*

Ch. 17:1ff *26 31 71 248 263*, 1f *71*, 1 *42 44 70 226*, 2 *32 137 178 225*, 3 *59 197 224*, 4ff *71*, 4 *47 59 65f 178 224f 234*, 5 *55 70f*, 6ff *70 268*, 6 *32 47 59 70 74 131*

178, 7 *32 178*, 8 *59 65 71 131 178*, 9 *137 178*, 10 *70 72*, 11f *178*, 11 *45 137*, 13 *45 55*, 14ff *51 107*, 14 *65 131 178 268*, 17ff *72*, 17 *67 131 268*, 18 *67 231*, 19 *42 67 245*, 20 *73*, 21ff *42 267*, 21 *246f*, 22f *72*, 22 *70f 178f 248*, 24—26 *179*, 24 *32 70f 137 178*

Ch. 18:1ff *27*, 1 *28*, 2 *30 262*, 3 *57 126*, 4 *23 127 157 192 213*, 5 *30 144 192 262*, 6 *57 61 192*, 7 *144 157 219*, 8 *61 157 192*, 9 *178 262f 284*, 10 *57 262*, 11 *54 67 178 205 224f*, 12—27 *148*, 13f *262*, 14 *93 130 245 262*, 15f *94 110 273*, 15 *57 155*, 16 *57*, 17 *130*, 19 *57*, 20f *192*, 21 *29*, 22,24,26 *57*, 28ff *80 116 148 173*, 28 *23 150*, 29 *130*, 32 *69 262f 284*, 35 *57 130 193 245*, 37 *74 131 189*, 40 *48 262*,

Ch. 19:1ff *150*, 5 *130*, 6 *57*, 9 *59*, 10 *192*, 11 *137*, 13 *262f*, 14 *23 44 51 149f 152 262*, 15 *57*, 16b—37 *41*, 17 *262f*, 19 *144*, 20 *130*, 21 *57 61*, 23f *246f*, 24 *263*, 25—27 *30 41—43*, 25 *273*, 26 *40 41 43 94 110*, 27 *273*, 28—30 *54 67*, 28f *205 224f*, 28 *23 41 127 149f 227 263*, 29f *53*, 29 *48*, 30 *67 150 189 216 225 254*, 31 *23f 51 262*, 32 *155*, 34ff *222 273*, 34 *54 60 216 254*, 35 *262 273*, 36f *262f*, 36 *64 262*, 38 *23 31 58 73 131 149 262*, 39 *30 150 262*, 40 *93*, 42 *23f 50f 262*,

Ch. 20:1ff *80 273*, 1 *23f 150*, 2—10 *273*, 2 *94 110*, 3f *130 148*, 5 *48 157*, 6 *30 48*, 7 *48*, 8f *273*, 9 *59 93 128 262f 265*, 10 *219*, 11 *57*, 12 *48*, 13ff *174*, 13 *40*, 14 *265*, 15—18 *173*, 15 *157*, 16 *221 262f*, 17 *30 44 46*, 18 *127 219*, 19 *23f 150 219*, 20 *127 219*, 21 *67 231*, 22 *189 216*, 24 *31 190 262f*, 25 *127 219*, 26 *23f 149f 219*, 28 *127*, 29 *74*, 30f *31 64—66 100 122 250 262 272*, 30 *79 219*, 31 *101*

Ch. 21:1ff *29 54 57 80 115 116 246 273f*, 1 *23 70f 149 219*, 2 *26—28 110 190 262f*,

3ff *174*, 3f *150*, 3 *57*, 4 *157 219 265*, 5 *221*, 6f *57*, 6 *219 248*, 7 *110 127 262*, 8 *262*, 9 *57*, 11 *49 248*, 12 *127 157 219*, 14 *64 70f 219 262*, 15ff *173f 273*, 19 *69 262f*, 20 *94 110 262*, 21f *157*, 23 *30 61 93 262 273*, 24f *262*, 24 *131*, 25 *66*,

Acts

1—2 *20*, 1:18 *139*, 2—8 *288*, 2 *24 243 284*, 2:38 *178*, 3:8 *182*, 3:13 *56*, 3:22 *191*, 5:31 *132*, 6:1ff *45*, 7 *141 288*, 7:15f *140*, 7:22 *66*, 7:37 *191*, 7:38 *75*, 8 *122 232 278 284*, 8:20 *178*, 9:41 *61*, 10:7 *61*, 10:9,23f,40 *23*, 10:45, 11:17 *178*, 13:23, 14:10 *132*, 14:10 *182*, 14:20 *23*, 16:12 *27*, 18:24ff *125*, 20:7 *23*, 20:11 *129*, 21:8 *23*, 22:3 *27*, 22:30 *23*, 23:17ff *222*, 23:32, 25:6,23 *23*, 27:17 *129*, 28:25 *185*

Romans

5:17 *178*, 5:12—21 *16*, 8:1 *54*, 11:11ff,25ff *62*, 11:25ff *62*, 11:31 *54*,

1 Corinthians

3:2 *181*, 8:4 *221*, 10:4 *75 166f 217*, 14:24 *187*, 15:4 *23*,

2 Corinthians

7:11 *181*, 9:10 *221*, 9:15 *178*, 11:2 *26 61*,

Galatians

3:19 *75*

Ephesians

3:7, 4:7 *178*, 5:22f *61*, 5:23 *132*,

Philippians

1:18 *181*, 3:20 *132*,

2 Timothy

2:6 *232*

Titus

2:13 *132*

Hebrews

2:2f *75*, 4:6 *62*, 6:4f *57*, 6:4 *178*, 9:19ff *105*, 11:27 *127*, 11:39f *62*

James

4:13 5:1 *54*

1 Peter

1—5 *108*, 2:2 *51*, 2:3 *57*

1 John

1—5 *108 214*, 1:1 *131*, 1:2 *70*, 1:3 *131*, 1:5 *131 189*, 1:7 *51 107 132*, 1:9 *51 107*, 2:2 *131f*, 2:3f *47*, 2:3,4,5 *229*, 2:7f *47*, 2:19 *70*, 2:23 *185*, 2:27 *269*, 2:28 *70*, 3:2 *70 131*, 3:5 *70 132*, 3:8 *70*, 3:9 *181*, 3:10 *229*, 3:14 *131*, 3:16 *229*, 3:18 *189*, 3:19 *229*, 3:22ff *47*, 3:24, 4:2 *229*, 4:6 *268*, 4:8 *189*, 4:9f *132*, 4:9 *70 131 229*, 4:10,13 *229*, 4:14 *131f*, 4:17 *229*, 4:21 5:2f *47*, 5:2 *229*, 5:6 *268*, 5:15 *131 177*, 5:16 *181*, 5:18 *131*, 5:19 *131*, 5:20 *131 224*,

2 John

3 *189*, 9 *185*, 12 *222*,

3 John

3 *222*, 10 *180*

Jude

25 *132*,

Revelation

1:12 *157*, 2:7 *176*, 3:4f,18 106, 4:1 *157*, 6:11, 7:9,14 *106*, 7:17 *213*, 10:8 *157*, 12 *41 112*, 12:5,17 *42*, 14:5 *51*, 14:14ff *242*, 17:1 *157*, 19:7 *26 61*, 19:9 *30 61*, 21:2 *26 61*, 21:6 *213*, 21:9 *61 157*, 22 *216*, 22:1 *213*, 22:17 *61 213*.

OTHER TEXTS
The Samaritan Pentateuch on Ex 20:21 *191*

Did Ɔ:4 *243*

Od Sal 6:8f
4   *50*

Ps Clem Rec. I, 54*191*

Corp Herm XI.21 *36*

Isocrates, Panegry *38 68*

Heocritus 10,12*55*

Dioscurides V. 86 *33*

Epietetus diss
I.1,16, I.22,15, I.27,13 *36,* II.19,16 36,40

Heliodorus 7,27,7*45*

Pap. Oxyr. 1088*176*